Developing Managerial Skills
in Organizational Behavior

DEVELOPING MANAGERIAL SKILLS IN ORGANIZATIONAL BEHAVIOR

Exercises, Cases, and Readings

SECOND EDITION

Lisa A. Mainiero and Cheryl L. Tromley
Fairfield University

Prentice Hall, Englewood Cliffs, New Jersey 07632

Library of Congress Cataloging-in-Publication Data

MAINIERO, LISA A.
  Developing managerial skills in organizational behavior :
exercises, cases, and readings / Lisa A. Mainiero and Cheryl L.
Tromley. -- 2nd ed.
      p.   cm.
  Includes bibliographical references and index.
  ISBN 0-13-208190-3
  1. Organizational behavior. 2. Organizational behavior--Case
studies. 3. Organizational behavior--Problems, exercises, etc.
I. Tromley, Cheryl L. II. Title.
HD58.7.M325 1993
302.3'5--dc20
                                            93-5071
                                               CIP

Acquisitions Editor: Valerie Ashton
Copy Editor: Rene Lynch
Cover Designer: Design Solutions
Manufacturing Buyer: Patrice Fraccio
Prepress Buyer: Trudy Pisciotti

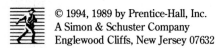
Printed in the United States of America
10 9 8 7 6 5 4 3 2 1

ISBN 0-13-208190-3

Prentice-Hall International (UK) Limited, *London*
Prentice-Hall of Australia Pty. Limited, *Sydney*
Prentice-Hall Canada Inc., *Toronto*
Prentice-Hall Hispanoamericana, S.A., *Mexico*
Prentice-Hall of India Private Limited, *New Delhi*
Prentice-Hall of Japan, Inc., *Tokyo*
Simon & Schuster Asia Pte. Ltd., *Singapore*
Editora Prentice-Hall do Brasil, Ltda., *Rio de Janeiro*

To **David M. Mangini** and **Arnold W. Shaw,**
without whose love, support, and patience
we could not have successfully accomplished
this task.

CONTENTS

PREFACE

Quite honestly, we were surprised with the positive reaction to the first edition of this book. We thought we were developing a supplementary reader for our own classes that a few other professors might also appreciate. We hoped that a few students might learn something from our efforts. Never did we expect such a warm, widespread reaction to our original collection of readings, cases, and exercises. We thank you for all the letters and words of encouragement we have received since the original publication of this book. We hope that this second edition does not disappoint any of the book's fans.

The second edition of *Developing Managerial Skills in Organizational Behavior: Exercises, Cases, and Readings* continues to be a collection of new and classic readings in organizational behavior, coupled with action-oriented, skill-building experiential exercises and cases. Although targeted for a graduate level management audience, it also is appropriate for advanced undergraduates. The book is now organized into ten chapters that include topics such as "Managing Diversity, Ethics in International Issues, and Corporate Social Responsibilities," "Careers and Stress," and "Intergroup Dynamics." Each chapter, as before, is an integrated package, combining

1. *Readings* that present the concepts and theories

2. *Experiential exercises* that give students an opportunity to practice their skills

3. *Cases* that allow students to apply the concepts and theories in a management situation

4. *Memo assignments* in which students analyze the concepts and theories vis-à-vis their own experience.

Readings. For the second edition, we selected readings that contribute to students' conceptual knowledge and support their skill development. We continued to remain sensitive to the relationship between the readings and the cases and exercises presented in each chapter. We have attempted to identify what we consider to be classic readings, but ultimately, as with the original edition, we chose the readings based on what we wanted our students to learn. We received a number of comments regarding the sexist language that appears in some of the older classic articles in the first edition. Because removal of this language was beyond our control due to copyright restrictions, we sincerely hope our readers will understand and accept the context in which these particular articles were written.

Experiential Exercises. The experiential exercises include a mix of self-assessment questionnaires, skill practice sessions, and theory application group work that help students to apply the theories and concepts to their own knowledge of management. Many of the exercises have three or more parts that can be used separately or as a package. For example, students may be asked to (1) diagnose their skills through the use of a self-assessment questionnaire, (2) practice their skills during a role play or group experience, and (3) develop an action plan that relates what they have learned to their ongoing management or part-time work experiences. The mix of exercises in this second edition continues to be flexible so that any exercise can be easily tailored to fit varying time limits and pedagogical needs. We also have included additional information in the *Instructor's Manual* that accompanies this book for further reference in teaching any of the experiential exercises located herein.

Cases. Cases have been included to give students the opportunity to integrate and use the theories and concepts from the readings in solving typical managerial problems. We have found that management students appreciate the opportunity to explore problem situations from a safe distance via "Monday morning quarterbacking." Some of the cases have never been published, while others are well known and widely used. Still others are based on news events, such as the NASA/Challenger disaster or the Saturn General Motors plant. For the second edition, we have updated some of the cases and added a few new ones.

Memo Assignments. Each chapter concludes with a brief written assignment that closes the learning loop by giving students the occasion to apply what they have learned to their own experiences. For example, in the chapter on "Group Dynamics," students are asked to evaluate their department or a group to which they belong according to the theories for group effectiveness presented in the chapter. Some memos are written as actual on-the-job assignments; others are more reflective of the students' skills and abilities. In the second edition, we have sought to rewrite some of the memos that required on-the-job experience so that students without much prior work experience also could handle the assignments meaningfully and easily.

As with the original book, we have sought to integrate each chapter so that the readings, exercises, cases, and memo assignments form a coherent unit. We hope that instructors will assign particular readings in conjunction with the chapter exercises so that the learning experience can be as integrative and meaningful as possible. Teaching notes on how to accomplish these aims are located in a separate supplement to this book, available from the publisher. In the teaching notes, you will find information on teaching objectives, time requirements, procedural instructions, teaching guidelines, and wrap-up discussion questions.

Since the publication of the original edition, the Yale doctoral program that trained us has been discontinued. This book represents, but does not pretend to be, an example of the Yale experiential teaching method by which we were taught the concepts and theories of organizational behavior. We thank all of our former Yale professors, notably Victor H. Vroom, Rosabeth Moss Kanter, and J. Richard Hackman, for their impact on us as teachers and researchers. We also would like to thank our direct contributors to the experiential exercises in this edition, specifically William P. Ferris of Western New England College, Jack Veiga and John Yanouzas of The University of Connecticut, Judi Babcock of Rhode Island College, Bonnie Betters-

Reed of Simmons College, Joel R. DeLuca, and C. Brooklyn Derr, as well as all the other contributors to this volume. But in particular, we thank those who have used the book and provided us with guidance for this second edition. Without their help, support, and advice, our task would have been much more difficult, and we gratefully express our thanks.

Lisa Mainiero
Cheryl Tromley

Developing Managerial Skills
in Organizational Behavior

CHAPTER 1

Managerial Work

INTRODUCTION

What is managerial work? What do managers do? If you are currently a manager, have been one in the past, or hope to be one in the future, you probably think you know the answer to these questions. Some people might say that managerial work involves finance, strategic planning, marketing, or manufacturing. They would be right. Most managers spend at least part of their time involved in tasks related to these areas. But if they are truly managers, none of these activities is their major responsibility.

What all managers have in common is that they manage and interact with people. New managers often are quite surprised by the time and effort they spend coping with people issues in their jobs. Coaching low performers to improve their work, organizing job tasks, settling disputes, and developing career paths for individual employees are only some of the activities in which managers become heavily involved. These tasks, combined with the challenges that dealing with people often provide, account for the majority of time spent in most managers' jobs.

Because the management of people is not a cut-and-dried subject, there are few hard-and-fast answers to the question "What do managers do?" Many people believe that managers spend their time planning, organizing, directing, and controlling the activities of their departments. From this perspective, managerial work is depicted as orderly, systematic, direct, static, and rigid. However, any reader who has had management experience knows first-hand that managerial work is anything but systematic. The "real world" of management is chaotic, challenging, and creative. Idealistic views of what management involves—perhaps sitting at an office desk, having productive, caring discussions with employees—fall quickly by the wayside with a little experience.

READINGS

This chapter offers a series of readings and exercises that will help you understand more realistically the nature of managerial work. In the first article, "Managerial Work: Analysis from Observation," Henry Mintzberg explodes some of the myths upon which many of us base our ideas about managerial work. Based on his research, he describes six characteristics of managerial work that present a clear picture of how managers actually spend their time. Managers have a heavy workload comprising predominately current, specific, and ad hoc issues. Their work is accomplished at an unrelenting pace and is characterized by variety, fragmentation, and brevity. Mintzberg also shows that managers typically portray a variety of roles in the course of performing their jobs. He introduces a typological framework to illustrate the distinct components of managerial work.

The second reading, "The Human Side of Enterprise," by Douglas Murray McGregor is considered a classic. It examines the assumptions that managers hold about people and identifies the impact these assumptions have on the behavior and attitudes of subordinates. McGregor presents these assumptions as Theory X and Theory Y management. A manager who holds Theory X assumptions takes the conventional view that employees are basically unwilling to work in the best interests of the company, cannot handle responsibility, and must be tightly controlled, prodded, and punished to get their work done. By contrast, managers who hold Theory Y assumptions believe that employees are inherently willing to accept responsibility, to do a good job, and to work in the best interests of the company.

In "The Coming of the New Organization," veteran author Peter F. Drucker offers his viewpoint on the organization of the future. He suggests that businesses 20 years from now will bear little resemblance to the manufacturing firms of today. Streamlined levels of management will make way for a set of new knowledge-based specialists who will direct and discipline their own work. Management in the future, he argues, can be likened to that of a conductor of a symphony orchestra. The information-based organization will place a premium on negotiating, conflict resolution, and communication skills.

These three readings examine some of the basic considerations of managerial work, including (1) what it is, (2) what assumptions we bring to it, (3) how these assumptions influence our behavior and the behavior of those we manage, and (4) what effective management will be like in the future.

EXERCISES AND CASES

The three chapter exercises will give you the opportunity to apply concepts presented in the readings. The first exercise, "Managerial Roles," is based on Mintzberg's article, "Managerial Work: Analysis from Observation." You will analyze your current job, the tasks you perform, and the roles you portray as a manager (or as a would-be manager). This exercise will help you understand first-hand the complexity of managerial work and the demands of its tasks.

In the second exercise, "Your Philosophy of Management," you will fill out a questionnaire based on McGregor's article, "The Human Side of Enterprise." This questionnaire will help you identify Theory X and Theory Y assumptions that you may make about people who work for you (or who may work for you in the future). By understanding your philosophy of management and some of its consequences, you will be in a better position to bring about the results you desire.

The final exercise, "Forecasting the Future Organization," is developed from Drucker's article, "The Coming of the New Organization." In this exercise you will revisit the planet Earth in the year 2020 to assess the state of corporate organization. As a visitor you will develop a commentary on the impact of information-based management, the internationalization of the corporation, and the requirements of managerial work in the future.

MEMO

In the memo assignment, *"Managing Your Job"* (located at the back of this book), you will have an opportunity to apply some of the knowledge learned in this chapter. This assignment, the first of ten such assignments that may be required by your instructor, will ask you to assess your job situation and determine a plan of action to improve the proportion of time spent on various managerial activities. You will also determine how you can improve your skills as a manager. Organizing the demands of your roles as a manager to the skills you must perform is the first step in what should become an ongoing process of improvement.

By the time you finish this chapter, you will understand the characteristics of managerial work, your philosophy of management, and how management will change in the future. You will have begun the process of self-assessment and skill development that will continue throughout this term. You will also better understand some of the ways you can become a more effective manager. Through this knowledge, you will develop a framework within which to organize the information and experiences that will follow.

Managerial Work: Analysis from Observation

Henry Mintzberg

The progress of management science is dependent on our understanding of the manager's working processes. A review of the literature indicates that this understanding is superficial at best. Empirical study of the work of five managers (supported by those research findings that are available) led to the following description: Managers perform the basic roles which fall into three groupings. The interpersonal roles describe the manager as figurehead, external liaison, and leader; the information processing roles describe the manager as the nerve center of his organization's information system; and the decision-making roles suggest that the manager is at the heart of the system by which organizational resource allocation, improvement, and disturbance decisions are made. Because of the huge burden of responsibility for the operation of these systems, the manager is called upon to perform his work at an unrelenting pace, work that is characterized by variety, discontinuity and brevity. Managers come to prefer issues that are current, specific, and ad hoc, and that are presented in verbal form. As a result, there is virtually no science in managerial work. The management scientist has done little to change this. He has been unable to understand work which has never been adequately described, and he has poor access to the manager's information, most of which is never documented. We must describe managerial work more precisely, and we must model the manager as a programmed system. Only then shall we be able to make a science of management.

What do managers do? Ask this question and you will likely be told that managers plan, organize, coordinate, and control. Since Henri Fayol (9) first proposed these words in 1916, they have dominated the vocabulary of management. (See, for example, [8], [12], [17].) How valuable are they in describing managerial work? Consider one morning's work of the president of a large organization:

> As he enters his office at 8:23, the manager's secretary motions for him to pick up the telephone, "Jerry, there was a bad fire in the plant last night, about $30,000 damage. We should be back in operation by Wednesday. Thought you should know."
> At 8:45, a Mr. Jamison is ushered into the manager's office. They discuss Mr. Jamison's retirement plans and his cottage in New Hampshire. Then the manager presents a plaque to him commemorating his thirty-two years with the organization.

Reprinted by permission of Henry Mintzberg, "Managerial Work: Analysis from Observation," *Management Science,* Vol. 18, Number 2, 1971. Copyright 1971 by The Institute of Management Sciences.

Mail processing follows: An innocent-looking letter, signed by a Detroit lawyer, reads: "A group of us in Detroit has decided not to buy any of your products because you used that anti-flag, anti-American pinko, Bill Lindell, upon your Thursday night TV show." The manager dictates a restrained reply.

The 10:00 meeting is scheduled by a professional staffer. He claims that his superior, a high-ranking vice president of the organization, mistreats his staff, and that if the man is not fired, they will all walk out. As soon as the meeting ends, the manager rearranges his schedule to investigate the claim and to react to this crisis.

Which of these activities may be called planning, and which may be called organizing, coordinating, and controlling? Indeed, what do words such as "coordinating" and "planning" mean in the context of real activity? In fact, these four words do not describe the actual work of managers at all; they describe certain vague objectives of managerial work ". . . they are just ways of indicating what we need to explain." [1, p. 537]

Other approaches to the study of managerial work have developed, one dealing with managerial decision-making and policy-making processes, another with the manager's interpersonal activities. (See, for example, [2] and [10].) And some empirical researchers, using the "diary" method, have studied, what might be called, managerial "media"—by what means, with whom, how long, and where managers spend their time.[1] But in no part of this literature is the actual content of managerial work systematically and meaningfully described.[2] Thus, the question posed at the start—what do managers do?—remains essentially unanswered in the literature of management.

This is indeed an odd situation. We claim to teach management in schools of both business and public administration; we undertake major research programs in management; we find a growing segment of the management science community concerned with the problems of senior management. Most of these people—the planners, information and control theorists, systems analysts, etc.—are attempting to analyze and change working habits that they themselves do not understand. Thus, at a conference called at M.I.T. to assess the impact of the computer on the manager, and attended by a number of America's foremost management scientists, a participant found it necessary to comment after lengthy discussion [20, p. 198]:

I'd like to return to an earlier point. It seems to me that until we get into the question of what the top manager does or what the functions are that define the top manage-

ment job, we're not going to get out of the kind of difficulty that keeps cropping up. What I'm really doing is leading up to my earlier question which no one really answered. And that is: Is it possible to arrive at a specification of what constitutes the job of a top manager?

His question was not answered.

RESEARCH STUDY ON MANAGERIAL WORK

In late 1966, I began research on this question, seeking to replace Fayol's words by a set that would more accurately describe what managers do. In essence, I sought to develop by the process of induction a statement of managerial work that would have empirical validity. Using a method called "structured observation," I observed for one-week periods the chief executives of five medium to large organizations (a consulting firm, a school system, a technology firm, a consumer goods manufacturer, and a hospital).

Structured as well as unstructured (i.e., anecdotal) data were collected in three "records." In the *chronology record,* activity patterns throughout the working day were recorded. In the *mail record,* for each of 890 pieces of mail processed during the five weeks, were recorded its purpose, format and sender, the attention it received and the action it elicited. And, recorded in the *contact record,* for each of the 368 verbal interactions, were the purpose, the medium (telephone call, scheduled or unscheduled meeting, tour), the participants, the form of initiation, and the location. It should be noted that all categorizing was done during and after observation so as to ensure that the categories reflected only the work under observation. [19] confirms a fuller description of this methodology and a tabulation of the results of the study.

Two sets of conclusions are presented below. The first deals with certain characteristics of managerial work, as they appeared from analysis of the numerical data (e.g., How much time is spent with peers? What is the average duration of meetings? What proportion of contacts are initiated by the manager himself?). The second describes the basic content of managerial work in terms of ten roles. This description derives from an analysis of the data on the recorded *purpose* of each contact and piece of mail.

The liberty is taken of referring to these findings as descriptive of managerial, as opposed to chief executive, work. This is done because many of the findings are supported by studies of other types of managers. Specifically, most of the conclusions on work characteristics are to be found in the combined results of a group of studies of foremen [11], [16], middle managers [4], [5], [15], [25], and chief executives [6]. And although there is little useful material on managerial roles, three studies do provide some evidence of the applicability of the role set. Most important, Sayles' empirical study of production managers [24] suggests that at least five of the ten roles are performed at the lower end of the managerial hierarchy. And some further evidence is provided by comments in Whyte's study of leadership in a street gang [26] and Neustadt's study of three U.S. presidents [21]. (Reference is made to these findings where appropriate.) Thus, although most of the illustrations are drawn from my study of chief executives, there is some justification in asking the reader to consider when he sees the terms "manager" and his "organization" not only "presidents" and their "companies," but also "foremen" and their "shops," "directors" and their "branches," "vice presidents" and their "divisions." The term *manager* shall be used

---

1. Carlson [6] carried out the classic study just after World War II. He asked nine Swedish managing directors to record on diary pads details of each activity in which they engaged. His method was used by a group of other researchers, many of them working in the U.K. (See [4], [5], [15], [25].)

2. One major project, involving numerous publications, took place at Ohio State University and spanned three decades. Some of the vocabulary used followed Fayol. The results have generated little interest in this area. (See, for example, [13]).

with reference to all those people in charge of formal organizations or their subunits.

SOME CHARACTERISTICS OF MANAGERIAL WORK

Six sets of characteristics of managerial work derive from analysis of the data of this study. Each has a significant bearing on the manager's ability to administer a complex organization.

Characteristic 1. The Manager Performs a Great Quantity of Work at an Unrelenting Pace

Despite a semblance of normal working hours, in truth managerial work appears to be very taxing. The five men in this study processed an average of thirty-six pieces of mail each day, participated in eight meetings (half of which were scheduled), engaged in five telephone calls, and took one tour. In his study of the foremen, Guest [11] found that the number of activities per day averaged 583, with no real break in the pace.

Free time appears to be very rare. If by chance a manager has caught up with the mail, satisfied the callers, dealt with all the disturbances, and avoided scheduled meetings, a subordinate will likely show up to usurp the available time. It seems that the manager cannot expect to have much time for leisurely reflection during office hours. During "off" hours, our chief executives spent much time on work-related reading. High-level managers appear to be able to escape neither from an environment which recognizes the power and status of their positions nor from their own minds which have been trained to search continually for new information.

Characteristic 2. Managerial Activity Is Characterized by Variety, Fragmentation, and Brevity

There seems to be no pattern to managerial activity. Rather, variety and fragmentation appear to be characteristic, as successive activities deal with issues that differ greatly both in type and in content. In effect the manager must be prepared to shift moods quickly and frequently.

A typical chief executive day may begin with a telephone call from a director who asks a favor (a "status request"); then a subordinate calls to tell of a strike at one of the facilities (fast movement of information, termed "instant communication"); this is followed by a relaxed scheduled event at which the manager speaks to a group of visiting dignitaries (ceremony); the manager returns to find a message from a major consumer who is demanding the renegotiation of a contract (pressure); and so on. Throughout the day, the managers of our study encountered this great variety of activity. Most surprisingly, the significant activities were interspersed with the trivial in no particular pattern.

Furthermore, these managerial activities were characterized by their brevity. Half of all the activities lasted less than nine minutes and only ten percent exceeded one hour's duration. Guest's foremen averaged 48 seconds per activity, and Carlson [6] stressed that his chief executives were unable to work without frequent interruption.

In my own study of chief executives, I felt that the managers demonstrated a preference for tasks of short duration and encouraged interruption. Perhaps the manager becomes accustomed to variety, or perhaps the flow of "instant communication" cannot be delayed. A more plausible explanation might be that the manager becomes conditioned by his workload. He develops a sensitive appreciation for the opportunity cost of his own time. Also, he is aware of the ever present assortment of obligations associated with his job—accumulations of mail that cannot be delayed, the callers that must be attended to, the meetings that require his participation. In other words, no matter what he is doing, the manager is plagued by what he must do and what he might do. Thus, the manager is forced to treat issues in an abrupt and superficial way.

Characteristic 3. Managers Prefer Issues That Are Current, Specific, and Ad Hoc

Ad hoc operating reports received more attention than did routine ones; current, uncertain information—gossip, speculation, hearsay—which flows quickly was preferred to historical, certain information; "instant communication" received first consideration; few contacts were held on a routine or "clocked" basis; almost all contacts concerned well-defined issues. The managerial environment is clearly one of stimulus-response. It breeds, not reflective planners, but adaptable information manipulators who prefer the live, concrete situation, men who demonstrate a marked action-orientation.

Characteristic 4. The Manager Sits Between His Organization and a Network of Contacts

In virtually every empirical study of managerial time allocation, it was reported that managers spent a surprisingly large amount of time in horizontal or lateral (nonline) communications. It is clear from this study and from that of Sayles [24] that the manager is surrounded by a diverse and complex web of contacts which serves as his self-designed external information system. Included in this web can be clients, associates and suppliers, outside staff experts, peers (managers of related or similar organizations), trade organizations, government officials, independents (those with no relevant organizational affiliation), and directors or superiors. (Among these, directors in this study and superiors in other studies did *not* stand out as particularly active individuals.)

The managers in this study received far more information than they emitted, much of it coming from contacts, and more from subordinates who acted as filters. Figuratively, the manager appears as the neck of an hourglass, sifting information into his own organization from its environment.

Characteristic 5. The Manager Demonstrates a Strong Preference for the Verbal Media

The manager has five media at his command—mail (documented), telephone (purely verbal), unscheduled meeting (informal face-to-face), scheduled meeting (formal face-to-face), and tour (observation). Along with all the other empirical studies of work characteristics, I found a strong predominance of verbal forms of communication.

Mail. By all indications, managers dislike the documented form of communication. In this study, they gave cursory attention to such items as operating reports and periodicals. It was estimated that only thirteen percent of the input mail was of specific and immediate use to the managers. Much of the rest dealt with formalities and provided general reference data. The managers studied initiated very little mail, only twenty-five pieces in the five weeks. The rest of the outgoing mail was sent in reaction to mail received—a reply to a request, an acknowledgement, some information forwarded to a part of the organization. The managers appeared to dislike this form of communication, perhaps because the mail is a relatively slow and tedious medium to use.

Telephone and Unscheduled Meetings. The less formal means of verbal communication—the telephone, a purely verbal form, and the unscheduled meeting, a face-to-face form—were used frequently (two-thirds of the contracts in the study) but for brief encounters (average duration of six and twelve minutes respectively). They were used primarily to deliver requests and to transmit pressing information to those outsiders and subordinates who had informal relationships with the manager.

Scheduled Meetings. These tended to be of long duration, averaging sixty-eight minutes in this study, and absorbing over half the managers' time. Such meetings provided the managers with their main opportunities to interact with large groups and to leave the confines of their own offices. Scheduled meetings were used when the participants were unfamiliar to the manager (e.g., students who request that he speak at a university), when a large quantity of information had to be transmitted (e.g., presentation of a report), when ceremony had to take place, and when complex strategy-making or negotiation had to be undertaken. An important feature of the scheduled meeting was the incidental, but by no means irrelevant, information that flowed at the start and end of such meetings.

Tours. Although the walking tour would appear to be a powerful tool for gaining information in an informal way, in this study tours accounted for only three percent of the managers' time.

In general, it can be concluded that the manager uses each medium for particular purposes. Nevertheless, where possible, he appears to gravitate to verbal media since these provide greater flexibility, require less effort, and bring faster response. It should be noted here that the manager does not leave the telephone or the meeting to get back to work. Rather, communication is his work, and these media are his tools. The operating work of the organization—producing a product, doing research, purchasing a part—appears to be undertaken infrequently by the senior manager. The manager's productive output must be measured in terms of information, a great part of which is transmitted verbally.

Characteristic 6. Despite the Preponderance of Obligations, the Manager Appears to Be Able to Control His Own Affairs

Carlson suggested in his study of Swedish chief executives that these men were puppets, with little control over their own affairs. A cursory examination of our data indicates that this is true. Our managers were responsible for the initiation of only thirty-two percent of their verbal contacts and a smaller proportion of their mail. Activities were also classified as to the nature of the managers' participation, and the active ones were outnumbered by the passive

ones (e.g., making requests vs. receiving requests). On the surface, the manager is indeed a puppet, answering requests in the mail, returning telephone calls, attending meetings initiated by others, yielding to subordinates' requests for time, reacting to crises.

However, such a view is misleading. There is evidence that the senior manager can exert control over his own affairs in two significant ways: (1) It is he who defines many of his own long-term commitments, by developing appropriate information channels which later feed him information, by initiating projects which later demand his time, by joining committees or outside boards which provide contacts in return for his services, and so on. (2) The manager can exploit situations that appear as obligations. He can lobby at ceremonial speeches; he can impose his values on his organization when his authorization is requested; he can motivate his subordinates whenever he interacts with them; he can use the crisis situation as an opportunity to innovate.

Perhaps these are two points that help distinguish successful and unsuccessful managers. All managers appear to be puppets. Some decide who will pull the strings and how, and they then take advantage of each move that they are forced to make. Others, unable to exploit this high-tension environment, are swallowed up by this most demanding of jobs.

THE MANAGER'S WORK ROLES

In describing the essential content of managerial work, one should aim to model managerial activity, that is, to describe it as a set of programs. But an undertaking as complex as this must be preceded by the development of a useful typological description of managerial work. In other words, we must first understand the distinct components of managerial work. At the present time we do not.

In this study, 890 pieces of mail and 368 verbal contacts were categorized as to purpose. The incoming mail was found to carry acknowledgements, requests and solicitations of various kinds, reference data, news, analytical reports, reports on events and on operations, advice on various situations, and statements of problems, pressures, and ideas. In reacting to mail, the managers acknowledged some, replied to the requests (e.g., by sending information), and forwarded much to subordinates (usually for their information). Verbal contacts involved a variety of purposes. In 15% of them activities were scheduled, in 6% ceremonial events took place and a few involved external board work. About 34% involved requests of various kinds, some insignificant, some for information, some for authorization of proposed actions. Another 36% essentially involved the flow of information to and from the manager, while the remainder dealt specifically with issues of strategy and with negotiations. (For details, see [19].)

In this study, each piece of mail and verbal contact categorized in this way was subjected to one question: Why did the manager do this? The answers were collected and grouped and regrouped in various ways (over the course of three years) until a typology emerged that was felt to be satisfactory. While an example, presented below, will primarily explain this process to the reader, it must be remembered that (in the words of Bronowski [3, p. 62]): "Every induction is a speculation and it guesses at a unity which the facts present but do not strictly imply."

Consider the following sequence of two episodes: A chief executive attends a meeting of an external board on which he sits. Upon his return to his organization, he immediately goes to the office of a subordinate, tells of a conversation he had with a fellow board member, and concludes with the statement: "It looks like we shall get the contract."

The purposes of these two contacts are clear—to attend an external board meeting, and to give current information (instant communication) to a subordinate. But why did the manager attend the meeting? Indeed, why does he belong to the board? And why did he give this particular information to his subordinate?

Basing analysis on this incident, one can argue as follows: The manager belongs to the board in part so that he can be exposed to special information which is of use to his organization. The subordinate needs the information but has not the status which would give him access to it. The chief executive does. Board memberships bring chief executives in contact with one another for the purpose of trading information.

Two aspects of managerial work emerge from this brief analysis. The manager serves in a "liaison" capacity because of the status of his office, and what he learns here enables him to act as "disseminator" of information into his organization. We refer to these as *roles*—organized sets of behaviors belonging to identifiable offices or positions [23]. Ten roles were chosen to capture all the activities observed during this study.

All activities were found to involve one or more of three basic behaviors—interpersonal contact, the processing of information, and the making of decisions. As a result, our ten roles are divided into three corresponding groups. Three roles—labelled *figurehead, liaison,* and *leader*—deal with behavior that is essentially interpersonal in nature. Three others—*nerve center, disseminator,* and *spokesman*—deal with information-processing activities performed by the manager. And the remaining four—*entrepreneur, disturbance handler, resource allocator,* and *negotiator*—cover the decision-making activities of the manager. We describe each of these roles in turn, asking the reader to note that they form a *gestalt,* a unified whole whose parts cannot be considered in isolation.

The Interpersonal Roles

Three roles relate to the manager's behavior that focuses on interpersonal contact. These roles derive directly from the authority and status associated with holding managerial office.

Figurehead. As legal authority in his organization, the manager is a symbol, obliged to perform a number of duties. He must preside at ceremonial events, sign legal documents, receive visitors, make himself available to many of those who feel, in the words of one of the men studied, "that the only way to get something done is to get to the top." There is evidence that this role applies at other levels as well. Davis [7, pp. 43–44] cites the case of the field sales manager who must deal with those customers who believe that their accounts deserve his attention.

Leader. Leadership is the most widely recognized of managerial roles. It describes the manager's relationship with his subordinates—his attempts to motivate them and his development of the milieu in which they work. Leadership actions pervade all activity—in contrast to most roles, it is possible to designate only a few activities as dealing exclusively with leadership (these mostly related to staffing duties). Each time a manager encourages a subordinate, or meddles in his affairs, or replies to one of his requests, he is playing the *leader* role. Subordinates seek out and react to

these leadership clues, and, as a result, they impart significant power to the manager.

Liaison. As noted earlier, the empirical studies have emphasized the importance of lateral or horizontal communication in the work of managers at all levels. It is clear from our study that this is explained largely in terms of the *liaison* role. The manager establishes his network of contacts essentially to bring information and favors to his organization. As Sayles notes in his study of production supervisors [24, p. 258], "The one enduring objective [of the manager] is the effort to build and maintain a predictable, reciprocating system of relationships. . . ."

Making use of his status, the manager reacts with a variety of peers and other people outside his organization. He provides time, information, and favors in return for the same from others. Foremen deal with staff groups and other foremen; chief executives join boards of directors, and maintain extensive networks of individual relationships. Neustadt notes this behavior in analyzing the work of President Roosevelt [21, p. 150]:

> His personal sources were the product of a sociability and curiosity that reached back to the other Roosevelt's time. He had an enormous acquaintance in various phases of national life and at various levels of government; he also had his wife and her variety of contacts. He extended his acquaintanceships abroad; in the war years Winston Churchill, among others, became a "personal source." Roosevelt quite deliberately exploited these relationships and mixed them up to widen his own range of information. He changed his sources as his interests changed, but no one who ever had interested him was quite forgotten or immune to sudden use.

The Informational Roles

A second set of managerial activities relate primarily to the processing of information. Together they suggest three significant managerial roles, one describing the manager as a focal point for a certain kind of organizational information, the other two describing relatively simple transmission of this information.

Nerve Center. There is indication, both from this study and from those by Neustadt and Whyte, that the manager serves as the focal point in his organization for the movement of nonroutine information. Homans, who analyzed Whyte's study, draws the following conclusions [26, p. 187]:

> Since interaction flowed toward [the leaders], they were better informed about the problems and desires of group members than were any of the followers and therefore better able to decide on an appropriate course of action. Since they were in close touch with other gang leaders, they were also better informed than their followers about conditions in Cornerville at large. Moreover, in their positions at the focus of the chains of interaction, they were better able than any follower to pass on to the group decisions that had been reached.

The term *nerve center* is chosen to encompass those many activities in which the manager receives information.

Within his own organization, the manager has legal authority that formally connects him—and only him—to *every* member. Hence, the manager emerges as *nerve center* of internal information. He may not know as much about any one function as the subordinate who specializes in it, but he comes to know more about his total organization than any other member. He is the information generalist. Furthermore, because of the manager's status and its manifestation in the *liaison* role, the manager gains unique access to a variety of knowledgeable outsiders including peers who are themselves *nerve centers* of their own organizations. Hence, the manager emerges as his organization's *nerve center* of external information as well.

As noted earlier, the manager's nerve center information is of a special kind. He appears to find it most important to get his information quickly and informally. As a result, he will not hesitate to bypass formal information channels to get it, and he is prepared to deal with a large amount of gossip, hearsay, and opinion which has not yet become substantiated fact.

Disseminator. Much of the manager's information must be transmitted to subordinates. Some of this is of a *factual* nature, received from outside the organization or from other subordinates. And some is of a *value* nature. Here, the manager acts as the mechanism by which organizational influencers (owners, governments, employee groups, the general public, etc., or simply the "boss") make their preferences known to the organization. It is the manager's duty to integrate these value positions, and to express general organizational preferences as a guide to decisions made by subordinates. One of the men studied commented: "One of the principal functions of this position is to integrate the hospital interests with the public interests." Papandreou describes this duty in a paper published in 1952, referring to management as the "peak coordinator" [22].

Spokesman. In his *spokesman* role, the manager is obliged to transmit his information to outsiders. He informs influencers and other interested parties about his organization's performance, its policies, and its plans. Furthermore, he is expected to serve outside his organization as an expert in its industry. Hospital administrators are expected to spend some time serving outside as public experts on health, and corporation presidents, perhaps as chamber of commerce executives.

The Decisional Roles

The manager's legal authority requires that he assume responsibility for all of his organization's important actions. The *nerve center* role suggests that only he can fully understand complex decisions, particularly those involving difficult value tradeoffs. As a result, the manager emerges as the key figure in the making and interrelating of all significant decisions in his organization, a process that can be referred to as *strategy-making*. Four roles describe the manager's control over the strategy-making system in his organization.

Entrepreneur. The *entrepreneur* role describes the manager as initiator and designer of much of the controlled change in his organization. The manager looks for opportunities and potential problems which may cause him to initiate action. Action takes the form of *improvement projects*—the marketing of a new product, the

strengthening of a weak department, the purchasing of new equipment, the reorganization of formal structure, and so on.

The manager can involve himself in each improvement project in one of three ways: (1) He may *delegate* all responsibility for its design and approval, implicitly retaining the right to replace that subordinate who takes charge of it. (2) He may delegate the design work to a subordinate, but retain the right to *approve* it before implementation. (3) He may actively *supervise* the design work himself.

Improvement projects exhibit a number of interesting characteristics. They appear to involve a number of subdecisions, consciously sequenced over long periods of time and separated by delays of various kinds. Furthermore, the manager appears to supervise a great many of these at any one time—perhaps fifty to one hundred in the case of chief executives. In fact, in his handling of improvement projects, the manager may be likened to a juggler. At any one point, he maintains a number of balls in the air. Periodically, one comes down, receives a short burst of energy, and goes up again. Meanwhile, an inventory of new balls waits on the sidelines and, at random intervals, old balls are discarded and new ones added. Both Lindblom [2] and Marples [18] touch on these aspects of strategy-making, the former stressing the disjointed and incremental nature of the decisions, and the latter depicting the sequential episodes in terms of a stranded rope made up of fibres of different lengths each of which surfaces periodically.

Disturbance Handler. While the *entrepreneur* role focuses on voluntary change, the *disturbance handler* role deals with corrections which the manager is forced to make. We may describe this role as follows: The organization consists basically of specialist operating programs. From time to time, it experiences a stimulus that cannot be handled routinely, either because an operating program has broken down or because the stimulus is new and it is not clear which operating program should handle it. These situations constitute disturbances. As generalist, the manager is obliged to assume responsibility for dealing with the stimulus. Thus, the handling of disturbances is an essential duty of the manager.

There is clear evidence for this role both in our study of chief executives and in Sayles' study of production supervisors [24, p. 162]:

> The achievement of this stability, which is the manager's objective, is a never-to-be-attained ideal. He is like a symphony orchestra conductor, endeavoring to maintain a melodious performance in which contributions of the various instruments are coordinated and sequenced, patterned and paced, while the orchestra members are having various personal difficulties, stage hands are moving music stands, alternating excessive heat and cold are creating audience and instrument problems, and the sponsor of the concert is insisting on irrational changes in the program.

Sayles goes further to point out the very important balance that the manager must maintain between change and stability. To Sayles, the manager seeks "a dynamic type of stability" (p. 162). Most disturbances elicit short-term adjustments which bring back equilibrium; persistent ones require the introduction of long-term structural change.

Resource Allocator. The manager maintains ultimate authority over his organization's strategy-making system by controlling the allocation of its resources. By deciding who will get what (and who will do what), the manager directs the course of his organization. He does this in three ways:

1. *In scheduling his own time,* the manager allocates his most precious resource and thereby determines organizational priorities. Issues that receive low priority do not reach the *nerve center* of the organization and are blocked for want of resources.

2. In designing the organizational structure and in carrying out many improvement projects, the manager *programs the work of his subordinates.* In other words, he allocates their time by deciding what will be done and who will do it.

3. Most significantly, the manager maintains control over resource allocation by the requirement that he *authorize all significant decisions* before they are implemented. By retaining this power, the manager ensures that different decisions are interrelated—that conflicts are avoided, that resource constraints are respected, and that decisions complement one another.

Decisions appear to be authorized in one of two ways. Where the costs and benefits of a proposal can be quantified, where it is competing for specified resources with other known proposals, and where it can wait for a certain time of year, approval for a proposal is sought in the context of a formal *budgeting* procedure. But these conditions are most often not met—timing may be crucial, nonmonetary costs may predominate, and so on. In these cases, approval is sought in terms of an *ad hoc request for authorization.* Subordinate and manager meet (perhaps informally) to discuss one proposal alone.

Authorization choices are enormously complex ones for the manager. A myriad of factors must be considered (resource constraints, influencer preferences, consistency with other decisions, feasibility, payoff, timing, subordinate feelings, etc.). But the fact that the manager is authorizing the decision rather than supervising its design suggests that he has little time to give to it. To alleviate this difficulty, it appears that managers use special kinds of *models* and *plans* in their decision making. These exist only in their minds and are loose, but they serve to guide behavior. Models may answer questions such as, "Does this proposal make sense in terms of the trends that I see in tariff legislation?" or "Will the EDP department be able to get along with marketing on this?" Plans exist in the sense that, on questioning, managers reveal images (in terms of proposed improvement projects) of where they would like their organizations to go: "Well, once I get these foreign operations fully developed, I would like to begin to look into a reorganization," said one subject of this study.

Negotiator. The final role describes the manager as participant in negotiation activity. To some students of the management process [8, p. 343], this is not truly part of the job of managing. But such distinctions are arbitrary. Negotiation is an integral part of managerial work, as this study notes for chief executives and as that of Sayles made very clear for production supervisors [24, p. 131]: "Sophisticated managers place great stress on negotiations as a way of life. They negotiate with groups who are setting standards for their work, who are performing support activity for them, and to whom they wish to 'sell' their services."

The manager must participate in important negotiation sessions because he is his organization's legal authority, its *spokesman* and its *resource allocator.* Negotiation is resource trading in real time. If the resource commitments are to be large, the legal authority must be present.

These ten roles suggest that the manager of an organization bears a great burden of responsibility. He must oversee his organization's status system; he must serve as a crucial informational link between it and its environment; he must interpret and reflect its basic values; he must maintain the stability of its operations; and he must adapt it in a controlled and balanced way to a changing environment.

MANAGEMENT AS A PROFESSION AND AS A SCIENCE

Is management a profession? To the extent that different managers perform one set of basic roles, management satisfies one criterion for becoming a profession. But a profession must require, in the words of the Random House Dictionary, "knowledge of some department of learning or science." Which of the ten roles now requires specialized learning? Indeed, what school of business or public administration teaches its students how to disseminate information, allocate resources, perform as figurehead, make contacts, or handle disturbances? We simply know very little about teaching these things. The reason is that we have never tried to document and describe in a meaningful way the procedures (or programs) that managers use.

The evidence of this research suggests that there is as yet no science in managerial work—that managers do not work according to procedures that have been prescribed by scientific analysis. Indeed, except for his use of the telephone, the airplane, and the dictating machine, it would appear that the manager of today is indistinguishable from his predecessors. He may seek different information, but he gets much of it in the same way—from word-of-mouth. He may make decisions dealing with modern technology but he uses the same intuitive (that is, nonexplicit) procedures in making them. Even the computer, which has had such a great impact on other kinds of organizational work, has apparently done little to alter the working methods of the general manager.

How do we develop a scientific base to understand the work of the manager? The description of roles is a first and necessary step. But righter forms of research are necessary. Specifically, we must attempt to model managerial work—to describe it as a system of programs. First, it will be necessary to decide what programs managers actually use. Among a great number of programs in the manager's repertoire, we might expect to find a time scheduling program, an information disseminating program, and a disturbance-handling program. Then, researchers will have to devote a considerable amount of effort to studying and accurately describing the content of each of these programs—the information and heuristics used. Finally, it will be necessary to describe the interrelationships among all of these programs so that they may be combined into an integrated descriptive model of managerial work.

When the management scientist begins to understand the programs that managers use, he can begin to design meaningful systems and provide help for the manager. He may ask: Which managerial activities can be fully reprogrammed (i.e., automated)? Which cannot be reprogrammed because they require human responses? Which can be partially reprogrammed to operate in a man-machine system? Perhaps scheduling, information collecting, and resource allocating activities lend themselves to varying degrees of reprogramming. Management will emerge as a science to the extent that such efforts are successful.

IMPROVING THE MANAGER'S EFFECTIVENESS

Fayol's fifty year old description of managerial work is no longer of use to us. And we shall not disentangle the complexity of managerial work if we insist on viewing the manager simply as a decision-maker or simply as a motivator of subordinates. In fact, we are unlikely to overestimate the complexity of the manager's work, and we shall make little headway if we take overly simple or narrow points of view in our research.

A major problem faces today's manager. Despite the growing size of modern organizations and the growing complexity of their problems (particularly those in the public sector), the manager can expect little help. He must design his own information system, and he must take full charge of his organization's strategy-making system. Furthermore, the manager faces what might be called the *dilemma of delegation.* He has unique access to much important information but he lacks a formal means of disseminating it. As much of it is verbal, he cannot spread it around in an efficient manner. How can he delegate a task with confidence when he has neither the time nor the means to send the necessary information along with it?

Thus, the manager is usually forced to carry a great burden of responsibility in his organization. As organizations become increasingly large and complex, this burden increases. Unfortunately, the man cannot significantly increase his available time or significantly improve his abilities to manage. Hence, in the large, complex bureaucracy, the top manager's time assumes an enormous opportunity cost and he faces the real danger of becoming a major obstruction in the flow of decisions and information.

Because of this, as we have seen, managerial work assumes a number of distinctive characteristics. The quantity of work is great; the pace is unrelenting; there is great variety, fragmentation, and brevity in the work activities; the manager must concentrate on issues that are current, specific, and ad hoc, and to do so, he finds that he must rely on verbal forms of communications. Yet it is on this man that the burden lies for designing and operating strategy-making and information processing systems that are to solve his organization's (and society's) problems.

The manager can do something to alleviate these problems. He can learn more about his own roles in his organization, and he can use this information to schedule his time in a more efficient manner. He can recognize that only he has much of the information needed by his organization. Then, he can seek to find better means of disseminating it into the organization. Finally, he can turn to the skills of his management scientists to help reduce his workload and to improve his ability to make decisions.

The management scientist can learn to help the manager to the extent he can develop an understanding of the manager's work and the manager's information. To date, strategic planners, operations researchers, and information system designers have provided little help for the senior manager. They simply have had no framework available by which to understand the work of the men who employed them, and they have had poor access to the information which has never been documented. It is folly to believe that a man with poor access to the organization's true *nerve center* can design a formal management information system. Similarly, how can the long-range planner, a man usually uninformed about many of the *current* events that take place in and around his organization, design meaningful strategic plans? For good reason, the literature docu-

ments many manager complaints of naive planning and many planner complaints of disinterested managers. In my view, our lack of understanding of managerial work has been the greatest block to the progress of management science.

The ultimate solution to the problem—to the overburdened manager seeking meaningful help—must derive from research. We must observe, describe, and understand the real work of managing; then and only then shall we significantly improve it.

REFERENCES

1. Braybrooke, David, "The Mystery of Executive Success Reexamined," *Administrative Science Quarterly,* Vol. 8 (1964), pp. 533–560.

2. ———— and Lindblom, Charles E., *A Strategy of Decision,* Free Press, New York, 1963.

3. Bronowski, J., "The Creative Process," *Scientific American,* Vol. 199 (September 1958), pp. 59–65.

4. Burns, Tom, "The Directions of Activity and Communications in a Departmental Executive Group," *Human Relations,* Vol. 7 (1954), pp. 73–97.

5. ————, "Management in Action," *Operational Research Quarterly,* Vol. 8 (1957), pp. 45–60.

6. Carlson, Sune, *Executive Behavior,* Strömbergs, Stockholm, 1951.

7. Davis, Robert T., *Performance and Development of Field Sales Managers,* Division of Research, Graduate School of Business Administration, Harvard University, Boston, 1957.

8. Drucker, Peter F., *The Practice of Management,* Harper and Row, New York, 1954.

9. Fayol, Henri, *Administration industrielle et générale,* Dunods, Paris, 1950 (first published 1916).

10. Gibb, Cecil A., "Leadership," Chapter 31 in Gardner Lindzey and Elliot A. Aronson (editors), *The Handbook of Social Psychology,* Vol. 4, Second edition, Addison-Wesley, Reading, Mass., 1969.

11. Guest, Robert H., "Of Time and the Foreman," *Personnel,* Vol. 32 (1955–56), pp. 478–486.

12. Gulick, Luther H., "Notes on the Theory of Organization," in Luther Gulick and Lyndall Urwick (editors), *Papers on the Science of Administration,* Columbia University Press, New York, 1937.

13. Hemphill, John K., *Dimensions of Executive Positions,* Bureau of Business Research Monograph Number 98, The Ohio State University, Columbus, 1960.

14. Homans, George C., *The Human Group,* Harcourt, Brace, New York, 1950.

15. Horne, J. H. and Lupton, Tom, "The Work Activities of Middle Managers—An Exploratory Study," *The Journal of Management Studies,* Vol. 2 (February 1965), pp. 14–33.

16. Kelly, Joe, "The Study of Executive Behavior by Activity Sampling," *Human Relations,* Vol. 17 (August 1964), pp. 277–287.

17. Mackenzie, R. Alex, "The Management Process in 3D," *Harvard Business Review* (November–December 1969), pp. 80–87.

18. Marples, D. L., "Studies of Managers—A Fresh Start?," *The Journal of Management Studies,* Vol. 4 (October 1967), pp. 282–299.

19. Mintzberg, Henry, "Structured Observation as a Method to Study Managerial Work," *The Journal of Management Studies,* Vol. 7 (February 1970), pp. 87–104.

20. Myers, Charles A. (Editor), *The Impact of Computers on Management,* The M.I.T. Press, Cambridge, Mass., 1967.

21. Neustadt, Richard E., *Presidential Power: The Politics of Leadership,* The New American Library, New York, 1964.

22. Papandreou, Andreas G., "Some Basic Problems in the Theory of the Firm," in Bernard F. Haley (editor), *A Survey of Contemporary Economics,* Vol. II, Irwin, Homewood, Illinois, 1952, pp. 183–219.

23. Sarbin, T. R. and Allen, V. L., "Role Theory," in Gardner Lindzey and Elliot A. Aronson (editors), *The Handbook of Social Psychology,* Vol. I, Second edition, Addison-Wesley, Reading, Mass., 1968, pp. 488–567.

24. Sayles, Leonard R., *Managerial Behavior: Administration in Complex Enterprises,* McGraw-Hill, New York, 1964.

25. Stewart, Rosemary, *Managers and Their Jobs,* Macmillan, London, 1967.

26. Whyte, William F., *Street Corner Society,* Second edition, University of Chicago Press, Chicago, 1955.

The Human Side of Enterprise

Douglas Murray McGregor

It has become trite to say that industry has the fundamental know-how to utilize physical science and technology for the material benefit of mankind, and that we must now learn how to utilize the social sciences to make our human organizations truly effective.

To a degree, the social sciences today are in a position like that of the physical sciences with respect to atomic energy in the thirties. We know that past conceptions of the nature of man are inadequate and, in many ways, incorrect. We are becoming quite certain that, under proper conditions, unimagined resources of creative human energy could become available within the organizational setting.

We cannot tell industrial management how to apply this new knowledge in simple, economic ways. We know it will require years of exploration, much costly development research, and a substantial amount of creative imagination on the part of management to discover how to apply this growing knowledge to the organization of human effort in industry.

MANAGEMENT'S TASK:
THE CONVENTIONAL VIEW

The conventional conception of management's task in harnessing human energy to organizational requirements can be stated broadly in terms of three propositions. In order to avoid the complications introduced by a label, let us call this set of propositions "Theory X":

This article is based on an address by Dr. McGregor before the Fifth Anniversary Convocation of the MIT School of Industrial Management. Reprinted, by permission of the publisher, from *Management Review,* November, 1957. Copyright © 1957 American Management Association, New York. All rights reserved.

1. Management is responsible for organizing elements of productive enterprise—money, materials, equipment, people—in the interest of economic ends.

2. With respect to people, this is a process of directing their efforts, motivating them, controlling their actions, modifying their behavior to fit the needs of the organization.

3. Without this active intervention by management, people would be passive—even resistant—to organizational needs. They must therefore be persuaded, rewarded, punished, controlled—their activities must be directed. This is management's task. We often sum it up by saying that management consists of getting things done through other people.

Behind this conventional theory there are several additional beliefs—less explicit, but widespread:

4. The average man is by nature indolent—he works as little as possible.

5. He lacks ambition, dislikes responsibility, prefers to be led.

6. He is inherently self-centered, indifferent to organizational needs.

7. He is by nature resistant to change.

8. He is gullible, not very bright, the ready dupe of the charlatan and the demagogue.

The human side of economic enterprise today is fashioned from propositions and beliefs such as these. Conventional organizational structures and managerial policies, practices, and programs reflect these assumptions.

In accomplishing its task—with these assumptions as guides—management has conceived of a range of possibilities.

At one extreme, management can be "hard" or "strong." The methods for directing behavior involve coercion and threat (usually disguised), close supervision, tight controls over behavior. At the other extreme, management can be "soft" or "weak." The methods for directing behavior involve being permissive, satisfying people's demands, achieving harmony. Then they will be tractable, accept direction.

This range has been fairly completely explored during the past half century, and management has learned some things from the exploration. There are difficulties in the "hard" approach. Force breeds counter-forces: restriction of output, antagonism, militant unionism, subtle but effective sabotage of management objectives. This "hard" approach is especially difficult during times of full employment.

There are also difficulties in the "soft" approach. It leads frequently to the abdication of management—to harmony, perhaps, but to indifferent performance. People take advantage of the soft approach. They continually expect more, but they give less and less.

Currently, the popular theme is "firm but fair." This is an attempt to gain the advantages of both the hard and the soft approaches. It is reminiscent of Teddy Roosevelt's "speak softly and carry a big stick."

IS THE CONVENTIONAL VIEW CORRECT?

The findings which are beginning to emerge from the social sciences challenge this whole set of beliefs about man and human nature and about the task of management. The evidence is far from conclusive, certainly, but it is suggestive. It comes from the laboratory, the clinic, the schoolroom, the home, and even to a limited extent from industry itself.

The social scientist does not deny that human behavior in industrial organization today is approximately what management perceives it to be. He has, in fact, observed it and studied it fairly extensively. But he is pretty sure that this behavior is *not* a consequence of man's inherent nature. It is a consequence rather of the nature of industrial organizations, of management philosophy, policy, and practice. The conventional approach of Theory X is based on mistaken notions of what is cause and what is effect.

Perhaps the best way to indicate why the conventional approach of management is inadequate is to consider the subject of motivation.

PHYSIOLOGICAL NEEDS

Man is a wanting animal—as soon as one of his needs is satisfied, another appears in its place. This process is unending. It continues from birth to death.

Man's needs are organized in a series of levels—a hierarchy of importance. At the lowest level, but pre-eminent in importance when they are thwarted, are his *physiological needs.* Man lives for bread alone, when there is no bread. Unless the circumstances are unusual, his needs for love, for status, for recognition are inoperative when his stomach has been empty for a while. But when he eats regularly and adequately, hunger ceases to be an important motivation. The same is true of the other physiological needs of man—for rest, exercise, shelter, protection from the elements.

A satisfied need is not a motivator of behavior! This is a fact of profound significance that is regularly ignored in the conventional approach to the management of people. Consider your own need for air: Except as you are deprived of it, it has no appreciable motivating effect upon your behavior.

SAFETY NEEDS

When the physiological needs are reasonably satisfied, needs at the next higher level begin to dominate man's behavior—to motivate him. These are called *safety needs.* They are needs for protection against danger, threat, deprivation. Some people mistakenly refer to these as needs for security. However, unless man is in a dependent relationship where he fears arbitrary deprivation, he does not demand security. The need is for the "fairest possible break." When he is confident of this, he is more than willing to take risks. But when he feels threatened or dependent, his greatest need is for guarantees, for protection, for security.

The fact needs little emphasis that, since every industrial employee is in a dependent relationship, safety needs may assume considerable importance. Arbitrary management actions, behavior which arouses uncertainty with respect to continued employment or which reflects favoritism or discrimination, unpredictable administration of policy—these can be powerful motivators of the safety needs in the employment relationship *at every level,* from worker to vice president.

SOCIAL NEEDS

When man's physiological needs are satisfied and he is no longer fearful about his physical welfare, his *social needs* become important motivators of his behavior—needs for belonging, for association, for acceptance by his fellows, for giving and receiving friendship and love.

Management knows today of the existence of these needs, but it often assumes quite wrongly that they represent a threat to the organization. Many studies have demonstrated that the tightly knit, cohesive work group may, under proper conditions, be far more effective than an equal number of separate individuals in achieving organizational goals.

Yet management, fearing group hostility to its own objectives, often goes to considerable lengths to control and direct human efforts in ways that are inimical to the natural "groupiness" of human beings. When man's social needs—and perhaps his safety needs, too—are thus thwarted, he behaves in ways which tend to defeat organizational objectives. He becomes resistant, antagonistic, uncooperative. But this behavior is a consequence, not a cause.

EGO NEEDS

Above the social needs—in the sense that they do not become motivators until lower needs are reasonably satisfied—are the needs of greatest significance to management and to man himself. They are the *egoistic needs,* and they are of two kinds:

1. Those needs that relate to one's self-esteem—needs for self-confidence, for independence, for achievement, for competence, for knowledge.

2. Those needs that relate to one's reputation—needs for status, for recognition, for appreciation, for the deserved respect of one's fellows.

Unlike the lower needs, these are rarely satisfied; man seeks indefinitely for more satisfaction of these needs once they have become important to him. But they do not appear in any significant way until physiological, safety, and social needs are all reasonably satisfied.

The typical industrial organization offers few opportunities for the satisfaction of these egoistic needs to people at lower levels in the hierarchy. The conventional methods of organizing work, particularly in mass-production industries, give little heed to these aspects of human motivation. If the practices of scientific management were deliberately calculated to thwart these needs, they could hardly accomplish this purpose better than they do.

SELF-FULFILLMENT NEEDS

Finally—a capstone, as it were, on the hierarchy of man's needs—there are what we may call the *needs for self-fulfillment.* These are the needs for realizing one's own potentialities, for continued self-development, for being creative in the broadest sense of that term.

It is clear that the conditions of modern life give only limited opportunity for these relatively weak needs to obtain expression. The deprivation most people experience with respect to other lower-level needs, and the needs for self-fulfillment remain dormant.

MANAGEMENT AND MOTIVATION

We recognize readily enough that a man suffering from a severe dietary deficiency is sick. The deprivation of physiological needs has behavioral consequences. The same is true—although less well recognized—of deprivation of higher-level needs. The man whose needs for safety, association, independence, or status are thwarted is sick just as surely as the man who has rickets. And his sickness will have behavioral consequences. We will be mistaken if we attribute his resultant passivity, his hostility, his refusal to accept responsibility to his inherent "human nature." These forms of behavior are *symptoms* of illness—of deprivation of his social and egoistic needs.

The man whose lower-level needs are satisfied is not motivated to satisfy those needs any longer. For practical purposes they exist no longer. Management often asks, "Why aren't people more productive? We pay good wages, provide good working conditions, have excellent fringe benefits and steady employment. Yet people do not seem to be willing to put forth more than minimum effort."

The fact that management has provided for these physiological and safety needs has shifted the motivational emphasis to the social and perhaps to the egoistic needs. Unless there are opportunities *at work* to satisfy these higher-level needs, people will be deprived; and their behavior will reflect this deprivation. Under such conditions, if management continues to focus its attention on physiological needs, its efforts are bound to be ineffective.

People *will* make insistent demands for more money under these conditions. It becomes more important than ever to buy the material goods and services which can provide limited satisfaction of the thwarted needs. Although money has only limited value in satisfying many higher-level needs, it can become the focus of interest if it is the *only* means available.

THE CARROT-AND-STICK APPROACH

The carrot-and-stick theory of motivation (like Newtonian physical theory) works reasonably well under certain circumstances. The *means* for satisfying man's physiological and (within limits) his safety needs can be provided or withheld by manage-

ment. Employment itself is such a means, and so are wages, working conditions, and benefits. By these means the individual can be controlled so long as he is struggling for subsistence.

But the carrot-and-stick theory does not work at all once man has reached an adequate subsistence level and is motivated primarily by higher needs. Management cannot provide a man with self-respect, or with the respect of his fellows, or with the satisfaction of needs for self-fulfillment. It can create such conditions that he is encouraged and enabled to seek such satisfactions for *himself,* or it can thwart him by failing to create those conditions.

But this creation of conditions is not "control." It is not a good device for directing behavior. And so management finds itself in an odd position. The high standard of living created by our modern technological know-how provides quite adequately for the satisfaction of physiological and safety needs. The only significant exception is where management practices have not created confidence in a "fair break"—and thus where safety needs are thwarted. But by making possible the satisfaction of low-level needs, management has deprived itself of the ability to use as motivators the devices on which conventional theory has taught it to rely—rewards, promises, incentives, or threats and other coercive devices.

The philosophy of management by direction and control—*regardless of whether it is hard or soft*—is inadequate to motivate because the human needs on which this approach relies are today unimportant motivators of behavior. Direction and control are essentially useless in motivating people whose important needs are social and egoistic. Both the hard and the soft approach fail today because they are simply irrelevant to the situation.

People, deprived of opportunities to satisfy at work the needs which are now important to them, behave exactly as we might predict—with indolence, passivity, resistance to change, lack of responsibility, willingness to follow the demagogue, unreasonable demands for economic benefits. It would seem that we are caught in a web of our own weaving.

A NEW THEORY OF MANAGEMENT

For these and many other reasons, we require a different theory of the task of managing people based on more adequate assumptions about human nature and human motivation. I am going to be so bold as to suggest the broad dimensions of such a theory. Call it "Theory Y," if you will.

1. Management is responsible for organizing the elements of productive enterprise—money, materials, equipment, people—in the interest of economic ends.

2. People are *not* by nature passive or resistant to organizational needs. They have become so as a result of experience in organizations.

3. The motivation, the potential for development, the capacity for assuming responsibility, the readiness to direct behavior toward organizational goals are all present in people. Management does not put them there. It is a responsibility of management to make it possible for people to recognize and develop these human characteristics for themselves.

4. The essential task of management is to arrange organizational conditions and methods of operation so that people can achieve their own goals *best* by directing *their own* efforts toward organizational objectives.

This is a process primarily of creating opportunities, releasing potential, removing obstacles, encouraging growth, providing guidance. It is what Peter Drucker has called "management by objectives" in contrast to "management by control." It does *not* involve the abdication of management, the absence of leadership, the lowering of standards, or the other characteristics usually associated with the "soft" approach under Theory X.

SOME DIFFICULTIES

It is no more possible to create an organization today which will be a full, effective application of this theory than it was to build an atomic power plant in 1945. There are many formidable obstacles to overcome.

The conditions imposed by conventional organization theory and by the approach of scientific management for the past half century have tied men to limited jobs which do not utilize their capabilities, have discouraged the acceptance of responsibility, have encouraged passivity, have eliminated meaning from work. Man's habits, attitudes, expectations—his whole conception of membership in an industrial organization—have been conditioned by his experience under these circumstances.

People today are accustomed to being directed, manipulated, controlled in industrial organizations and to finding satisfaction for their social, egoistic, and self-fulfillment needs away from the job. This is true of much of management as well as of workers. Genuine "industrial citizenship"—to borrow again a term from Drucker—is a remote and unrealistic idea, the meaning of which has not even been considered by most members of industrial organizations.

Another way of saying this is that Theory X places exclusive reliance upon external control of human behavior, while Theory Y relies heavily on self-control and self-direction. It is worth noting that this difference is the difference between treating people as children and treating them as mature adults. After generations of the former, we cannot expect to shift to the latter overnight.

STEPS IN THE RIGHT DIRECTION

Before we are overwhelmed by the obstacles, let us remember that the application of theory is always slow. Progress is usually achieved in small steps. Some innovative ideas which are entirely consistent with Theory Y are today being applied with some success.

Decentralization and Delegation

There are ways of freeing people from the too-close control of conventional organization, giving them a degree of freedom to direct their own activities, to assume responsibility, and, importantly, to satisfy their egoistic needs. In this connection, the flat organization of Sears, Roebuck and Company provides an interesting example. It forces "management by objectives," since it enlarges the number of people reporting to a manager until he cannot direct and control them in the conventional manner.

Job Enlargement

This concept, pioneered by I.B.M. and Detroit Edison, is quite consistent with Theory Y. It encourages the acceptance of responsibility at the bottom of the organization; it provides opportunities for satisfying social and egoistic needs. In fact, the reorganization of work at the factory level offers one of the more challenging opportunities for innovation consistent with Theory Y.

Participation and Consultative Management

Under proper conditions, participation and consultative management provide encouragement to people to direct their creative energies toward organizational objectives, give them some voice in decisions that affect them, provide significant opportunities for the satisfaction of social and egoistic needs. The Scanlon Plan is the outstanding embodiment of these ideas in practice.

Performance Appraisal

Even a cursory examination of conventional programs of performance appraisal within the ranks of management will reveal how completely consistent they are with Theory X. In fact, most such programs tend to treat the individual as though he were a product under inspection on the assembly line.

A few companies—among them General Mills, Ansul Chemical, and General Electric—have been experimenting with approaches which involve the individual in setting "targets" or objectives *for himself,* and in a *self*-evaluation of performance semiannually or annually. Of course, the superior plays an important leadership role in this process—one, in fact, which demands substantially more competence than the conventional approach. The role is, however, considerably more congenial to many managers than the role of "judge" or "inspector" which is usually forced upon them. Above all, the individual is encouraged to take a greater responsibility for planning and appraising his own contribution to organizational objectives; and the accompanying effects on egoistic and self-fulfillment needs are substantial.

APPLYING THE IDEAS

The not infrequent failure of such ideas as these to work as well as expected is often attributable to the fact that a management has "bought the idea" but applied it within the framework of Theory X and its assumptions.

Delegation is not an effective way of exercising management by control. Participation becomes a farce when it is applied as a sales gimmick or a device for kidding people into thinking they are important. Only the management that has confidence in human capacities and is itself directed toward organizational objectives rather than toward the preservation of personal power can grasp the implications of this emerging theory. Such management will find and apply successfully other innovative ideas as we move slowly toward the full implementation of a theory like Y.

THE HUMAN SIDE OF ENTERPRISE

It is quite possible for us to realize substantial improvements in the effectiveness of industrial organizations during the next decade or two. The social sciences can contribute much to such developments; we are only beginning to grasp the implications of the growing body of knowledge in these fields. But if this conviction is to become a reality instead of a pious hope, we will need to view the process much as we view the process of releasing the energy of the atom for constructive human ends—as a slow, costly, sometimes discouraging approach toward a goal which would seem to many to be quite unrealistic.

The ingenuity and the perseverance of industrial management in the pursuit of economic ends have changed many scientific and technological dreams into commonplace realities. It is now becoming clear that the application of these same talents to the human side of enterprise will not only enhance substantially these materialistic achievements, but will bring us one step closer to "the good society."

The Coming of the New Organization

Peter F. Drucker

The typical large business 20 years hence will have fewer than half the levels of management of its counterpart today, and no more than a third the managers. In its structure, and in its management problems and concerns, it will bear little resemblance to the typical manufacturing company, circa 1950, which our textbooks still consider the norm. Instead it is far more likely to resemble organizations that neither the practicing manager nor the management scholar pays much attention to today: the hospital, the university, the symphony orchestra. For like them, the typical business will be knowledge-based, an organization composed largely of specialists who direct and discipline their own performance through organized feedback from colleagues, customers, and headquarters. For this reason, it will be what I call an information-based organization.

Businesses, especially large ones, have little choice but to become information-based. Demographics, for one, demands the shift. The center of gravity in employment is moving fast from manual and clerical workers to knowledge workers who resist the command-and-control model that business took from the military 100 years ago. Economics also dictates change, especially the need for large businesses to innovate and to be entrepreneurs. But above all, information technology demands the shift.

Advanced data-processing technology isn't necessary to create an information-based organization, of course. As we shall see, the British built just such an organization in India when "information technology" meant the quill pen, and barefoot runners were the "telecommunications" systems. But as advanced technology becomes more and more prevalent, we have to engage in analysis and diagnosis—that is, in "information"—even more intensively or risk being swamped by the data we generate.

So far most computer users still use the new technology only to do faster what they have always done before, crunch conventional numbers. But as soon as a company takes the first tentative steps from data to information, its decision processes, management structure, and even the way its work gets done begin to be transformed. In fact, this is already happening, quite fast, in a number of companies throughout the world.

We can readily see the first step in this transformation process when we consider the impact of computer technology on capital-investment decisions. We have known for a long time that there is no one right way to analyze a proposed capital investment. To understand it we need at least six analyses: the expected rate of return; the payout period and the investment's expected productive life; the discounted present value of all returns through the productive lifetime of the investment; the risk in not making the investment or deferring it; the cost and risk in case of failure; and finally, the opportunity cost. Every accounting student is taught these concepts. But before the advent of data-processing capacity, the actual analyses would have taken man-years of clerical toil to complete. Now anyone with a spreadsheet should be able to do them in a few hours.

The availability of this information transforms the capital-investment analysis from opinion into diagnosis, that is, into the rational weighing of alternative assumptions. Then the information transforms the capital-investment decision from an opportunistic, financial decision governed by the numbers into a business decision based on the probability of alternative strategic assumptions. So the decision both presupposes a business strategy and challenges that strategy and its assumptions. What was once a budget exercise becomes an analysis of policy.

The second area that is affected when a company focuses its data-processing capacity on producing information is its organization structure. Almost immediately, it becomes clear that both the number of management levels and the number of managers can be sharply cut. The reason is straightforward: it turns out that whole layers of management neither make decisions nor lead. Instead, their main, if not their only, function is to serve as "relays"—human boosters for the faint, unfocused signals that pass for communication in the traditional pre-information organization.

One of America's largest defense contractors made this discovery when it asked what information its top corporate and operating managers needed to do their jobs. Where did it come from? What form was it in? How did it flow? The search for answers soon revealed that whole layers of management—perhaps as many as 6 out of a total of 14—existed only because these questions had not been asked before. The company had had data galore. But it had always used its copious data for control rather than for information.

Information is data endowed with relevance and purpose. Converting data into information thus requires knowledge. And knowledge, by definition, is specialized. (In fact, truly knowledgeable people tend toward overspecialization, whatever their field, precisely because there is always so much more to know.)

The information-based organization requires far more specialists overall than the command-and-control companies we are accustomed to. Moreover, the specialists are found in operations, not at corporate headquarters. Indeed, the operating organization tends to become an organization of specialists of all kinds.

Information-based organizations need central operating work such as legal counsel, public relations, and labor relations as much as ever. But the need for service staffs—that is, for people without operating responsibilities who only advise, counsel, or coordinate—shrinks drastically. In its *central* management, the information-based organization needs few, if any, specialists.

Because of its flatter structure, the large, information-based organization will more closely resemble the businesses of a century ago than today's big companies. Back then, however, all the knowledge, such as it was, lay with the very top people. The rest were helpers or hands, who mostly did the same work and did as they were told. In the information-based organization, the knowledge will be primarily at the bottom, in the minds of the specialists who do different work and direct themselves. So today's typical organization in which knowledge tends to be concentrated in service staffs, perched rather insecurely between top management and the operating people, will likely be labeled a phase, an attempt to infuse knowledge from the top rather than obtain information from below.

Finally, a good deal of work will be done differently in the information-based organization. Traditional departments will serve as guardians of standards, as centers for training and the assignment of specialists; they won't be where the work gets done. That will happen largely in task-focused teams.

This change is already under way in what used to be the most clearly defined of all departments—research. In pharmaceuticals, in telecommunications, in papermaking, the traditional *sequence* of research, development, manufacturing, and marketing is being replaced by *synchrony:* specialists from all these functions work together as a team, from the inception of research to a product's establishment in the market.

How task forces will develop to tackle other business opportunities and problems remains to be seen. I suspect, however, that the need for a task force, its assignment, its composition, and its leadership will have to be decided on case by case. So the organization that will be developed will go beyond the matrix and may indeed be quite different from it. One thing is clear, though: it will require greater self-discipline and even greater emphasis on individual responsibility for relationships and for communications.

To say that information technology is transforming business enterprises is simple. What this transformation will require of companies and top managements is much harder to decipher. That is why I find it helpful to look for clues in other kinds of information-based organizations, such as the hospital, the symphony orchestra, and the British administration in India.

A fair-sized hospital of about 400 beds will have a staff of several hundred physicians and 1,200 to 1,500 paramedics divided among some 60 medical and paramedical specialties. Each specialty has its own knowledge, its own training, its own language. In each specialty, especially the paramedical ones like the clinical lab and physical therapy, there is a head person who is a working specialist rather than a full-time manager. The head of each specialty reports directly to the top, and there is little middle management. A good deal of the work is done in ad hoc teams as required by an individual patient's diagnosis and condition.

A large symphony orchestra is even more instructive, since for some works there may be a few hundred musicians on stage playing together. According to organization theory then, there should be several group vice president conductors and perhaps a half-dozen division VP conductors. But that's not how it works. There is only the conductor-CEO—and every one of the musicians plays directly to that person without an intermediary. And each is a high-grade specialist, indeed an artist.

But the best example of a large and successful information-based organization, and one without any middle management at all, is the British civil administration in India.[1]

The British ran the Indian subcontinent for 200 years, from the middle of the eighteenth century through World War II, without making any fundamental changes in organization structure or administrative policy. The Indian civil service never had more than 1,000 members to administer the vast and densely populated subcontinent—a tiny fraction (at most 1%) of the legions of Confucian mandarins and palace eunuchs employed next door to administer a not-much-more populous China. Most of the Britishers were quite young; a 30-year-old was a survivor, especially in the early years. Most lived alone in isolated outposts with the nearest countryman a day or two of travel away, and for the first hundred years there was no telegraph or railroad.

The organization structure was totally flat. Each district officer reported directly to the "Coo," the provincial political secretary. And since there were nine provinces, each political secretary had at least 100 people reporting directly to him, many times what the doctrine of the span of control would allow. Nevertheless, the system worked remarkably well, in large part because it was designed to ensure that each of its members had the information he needed to do his job.

Each month the district officer spent a whole day writing a full report to the political secretary in the provincial capital. He discussed each of his principal tasks—there were only four, each clearly delineated. He put down in detail what he had expected would happen with respect to each of them, what actually did happen, and why, if there was a discrepancy, the two differed. Then he wrote down what he expected would happen in the ensuing month with respect to each key task and what he was going to do about it, asked questions about policy, and commented on long-term opportunities, threats, and needs. In turn, the political secretary "minuted" every one of those reports—that is, he wrote back a full comment.

On the basis of these examples, what can we say about the requirements of the information-based organization? And what are its management problems likely to be? Let's look first at the requirements. Several hundred musicians and their CEO, the conductor, can play together because they all have the same score. It tells both flutist and timpanist what to play and when. And it tells the conductor what to expect from each and when. Similarly, all the specialists in the hospital share a common mission: the care and cure of the sick. The diagnosis is their "score"; it dictates specific action for the X-ray lab, the dietitian, the physical therapist, and the rest of the medical team.

---

1. The standard account is Philip Woodruff, *The Men Who Ruled India,* especially the first volume, *The Founders of Modern India* (New York: St. Martin's, 1954). How the system worked day by day is charmingly told in *Sowing* (New York: Harcourt Brace Jovanovich, 1962), volume one of the autobiography of Leonard Woolf (Virginia Woolf's husband).

Information-based organizations, in other words, require clear, simple, common objectives that translate into particular actions. At the same time, however, as these examples indicate, information-based organizations also need concentration on one objective or, at most, on a few.

Because the "players" in an information-based organization are specialists, they cannot be told how to do their work. There are probably few orchestra conductors who could coax even one note out of a French horn, let alone show the horn player how to do it. But the conductor can focus the horn player's skill and knowledge on the musicians' joint performance. And this focus is what the leaders of an information-based business must be able to achieve.

Yet a business has no "score" to play by except the score it writes as it plays. And whereas neither a first-rate performance of a symphony nor a miserable one will change what the composer wrote, the performance of a business continually creates new and different scores against which its performance is assessed. So an information-based business must be structured around goals that clearly state management's performance expectations for the enterprise and for each part and specialist and around organized feedback that compares results with these performance expectations so that every member can exercise self-control.

The other requirement of an information-based organization is that everyone take information responsibility. The bassoonist in the orchestra does so every time she plays a note. Doctors and paramedics work with an elaborate system of reports and an information center, the nurse's station on the patient's floor. The district officer in India acted on this responsibility every time he filed a report.

The key to such a system is that everyone asks: Who in this organization depends on me for what information? And on whom, in turn, do I depend? Each person's list will always include superiors and subordinates. But the most important names on it will be those of colleagues, people with whom one's primary relationship is coordination. The relationship of the internist, the surgeon, and the anesthesiologist is one example. But the relationship of a biochemist, a pharmacologist, the medical director in charge of clinical testing, and a marketing specialist in a pharmaceutical company is no different. It, too, requires each party to take the fullest information responsibility.

Information responsibility to others is increasingly understood, especially in middle-sized companies. But information responsibility to oneself is still largely neglected. That is, everyone in an organization should constantly be thinking through what information he or she needs to do the job and to make a contribution.

This may well be the most radical break with the way even the most highly computerized businesses are still being run today. There, people either assume the more data, the more information—which was a perfectly valid assumption yesterday when data were scarce, but leads to data overload and information blackout now that they are plentiful. Or they believe that information specialists know what data executives and professionals need in order to have information. But information specialists are tool makers. They can tell us what tool to use to hammer upholstery nails into a chair. We need to decide whether we should be upholstering a chair at all.

Executives and professional specialists need to think through what information is for them, what data they need: first, to know what they are doing; then, to be able to decide what they should be doing; and finally, to appraise how well they are doing. Until this happens MIS departments are likely to remain cost centers rather than become the result centers they could be.

Most large businesses have little in common with the examples we have been looking at. Yet to remain competitive—maybe even to survive—they will have to convert themselves into information-based organizations, and fairly quickly. They will have to change old habits and acquire new ones. And the more successful a company has been, the more difficult and painful this process is apt to be. It will threaten the jobs, status, and opportunities of a good many people in the organization, especially the long-serving, middle-aged people in middle management who tend to be the least mobile and to feel most secure in their work, their positions, their relationships, and their behavior.

The information-based organization will also pose its own special management problems. I see as particularly critical:

1. Developing rewards, recognition, and career opportunities for specialists.

2. Creating unified vision in an organization of specialists.

3. Devising the management structure for an organization of task forces.

4. Ensuring the supply, preparation, and testing of top management people.

Bassoonists presumably neither want nor expect to be anything but bassoonists. Their career opportunities consist of moving from second bassoon to first bassoon and perhaps of moving from a second-rank orchestra to a better, more prestigious one. Similarly, many medical technologists neither expect nor want to be anything but medical technologists. Their career opportunities consist of a fairly good chance of moving up to senior technician, and a very slim chance of becoming lab director. For those who make it to lab director, about 1 out of every 25 or 30 technicians, there is also the opportunity to move to a bigger, richer hospital. The district officer in India had practically no chance for professional growth except possibly to be relocated, after a three-year stint, to a bigger district.

Opportunities for specialists in an information-based business organization should be more plentiful than they are in an orchestra or hospital, let alone in the Indian civil service. But as in these organizations, they will primarily be opportunities for advancement within the specialty, and for limited advancement at that. Advancement into "management" will be the exception, for the simple reason that there will be far fewer middle-management positions to move into. This contrasts sharply with the traditional organization where, except in the research lab, the main line of advancement in rank is out of the specialty and into general management.

More than 30 years ago General Electric tackled this problem by creating "parallel opportunities" for "individual professional contributors." Many companies have followed this example. But professional specialists themselves have largely rejected it as a solution. To them—and to their management colleagues—the only meaningful opportunities are promotions into management. And the prevailing compensation structure in practically all businesses reinforces this attitude because it is heavily biased toward managerial positions and titles.

There are no easy answers to this problem. Some help may come from looking at large law and consulting firms, where even the most senior partners tend to be specialists, and associates who will not make partners are outplaced fairly early on. But whatever scheme is eventually developed will work only if the values and compensation structure of business are drastically changed.

The second challenge that management faces is giving its organization of specialists a common vision, a view of the whole.

In the Indian civil service, the district officer was expected to see the "whole" of his district. But to enable him to concentrate on it, the government services that arose one after the other in the nineteenth century (forestry, irrigation, the archaeological survey, public health and sanitation, roads) were organized outside the administrative structure, and had virtually no contact with the district officer. This meant that the district officer became increasingly isolated from the activities that often had the greatest impact on—and the greatest importance for—his district. In the end, only the provincial government or the central government in Delhi had a view of the "whole," and it was an increasingly abstract one at that.

A business simply cannot function this way. It needs a view of the whole and a focus on the whole to be shared among a great many of its professional specialists, certainly among the senior ones. And yet it will have to accept, indeed will have to foster, the pride and professionalism of its specialists—if only because, in the absence of opportunities to move into middle management, their motivation must come from that pride and professionalism.

One way to foster professionalism, of course, is through assignments to task forces. And the information-based business will use more and more smaller self-governing units, assigning them tasks tidy enough for "a good man to get his arms around," as the old phrase has it. But to what extent should information-based businesses rotate performing specialists out of their specialties and into new ones? And to what extent will top management have to accept as its top priority making and maintaining a common vision across professional specialties?

Heavy reliance on task-force teams assuages one problem. But it aggravates another: the management structure of the information-based organization. Who will the business's managers be? Will they be task-force leaders? Or will there be a two-headed monster—a specialist structure, comparable, perhaps, to the way attending physicians function in a hospital, and an administrative structure of task-force leaders?

The decisions we face on the role and function of the task-force leaders are risky and controversial. Is theirs a permanent assignment, analogous to the job of the supervisory nurse in the hospital? Or is it a function of the task that changes as the task does? Is it an assignment or a position? Does it carry any rank at all? And if it does, will the task-force leaders become in time what the product managers have been at Procter & Gamble: the basic units of management and the company's field officers? Might the task-force leaders eventually replace department heads and vice presidents?

Signs of every one of these developments exist, but there is neither a clear trend nor much understanding as to what each entails. Yet each would give rise to a different organizational structure from any we are familiar with.

Finally, the toughest problem will probably be to ensure the supply, preparation, and testing of top management people. This is, of course, an old and central dilemma as well as a major reason for the general acceptance of decentralization in large businesses in the last 40 years. But the existing business organization has a great many middle-management positions that are supposed to prepare and test a person. As a result, there are usually a good many people to choose from when filling a senior management slot. With the number of middle-management positions sharply cut, where will the information-based organization's top executives come from? What will be their preparation? How will they have been tested?

Decentralization into autonomous units will surely be even more critical than it is now. Perhaps we will even copy the German *Gruppe* in which the decentralized units are set up as separate companies with their own top managements. The Germans use this model precisely because of their tradition of promoting people in their specialties, especially in research and engineering; if they did not have available commands in near-independent subsidiaries to put people in, they would have little opportunity to train and test their most promising professionals. These subsidiaries are thus somewhat like the farm teams of a major-league baseball club.

We may also find that more and more top management jobs in big companies are filled by hiring people away from smaller companies. This is the way that major orchestras get their conductors—a young conductor earns his or her spurs in a small orchestra or opera house, only to be hired away by a larger one. And the heads of a good many large hospitals have had similar careers.

Can business follow the example of the orchestra and hospital where top management has become a separate career? Conductors and hospital administrators come out of courses in conducting or schools of hospital administration respectively. We see something of this sort in France, where large companies are often run by men who have spent their entire previous careers in government service. But in most countries this would be unacceptable to the organization (only France has the *mystique* of the *grandes écoles*). And even in France, businesses, especially large ones, are becoming too demanding to be run by people without first-hand experience and a proven success record.

Thus the entire top management process—preparation, testing, succession—will become even more problematic than it already is. There will be a growing need for experienced businesspeople to go back to school. And business schools will surely need to work out what successful professional specialists must know to prepare themselves for high-level positions as *business* executives and *business* leaders.

Since modern business enterprise first arose, after the Civil War in the United States and the Franco-Prussian War in Europe, there have been two major evolutions in the concept and structure of organizations. The first took place in the ten years between 1895 and 1905. It distinguished management from ownership and established management as work and task in its own right. This happened first in Germany, when Georg Siemens, the founder and head of Germany's premier bank, *Deutsche Bank,* saved the electrical apparatus company his cousin Werner had founded after Werner's sons and heirs had mismanaged it into near collapse. By threatening to cut off the bank's loans, he forced his cousins to turn the company's management over to professionals. A little later, J. P. Morgan, Andrew Carnegie, and John D. Rockefeller, Sr. followed suit in their massive restructurings of U.S. railroads and industries.

The second evolutionary change took place 20 years later. The development of what we still see as the modern corporation began with Pierre S. du Pont's restructuring of his family company in the early twenties and continued with Alfred P. Sloan's redesign of General Motors a few years later. This introduced the command-and-control organization of today, with its emphasis on decentralization, central service staffs, personnel management, the whole apparatus of budgets and controls, and the important distinction between policy and operations. This stage culminated in the massive reorganization of General Electric in the early 1950s, an action that perfected the model most big businesses around the world (including Japanese organizations) still follow.[2]

2. Alfred D. Chandler, Jr. has masterfully chronicled the process in his two books *Strategy and Structure* (Cambridge: MIT Press, 1962) and *The Visible Hand* (Cambridge: Harvard University Press, 1977)—surely the best studies of the administrative history of any major institution. The process itself and its results were presented and analyzed in two of my books: *The Concept of the Corporation* (New York: John Day, 1946) and *The Practice of Management* (New York: Harper Brothers, 1954).

Now we are entering a third period of change: the shift from the command-and-control organization, the organization of departments and divisions, to the information-based organization, the organization of knowledge specialists. We can perceive, though perhaps only dimly, what this organization will look like. We can identify some of its main characteristics and requirements. We can point to central problems of values, structure, and behavior. But the job of actually building the information-based organization is still ahead of us—it is the managerial challenge of the future.

Exercise: Managerial Roles

PURPOSE

The purpose of this exercise is to help you understand what roles you routinely fulfill in your current position. By the time you complete this exercise, you will

1. Identify how you (or another manager) portray managerial roles in his or her job

2. Determine whether or not appropriate amounts of time are spent portraying particular managerial roles

3. Develop strategies to improve the fit between how you spend your time and the demands of your job

INTRODUCTION

According to Mintzberg (1971), there are ten roles that characterize managerial work. Among the roles identified in the *Interpersonal* category are *figurehead, leader,* and *liaison. Informational* roles include *nerve center, disseminator,* and *spokesperson.* Finally, *decisional* roles are categorized as *entrepreneur, disturbance handler, resource allocator,* and *negotiator.*

What surprises many managers is that their jobs can be analyzed in terms of these roles. Managers often view their responsibilities throughout the day as chaotic, fragmented, and erratic. Rarely do managers reflect upon the demands of their jobs as an organized set of role responsibilities that continually must be fulfilled. Understanding how these role responsibilities take place can help managers fulfill their job duties more completely.

The original version of this exercise was developed by Cheryl L. Tromley and presented at the Eastern Academy of Management, Portland, ME, 1989. This version was revised by Lisa A. Mainiero.

This exercise has that purpose. According to Mintzberg (1971), the role descriptions are defined as follows:

Interpersonal Roles

1. *Figurehead:* Acting as a representative of the organization by performing symbolic duties, such as presiding at ceremonial events and receiving visitors

2. *Leader:* Interacting with subordinates, including but not limited to motivating, directing, guiding, staffing, helping, encouraging, evaluating others

3. *Liaison:* Establishing and maintaining a network of contacts and relationships outside and inside the organization.

Informational Roles

1. *Nerve Center:* Collecting information from formal and informal channels both inside and outside the organization

2. *Disseminator:* Integrating information and transmitting it to subordinates

3. *Spokesperson:* Integrating information and transmitting it to outsiders.

Decisional Roles

1. *Entrepreneur:* Seeking, initiating, and designing innovative improvement projects

2. *Disturbance Handler:* Making short-term adjustments and long-term structural changes to maintain the equilibrium of the organization

3. *Resource Allocator:* Controlling allocation of own and subordinates' time, as well as authorizing all significant resource decisions

4. *Negotiator:* Negotiating with suppliers, banks, customers, clients, and the government in the external environment.

In this exercise, you will have the opportunity to analyze these roles as you portray them in your job. Alternatively, if you are not currently employed as a manager, you will have the opportunity to interview someone who is, to complete the exercise.

INSTRUCTIONS

1. Review the article by Mintzberg, "Managerial Work: Analysis by Observation," and role descriptions as listed in the Introduction.

2. Option 1. *If currently employed as a manager:* Answer the questions that follow in terms of your current job. Follow the *Role Decision Tree* and *Role Analysis Forms* as instructed. Complete the *Action Plan* that follows.

3. Option 2. *If not currently employed as a manager:* Interview someone who is currently employed as a manager. You may interview a manager at a large company or a small business concern, but make certain that this person supervises others as a component of his or her job. Use the questions that follow as your interview questions. Define the roles for your interview participant prior to the interview.

4. Report your findings to the class.

5. Participate in a class discussion.

Option 1

Role Decision Tree

Directions: For each role (i.e., Figurehead, Leader, Liaison, Nerve Center, Disseminator, Spokesperson, Entrepreneur, Disturbance Handler, Resource Allocator, Negotiator) follow the *Role Decision Tree,* answering the questions as you go, until you reach a terminal statement.

If you reach a *Maintain* statement on the decision tree, write *maintain* under the *DESIRED ACTION* column of the *Action Plan.* If you reach a terminal statement other than *Maintain,* fill out a *Role Analysis Form.*

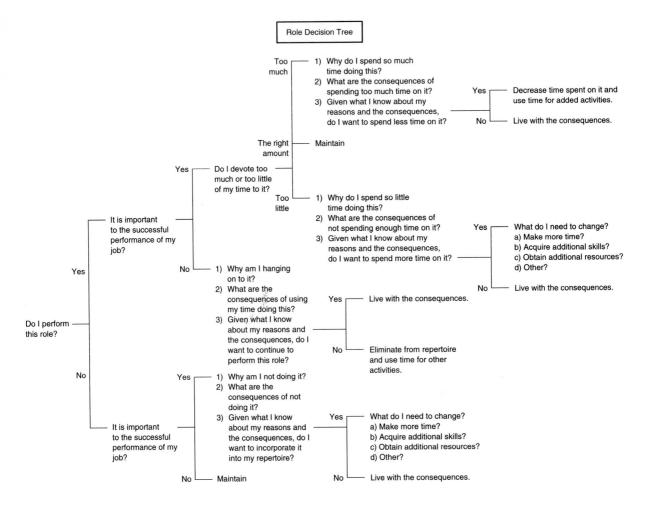

Role Analysis Form

Directions: Complete a *Role Analysis Form* for every role for which you do not reach a *Maintain* terminal statement on the *Role Decision Tree*. On this form you will be asked

1. Why you spend too little, too much, or no time on this role. Some possible reasons include habit, skills, time.

2. What the consequences are. Some possible consequences include other more important activities for which you do not have time, less leisure time, negative impact on career advancement, negative impact on employees.

3. Whether, given your reasons and the consequences you have identified, you want to make a change.

4. What the desired action is: increase, decrease, add, eliminate, none (if you have decided not to make a change).

5. If you decide not to make a change, why not? At this point you will know the consequences of your decision and the trade-offs you are making.

6. If you decide to make a change, what steps will you take? The steps may include improve skills, delegate authority, take time from other activities, get additional resources. Your analysis of why you are spending too little, too much, or no time on this role may help you answer this question. After you decide what you must do to make the change, you may decide that it is not worth the effort. If this happens, return to Step 4.

See Role Analysis Form that follows.

Action Plan

Directions: Transfer your *DESIRED ACTION* from the *Role Analysis Form* to the *Action Plan*. If your *DESIRED ACTION* is *increase, decrease, add,* or *eliminate,* review Step 6 of the *Role Analysis Form*. Determine what specific actions you will have to take. For example, you may think you need to improve your interpersonal skills in order to increase the amount of time you spend on leadership. You should determine exactly how you plan to improve these skills. Do you want to attend a training program? If so, which one? If you are not sure, how are you going to find out? Will you have to obtain additional resources to fulfill this objective? Which ones? Time? Money? How do you plan to obtain these needed resources? It is important that you be specific. Enter these actions under *SPECIFIC BEHAVIORS* on the *Action Plan*. Decide how long you expect each of these actions to take and commit yourself to a *TIME FRAME*. Enter this on the *Action Plan*. Decide how you plan to *MONITOR* your progress. That is, how will you know whether you are making progress toward your *DESIRED ACTION?* Enter this on the *Action Plan*. Look at the roles that you want to change. Which change is the most important for the successful performance of your job? Enter a 1 in the *PRIORITY* column of the *Action Plan*. Enter a 2 for the change that you feel is next in importance, and so on for all of the changes.

The completed plan will give you an overview of

1. What is currently working for you

2. What you want to change

3. Exactly how and when you plan to make these changes

4. How you plan to monitor these changes

5. Where you can most productively concentrate your energy

6. Where you will be gaining and losing time

Role Analysis Form

ROLE: _____

1. Why am I spending too much, too little, or no time on this role?

2. What are the consequences?

3. Make change? (yes or no)   4. Desired action:

5. If no, why not?

6. If yes, what do I have to do to make the change happen?

Action Plan

Role	Desired Action	Specific Behaviors	Time Frame	Monitor	Priority
Figurehead					
Leader					
Liaison					
Nerve Center					
Disseminator					
Spokesperson					
Entrepreneur					
Disturbance Handler					
Resource Allocator					
Negotiator					

Option 2

Managerial Role Interview Questions

(Note: If you are interviewing a manager, please read the role descriptions to him or her prior to the interview. You may want to provide a written list of the role descriptions to facilitate your discussion.)

1. Which roles do you spend the most time fulfilling in the course of doing your job? The least time?

2. Which roles are most important to the successful performance of your job? The least important?

3. Are you focusing your energy on the roles that are most important to the successful performance of your job?

4. On which roles are you spending too much time? Too little time?

5. What are the consequences of spending too much or too little time on the roles you have identified?

6. Which roles would your boss say are the most important to the successful performance of your job?

7. Do you and your boss agree or disagree? Why?

8. What steps will you have to take to enable you to spend time on the roles most critical to the performance of your job?

DISCUSSION QUESTIONS

1. To what extent do you agree with Mintzberg's (1971) depictions of managerial roles? Do they accurately portray what goes on in your job on a daily or weekly basis?

2. How does the proportion of time spent on particular roles vary by level in the organization? In other words, do upper-level managers spend more time in certain roles than do first-line supervisors?

3. How does the proportion of time spent on particular roles vary by function in the organization? In other words, do staff managers spend more time in certain roles than do line supervisors?

4. If you and your boss disagree regarding the proportion of time spent in certain roles, how should that disagreement be resolved?

REFERENCE

H. Mintzberg. "Managerial Work: Analysis from Observation." *Management Science,* 1971, Vol. 18, 97–110.

Exercise: Understanding Your Philosophy of Management

PURPOSE

The purpose of this exercise is to help you understand your philosophy of management. By the time you finish this exercise, you will

1. Identify your basic assumptions about subordinates

2. Learn how strongly you hold these assumptions

3. Develop a basis for understanding the consequences of your assumptions

INTRODUCTION

Many people have a story to tell about a job in which they were productive and satisfied. Equally often, people have a story about a job in which they were unproductive and dissatisfied. While many factors may have contributed to these experiences, a common thread is usually the treatment these individuals received from their

---

This exercise was developed by Cheryl L. Tromley. The exercise is based on the ideas presented in D. M. McGregor, "The Human Side of Enterprise," *Management Review,* 1957, November, 22–28, 88–92.

bosses. If you ever had a boss who caused you to feel dissatisfied with your job, you probably swore that when you achieved a position of authority you would treat your subordinates differently. Unfortunately, events do not always unfold the way we plan.

Managers vary widely in their attitudes and behaviors toward subordinates. These attitudes and behaviors are based on the assumptions that managers hold about people in general, employees of a company in particular, and the role of management. These assumptions, in turn, form the basis of a philosophy of management that can affect subordinates' satisfaction and productivity.

Managers' assumptions about people arise from a complex mix of personality and experience. They shape the attitudes toward subordinates that we bring to our first job. During the course of our experiences at work, our assumptions and attitudes are modified by our interactions with subordinates, superiors, and peers. These interactions all occur in the context of an organizational culture with norms about how we should treat subordinates.

This process takes place continually over our working lives. It is so subtle that we are often unaware that it is occurring. The result is that we may find, to our dismay, that we sometimes treat our subordinates in precisely the way we had sworn not to do. Why? Most of us are relatively unaware of our assumptions about subordinates and how these assumptions may have changed. Therefore, understanding your assumptions and attitudes can be the first step in becoming the manager that you want to be.

INSTRUCTIONS

1. Read the directions and complete the Philosophy of Management Questionnaire.

2. Transfer your responses to the Scoring Key.

3. Find your score.

4. Read the descriptions provided and interpret your score.

5. Participate in a class discussion.

Philosophy of Management Questionnaire

Directions: Carefully read each of the following statements and decide how strongly you agree or disagree with each according to the scale provided. Indicate your response in the space provided beside each statement.

1	2	3	4	5	6	7
STRONGLY DISAGREE	DISAGREE	SLIGHTLY DISAGREE	NEITHER AGREE NOR DISAGREE	SLIGHTLY AGREE	AGREE	STRONGLY AGREE

_____ 1. Employees should be involved in setting their goals.

_____ 2. Employees need something beyond enough money and a secure job.

_____ 3. Most people resist change.

_____ 4. Managers should guide rather than control.

_____ 5. Most people do not like to work.

_____ 6. The average person is easily deceived.

_____ 7. Groups of employees spell trouble for the organization.

_____ 8. People enjoy having greater variety in their work.

_____ 9. Managers should try to achieve harmony in their departments at all costs.

_____ 10. The organization should provide employees with the opportunity to gain self-confidence and realize their potentials.

_____ 11. The average employee does not care about the organization's needs or goals.

_____ 12. People enjoy being creative.

_____ 13. Good wages, working conditions, fringe benefits, and steady employment are enough to satisfy most people.

_____ 14. The average employee dislikes responsibility.

_____ 15. People need to feel a sense of achievement and competence.

_____ 16. Employees can learn to direct their own activities.

_____ 17. The fewer tasks employees' jobs entail, the more productive they will be.

_____ 18. It is management's responsibility to develop an employee's capacity for responsibility.

_____ 19. Employees are basically children and should be treated that way.

_____ 20. Groups are a natural and positive outgrowth of human interaction.

_____ 21. Managers should set goals for employees.

_____ 22. Managers should closely supervise subordinates' behavior.

_____ 23. People naturally try to increase their knowledge.

_____ 24. Most employees do not work any harder than they have to.

_____ 25. Recognition and appreciation may make employees work harder than money.

_____ 26. Management philosophy, policy, and practice can influence the productivity of employees.

_____ 27. Employees are adults capable of self-direction and self-control.

_____ 28. Employees are happiest when they do not have to think about their jobs.

_____ 29. People are not naturally passive.

_____ 30. Groups tend to make people more resistant, antagonistic, and uncooperative.

_____ 31. People want to develop their talents and abilities to their fullest extent.

_____ 32. Employees need to directed and controlled.

_____ 33. Employees can be motivated to work in the best interest of the organization.

_____ 34. Managers should create opportunities for people to realize their full potential.

_____ 35. Most people have very little ambition.

_____ 36. A main responsibility of management is to get subordinates to accept direction.

_____ 37. Managers should strive to help employees become self-directed.

_____ 38. When employees are unproductive, it is because they are basically lazy.

_____ 39. Groups can often be more effective than individuals at performing organizational tasks.

_____ 40. Most employees want to be told what to do.

_____ 41. People will learn things only if they are forced to.

_____ 42. In general, employees care about how well they perform their jobs.

_____ 43. People need independence.

_____ 44. Employees are primarily motivated by money.

_____ 45. Managers should exercise tight control over their departments.

_____ 46. People enjoy assuming responsibility.

_____ 47. Managers should try to keep tight, cohesive groups of employees from forming.

_____ 48. Employees should have a voice in the decisions that affect them.

Scoring

Directions: Transfer each of your answers from the questionnaire to the scoring key below. The numbers on the scoring key correspond to the numbers next to each statement of the questionnaire. For example, if you answered 6 to statement 3, you would put a 6 in the first row of Column 2. When you have completed the scoring key, add up all your scores in Columns 1 and 2. Next, subtract your Column 2 total from your Column 1 total. Place an *X,* on the scale provided, corresponding to this score.

Column 1	*Column 2*
1. _____	3. _____
2. _____	5. _____
4. _____	6. _____
8. _____	7. _____
10. _____	9. _____
12. _____	11. _____
15. _____	13. _____
16. _____	14. _____
18. _____	17. _____
20. _____	19. _____
23. _____	21. _____
25. _____	22. _____
26. _____	24. _____
27. _____	28. _____
29. _____	30. _____
31. _____	32. _____
33. _____	35. _____
34. _____	36. _____
37. _____	38. _____
39. _____	40. _____
42. _____	41. _____
43. _____	44. _____
46. _____	45. _____
48. _____	47. _____

Column 1 total _____   Column 2 total _____

Column 1 total – Column 2 total = _____

144	124	104	84	64	44	24	0	−24	−44	−64	−84	−104	−124	−144

STRONG
THEORY Y

STRONG
THEORY X

INTERPRETATION

Directions: Read the following descriptions to get an indication of your management philosophy and how strongly you hold the assumptions associated with it. Read McGregor's article, "The Human Side of Enterprise," to learn more about your management philosophy and some of the consequences of the related assumptions.

❏ If your score falls between +144 and 0, your management philosophy is based on Theory Y assumptions. The closer you fall to 144, the more strongly you hold these assumptions and the fewer Theory X assumptions you hold. The closer your score is to 0, the more your management philosophy reflects a mix of Theory Y and Theory X assumptions.

❏ If your score falls between 0 and −144, your management philosophy is based on Theory X assumptions. The closer you fall to −144, the more strongly you hold these assumptions, and the fewer Theory Y assumptions you hold. The closer your score is to 0, the more your management philosophy reflects a mix of Theory X and Theory Y assumptions.

Theory Y

You believe that:

❏ Management should create conditions that enable and encourage employees to attain their own goals by working toward the goals of the organization.

❏ Employees are inherently ready to accept responsibility, do a good job, and work in the best interests of the company.

❏ It is management's responsibility to create the conditions that will allow employees to develop their fullest potential.

Theory X

You believe that:

❏ Management's only responsibility is to improve the company's "bottom line."

❏ The employees of an organization are tools to be used to meet this goal.

❏ People are basically unwilling to work in the best interests of the company, cannot handle responsibility, and must be tightly controlled, prodded, and punished to get their work done.

DISCUSSION QUESTIONS

1. What do the results of this questionnaire tell you about your philosophy of management?

2. What are some of the consequences of your assumptions? Have you seen any evidence of these consequences in your job?

3. Which philosophy of management characterizes your boss in his or her interactions with you as a subordinate? Which philosophy of management characterizes top management at your company? What impact has this had on you?

4. Is it likely, in your opinion, that people can learn to change their philosophy of management? Which changes would you like to make? Why?

REFERENCE

D. M. McGregor. "The Human Side of Enterprise." *Management Review,* November 1957, 22–28, 88–92.

Exercise: Forecasting the Future Organization

PURPOSE

The purpose of this exercise is to prepare you to work for the organization of the future. By the time you finish this exercise, you will

1. Identify the characteristics of future organizations

2. Assess the skills required to work for such an organization

3. Contemplate what it will be like to manage the organization of the future

INTRODUCTION

In his article, "The Coming of the Future Organization," Peter F. Drucker suggests that information-based systems will dominate future organizations. The premium placed on information will breed a new type of organizational structure. Fewer levels of management will be needed to accomplish work tasks. Traditional departments will soften their boundaries. Workers will discipline their own expertise. In fact, subject matter experts, rather than managers, will predominate.

These changes will require that the role of management within the context of the large organization be entirely rewritten. Drucker (1988) likens the new role of the manager to that of a conductor in charge of a symphony orchestra, a leader who coordinates the team and its subelements. The flatter structure of the organization of the future will more closely resemble businesses that predate the industrial revolution. The need for service staffs, and the middle management that supplies them, will shrink dramatically.

It is important, therefore, to begin to examine managerial work vis-à-vis such futuristic changes. What will the role of the manager be like in the year 2020? Would

This exercise was developed by Lisa A. Mainiero.

you prefer to work as a highly trained specialist, perhaps from home? Or would you still prefer to train for future management?

INSTRUCTIONS

1. Review Drucker's (1988) article, "The Coming of the New Organization."

2. Complete the questions that follow.

3. Join a small group as directed by your instructor. Report your comments to the members of your group.

4. Report your group's summary of the organization of the future.

5. Participate in a class discussion.

Forecasting the Future Organization

Part I

Directions: Assume it is the year 2020 and that you have been sent to the future. What will it be like to work for a future organization? How will companies have changed? On a sheet of paper, write out your descriptions of the following:

1. A typical day in the life of a specialist who works for a modern manufacturing company

2. A typical day in the life of a manager in that same company

Part II

Directions: In a small group, share your descriptions of the future. Identify the most compelling elements among the future projections developed by individual members. Using whatever creative skills that exist among your group members, visualize a team approach to the organization of the future. Have one group member write out your team's description. Be prepared to read your team's suggestion to the class at the conclusion of this exercise.

1. *Team Approach:* A typical day in the life of a specialist who works for a modern manufacturing company

2. *Team Approach:* A typical day in the life of a manager in that same company

Part III

(Optional. Complete only if directed to do so by your instructor.)

Directions: Form two groups. One group will demonstrate how work will be accomplished in a *circular* organization. The other group will demonstrate how work will be completed in a *diamond* organization.

1. Your mission is to improvise and demonstrate in front of the class how work will be accomplished using one of the organizational geometries that will be assigned to you by your instructor. Your instructor will assign you one of the two tasks listed below.

2. Once your task is assigned, plan out how you will organize your work. Appoint leader/manager/coordinators, assign knowledge specialists, and define how the work will be accomplished before you begin. Reorganize the room so that you can accomplish your work in the manner in which you think it should be done.

Keep in mind that the other group in class will observe how you conduct your work once your planning session is completed. Review the chart that details the characteristics of diamond and circular organizational geometries before you begin.

For Diamond-Shaped Geometries: The Design

Nolan and Pollack (1986), two information-system theorists, suggest that the organization of the future will more closely resemble a *networked diamond* than a pyramid. They theorize that the computer revolution has created an ease of communication and information sharing that will eventually break down traditional hierarchies. Strategic and tactical decisions will be made by a "leadership wedge" that crosses from the top down into the middle and lower levels of the organization. The middle levels of management will primarily be staffed with knowledge-based workers who will share information independently and interdependently on project assignments as needed.

In this organizational design, most workers will work independently from one another, perhaps even at home, assembling and organizing project information. As the need arises, workers will work interdependently, using modern technology, in a way that allows them to share necessary information across computers. As further needs arise, workers will hold meetings to discuss general direction, vision, and objectives for project assignments. Workers may also meet to evaluate their efforts and assess project quality before moving on to other assignments.

For Diamond-Shaped Geometries: The Task

You are employees of FutureDesign, a firm that packages containers for other firms' products. One of your firm's newest clients is a major household products manufacturer. The client organization would like you to develop new packaging for one of their toothpaste products. FutureDesign received the contract for this new design by offering to package the toothpaste product in a "breakthrough" type of package. It is the mission of your group to develop a new product design.

For Circular-Shaped Geometries: The Design

Ackoff (1989) suggests that a *circular* organization will operationalize organizational democracy and improve the quality of working life. The central idea in a circular organization is that every person is in a position of authority. In this design, each manager and supervisor is provided with a board. At a minimum, the board at every level of the organization except at the top includes the manager whose board it is, his or her immediate superior, and his or her immediate subordinates. For any manager who has more than two subordinates, the subordinates constitute a majority on the board. Any board has the right to add additional managers drawn from inside or outside the organization as needed.

It is the responsibility of the board to (1) engage in planning and policymaking activities, (2) integrate and aid decision making, and (3) evaluate the performance of the manager whose board it is and remove him or her from the position if necessary. Boards intersect with other boards, and membership is crossed across boards so that the organization appears to be a series of joined concentric circles rather than the traditional pyramid that fosters linear decision making.

For Circular-Shaped Geometries: The Task

You are employees of EnviroAds, an advertising firm that specializes in accentuating the environmental concerns in the advertising of its clients' products. One of your firm's newest clients is a carpet manufacturer that recently eliminated formaldehyde from its manufacturing process. The client organization would like you to develop an advertising campaign that highlights this fact. It is the mission of your group to develop a new advertising campaign.

Characteristics of Circular- and Diamond-Shaped Organizations

Circular[1]

Diamond[2]

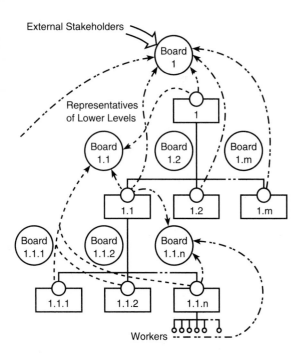

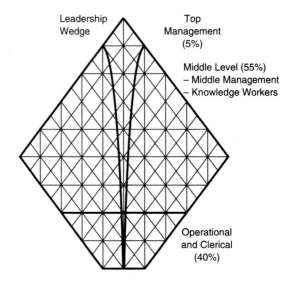

Elements of Circular Organizations

Cooperative task accomplishment

Egalitarian, democratic decision making

Each person is a point of authority

Opportunity to evaluate manager

Concentric boards interact to accomplish goal

Elements of Diamond Organizations

Independent then interactive task accomplishment

Meritocracy-oriented decision making

Each person is a knowledge-based specialist

Assessment of peer's independent work efforts

Each person a part of a larger network

1. *Source:* R. L. Ackoff. "The Circular Organization: An Update." *Academy of Management Executive,* 1989, *3*(1), p. 12.

2. *Source:* R. L. Nolan and A. J. Pollack. "Organization and Architecture, or Architecture and Organization." Unpublished journal manuscript, Nolan, Norton & Company Working Papers Series, 1986, p. 6.

DISCUSSION QUESTIONS

1. To what extent do you think these organizational designs model what the workplace will be like in the future? Will the organizational pyramid be replaced by these new designs?

2. Changes in organizational design often bring about unintended problems. What specific challenges for management do you see resulting from any of these new concepts and designs?

3. Many of the futuristic organizational concepts place a premium on peer relationships. What implications does this suggest for traditional authority relationships in the workplace?

REFERENCES

R. L. Ackoff. "The Circular Organization: An Update." *Academy of Management Executive,* 1989, *3*(1), 11–16.

P. F. Drucker. "The Coming of the New Organization." *Harvard Business Review,* Jan.–Feb. 1988, 45–53.

R. L. Nolan and A. J. Pollack. "Organization and Architecture, or Architecture and Organization." Unpublished journal manuscript, Nolan, Norton & Company Working Papers Series, 1986.

CHAPTER 2

Interpersonal Relations, Communication, and Conflict

INTRODUCTION

As mentioned in Chapter One, a manager's major responsibility is managing people. But sometimes there is a tendency to discount the importance of managing others. Many students naively believe that they can be effective managers if they simply perform the technical aspects of their jobs well. Although technical skills are important, no manager, no matter how technically competent, will be successful without knowing how to manage interpersonal relations. Developing and maintaining effective interpersonal relationships is a key ingredient for managerial success.

This requires that managers practice effective communication skills daily. Managers must know how to get the information they need from others and to make others understand them. Managers also must display a sensitivity toward the issues that may lead to hurt feelings among employees. Dissatisfied employees are nonproductive employees, and unresolved conflicts may hamper a manager's ability to create a departmental climate in which all employees can perform effectively.

When issues are not communicated effectively, conflict is likely to erupt. Decisions regarding work schedules, task assignments, resource allocation, and even the organization of office space all may potentially breed conflict. But many managers prefer to avoid or ignore conflict situations because they are uneasy with the resulting emotions. While this strategy may work in the short term, it can lead to worse problems in the long run. Learning how to handle conflict effectively in a way that provides a fair settlement for all parties is a vital skill that managers must practice daily to ensure their success.

READINGS

Because there is no single best way to manage interpersonal conflict, an analysis of the situation is usually the first step. In "Managing Conflict in Today's Organizations," author Gordon L. Lippitt explores how conflict can be more effectively managed. He discusses the pros and cons of conflict, typical conflict management styles, and how the management of agreement takes place. This article will help you feel less uncomfortable the next time you are confronted with a situation involving interpersonal conflict. You will understand the dynamics and the options available to you.

John J. Gabarro and John P. Kotter, in "Managing Your Boss," discuss how to improve what can be a particularly difficult relationship—the one with your boss. They argue that effective management not only involves managing subordinates but also superiors. They emphasize the notion that boss and subordinate are mutually dependent. To improve your relationship with your boss, you must understand your own and your boss's strengths, weaknesses, work styles, and needs. Once you have this information you can develop a mutually productive understanding that will help you to work together more effectively.

The final article in this chapter, "Face Your Problem Subordinates Now!," by John F. Veiga, discusses the challenges of managing subordinates. Veiga suggests that too often managers ignore their problem subordinates. Although it is tempting to manage only top performers, this strategy represents a vast waste of resources and talent. Veiga identifies four types of problem subordinates: *talented but abrasive, charming but unreliable, ideal, and plateaued but indifferent.* He directs the reader to become more sensitive to the interpersonal challenges involved in managing problem subordinates and offers ideas for coping with the particular conflicts, stresses, and strains that may arise from managing each particular situation.

Interpersonal relations is a vast area to attempt to cover in one chapter with three readings. Within our space limitations, we selected readings that we felt would provide you with a solid foundation on which to build your skills. The information in these articles will provide the groundwork for the exercises and case that follow.

EXERCISES AND CASES

The first exercise, "Developing Conflict-Resolution Skills," is designed to give you the opportunity to understand how you normally resolve conflict situations. The first step in improving your conflict-resolution skills is to understand how you typically approach conflict situations. The next step is to practice alternative conflict-resolution skills. This exercise is an opportunity for you to begin this process.

The "Bob Knowlton" case illustrates how *not* to manage the relationship with your boss. This case, in which poor communication and conflict resolution led to disaster, clearly illustrates how important the development of interpersonal skills is to managerial success. By the time you finish this case, you should be more aware of the importance of expending the effort to create and maintain successful interpersonal relations. Do not discount its importance; this can be the difference between success and failure as a manager.

The third exercise, "Dealing with Problem Subordinates," offers practice in resolving subordinate performance problems. In this exercise you will categorize and evaluate six vignettes that describe particular subordinate difficulties. You will be asked to create a development plan to improve the performance of each of these subordinates. It is a manager's prime responsibility to ensure the productivity of all employees. This exercise challenges your management skills to creatively manage all of your employees, even those whom you view as problem performers.

MEMO

The memo assignment for this chapter, *"Resolving Personal and Professional Conflicts"* (located at the back of this book), will enable you to apply what you have learned about interpersonal relations to your own situation. You will be asked to identify two problematic relationships in your life—one personal, the other professional—and to write a letter to one of these individuals involved describing your viewpoints. Part of your letter will include an action plan for improvement. By completing this plan, you may find a way to enhance your interpersonal relationships and to practice communication and conflict-resolution skills to increase your future success as a manager.

By the time you finish this chapter, you will have had an opportunity to practice two of the most vital interpersonal skills: communication and conflict resolution. You will also have an idea of your current strengths and weaknesses in this area so that you will know what you already do well and what you need to improve.

Managing Conflict in Today's Organizations

Gordon L. Lippitt

One of the key elements in modern management is the realization that conflict management and resolution has become an increasingly important competency of organizational managers.

The American Management Association recently sponsored a survey of managerial interests in conflict management. The respondents in the survey included 116 chief executive officers, 76 vice presidents and 66 middle managers. Their responses strongly suggest that conflict is a topic of growing importance:[1]

❒ They spend about 24 percent of their time dealing with conflict;

❒ Their conflict-management ability has become more important over the past ten years;

❒ They rate conflict management as a topic of equal or slightly higher importance than planning, communication, motivation and decision making;

❒ Their interests in the sources of conflict emphasize psychological factors, such as misunderstanding, communication failure, personality clashes and value differences;

From *Training and Development Journal*, July 1982, pp. 67–74. Reprinted with the permission of the Gordon Lippitt Foundation, Potomac, MD.

1. Thomas, K. W. & Schmidt, W. H. A survey of managerial interests with respect to conflict. *Academy of Management Journal*, 1976, *19*(2), 315–318.

❒ They feel the conflict level in their organization is about right—not too low or too high.

These executives and managers also revealed what they considered to be the principal causes of conflict within organizations: misunderstanding (communication failure), personality clashes, value and goal differences, substandard performance, differences over method, responsibility issues, lack of cooperation, authority issues, frustration and irritability, competition for limited resources and noncompliance with rules and policies.

Nevertheless corporate executives and managers devote 24 percent of their working time to conflict management. School and hospital administrators, mayors and city managers consider this quite low. In these and similar fields, conflict resolution commands nearly 49 percent of the attention of such officials. The causes of conflict usually are the same as those cited above, but in a different rank order.

It is obvious that one relevant management development activity should include helping managers *manage conflict*—the reality that conflict should sometimes be encouraged, tolerated and creatively channeled into effective problem-solving. Managers should know the causes of conflict, ways to diagnose the type of conflict and methods to cope with differences.

CONFLICT—AN EVERYDAY FARE

Fighting, hostility and controversy, all of which can be called conflict, are nearly everyday fare for individuals and groups, although they are not always evident. Too often, emotional effort and involvement goes largely unrewarded because people move in restrictive rather than constructive channels. Also, conflict releases energy at every level of human affairs—energy that can produce positive, constructive results. Two things should be recognized here: conflict is an absolutely predictable social phenomenon, and it should be channeled to useful purposes. Both of these facts lie at the heart of effective management. The goal of organizational leadership is not to eliminate conflict, but to use it—to turn the released energy to good advantage.

Conflict is almost always caused by unlike points of view. Because we do not learn exactly alike, and because we therefore see and value things differently, we vary in our beliefs. Because conflict, large or small, is inevitable, the extreme result at either end is an undesirably abrasive situation or dialogue that is creatively productive.

Most leaders look upon conflict as a negative experience. This is the key to the problem. We should take pains to see that conflict is a creative and positive occurrence; otherwise, we must recognize the destructive nature of conflict carried too far, too long. It:

❑ Diverts energy from the real task;

❑ Destroys morale;

❑ Polarizes individuals and groups;

❑ Deepens differences;

❑ Obstructs cooperative action;

❑ Produces irresponsible behavior;

❑ Creates suspicion and distrust;

❑ Decreases productivity.

But the list of positive and creative values inherent in conflict is equally long. Conflict:

❑ Opens up an issue in a confronting manner;

❑ Develops clarification of an issue;

❑ Improves problem-solving quality;

❑ Increases involvement;

❑ Provides more spontaneity in communication;

❑ Initiates growth;

❑ Strengthens a relationship when creatively resolved;

❑ Helps increase productivity.

Parties to conflict, for the most part, find themselves in one (or more) of four areas of disagreement: *facts* (the present situation or problem), *methods* (the best way to achieve our goals), *goals* (how we want things to be) and *values* (long-term goals and qualities we support). Generally, it is easiest to resolve differences over facts and most difficult to settle differences over values.

Conflict is a state of real difference between two or more persons where overt behavior is characterized by differing perceptions toward goals that, in turn, create tension and disagreement and tend to polarize those involved. Conflict is of increasing importance to management. Many reasons for this exist, including the growing scarcity of natural resources; the complexity and increasing interdependence of relationships between individuals, groups, organizations and nations; the values and life-style pluralism that characterize people of all ages, sexes and races; and the rising expectations and psychology of entitlement reflected in the motivation of employees, managers, owners, customers and all others who interact with the organization.[2]

CONFLICT RESOLUTION

In a study of the constructive use of conflict, in which 57 managers were interviewed, five principal methods of interpersonal conflict resolution were identified:

❑ *Withdrawal:* retreating from an actual or potential conflict situation;

❑ *Smoothing:* emphasizing areas of agreement and deemphasizing areas of difference over conflictual areas;

❑ *Compromising:* searching for solutions that bring some degree of satisfaction to the conflicting parties;

❑ *Forcing:* exerting one's viewpoint at the potential expense of another—often open competition and a win-lose situation;

❑ *Confrontation:* addressing a disagreement directly and in a problem-solving mode—the affected parties work through their disagreement.

It is important to depersonalize conflict by ensuring that the disputants do not judge each other and to focus the conflict on the basic issues by concentrating disagreement on facts. Progress in this direction, however slight, is usually self-continuing and tends to reduce wholesale indictment to retail packaging. This limits conflict to manageable areas that are more likely to be subject to negotiation, accommodation or compromise. When people are introduced to what they recognize as fact, they tend to become more objective. Unsupported opinion and implication generally cause an opposite effect. The leader, as a rule, should look at the issues coldly and at the people involved warmly.

Leadership in resolving organizational conflict creatively also requires empathy and equality, but not neutrality. The neutrality position is damaging because, by nature, it recognizes nothing. Empathy, on the other hand, means that leadership recognizes both the plight and the ideas of both sides in conflict, without necessarily agreeing totally with either. Equality means that neither of the conflicting parties will be made to feel inferior, for the alternative is greater jealousy and heightened competition.

Finally, adopting an attitude of one side winning and the other side losing is like pouring gasoline on a fire. On the other hand, the provisional try—honest fact-finding (all the facts), exhaustive exploration (both parties working together) and meaningful problem-solving (with a lot of "what if we try this . . . ?")—pries open the door to constructive creativity.

These are, of course, fundamental rules. The experienced leader knows that they do not always work as they should. It is necessary to contend with counterforces between those who passively refuse to engage in conflict and those who deliberately develop conflict as a battleground for hatreds and greeds, as well as

---

2. Albanese, R. *Managing: Toward accountability for performance* (rev.). Homewood, IL: Richard D. Irwin, Inc., 1978, pp. 421–422.

those who view conflict as a healthy challenge for betterment. Nevertheless, management of human conflict is an objective of organizational renewal.

A helpful way to comprehend two particular styles of conflict management—that of assertiveness and cooperativeness—is illustrated in Figure 1. Each style has both positive and negative factors:[3]

Competitor. A competing style is high on assertiveness and low on cooperativeness. This style is power-oriented and approaches conflict in terms of a win-lose strategy. On the negative side, a competitor may suppress, intimidate or coerce the other parties into conflict.

On the positive side, a competing style may be necessary when a quick, decisive action is required, or when important but unpopular courses of action may be taken. In addition, competing may be required when "you know you're right" on an issue. An avoiding style, however, can make sense when a conflict situation has relatively minor implications for managerial effectiveness, when there appears to be little chance for a person to "win" and when the benefits of confronting a conflict situation are overshadowed by the potential damage of confrontation.

3. Thomas, K. W. Conflict and conflict management. In M. D. Dunnette (Ed.), *The handbook of industrial and organizational psychology.* Chicago: Rand McNally College Publishing Company, 1976, p. 900.

Accommodator. The accommodating style is low in assertiveness and high in cooperativeness. A person who uses an accommodating style as the primary approach to conflict management may be showing too little concern for personal goals. Such a lack of concern may lead to lack of influence and recognition. It means that conflicts are resolved without each party to the conflict presenting his or her view in a forceful and meaningful way.

Like the other conflict management styles, however, the accommodating style has its uses. It is useful when a conflict issue is more important to the other person; when another style's disadvantages outweigh those of the accommodating style; when maintaining harmony is important; when it is advantageous to allow the other person to experience winning; and when an accommodating style on an issue may make the other person more receptive on another, more important issue.

Compromiser. To some people, the word "compromise" suggests weakness and lack of commitment to a position. A compromiser may be thought of as a person who puts expediency above principle or who seeks short-term solutions at the expense of long-term objectives. A compromising style results in each conflict participant sharing in some degree of winning and losing.

It is important, however, to recognize the potential value of compromise. Compromise is a common and practical approach to conflict management because it often fits the realities of organizational life. This "fit" occurs when a conflict is not important enough to either party to warrant the time and psychological investment in one of the more assertive modes of conflict management. In addition, compromise may be the only practical way of handling a

FIGURE 1

Conflict-management styles. [Adapted from Kenneth Thomas' "Conflict and Conflict Management" in M. Dunnette (ed.), The Handbook of Industrial and Organizational Psychology, *Chicago: Rand McNally College Publishing Company, 1976, p. 900.]*

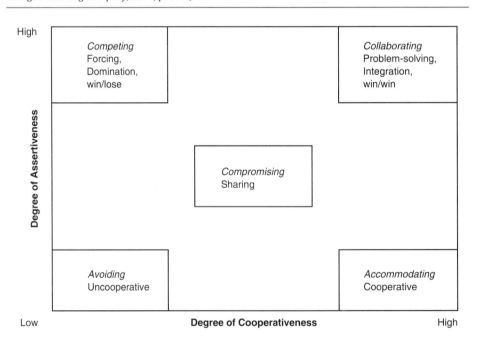

conflict situation in which two equally strong and persuasive parties attempt to work out a solution.

Avoider. At first glance, an avoiding style may appear to have no value as a mode of managing conflict. An avoiding style may reflect a failure to address important issues and a tendency to remain neutral when there is a need to take a position. An avoider may also exhibit detachment from conflict and a readiness to comply or conform, based on indifference.

Collaborator. Given the two dimensions of cooperativeness and assertiveness shown in Figure 1, the collaborating style is high on both dimensions. How is it possible to be both assertive about personal goals and cooperative about others' goals? It is possible only if the parties to a conflict recast it as a problem-solving situation. A problem-solving approach requires the following conditions:

❒ There is an attempt to depersonalize the conflict. That is, the parties to the conflict channel their energies to solving the problem rather than defeating each other.

❒ The goals, opinions, attitudes and feelings of all parties are accepted as legitimate concerns, and all parties play a constructive role.

❒ The parties realize that a conflict issue can make a constructive contribution to the quality of human relationships if the issue is worked through in a supportive and trusting climate in which opinions and differences are freely aired.

By developing an awareness of conflict elements and the conditions that foster them, you can maintain a low-conflict setting with your associates. Some of the factors in the work setting that predispose individuals to engage in unnecessary conflict are:[4]

❒ Poorly defined jobs, tasks, responsibilities and ranges of authority.

❒ Prior history of conflict between two or more people or groups.

❒ Interdepartmental relationships that frequently place members at cross purposes; traditional adversary relationships such as sales versus engineering, production versus quality assurance, nursing versus administration or district office versus regional headquarters.

❒ Unreasonable levels of pressure and pace in the organization.

❒ Severe economic downturn that jeopardizes the job security of organization members.

❒ Overly competitive climate fostered by top management and managers at various levels.

❒ Favoritism shown by managers to one or two employees.

❒ Punitive or threatening style of treatment by a unit manager, leading to escapist behavior, such as blaming others and shifting responsibility.

❒ Unclear or arbitrary standards for advancement and promotion in the organization; inconsistent patterns of rewarding accomplishment; overly secretive and competitive organizational politics.

❒ Great confusion or uncertainty about upcoming major changes or upheavals in the organization; inability of employees to define their future roles and interactions.

By anticipating it, an effective manager tries to lessen the chance of open conflict. It can be observed that the evolution of open conflict passes through five distinct stages:[5]

❒ *Anticipation.* A change is to be made and problems are forecast.

❒ Conscious but unexpressed *difference.* Rumors are out, but there is no confirmation. People do not like what they hear.

❒ *Discussion.* Information is presented. Questions are asked. Sides of the questions become open.

❒ Open *dispute.* The principals in the situation confront the sides of the argument. Differing opinions become clear.

❒ Open *conflict.* The conflict sharpens up, with forces mobilizing behind each side of the argument.

A good general approach to minimizing and resolving conflicts consists of the following three basic steps:[6]

❒ Establish and maintain a low-conflict, low-stress climate, with cooperation as the norm.

❒ Isolate each significant conflict to a single, specific task issue or family of issues. Don't accept personality clashes, but insist that the protagonists focus on a concrete issue and its rational elements.

❒ Help the protagonists apply a rational problem-solving model or procedure to the issue; go for a workable compromise.

One aspect of management differences is also the management of agreement. Frequently, an organization does not confront and openly deal with how people might feel about an issue, problem or situation.

MANAGEMENT OF AGREEMENT

The essence of conflict management through confrontation, negotiation and collaboration is to come to agreement. In many cases, however, a condition of agreement may already exist—unrecognized, unspoken, unrealized. It has been well hypothesized that members of groups and organizations—as individuals—may be in agreement as to the nature of a situation or problem, but that no one individual has seen fit to present his or her agreement:

> Organizations frequently take actions in contradiction to what they really want to do and therefore defeat the very purposes they are trying to achieve. This also deals with

4. Albrecht, K. *Stress and the manager.* Englewood Cliffs, NJ: Prentice-Hall, Inc., 1979, pp. 273–274.

5. Rumley, J. *The management of difference.* Washington, DC: Development Publications, 1977.

6. Albrecht, K. *Stress and the manager.* p. 274.

a major corollary of the paradox, which is that the inability to manage agreement is a major source of organization dysfunction.[7]

Frequently, people in organizations know how to cope with a problem, but they do not share this knowledge with those in positions of authority or leadership—evidence of an unwillingness to communicate openly. As a result, all too often, invalid or inaccurate information leads to action that is contrary to the best interest of the organization. Members of the organization experience frustration, anger, irritation, and dissatisfaction—whereupon the cycle repeats itself. Jerry Harvey identifies six reasons why this occurs:[8]

❒ *Action anxiety.* People tend to be anxious about acting in accordance with their beliefs.

❒ *Negative fantasies.* If we openly and positively correct a wrong, we may create new problems.

❒ *Real risk.* The reality of life whenever we confront others; it might affect job security and one's role.

❒ *Fear of separation.* If a person "opens up," it might threaten his or her acceptance in the group.

❒ *Fear of conflict* (real or artificial). Real conflict occurs when people have real differences. Artificial conflict, on the other hand, occurs when people agree on the actions they want to take and then do the opposite. The resulting anger, frustration and blaming behavior, generally termed "conflict" is not based on real differences. It stems from the protective reactions that occur when a decision that no one originally believed in or was committed to goes sour. As a paradox within a paradox, such conflict is symptomatic of agreement.

❒ *Group think.* A conforming pattern of group action that resists innovation, creativity and deviation.

All this brings us once again to the conclusion that the management of agreement is a matter of confrontation, search and coping. Confrontation has been called a process of interpersonal relating in which the behavior, the presence or the mere existence of one person makes a difference in the behavior of another because they openly "face up" to the situation in which they are involved.

To be productive, this process relies on all the individuals involved communicating honestly and with integrity; but even so it generally tends to be inversely related to the intensity of domination which the involved individuals bring to bear. The highest levels of confrontation are found in human interaction in which conflict, threat and domination—and hence the psychological necessity for defense—are negligible. Conflict, of course, is a kind of interacting, and little interacting takes place that is totally void of conflict, domination or attempts to influence. "Direct confrontation of relevant situations in an organization is essential. If we do not confront one another we keep the trouble within ourselves and we stay in trouble."[9]

All concerned must look for an understanding of the position taken by the other person or group. Each person must do this in his or her own way, communicating clearly and avoiding judgmental behavior to help establish a relationship of trust. If each person's autonomy and independence is to be preserved, there must be a minimal attempt by someone to control someone else. A problem-solving, goal-oriented, continuously experimental approach must be adopted, and there must be considerable flexibility with respect to the acceptance or rejection of the ideas of others.

Contrasted to the questions of attitude and procedure, coping brings us to the action in managing conflict and agreement. To cope requires an appropriate response to the situation, issue, problem or relationship that has been confronted. Appropriateness may be in the "eye of the beholder," but in the context of organization renewal, appropriate management of conflict or agreement is related to solving the problem in such a way that the person involved learns from the process; the human subsystems are strengthened by the coping; the organization is aided in its growth; and in some minor or major way, the resolution or solution contributes to the environmental forces affecting the organization.

The importance of managing conflict and agreement has been presented not because they are negative forces, but rather because they are positive aspects of human system renewal:

> Diversity of orientation and differences in point of view—"fruitful friction"—are essential if one seeks creative and effective organizations. Differences, of course, can result in irreconcilable, costly conflict unless the interaction-influence network and the problem-solving processes or organizations channel the differences to productive and not destructive ends. There is need to develop more sophisticated social institutions and organizations that have the capacity to deal constructively with the conflicts caused by change or by diversity.[10]

If the conflict situation is in the healthy zone, skills and techniques for successful management can be learned and applied effectively. If the conflict situation is in the unhealthy zone, a different set of analytic skills and insights is needed. This is more complex and often a longer process. It is important to know the unhealthy conflict can be managed as successfully as healthy conflict if there is clear understanding of its nature and the factors underlying it.

The management of conflict has assumed greater importance among managers. It should be an essential part of the management development process. Human resource development planners should initiate skill training opportunities for supervisors, managers and technical specialists in effective conflict resolution to allow for more effective problem-solving and planning.

7. Harvey, J. B. The abilene paradox: The management of agreement. *Organizational Dynamics,* 1974, *3*(1), 66.

8. *Ibid.,* p. 75.

9. Davis, S. A. An organic problem-solving method of organizational change. *Journal of Applied Behavioral Science,* 1967, *3*(1), 13.

10. Likert, R. & Likert, J. G. *New ways of managing conflict.* New York: McGraw-Hill, 1976, p. 23.

Managing Your Boss

John J. Gabarro

John P. Kotter

To many the phrase *managing your boss* may sound unusual or suspicious. Because of the traditional top-down emphasis in organizations, it is not obvious why you need to manage relationships upward—unless, of course, you would do so for personal or political reasons. But in using the expression *managing your boss,* we are not referring to political maneuvering or apple polishing. Rather, we are using the term to mean the process of consciously working with your superior to obtain the best possible results for you, your boss, and the company.

Recent studies suggest that effective managers take time and effort to manage not only relationships with their subordinates but also those with their bosses.[1] These studies show as well that this aspect of management, essential though it is to survival and advancement, is sometimes ignored by otherwise talented and aggressive managers. Indeed, some managers who actively and effectively supervise subordinates, products, markets, and technologies, nevertheless assume an almost passive reactive stance vis-à-vis their bosses. Such a stance practically always hurts these managers and their companies.

If you doubt the importance of managing your relationship with your boss or how difficult it is to do so effectively, consider for a moment the following sad but telling story:

Frank Gibbons was an acknowledged manufacturing genius in his industry and, by any profitability standard, a very effective executive. In 1973, his strengths propelled him into the position of vice president of manufacturing for the second largest and most profitable company in its industry. Gibbons was not, however, a good manager of people. He knew this, as did others in his company and his industry. Recognizing this weakness, the president made sure that those who reported to Gibbons were good at working with people and could compensate for his limitations. The arrangement worked well.

In 1975, Philip Bonnevie was promoted into a position reporting to Gibbons. In keeping with the previous pattern, the president selected Bonnevie because he had an excellent track record and a reputation for being good with people. In making that selection, however, the president neglected to notice that, in his rapid rise through the organization, Bonnevie himself had never reported to anyone who was poor at managing subordinates. Bonnevie had always had good-to-excellent bosses. He had never been forced to manage a relationship with a difficult boss. In retrospect, Bonnevie

1. See, for example, John J. Gabarro, "Socialization at the Top: How CEOs and Their Subordinates Develop Interpersonal Contracts," *Organizational Dynamics,* Winter 1979; and John P. Kotter, *Power in Management,* AMACOM, 1979.

admits he had never thought that managing his boss was a part of his job.

Fourteen months after he started working for Gibbons, Bonnevie was fired. During that same quarter, the company reported a net loss for the first time in seven years. Many of those who were close to these events say that they don't really understand what happened. This much is known, however: while the company was bringing out a major new product—a process that required its sales, engineering, and manufacturing groups to coordinate their decisions very carefully—a whole series of misunderstandings and bad feelings developed between Gibbons and Bonnevie.

For example, Bonnevie claims Gibbons was aware of and had accepted Bonnevie's decision to use a new type of machinery to make the new product; Gibbons swears he did not. Furthermore, Gibbons claims he made it clear to Bonnevie that introduction of the product was too important to the company in the short run to take any major risks.

As a result of such misunderstandings, planning went awry: a new manufacturing plant was built that could not produce the new product designed by engineering, in the volume desired by sales, at a cost agreed on by the executive committee. Gibbons blamed Bonnevie for the mistake. Bonnevie blamed Gibbons.

Of course, one could argue that the problem here was caused by Gibbons' inability to manage his subordinates. But one can make just as strong a case that the problem was related to Bonnevie's inability to manage his boss. Remember, Gibbons was not having difficulty with any other subordinates. Moreover, given the personal price paid by Bonnevie (being fired and having his reputation within the industry severely tarnished), there was little consolation in saying the problem was that Gibbons was poor at managing subordinates. Everyone already knew that.

We believe that the situation could have turned out differently had Bonnevie been more adept at understanding Gibbons and at managing his relationship with him. In this case, an inability to manage upward was unusually costly. The company lost $2 to $5 million, and Bonnevie's career was, at least temporarily, disrupted. Many less costly cases like this probably occur regularly in all major corporations, and the cumulative effect can be very destructive.

MISREADING THE BOSS-SUBORDINATE RELATIONSHIP

People often dismiss stories like the one we just related as being merely cases of personality conflict. Because two people can on occasion be psychologically or temperamentally incapable of working together, this can be an apt description. But more often, we have found, a personality conflict is only a part of the problem—sometimes a very small part.

Bonnevie did not just have a different personality from Gibbons; he also made or had unrealistic assumptions and expectations about the very nature of boss-subordinate relationships. Specifically, he did not recognize that his relationship to Gibbons involved *mutual dependence* between two *fallible* human beings. Failing to recognize this, a manager typically either avoids trying to manage his or her relationship with a boss or manages it ineffectively.

Some people behave as if their bosses were not very dependent on them. They fail to see how much the boss needs their help and cooperation to do his or her job effectively. These people refuse to acknowledge that the boss can be severely hurt by their actions and needs cooperation, dependability, and honesty from them.

Some see themselves as not very dependent on their bosses. They gloss over how much help and information they need from the boss in order to perform their own jobs well. This superficial view is particularly damaging when a manager's job and decisions affect other parts of the organization, as was the case in Bonnevie's situation. A manager's immediate boss can play a critical role in linking the manager to the rest of the organization, in making sure the manager's priorities are consistent with organizational needs, and in securing the resources the manager needs to perform well. Yet some managers need to see themselves as practically self-sufficient, as not needing the critical information and resources a boss can supply.

Many managers, like Bonnevie, assume that the boss will magically know what information or help their subordinates need and provide it to them. Certainly, some bosses do an excellent job of caring for their subordinates in this way, but for a manager to expect that from all bosses is dangerously unrealistic. A more reasonable expectation for managers to have is that modest help will be forthcoming. After all, bosses are only human. Most really effective managers accept this fact and assume primary responsibility for their own careers and development. They make a point of seeking the information and help they need to do a job instead of waiting for their bosses to provide it.

In light of the foregoing, it seems to us that managing a situation of mutual dependence among fallible human beings requires the following:

❐ That you have a good understanding of the other person and yourself, especially regarding strengths, weaknesses, work styles, and needs.

❐ That you use this information to develop and manage a healthy working relationship—one which is compatible with both persons' work styles and assets, is characterized by mutual expectations, and meets the most critical needs of the other person. And that is essentially what we have found highly effective managers doing.

UNDERSTANDING THE BOSS AND YOURSELF

Managing your boss requires that you gain an understanding of both the boss and his context as well as your own situation and needs. All managers do this to some degree, but many are not thorough enough.

The Boss's World

At a minimum, you need to appreciate your boss's goals and pressures, his or her strengths and weaknesses. What are your boss's organizational and personal objectives, and what are the pressures on him, especially those from his boss and others at his level? What are your boss's long suits and blind spots? What is his or her preferred style of working? Does he or she like to get information through memos, formal meetings, or phone calls? Does your boss thrive on conflict or try to minimize it?

Without this information, a manager is flying blind when dealing with his boss, and unnecessary conflicts, misunderstandings, and problems are inevitable.

Goals & Pressures. In one situation we studied, a top-notch marketing manager with a superior performance record was hired into a company as a vice president "to straighten out the marketing and sales problems." The company, which was having financial difficulties, had been recently acquired by a larger corporation. The president was eager to turn it around and gave the new marketing vice president free rein—at least initially. Based on his previous experience, the new vice president correctly diagnosed that greater market share was needed and that strong product management was required to bring that about. As a result, he made a number of pricing decisions aimed at increasing high-volume business.

When margins declined and the financial situation did not improve, however, the president increased pressure on the new vice president. Believing that the situation would eventually correct itself as the company gained back market share, the vice president resisted the pressure.

When by the second quarter margins and profits had still failed to improve, the president took direct control over all pricing decisions and put all items on a set level of margin, regardless of volume. The new vice president began to find himself shut out by the president, and their relationship deteriorated. In fact, the vice president found the president's behavior bizarre. Unfortunately, the president's new pricing scheme also failed to increase margins, and by the fourth quarter both the president and the vice president were fired.

What the new vice president had not known until it was too late was that improving marketing and sales had been only *one* of the president's goals. His more immediate goal had been to make the company more profitable—quickly.

Nor had the new vice president known that his boss was invested in this short-term priority for personal as well as business reasons. The president had been a strong advocate of the acquisition within the parent company, and his personal credibility was at stake.

The vice president made three basic errors. He took information supplied to him at face value, he made assumptions in areas where he had no information, and—most damaging—he never actively tried to clarify what his boss's objectives were. As a result, he ended up taking actions that were actually at odds with the president's priorities and objectives.

Managers who work effectively with their bosses do not behave this way. They seek out information about the boss's goals and problems and pressures. They are alert for opportunities to question the boss and others around him to test their assumptions. They pay attention to clues in the boss's behavior. Although it is imperative they do this when they begin working with a new boss, effective managers also do this on an ongoing basis because they recognize that priorities and concerns change.

Strengths, Weaknesses & Work Styles. Being sensitive to a boss's work style can be crucial, especially when the boss is new. For example, a new president who was organized and formal in his approach replaced a man who was informal and intuitive. The new president worked best when he had written reports. He also preferred formal meetings with set agendas.

One of his division managers realized this need and worked with the new president to identify the kinds and frequency of information and reports the president wanted. This manager also made a point of sending background information and brief agendas for their discussions. He found that with this type of preparation their meetings were very useful. Moreover, he found that with adequate preparation his new boss was even more effective at brainstorming problems than his more informal and intuitive predecessor had been.

In contrast, another division manager never fully understood how the new boss's work style differed from that of his predecessor. To the degree that he did sense it, he experienced it as too much control. As a result, he seldom sent the new president the background information he needed, and the president never felt fully prepared for meetings with the manager. In fact, the president spent much of his time when they met trying to get information that he felt he should have had before his arrival. The boss experienced these feelings as frustrating and inefficient, and the subordinate often found himself thrown off guard by the questions that the president asked. Ultimately, this division manager resigned.

The difference between the two division managers just described was not so much one of ability or even adaptability. Rather, the difference was that one of the men was more sensitive to his boss's work style than the other and to the implications of his boss's needs.

You and Your Needs

The boss is only one-half of the relationship. You are the other half, as well as the part over which you have more direct control. Developing an effective working relationship requires, then, that you know your own needs, strengths and weaknesses, and personal style.

Your Own Style. You are not going to change either your basic personality structure or that of your boss. But you can become aware of what it is about you that impedes or facilitates working with your boss and, with that awareness, take actions that make the relationship more effective.

For example, in one case we observed, a manager and his superior ran into problems whenever they disagreed. The boss's typical response was to harden his position and overstate it. The manager's reaction was then to raise the ante and intensify the forcefulness of his argument. In doing this, he channeled his anger into sharpening his attacks on the logical fallacies in his boss's assumptions. His boss in turn would become even more adamant about holding his original position. Predictably, this escalating cycle resulted in the subordinate avoiding whenever possible any topic of potential conflict with his boss.

In discussing this problem with his peers, the manager discovered that his reaction to the boss was typical of how he generally reacted to counterarguments—but with a difference. His response would overwhelm his peers, but not his boss. Because his attempts to discuss this problem with his boss were unsuccessful, he concluded that the only way to change the situation was to deal with his own instinctive reactions. Whenever the two reached an impasse, he would check his own impatience and suggest that they break up and think about it before getting together again. Usually when they renewed their discussion, they had digested their differences and were more able to work them through.

Gaining this level of self-awareness and acting on it are difficult but not impossible. For example, by reflecting over his past experiences, a young manager learned that he was not very good at dealing with difficult and emotional issues where people were involved. Because he disliked those issues and realized that his instinctive responses to them were seldom very good, he developed a habit of touching base with his boss whenever such a problem arose. Their discussions always surfaced ideas and approaches the manager had not considered. In many cases, they also identified specific actions the boss could take to help.

Dependence on Authority Figures. Although a superior-subordinate relationship is one of mutual dependence, it is also one in which the subordinate is typically more dependent on the boss than the other way around. This dependence inevitably results in the subordinate feeling a certain degree of frustration, sometimes anger, when his actions or options are constrained by his boss's decisions. This is a normal part of life and occurs in the best of relationships. The way in which a manager handles these frustrations largely depends on his or her predisposition toward dependence on authority figures.

Some people's instinctive reaction under these circumstances is to resent the boss's authority and to rebel against the boss's decisions. Sometimes a person will escalate a conflict beyond what is appropriate. Seeing the boss almost as an institutional enemy, this type of manager will often, without being conscious of it, fight with the boss just for the sake of fighting. His reactions to being constrained are usually strong and sometimes impulsive. He sees the boss as someone who, by virtue of his role, is a hindrance to progress, an obstacle to be circumvented or at best tolerated.

Psychologists call this pattern of reactions counterdependent behavior. Although a counterdependent person is difficult for most superiors to manage and usually has a history of strained relationships with superiors, this sort of manager is apt to have even more trouble with a boss who tends to be directive or authoritarian. When the manager acts on his or her negative feelings, often in subtle and nonverbal ways, the boss sometimes *does* become the enemy. Sensing the subordinate's latent hostility, the boss will lose trust in the subordinate or his judgment and behave less openly.

Paradoxically, a manager with this type of predisposition is often a good manager of his own people. He will often go out of his way to get support for them and will not hesitate to go to bat for them.

At the other extreme are managers who swallow their anger and behave in a very compliant fashion when the boss makes what they know to be a poor decision. These managers will agree with the boss even when a disagreement might be welcome or when the boss would easily alter his decision if given more information. Because they bear no relationship to the specific situation at hand, their responses are as much an overreaction as those of counterdependent managers. Instead of seeing the boss as an enemy, these people deny their anger—the other extreme—and tend to see the boss as if he or she were an all-wise parent who should know best, should take responsibility for their careers, train them in all they need to know, and protect them from overly ambitious peers.

Both counterdependence and overdependence lead managers to hold unrealistic views of what a boss is. Both views ignore that most bosses, like everyone else, are imperfect and fallible. They don't have unlimited time, encyclopedic knowledge, or extrasensory perception; nor are they evil enemies. They have their own pressures and concerns that are sometimes at odds with the wishes of the subordinate—and often for good reason.

Altering predispositions toward authority, especially at the extremes, is almost impossible without intensive psychotherapy (psychoanalytic theory and research suggest that such predispositions are deeply rooted in a person's personality and upbringing). However, an awareness of these extremes and the range between them can be very useful in understanding where your own predispositions fall and what the implications are for how you tend to behave in relation to your boss.

If you believe, on the one hand, that you have some tendencies toward counterdependence, you can understand and even predict what your reactions and overreactions are likely to be. If, on the other hand, you believe you have some tendencies toward overdependence, you might question the extent to which your overcompliance or inability to confront real differences may be making both you and your boss less effective.

DEVELOPING AND MANAGING THE RELATIONSHIP

With a clear understanding of both your boss and yourself, you can—usually—establish a way of working together that fits both of you, that is characterized by unambiguous mutual expectations, and that helps both of you to be more productive and effective. We have already outlined a few things such a relationship consists of, which are itemized in the *Exhibit,* and here are a few more.

Compatible Work Styles

Above all else, a good working relationship with a boss accommodates differences in work style. For example, in one situ-

EXHIBIT
Managing the Relationship with Your Boss

Make sure you understand your boss and his context, including:

His goals and objectives

The pressures on him

His strengths, weaknesses, blind spots

His preferred work style

Assess yourself and your needs, including:

Your own strengths and weaknesses

Your personal style

Your predisposition toward dependence on authority figures

Develop and maintain a relationship that:

Fits both your needs and styles

Is characterized by mutual expectations

Keeps your boss informed

Is based on dependability and honesty

Selectively uses your boss's time and resources

ation we studied, a manager (who had a relatively good relationship with his superior) realized that during meetings his boss would often become inattentive and sometimes brusque. The subordinate's own style tended to be discursive and exploratory. He would often digress from the topic at hand to deal with background factors, alternative approaches, and so forth. His boss, instead, preferred to discuss problems with a minimum of background detail and became impatient and distracted whenever his subordinate digressed from the immediate issue.

Recognizing this difference in style, the manager became terser and more direct during meetings with his boss. To help himself do this, before meetings with the boss he would develop brief agendas that he used as a guide. Whenever he felt that a digression was needed, he explained why. This small shift in his own style made these meetings more effective and far less frustrating for them both.

Subordinates can adjust their styles in response to their bosses' preferred method for receiving information. Peter Drucker divides bosses into "listeners" and "readers." Some bosses like to get information in report form so that they can read and study it. Others work better with information and reports presented in person so that they can ask questions. As Drucker points out, the implications are obvious. If your boss is a listener, you brief him in person, then follow it up with a memo. If your boss is a reader, you cover important items or proposals in a memo or report, *then* discuss them with him.

Other adjustments can be made according to a boss's decision-making style. Some bosses prefer to be involved in decisions and problems as they arise. These are high-involvement managers who like to keep their hands on the pulse of the operation. Usually their needs (and your own) are best satisfied if you touch base with them on an ad hoc basis. A boss who has a need to be involved will become involved one way or another, so there are advantages to including him at your initiative. Other bosses prefer to delegate—they don't want to be involved. They expect you to come to them with major problems and inform them of important changes.

Creating a compatible relationship also involves drawing on each other's strengths and making up for each other's weaknesses. Because he knew that his boss—the vice president of engineering—was not very good at monitoring his employees' problems, one manager we studied made a point of doing it himself. The stakes were high: the engineers and technicians were all union members, the company worked on a customer-contract basis, and the company had recently experienced a serious strike.

The manager worked closely with his boss, the scheduling department, and the personnel office to ensure that potential problems were avoided. He also developed an informal arrangement through which his boss would review with him any proposed changes in personnel or assignment policies before taking action. The boss valued his advice and credited his subordinate for improving both the performance of the division and the labor-management climate.

Mutual Expectations

The subordinate who passively assumes that he or she knows what the boss expects is in for trouble. Of course, some superiors will spell out their expectations very explicitly and in great detail. But most do not. And although many corporations have systems that provide a basis for communicating expectations (such as formal planning processes, career planning reviews, and performance appraisal reviews), these systems never work perfectly. Also, between these formal reviews expectations invariably change.

Ultimately, the burden falls on the subordinate to find out what the boss's expectations are. These expectations can be both broad (regarding, for example, what kinds of problems the boss wishes to be informed about and when) as well as very specific (regarding such things as when a particular project should be completed and what kinds of information the boss needs in the interim).

Getting a boss who tends to be vague or nonexplicit to express his expectations can be difficult. But effective managers find ways to get that information. Some will draft a detailed memo covering key aspects of their work and then send it to their bosses for approval. They then follow this up with a face-to-face discussion in which they go over each item in the memo. Their discussion often surfaces virtually all of the boss's relevant expectations.

Other effective managers will deal with an inexplicit boss by initiating an ongoing series of informal discussions about "good management" and "our objectives." Still others find useful information more indirectly through those who used to work for the boss and through the formal planning systems in which the boss makes commitments to his superior. Which approach you choose, of course, should depend on your understanding of your boss's style.

Developing a workable set of mutual expectations also requires that you communicate your own expectations to the boss, find out if they are realistic, and influence the boss to accept the ones that are important to you. Being able to influence the boss to value your expectations can be particularly important if the boss is an overachiever. Such a boss will often set unrealistically high standards that need to be brought into line with reality.

A Flow of Information

How much information a boss needs about what a subordinate is doing will vary significantly depending on the boss's style, the situation he is in, and the confidence he has in the subordinate. But it is not uncommon for a boss to need more information than the subordinate would naturally supply or for the subordinate to think the boss knows more than he really does. Effective managers recognize that they probably underestimate what the boss needs to know and make sure they find ways to keep him informed through a process that fits his style.

Managing the flow of information upward is particularly difficult if the boss does not like to hear about problems. Although many would deny it, bosses often give off signals that they want to hear only good news. They show great displeasure—usually non-verbally—when someone tells them about a problem. Ignoring individual achievement, they may even evaluate more favorably subordinates who do not bring problems to them.

Nevertheless—for the good of the organization, boss, and subordinate—a superior needs to hear about failures as well as successes. Some subordinates deal with a good-news-only boss by finding indirect ways to get the necessary information to him, such as a management information system in which there is no messenger to be killed. Others see to it that potential problems, whether in the form of good surprises or bad news, are communicated immediately.

Dependability and Honesty

Few things are more disabling to a boss than a subordinate on whom he cannot depend, whose work he cannot trust. Almost no one is intentionally undependable, but many managers are inadvertently so because of oversight or uncertainty about the boss's priorities. A commitment to an optimistic delivery date may please a superior in the short term but be a source of displeasure if not honored. It's difficult for a boss to rely on a subordinate who repeatedly slips deadlines. As one president put it (describing a subordinate): "When he's great, he's terrific, but I can't depend on him. I'd rather he be more consistent even if he delivered fewer peak successes—at least I could rely on him."

Nor are many managers intentionally dishonest with their bosses. But it is so easy to shade the truth a bit and play down concerns. Current concerns often become future surprise problems. It's almost impossible for bosses to work effectively if they cannot rely on a fairly accurate reading from their subordinates. Because it undermines credibility, dishonesty is perhaps the most troubling trait a subordinate can have. Without a basic level of trust in a subordinate's word, a boss feels he has to check all of a subordinate's decisions, which makes it difficult to delegate.

Good Use of Time and Resources

Your boss is probably as limited in his store of time, energy, and influence as you are. Every request you make of him uses up some of these resources. For this reason, common sense suggests drawing on these resources with some selectivity. This may sound obvious, but it is surprising how many managers use up their boss's time (and some of their own credibility) over relatively trivial issues.

In one instance, a vice president went to great lengths to get his boss to fire a meddlesome secretary in another department. His boss had to use considerable effort and influence to do it. Understandably, the head of the other department was not pleased. Later, when the vice president wanted to tackle other more important problems that required changes in the scheduling and control practices of the other department, he ran into trouble. He had used up many of his own as well as his boss's blue chips on the relatively trivial issue of getting the secretary fired, thereby making it difficult for him and his boss to meet more important goals.

WHOSE JOB IS IT?

No doubt, some subordinates will resent that on top of all their other duties, they also need to take time and energy to manage their relationships with their bosses. Such managers fail to realize the importance of this activity and how it can simplify their jobs by eliminating potentially severe problems. Effective managers recognize that this part of their work is legitimate. Seeing themselves as ultimately responsible for what they achieve in an organization, they know they need to establish and manage relationships with everyone on whom they are dependent, and that includes the boss.

Face Your Problem Subordinates Now!

John F. Veiga

Ask any manager the question, "Do you have problem subordinates?" and the reply is generally an emphatic "Yes!" or a more cynical "You *must* be kidding!" If there is one universal truth about managers, it is that all of them have problem subordinates. If there is a second truth, it is that the stories they have to tell about these subordinates often reflect a good deal of disparagement and despair.

Here are a few typical tales of woe:

> ". . . Talking to that man is like talking to a rock! I know he's very bright, some say an electronic genius, [but] he must have been brought up in a test tube. He never smiles and it's impossible to carry on a normal conversation with him. He intimidates the hell out of most people by just staring at them."
>
> "This woman is very charming and personable. She seems to have talent and yet more often than not, she disappoints me. I give her a major assignment and she comes up short. Quite often, I end up picking up the pieces. Surprisingly, she always seems to land on her feet . . . she generally has a plausible excuse for what she's done, or not done. . . . I'm never sure how much I can count on her."
>
> "He seems to be unplugged from the socket. I mean, really, he seems to be disconnected from the realities of his job. He tells me things that make no sense whatsoever and I really can't rely on him to complete a job of any importance. If he weren't so close to retirement age I might do something—maybe put a bomb under his chair?" (laughs)

On first reading, one feels that these subordinates have chronic defects and that their bosses would be much better off just getting rid of them than dealing with them. After all, who would want to put up with any one of them?

But are they really as unsalvageable as they are portrayed? Certainly, in the opinions of their exasperated bosses, they are. One thing is clear, however: Unless and until some corrective action is taken, the prognosis is not encouraging.

How can such individuals thrive in today's corporate world? How can they be tolerated, or even ignored, in light of the potential havoc they can and do wreak on the organization? Perhaps the answer is that they have become so pervasive, they are an accepted fact of life. As one CEO explained, "I just assume there are a certain percentage of subordinates who, regardless of the amount of human relations training we force on them, are difficult to get along with by nature." Or, as another executive mused, "Maybe it is because all of us have been problematic from time to time; therefore, we make allowances. After all, nobody is perfect." Although such arguments have a ring of truth, they tend to mask the real problem: Too many managers are unwilling to confront problem subordinates.

Who is the real victim here? Is it the boss, for having to live with such a difficult subordinate? Or is it the subordinate, who no doubt is doing something that causes problems but who may also suffer from his or her boss's reluctance to confront and try to correct such behavior?

In many cases, problem subordinates are as much a result of mismanagement (or failure to manage) as they are of personal shortcomings. Hence, both parties are victims *and* both are to blame. The tragedy is that because no action is taken—a strategy the vast majority of the executives I surveyed admitted having followed—matters get worse. Clearly, managers at all levels need to examine their role in creating problem subordinates and determine preventive measures to be taken. Senior managers who are derelict must take the lead.

NAME CALLING IS THE EASY PART

What was said about the subordinates described above are but a few printable examples of the "rogues' gallery" of problem subordinates uncovered in my research.[1] No attempt was made to cover the entire spectrum of problem subordinates at all levels in the organization; classifying all the possibilities would be a herculean task. The search was limited to those long-term cases that senior executives found exasperating to manage—where tough but seldom-made calls are involved. I omitted cases outside the manager's control, such as alcoholism or drug abuse, where outside help or referral to an employee assistance program is called for, and clear-cut cases of total incompetence or dishonesty, where termination is the only answer.

In gathering the survey data, I asked executives taking part in one of several seminars I conducted to write detailed case histories of problem subordinates who worked for them. During this process, many participants would look up, chuckle to themselves and ask, "You want us to describe only one? I can think of several,

---

1. The findings presented here are based on a formal survey of 150 executives from over 100 firms, who attended one of several Executive Development programs in which I was a faculty member, and on informal surveys of over 2,000 managers who have attended my "Working with Problem Subordinates" seminars over the past 10 years. These individuals were kind enough to share their frustrations and remedies with me. In addition, I did extensive in-depth, follow-up interviews with 15 executives. The participants in the formal survey averaged 49 years of age and held positions from vice president to CEO (86% were males, 14% females). The typical problem manager averaged 44 years of age; 64% were male, 36% were female. Both sexes were equally scathed by their bosses, except in the choice of adjectives used. Thus, gender per se played no unique role in the name calling.

Reprinted with permission from *The Academy of Management Executive,* 1988, Vol. 2 (2), pp. 145–152.

and I'm having trouble deciding which one to nominate." Virtually every executive had a story to tell and, in many cases, the story telling seemed to have a cathartic effect.

As these executives soon found out, describing a problem subordinates turned out to be very difficult. Name calling was the easy part: "He's an SOB," or "She's a game player." Going beyond the superficial and describing how these people actually behaved proved difficult but enlightening. In some cases, the executives were amazed at how little evidence they could muster. In others, the evidence often involved very subtle behavior; some easy to describe, some not. The initial descriptions were usually based on how the problem subordinates made their bosses feel—"She drives me nuts!"—and not in terms of behaviors that caused the feelings. This exercise illustrated that while problem subordinates are discussed and thought about frequently, such musing rarely produces useful information for providing effective feedback. And operating on pejoratives and half-truths only makes matters worse. In many cases, these executives found themselves in a classic perceptual trap. Using limited and selectively perceived information they focused on a single trait, to the exclusion of many positive attributes the problem subordinates might have had.

Not too surprisingly, when the executives attempted to reconcile their stories with what they reported at performance appraisal time, the gap was significant. One executive said:

> "We keep two sets of books. One is the public record, which is generally circumspect and vague, and the other [is] the private record, which contains how we really feel. And it is the latter one which we rarely share, except with confidantes, but which influences our thinking when we make decisions that affect the individual's career."

WHY ARE PROBLEM SUBORDINATES AVOIDED?

Most executives readily admitted that the problem subordinates they described were not as problematic or ineffective as their expletive-laced portraits had suggested. However, when the emotions generated by these individuals were tapped, it was very easy to overreact. At times, problem subordinates took on an almost surreal existence to their frustrated bosses. During a spare moment, freed of the daily stresses—perhaps during the evening commute or just before going to sleep—reflecting on the problem subordinate often produced a kind of autistic hostility, an emotion not entirely grounded in reality, but still painfully real. As one manager explained:

> "On the drive home, he would be on my mind . . . I would get so damned mad at him and myself for not saying anything that I would work myself into a rage. Sometimes it would take me over an hour to calm down. And then I'd come back to the all-too-familiar dilemma: Do I take some action or do I try to put it out of my mind for now?"

For these distraught bosses, their anger was, in effect, feeding upon *itself*—the subordinates need not have done anything at all. The angrier these bosses became about their own inability to confront the problem, the more they blamed their subordinates for "making" them feel that way.[2]

Although such feelings are common, they are often exaggerated by the intense anxiety a manager experiences when thinking about confronting a problem subordinate. Ideally, such feelings need to be transformed into constructive action. Unfortunately, however, they often are rationalized away, further exacerbating an already difficult situation. Thus, while anger often plays an integral role, such self-inflicted misery begs the question: Why do managers from the executive ranks down to first-line supervisors avoid confronting the source of their pain? Could it be that managers, especially top executives, just do not have the guts to talk to their people face to face?[3] Perhaps. However, upon closer examination, I found a variety of reasons for avoidance.

First of all, it is too simplistic to attribute "being chicken" as the primary reason for such avoidance behavior. Certainly, some bosses avoid confrontation because they are afraid that they will jeopardize a long-term friendship—the most common reason given—or they are afraid they might create an even worse relationship: "She's so defensive that if I confront her, she could just get worse or even turn on me." Others experience guilt:

> "Just after Jim's wife died we decided not to promote him as planned. I felt he needed some space to get his life in order. As I look back on it now, it was shortly after these events that Jim's attitude turned sour and I never—well, I never knew how to approach him after he blamed me. . . . I know I should have, but I hoped that time would straighten him out."

In almost all cases, bosses feel frustrated—"I have tried repeatedly to point out to her that she has to be more sensitive to other managers' feelings, but after a few weeks, she's right back into bulldozing everyone. . . . I don't see how I can change her personality"—or hopeless—"If you want legal backing, the person has to be more than a pain-in-the-neck to get fired in my shop, so what's the point of trying?" Sometimes bosses are insecure: "She knows more about running this place than I do!"—or are reluctant to "play God"—"I don't want to be the one to push him over the edge. This wouldn't be the first time someone has considered suicide or gone on a rampage after a poor performance review."[4]

Avoidance also results from a tendency on the part of managers to want overwhelming proof before taking action against a problem employee—a tendency often reinforced by personnel

---

2. The paradoxical behavior involved in autistic hostility is further explained in T. M. Newcomb's "Autistic Hostility and Social Reality," *Human Relations,* 1947, 1, 69–86.

3. This case was made the strongest in Walter Kiechel III's "No Words From On High," *Fortune,* January 6, 1986, 125–126.

4. The front-page story of the *New York Times* on August 21, 1986, "Oklahoma Letter Carrier Kills 14 and Then Himself," is a chilling reminder to all managers as to what could happen when poor performance is confronted. However, it should be noted that according to the newspaper account, this was a rare case involving an employee with a history of instability *and* a management that allegedly had engaged in verbal abuse of employees and other forms of harassment.

policies designed to avoid litigation and thus severely restrict managerial response. One manager from a major U.S. corporation confided in me the major reason he had not confronted a problem subordinate:

> "If I screw up in following to the letter corporate procedure, it's my butt on the line.... Personnel expects me to maintain detailed contemporaneous notes on all discussions I have with the employee and a carefully documented history of any infractions.... What I want to know is how the hell are you supposed to do that with a subordinate whose primary fault is being arrogant and insensitive?"

Thus, gathering detailed evidence is often perceived as so onerous that it rarely is done. In the absence of convincing evidence, and the desire to avoid a libelous confrontation, managers feel their hands are tied and therefore continue to give conflicting signals to problem subordinates. Quite often the feedback is inconsistent with how managers feel—sometimes it is a complete fabrication—but it is justified as reasonable given the lack of hard evidence. Having thus committed to a course of faulty and erroneous feedback, managers often believe there is no turning back and, in an effort to reduce their feelings of dissonance, they begin to justify a continued strategy of avoidance, thereby becoming trapped in a self-reinforcing pattern of behavior.

TYPES OF PROBLEM SUBORDINATES

In my examination of the case histories of problem subordinates, two recurring themes emerged. The first theme related to job performance; that is, whether or not the individual performed above or below the boss's expectation. The second related to interpersonal skills; that is, whether or not the individual worked effectively with others.[5] Combining these two themes resulted in the grid shown in Exhibit 1.

I also attempted to classify the hundreds of reported cases in the hope of identifying some common ground. Therefore, the most pervasive problem subordinates were classified into three types: the talented but abrasive (cited by 40% of the executives), the charming but unreliable (cited by 33%), and the plateaued but indifferent (cited by 20%). The fourth type on the grid, the ideal subordinate, represents the talent mix that managers desire—one who performs up to expectation and works effectively with others.

Talented but abrasive subordinates were generally described as very bright and gifted performers who were insensitive to others and lacked interpersonal skills. Most were perceived as "superstars" or "comers," and yet because they played solely to their strengths and were either unaware of or ignored their weaknesses, they were eventually labeled everything from "arrogant know-it-alls" and "pushy, unfeeling SOBs" to "smart asses." In some instances their behavior was excused: "She is always willing to take more responsibility" or justified: "We needed some asses kicked, and he was the man for the job." Some of them were similar to what Harry Levinson labeled the "abrasive personality,"[6] although the term "personality" often connotes to the layperson a permanent and therefore unalterable condition, which in these cases was often not so. Because abrasive subordinates were usually quite good at their jobs, they

---

5. These themes are similar to the "technical" and "human skills" discussed in Robert I. Katz's "Skills of an Effective Administrator," *Harvard Business Review,* September–October 1974, 90–102.

6. Harry Levinson. "The Abrasive Personality," *Harvard Business Review,* May–June 1978, 86–94.

EXHIBIT 1
How Managers Classify Subordinates

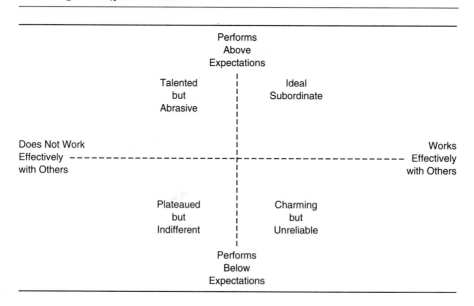

tended to become impatient with anyone who could not keep up. In some cases, this impatience showed itself in both verbal and non-verbal behaviors such as the caustic remark or the silent stare. These individuals were also perceived as having a talent for making politically insensitive remarks, which was often further exacerbated by their general unwillingness to concern themselves with issues of political sensitivity. Paradoxically, by trying to avoid encounters or tune out abrasive individuals, bosses and co-workers often unwittingly reinforced such unwanted behavior.

Charming but unreliable subordinates were in many ways the exact opposites of the abrasive individuals. The former were perceived as interpersonally skillful—what one executive called "personality plus"—but their job performance was problematic. Although they were not incompetent, they seemed to have a penchant for not delivering what they promised. Generally, they got the job done, but often it was because others, including their bosses, picked up the pieces or because they were able to talk their way out of doing all that was asked of them. Their bosses often marvelled at their uncanny ability to survive ("He always comes out smelling like a rose" or "She always lands on her feet"). Unfortunately, because the real deficit went unaddressed, their major strength eventually became a liability ("He's nothing but a game player"; "She's a real smoothie—all style and no substance").

Plateaued but indifferent subordinates did not merely combine the flaws of the other two problem types.[7] At some point in their pasts, many of these individuals would have been classified as either talented but abrasive or charming but unreliable—a time when they should have been dealt with. They were typically viewed as interpersonally ineffective because others refused to take them seriously. Traits that at one time would have produced pejoratives were now seen as harmless; e.g., "Her bark is worse than her bite." And while their performance was below expectations, it wasn't because they made promises they couldn't keep; rather, they were perceived as preretirement-aged plodders who either hadn't kept up, or couldn't be counted on because they were past their prime. Because of this "deadwood" status, then, they were generally given unimportant, make-work assignments or expected to do the bare minimum. Their indifference was as much the result of how they were treated as it was a chosen state of mind. Although their co-workers accepted that these individuals were just biding their time until retirement, they were far less forgiving when asked to carry part of what should have been the indifferent subordinate's work load—much to the boss's chagrin.

WHAT'S A BOSS TO DO?

In my consultations with hundreds of managers over the last 10 years, no easy answers have emerged. No one can guide you with complete confidence. One thing is clear, however: There are many alternatives a manager can exercise besides getting rid of a problem subordinate or just doing nothing. Just because certain individuals are talented does not mean you must tolerate abrasiveness or treat such individuals as special; neither is there any reason to avoid straight talk with the unreliable peformer, plausible excuses or not.

While the executives I surveyed spoke of many different company-sponsored programs to assist managers in dealing with problem subordinates, they all agreed that ultimate responsibility for initiating action lies squarely on the boss's shoulders. Following are some maxims for dealing with problem subordinates, offered by these executives, which all managers must heed.

Confrontation Must Be Direct

Contrary to the usual prescriptions for helping a person with a problem, most of the executives queried believed that candor promotes credibility and that problematic individuals cannot be handled with kid gloves or in a detached, counseling-like way. This is no time to offer a "positive sandwich"—praise followed by criticism, followed by praise again—because most subordinates are smart enough to perceive its contents as "baloney." The goal is to clarify the unwanted behaviors and the consequences. From the start, be prepared to take a tough stand; take the risk of owning up to your position first, then be prepared to be receptive.[8] Blaming and fault finding will not work. Both parties must accept the fact that each is responsible at some level for allowing the situation to continue. Remember that you are dealing with individuals who probably know they disappoint you. Thus, your attempt to unravel this illusion about their performance calls for straight talk. Clear-cut expectations must be established; make clear what is wrong and what you expect to see changed. Offering psychological safety and support to encourage a small but new step is essential. Help these individuals face the central question: Why do they behave as they do? Are they unsure of themselves? Are they having trouble managing their time or establishing priorities? Are there legitimate, personal reasons or priorities that have caused them to behave as they do? Or are they having trouble admitting that they are not well suited to their jobs? As the following two cases illustrate, a big first step is starting with some honest dialogue.

The Talented but Abrasive Engineer. "Jack was a very bright industrial engineer; he had a master's degree in engineering and had been promoted to senior engineer at the age of 25. The problem was that every time he worked on a project with manufacturing personnel, he caused trouble. He 'knew' more than the foremen he worked with and let them know it in many ways. Since his ideas were too good to waste, I had to run interference for him. I would present Jack's ideas to the foremen, drop a lot of his statistical analysis, and

---

7. There is a growing body of research on the nature of the plateaued performer. See especially Thomas P. Ference, James A. F. Stoner, and E. Kirby Warren's "Managing the Career Plateau," *Academy of Management Review,* 1977, 2(4), 602–612, and John F. Veiga's "Plateaued Versus Non-plateaued Managers: Career Patterns, Attitudes, and Path Potential," *Academy of Management Journal,* 1981, 24(3), 566–578.

8. For the manager interested in more information on how to coach managers effectively, see Ferdinand F. Fournies' *Coaching for Improved Work Performance,* New York: Van Nostrand Reinhold Company, Inc., 1978; Michael Beer's "Performance Appraisal," in Jay W. Lorsch (Ed.) *Handbook of Organizational Behavior,* Englewood Cliffs, NJ: Prentice-Hall, Inc., 1987; and Charles D. Orth, Harry E. Wilkinson, and Robert C. Benfari's "The Manager's Role as Coach and Mentor," *Organizational Dynamics,* Spring 1987, 66–74.

generally win their acceptance. Even though I valued Jack's contributions, I seemed to be running interference more frequently. When I called Jack in for his annual performance review, I decided it was time to confront him. At first he told me it wasn't his fault that there were so many 'stupid people' in manufacturing. I told him that's why we hire 'smart' engineers: to help those less fortunate. I also told him his ideas were no better than his ability to implement them; that was what he was paid for, and I would no longer smooth the way. Jack wanted to focus on what was wrong with the manufacturing personnel, but I reminded him that if I could get his ideas accepted it must have something to do with how he presented his ideas. He reluctantly agreed to meet the next day with me and one of the foremen he had trouble with to explore his problem. In that meeting, he found out that his attempts to impress the foreman with his statistical prowess were seen as an attempt to put the foreman down. The foreman told Jack, 'I don't need to take crap from a smart-mouthed college graduate. I know my job and I do it well. When you accept that fact, you might be able to see that I have just as much to contribute as you do. Sure, I don't understand the numbers, but I do know my people and how things work, and you don't.'

"When the meeting was over, Jack was angry. He didn't say anything but it was clear that he felt ganged up on. I thought I might lose him until about two weeks after the meeting when he asked to see me. When we met, he asked my advice on how he could present a new cost-cutting idea to the plant manager. While he never talked about the earlier meeting, it was clear that he had heard the message. As it turned out, this was one of several meetings he and I would have."

The Charming but Unreliable Plant Manager. "Tom is the manager of one of our five assembly plants and reports to me. He's been in the job for five years. I had managed the plant before him and supported his promotion. He had always struck me as a personable guy and I liked him . . . he was honest and loyal. After one year, Tom's plant became the poorest performer in my division. When I ran this plant it had regularly been number one or two out of the five.

"When I noticed this slippage in productivity, I began to question Tom. In the beginning he made promises to turn things around. He told me how some things he was working on showed real promise. He sold me. I believed. During this same time, he had also made a lot of friends in the company. Everyone liked him, everyone talked to him . . . he knew more about what was going on in the company than I did. But his promises never materialized. He was getting on my nerves. There were times when I would see him going to lunch with corporate staff people and I'd think, 'Why the hell isn't he back in his plant fixing things instead of spending his time B-S'ing with staff people?' On more than one occasion, my wife listened to my tale. But invariably I did nothing. Because we were good friends, some of the other plant managers believed I was protecting an old buddy.

"Initially, when my boss would question Tom's performance I would make excuses for him. Soon it became clear that my ability to manage Tom was being called into question. I began to cut his annual salary increments. He said he understood but still nothing. Finally, about a year ago I decided I had to take some action. I knew that if I got angry with him that that would do no good . . . but I felt the need to lay all my cards on the table. I can't tell how many dress rehearsals I went through in my mind. But when the time came I was surprisingly calm. I talked and he listened. I told him how I had grappled with the problem and had tried to avoid it; how I felt he and I had to begin addressing what was happening. You know what? He agreed. He told me how lousy he felt that he was unable to get his plant moving. How he hated to come to plant manager meetings, especially when performance issues were talked about. How he had begun to seriously doubt his career choice. We met again and talked some more. At that time I asked him to develop a plan that would improve his performance over the next two years. We agreed that this would be a good way to test his potential as a plant manager and a way to provide the evidence as to whether he should continue on his present career track or look for a reassignment more suited to his ability. One year has gone by since the plan was developed. So far the results are not too encouraging. I have serious doubts that he will improve. But two things are different now. First, we are talking openly about what's happening and secondly, I am convinced that he will be much more receptive to a job change. In the meantime, my boss is very pleased with my approach to managing Tom."

Unfortunately, attempts such as these are rare. Instead, managers often bungle the job by exerting subtle pressure on the subordinate to leave rather than directly confronting him or her. In many cases, the subtle pressure—such as irrelevant or undesirable assignments or excluding the subordinate from management seminars and retreats—eventually are escalated to the not so subtle—such as holding back on salary increases or other tangible perks. Unfortunately, these kinds of pressures drive a wedge between boss and subordinate. On the surface, relations between the two appear cordial, polite, even friendly, but beneath the surface, both are getting further mired in the deception. Clearly, action must be taken to break this self-reinforcing pattern of behavior. As we saw in the above cases, both parties benefited from confronting the situation, even if the final resolution was uncertain.

Frozen Evaluations Can Get in the Way

All too often, ability and potential become inextricably tied to past performance. This is especially true when subordinates do not live up to their bosses' expectations. As one executive observed: "In organizations we label people. . . . It's a gradual, insidious kind of process . . . but, over time, labels stick and become well-known, unspoken fact." Such labeling gradually reduces the confidence a boss will show in a subordinate and eventually may threaten the subordinate's self-worth. Once this happens, both the charming but unreliable performers and the talented but abrasive individuals are likely to start making extra efforts to prove their value by engaging in activities that place greater emphasis on their strengths—in most cases, whatever they do well they will try to do more of. In turn, the boss will assign them less important projects or compensate by monitoring their work more frequently. As one engineering manager told me:

"When I took over the engineering department, there was one engineer who spent several hours a week running a sports pool all over the plant. Everyone liked this guy. He had helped the department many times by greasing the skids with other units. Anytime a 'sell job' was needed, we used him. Unfortunately, I had to check his work all the time. Eventually, I had to put him on unimportant projects to avoid serious mistakes and save my time."

Labeling subordinates based solely on past performance rests on the faulty assumption that people are unable to change over time. Who is to say that the engineer described above would not make an excellent customer service representative or a liaison with purchasing? Moreover, such unchanged or "frozen evaluations" are unfair and in many cases are merely excuses for the boss to do nothing.[9] Once previously held views are put aside, the potential for new insights can be enormous. As one boss explained:

"I used to tune this woman out because she grated on me. The more I tuned out, the more she would push her point. Finally, one day I started to listen. As painful as it was, I kept telling myself, 'This woman is bright; just try to see her point of view.' Eventually, I got past my negative reaction and she started to behave less abrasively. What I need to do now is to help her to see how her desire to be heard and have her ideas appreciated is causing her to be too pushy and triggering many of the problems she has with others."

Early Warning Signals Are Easily Missed or Ignored

Many problem subordinates start out with great promise. Some are so likeable that in early career their shortcomings are

9. For more information on avoiding "frozen evaluations," see Chapter 13 of William V. Haney's *Communication and Interpersonal Relations: Text and Cases,* 5th Edition, Homewood, IL: Richard D. Irwin, Inc., 1986, pp. 408–432.

easily overlooked: "She's so pleasant to work with I'm sure it's only a matter of time before she comes up to speed." Others are so talented that a few eccentricities are hardly noticed: "He's just a little strong willed." Thus, the insidious thing about looking for warning signs is that they are easily missed or ignored. All too often, bright and/or charming young subordinates seem to be given a special dispensation by their seniors. Indeed, many of the problem subordinates described in the survey were not perceived as problematic until after they turned 40 and took on a major management responsibility. As one CEO from an electronics firm observed: "What passes for hard-driving, mover-and-shaker behavior at age 30 is quite often perceived as arrogance and insensitivity at 45." And yet, the prognosis is likely to be more promising in early career when the individual is the most malleable and the damage minimal. This is the time when they are most easily turned around or redirected.

Accept the fact that it is going to be difficult to challenge youthful brashness because such attempts can backfire. If your efforts become too threatening, you could be faced with a hostile and uncooperative subordinate. You might also find yourself trying to convince him or her to stay or, worse, you could stand accused of causing the problem. Don't wait for all the evidence to accumulate before you start a dialogue. When in doubt, trust your instincts. Most managers have good instincts but often fail to follow them. Early coaching can make a difference; waiting until the warning signs can no longer be ignored is a mistake.

There Is No Excuse for Continued Neglect

Shelving an individual in midcareer because of shortcomings that should have been dealt with years before is inexcusable, but continuing to write him or her off as "deadwood" is also wrong. In many of these cases, an attitude of "why bother" prevails, leaving both boss and subordinate feeling helpless, believing the situation is outside their control and seeing little hope of escape. Given the long history of neglect from which such cases have evolved, both parties are right; little can be done to change what has already happened, and little can be done at this stage in the individual's career to offer major redirection. But does that mean that these individuals deserve continued neglect? Hardly.

Often the plateaued but indifferent subordinate has potential and talent; your job is to identify it. Just as you would be unwilling to drive an automobile running on fewer than all its cylinders, you should also be unwilling to allow any human resource to be underutilized. In the beginning, these indifferent individuals must be involved in mainstream activity, no matter how trivial their part. At a minimum, they should be expected to carry their fair share of the workload. Find out what interests them and encourage them to follow through. Not all your people have to do the same thing. Try to juggle the workload to match individual interests and talents. (These subordinates may be ideal candidates for retraining or job rotation.) As the following case illustrates, sometimes a small effort, even in late career, can make a difference:

> "I manage a group of designers. Many of them love creating new ideas but lack the patience for the detail work after the initial design is accepted. One of my designers, an older woman named Mary, hadn't been assigned any major projects for several years. Mary was considered good in her day but she had not kept pace with the times. Other designers refused to work with her because she was considered a 'nit-picker' and that disturbed their creative flow. As a consequence, I had to assign her to minor projects.
>
> "One day a couple of my best designers approached me with a complaint. . . . They felt it was unfair that they had to do projects that Mary should be doing. They were especially unhappy about doing the additional burdensome detail work. . . . That meeting gave me an idea. I decided to experiment by assigning Mary to do the follow-up detail work on accepted designs. This would free up the other designers to do what they loved to do best. It turned out to be a perfect marriage after some encouraging and nudging on my part. Mary's attention to detail resulted in her finding minor flaws in the accepted designs and saved us production glitches. The other designers began to respect her 'eye for detail' and seek her advice during the preliminary stages of design. This gave Mary a greater sense of ownership in the project."

To be sure, there are also a number of plateaued but indifferent workers who, for whatever reasons—cynicism, despair, or apathy—are less willing to respond to such change attempts. Before you throw in the towel, however, recognize that helplessness conditioned by years of neglect requires a patient response on your part; don't give up too easily.[10] As one executive summed up, "There are no easy answers when you deal with human beings. . . . If there were, we wouldn't need managers."

Own Up to the Part You've Played

Regardless of the type of problem subordinate you face, the place to start is with yourself. How big a part have you played in creating the problem or allowing it to continue? When is the last time you paid attention to a problem subordinate or took the time to find out how he or she feels about the job? In all likelihood, it has been a long time. Sadly, such attempts are frequently affected by a simplistic cost/benefit decision: Managers will invest energy in a subordinate when the payoff is substantial, but are unwilling to do so when it is not. However, writing off another human being as a bad investment is not only a dereliction of a manager's responsibility to develop human resources—it is dehumanizing as well. Although you cannot undo past practices or necessarily fix what is broken, there are many instances where effective interventions have made a difference.

You can also begin by recognizing that the metaphors used to describe problem subordinates often create more hostility and frustration in you that is warranted, and that such metaphors, whether derogatory or despairing, tend to guide and shape how you respond. Recognize, too, that such actions detract from your primary mission of developing productive human beings.

When Don Quixote thrust his lance at "monsters" created out of windmills, it was funny; when managers allow themselves to be hassled by "monstrous" kinds of behavior, some real and some imagined, it is not. Perhaps it is time to recast these metaphors to produce more positive images: A subordinate with a problem, rather than a problem subordinate, could become a potential challenge and not a threat, a mismatch and not a misfit. And perhaps it is time to stop passing the buck, arguing that "It's not my fault, I inherited him (or her)." Managers don't "inherit" people, but they do inherit responsibility for their performance and development, a rule to which most managers subscribe but for which few are willing to foot the bill.

POSTSCRIPT

Bear in mind that no one expects you to be a miracle worker. There are no quick fixes or guarantees. One week of training is not the answer, nor is a simple heart-to-heart talk. You must accept the fact that this will be a long haul. Establishing a pattern of coaching and feedback, perhaps supplemented with training, takes time. In some situations, the behavior patterns are well entrenched, if not permanent. In these cases, it may be nearly impossible to promote change or it may take some major crisis to break the pattern. As one CEO explained: "The threat of a takeover made us all pull together . . . survival was at stake. Each of us learned a valuable lesson in humility and teamwork." Some changes take time to be implemented; others will never occur. Sometimes you may be too big a part of the problem and might have to change as well; other times, the only answer is reassignment or termination.

In the final analysis, managerial vitality depends on the ability to see something new in the old and the familiar. Therefore, all managers must be willing to take another hard look at problem subordinates *and* themselves and be prepared to face both. Unless and until managers accept this charge, they will continue to be victimized and continue to be blameworthy.

---

10. The consequences of failure to give individuals effective career feedback are clearly highlighted in John F. Veiga's "Do Managers on the Move Get Anywhere?" *Harvard Business Review,* March–April 1981, 20–38, and Jay W. Lorsch and Haruo Takagi's "Keeping Managers Off the Shelf," *Harvard Business Review,* July–August 1986, 60–65.

Exercise: Developing Conflict-Resolution Skills

PURPOSE

The purpose of this exercise is to help you to identify your personal conflict-resolution style. By the time you complete this exercise, you will

1. Identify your personal style of conflict resolution

2. Determine the potential dysfunctional outcomes associated with conflict resolution

3. Understand the pros and cons of conflict-resolution styles

INTRODUCTION

Conflict management is a vital part of effective managerial performance. As managers portray the roles of "disturbance handler" and "negotiator," many situations require them to resolve conflicts effectively and productively.

However, most managers find that handling conflicts productively can be a difficult proposition. Rather than solving the conflict directly, those people who are involved in the conflict are typically labeled as "troublemakers." Managers are more likely to dismiss such individuals as having personality deficiencies that contribute to poor performance on the job rather than find a way to resolve the conflict. When confronted with a problem, managers need to guard against the tendency to assume that bad behaviors imply bad persons. Instead, managers should learn productive ways in which conflicts can be objectively resolved.

INSTRUCTIONS

In Part I of this exercise, you will complete a questionnaire that will help you understand your own conflict-resolution style. In Part II, you will learn how to productively confront conflict through a role-play practice session that will help you to improve your conflict-management skills.

Part I

1. Complete the conflict-resolution questionnaire that follows.

2. Score the questionnaire to determine your style of conflict resolution.

3. Read "Conflict-Resolution Styles."

4. Participate in a class discussion. Your instructor will provide a worksheet with confrontational responses to the situations described in the questionnaire.

This exercise was developed by Lisa A. Mainiero.

Part II

   1. Choose a partner for the role-play session. One individual should play the role of Mike, the owner, while the other individual portrays the role of Julia, the sales manager.

   2. Utilize consensual methods to resolve the conflict. Your instructor will ask you to report on your solution.

   3. Participate in a class discussion.

Part I: Conflict Styles Questionnaire

Directions: Rank order the following responses on a 1–4 scale, with number 1 indicating your most likely response to the situation and 4 indicating your least likely response to the situation. Try to consider how you would actually react if faced with the situation described, rather than how you think you *should* react.

1. One of your subordinates has recently been asking for a raise. Money is available within the budget for exceptional performers, but in your opinion this subordinate does not fall into that category. You would be most likely to

_____ a. Tell him or her that you do not feel that his/her recent performance warrants a raise

_____ b. Avoid the discussion

_____ c. Compromise by saying that you will grant a raise but for a smaller percentage than requested

_____ d. Tell him or her that you would like to grant the raise, but your hands are tied

2. George is a valued technical expert in your department, but lately he has been telling everyone what to do in their jobs. His opinion is respected in his area of expertise, but his recent behavior is causing much resentment. You would be most likely to

_____ a. Assume the situation will resolve itself shortly

_____ b. Tell George to back off—he's causing more problems than he's worth

_____ c. Tell your subordinates that George is a valued employee but at the same time tell George that he should only concentrate on areas where he can make an appropriate contribution

_____ d. Remind everyone that George is a valued employee and the group should be like a family

3. One of your peers has recently accepted a new project that crosses your area. He/she has visited your department and asked for help from your subordinates. At first you agreed to lend your people, but it is now becoming excessive. You would be most likely to

_____ a. Tell him or her to use his or her own people on the project

_____ b. Assume the problem will resolve itself when the project is completed in a few months

_____ c. Tell him or her he or she can have your people only for a limited time and only if he or she agrees to an exchange with some of his or her employees to do the work in your department

_____ d. Let him or her continue using your people; after all, your department does have the necessary expertise

4. You have had a service order into the Purchasing Department for the past three months, and you should have received your equipment by now. The equipment is not urgent, however. You call the Purchasing Department, only to find that the equipment had never been ordered. This is a situation that has occurred previously with this department. You would be most likely to

_____ a. Accept the response as being "par for the course"

_____ b. Tell them you are furious and that you will take this matter to their boss immediately

_____ c. Compromise by saying if they can get you the equipment in a few weeks, you won't call their boss

_____ d. Understand their pressures and let them know you will give them a second chance

5. Your boss has just given you another new project to work on over the next few months. You feel you are already overburdened and just can't take on any more work. You would be most likely to

_____ a. Resignedly accept the project; after all, you don't want any hard feelings between you and your boss

_____ b. Decide not to work on the project and hope your boss forgets about it

_____ c. Suggest to your boss that you are willing to work on the project if your workload is reduced in other areas

_____ d. Tell your boss you just can't do it and that he or she is being unfair by requesting this extra work

6. You gave a coveted work assignment to one of your subordinates who has recently shown much promise, but your top performer has been acting hurt since the situation occurred. You would be most likely to

_____ a. Force the issue with your top performer by asking him or her to tell you what is bothering him or her

_____ b. Ignore the problem

_____ c. Let your top performer know he or she is still a valued employee

_____ d. Have your top performer work with your other employees on the project to provide whatever assistance is needed

7. Your boss has just given you an assignment that would require you to work over the weekend. In his or her mind, it is a top priority assignment and should be accomplished quickly and efficiently. You feel that more time is necessary for you to do your best, and you don't particularly want to work over the weekend. You would be most likely to

_____ a. Negotiate time off on Monday for having worked the weekend

_____ b. Tell your boss that you are unwilling to work the weekend and that you don't feel the project is really that urgent

_____ c. Decide not to work the weekend on your own but work early next week on the project. If your boss questions you, you can pretend that there was too much to do over the weekend and you are still working

_____ d. Accept the assignment so as not to cause conflict between you and your boss

8. Being part of an internal auditing team, you've discovered a misappropriation of funds in another department. The head of this department has been with the company for many years and is considered a valued employee. You would be most likely to

_____ a. Say nothing

_____ b. Tell your superior immediately

_____ c. Confront him or her with your knowledge, but allow him or her to replace the money

_____ d. Assume that he or she must have financial difficulties at home and that he or she will soon change his or her behavior

9. You have just given an important assignment to a group of young promising executives. While they have never handled such an assignment, you firmly believe they have the skills to do the job well. The members of a more experienced group, who have a long history of service to the company, resent your decisions and have started to slack off on the job. You would be most likely to

_____ a. Tell them to go back and redo the work more carefully

_____ b. Say nothing, because they have always done their work well in the past. Assume they will come around

_____ c. Give the assignment to the more experienced group

_____ d. Give the more experienced group part of a different coveted assignment

10. You are the controller of a manufacturing firm. You have recently adopted the policy of restrained purchasing because of budget constraints. The Purchasing Department, however, continues to produce an excessive number of requisitions for purchases that is throwing your budget calculations off balance. You would be most likely to

_____ a. Ignore the situation

_____ b. Refuse to honor the most recent purchase orders

_____ c. Tell the head of Purchasing that, although you understand his or her needs, you cannot accommodate him or her during the present fiscal year but might be able to do something for him or her in the budget next year

_____ d. Assume that Purchasing must be in a crisis situation, and allocate more monies to their budget fund from other departmental allocations

Scoring Key

Directions: To determine your most likely conflict-resolution style, write in your rank for each response. Then total the numbers in each column to determine your particular conflict-resolution style.

Forcing	*Avoiding*	*Accommodating*	*Compromising*
1a _____	1b _____	1d _____	1c _____
2b _____	2a _____	2d _____	2c _____
3a _____	3b _____	3d _____	3c _____
4b _____	4a _____	4d _____	4c _____
5d _____	5b _____	5a _____	5c _____
6a _____	6b _____	6c _____	6d _____
7b _____	7d _____	7c _____	7a _____
8b _____	8a _____	8d _____	8c _____
9a _____	9b _____	9c _____	9d _____
10b _____	10a _____	10d _____	10c _____

Totals

_____   _____   _____   _____

INTERPRETATION

Total your scores in each column. Your *lowest* total represents your likely method of conflict resolution. Then read "Conflict-Resolution Styles" to learn more about your particular style of conflict resolution.

Conflict-Resolution Styles

Managers' responses to interpersonal confrontations fall into four categories: forcing, accommodating, avoiding, and compromising.

❐ The *forcing* response is an attempt to satisfy your own needs at the expenses of others. Forcing involves the use of formal authority, physical threats, intimidation, or even majority rule.

❐ *Accommodating* satisfies another person's concerns while neglecting your own. Individuals who respond to conflict situations by using an accommodating style frequently find they are being taken advantage of by allowing other parties to get their way.

❐ The *avoiding* style characterizes individuals who neglect the interests of both parties by postponing a decision on the conflict. This is often the response of managers who are not well prepared emotionally to handle a conflict situation; they seem to believe by ignoring the situation and postponing a decision, the conflict will go away.

❐ Finally, *compromising* involves asking both parties to make a sacrifice to achieve a mutually workable solution to the problem. Those who use the compromising style may be able to find a way to solve the problem on a short-term basis, but in the long run they may find that their original compromise breeds latent hostility and frustration.

Each style has its own distinct effect:

❐ *Forcing* creates hostility and resentment against those who use the style because those who feel closed out of a decision process will naturally react against that decision.

❐ *Accommodating* leads to a situation in which the individual preserves harmonious relationships at the expense of his or her own rights in the conflict situation.

❐ *Avoiding* causes frustration and anger because individuals who must wait for a decision waste time and energy until their problem is resolved.

❐ *Compromising* offers only partial satisfaction to both parties since it forces each party to give up something to gain something in the interchange. Someone wins, and someone loses—a "win-lose" method.

The ideal style is a *consensual* or *collaborative* method of conflict resolution in which the views of both parties are treated as equally valid. Equal emphasis is placed on the quality of the outcome and the fairness of the decision-making process. Consensual/collaborative methods require that you identify a *superordinate goal* that organizes your priorities and expectations. Focusing on what is in common, rather than the disparate viewpoints, helps you determine options that create a "win-win" solution.

Part II: Role Play Exercise on Managing Conflict

Directions: The purpose of this role play is to practice conflict-resolution skills. Choose a partner with whom you will work during this exercise. One individual will play Mike, the owner of the small business. The other person will play Julia, the sales manager. You may read both roles as preparation for the role play.

To prepare for your discussion, think about what you want to achieve in the role-play session. What will you give up? What do you want to gain in return? How would you like to see the conflict resolved? Determine tentative answers to these questions:

1. What is the root cause or source of the conflict?
2. Which emotions may surface?
3. Is there a superordinate goal that both parties hold in common?
4. How can the conflict be resolved in a way that meets each person's objectives?

Your instructor will ask you to report on your solution.

Role of Mike, Small Business Owner

As the owner of this small business, I have to make the tough decisions. All the responsibility of the business, and all of its funding, reside with me. I knew that owning a small business could be stressful. But I had no idea that most of the stress would come from personnel problems!

Sales were down during the months of November and December. Things have gone from bad to worse. Now I have to decide if I am going to put in more money to keep the business going or simply shut it down altogether. I know this business has some real potential if I can just hang in there. But with this latest crisis with Julia, I really wonder if it is worth all the hassle.

I thought Julia was happy with her job. She has been my most motivated sales worker. She seemed to really enjoy the sales challenges associated with a start-up venture. But two months ago she developed a different attitude. She started complaining that she could no longer make her sales quotas to earn enough income to support her family. So I sat her down and we discussed putting her on part salary in exchange for new training responsibilities as well as on a commission basis for her regular sales work. She seemed satisfied—at first. Now she is complaining about having to do sales promotion and sales training on top of her regular sales job. I spoke to her and gave her a lecture about how it is necessary in a fledgling business to do several jobs at once. She nodded and seemed to agree.

But just before I took my vacation, she stormed into the office, saying she had to have more money in her budget. She wanted to hire top-quality sales personnel to make the business flourish. I explained this just wasn't realistic at the present time; sales were down and there just wasn't any extra money to go around. For the moment we will need to hire sales employees whom we can train ourselves at less of a cost. She stormed out.

Afterward, her husband, who is a good friend of mine, called me to say that Julia was having a difficult time lately. He indicated that she was upset because she needed to feel appreciated and supported in her work. So I tried to mend fences and let her know her work was first-rate. I've tried to do what I could but with all the details involved in running a start-up, there just isn't enough time to give her the kind of attention she needs.

Julia is my best worker—and she has been with me from the start—so I want her to stay around. But lately her attitude has been impossible. She has been creating havoc in the office with her pouting. In a small office, when one person is having a bad day, everyone suffers. I'm just not sure how long I can allow her to destroy morale.

I used to be confident that Julia would develop a more realistic notion about the business. But after two more arguments on this subject, I am not certain she really understands the issues. I heard from one of the other sales employees that Julia has been threatening to quit. I just don't know what I should do.

Role of Julia, Sales Manager

Well, I've had it. No more. I'm not going to be taken advantage of any longer. I know I can make a lot more money elsewhere, and that's what I'm going to do. I'm not going to stand for this treatment any longer.

I really believed in this business. That's why I thought it would be a lot more worthwhile to get involved in a small entrepreneurial business of this type—you know, see it grow, right from the start. But Mike won't capitalize the business the way it should be capitalized. He's such a tightwad. And then he goes and takes a vacation for a week, clear across the country! If things were really that bad, he wouldn't have been able to afford the trip.

I tried my best in November and December, but it was just a bad time of year. There was nothing I could do, really. So I lost money in absent commissions. And Mike wanted me to hire, train, and develop new salespeople—and do sales promotion—all at the same time! It was impossible—especially for the pay I get. Because I am paid now on a part salary-part commission basis, my pay really dipped when sales went down. In six months, when my husband goes back to school, I'm going to have to be the primary breadwinner in our family. I can't accept this low-level pay—and backslides—when I'm doing so much more work.

The problem is that Mike won't let go of the money. I wanted to hire two terrific salespeople in December, but they wanted more than he could offer. So I lost them. The only way that we are ever going to get this business off the ground is if we hire good salespeople up front to get the sales that we need. This business will suffer without good salespeople. Three good salespeople could do the work of seven part-timers! But he won't hear of it.

And he won't share any of the credit or ownership of the business. Mike keeps talking about providing medical benefits and profit sharing possibilities, but it's all just talk. He'll never let go of control. The thing that really gets to me is that he doesn't seem to care—or even notice—how much of myself I have put into his business. That's what he's always saying: that it's *his* business, that *he's* the one who has to make the bottom-line decisions.

I have really sacrificed, right along with him, for the past year, but he treats me like a piece of furniture. I have a lot of good ideas, and if he would just listen to them, I know he could make a go of the business. But he's so stubborn and so tightfisted I'm not sure it would work. It's for all these reasons that I'm thinking of quitting. I like the business, and I really want to stay on, but I'm just not sure all the hassle is worth it.

The Setting

Mike has asked Julia to come into his office for a discussion. Julia has just arrived, and both are ready to share their perspectives.

DISCUSSION QUESTIONS

1. What is the root source of the conflict between Mike and Julia? How do both parties really feel about the situation?

2. How did you resolve the conflict? Was the conflict resolved successfully to both parties' mutual satisfaction? Or did you "force" a solution due to the pressures of time?

3. What are the differences between compromise and collaboration? Why are these differences so important?

4. Are conflict styles a function of personality or an adaptation to the situation? Explain.

REFERENCE

D. A. Whetten and K. S. Cameron. *Developing Management Skills.* Glenview, IL: Scott, Foresman, 1984, Chapter 8.

Case: Bob Knowlton

PURPOSE

The Bob Knowlton case highlights a classic management dilemma—a misunderstanding between a subordinate and his boss. By the time you finish this case assignment, you will

1. Understand how miscommunication and poor conflict resolution can affect real organizational situations

2. Diagnose the problems associated with managing your boss

3. Learn how to diagnose organizational situations to gain the appropriate skills for similar situations you may encounter as a manager

INTRODUCTION

The Bob Knowlton case illustrates how poor interpersonal communications, misjudgments, and poor conflict-resolution skills can significantly affect workplace situations. In the case, a new player, Simon Fester, is introduced as an unknown to Bob Knowlton, causing misjudgments and misperceptions. A conflict arises that ultimately leads to Bob Knowlton's resignation. As you read the case, keep in mind the reading by Gabarro and Kotter, "Managing Your Boss."

INSTRUCTIONS

1. Read all three articles in the chapter as preparation for this case.
2. Read the Bob Knowlton case. Answer these questions:
   a. What attitudes, misjudgments, assumptions, and misperceptions are generated on the part of the three key individuals in the case?
   b. How could this conflict have been easily resolved?
3. Participate in a class discussion.

Bob Knowlton

Bob Knowlton was sitting alone in the conference room of the laboratory. The rest of the group had gone. One of the secretaries had stopped and talked for a while about her husband's coming induction into the Army and had finally left. Bob, alone in the laboratory, slid a little further down in his chair, looking with satisfaction at the results of the first test run of the new photon unit.

He liked to stay after the others had gone. His appointment as project head was still new enough to give him a deep sense of pleasure. His eyes were on the graphs before him, but in his mind he could hear Dr. Jerrold, the head of the laboratory, saying again, "There's one thing about this place that you can bank on. The sky is the limit for the person who can produce!" Knowlton felt again the tingle of happiness and embarrassment. Well, dammit, he said to himself, he had produced. He wasn't kidding anybody. He had come to the Simmons Laboratories 2 years ago. During a routine testing of some rejected Clanson components, he had stumbled onto the idea of the photon correlator, and the rest had just happened. Jerrold had been enthusiastic; a separate project had been set up for further research and development of the device, and he had gotten the job of running it. The whole sequence of events still seemed a little miraculous to Knowlton.

He shrugged out of the reverie and bent determinedly over the sheets when he heard someone come into the room behind him. He looked up expectantly; Jerrold often stayed late himself, and now and then dropped in for a chat. This always made the day's end especially pleasant for Bob. It wasn't Jerrold. The man who had come in was a stranger. He was tall, thin, and rather dark. He wore steel-rimmed glasses and had on a very wide leather belt with a large brass buckle. (His wife remarked later that it was the kind of belt the pilgrims must have worn.)

The stranger smiled and introduced himself, "I'm Simon Fester. Are you Bob Knowlton?" Bob said yes, and they shook hands. "Doctor Jerrold said I might find you in. We were talking about your work, and I'm very much interested in what you are doing." Bob waved to a chair.

Fester didn't seem to belong in any of the standard categories of visitors: customer, visiting foreman, stockholder. Bob pointed to the sheets on the table. "There are the preliminary results of a test we're running. We've got a new gadget by the tail and we're trying to understand it. It's not finished, but I can show you the section that we're testing."

He stood up, but Fester was deep in the graphs. After a moment, he looked up with an odd grin. "These look like plots of a Jennings surface. I've been playing around with some autocorrelation functions of surfaces—you know that stuff." Bob, who had no idea what he was referring to, grinned back and nodded, and immediately felt uncomfortable. "Let me show you the monster," he said, and led the way to the work room.

After Fester left, Knowlton slowly put the graphs away, feeling vaguely annoyed. Then, as if he had made a decision, he quickly locked up and took the long way out so that he would pass Jerrold's

office. But the office was locked. Knowlton wondered whether Jerrold and Fester had left together.

The next morning, Knowlton dropped into Jerrold's office, mentioned that he had talked with Fester, and asked who he was. "Sit down for a minute," Jerrold said. "I want to talk to you about him. What do you think of him?" Knowlton replied truthfully that he thought Fester was very bright and probably very competent. Jerrold looked pleased.

"We're taking him on," he said. "He's had a very good background in a number of laboratories, and he seems to have ideas about the problems we're tackling here." Knowlton nodded in agreement, instantly wishing that Fester would not be placed with him.

"I don't know yet where he will finally land," Jerrold continued, "but he seems interested in what you are doing. I thought he might spend a little time with you by way of getting started." Knowlton nodded thoughtfully. "If his interest in your work continues, you can add him to your group."

"Well, he seemed to have some good ideas even without knowing exactly what we are doing," Knowlton answered. "I hope he stays; we'd be glad to have him."

Knowlton walked back to the laboratory with mixed feelings. He told himself that Fester would be good for the group. He was no dunce; he'd produce. Knowlton thought again of Jerrold's promise when he had promoted him—"the person who produces gets ahead in this outfit." The words seemed to carry the overtones of a threat now.

The next day, Fester didn't appear until mid-afternoon. He explained that he had had a long lunch with Jerrold, discussing his place in the laboratory. "Yes," said Knowlton, "I talked with Jerry this morning about it, and we both thought you might work with us for a while." Fester smiled in the same knowing way that he had smiled when he mentioned the Jennings surfaces. "I'd like to," he said.

Knowlton introduced Fester to the other members of the laboratory. Fester and Link, the mathematician of the group, hit it off well together and spent the rest of the afternoon discussing a method of analysis of patterns that Link had been worrying over for the last month.

It was 6:30 when Knowlton left the laboratory that night. He had waited almost eagerly for the end of the day to come—when everyone would be gone and he could sit in the quiet rooms, relax, and think it over. "Think what over?" he asked himself. He didn't know. Shortly after 5 p.m. everyone had gone except Fester, and what followed was almost a duel. Knowlton was annoyed that he was being cheated out of his quiet period and finally resentfully determined that Fester should leave first.

Fester was reading at the conference table, and Knowlton was sitting at his desk in the little glass-enclosed cubicle that he used during the day when he needed to be undisturbed. Fester was carefully studying the last year's progress reports. The time dragged. Knowlton doodled on a pad, the tension growing inside him. What the hell did Fester think he was going to find in the reports?

Knowlton finally gave up and they left the laboratory together. Fester took several reports with him to study in the evening. Knowlton asked him if he thought the reports gave a clear picture of the laboratory's activities.

"They're excellent," Fester answered with obvious sincerity. "They're not only good reports; what they report is damn good, too!" Knowlton was surprised at the relief he felt and grew almost jovial as he said goodnight.

Driving home, Knowlton felt more optimistic about Fester's presence in the laboratory. He had never fully understood the analysis that Link was attempting. If there was anything wrong with Link's approach, Fester would probably spot it. "And if I'm any judge," he murmured, "he won't be especially diplomatic about it."

He described Fester to his wife, who was amused by the broad leather belt and the brass buckle. "It's the kind of belt that pilgrims must have worn," she laughed.

"I'm not worried about how he holds his pants up," Knowlton laughed with her. "I'm afraid that he's the kind that just has to make like a genius twice each day. And that can be pretty rough on the group."

Knowlton had been asleep for several hours when he was abruptly awoken by the telephone. He realized it had rung several times. He swung off the bed muttering about damn fools and telephones. It was Fester. Without any excuses, apparently oblivious of the time, he plunged into an excited recital of how Link's patterning problems could be resolved.

Knowlton covered the mouthpiece to answer his wife's stage-whispered "Who is it?" "It's the genius," replied Knowlton.

Fester, completely ignoring that it was 2 a.m., proceeded excitedly to start in the middle of an explanation of a completely new approach to certain photon laboratory problems that he had stumbled onto while analyzing past experiments. Knowlton managed to put some enthusiasm in his own voice and stood there, half-dazed and very uncomfortable, listening to Fester talk endlessly about what he had discovered. It was probably not only a new approach but also an analysis that showed the inherent weakness of the previous experiment and how experimentation along that line would certainly have been inconclusive. The following day Knowlton spent the entire morning with Fester and Link, the mathematician, the morning meeting having been called off so that Fester's work of the previous night could be gone over intensively. Fester was very anxious that this be done and Knowlton was not too unhappy to suspend the meeting for reasons of his own.

For the next several days, Fester sat in the back office that had been turned over to him and did nothing but read the progress reports of the work that had been done in the last 6 months. Knowlton felt apprehensive about the reaction that Fester might have to some of his work. He was a little surprised at his own feelings. He had always been proud (although he had put on a convincingly modest face) of the way in which new ground had been broken in his group. Now he wasn't sure, and it seemed to him that Fester might easily show that the line of research they had been following was unsound or even unimaginative.

The next morning, as was the custom in Bob's group, the members of the laboratory, including the secretaries, sat around the conference table. Bob always prided himself on the fact that the work of the laboratory was guided and evaluated by the group as a whole, and he was fond of repeating that it was not a waste of time to include secretaries in such meetings. Often, what started out as a boring recital of fundamental assumptions to a naive listener uncovered new ways of regarding these assumptions that would not have occurred to the researcher who had long ago accepted them as a necessary basis for his or her work.

These group meetings also served Bob in another sense. He admitted to himself that he would have felt far less secure if he had had to direct the work out of his own mind, so to speak. With the group meeting as the principle of leadership, it was always possible to justify the exploration of blind alleys because of the general educative effect on the team. Fester was there. Lucy Jones and Martha Smith, the laboratory secretaries, were there. Link was sitting next to Fester, their conversation concerning Link's mathematical study apparently continuing from yesterday. The other members, Bob Davenport, George Thurlow, and Arthur Oliver, were waiting quietly.

Knowlton, for reasons that he didn't quite understand, proposed for discussion this morning a problem that all of them had spent considerable time on previously, with the conclusion that a solution was impossible, that there was no feasible way to treat it in an experimental fashion. When Knowlton proposed the problem, Davenport remarked that there was hardly any use in reviewing it again, that he was satisfied that there was no way to approach the problem with the equipment and the physical capacities of the laboratory.

This statement had the effect of a shot of adrenalin on Fester. He said he would like to know about the problem in detail, and walking to the blackboard, began to write the "factors" as various members of the group began to discuss the problem and simultaneously list the reasons for its abandonment.

Very early in the description of the problem, it was evident that Fester would disagree about the impossibility of attacking it. The group realized this and finally the descriptive materials and their recounting of the reasoning that had led to its abandonment dwindled away. Fester began his statement which, as it proceeded, might well have been prepared the previous night although Knowlton knew this was impossible. He could not help being impressed with the organized, logical way that Fester was presenting ideas that must have occurred to him only a few minutes before.

Fester had some things to say, however, that left Knowlton with a mixture of annoyance, irritation and, at the same time, a rather smug feeling of superiority over Fester in at least one area. Fester thought that the way the problem had been analyzed was really typical of group thinking and, with an air of sophistication that made it difficult for a listener to dissent, he proceeded to comment on the American emphasis on team ideas, satirically describing the ways in which they had led to a "high level of mediocrity."

During this time, Knowlton observed that Link stared studiously at the floor, and he was very conscious of Thurlow's and Davenport's glances toward him at several points during Fester's speech. Inwardly, Knowlton couldn't help feeling that this was one point at least in which Fester was off on the wrong foot. The whole laboratory, following Jerry's lead, talked if not practiced the theory of small research teams as the basic organization for effective research. Fester insisted that the problem could be approached and that he would like to study it for a while himself.

Knowlton ended the morning session by remarking that the meetings would continue and that the very fact that a supposedly insoluble experimental problem was now going to receive another chance was another indication of the value of such meetings. Fester immediately remarked that he was not at all averse to meetings for the purpose of informing the group of the progress of its members— that the point he wanted to make was that creative advances were seldom accomplished in such meetings, that they were made by the individual "living with" the problem closely and continuously, a sort of personal relationship to it.

Knowlton went on to say to Fester that he was very glad that Fester had raised these points and that he was sure the group would profit by reexamining the basis on which they had been operating. Knowlton agreed that individual effort was probably the basis for making the major advances, but that he considered the group meetings useful primarily because of the effect they had on keeping the group together and on helping the weaker members of the group keep up with the members who were able to advance more easily and quickly in the analysis of problems.

It was clear as days went by and meetings continued as they did that Fester came to enjoy them because of the pattern that the meetings assumed. It became typical for Fester to hold forth and it was unquestionably clear that he was more brilliant, better prepared on the various subjects that were germane to the problems being studied, and more capable of progress than anyone there. Knowlton grew increasingly disturbed as he realized that his leadership of the group had been, in fact, taken over.

Whenever the subject of Fester was mentioned in occasional meetings with Jerrold, Knowlton would comment only on Fester's ability and obvious capacity for work. Somehow he never felt that he could mention his own discomforts, not only because they revealed a weakness on his part but also because it was quite clear that Jerrold himself was considerably impressed with Fester's work and with the contacts he had with him outside the photon laboratory.

Knowlton now began to feel that perhaps the intellectual advantages that Fester had brought to the group did not quite compensate for what he felt were evidences of a breakdown in the cooperative spirit that he had seen in the group before Fester's coming. More and more of the morning meetings were skipped. Fester's opinion of the abilities of other group members, with the exception of Link, was obviously low. At times, during the morning meetings or in smaller discussions, he had been on the point of rudeness, refusing to pursue an argument when he claimed it was based on the other person's ignorance of the facts involved. His impatience with others led him to make similar remarks to Jerrold. Knowlton inferred this from a conversation with Jerrold in which Jerrold asked whether Davenport and Oliver were going to be continued on; and his failure to mention Link led Knowlton to believe that this was the result of private conversations between Fester and Jerrold.

It was not difficult for Knowlton to make a quite convincing case on whether the brilliance of Fester was sufficient compensation for the beginning of the breakup of the group. He took the opportunity to speak privately with Davenport and Oliver, and it was quite clear that both were uncomfortable because of Fester. Knowlton didn't press the discussion beyond the point of hearing them in one way or another say that they did feel awkward and that it was sometimes difficult for them to understand the arguments Fester advanced, but often embarrassing to ask him to provide the background on which his arguments were based. Knowlton did not interview Link.

About 6 months after Fester came to the photon laboratory, a meeting was scheduled in which the sponsors of the research would visit the laboratory to get an idea of the work and its progress. It was customary at these meetings for project heads to present the research being conducted in their groups. The members of each group were invited to other meetings, which were held later in the day and open to all, but the special meetings were usually attended only by project heads, the head of the laboratory, and the sponsors.

As the time for the special meeting approached, it seemed to Knowlton that he must avoid the presentation at all cost. He felt that he could not trust himself to present the ideas and work that Fester had advanced, because of his apprehension as to whether he could present them in sufficient detail and answer questions correctly. On the other hand, he did not feel he could ignore these newer lines of work and present only the material that he had done or had been started before Fester's arrival. He also felt that it would not be beyond Fester at all, in his blunt and undiplomatic way (if he were present at the meeting, that is) to comment on his own presentation and reveal the inadequacy that Knowlton felt he had. It also seemed quite clear that it would not be easy to keep Fester from attending the meeting, even though he was not on the administrative level that was invited.

Knowlton found an opportunity to speak to Jerrold and raised the question. He remarked to Jerrold that, with the meetings coming up and with the interest in the work and with the contributions that Fester had been making, Fester would probably like to attend these meetings, but that there was a question of the feelings of the others in the group if Fester alone were invited. Jerrold dismissed this very lightly by saying that he didn't think the group would fail to understand Fester's rather different position, and that he thought Fester by all means should be invited. Knowlton then immediately agreed, adding that Fester should present the work because much of it had been done by him and that, as Knowlton put it, this would be an opportune way to recognize Fester's contributions and to reward him since he was eager to be recognized as a productive member of the laboratory. Jerrold agreed and so the matter was decided.

Fester's presentation was very successful and in some ways dominated the meeting. He attracted the interest and attention of many in attendance, and a long discussion followed his presentation. Later in the evening, with the entire laboratory staff present, a small circle of people formed about Fester in the cocktail period before the dinner. One of them was Jerrold himself, and a lively discussion took place concerning the application of Fester's theory. All of this disturbed Knowlton and his reaction and behavior were characteristic. He joined the circle, praised Fester to Jerrold and to the others, and remarked on the brilliance of the work.

Without consulting anyone, Knowlton began to take an interest in the possibility of a job elsewhere. After a few weeks he found that a new laboratory of considerable size was being organized in a nearby city, and that his training would enable him to secure a project-head job equivalent to his present one, with slightly more money.

He immediately accepted it and notified Jerrold by a letter, which he mailed on a Friday night to Jerrold's home. The letter was quite brief and Jerrold was stunned. The letter merely said he had found a better position; that there were personal reasons why he didn't want to appear at the laboratory anymore; and that he would be glad to return at a later time from where he would be some 40 miles away, to assist if there was any mixup at all in the past work. It also mentioned that he felt sure that Fester could supply any leadership for the group, and that his decision to leave so suddenly was based on some personal problems; he hinted at problems of health in his family, his mother and father. All of this was fictitious, of course. Jerrold took it at face value but still felt that this was very strange behavior and quite unaccountable since he had always felt his relationship with Knowlton had been warm and that Knowlton was satisfied and, as a matter of fact, quite happy and productive.

Jerrold was considerably disturbed, because he had already decided to place Fester in charge of another project that was going to be set up very soon. He had been wondering how to explain to Knowlton, in light of the obvious help and value Knowlton was getting from Fester and the high regard in which he held him. He had, as a matter of fact, considered the possibility that Knowlton could add to his staff another person with Fester's kind of background and training, which had proven so valuable.

Jerrold did not make any attempt to meet Knowlton. In a way, he felt aggrieved about the situation. Fester, too, was surprised at the suddenness of Knowlton's departure and when Jerrold asked him whether he had reasons to prefer to stay with the photon group instead of the impending Air Force project, he chose the Air Force project and went on to that job the following week. The photon laboratory was hard hit. The leadership of the laboratory was temporarily given to Link until someone could be hired to take charge.

DISCUSSION QUESTIONS

1. To what extent did Bob Knowlton contribute to his downfall? Was Bob a captive of his own assumptions and perceptions?

2. Diagnose the relationship between Bob Knowlton and his boss. Where did the relationship go wrong? How could it have been salvaged?

3. To what extent did the lack of communication among the three players in the case, and the type of evaluative or ambiguous communication that did occur, contribute to the problems associated with the case?

4. What was Bob's preferred style of conflict resolution? How did his style of conflict resolution contribute to his problems?

Exercise: Dealing with Problem Subordinates

PURPOSE

The purpose of this exercise is to help you become more aware of the challenges of subordinate performance problems. By the time you complete this exercise, you will

1. Learn how to categorize typical performance problems

2. Develop strategies with which to manage such performance problems

3. Understand the challenges of managing subordinates

INTRODUCTION

If there is one universal truth among managers, it is that all of them have subordinates with performance problems. Motivating and leading "ideal" subordinates is a simple

---

This exercise was developed by Lisa A. Mainiero with John F. Veiga and presented at the Eastern Academy of Management, Hartford, CT, 1991.

task, but coping with the realities of problem subordinates is an entirely different matter. In many cases, ignorance on the part of the manager of how to handle a problem subordinate causes the manager to neglect the problem. This, in turn, leads to exasperation, dissatisfaction, lowered performance, and depressed morale.

According to Veiga's (1988) article, "Face Your Problem Subordinates Now!", two recurring themes—*job performance* and *interpersonal relations*—emerged in his classification of problem subordinates. Employees who perform above job expectations but who are perceived as not working effectively with others are classified as **"talented but abrasive."** Employees who perform below expectations and who are viewed as having difficulty working with others are categorized as **"plateaued but indifferent."** Employees who work effectively with others yet perform below expectations are seen as **"charming but unreliable."** Finally, employees who perform above expectations and work effectively with others are viewed as **"ideal"** subordinates.

It can be argued that a subordinate's classification into one of these categories may suggest levers for change. For example, if a manager is dealing with a **"talented but abrasive"** subordinate, coaching in terms of communication and political skills might be recommended. **"Plateaued but indifferent"** subordinates might benefit from career counseling or work redesign, while **"charming but unreliable"** subordinates might require additional technical training to help them perform job tasks more effectively. Veiga (1988) argues that there are no quick fixes or guarantees with problem subordinates. Managers must accept the fact that a pattern of coaching and feedback, supplemented with training, is necessary to improve performance.

This experiential exercise has been developed to help you recognize subordinate performance problems and determine strategies to manage them. You will be given six case vignettes of problem subordinates to evaluate independently and in groups. Skills in diagnosis and implementation are practiced so that students (1) categorize problem subordinates and (2) determine strategies to improve performance.

INSTRUCTIONS

1. Review John F. Veiga's article, "Face Your Problem Subordinates Now!" *The Academy of Management Executive,* 1988, Vol. II(2), 145–152.

2. Read the *Management Problems* case vignettes and complete them independently.

3. In a small group, discuss how you each independently classified subordinates in the six case vignettes. Attempt to reach a consensus decision on each vignette.

4. Together as a group, prepare a developmental plan for performance improvement for each vignette. The *Skills and Development Activities Guide* may facilitate your group discussion.

5. Report out your group's strategies for dealing with selected cases to the class as directed by your instructor.

6. Participate in a class discussion on "real-life" problem subordinates.

Part I: Management Problem Case Vignettes

Case A: Recently, you were promoted to the position of manager of your department. One member of your group who now reports to you, Fred, is upset that you were given the promotion over him. Although he is known as the company expert on technical matters in his field, lately his work has been slipping. On more than one occasion he has left work early, arrived late, and missed several deadlines on monthly reports. You are concerned because you consider him a valuable employee on your staff and an asset to the company. Since you are new to your position, you know you must depend on his expertise to keep the group on track as you learn more about your new responsibilities. Fred has been known to be difficult to deal with and has developed a reputation as a scientific "primadonna." In a meeting the other day, several of your peers (and your boss) were joking about Fred's occasional superior attitude toward others. His attitude and behavior on the job are not consistent with the norms your company associates with its management staff. Fred seems to believe that he's put in his time and that the company "owes it to him" to grant him a promotion. You believe he has the talent, skills, and knowledge to make excellent contributions if his attitude improves.

1. If this situation were left unchecked, what category might this subordinate represent?

_____ Talented but Abrasive   _____ Charming but Unreliable

_____ Plateaued but Indifferent   _____ Ideal

2. How would you manage this situation?
3. What strategies would you use to coach and guide this subordinate's development?

Case B: Your assistant, Ann, has worked for you over the past two years. During that time, you have learned to respect the clerical and word processing skills she demonstrates. However, you are concerned about other areas of her job that, in your view, reflect substandard performance. On occasion, it seems that she does not hear your requests, or if she does hear, she does not follow through on them. Occasionally she performs tasks different from those you have assigned. For example, just yesterday you asked that she make arrangements for a temp to handle a special project. No temporary turned up this morning to take on the assignment. When you asked Ann about the situation, she said she forgot to make the phone call because she was so busy preparing a lengthy mailing that you had given her the day before. You became frustrated by her response, as similar incidents had happened many times in the past. You wonder if the reason incidents like these keep happening is due to a lack of listening skills on her part or a result of poor time management skills. You have heard complaints from others who must work with her from time to time, so you are confident that your judgment is accurate in this matter. Whatever the cause, you have decided that now is the time to discuss this with her.

1. If this situation were left unchecked, what category might this subordinate represent?

_____ Talented but Abrasive   _____ Charming but Unreliable

_____ Plateaued but Indifferent   _____ Ideal

2. How would you manage this situation?
3. What strategies would you use to coach and guide this subordinate's development?

Case C: For several months you have been upset that one of your staff members, George, has placed you in more than one embarrassing situation. The situation just described to you in a phone call from a former customer, however, takes the cake. This former customer wanted to know who in your group now had responsibility for handling his account. You went to great lengths to cultivate this customer when you were a member of the sales team; fortunately, through your efforts the company won a major share of his business. Several months ago you specifically assigned account responsibility for this customer to George. You chose George because he is very effective in meetings with customers due to his strong interpersonal skills. Reports from the field indicate that George is one of the most beloved salespeople that your company has to offer. When pursuing a new customer, George has been known to put on quite a sales show, taking new customers out for expensive dinners, providing them with theater tickets, and driving them to the theater in limousines. However, George does not demonstrate strong customer follow-up skills, and he also has been known to neglect sales quota deadlines. You had asked George to follow through on arrangements with this particular customer; the phone call alerted you to the fact that the customer has not been contacted for follow-up. Fuming, you leave your office and head straight for George's desk.

1. If this situation were left unchecked, what category might this subordinate represent?

_____ Talented but Abrasive   _____ Charming but Unreliable

_____ Plateaued but Indifferent   _____ Ideal

2. How would you manage this situation?

3. What strategies would you use to coach and guide this subordinate's development?

Case D: It's Monday morning, and you have just returned to your office after traveling for two weeks. You check in with each of your direct reports to discuss their activities in your absence. One member of your staff, Greg, is frustrated and furious. After letting him vent his frustration, you discover the problem. While you were gone, your boss agreed to an arrangement with another function that will change record-keeping procedures significantly for your department. You will now have to organize information by project number instead of alphabetically by project name. Your boss decided not to tell your staff, preferring to wait for you to return so that he could talk to you and let you handle the announcement. From one point of view, the change makes sense. The new approach will make it much easier to track project costs by category. However, your people will now have to create and learn an entirely new system. This will require the reorganization of all existing files and records. Greg heard rumors of the change late last Friday and became quite upset. He took it upon himself to confront your boss about the problem. A messy argument erupted in your absence. Now one of your best people is angry and your boss is upset. This is particularly difficult for you as Greg is one of your most talented performers and you had hoped he would be promoted soon.

1. If this situation were left unchecked, what category might this subordinate represent?

_____ Talented but Abrasive   _____ Charming but Unreliable

_____ Plateaued but Indifferent   _____ Ideal

2. How would you manage this situation?

3. What strategies would you use to coach and guide this subordinate's development?

Case E: Due to organizational restructuring, the members of your department will now be assigned responsibility for making regular telephone contact with customers to alert customers to the availability of new promotional material and to monitor local sales efforts. You are pleased with the change in assignments. However, when you discussed plans for the change with individual subordinates, one employee, Lillian, expressed a great deal of reluctance and uncertainty. You are concerned whether Lillian will be able to adjust to the change at all. She has grown comfortable with the administrative tasks she has performed over the years and is not happy about changing her job duties. Lillian does not have the skills appropriate to the selling assignment, and she is not motivated to make the change. Lillian is an average but solid performer. She has strong interpersonal skills but is uncomfortable dealing directly with customers. If pushed, you are certain that Lillian would gain the confidence she needs to handle the new assignment, but you are not certain whether this is the right course of action. Somehow you must make a decision about her new role in the department.

1. If this situation were left unchecked, what category might this subordinate represent?

_____ Talented but Abrasive   _____ Charming but Unreliable

_____ Plateaued but Indifferent   _____ Ideal

2. How would you manage this situation?

3. What strategies would you use to coach and guide this subordinate's development?

Case F: One of the employees who reports to you, Sally, seems to think she is destined for great things at the company where you work. The problem is that you don't agree with Sally's assessment of her potential. Nor does your boss. Sally has seen her peers promoted and considers herself ready for advancement. Sally has an outgoing personality and generally gets along well with people. However, she has a tendency to get on everyone's nerves in the department with her hour-long personal phone calls. She also has a tendency to blow events out of proportion. For example, she was quite upset with the comments you made during her last performance review. You reviewed a number of her shortcomings concerning missed deadlines and substandard work, yet she had an excuse for every example offered. Since that discussion, she has avoided talking to you on matters that do not require your direct approval. Recently another staff member let you know that Sally has told others that you feel threatened by her and have reacted by giving her an unfair performance review. You are concerned about this news and feel that it is just another example of Sally's lack of readiness for promotion. Of particular concern is that lately her work has been slipping and she no longer is motivated to do her best.

1. If this situation were left unchecked, what category might this subordinate represent?

_____ Talented but Abrasive   _____ Charming but Unreliable

_____ Plateaued but Indifferent   _____ Ideal

2. How would you manage this situation?

3. What strategies would you use to coach and guide this subordinate's development?

Part II: Group Discussion Action Planning

Skills That Require Improvement	*Action Planning Strategies*

Case A

Case B

Case C

Case D

Case E

Case F

How Managers Classify Subordinates

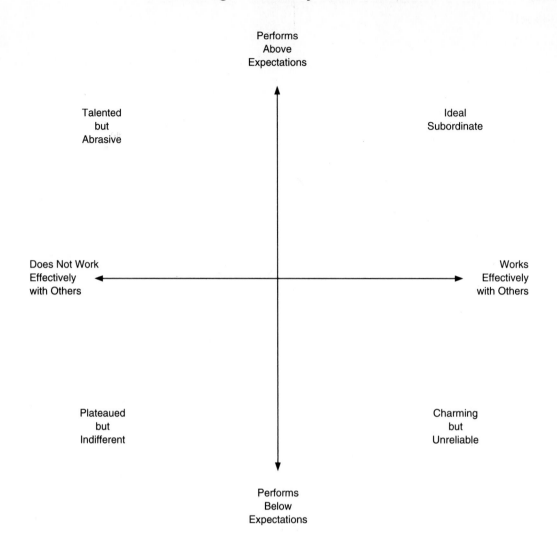

Performs
Above
Expectations

Talented
but
Abrasive

Ideal
Subordinate

Does Not Work
Effectively
with Others

Works
Effectively
with Others

Plateaued
but
Indifferent

Charming
but
Unreliable

Performs
Below
Expectations

John F. Veiga. "Face Your Problem Subordinates Now!" *The Academy of Management Executive,* 1988, Vol. II(2), 145–152.

Skills and Developmental Activities Guide

SKILL AREA: PLANNING AND ORGANIZING

Sample Developmental Activities

1. Give the employee a project to plan using a PERT chart or some other scheduling device.

2. Ask the employee to provide you with a monthly report of job activities that include a plan for the upcoming month.

3. Have employee develop priorities for the work that needs to be accomplished.

4. Request that employee prepare a report that outlines how work activities can be consolidated.

5. Have employee keep a daily work journal and review how she or he completes tasks: in chunks or in sporadic pieces.

6. Utilize weekly planning sessions that help the employee plan out his or her weekly and/or monthly activities.

7. Require that the employee attend a training seminar on this topic.

How to Coach, Advise, and Guide

1. Encourage the use of planning calendars and schedule books on a daily, weekly, and monthly basis.

2. Set clear target dates that cannot be changed.

3. Establish milestones to check progress.

4. Suggest that employee talk to others who have performed similar tasks and projects to determine appropriate lead times and resources.

5. Show the employee how you personally organize your own work.

Your Own Ideas

1.

2.

3.

SKILL AREA: INTERPERSONAL RELATIONS AND CONFLICT RESOLUTION

Sample Developmental Activities

1. Have employee serve as the department's channel for employee complaints and problems.

2. Have employee initiate discussions with employees who you sense need to discuss a problem or concern.

3. Assign employee a task force assignment that is bound to require conflict resolution among the parties.

4. Encourage employee to deal with angry customers or vendors.

5. Have employee attend a training seminar on this topic.

How to Coach, Advise, and Guide

1. Encourage employee to listen and respond to others with empathy.

2. Encourage employee not to judge but understand others.

3. Serve as a role model for employee in dealing with others and handling employee conflicts.

4. Help employee understand how to create "win-win" solutions to problems.

5. After a sensitive discussion with another upset employee, have the employee discuss that person's feelings with you.

Your Own Ideas

1.

2.

3.

SKILL AREA: ORAL AND WRITTEN COMMUNICATION

Sample Developmental Activities

1. Have employee make presentations to the work group about activities, products, and problems.

2. Have employee write weekly reports, memos, and letters and critique them for style and substance.

3. Videotape employee: daily actions with others and presentations.

4. Allow employee to conduct a meeting and let the group give him or her written feedback on skills.

5. Have employee attend a training seminar on this topic.

How to Coach, Advise, and Guide

1. Call on employee to present views in meetings.

2. Have employee develop an outline prior to writing letters, reports, and memos.

3. Ask employee to summarize views, in oral and/or written form, as much as possible.

4. As presentations are made, encourage employee to critique them.

5. Encourage employee to get multiple sources of feedback.

Your Own Ideas

1.

2.

3.

SKILL AREA: FOLLOW-UP AND VERIFICATION

Sample Developmental Activities

1. Have employee prepare a list of tasks and corresponding target dates.

2. Assign employee the responsibility of submitting weekly or monthly project reports and critique them.

3. Require employee to have oral discussions with you on a periodic basis about progress.

4. Assign employee a task force responsibility that will require follow-up and verification.

5. Have employee attend a training seminar on this topic.

How to Coach, Advise, and Guide

1. Encourage employee to utilize daily calendars.

2. Provide employee with a "Things to Do" pad to schedule and plan target dates.

3. Insist that employee communicate with you about project progress frequently.

4. Serve as a role model by following up with employee about progress.

5. Ensure that target dates are never changed or altered.

Your Own Ideas

1.

2.

3.

SKILL AREA: STRATEGIZING AND POLITICKING

Sample Developmental Activities

1. Have employee analyze the elements of your company's corporate culture.

2. Have employee prepare a report on the key individuals whose support will be required in developing and implementing a new project.

3. Have employee analyze the adverse effects a particular decision or action might have on other departments or areas.

4. Assign the employee the task of collecting data about how he or she is perceived by others—the employee's corporate "image"—and report back to you.

5. Have employee attend a training seminar on this topic.

How to Coach, Advise, and Guide

1. Continually highlight aspects of the organizational culture as it applies to behavior, norms, attitudes of employees.

2. Provide your own insights on the impact of a given decision on other departments and areas.

3. Discuss with employees your own ideas for strategy implementation.

4. Provide feedback to employee on his or her "image" in the company, and request that others do the same.

5. Encourage employees to spin out scenarios for possible courses of implementation.

Your Own Ideas

1.

2.

3.

SKILL AREA: INITIATING AND CREATING

Sample Developmental Activities

1. Ask employees to submit ideas for changing work procedures and policies on a periodic basis.

2. Assign employee the task of designing a project from start to finish.

3. Have employee prepare a report to initiate a change in work-flow relationships.

4. Assign employee the responsibility of developing a creative solution to long-standing departmental problems.

5. Have employee attend a training seminar on this topic.

How to Coach, Advise, and Guide

1. Encourage employees to dream up "crazy" solutions to problems.

2. Require employee to find own answers to questions brought to you.

3. Serve as a role model for employee in initiating change.

4. Insist that employees act independently from you.

5. Require that employees do not come to you with complaints about a problem unless they have already thought of a solution to the problem on their own.

Your Own Ideas

1.

2.

3.

DISCUSSION QUESTIONS

1. Why is it so easy to label a problem subordinate but so difficult to find developmental activities to coach that subordinate? Explain.

2. What relationship should there be between the developmental activities suggested by this exercise and that employee's formal performance appraisal?

3. Many argue that the sign of a good manager is that he or she takes the time to develop his or her lowest performers into promotable employees. But this can take inordinate amounts of the manager's valuable time. How do you reconcile these two perspectives?

REFERENCE

J. F. Veiga. "Face Your Problem Subordinates Now!" *The Academy of Management Executive,* 1988, Vol. II(2), 145–152.

CHAPTER 3

Motivation, Job Design, and Performance

INTRODUCTION

What is motivation? Although a great deal has been written about this subject, there is no cookbook answer. What we do know is that motivation arises from a complex interaction of personality traits and situational determinants. We also suspect that what makes the difference between an effective manager and an average manager is the manager's ability to motivate subordinates to perform well in their jobs.

The basic question that many managers face is, "How can I get my subordinates to become more motivated and productive?" Conflicting theories abound regarding exactly what it is that creates the greatest improvements in employee performance. Employees can be motivated as a result of their own internal ambitions to perform well on the job, but if the tasks they perform in their jobs are not sufficiently challenging or interesting, they will be less willing to be productive.

Simply put, managers can motivate their subordinates in two ways: (1) by managing subordinates to bring out the needs, drives, and ambitions of each individual and tie performance to the achievement of individual goals, and (2) by creating the proper conditions for motivation to occur through job design and task assignments. It is the manager's task to survey the situation and make changes accordingly.

READINGS

Many managers believe that the way to motivate subordinates is to pay them well. The first article, "One More Time: How Do You Motivate Employees?," by Frederick Herzberg, questions this assumption. Herzberg describes a key difference between the factors that contribute to job dissatisfaction and those that influence motivational processes. He argues that job context factors, such as managerial style, pay, working conditions, and benefits, contribute to employee satisfaction or dissatisfaction, but that motivation is enhanced only by job content—the opportunity for recognition, achievement, and challenge. This theory has touched off a debate on the subject that continues even today.

The second article, "Designing Work for Individuals and for Groups," by J. Richard Hackman, focuses on ways to design jobs to enhance motivation and productivity. The article describes the Job Characteristics Model of motivation, which suggests that a well-designed job may enhance employee motivation. Motivation may increase when employees achieve three critical psychological states: (1) experienced meaningfulness, (2) experienced responsibility, and (3) knowledge of results. Five job characteristics contribute to motivation: (1) skill variety, (2) task identity, (3) task significance, (4) autonomy, and (5) feedback from the job.

The third article, "A Solution to the Performance Appraisal Feedback Enigma," by Herbert H. Meyer, is an updated version of a classic article by the same author on the difficulties associated with giving performance reviews to subordinates. The author reports on the original General Electric study that suggested that split roles played by the boss—as a coach and an evaluator—can hamper the performance appraisal discussion. Performance reviews can be made more effective if participants learn to listen to one another and provide proper feedback. Giving performance reviews is a genuine skill and communication is the key to success.

EXERCISES AND CASES

To help you practice your motivational skills, two exercises and one case are presented. The first exercise, "Enlivening the Job Characteristics Model: A Job Redesign Project" asks you to apply the Hackman & Oldham model of work motivation. By taking the questionnaire, you will learn how well designed (or poorly designed) jobs can be. The principles of work redesign will be used on a class member's job to illustrate how jobs can be redesigned to enhance their motivating properties.

The second exercise is a case entitled, "Saturn Rising: Work Redesign on the Factory Shop Floor." This case is a report on two *Business Week* articles that discuss how the General Motors Saturn automotive plant utilizes state-of-the-art behavioral science concepts such as semiautonomous work teams, motivation-enhanced compensation, and innovative reporting structures to improve product quality. The case offers a follow-up article concerning labor-management relations a few years later so that you can assess the efficacy of these innovations.

The third exercise, "Giving and Receiving Feedback," focuses on feedback skills in managing others' performance. You will participate in a mock performance appraisal situation in which you must provide feedback—positive and negative—to an employee with performance problems. This exercise will teach you how to conduct a more effective performance appraisal as well as provide feedback to others.

MEMO

Finally, the memo assignment for this chapter, *"Redesigning Your Job"* (located at the end of this book), asks you to think about the material learned in this chapter and apply it to your job. You will consider your job as currently designed and determine ways in which it can be made more motivating. You will also consider the jobs of your subordinates (if you have them) and think about ways in which you can rearrange the work so that your employees can have more motivating jobs.

By the time you finish this chapter, you will have a better understanding of motivational processes, the role of job design, and appraising performance. You will begin to practice using these motivational theories to improve your skills in these areas as a manager.

One More Time:
How Do You Motivate Employees?

Frederick Herzberg

FOREWORD

KITA—the externally imposed attempt by management to "install a generator" in the employee—has been demonstrated to be a total failure, the author says. The absence of such "hygiene" factors as good supervisor-employee relations and liberal fringe benefits can make a worker unhappy, but their presence will not make him want to work harder. Essentially meaningless changes in the tasks that workers are assigned to do have not accomplished the desired objective either. The only way to motivate the employee is to give him challenging work in which he can assume responsibility.

Frederick Herzberg, who is Professor and Chairman of the Psychology Department at Case Western Reserve University, has devoted many years to the study of motivation in the United States and abroad. He is the author of *Work and the Nature of Man* (World Publishing Company, 1966).

How many articles, books, speeches, and workshops have pleaded plaintively, "How do I get an employee to do what I want him to do?"

The psychology of motivation is tremendously complex, and what has been unraveled with any degree of assurance is small indeed. But the dismal ratio of knowledge to speculation has not dampened the enthusiasm for new forms of snake oil that are constantly coming on the market, many of them with academic testimonials. Doubtless this article will have no depressing impact on the market for snake oil, but since the ideas expressed in it have been tested in many corporations and other organizations, it will help—I hope—to redress the imbalance in the aforementioned ratio.

'MOTIVATING' WITH KITA

In lectures to industry on the problem, I have found that the audiences are anxious for quick and practical answers, so I will begin with a straightforward, practical formula for moving people.

What is the simplest, surest, and most direct way of getting someone to do something? Ask him? But if he responds that he does not want to do it, then that calls for a psychological consultation to determine the reason for his obstinacy. Tell him? His response shows that he does not understand you, and now an expert in communication methods has to be brought in to show you how to get through to him. Give him a monetary incentive? I do not need to remind the reader of the complexity and difficulty involved in setting up and administering an incentive system. Show him? This means a costly training program. We need a simple way.

Every audience contains the "direct action" manager who shouts, "Kick him!" And this type of manager is right. The surest and least circumlocuted way of getting someone to do something is to kick him in the pants—give him what might be called the KITA.

There are various forms of KITA, and here are some of them:

Negative Physical KITA. This is a literal application of the term and was frequently used in the past. It has, however, three major drawbacks: (1) it is inelegant; (2) it contradicts the precious image of benevolence that most organizations cherish; and (3) since it is a physical attack, it directly stimulates the autonomic nervous system, and this often results in negative feedback—the employee may just kick you in return. These factors give rise to certain taboos against negative physical KITA.

The psychologist has come to the rescue of those who are no longer permitted to use negative physical KITA. He has uncovered infinite sources of psychological vulnerabilities and the appropriate methods to play tunes on them. "He took my rug away"; "I wonder what he meant by that"; "The boss is always going around me"—these symptomatic expressions of ego sores that have been rubbed raw are the result of application of:

Negative Psychological KITA. This has several advantages over negative physical KITA. First, the cruelty is not visible; the bleeding is internal and comes much later. Second, since it affects the higher cortical centers of the brain with its inhibitory powers, it reduces the possibility of physical backlash. Third, since the number of psychological pains that a person can feel is almost infinite, the direction and site possibilities of the KITA are increased many times. Fourth, the person administering the kick can manage to be above it all and let the system accomplish the dirty work. Fifth, those who practice it receive some ego satisfaction (oneupmanship), whereas they would find drawing blood abhorrent. Finally, if the employee does complain, he can always be accused of being paranoid, since there is no tangible evidence of an actual attack.

Now, what does negative KITA accomplish? If I kick you in the rear (physically or psychologically), who is motivated? *I* am motivated; *you* move! Negative KITA does not lead to motivation, but to movement. So:

Positive KITA. Let us consider motivation. If I say to you, "Do this for me or the company, and in return I will give you a reward, an incentive, more status, a promotion, all the quid pro quos that exist in the industrial organization," am I motivating you? The overwhelming opinion I receive from management people is, "Yes, this is motivation."

I have a year-old Schnauzer. When it was a small puppy and I wanted it to move, I kicked it in the rear and it moved. Now that I have finished its obedience training, I hold up a dog biscuit when I want the Schnauzer to move. In this instance, who is motivated—I or the dog? The dog wants the biscuit, but it is I who want it to move. Again, I am the one who is motivated, and the dog is the one who moves. In this instance all I did was apply KITA frontally; I exerted a pull instead of a push. When industry wishes to use positive KITAs, it has available an incredible number and variety of dog biscuits (jelly beans for humans) to wave in front of the employee to get him to jump.

Why is it that managerial audiences are quick to see that negative KITA is *not* motivation, while they are almost unanimous in their judgment that positive KITA *is* motivation? It is because negative KITA is rape, and positive KITA is seduction. But it is infinitely worse to be seduced than to be raped; the latter is an unfortunate occurrence, while the former signifies that you were a party to your own downfall. This is why positive KITA is so popular: it is a tradition; it is in the American way. The organization does not have to kick you; you kick yourself.

Myths About Motivation

Why is KITA not motivation? If I kick my dog (from the front or the back), he will move. And when I want him to move again, what must I do? I must kick him again. Similarly, I can charge a man's battery, and then recharge it, and recharge it again. But it is only when he has his own generator that we can talk about motivation. He then needs no outside stimulation. He *wants* to do it.

With this in mind, we can review some positive KITA personnel practices that were developed as attempts to instill "motivation":

1. *Reducing time spent at work*—This represents a marvelous way of motivating people to work—getting them off the job! We have reduced (formally and informally) the time spent on the job over the last 50 or 60 years until we are finally on the way to the "6½-day weekend." An interesting variant of this approach is the development of off-hour recreation programs. The philosophy here seems to be that those who play together, work together. The fact is that motivated people seek more hours of work, not fewer.

2. *Spiraling wages*—Have these motivated people? Yes, to seek the next wage increase. Some medievalists still can be heard to say that a good depression will get employees moving. They feel

that if rising wages don't or won't do the job, perhaps reducing them will.

3. *Fringe benefits*—Industry has outdone the most welfare-minded of welfare states in dispensing cradle-to-the-grave succor. One company I know of had an informal "fringe benefit of the month club" going for a while. The cost of fringe benefits in this country has reached approximately 25% of the wage dollar, and we still cry for motivation.

People spend less time working for more money and more security than ever before, and the trend cannot be reversed. These benefits are no longer rewards; they are rights. A 6-day week is inhuman, a 10-hour day is exploitation, extended medical coverage is a basic decency, and stock options are the salvation of American initiative. Unless the ante is continuously raised, the psychological reaction of employees is that the company is turning back the clock.

When industry began to realize that both the economic nerve and the lazy nerve of their employees had insatiable appetites, it started to listen to the behavioral scientists who, more out of a humanist tradition than from scientific study, criticized management for not knowing how to deal with people. The next KITA easily followed.

4. *Human relations training*—Over 30 years of teaching and, in many instances, of practicing psychological approaches to handling people have resulted in costly human relations programs and, in the end, the same question: How do you motivate workers? Here, too, escalations have taken place. Thirty years ago it was necessary to request, "Please don't spit on the floor." Today the same admonition requires three "please"s before the employee feels that his superior has demonstrated the psychologically proper attitudes toward him.

The failure of human relations training to produce motivation led to the conclusion that the supervisor or manager himself was not psychologically true to himself in his practice of interpersonal decency. So an advanced form of human relations KITA, sensitivity training, was unfolded.

5. *Sensitivity training*—Do you really, really understand yourself? Do you really, really, really trust the other man? Do you really, really, really, really cooperate? The failure of sensitivity training is now being explained, by those who have become opportunistic exploiters of the technique, as a failure to really (five times) conduct proper sensitivity training courses.

With the realization that there are only temporary gains from comfort and economic and interpersonal KITA, personnel managers concluded that the fault lay not in what they were doing, but in the employee's failure to appreciate what they were doing. This opened up the field of communications, a whole new area of "scientifically" sanctioned KITA.

6. *Communications*—The professor of communications was invited to join the faculty of management training programs and help in making employees understand what management was doing for them. House organs, briefing sessions, supervisory instruction on the importance of communication, and all sorts of propaganda have proliferated until today there is even an International Council of Industrial Editors. But no motivation resulted, and the obvious thought occurred that perhaps management was not hearing what the employees were saying. That led to the next KITA.

7. *Two-way communication*—Management ordered morale surveys, suggestion plans, and group participation programs. Then

both employees and management were communicating and listening to each other more than ever, but without much improvement in motivation.

The behavioral scientists began to take another look at their conceptions and their data, and they took human relations one step further. A glimmer of truth was beginning to show through in the writings of the so-called higher-order-need psychologists. People, so they said, want to actualize themselves. Unfortunately the "actualizing" psychologists got mixed up with the human relations psychologists, and a new KITA emerged.

8. *Job participation*—Though it may not have been the theoretical intention, job participation often became a "give them the big picture" approach. For example, if a man is tightening 10,000 nuts a day on an assembly line with a torque wrench, tell him he is building a Chevrolet. Another approach had the goal of giving the employee a *feeling* that he is determining, in some measure, what he does on his job. The goal was to provide a *sense* of achievement rather than a substantive achievement in his task. Real achievement, of course, requires a task that makes it possible.

But still there was no motivation. This led to the inevitable conclusion that the employees must be sick, and therefore to the next KITA.

9. *Employee counseling*—The initial use of this form of KITA in a systematic fashion can be credited to the Hawthorne experiment of the Western Electric Company during the early 1930s. At that time, it was found that the employees harbored irrational feelings that were interfering with the rational operation of the factory. Counseling in this instance was a means of letting the employers unburden themselves by talking to someone about their problems. Although the counseling techniques were primitive, the program was large indeed.

The counseling approach suffered as a result of experiences during World War II, when the programs themselves were found to be interfering with the operation of the organizations; the counselors had forgotten their role of benevolent listeners and were attempting to do something about the problems that they heard about. Psychological counseling, however, has managed to survive the negative impact of World War II experiences and today is beginning to flourish with renewed sophistication. But, alas, many of these programs, like all the others, do not seem to have lessened the pressure of demands to find out how to motivate workers.

Since KITA results only in short-term movement, it is safe to predict that the cost of these programs will increase steadily and new varieties will be developed as old positive KITAs reach their satiation points.

HYGIENE VS. MOTIVATORS

Let me rephrase the perennial question this way: How do you install a generator in an employee? A brief review of my motivation-hygiene theory of job attitudes is required before theoretical and practical suggestions can be offered. The theory was first drawn from an examination of events in the lives of engineers and accountants. At least 16 other investigations, using a wide variety of populations (including some in the Communist countries), have since been completed, making the original research one of the most replicated studies in the field of job attitudes.

The findings of these studies, along with corroboration from many other investigations using different procedures, suggest that the factors involved in producing job satisfaction (and motivation) are separate and distinct from the factors that lead to job dissatisfaction. Since separate factors need to be considered, depending on whether job satisfaction or job dissatisfaction is being examined, it follows that these two feelings are not opposites of each other. The opposite of job satisfaction is not job dissatisfaction but, rather, *no* job satisfaction; and, similarly, the opposite of job dissatisfaction.

Stating the concept presents a problem in semantics, for we normally think of satisfaction and dissatisfaction as opposites—i.e., what is not satisfying must be dissatisfying, and vice versa. But when it comes to understanding the behavior of people in their jobs, more than a play on words is involved.

Two different needs of man are involved here. One set of needs can be thought of as stemming from his animal nature—the built-in drive to avoid pain from the environment, plus all the learned drives which become conditioned to the basic biological needs. For example, hunger, a basic biological drive, makes it necessary to earn money, and then money becomes a specific drive. The other set of needs relates to that unique human characteristic, the ability to achieve and, through achievement, to experience psychological growth. The stimuli for the growth needs are tasks that induce growth; in the industrial setting, they are the *job content*. Contrariwise, the stimuli inducing pain-avoidance behavior are found in the *job environment*.

The growth or *motivator* factors that are intrinsic to the job are: achievement, recognition for achievement, the work itself, responsibility, and growth or advancement. The dissatisfaction-avoidance or *hygiene* (KITA) factors that are extrinsic to the job include: company policy and administration, supervision, interpersonal relationships, working conditions, salary, status, and security.

A composite of the factors that are involved in causing job satisfaction and job dissatisfaction, drawn from samples of 1,685 employees, is shown in *Exhibit I*. The results indicate that motivators were the primary cause of satisfaction, and hygiene factors the primary cause of unhappiness on the job. The employees, studied in 12 different investigations, included lower-level supervisors, professional women, agricultural administrators, men about to retire from management positions, hospital maintenance personnel, manufacturing supervisors, nurses, food handlers, military officers, engineers, scientists, housekeepers, teachers, technicians, female assemblers, accountants, Finnish foremen, and Hungarian engineers.

They were asked what job events had occurred in their work that had led to extreme satisfaction or extreme dissatisfaction on their part. Their responses are broken down in the exhibit into percentages of total "positive" job events and of total "negative" job events. (The figures total more than 100% on both the "hygiene" and "motivators" sides because often at least two factors can be attributed to a single event; advancement, for instance, often accompanies assumption of responsibility.)

To illustrate, a typical response involving achievement that had a negative effect for the employee was, "I was unhappy because I didn't do the job successfully." A typical response in the small number of positive job events in the Company Policy and Administration grouping was, "I was happy because the company reorganized the section so that I didn't report any longer to the guy I didn't get along with."

As the lower right-hand part of the exhibit shows, of all the factors contributing to job satisfaction, 81% were motivators. And of all the factors contributing to the employees' dissatisfaction over their work, 69% involved hygiene elements.

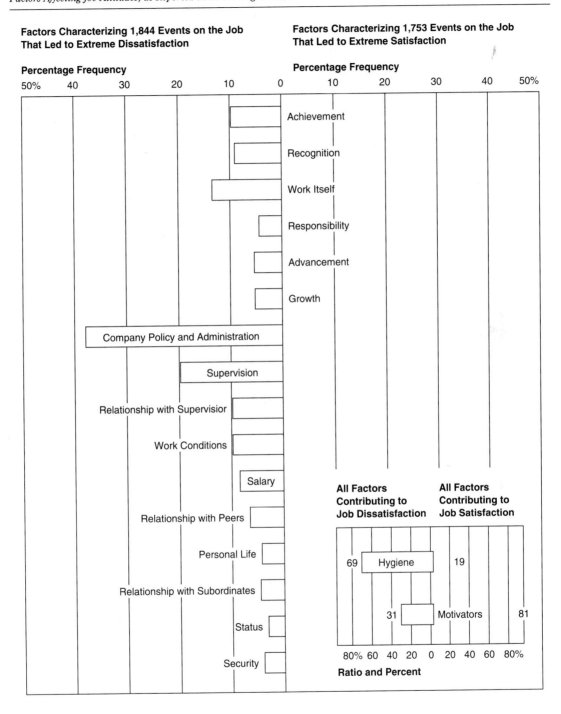

Factors Characterizing 1,844 Events on the Job That Led to Extreme Dissatisfaction

Factors Characterizing 1,753 Events on the Job That Led to Extreme Satisfaction

Percentage Frequency

50% 40 30 20 10 0 10 20 30 40 50%

Percentage Frequency

- Achievement
- Recognition
- Work Itself
- Responsibility
- Advancement
- Growth
- Company Policy and Administration
- Supervision
- Relationship with Supervisior
- Work Conditions
- Salary
- Relationship with Peers
- Personal Life
- Relationship with Subordinates
- Status
- Security

All Factors Contributing to Job Dissatisfaction

All Factors Contributing to Job Satisfaction

69 Hygiene 19

31 Motivators 81

80% 60 40 20 0 20 40 60 80%

Ratio and Percent

Eternal Triangle

There are three general philosophies of personnel management. The first is based on organizational theory, the second on industrial engineering, and the third on behavioral science.

The organizational theorist believes that human needs are either so irrational or so varied and adjustable to specific situations that the major function of personnel management is to be as pragmatic as the occasion demands. If jobs are organized in a proper manner, he reasons, the result will be the most efficient job structure, and the most favorable job attitudes will follow as a matter of course.

The industrial engineer holds that man is mechanistically oriented and economically motivated and his needs are best met by attuning the individual to the most efficient work process. The goal of personnel management therefore should be to concoct the most appropriate incentive system and to design the specific working conditions in a way that facilitates the most efficient use of the human machine. By structuring jobs in a manner that leads to the most efficient operation, the engineer believes that he can obtain the optimal organization of work and the proper work attitudes.

The behavioral scientist focuses on group sentiments, attitudes of individual employees, and the organization's social and psychological climate. According to his persuasion, he emphasizes one or more of the various hygiene and motivator needs. His approach to personnel management generally emphasizes some form of human relations education, in the hope of instilling healthy employee attitudes and an organizational climate which he considers to be felicitous to human values. He believes that proper attitudes will lead to efficient job and organizational structure.

There is always a lively debate as to the overall effectiveness of the approaches of the organizational theorist and the industrial engineer. Manifestly they have achieved much. But the nagging question for the behavioral scientist has been: What is the cost in human problems that eventually cause more expenses to the organization—for instance, turnover, absenteeism, errors, violation of safety rules, strikes, restriction of output, higher wages, and greater fringe benefits? On the other hand, the behavioral scientist is hard put to document much manifest improvement in personnel management, using his approach.

The three philosophies can be depicted as a triangle, as is done in *Exhibit II,* with each persuasion claiming the apex angle. The motivation-hygiene theory claims the same angle as industrial engineering, but for opposite goals. Rather than rationalizing the work to increase efficiency, the theory suggests that work be *enriched* to bring about effective utilization of personnel. Such a systematic attempt to motivate employees by manipulating the motivator factors is just beginning.

The term *job enrichment* describes this embryonic movement. An older term, job enlargement, should be avoided because it is associated with past failures stemming from a misunderstanding of the problem. Job enrichment provides the opportunity for the employee's psychological growth, while job enlargement merely makes a job structurally bigger. Since scientific job enrichment is very new, this article only suggests the principles and practical steps that have recently emerged from several successful experiments in industry.

Job Loading

In attempting to enrich an employee's job, management often succeeds in reducing the man's personal contribution, rather than giving him an opportunity for growth in his accustomed job. Such an endeavor, which I shall call horizontal job loading (as opposed to vertical loading or providing motivator factors), has been the problem of earlier job enlargement programs. This activity merely enlarges the meaninglessness of the job. Some examples of this approach, and their effect, are:

EXHIBIT II
'Triangle' of Philosophies of Personnel Management.

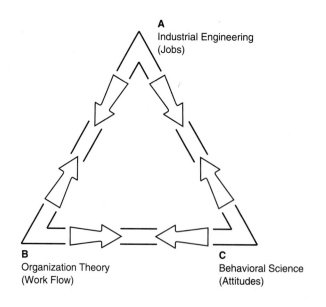

A
Industrial Engineering
(Jobs)

B
Organization Theory
(Work Flow)

C
Behavioral Science
(Attitudes)

EXHIBIT III
Principles of Vertical Job Loading.

Principle	Motivators Involved
A. Removing some controls while retaining accountability	Responsibility and personal achievement
B. Increasing the accountability of individuals for own work	Responsibility and recognition
C. Giving a person a complete natural unit of work (module, division, area, and so on)	Responsibility, achievement, and recognition
D. Granting additional authority to an employee in his activity, job freedom	Responsibility, achievement, and recognition
E. Making periodic reports directly available to the worker himself rather than to the supervisor	Internal recognition
F. Introducing new and more difficult tasks not previously handled	Growth and learning
G. Assigning individuals specific or specialized tasks, enabling them to become experts	Responsibility, growth and advancement

❒ Challenging the employee by increasing the amount of production expected of him. If he tightens 10,000 bolts a day, see if he can tighten 20,000 bolts a day. The arithmetic involved shows that multiplying zero by zero still equals zero.

❒ Adding another meaningless task to the existing one, usually some routine clerical activity. The arithmetic here is adding zero to zero.

❒ Rotating the assignments of a number of jobs that need to be enriched. This means washing dishes for a while, then washing silverware. The arithmetic is substituting one zero for another zero.

❒ Removing the most difficult parts of the assignment in order to free the worker to accomplish more of the less challenging assignments. This traditional industrial engineering approach amounts to subtraction in the hope of accomplishing addition.

These are common forms of horizontal loading that frequently come up in preliminary brainstorming sessions on job enrichment. The principles of vertical loading have not all been worked out as yet, and they remain rather general, but I have furnished seven useful starting points for consideration in *Exhibit III.*

A Successful Application

An example from a highly successful job enrichment experiment can illustrate the distinction between horizontal and vertical loading of a job. The subjects of this study were the stockholder correspondents employed by a very large corporation. Seemingly, the task required of these carefully selected and highly trained correspondents was quite complex and challenging. But almost all indexes of performance and job attitudes were low, and exit interviewing confirmed that the challenge of the job existed merely as words.

A job enrichment project was initiated in the form of an experiment with one group, designated as an achieving unit, having its job enriched by the principles described in *Exhibit III.* A control group continued to do its job in the traditional way. (There were also two "uncommitted" groups of correspondents formed to measure the so-called Hawthorne Effect—that is, to gauge whether productivity and attitudes toward the job changed artificially merely because employees sensed that the company was paying more attention to them in doing something different or novel. The results for these groups were substantially the same as for the control group, and for the sake of simplicity I do not deal with them in this summary.) No changes in hygiene were introduced for either group other than those that would have been made anyway, such as normal pay increases.

The changes for the achieving unit were introduced in the first two months, averaging one per week of the seven motivators listed in *Exhibit III.* At the end of six months the members of the achieving unit were found to be outperforming their counterparts in the control group, and in addition indicated a marked increase in their liking for their jobs. Other results showed that the achieving group had lower absenteeism and, subsequently, a much higher rate of promotion.

Exhibit IV illustrates the changes in performance, measured in February and March, before the study period began, and at the end of each month of the study period. The shareholder service index represents quality of letters, including accuracy of information, and speed of response to stockholders' letters of inquiry. The index of a current month was averaged into the average of the two prior months, which means that improvement was harder to obtain if the indexes of the previous months were low. The "achievers" were performing less well before the six-month period started, and their performance service index continued to decline after the introduction of the motivators, evidently because of uncertainty over their newly granted responsibilities. In the third month, however, performance improved, and soon the members of this group had reached a high level of accomplishment.

Exhibit V shows the two groups' attitudes toward their job, measured at the end of March, just before the first motivator was introduced, and again at the end of September. The correspondents were asked 16 questions, all involving motivation. A typical one was, "As you see it, how many opportunities do you feel that you have in your job for making worthwhile contributions?" The answers were scaled from 1 to 5, with 80 as the maximum possible score. The achievers became much more positive about their job, while the attitude of the control unit remained about the same (the drop is not statistically significant).

EXHIBIT IV
Shareholder Service Index in Company Experiment.
[Three-Month Cumulative Average]

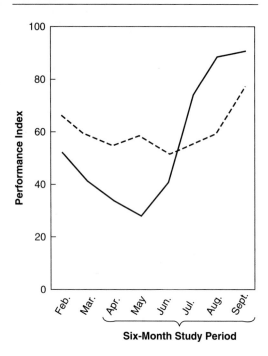

Six-Month Study Period

EXHIBIT V
Changes in Attitudes Toward Tasks in Company Experiment.
[Changes in Mean Scores over Six-Month Period]

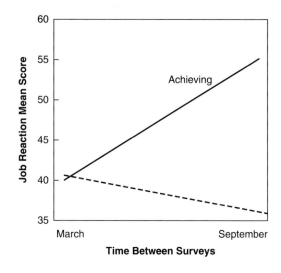

Time Between Surveys

How was the job of these correspondents restructured? *Exhibit VI* lists the suggestions made that were deemed to be horizontal loading, and the actual vertical loading changes that were incorporated in the job of the achieving unit. The capital letters under "Principle" after "Vertical loading" refer to the corresponding letters in *Exhibit III*. The reader will note that the rejected forms of horizontal loading correspond closely to the list of common manifestations of the phenomenon on page 91, left column.

STEPS TO JOB ENRICHMENT

Now that the motivator idea has been described in practice, here are the steps that managers should take in instituting the principle with their employees.

1. Select those jobs in which (a) the investment in industrial engineering does not make changes too costly, (b) attitudes are poor, (c) hygiene is becoming very costly, and (d) motivation will make a difference in performance.

2. Approach these jobs with the conviction that they can be changed. Years of tradition had led managers to believe that the content of the jobs is sacrosanct and the only scope of action that they have is in ways of stimulating people.

3. Brainstorm a list of changes that may enrich the jobs, without concern for their practicality.

4. Screen the list to eliminate suggestions that involve hygiene, rather than actual motivation.

5. Screen the list for generalities, such as "give them more responsibility," that are rarely followed in practice. This might seem obvious, but the motivator words had never left industry; the substance has just been rationalized and organized out. Words like "responsibility," "growth," "achievement," and "challenge," for example, have been elevated to the lyrics of the patriotic anthem for all organizations. It is the old problem typified by the pledge of allegiance of the flag being more important than contributions to the country—of following the form, rather than the substance.

6. Screen the list to eliminate any *horizontal* loading suggestions.

7. Avoid direct participation by the employees whose jobs are to be enriched. Ideas they have expressed previously certainly constitute a valuable source for recommended changes, but their direct involvement contaminates the process with human relations *hygiene* and, more specifically, gives them only a *sense* of making a contribution. The job is to be changed, and it is the content that will produce the motivation, not attitudes about being involved or the challenge inherent in setting up a job. That process will be over shortly, and it is what the employees will be doing from then on that will determine their motivation. A sense of participation will result only in short-term movement.

8. In the initial attempts at job enrichment, set up a controlled experiment. At least two equivalent groups should be chosen, one an experimental unit in which the motivators are systematically introduced over a period of time, and the other one a control group in which no changes are made. For both groups, hygiene should be allowed to follow its natural course for the duration of the experiment. Pre- and post-installation tests of performance and job attitudes are necessary to evaluate the effectiveness of the job enrichment program. The attitude test must be limited to motivator items in order to divorce the employee's view of the job he is given from all the surrounding hygiene feelings that he might have.

9. Be prepared for a drop in performance in the experimental group the first few weeks. The changeover to a new job may lead to a temporary reduction in efficiency.

10. Expect your first-line supervisors to experience some anxiety and hostility over the changes you are making. The anxiety comes from their fear that the changes will result in poorer performance for their unit. Hostility will arise when the employees start assuming what the supervisors regard as their own responsibility for performance. The supervisor without checking duties to perform may then be left with little to do.

After a successful experiment, however, the supervisor usually discovers the supervisory and managerial functions he has neglected, or which were never his because all his time was given over to checking the work of his subordinates. For example, in the R&D division of one large chemical company I know of, the supervisors of the laboratory assistants were theoretically responsible for their training and evaluation. These functions, however, had come to be performed in a routine, unsubstantial fashion. After the job enrichment program, during which the supervisors were not merely passive observers of the assistants' performance, the supervisors actually were devoting their time to reviewing performance and administering thorough training.

What has been called an employee-centered style of supervision will come about not through education of supervisors, but by changing the jobs that they do.

CONCLUDING NOTE

Job enrichment will not be a one-time proposition, but a continuous management function. The initial changes, however, should last for a very long period of time. There are a number of reasons for this:

❒ The changes should bring the job up to the level of challenge commensurate with the skill that was hired.

❒ Those who have still more ability eventually will be able to demonstrate it better and win promotion to higher-level jobs.

❒ The very nature of motivators, as opposed to hygiene factors, is that they have a much longer-term effect on employees' attitudes. Perhaps the job will have to be enriched again, but this will not occur as frequently as the need for hygiene.

Not all jobs can be enriched, nor do all jobs need to be enriched. If only a small percentage of the time and money that is

EXHIBIT VI

Enlargement vs. Enrichment of Correspondents' Tasks in Company Experiment.

Horizontal Loading Suggestions (Rejected)	*Vertical Loading Suggestions (Adopted)*	*Principle*
Firm quotas could be set for letters to be answered each day, using a rate which would be hard to reach.	Subject matter experts were appointed within each unit for other members of the unit to consult with before seeking supervisory help. (The supervisor had been answering all specialized and difficult questions.)	G
The women could type the letters themselves, as well as compose them, or take on any other clerical functions.	Correspondents signed their own names on letters. (The supervisor had been signing all letters.)	B
All difficult or complex inquiries could be channeled to a few women so that the remainder could achieve high rates of output. These jobs could be exchanged from time to time.	The work of the more experienced correspondents was proofread frequently by supervisors and was done at the correspondents' desks, dropping verification from 100% to 10%. (Previously, all correspondents' letters had been checked by the supervisor.)	A
The women could be rotated through units handling different customers, and then sent back to their own units.	Production was discussed, but only in terms such as "a full day's work is expected." As time went on, this was no longer mentioned. (Before, the group had been constantly reminded of the number of letters that needed to be answered.)	D
	Outgoing mail went directly to the mailroom without going over supervisors' desks. (The letters had always been routed through the supervisors.)	A
	Correspondents were encouraged to answer letters in a more personalized way. (Reliance on the form-letter approach had been standard practice.)	C
	Each correspondent was held personally responsible for the quality and accuracy of letters. (This responsibility had been the province of the supervisor and the verifier.)	B, E

now devoted to hygiene, however, were given to job enrichment efforts, the return in human satisfaction and economic gain would be one of the largest dividends that industry and society have ever reaped through their efforts at better personnel management.

The argument for job enrichment can be summed up quite simply: If you have someone on a job, use him. If you can't use him on the job, get rid of him, either via automation or by selecting someone with lesser ability. If you can't use him and you can't get rid of him, you will have a motivation problem.

Designing Work for Individuals and for Groups

J. Richard Hackman

As yet there are no simple or generally accepted criteria for a well-designed job, nor is a single technology acknowledged as the proper way to go about redesigning work. Moreover, it often is unclear in specific circumstances whether work should be structured to be performed by individual employees, or whether it should be designed to be carried out by a *group* of employees working together.

The first part of this selection reviews one current model for work design that focuses on the individual performer. In the second part, discussion turns to a number of issues that must be dealt with when work is designed for interacting teams of employees.

DESIGNING WORK FOR INDIVIDUALS

A model specifying how job characteristics and individual differences interact to affect the satisfaction, motivation, and productivity of individuals at work has been proposed by Hackman and Oldham (1976). The model is specifically intended for use in planning and carrying out changes in the design of jobs. It is described below, and then is used as a guide for a discussion of diagnostic procedures and change principles that can be used in redesigning the jobs of individuals.

The Job Characteristics Model

The basic job characteristics model is shown in Figure 1. As illustrated in the figure, five core job dimensions are seen as creating three critical psychological states which, in turn, lead to a number of beneficial personal and work outcomes. The links among the job dimensions, the psychological states, and the outcomes are shown to be moderated by the strength of individuals' growth needs. The major classes of variables in the model are reviewed briefly below.

Psychological States. The three following psychological states are postulated as critical in affecting a person's motivation and satisfaction on the job:

1. Experienced meaningfulness: The person must experience the work as generally important, valuable, and worthwhile.

2. Experienced responsibility: The individual must feel personally responsible and accountable for the results of the work he or she performs.

3. Knowledge of results: The individual must have understanding, on a fairly regular basis, of how effectively he or she is performing on the job.

The more these three conditions are present, the more people will feel good about themselves when they perform well. Or, following Hackman and Lawler (1971), the model postulates that internal rewards are obtained by individuals when they *learn* (knowledge of results) that they *personally* (experienced responsibility) have performed well on a task that they *care about* (experienced meaningfulness). These internal rewards are reinforcing to the individual, and serve as incentives for continued efforts to perform well in the future. When the persons do not perform well, they do not experience a reinforcing state of affairs, and may elect to try harder in the future so as to regain the rewards that good performance brings. The net result is a self-perpetuating cycle of positive work motivation powered by self-generated rewards, that is predicted to continue until one or more of the three psychological states is no longer present—or until the individual no longer values the internal rewards that derive from good performance.

Job Dimensions. Of the five job characteristics shown in Figure 1 as fostering the emergence of the psychological states, three contribute to the experienced meaningfulness of the work, and one each contributes to experienced responsibility and to knowledge of results.

The three job dimensions that contribute to a job's *meaningfulness* are:

1. *Skill variety* The degree to which a job requires a variety of different activities in carrying out the work, which involve the use of a number of different skills and talents of the person.

When a task requires a person to engage in activities that challenge or stretch his or her skills and abilities, that task almost invariably is experienced as meaningful by the individual. Many parlor games, puzzles, and recreational activities, for example, achieve much of their fascination because they tap and test the intellective or motor skills of the people who do them. When a job draws upon several skills of an employee, that individual may find

Reprinted with permission from J. R. Hackman, E. E. Lawler III, and L. W. Porter (eds.), *Perspectives on Behavior in Organizations* (New York: McGraw-Hill Book Company, 1977).

FIGURE 1
The Job Characteristics Model of Work Motivation.

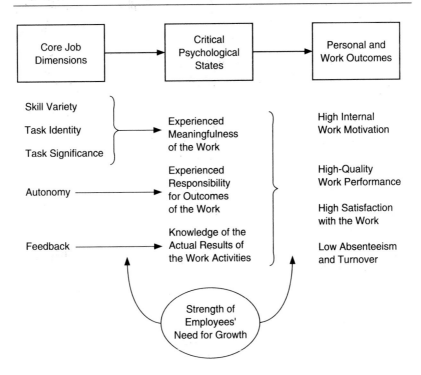

the job to be of very high personal meaning—even if, in any absolute sense, it is not of great significance or importance.

2. *Task identity* The degree to which the job requires completion of a "whole" and identifiable piece of work—that is, doing a job from beginning to end with a visible outcome.

If an employee assembles a complete product or provides a complete product of service he or she should find the work more meaningful than if he or she were responsible for only a small part of the whole job—other things (such as skill variety) being equal.

3. *Task significance* The degree to which the job has a substantial impact on the lives or work of other people—whether in the immediate organization or in the external environment.

When individuals understand that the results of their work may have a significant effect on the well-being of other people, the experienced meaningfulness of the work usually is enhanced. Employees who tighten nuts on aircraft brake assemblies, for example, are more likely to perceive their work as meaningful than are workers who fill small boxes with paper clips—even though the skill levels involved may be comparable.

The job characteristic predicted to prompt feelings of personal *responsibility* for the work outcomes is autonomy. "Autonomy" is defined as the degree to which the job provides substantial freedom, independence, and discretion to the individual in scheduling the work and in determining the procedures to be used in carrying it out.

To the extent that autonomy is high, work outcomes will be viewed by workers as depending substantially on their *own* efforts,

initiatives, and decisions, rather than on the adequacy of instructions from the boss or on a manual of job procedures. In such circumstances, individuals should feel a strong personal responsibility for the successes and failures that occur on the job.

The job characteristic that fosters *knowledge of results* is "feedback," which is defined as the degree to which carrying out the work activities required by the job results in the individual's obtaining direct and clear information about the effectiveness of his or her performance.

It often is useful to combine the scores of a job on the five dimensions described above into a single index reflecting the overall potential of the job to prompt self-generated work motivation on the part of job incumbents. Following the model diagrammed in Figure 1, a job high in motivating potential must be high on at least one (and hopefully more) of the three dimensions that lead to experienced meaningfulness, *and* high on autonomy and feedback as well—thereby creating conditions for all three of the critical psychological states to be present. Arithmetically, scores of jobs on the five dimensions are combined as follows to meet this criterion:

$$\text{Motivating potential score (MPS)} =$$

$$\left(\frac{\text{skill variety} + \text{task identity} + \text{task significance}}{3} \right)$$

$$\leftarrow \times \ \text{autonomy} \times \ \text{job feedback}$$

As can be seen from the formula, a near-zero score of a job on either autonomy or feedback will reduce the overall MPS to near-zero; whereas a near-zero score on one of the three job dimensions that contribute to experienced meaningfulness cannot, by itself, do so.

Strength of the Individual's Need for Growth. The strength of a person's need for growth is postulated to moderate how people react to complex, challenging work at two points in the model shown in Figure 1: first, at the link between the objective job dimensions and the psychological states, and again between the psychological states and the outcome variables. The first link means that persons with a high need for growth are more likely (or better able) to *experience* the psychological states when an objective job is enriched than persons with a low need for growth. The second link means that individuals with a high need for growth will respond more positively to the psychological states, when they are present, than persons with a low need for growth.

Outcome Variables. Also shown in Figure 1 are several outcomes that are affected by the level of self-generated motivation experienced by people at work. Of special interest as an outcome variable is internal work motivation (Lawler & Hall, 1970; Hackman & Lawler, 1971), because it taps directly the contingency between effective performance and self-administered affective rewards. Typically questionnaire items measuring internal work motivation include: (1) I feel a great sense of personal satisfaction when I do this job well; (2) I feel bad and unhappy when I discover that I have performed poorly on this job; and (3) My own feelings are *not* affected much one way or the other by how well I do on this job (reversed scoring).

Other outcomes listed in Figure 1 are the quality of work performance, job satisfaction (especially satisfaction with opportunities for personal growth and development on the job), absenteeism, and turnover. All these outcomes are predicted to be affected positively by a job high in motivating potential.

Validity of the Job Characteristics Model

Empirical testing of the job characteristics model of work motivation is reported in detail elsewhere (Hackman & Oldham, 1976). In general, results are supportive, as suggested by the following overview:

1. People who work on jobs high on the core job characteristics are more motivated, satisfied, and productive than people who work on jobs that score low on these characteristics. The same is true for absenteeism, although less strongly so.

2. Responses to jobs high in objective motivating potential are more positive for people who have strong needs for growth than for people with weak needs for growth. The moderating effect of an individual's need for growth occurs both at the link between the job dimensions and the psychological states and at the link between the psychological states and the outcome measures, as shown in Figure 1. (This moderating effect is not, however, obtained for absenteeism.)

3. The job characteristics operate *through* the psychological states in influencing the outcome variables, as predicted by the model, rather than influencing the outcomes directly. Two anomalies have been identified, however: (1) results involving the feedback dimension are in some cases less strong than for those obtained for the other dimensions (perhaps in part because individuals receive feedback at work from many sources—not just the job), and (2) the linkage between autonomy and experienced responsibility does not operate exactly as specified by the model in affecting the outcome variables (Hackman & Oldham, 1976).

Diagnostic Use of the Model

The job characteristics model was designed so that each major class of variables (objective job characteristics, mediating psychological states, strength of the individual's need for growth, and work motivation and satisfaction) can be directly measured in actual work situations. Such measurements are obtained using the Job Diagnostic Survey (JDS), which is described in detail elsewhere (Hackman & Oldham, 1975). The major intended uses of the JDS are (1) to diagnose existing jobs before planned work redesign, and (2) to evaluate the effects of work redesign—for example, to determine which job dimensions did and did not change, to assess the impact of the changes on the motivation and satisfaction of employees, and to test for any possible alterations after the change in the need for growth of people whose jobs were redesigned.

In the paragraphs to follow, several steps are presented that might be followed by a change agent in carrying out a diagnosis using the JDS.

Step 1: Are Motivation and Satisfaction Really Problems? Sometimes organizations undertake job enrichment or work redesign to improve work motivation and satisfaction when in fact the real problem with work performance lies elsewhere—for example, in the equipment or technology of the job. It is important, therefore, to examine the level of employees' motivation and satisfaction at an early stage in a job diagnosis. If motivation and satisfaction are problems, and are accompanied by documented problems in work performance, absenteeism, or turnover as revealed by independent organizational indices, the change agent would continue to step 2. If not, the agent presumably would look to other aspects of the work situation (e.g., the technology, the workflow) to identify and understand the reasons for the problem which gave rise to the diagnostic activity.

Step 2: Is the Job Low in Motivating Potential? To answer this question, the change agent would examine the Motivating Potential Score of the target job, and compare it with the MPS scores of other jobs to determine whether or not the *job itself* is a probable cause of the motivational problems documented in step 1. If the job turns out to be low on MPS, he would continue to step 3; if it scores high, he would look for other reasons for the motivational difficulties (e.g., the pay plan, the nature of supervision, and so on).

Step 3: What Specific Aspects of the Job Are Causing the Difficulty? This step involves examination of the job on each of the five core job dimensions, to pinpoint the specific strengths and weaknesses of the job as it currently exists. It is useful at this stage to construct a profile of the target job, to make visually apparent where improvements need to be made. An illustrative profile for two jobs (one "good" job and one job needing improvement) is shown in Figure 2.

FIGURE 2
JDS Profile of a "Good" Job and a "Bad" Job.

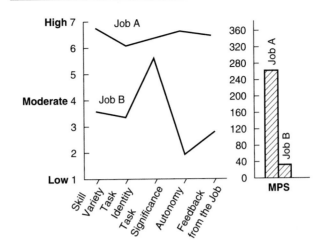

Job A is an engineering maintenance job, and is high on all of the core dimensions; the MPS of this job is very high: 260.[1] Job enrichment would not be recommended for this job; if employees working on the job are unproductive and unhappy, the reasons probably have little to do with the design of the work itself.

Job B, on the other hand, has many problems. This job involves the routine and repetitive processing of checks in a bank. The MPS of 30—which is quite low—would be even lower if it were not for the moderately high task significance of the job. (Task significance is moderately high because the people are handling large amounts of other people's money, and their efforts potentially have important consequences for the unseen clients.) The job provides the individuals with very little direct feedback about how effectively they are performing; the employees have little autonomy in how they go about doing the job; and the job is moderately low in both skill variety and task identity.

For Job B, then, there is plenty of room for improvement, and many avenues to consider in planning job changes. For still other jobs, the avenues for change may turn out to be considerably more specific: for example, feedback and autonomy may be reasonably high, but one or more of the core dimensions which contribute to the experienced meaningfulness of the work (i.e., skill variety, task identity, and task significance) may be low. In such a case, attention would turn to ways to increase the standing of the job on these latter three dimensions.

Step 4: How Ready Are the Employees for Change? Once it has been documented that there is need for improvement in the focal job, and the particularly troublesome aspects of the job have been identified, then it is appropriate to begin planning the specific action steps which will be taken to enrich the job. An important factor in such planning is determining the strength of the employees' needs

for growth, since employees whose needs for growth are strong should respond more readily to job enrichment than employees whose needs are weak. The measure of the need for growth provided by the JDS can be helpful in identifying which employees should be among the first to have jobs changed (i.e., those whose needs for growth are strong), and how such changes should be introduced (e.g., perhaps with more caution for individuals whose needs for growth are weak).

Step 5: What Special Problems and Opportunities Are Present in the Existing Work System? Before undertaking actual job changes, it is always advisable to search for any special roadblocks that may exist in the organizational unit as it currently exists, and for special opportunities that may be built upon in the change program.

Frequently of special importance in this regard is the level of *satisfaction* employees currently experience with various aspects of their organizational life. For example, the JDS provides measures of satisfaction with pay, job security, co-workers, and supervision. If the diagnosis reveals high dissatisfaction in one or more of these areas, then it may be very difficult to initiate and maintain a successful job redesign project (Oldham, 1976; Oldham, Hackman & Pearce, 1976). On the other hand, if satisfaction with supervision is especially high, then it might be wise to build an especially central role for supervisors in the initiation and management of the change process.

Other examples could be given as well. The point is simply that such supplementary measures (especially those having to do with aspects of employee satisfaction) may be helpful in highlighting special problems and opportunities that deserve explicit recognition and attention as part of the diagnosis of an existing work system.

Principles for Enriching Jobs

The core job dimensions specified in the job-characteristics model are tied directly to a set of action principles for redesigning jobs (Hackman, Oldham, Janson & Purdy, 1975; Walters & Associ-

---

1. MPS scores can range from 1 to 343. The average is about 125.

ates, 1975). As shown in Figure 3, these principles specify what types of changes in jobs are most likely to lead to improvements in each of the five core job dimensions, and thereby to an increase in the motivating potential of the job as a whole.

Principle 1: Forming Natural Work Units. A critical step in the design of any job is the decision about how the work is to be distributed among the people who do it. Consider, for example, a typing pool—consisting of one supervisor and ten typists—that does all the typing for one division of an organization. Jobs are delivered in rough draft or dictated form to the supervisor, who distributes them as evenly as possible among the typists. In such circumstances the individual letters, reports, and other tasks performed by a given typist in one day or week are randomly assigned. There is no basis for identifying with the work or the person or department for whom it is performed, or for placing any personal value upon it.

By contrast, creating natural units of work increases employees' "ownership" of the work, and therefore improves the chances that employees will view it as meaningful and important rather than as irrelevant and boring. In creating natural units of work, one must first identify what the basic work items are. In the typing pool example, that might be "pages to be typed." Then these items are grouped into natural and meaningful categories. For example, each typist might be assigned continuing responsibility for all work requested by a single department or by several smaller departments. Instead of typing one section of a large report, the individual will type the entire piece of work, with the knowledge of exactly what the total outcome of the work is. Furthermore, over a period of time the typists will develop a growing sense of how the work affects co-workers or customers who receive the completed product. Thus, as shown in Figure 3, forming natural units of work increases two of the core job dimensions that contribute to experienced meaningfulness—task identity and task significance.

It is still important that work be distributed so that the system as a whole operates efficiently, of course, and workloads must be arranged so that they are approximately equal among employees.

The principle of natural work units simply requires that these traditional criteria be supplemented so that, insofar as possible, the tasks that arrive at an employee's work station form an identifiable and meaningful whole.

Principle 2: Combining Tasks. The very existence of a pool made up entirely of persons whose sole function is typing, reflects a fractionalization of jobs that sometimes can lead to such hidden costs as high absenteeism and turnover, extra supervisory time, and so on. The principle of combining tasks is based on the assumption that such costs often can be reduced by simply taking existing and fractionalized tasks and putting them back together again to form a new and larger module of work. At the Medfield, Massachusetts, plant of Corning Glass Works, for example, the job of assembling laboratory hotplates was redesigned by combining a number of previously separate tasks. After the change, each hotplate was assembled from start to finish by one operator, instead of going through several separate operations performed by different people.

Combining tasks (like forming natural work units) contributes in two ways to experienced meaningfulness of the work. First, task identity is increased. The hotplate assembler, for example, can see and identify with a finished product ready for shipment—rather than a nearly invisible junction of solder. Moreover, as more tasks are combined into a single worker's job, the individual must use a greater variety of skills in performing the job, further increasing the meaningfulness of the work.

Principle 3: Establishing Relationships with Clients. By establishing direct relationships between workers and their clients, jobs often can be improved in three ways. First, feedback increases because additional opportunities are created for the employees to receive direct praise or criticism of their work outputs. Second, skill variety may increase, because of the need to develop and exercise one's interpersonal skills in managing and maintaining the relationship with the client. Finally, autonomy will increase to the degree that individuals are given real personal responsibility for deciding

FIGURE 3
Principles for Changing Jobs.

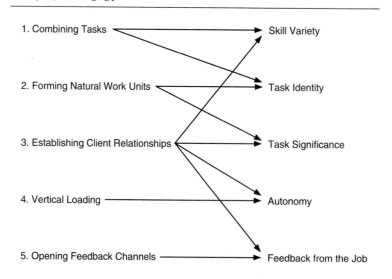

how to manage their relationships with the people who receive the outputs of their work.

Creating relationships with clients can be viewed as a three-step process: (1) identification of who the client actually is; (2) establishing the most direct contact possible between the worker and the client; and (3) establishing criteria and procedures so that the client can judge the quality of the product or service received and relay his judgments directly back to the worker. Especially important (and, in many cases, difficult to achieve) is identification of the specific criteria by which the work output is assessed by the client—and ensuring that both the worker and the client understand these criteria and agree with them.

Principle 4: Vertical Loading. In vertical loading, the intent is to partially close the gap between the "doing" and the "controlling" aspects of the job. Thus, when a job is vertically loaded, responsibilities and controls that formerly were reserved for management are given to the employee as part of the job. Among ways this might be achieved are the following:

❏ Giving the job incumbents responsibility for deciding on work methods, and for advising or helping train less experienced workers.

❏ Providing increased freedom in time management, including decisions about when to start and stop work, when to take a break, and how to assign work priorities.

❏ Encouraging workers to do their own trouble-shooting and manage work crises, rather than calling immediately for a supervisor.

❏ Providing workers with increased knowledge of the financial aspects of the job and the organization, and increased control over budgetary matters that affect their own work.

When a job is vertically loaded, it inevitably increases in *autonomy.* And, as shown in Figure 1, this should lead to increased feelings of personal responsibility and accountability for the work outcomes.

Principle 5: Opening Feedback Channels. In virtually all jobs there are ways to open channels of feedback to individuals to help them learn not only how well they are performing their jobs, but also whether their performance is improving, deteriorating, or remaining at a constant level. While there are various sources from which information about performance can come, it usually is advantageous for workers to learn about their performance *directly as they do the job* rather than from management on an occasional basis.

Feedback provided by the job itself is more immediate and private than feedback provided by its supervisor, and can also increase workers' feelings of personal control over their work. Moreover, it avoids many of the potentially disruptive interpersonal problems which can develop when workers can find out how they are doing only by means of direct messages or subtle cues from the boss.

Exactly what should be done to open channels for feedback from the job varies from job to job and organization to organization. In many cases, the changes involve simply removing existing blocks which isolate the individual from naturally occurring data about performance, rather than generating entirely new feedback mechanisms. For example:

Establishing direct relationships with clients (discussed above) often removes blocks between the worker and natural external sources of data about the work.

Quality control in many organizations often eliminates a natural source of feedback, because all quality checks are done by people other than the individuals responsible for the work. In such cases, feedback to the workers, if there is any, may be belated and diluted. By placing most quality-control functions in the hands of workers themselves, the quantity and quality of data available to them about their own performance will dramatically increase.

Tradition and established procedure in many organizations dictate that records about performance be kept by a supervisor and transmitted up (not down) the organizational hierarchy. Sometimes supervisors even check the work and correct any errors themselves. The worker who made the error never knows it occurred and is therefore denied the very information which can enhance both internal work motivation and the technical adequacy of his performance. In many cases, it is possible to provide standard summaries of performance records directly to the workers (and perhaps also to their superiors), thereby giving employees personally and regularly the data they need to improve their effectiveness.

Computers and other automated machines sometimes can be used to provide individuals with data now blocked from them. Many clerical operations, for example, are now performed on computer consoles. These consoles often can be programmed to provide the clerk with immediate feedback in the form of a CRT display or a printout indicating that an error has been made. Some systems even have been programmed to provide the operator with a positive feedback message when a period of error-free performance has been sustained.

Conclusion. The principles for redesigning jobs reviewed above, while illustrative of the kinds of changes that can be made to improve the jobs of individuals in organizations, obviously are not exhaustive. They were selected for attention here because of the links (Figure 3) between the principles and the core job dimensions in the motivational model presented earlier. Other principles for enriching jobs (which, although often similar to those presented here, derive from alternative conceptual frameworks) are presented by Ford (1969), Glaser (1975), Herzberg (1974), and Katzell and Yankelovich (1975, chap. 6).

DESIGNING WORK FOR TEAMS

Often it is easier or more appropriate, given the nature of the work to be done and the organizational circumstances under which it is to be done, to design work for interacting teams rather than for individuals working alone. In such cases, the ultimate aim generally is similar to that sought when individual job enrichment is carried out: that is, to improve the quality of the work experience of the people involved, and simultaneously to increase the quality and quantity of the work produced. The difference is that the work is defined and implemented as a *group* task, rather than as an interconnected set of individual tasks. Because of this, a larger chunk of work can be included within the boundaries of the task, thereby increasing the intrinsic meaningfulness of the work. Moreover, the possibility is increased for the development of close, socially satisfying work relationships among team members. Such relationships are highly valued by many people, but difficult or impossible to achieve by means of redesign of individual jobs in such work settings as assembly lines, where individual work stations may be fixed and so widely separated that meaningful social interaction with others is (for all practical purposes) precluded.

Until relatively recently, most work design for teams has been carried out from the perspective of sociotechnical systems theory, and has involved the creation of autonomous or semi-autonomous work groups. Specific arrangements (e.g., how the group task itself is designed, the size and composition of the work group, the nature of the reward system) have varied from project to project, but the following attributes are characteristic of most autonomous work groups:[2]

1. A "whole" task for the group, in which the mission of the group is sufficiently identifiable and significant that members find the work of the group meaningful.

2. Workers who each have a number of the skills required for completion of the group task, thereby increasing the flexibility of the group in carrying out the task. When individuals do not have a robust repertoire of skills initially, procedures are developed to encourage cross-training among members.

3. Autonomy for the group to make decisions about the methods by which the work is carried out, the scheduling of various activities, the assignment of different individuals to different tasks, and (sometimes) the selection of new group members.

4. Compensation based on the performance of the group as a whole, rather than on the contributions of individual group members.

It should be emphasized that these four ingredients are simply summary statements of the kinds of changes that often are made when work is redesigned for interacting teams. They do not represent the only way to design work for groups, nor are these ingredients necessarily the most appropriate ones for any given instance. Therefore, it may be useful to step back from specific change principles and attempt to identify the major *general* criteria for the design of work for teams—and then to explore alternative strategies for attempting to achieve those criteria.

Design Criteria for Interacting Work Groups

The two criteria listed below appear to be the minimum requirements for the design of interacting work teams if high productivity by the team and the satisfaction of its members are to be achieved simultaneously.

1. The team itself should be a cohesive group, in which members feel committed to the goals of the group, and in which they can experience significant personal satisfaction through their interactions with teammates.

In a highly cohesive group, members greatly value the rewards (usually interpersonal) that fellow members can provide. This means that the quality of the social experience of members in cohesive groups is likely to be high rather than low. It also means

---

2. See, for example, Bucklow (1966), Davis (1966, p. 44), Davis and Trist (1974), Gulowsen (1972, pp. 375–378), and Trist, Higgin, Murray, and Pollock (1963, chap. 9).

that cohesive groups usually have a considerable leverage in enforcing member compliance with group norms. That is, since members of cohesive groups strongly value the rewards controlled by their peers, they are especially likely to engage in behavior that is congruent with group norms. Failure to do so can result in those rewards being made unavailable to them (e.g., being "frozen out") or can lead other group members to negatively sanction their actions (Hackman, 1976).

The problem is that while cohesive groups have been shown to generate a high degree of uniformity of behavior in terms of group norms, the *direction* of those norms is unrelated to the level of cohesiveness of the group (Berkowitz, 1954; Schachter, Ellertson, McBride, & Gregory, 1951; Seashore, 1954). Sometimes highly cohesive groups enforce a norm of low performance; at other times they encourage and support members' efforts toward high performance. Relatively little is known about what factors determine whether group norms will encourage high or low performance (e.g., Lawler & Cammann, 1972; Vroom, 1969, pp. 226–227). It is necessary, therefore, to propose an additional criterion for the design of work teams in organizations.

2. The environment of the work group, including its task, must be such that the group norms that emerge and are enforced are consistent with the two aims of high productivity and satisfying interpersonal relationships.

Approaches to Work Design for Interacting Groups

Meeting the two design criteria identified above requires, at minimum, attention to (1) the composition and dynamics of the group itself, (2) reward contingencies in the organizational environment, and (3) the structure of the group task. These matters are explored below.

Design and Maintenance of the Group qua Group. It is important that members of an interacting work team be able to experience themselves as part of a group that is *psychologically meaningful* to them. Usually this requires that the group be moderately small (usually less than fifteen members, although apparently successful autonomous work groups of larger size have been reported), and that members occupy a single workplace (or at least contiguous workplaces with easy access to one another). Merely calling a set of people a "group" for reasons other than the nature of their relationships with each other (e.g., a set of flight attendants who have the same supervisor but who literally fly all over the country and rarely see one another) does not meet the conditions for creation of an effective work team.

Moreover, while reasonably close and meaningful interpersonal relationships can be important to the success of interacting work teams, group process interventions (e.g., "team building") that focus *exclusively* on relationships among group members—or on the social climate of the group as a whole—should be used with caution. Direct interpersonal interventions can be quite powerful in altering social behavior in a group, and for this reason they may be very useful in increasing the capability and willingness of members to share with one another special skills that are needed for work on the group task. Yet research also shows that when such interventions are used alone, the group's task effectiveness rarely is enhanced (and often suffers) as a result (cf. Hackman & Morris, 1975;

Herold, in press). Thus, while process interventions can be of great use as part of a broader intervention package aimed at creating effective work teams, total reliance on such interventions appears inappropriate if the goal is to work toward simultaneous improvement of the social experience of the members *and* their collective task productivity.

Design of Environmental Contingencies. The way the organizational environment of the group is arranged can affect whether or not it is in the best interest of group members to work together effectively and, indeed, whether or not it is *possible* for them to do so. Especially important in this regard are the compensation system and the role of the first-line supervisor.

In almost every case in which autonomous work groups have been successfully created in organizations, pay systems have been arranged so that members were paid on a basis of the performance of the group as a whole, rather than in terms of the level of performance of individual employees. Moving to a group-based compensation system increases the chances that internal cooperation and cohesiveness will increase as members work together to obtain the group-level rewards. Moreover, dysfunctional group interaction that grows from the fear (or the fact) of pay inequities among members should diminish when compensation is tied directly to the output of the group as a whole. It should be noted, however, that simply moving to a group-level compensation system does *not* eliminate the possibility of less than optimal productivity norms. When group members mistrust management, for example, norms enforcing low productivity may emerge to protect the group against possible changes of performance standards by management. Thus, while group-level compensation plans play an important part in the design of work for interacting teams, they in no way guarantee high group productivity.

Also critical to the design of work for teams is the new role that first-line supervisors play under such arrangements. In many applications, the supervisor moves from having day-to-day (even minute-to-minute) responsibility for the work behavior and productivity of individual employees to a role that primarily involves managing the *boundaries* of the group—not what goes on within those boundaries (Taylor, 1971). Thus, the supervisor assists the group in liaison with other groups, and may serve as the advocate of the group in discussion with higher management, but routine decision-making about the work and management of work crises is left to the group. Under such conditions, group members should experience substantially more ownership of their work activities and output, thereby creating the conditions required for members to experience collective responsibility for—and commitment to—their shared task.

Design of the Group Task. One of the greatest determinants of whether a group develops a norm of high or low productivity is the design of the group task itself. What task characteristics are likely to prompt high group commitment to effective performance? As a start, the five core dimensions used in the job characteristics model of individual work motivation would seem useful (i.e., skill variety, task identity, task significance, autonomy, and feedback). There is no reason why such dimensions could not be applied to the analysis of group tasks just as they are to individual tasks.

If group tasks were designed to be high on these or similar job dimensions, then an increase in the task-relevant motivation of group members would be expected—and, over time, group norms about productivity should become consistent with the increased motivation of individual group members. Yet, such positive outcomes should come about only (1) if the individual group members identify with and feel commitment to the group as a whole (it is, after all, a *group* task), and (2) if the internal process of the group facilitates and reinforces (rather than impairs) concerted action toward shared group goals.

The core job dimensions have little to offer toward the creation of these two conditions. How, for example, could a group task be designed so that all members see it as providing high autonomy—and therefore experience substantial *personal* responsibility for the outcomes of the *group?* Moreover, given that it is now well documented that how group tasks are designed affects not only the motivation of group members, but also the patterns of social interaction that develop among them (Hackman & Morris, 1975), how can group tasks be structured so that they prompt task-effective rather than dysfunctional interaction among members?

Such questions have no simple answers. And while task design *per se* potentially can contribute to their solution, the issues raised also are affected by the environmental contingencies that are operative, and by the design and composition of the group itself. Thus, once again, it must be concluded that no single approach can create an effective design for work to be done by interacting teams. Instead, such a goal requires simultaneous use of a number of different handles for change—some of which have to do with the group, some with the task, and some with the broader organizational contexts.

Group versus Individual Task Design: Which When?

Choices for designing work for individuals or for groups are complex, and in many cases depend on factors idiosyncratic to a given situation. In general, however, a group-based design seems indicated when one or more of the following conditions is present:

1. When the product, service, or technology is such that meaningful individual work is not realistically possible (e.g., when a large piece of heavy equipment is being produced). In such cases it often is possible for a group to take autonomous responsibility for an entire product or service—while the only possible job design for individuals would involve small segments of the work (cf. Walton, 1975).

2. When the technology or physical work setting is such that high interdependence among workers is required. For example, Susman (1970) has suggested that one effect of increased automation (especially in continuous process production) is to increase interdependence among workers. The creation of autonomous work groups under such circumstances would seem to be a rather natural extension of the imperatives of the technology itself. When, on the other hand, there are no required interdependencies (e.g., telephone installers who operate their own trucks, coordinating only with a foreman or dispatcher), then there would seem to be no real basis on which meaningful work teams could be formed, and enrichment of individual jobs might be a better alternative.

3. When individuals have strong social needs—and the enrichment of individual jobs would run significant risk of breaking up existing groups of workers that provide social satisfactions to

their members. In such cases, designing work for teams would capitalize on the needs of employees, whereas individual-oriented job enrichment might require that individuals give up important social satisfactions to obtain a better job (Reif & Luthans, 1972).

4. When the overall motivating potential of employees' jobs would be expected to be *considerably* higher if the work were arranged as a group task rather than as a set of individual tasks. Probably in most cases the standing of a job on the core dimensions would increase if the job were designed as a group task, simply because a larger piece of work can be done by a group than by an individual. This should not, however, automatically tilt the decision toward group work design—there are numerous interpersonal factors that must be attended to in effectively designing work for interacting groups. Sometimes the risk or effort required to deal with such factors may make it more appropriate to opt for individual task design, even though a group task might be expected to be somewhat better *as a task* than would be any of the individual tasks.

Cautions in Designing Work for Groups

In conclusion, three caveats about the design of work for groups are suggested:

1. Existing evidence suggests that the work must provide group members with *substantial* autonomy if they are to experience high responsibility for it. Just as "pseudo-participation" in organizations may be worse than no participation at all, so it is that autonomous work groups should not be formed unless there is reasonable assurance that the result will not be a potentially frustrating state of "pseudo-autonomy." This, of course, requires careful attention to issues of management and supervision, to ensure that managers are both willing and able to provide the group with sufficient real autonomy to carry out the proposed group task (cf. Gulowsen, 1972).

2. The needs of employees who will make up the groups must be carefully attended to, because work in interacting teams on a complex task will not be satisfying or motivating to all people. Optimally, the need of group members for both social interaction and growth should be rather high. If the social needs of group members are high but their needs for growth are low, then there is risk that the group members will use the group solely as a source of social satisfaction. Even if the task were very high in objective motivating potential, members might find the group so much more involving than the task that productivity would suffer. When, on the other hand, members have a high need for growth but low needs for social interaction, then it might be better to consider designing the work for individuals, if technology permits. If employees have both low social needs and low needs for growth, then prospects for creating teams in which members work together effectively and productively on a challenging task would appear very dim indeed.

3. Finally, it should be noted that virtually all of the above discussion has focused on characteristics of groups and of tasks that are likely to generate high *motivation* to perform the task effectively. For some group tasks, the level of motivation (or effort) of group members is not critical to the success of the group; instead, the effectiveness of the performance varies simply with the level of knowledge and skill of the members, or with the performance strategies utilized by the group (cf. Hackman & Morris, 1975). In such circumstances, the attributes of the group, the task, and the environment that would be required for a high degree of group effectiveness would be quite different from those proposed here.

REFERENCES

Berkowitz, L. Group standards, cohesiveness and productivity. *Human Relations,* 1954, **7,** 509–519.

Bucklow, M. A new role for the work group. *Administrative Science Quarterly, 1966,* **11,** 59–78.

Davis, L. E. The design of jobs. *Industrial Relations,* 1966, **6,** 21–45.

Davis, L. E., & Trist, E. L. Improving the quality of work life: Sociotechnical case studies. In J. O'Toole (Ed.), *Work and the quality of life.* Cambridge, Mass.: MIT Press, 1974.

Ford, R. N. *Motivation through the work itself.* New York: American Management Association, 1969.

Glaser, E. M. *Improving the quality of worklife . . . And in the process, improving productivity.* Los Angeles: Human Interaction Research Institute, 1975.

Gulowsen, J. A measure of work group autonomy. In L. E. Davis & J. C. Taylor (Eds.), *Design of jobs.* Middlesex, England: Penguin, 1972.

Hackman, J. R. Group influences on individuals in organizations. In M. D. Dunnette (Ed.), *Handbook of industrial and organizational psychology.* Chicago: Rand McNally, 1976.

Hackman, J. R., & Lawler, E. E. Employee reactions to job characteristics. *Journal of Applied Psychology Monograph,* 1971, **55,** 259–286.

Hackman, J. R., & Morris, C. G. Group tasks, group interaction process, and group performance effectiveness: A review and proposed integration. In L. Berkowitz (Ed.), *Advances in experimental social psychology* (Vol. 8.). New York: Academic Press, 1975.

Hackman, J. R., & Oldham, G. R. Development of the Job Diagnostic Survey. *Journal of Applied Psychology,* 1975, **60,** 159–170.

Hackman, J. R., & Oldham, G. R. Motivation through the design of work: Test of a theory. *Organizational Behavior and Human Performance,* 1976, **16,** 250–279.

Hackman, J. R., Oldham, G., Janson, R., & Purdy, K. A new strategy for job enrichment. *California Management Review, 1975,* **17** (4), 57–71.

Herold, D. M. Group effectiveness as a function of task-appropriate interaction processes. In J. L. Livingstone (Ed.), *Managerial accounting: The behavioral foundations.* Columbus, Ohio: Grid Publishers, in press.

Herzberg, F. The wise old Turk. *Harvard Business Review,* 1974, **52,** 70–80.

Katzell, R. A., Yankelovich, D., et al. *Work, productivity and job satisfaction.* New York: The Psychological Corporation, 1975.

Lawler, E. E., & Cammann, C. What makes a work group successful? In A. J. Marrow (Ed.), *The failure of success.* New York: Amacom, 1972.

Lawler, E. E., & Hall, D. T. The relationship of job characteristics to job involvement, satisfaction and intrinsic motivation. *Journal of Applied Psychology,* 1970, **54,** 305–312.

Oldham, G. R. Job characteristics and internal motivation: The moderating effect of interpersonal and individual variables. *Human Relations,* 1976, **29,** 559–569.

Oldham, G. R., Hackman, J. R., & Pearce, J. L. Conditions under which employees respond positively to enriched work. *Journal of Applied Psychology,* 1976, **61,** 395–403.

Reif, W. E., & Luthans, F. Does job enrichment really pay off? *California Management Review,* 1972, **15,** 30–37.

Schachter, S., Ellertson, N., McBride, D., & Gregory, D. An experimental test of cohesiveness and productivity. *Human Relations,* 1951, **4,** 229–238.

Seashore, S. *Group cohesiveness in the industrial work group.* Ann Arbor: University of Michigan, 1954.

Susman, G. I. The impact of automation on work group autonomy and task specialization. *Human Relations,* 1970, **23,** 567–577.

Taylor, J. C. Some effects of technology in organizational change. *Human Relations,* 1971, **24,** 105–123.

Trist, E. L., Higgin, G. W., Murray, H., & Pollock, A. B. *Organizational choice.* London: Tavistock, 1963.

Vroom, V. H. Industrial social psychology. In G. Lindzey & E. Aronson (Eds.), *Handbook of social psychology* (2d ed.). Reading, Mass.: Addison-Wesley, 1969.

Walters, R. W., & Associates. *Job enrichment for results.* Reading, Mass.: Addison-Wesley, 1975.

Walton, R. E. From Hawthorne to Topeka and Kalmar. In E. L. Cass & F. G. Zimmer (Eds.), *Man and work in society.* New York: Van Nostrand-Reinhold, 1975.

A Solution to the Performance Appraisal Feedback Enigma

Herbert H. Meyer

To say that the performance appraisal feedback problem has been an enigma for managers and personnel specialists is probably a glaring understatement. Formal programs to evaluate and document the job performance of subordinates and then provide feedback to the respective subordinates have been around at least as long as there have been personnel departments in organizations. The appraisal and feedback program is one of the psychologists' and personnel specialists' popular topics in the personnel literature. There have been literally thousands of articles on this topic in journals in the personnel field during the last seventy-five years. Most of these articles generally applaud the virtues of the performance appraisal and feedback process, lament their lack of success, then present suggested solutions to the program. This format has not changed much over the years.

Problems experienced with performance appraisal programs are myriad. Significant evidence has shown that most managers find the program onerous and distasteful. The following scenario depicts a situation that many managers have probably faced in dealing with the performance appraisal feedback problem:

Jane Novak was preparing for the annual performance appraisal review discussion scheduled with Henry Buckner. She remembered the unpleasant experience she had in a similar discussion a year ago. Henry's performance since that discussion had been tolerable, but mediocre at best. While there were many aspects of the job where Henry's performance could be improved, she planned to focus on only two or three areas where improvement was especially needed.

Last year in her first appraisal discussion with Henry, he reacted very defensively to any suggestions she made for improving performance. He was especially annoyed by the fact that the overall rating she had assigned was only "Very Satisfactory." In fact, he appealed the rating, but fortunately Jane's boss supported her judgment. Customarily, most professionals in the company were rated as either "Outstanding" or "Excellent." While distributions weren't published, it was generally known that only a small percentage received ratings below "Excellent" on the scale. Yet, Jane couldn't in good conscience rate Henry above "Very Satisfactory," which was the midpoint on the scale.

Jane hated to conduct these annual review discussions, especially with those for whom she couldn't justify an "Outstanding" overall rating. The discussions often seemed to do more harm than good. Her relationships with Henry, for example, had been strained since their annual review discussion last year.

Is Jane's experience with the annual performance review discussion unusual? Do her reactions indicate that she is a poor manager? The answer to both questions is no.

Experience with appraisal programs shows that unless administrative pressures are applied to ensure that people are appraised and feedback given, the programs invariably die out very rapidly. Managers just do not carry out the process, even though departmental policy may call for it. Most organizations have found that a subordinate sign-off procedure must be used to guarantee that appraisals are completed and feedback is given.

IS APPRAISAL FEEDBACK USEFUL?

Starting about 30 years ago at G.E., we carried out an intensive series of studies on the performance appraisal and feedback

Reprinted with permission from the *Academy of Management Executive,* 1991, Vol. 5(1), pp. 68–76.

process. Followup surveys showed that the majority of employees expressed more uncertainty about the status of their performance in their managers' opinions after a performance appraisal interview than before. Evidently, in many cases the manager's formal feedback was discrepant with the informal signals they had been receiving about his or her view of their job performance. As Dave DeVries observed in a newsletter published by the Center for Creative Leadership a few years ago, most people get the feedback they consider to be really reliable in indirect, obscure ways. They judge the boss's mood, talk with the boss's secretary, note whether or not they are invited to important meetings, whether or not their opinion is sought on important matters, and so on.[1]

A great deal of evidence, from our General Electric research and that reported in the literature, has shown that there is a strong tendency to distort appraisals toward favorable reviews when feedback must be given. For example, the federal government introduced a merit pay plan for mid-level employees about ten years ago. A rating of "fully successful" or better is needed to qualify for a merit increase. A recent study showed that 99.5 percent were eligible.[2]

Managers learn through unpleasant experience that negative feedback not only results in the employee having negative feelings, but it also too often results in deteriorated rather than improved performance. Consequently, because of this positive distortion, subordinates may get misleading information which is often inconsistent with administrative decisions such as salary actions, promotion, and demotions. Such distorted ratings sometimes cause trouble when the manager wants to fire a poor performer. The manager may decide that a certain employee who has consistently performed inadequately should be demoted or fired. Yet, the record may show that this employee's performance has been consistently rated as "very satisfactory."

FEW "GOOD" PROGRAMS

Surveys of companies with appraisal programs have repeatedly revealed that few are satisfied with its performance appraisal program. A survey of 200 large companies conducted by Psychological Associates showed that 70 percent of employees said they were more confused than enlightened by the performance appraisal feedback they received. Similarly, an American Society of Personnel Administrators survey concluded that less than ten percent of companies have reasonably successful performance appraisal programs.

A recent nationwide survey of 3,500 companies showed that the most frequently mentioned human resource concern was the organization's performance appraisal system. Based on another survey reported in *Industry Week,* the author summarized that, "The handling of performance reviews is little short of disastrous—a periodic agony thrust on both bosses and subordinates."[3]

In a recent article in *Personnel Management,* after an exhaustive study of appraisal programs in the public sector the author observed, "The chances of failure in operating appraisal schemes far outweigh the chances of success. Many organizations have failed. Many others have systems which have degenerated into sterile paper chases, satisfying personnel departments' thirst for forms and justifying their existence but contributing little to the quality of organizational performance. Appraisal in practice tends to become a grand annual convulsion, more of a bureaucratic colossus than a means of insuring continuing development of people."[4]

R. E. Kopelman, in his book *Managing Productivity in Organizations* noted that most managers regard the performance appraisal interview as a fundamentally unpleasant situation—one to be avoided, postponed, or handled hurriedly.[5] A similar conclusion was reached by Napier and Latham based on their survey of appraisal programs in practice. They found that most appraisers saw little or no practical value in conducting performance appraisal interviews. No potential positive or negative consequences were generally foreseen, unless negative information was fed back and in those cases, the appraiser usually experienced aversive consequences.[6]

WHY ARE PROGRAMS RETAINED?

If the results of appraisal and feedback programs have been so negative, why have they persisted? Why do we keep butting our heads against the wall and continue the search for a solution when the quest for this utopia seems so hopeless? I am sure we persist because the idea seems so logical, so common-sensible. Appraisal and feedback should serve important administrative and developmental objectives.

Feedback regarding job performance seems necessary to justify administrative decisions, such as whether a salary increase is awarded and the size of the increase, or whether an employee should be transferred to another job or scheduled for promotion. Feedback should contribute to improved performance. The positive effect of feedback on performance has always been an accepted psychological principle.

---

1. See David DeVries' comments in the June 1978 Center for Creative Leadership Newsletter regarding his survey of 1,450 managers on their experiences with the communication of performance appraisals.

2. This finding was based on a federal government study which was cited in an article entitled, "Grading 'Merit Pay'," in the November 1988 issue of *Newsweek.*

3. The four survey results described here were cited in an article entitled "Performance Review: Examining the Eye of the Beholder" by Berkeley Rice in the December 1985 issue of *Across the Board* (a journal published by the Conference Board in New York).

4. J. George, "Appraisal in the Public Sector: Dispensing with the Big Stick," *Personnel Management,* May 1986, 32–35.

5. R. E. Kopelman, *Managing Productivity in Organizations: A Practical, People-Oriented Perspective* (New York: McGraw-Hill, 1986).

6. N. K. Napier and G. P. Latham, "Outcome Expectancies of People Who Conduct Performance Appraisals," *Personnel Psychology,* 1986, Vol. 39, No. 4, 827–837.

It is also well established that feedback designed to reinforce or alter behavior is most effective if provided when the behavior occurs. Daily coaching is more valuable for this purpose than a once-a-year discussion. However, most personnel managers insist that their managers schedule an annual, formally documented review to ensure that every employee gets at least some feedback about his or her job performance. This annual feedback interview is intended to provide a clear message to employees about their performance and to motivate them to improve.

SPLIT ROLES

In some organizations, administrative feedback, such as communicating planned salary action, is separated from motivational and developmental feedback. Norman Maier, a noted industrial psychologist, recommended this more than thirty years ago. He ascertained that when the supervisor appraises a subordinate for administrative purposes, he or she is serving as a judge. If the supervisor is to effectively motivate a subordinate and provide guidance for development, he or she must serve as a counselor. Maier maintained that being both judge and counselor is incompatible. A person being judged is likely to be defensive. For counseling to be effective, the employee must be receptive to advice and suggestion, not defensive.[7]

One of our G.E. studies in which almost 100 actual appraisal interviews were observed, supported Norm Maier's contention.[8] Managers were required to communicate a salary decision and suggestions for performance improvement in the same interview. We observed that subordinate's defensive reactions were so common, and the ego involvement in the salary decision so powerful, that attempts to counsel the employee about needed performance improvement were mostly futile.

Our recommendation that salary action appraisal and motivational and developmental appraisal be accomplished in separate programs has not been widely accepted—at least not in the United States. Surveys show that in most organizations, both types of appraisals are covered in the same interview. Evidently this is not true in Great Britain where a recent survey of appraisal practices in large companies revealed that appraisals for the two different purposes were separated in 85 percent of the responding companies.[9]

Based on my experience, I still maintain very strongly that appraisal for the two different purposes should be separated. I will focus here principally on motivational and developmental appraisal

---

7. Norman Maier's 1958 book on this subject, *The Appraisal Interview: Objectives, Methods, and Skills,* published by Wiley, is still widely used in training programs and frequently referred to by writers in the field.

8. This study was reported in a 1965 *Harvard Business Review* article entitled, "Split Roles in Performance Appraisal." A shortened version of the article was republished in 1989 as an "*HBR* Retrospect," since the original 1965 article was one of HBRs ten best-selling reprints.

9. This finding was reported in a 1985 article in the British journal, *Personnel Management.* The article, by H. Murlis and A. Wright, was entitled, "Rewarding the Performance of the Eager Beaver."

discussions. How can the process be more effective? I think the answer is to change our approach to the process.

CONTROL VERSUS INVOLVEMENT-ORIENTED MANAGEMENT

The traditional workforce management approach is to achieve efficiency by imposing management control over workers' behavior. However, it is becoming clear that a control-oriented approach to management is less effective. Our culture has changed. To remain competitive, organizations must elicit the commitment of employees at all levels. Commitment is not likely to be engendered in today's employees by interacting with them in a control-oriented manner. Employees want to be respected, to be in the know, involved, and to be treated as important individuals rather than as "hands."

The conventional approach to performance appraisal and feedback is certainly consistent with the control-oriented approach to management. It fits perfectly in a bureaucratically run organization. It is incompatible with an involvement-oriented management style.

A CHANGED APPROACH

The traditional approach to appraisal—where the manager completes an evaluation form and meets with the employee to communicate the appraisal—is becoming *anachronistic* in our culture. Performance appraisal conducted in the traditional manner is highly authoritarian. When a manager sits down with an employee for an appraisal, there is no doubt about who is the "boss" and who is in the subordinate or dependent role. It is a *parent-child* type of exchange.

Our culture has been moving away from authoritarianism for at least the last fifty years. Few people like a dictatorial boss and no one wants to have his or her dependence accentuated. People want to be involved, respected, treated as equals and for this reason, involvement-oriented management has become popular. Most performance appraisal programs are inconsistent with this management style.

THE USE OF SELF APPRAISAL

The conventional approach to performance appraisal is sometimes appropriate when the subordinate is dependent on the supervisor—for new employees, trainees, or perhaps for people in highly structured jobs. It is not appropriate, however, for most employees. It is certainly inappropriate for professionals and administrators. For employees who are not in an obviously dependent role, an appraisal discussion designed to serve communication, motivation, and development purposes should be based on the subordinate's *self appraisal.*

About twenty years ago, Glenn Bassett and I conducted another study at G.E. which demonstrated that appraisal discussions between manager and subordinate based on the subordinate's self-review were significantly more constructive and satisfying to both parties than those based on the manager's appraisal. It also resulted in significant improvement in job performance. Even though these discussions also communicated a salary decision, focussing on the subordinate's self-review was definitely more favorable.[10]

ADVANTAGES OF SELF-REVIEW

Self-review has several advantages. First, it enhances the subordinate's dignity and self-respect. The employee is not forced into a dependent role. Second, it places the manager into the role of counselor, not judge. Third, it is more likely to elicit employee commitment to any development plans or goals formulated in the discussion. That is, the subordinate is more likely to develop a feeling of ownership in plans and goals which he or she helped to create.

A fourth and major advantage of the self-review approach to the appraisal discussion was mentioned previously. That is, discussion based on the subordinate's review of his or her own performance is likely to be more satisfying to both parties and more productive than is the more traditional manager-to-subordinate review. Indeed, a number of studies seem to support that satisfaction with appraisal discussion results is strongly related to subordinate contribution and participation in the discussion.[11]

The biggest problem with this approach is that it violates traditional mores regarding the proper relationship between boss and subordinate. This is probably why the results of our experiment on self appraisals have not been widely applied. Certainly, supervisors participating in appraisal discussions based on subordinates' self-review have to some extent lost the value of their acquired credentials as the "superior."

Another disadvantage of self-review is the self-serving bias expected to inflate the self-appraisal. However, research has shown that this "leniency error" can be minimized by orienting the self analysis toward self development rather than appraisal for administrative purposes. In fact, self reviews have proved to be superior to supervisory reviews in identifying individual strengths and shortcomings.[12]

ELIMINATE THE "GRADING"

To improve the value of a feedback discussion based on self-review, the "grading" aspect should be eliminated. Assigning a numerical or adjectival grade, such as "satisfactory," "excellent," "adequate," "outstanding," or "poor" to overall performance or specific performance tends to obstruct rather than facilitate constructive discussion.

In addition, I recommend eliminating the formal grading aspect of a performance appraisal program used for administrative purposes. Most people in business find grading somewhat demeaning. It treats a mature person like a school child. The administrative action taken, such as the amount of salary increase or a promotion will communicate an overall appraisal better than will a grade. Recognition can certainly be given and improvement needs discussed without necessarily assigning grades to performance.

---

10. This study was reported in a 1968 article in *Personnel Psychology* entitled, "Performance Appraisal Based on Self-Review." Incidentally, recently a student, P. R. Simmons, in our Ph.D. program in industrial/organizational psychology at the University of South Florida, replicated this study with a few modifications for a dissertation project. His study sample consisted of clerical workers. I would expect their jobs to be fairly highly structured, so that perhaps the traditional top-down approach to appraisal might be appropriate. As an added twist, he obtained a measure of the degree to which each of the participating departments was run in a democratic or authoritarian manner. He found the self-review approach to appraisal to be especially effective in democratically run departments. Subordinate motivation to improve performance and supervisor satisfaction with the results of the appraisal program were significantly more favorable under the self-review condition.

11. The positive effects of subordinate participation in appraisal discussions have been documented in a number of articles relating to performance appraisal, including: D. J. Campbell and C. Lee, "Self-Appraisal in Performance Evaluation: Development Versus Evaluation," *Academy of Management Review,* 1988, Vol. 13, No. 2, 302–324; D. M. Herold, R. C. Liden, and M. L. Leatherwood, "Using Multiple Attributes to Assess Sources of Performance Feedback," *Academy of Management Journal,* 1987, Vol. 30, No. 4, 826–835; J. M. Ivancevich and J. T. McMahon, "The Effects of Goal Setting, External Feedback, and Self-Generated Feedback on Outcome Variables: A Field Experiment," *Academy of Management Journal,* 1982, Vol. 25, No. 2, 359–372; R. L. Dipboye and R. de Pontbriand, "Correlates of Employee Reactions to Performance Appraisals and Appraisal Systems," *Journal of Applied Psychology,* 1981, Vol. 66, No. 2, 248–251; C. C. Manz and H. P. Sims, Jr., "Self Management as a Substitute for

Leadership: A Social Learning Perspective," *Academy of Management Review,* 1980, Vol. 5, No. 3, 361–367; R. J. Burke, W. Weitzel, and T. Weir, "Characteristics of Effective Performance Review and Development Interviews: Replication and Extension," *Personnel Psychology,* 1978, Vol. 31, No. 4, 903–919; H. H. Meyer, "The Annual Performance Review Discussion—Making it Effective," *Personnel Journal,* October 1977; and M. M. Greller, "Subordinate Participation and Reactions to the Appraisal Interview," *Journal of Applied Psychology,* 1975, Vol. 6, No. 5, 544–549.

12. The superiority of self reviews over supervisory appraisals for self-development purposes was well documented by Paul Mabe and Stephen West in a June 1982 article in the *Journal of Applied Psychology* (Vol. 67, No. 3), which presented a summary of the results of 55 studies in which self-evaluations were compared with other measures of performance. In a similar survey of research on self appraisal, George Thornton found that self-appraisals showed less "halo" than ratings made by supervisors. In other words, subordinates rating their own performance identified specific strengths and shortcomings better than did their respective supervisors. This study was reported in an article entitled, "Psychometric Properties of Self-Appraisals of Job Performance," in the Summer 1980 issue of *Personnel Psychology* (Vol. 33, No. 2).

CONTENT OF THE DISCUSSION

Usually, formal performance appraisal discussions are scheduled annually. The major purpose is to provide a periodic summary of job performance and future possibilities. This discussion, if based on self-review, will provide the supervisor with the *subordinate's perspective* of the job, goals, problems, and responsibilities. Specifically, this annual discussion might cover:

1. Overall progress—an analysis of accomplishments and shortcomings.

2. Problems encountered in meeting job requirements.

3. Opportunities to improve performance.

4. Long range plans, opportunities—for the job and for the individual's career.

5. General discussion of possible plans and goals for the coming year.

If a goal setting program is being used, such as Management by Objectives, this annual review discussion is not the best place to establish detailed job goals for the year. To be effective, a goal-setting program must be a continuous process. Several meetings may be needed to propose, negotiate, and agree on goals. Review discussions should be held more than once a year. In many jobs, quarterly reviews may be appropriate, while in other jobs progress review discussions may be needed monthly or weekly.

THE SUPERVISOR'S ROLE

Even though the subordinate has the lead role in the annual review discussion, the supervisor is not passive. The supervisor should prepare by noting the points he or she would like to make and how to present them. Actually, the supervisor is in a better position to give the employee recognition and suggest changes in activities or behavior when reacting to instead of initiating all input. The supervisor's role becomes that of "counselor" rather than "judge" or "the boss."

NEED FOR TRAINING

If self-review is adopted as the medium for an annual review, it will not obviate the need for training. Training supervisors to handle this type of discussion could be valuable. It need not be any more extensive than the training given for conventional appraisal programs. I can envision, for example, a behavior modeling training program which covers such topics as how to deal with an overly favorable self appraisal, an unrealistically self-deprecating review, an important problem or development need not brought up by the subordinate, and so on.

In addition, employees will need guidance on how to prepare for and conduct a self-review discussion. As a minimum, instructional materials, perhaps in the form of a brief manual, should be provided.

HOW WILL ADMINISTRATIVE DECISIONS BE MADE?

Performance appraisal programs are often used as the basis for compensation and promotion decisions. If the type of performance review discussion proposed here is directed only to communication and development objectives, how should those administrative decisions be made and communicated?

As indicated earlier, I strongly believe that appraisal for development should be separated from appraisal for compensation or promotion. The annual discussion based on a self-review is designed to stimulate self development and to open communication channels to improve the working relationship between supervisor and subordinate. A performance appraisal discussion in which salary and/or promotion decisions are communicated does not provide a desirable climate for achieving communication and development objectives.[13]

Administrative decisions pertaining to merit raises or promotions are too important to the organization to be made by supervisors alone. Few supervisors are all-seeing, all-knowing persons. They have their own idiosyncrasies, failings, biases. In some cases, a supervisor may hide an especially effective employee to ensure continued achievement of his or her unit's objectives. Sometimes a supervisor is threatened by an unusually effective subordinate.

An administrative decision, such as on merit pay or promotion, almost always constitutes a zero-sum game. If differentiations are made, for each winner there must be one or more losers. Identifying the winners is extremely important to the organization as a whole, and therefore these should be organizational decisions, not decisions made by individual supervisors.

A growing trend in large organizations is to use an "annual human resources review" procedure to appraise the performance and potential of all employees. Peer-level managers in each division meet as a team with their manager to discuss the performance and potential of all employees who report to them. Using a team of people to evaluate individual performance provides a broader perspective in appraising employees than individual assessment. It not only provides a more comprehensive and objective evaluation of each employee's performance, potential, and development needs, but it also minimizes the effects of individual biases based on distorted emphases, prejudicial viewpoints, and limited perspectives.

---

13. The study referred to in footnote 8 showed quite clearly that the supervisor's role as "judge" in communicating an administrative decision, such as a scheduled merit raise, created an almost impossible climate for providing counseling or development planning effectively. More often than not, the subordinate's evaluation of his or her supervisor actually declined as a result of the dual-purpose appraisal discussion. This was probably because in the great majority of cases, the planned administrative action communicated, such as the size of the scheduled merit raise, fell short of the subordinate's expectation.

Even though some of the managers in this process may have minimal exposure to some of the employees, they can contribute by insisting that judgments are backed by objective and behavioral evidence. After all, each participating manager has an important stake in the process. If another manager's employee is identified as a winner, one or more of his or her "winners" might become losers.

Appraisals resulting from a team meeting of this kind are more likely to be accepted by employees. It is more difficult to challenge an appraisal formulated by group consensus. Moreover, when a supervisor communicates a merit pay decision to a subordinate, it is less likely that their working relationship will deteriorate. This is not the case when a merit pay decision is made by the supervisor acting alone.

The annual human resources review process has additional benefits that more than justify the investment of time. Each participating manager will become thoroughly familiar with the responsibilities and performance characteristics of each employee in the department. It may clarify expectations regarding responsibilities of specific individuals or positions. It often defines and solves departmental workflow problems. The participating managers may formulate strategy and action plans for more effectively using human resources to achieve department objectives.

SUMMARY

I think the administrative and developmental objectives of the performance appraisal process should be addressed in separate programs. To achieve communication, counseling, and development objectives, I believe very strongly that our traditional top-down approach to performance appraisal is anachronistic, passé, and obsolete. It is a parent-child type of exchange that is inconsistent with cultural values that have evolved in modern organizations. It often proves to be an embarrassing experience for both parties involved and it accentuates the dependent role of the subordinate. This relationship is appropriate only in a control-oriented management environment. Effective organizations are moving away from the control-oriented approach toward an involvement-oriented climate designed to elicit commitment on the part of employees at all levels. Even the term "subordinate" is eschewed in modern organizations.

In most organizations, if supervisors are constrained to use the traditional supervisor rating and feedback approach to the annual review discussion, it would be better to abandon the program altogether. Conversely, if one concedes that it is desirable for supervisors to have some sort of annual review discussion with each of their direct reports, a discussion based on self-review can be valuable and constructive.

Exercise: Enlivening the Job Characteristics Model: A Job Redesign Project

PURPOSE

The purpose of this exercise is to give you the opportunity to learn and use the principles of job redesign. By the time you complete this exercise, you will

1. Understand the Hackman and Oldham (1976) model of job redesign

2. Allow "objective outsiders" (your fellow students) to diagnose the "motivating potential" of your current job or any past job you may wish to have diagnosed

3. Practice your own diagnostic skills by analyzing others' jobs

4. Begin to consider the nature of changes that would enrich the jobs under consideration

This exercise was developed by William P. Ferris and was presented at the Eastern Academy of Management, Baltimore, MD, 1992. The sections of the Job Diagnostic Survey are used with permission from J. R. Hackman and G. R. Oldham, *Work Design,* Reading, MA: Addison-Wesley, 1980.

INTRODUCTION

According to Herzberg (1968) motivation in the workplace is associated with the *job content,* while dissatisfaction is associated with *job context* factors. Hackman and Oldham (1975), in their theory of job redesign, expanded upon this idea by identifying five job characteristics or "core job dimensions" that they felt contributed to motivation: (1) skill variety, (2) task identity, (3) task significance, (4) autonomy, and (5) feedback from the job itself. The model postulated that a job's motivating potential was measurable to the degree that its core job dimensions were capable of eliciting "critical psychological states," which would lead to "personal and work outcomes" that signaled growing "employee growth need strength." These critical psychological states—experienced meaningfulness of the work, experienced responsibility for outcomes of the work, and knowledge of the actual results of the work activities—affect employee job satisfaction. To the degree that they can be achieved, they help employees fulfill their growth needs such as the need to learn, be challenged, and achieve. In sum, a motivational potential score (MPS) for any job is available by applying the Hackman and Oldham formula shown below.

$$\text{Motivating Potential Score} = \frac{\text{Skill variety} + \text{Task identity} + \text{Task significance}}{3} \times \text{Autonomy} \times \text{Feedback}$$

This exercise allows you to participate in a job redesign process. Not every job incumbent has a pressing need to grow, despite having a job with a low MPS, so you will not necessarily be redesigning the job you present for diagnosis. However, at a minimum, this exercise will allow you to help others work on redesigning elements of the jobs that they present. First, you will help diagnose the motivating potential of your instructor's job or one selected by your instructor in order to gain familiarity with the process itself. Next, you will both help to diagnose a classmate's job and present a job of your own to be diagnosed. Finally, you will discuss possible ways to enrich some of the lower-scoring jobs, perhaps by utilizing design features of some of the higher-scoring jobs.

INSTRUCTIONS

1. Read the article by Hackman, "Designing Work for Individuals and for Groups."

2. Analyze the job of college professor as your instructor presents it in class discussion format and as indicated in the directions. *Option:* Instructor may choose to present a different job for demonstration purposes.

3. Divide into trios to present and analyze each others' jobs according to the direction in Part I. *Option:* Present one of your subordinates' jobs to be analyzed according to the model.

4. Complete Part II, which is a section of the Job Diagnostic Survey instrument used by Hackman and Oldham, to determine your level of satisfaction, internal work motivation, and growth need strength.

5. Following directions for Part III, share high and low MPS scores from trios in full class discussion.

6. Focus on a job volunteered for enrichment by a classmate for purposes of enhancing its motivation potential.

JOB REDESIGN EXERCISE

Directions: Your instructor will present a job everyone is relatively familiar with already, that of college professor. You will ask your instructor such questions as appear in the directions to Part I with a view to assessing the scores of the job presented according to the scale below on each of the five core job dimensions:

7 = very high
6 = high
5 = somewhat high
4 = moderate
3 = somewhat low
2 = low
1 = very low

Your instructor will take a quick poll of the class for each dimension and plug the appropriate class consensus number from 1 to 7 into the Job Characteristics formula written on the chalkboard. An MPS for the job of college professor (or such other job as the instructor may choose to present) will be calculated.

Part I: Individual Job Diagnosis

Directions: Following the demonstration above, divide into trios and take turns presenting a job you have held for analysis by your trio members. First, **briefly** explain the job, then answer questions as if you were being interviewed by a newspaper reporter. The two trio members doing the analysis will briefly confer after asking a few questions on each of the five core job dimensions and assess a score from 1 to 7 for each. Then, they will plug the numbers into the formula to arrive at a final MPS. Some sample questions to help you analyze each of the core job dimensions appear below. Feel free to call the instructor over to your group to help clarify an issue.

Skill Variety: Describe the different identifiable skills required to do your job. What is the nature of the oral, written, and/or quantitative skills needed? Physical skills? Do you get the opportunity to use all your skills?

Task Identity: What is your product? Are you involved in its production from beginning to end (including delivery)? If not, are you involved in a particular phase of its production from beginning to end?

Task Significance: How important is your product? How important is your role in producing it? How important is your job to the people you work with? If your job were eliminated, how inferior would your product be? Where does your product fit in the spectrum from "high end" to "low end"?

Autonomy: How much independence do you have on your job? Do you have to follow a strict schedule? If so, how much can you control it? Are you subject to the call of a beeper or a boss or a customer during your off hours? How much of your work is delegated to you to decide how to do it yourself? How closely are you supervised? To what degree are you held accountable?

Feedback: What feedback *systems* are in place concerning your job? Do you get regular feedback *from your job itself* on how you are doing? From your customers? From other stakeholders? From your peers and/or subordinates? From your supervisor?

Analysis of MPS scores

For diagnostic purposes:

❏ A score higher than 200 is a job in good shape with high motivating potential.

❏ A score lower than 100 means that the job would benefit from redesign.

❏ A score between 100 and 200 suggests possibilities in either direction.

Part II: The Job Diagnostic Survey (Short Form)

Section A

Directions: Now please indicate how *satisfied* you are with each aspect of your job listed below. Once again, write the appropriate number in the blank beside each statement.

How satisfied are you with this aspect of your job?

1	2	3	4	5	6	7
Extremely Dissatisfied	Dissatisfied	Slightly Dissatisfied	Neutral	Slightly Satisfied	Satisfied	Extremely Satisfied

_____ 1. The amount of job security I have

_____ 2. The amount of pay and fringe benefits I receive

_____ 3. The amount of personal growth and development I get in doing my job

_____ 4. The people I talk to and work with on my job

_____ 5. The degree of respect and fair treatment I receive from my boss

_____ 6. The feeling of worthwhile accomplishment I get from doing my job

_____ 7. The chance to get to know other people while on the job

_____ 8. The amount of support and guidance I receive from my supervisor

_____ 9. The degree to which I am fairly paid for what I contribute to this organization

_____ 10. The amount of independent thought and action I can exercise in my job

_____ 11. How secure things look for me in the future in this organization

_____ 12. The chance to help other people while at work

_____ 13. The amount of challenge in my job

_____ 14. The overall quality of the supervision I receive on my work

Section B

Directions: Listed below are a number of characteristics that could be present on any job. People differ about how much they would like to have each one present in their own jobs. We are interested in learning *how much you personally would like* to have each one present in your job.

Using the following scale, please indicate the *degree* to which you *would like* to have each characteristic present in your job. (*Note:* The numbers on this scale are different from those used in previous scales.)

4	5	6	7	8	9	10
Would like having this only a moderate amount (or less)			Would like having this very much			Would like having this *extremely* much

_____ 1. High respect and fair treatment from my supervisor

_____ 2. Stimulating and challenging work

_____ 3. Chances to exercise independent thought and action in my job

_____ 4. Great job security

_____ 5. Very friendly co-workers

_____ 6. Opportunities to learn new things from my work

_____ 7. High salary and good fringe benefits

_____ 8. Opportunities to be creative and imaginative in my work

_____ 9. Quick promotions

_____ 10. Opportunities for personal growth and development in my job

_____ 11. A sense of worthwhile accomplishment in my work

Scoring Key

A. *Affective Responses to the Job:* The private, affective reactions or feelings an employee gets from working on his or her job.

   Specific Satisfactions: These short scales tap several specific aspects of the employee's job satisfaction.

   1. "Pay" satisfaction. Average items #2 and #9 of Section A.

   $$\underline{\hspace{1cm}} + \underline{\hspace{1cm}} = 2\,\overline{\big|\underline{\hspace{2cm}}} = \underline{\hspace{1cm}}$$

   2. "Security" satisfaction. Average items #1 and #11 of Section A.

   $$\underline{\hspace{1cm}} + \underline{\hspace{1cm}} = 2\,\overline{\big|\underline{\hspace{2cm}}} = \underline{\hspace{1cm}}$$

   3. "Social" satisfaction. Average items #4, #7, and #12 of Section A.

   $$\underline{\hspace{1cm}} + \underline{\hspace{1cm}} + \underline{\hspace{1cm}} = 3\,\overline{\big|\underline{\hspace{2cm}}} = \underline{\hspace{1cm}}$$

   4. "Supervisory" satisfaction. Average items #5, #8, and #14 of Section A.

   $$\underline{\hspace{1cm}} + \underline{\hspace{1cm}} + \underline{\hspace{1cm}} = 3\,\overline{\big|\underline{\hspace{2cm}}} = \underline{\hspace{1cm}}$$

   5. "Growth" satisfaction. Average items #3, #6, #10, and #13 of Section A.

   $$\underline{\hspace{1cm}} + \underline{\hspace{1cm}} + \underline{\hspace{1cm}} + \underline{\hspace{1cm}} = 4\,\overline{\big|\underline{\hspace{2cm}}} = \underline{\hspace{1cm}}$$

B. *Individual Growth Need Strength:* This scale taps the degree to which an employee has strong or weak desire to obtain "growth" satisfactions from his or her work. Average items #2, #3, #6, #8, #10, #11 from Section B. Before averaging, subtract 3 from each item score; this will result in a summary scale ranging from one to seven.

$$\underline{\hspace{1cm}} + \underline{\hspace{1cm}} + \underline{\hspace{1cm}} + \underline{\hspace{1cm}} + \underline{\hspace{1cm}} + \underline{\hspace{1cm}}$$
$$-\ \ 3\ \ -\ \ 3\ \ -\ \ 3\ \ -\ \ 3\ \ -\ \ 3\ \ -\ \ 3$$
$$= \underline{\hspace{1cm}} + \underline{\hspace{1cm}} + \underline{\hspace{1cm}} + \underline{\hspace{1cm}} + \underline{\hspace{1cm}} + \underline{\hspace{1cm}} = 6\,\overline{\big|\underline{\hspace{2cm}}} = \underline{\hspace{1cm}}$$

Analysis of Part II

For diagnostic purposes

❏ *The GNS:* A score higher than 5 suggests you are ready for a redesign. A score lower than 3 suggests you may not be responsive. An in-between score suggests that you could move in either direction.

❏ *Satisfactions:* Scores higher than 4 suggest higher levels of satisfaction. Scores lower than 4 suggest there is room for change.

Part III: Job Redesign

Directions: Returning to full class discussion, trios report highest and lowest MPS scores. A few of the highest- and lowest-scoring jobs should be briefly described. Then, any student who wishes may present a job to the class for redesign. Students with high scores in the JDS items assessed in Part II above may be especially willing to present a job for redesign. Students should use information gathered from their trio work as well as Hackman (1977) to help inform discussion and brainstorm ways to enrich the job presented for redesign.

The Job Characteristics Model: Principles for Redesign

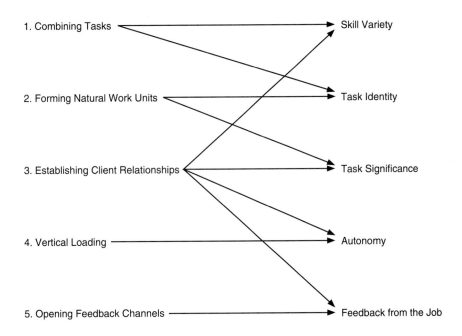

Diagnostic Questions for Redesign

1. Assuming improvement could be made in any of the five core job dimensions, where would you be likely to increase the MPS of the job under consideration the most? Explain your rationale.

2. How would you propose to begin (and continue) a dialogue with your employer or manager on the subject of improving the motivating potential of your job?

3. What aspects of your job, if any, can you enrich according to the job characteristics model without needing permissions or approvals?

4. How would you weigh the costs against the benefits of undertaking redesign for the job under consideration?

Option: Remember that this exercise can be very profitably done using a subordinate's job rather than your own. Job redesign can proceed from the top down as well as from the middle or bottom of an organization.

DISCUSSION QUESTIONS

1. How do power, politics, and "turf" issues influence the degree to which jobs can be redesigned?

2. What special requirements does job redesign of one's subordinates' jobs make of the manager? What is the responsibility of upper management that would like to see job redesign implemented to the mid-level and first-line managers who would be directly involved in such implementation?

3. What unintended consequences may occur when new procedures are introduced in one area and similar changes are not effected in other corresponding areas or departments? What are the alternatives for dealing with these consequences?

4. How can you use the information in this exercise directly as a way to improve subordinates' motivation at work?

5. What is the relationship between low employee growth needs and low motivating potential scores in the same workplace? How should you use the information in this exercise, if at all, to attempt job redesign when employee growth need strength is low?

REFERENCES

F. Herzberg. "One More Time: How Do You Motivate Employees?" *Harvard Business Review,* Sept.–Oct. 1987.

J. R. Hackman. "Designing Work for Individuals and for Groups." In J. R. Hackman, E. E. Lawler III, and L. W. Porter (eds.), *Perspectives on Behavior in Organizations.* Second edition. New York: McGraw-Hill, 1983.

J. R. Hackman, and G. Oldham. "Development of the Job Diagnostic Survey." *Journal of Applied Social Psychology,* 1975, pp. 60, 159–170.

Case: Saturn Rising:
Work Redesign on the Factory Shop Floor

PURPOSE

This case introduces you to the concept of semiautonomous work teams and demonstrates some of the unintended effects of job redesign programs. By the time you finish this case, you will:

1. Understand the concept of semiautonomous work teams

2. Identify the positive aspects of job redesign programs and their productivity benefits

3. Determine the conditions that can have a negative effect on job redesign programs

INTRODUCTION

The Hackman (1977) article, "Designing Work for Individuals and for Groups," suggests possibilities for redesigning jobs—including factory jobs—so that jobs can be made more motivating. One way in which this can be accomplished is by semiautonomous work teams. Semiautonomous work teams represent a radical change in how work is designed on the factory shop floor. As an alternative to the standard assembly line concept, these teams typically are responsible for a "chunk" of the work that is produced in the factory. Workers on each team make their own job assignments, interview prospective employees, schedule coffee breaks, determine pay raises, and generally manage themselves and their work. In this way, workers are motivated by the challenge of the job itself—the actual work over which they have some control. At the same time, some of the demotivating aspects of routine assembly line work are eliminated.

The following case excerpts from two *Business Week* articles illustrate how these concepts have been put into practice at the General Motors Saturn automotive plant. As you read the case, consider how successful you think the redesign efforts may be in the future.

INSTRUCTIONS

1. Read the article by Hackman, "Designing Work for Individuals and for Groups."

2. Read Part I of the case. Complete the analysis questions at the end of this section.

3. Read Part II of the case. Complete the discussion questions that follow.

4. Participate in a general class discussion.

Part I

How Power will be Balanced
on Saturn's Shop Floor

GM and Its Auto Workers Launch
a Bold Experiment in Self-Management

Imagine this: You apply for a job at General Motors Corp.'s new Saturn facility. You take a battery of tests to see if you can fit into the unconventional Saturn system. You pass muster and land the job. But there's still one hurdle to clear. Now you must be interviewed by teams of workers—the basic work group at the Saturn complex of plants. You make the rounds until you click with a group where your mechanical know-how, work ethic, and sense of humor make you well-accepted.

Incredible as it seems, such worker autonomy will permeate Saturn Corp., GM's $5 billion effort to build small cars in the U.S. at costs competitive with the Japanese. Saturn won't even start production until 1989, and the two sides are still finishing up a labor agreement. But negotiating documents and *Business Week* interviews have started to uncover the details of how Saturn may become the boldest experiment ever in self-management and consensus decision-making—going far beyond anything in Japanese or European factories.

Instead of cogs in a system, Saturn's workers will be full partners. Representatives of the United Auto Workers will sit in on all planning and operating committees. Work teams will operate without foremen. To emphasize the new equality, old job titles will be replaced with neutral ones (table), and blue-collar workers will earn a salary, just like managers. Both will earn bonuses based on performance. And although the UAW will keep the right to strike, it will try to agree on changes in pay by consensus with management instead of in formal bargaining. The union will have a say in managers' salaries, too.

BIG UNKNOWNS

Such ideas have big implications for the auto industry and for labor relations generally. In exchange for its new voice in management, the UAW will give GM an initial 20% break on guaranteed wages, plus less restrictive work rules. Along with Saturn's more efficient product design, manufacturing, and inventory systems, this should help halve the time needed to build a small car to 60 hours and close the cost gap with Japan of $2,000 per car. Chrysler Corp. and American Motors Corp. have already said they want Saturn-like deals. And while Ford Motor Co. and GM are mute now, they will likely push Saturn ideas in 1987 bargaining. As its influence spreads, Saturn could lift worker participation to a new plateau. "You see bits and pieces of this elsewhere," says Harry C. Katz, a management professor at the Massachusetts Institute of Technology, "but nothing so complete."

Business Week/August 5, 1985. By Maralyn Edid in Detroit.

Before any of this happens, GM and the UAW must conquer some big unknowns. Industry critics question whether Saturn is worth the loss of so many management prerogatives. And factions in the UAW think that turning workers into managers and de-emphasizing collective bargaining might undermine the union. "If the union climbs into bed with the company," says Peter Kelly, president of UAW Local 160 in Warren, Mich., and a chronic critic of union policies, "you don't have checks and balances."

OLD SAFEGUARDS

But UAW negotiators point to their strike weapon plus a new kind of check at Saturn: consensus. Whether a committee is dominated by GM or UAW representatives, nothing will get done unless everyone agrees. And the UAW is on every committee. "We're providing an opportunity to do things in a different fashion," says Donald F. Ephlin, a UAW vice-president and director of the GM Dept. "But we've built in the safeguards of the old way."

The basic groups in Saturn plants will be work units of 6 to 15 UAW members who will elect a "counselor" from their own ranks. The team will decide who does which job. It will also maintain equipment, order supplies, and set the relief and vacation schedules of its members. Each group will have a personal computer for keeping tabs on business data, ranging from production schedules to freight pickups and deliveries.

Like experimental teams already working in a few GM facilities, the Saturn units will be responsible for controlling variable costs and doing quality inspections. But they will have far more authority than that. If a team comes up with a better idea for a new piece of equipment, Saturn's finance and purchasing departments must respond. The experts can't shrug off suggestions, as they tended to before. They must reach a consensus with the team. Power, in a word, will rest with the workers.

The first management input will come at the next level, the work unit module. It will consist of up to six work units, and GM will assign an "adviser"—Saturn's version of a foreman—to each module as liaison with company experts in engineering, marketing, personnel, and the like. Work-unit advisers will also be the conduit for information to and from the committee that will manage an entire plant—the business unit. This group will also include the plant manager, probably with another title, plus one elected UAW representative.

The entire Saturn complex will be run by a fourth group, the manufacturing advisory committee. It will consist of top UAW and company officials from the business units, plus the manager of the Saturn complex and an elected UAW official. This is the committee that is supposed to reach consensus decisions on changes in salaries and benefits. It will answer on this and other decisions to the highest committee in Saturn, the strategic advisory committee. Made up of a top UAW official, plus Saturn's president and his staff, the committee will handle long-term planning for the company.

ETHOS LESSONS

UAW members will be taught to handle their new status during three to six months of company-paid training in problem solving, decision-making, business methods, and job skills. So they won't lose their allegiance to the UAW, they will also take classes in labor history and the union ethos.

For the most part, the 6,000 Saturn workers will have jobs for life. Some 80% of them will be protected from layoffs except in case of "catastrophic events." And even then, the joint committees can reject layoffs in favor of reduced work hours or a temporary shutdown. The job security plan illustrates Saturn's built-in flexibility. Both sides are sensitive to charges that the 20% of Saturn workers who will be vulnerable to layoffs—they'll be called "associate members"—will in essence be second-class citizens. "If it creates dissension," says one Saturn insider, "we'll scrap it."

Friction could also arise with Saturn's elimination of seniority rules. Many unionists are loathe to give up this traditional defense against favoritism when pink slips and higher-paying jobs are handed out. Saturn proponents say that because most workers will be in one job classification, no one will be bidding for better jobs. But there's still room for conflict. Skeptics note that team members might discriminate against women and minorities when assigning jobs. And pay bonuses, based on the performance of business units or work modules, could create pay disparities—and resentment.

But Saturn's framers think the potential gains are worth the risks. In the two years they spent traveling in Europe and Japan and devising the system, they learned that it's important to stay flexible. If Saturn workers and managers find the system too idealistic, they can always modify it to suit the real world.

DISCUSSION QUESTIONS: PART I

1. Does the General Motors Saturn automotive plant represent how factory work should be designed in the future? Why or why not?

2. Do you believe the job redesign changes at the Saturn plant will remain consistent over time? If not, which job redesign changes do you think will lose favor over time?

3. What recommendations would you offer to management to improve or sustain the job redesign changes at the plant?

Part II:

At Saturn, What Workers Want Is . . . Fewer Defects

After a new labor pact, plant output takes a backseat to quality

When General Motors Corp. Chairman Robert C. Stempel paid a visit to Saturn Corp.'s factory in Spring Hill, Tenn., on Oct. 4, he walked smack into a demonstration by the United Auto Workers. With negotiations under way for a new labor contract, plant workers had donned black-and-orange armbands and launched a work slowdown.

Another demand for higher pay? Not exactly. Saturn workers were complaining because management was trying to increase output of the popular compact at the expense of quality. Done right, high quality and high productivity should go hand in hand. But a year after the first car rolled out of the plant, Saturn is still rooting out manufacturing bugs, and working too fast can spoil quality. The workers knew that their jobs, in the long run, depended on making a top-notch product. Management seemed temporarily to have forgotten. "We were not going to sacrifice quality to get productivity," says Michael Bennett, president of UAW Local 1853.

The issue was settled on Nov. 13, when Saturn's 4,500 unionized workers approved their first labor pact since GM started the company in 1983. The union won a central demand: It delayed Saturn's plan to start tying 20% of workers' pay to aggressive quality and productivity goals. Management, in essence, conceded that Saturn's slow start, primarily its own fault, would have led to an immediate 20% pay cut. Saturn also eased off its production goal of 900 cars a day; it now produces 700. While these moves weren't good news for Saturn, they at least affirmed the revolutionary labor and management bond that has made the two sides working partners there. "In some cases, [the union] was absolutely right," concedes Saturn's president, Richard G. (Skip) LeFauve, who adds that the protests "refocused everyone to the sense of urgency to get the quality problems fixed."

Business Week/December 2, 1991. By David Woodruff in Spring Hill, Tenn.

The quality dispute comes at a critical time for Saturn. Former GM Chairman Roger B. Smith launched the company in an effort to do what no U.S. auto maker has accomplished in two decades: profitably build high-quality small cars that compete with Japanese models. But Saturn has been blocked by a series of setbacks since production began (table). Early on, it was unable to turn out enough sedans and coupes to meet demand. In the 1991 model year, Saturn built just 50,000 cars—one-third the original projection and well below capacity of 240,000.

WORD OF MOUTH

The problem with this is that Saturn buyers love their cars. A survey by California market researcher J. D. Power & Associates Inc. ranks Saturn sixth in customer satisfaction—just below cars such as Lincoln and Mercedes-Benz, which cost three times Saturn's average $11,000 sticker price. Power also says Saturn owners recommend their cars to more people than the owners of any other brand, even luxury lines. And nearly 95% of Saturn buyers have paid full retail. That's almost unheard-of in a market where rebates average $1,600 a car. "In our first four months, we probably could have sold another 500 cars," says James W. Lupient, president of Lupient Automotive Group, which runs a dozen Minneapolis dealerships.

Anxious Saturn managers hoped to capitalize on this ground swell in September, when they boosted production goals by 13%, to 900 cars a day. But as soon as they did, the plant's defect rate spiked up. For instance, Spring Hill's just-in-time inventory system, which delivers components to the assembly line just as they're needed, leaves little room for error. If a problem interrupts production in the building that casts, machines, and assembles Saturn's four-cylinder aluminum engines, the final assembly line next door grinds to a halt just six minutes later.

As a result, even minor snafus can shut down the whole line. And there have been a raft of such glitches. For instance, Saturn sprays body panels with a new, water-based paint to avoid the environmental drawbacks of solvent-based paints. But it's hard to keep the coating's viscosity constant, so the paint line sometimes slows to a crawl while workers ensure even coverage. In addition, the molds for Saturn's plastic fenders produce an unsightly seam along one edge. So the company ships fenders 15 miles to a small independent shop in Columbia, Tenn., for hand sanding, then back to Spring Hill for painting. And computerized spot-welding machines in Saturn's framing department conk out regularly, sometimes requiring a software fix. Indeed, these and other problems were reasons the union wanted production slowed.

HIGH-FLOWN IDEAS

Saturn's cooperative approach to labor relations—which includes involving workers—in decision-making from the plant floor to the board room—has caused other problems for management, too. The idea is to treat workers as co-owners who have as big a stake in the success of the company as executives or shareholders. This requires employees to work closely in production-line teams. But not everyone likes the practical application of such high-flown ideas. In a survey of union members last summer, about 6% said they were unhappy at Spring Hill and wanted out. The reasons varied. Some hadn't adjusted to teamwork. Others had personal problems, such as split families or unsold houses, that were caused when they transferred from other GM plants.

Although the proportion of workers who are disgruntled is small, GM went to extreme lengths in the new labor agreement not to let any dissatisfied employees poison the atmosphere. The contract offers severance pay for those who wish to leave, ranging from $15,000 to $50,000 depending on length of service at GM. Saturn officials figure that 25 to 100 of the plant's workers will opt to go. Such buyouts are expensive and usually are done only by companies trying to cut their work force. But Saturn decided that harmony was worth the price. "They don't want to be here, and they aren't very productive," says Thomas G. Manoff, Saturn's vice-president for finance, who doesn't plan to hire replacement workers.

Although Saturn managers are treading carefully in dealing with the company's startup woes, the pressure to move faster is growing. With GM's car sales mired in a yearlong slump, the company is careening toward a 1991 loss of $2.6 billion. And some $500 million of that is because of Saturn, analysts say. "We're all under the gun to help the mother ship," says Manoff. Union and management officials are confident that they can work out all of Saturn's kinks. If they do, it could be just in time to meet rising demand, assuming that Detroit's sales perk up next spring. Until then, GM's Stempel has little choice but to grit his teeth and bear the losses.

DISCUSSION QUESTIONS: PART II

1. Is quality being sacrificed to gain productivity? Do you agree with the perspective of labor or the perspective of management?

2. To what extent do you think the difficulties in the production of the Saturn car are a direct result of the job redesign changes in the plant or other (outside) factors?

3. Ten years from now, do you believe the Saturn plant will operate similarly to the way it operates today? Why or why not?

REFERENCES

M. Edid. "How Power Will Be Balanced on Saturn's Shop Floor." *Business Week,* August 5, 1985.

D. Woodruff. "At Saturn, What Workers Want Is . . . Fewer Defects." *Business Week,* December 2, 1991.

Exercise: Giving and Receiving Feedback

PURPOSE

This exercise is designed to give you the opportunity to practice giving and receiving feedback in a typical job situation—the performance appraisal. By the time you finish this exercise you will

1. Understand the guidelines for giving and receiving maximally useful feedback

2. Practice using these guidelines to give and receive feedback

3. Identify your strengths and weaknesses in this skill

4. Develop an action plan identifying additional sources of information

INTRODUCTION

The ability to give and receive feedback is a critical component of managerial success.

Giving Feedback

The basic task of a manager is managing people. As a result, managers spend a significant portion of their time providing subordinates with information about their performance. Giving feedback usually occurs in two contexts:

❏ Structured performance appraisal

❏ Day-to-day interaction

This exercise was developed by Cheryl L. Tromley. The guidelines for giving and receiving feedback in this exercise are based in part on those presented in C. R. Mill. "Feedback: The Art of Giving and Receiving Help." In L. Porter and C. R. Mill (eds.), *The Reading Book for Human Relations Training,* NTL Institute, 1976.

Knowing how to provide this information in a form that can be easily understood and used is a critical managerial skill.

It is equally important to be able to communicate with peers and superiors about the effects their behavior is having on us. Conflicts and misunderstandings seem endemic to organizational life. Many of these problems can be minimized or avoided with the increased use of effective feedback.

Receiving Feedback

We usually think about feedback skills in terms of giving feedback to others. However, learning how to receive feedback is an equally important skill. We are often woefully ignorant of the impact our behavior has on others. What we intend is often not the outcome. How many times have you been surprised to find out, years after the fact, that something you did was misinterpreted, often with negative consequences? By learning how to receive feedback and to elicit it when it is needed, you will be able to increase the likelihood of having the impact you desire.

Feedback—whether positive or negative, whether given or received—is often a source of anxiety for managers. The many and varied reasons for this anxiety are often rooted in a natural fear of hurting or being hurt. While it would be unrealistic to say this fear can be eliminated entirely, it is possible to reduce the anxiety many managers experience through knowledge and practice. This exercise is an opportunity for you to begin to learn the vital skills of giving and receiving feedback.

INSTRUCTIONS

This is a four-part exercise. In Part I you will evaluate how you normally give and receive feedback. In Part II you will have the opportunity to practice giving and receiving feedback in an organizational role-play. In Part III you will give and receive feedback about the feedback skills you displayed in Part II. In Part IV you will compare your perceptions from Part I with the feedback you received in Part III and develop an action plan.

Part I

1. Read the directions and complete the Feedback Skills Self-Assessment Questionnaire.

2. Find your score.

3. Read the Guidelines for Effective Feedback.

4. Compare your self-assessment results with the guidelines.

5. List your strengths and weaknesses on Action Plan I.

Part II

1. Read the directions and complete the Performance Appraisal Role-Play.

2. Complete the Performance Appraisal Role-Play Feedback Form.

Part III

1. Using the Performance Appraisal Role-Play Feedback Form, give your role-play partner feedback about the feedback skills he or she displayed during the role-play.

2. Receive feedback from your role-play partner about the feedback skills you displayed during the role-play.

3. Enter this information on Action Plan II.

Part IV

1. Complete Action Plan III.

2. Participate in a class discussion.

Part I: Feedback Skills Self-Assessment

Feedback Skills Self-Assessment Questionnaire

Directions: The following self-assessment questionnaire contains two sections: (1) giving feedback and (2) receiving feedback. Complete each section according to the instructions provided. Be honest with yourself. Unless you decide otherwise, no one else will see this evaluation. This is an opportunity for you to assess your own strengths and weaknesses; an opportunity for you to determine what you are already doing well and what you need to improve.

Section 1: Giving Feedback

Think back to a time when you gave someone feedback about their behavior. For each of the following pairs, check the statement that most closely matches what you *normally* do when you give feedback to someone else.

When I give feedback to someone else I

1. a.	Describe the behavior	_____ (a)
b.	Evaluate the behavior	_____ (b)
2. a.	Focus on the feelings that the behavior evokes	_____ (a)
b.	Tell the person what they should be doing differently	_____ (b)
3. a.	Give specific instances of the behavior	_____ (a)
b.	Generalize	_____ (b)
4. a.	Deal only with behavior that the person can control	_____ (a)
b.	Sometimes focus on something the person can do nothing about	_____ (b)
5. a.	Tell the person as soon as possible after the behavior	_____ (a)
b.	Sometimes wait too long	_____ (b)
6. a.	Focus on the effect the behavior has on me	_____ (a)
b.	Try to figure out why the individual did what he or she did	_____ (b)
7. a.	Balance negative feedback with positive feedback	_____ (a)
b.	Sometimes focus only on the negative	_____ (b)
8. a.	Do some soul searching to make sure that the reason I am giving the feedback is to help the other person or to strengthen our relationship	_____ (a)
b.	Sometimes give feedback to punish, win against, or dominate the other person	_____ (b)

Section 2: Receiving Feedback

Think back to a time when someone gave you feedback about your behavior. For each of the following pairs, check the statement that most closely matches what you *normally* do when someone gives you feedback.

1. a.	I sometimes ask for feedback about my behavior	_____ (a)
b.	I rarely elicit feedback about my behavior	_____ (b)

When someone else gives me feedback I

2. a. Listen carefully and concentrate on understanding what is being said   _____ (a)

   b. Let my mind wander, interrupt, or spend my time trying to formulate a response _____ (b)

3. a. Check to make sure I've understood what the person means   _____ (a)

   b. Just assume that I understand   _____ (b)

4. a. Ask for examples and clarification   _____ (a)

   b. Try to justify my behavior and defend myself   _____ (b)

5. a. Ask additional people for input when the feedback doesn't agree with my perceptions   _____ (a)

   b. Discount feedback that doesn't agree with my perceptions   _____ (b)

Feedback Skills Self-Assessment Scoring Key

Directions: On the scoring key below indicate

1. How many (a) responses you checked for giving feedback
2. How many (b) responses you checked for giving feedback
3. How many (a) responses you checked for receiving feedback
4. How many (b) responses you checked for receiving feedback

Scoring Key

Giving Feedback			*Receiving Feedback*	
(a)	*(b)*		*(a)*	*(b)*
_____	_____		_____	_____

INTERPRETATION

The (a) responses are your self-perceived strengths, and the (b) responses are your self-perceived weaknesses. By looking at the proportion of your (a) and (b) responses, you will be able to see an overview of

1. How effective you feel you are when giving and receiving feedback

2. Where you feel your strengths and weaknesses lie. That is, do your strengths and/or weaknesses involve giving or receiving feedback?

GUIDELINES FOR EFFECTIVE FEEDBACK

Directions: Review the following guidelines. Each guideline corresponds in order to one of the questions in the Self-Assessment Questionnaire.

❏ Compare each of your responses to the corresponding guideline. You will note that each guideline begins with two code words (such as *Descriptive* and *Eval-*

uative). One of these code words corresponds to a strength (in this case, *Descriptive*) and one corresponds to weakness (*Evaluative*). Each of these code words is also labeled as either (a) or (b), corresponding to the (a) or (b) responses in the Self-Assessment Questionnaire.

❏ For each (a) alternative that you checked in the Self-Assessment Questionnaire, circle the corresponding code word in Action Plan I, Part 1: Self-Assessment.

❏ Follow the same procedure for all of your (b) responses.

Example: If you checked *1. a. Describe the behavior* in Section 1 (giving feedback) of the Self-Assessment Questionnaire, go to guideline *1* in *Section 1: Giving Feedback* of the Guidelines for Effective Feedback. The code word corresponding to your response is *(a) Descriptive.* Circle *Descriptive* in the *Strength (a)—Giving* section of Action Plan I.

Section 1: Giving Feedback

1. (a) *Descriptive,* (b) *Evaluative*
Effective feedback describes the behavior rather than evaluates it. For example, it is more effective to say, "You have interrupted me ten times during this meeting" than "You're a loudmouthed, inconsiderate jerk." The descriptive statement describes only the behavior ("you did . . ."). The evaluative statement attacks the individual ("you are . . ."). While no one likes to hear that they have repeatedly interrupted you, they will be less defensive to a valid description than to a personal attack.

2. (a) *Feelings evoked,* (b) *Do it differently*
Effective feedback focuses on the feelings that the behavior evokes in the person giving the feedback; it is not a demand to change. For example, it is more effective to say, "When you interrupt me it makes me feel like you don't care about what I have to say" than "You have to stop interrupting people." The latter may be what you feel, but effective feedback does not demand change. Helpful feedback is given so the person can better understand the effect that his or her behavior has on you. It is up to the person receiving the feedback to decide what to do about it, if anything.

3. (a) *Specific,* (b) *General*
Effective feedback gives specific examples of the behavior rather than general ones. For example, it is more effective to say, "You have interrupted me ten times during this meeting" than "You always interrupt people." The more specific the feedback, the easier it is for the person receiving the feedback to understand exactly what you mean, to believe what you say, and to develop a plan for change.

4. (a) *Controllable,* (b) *Uncontrollable*
Effective feedback concerns behavior the individual can do something about. Telling someone about something over which they have no control will only frustrate them and create resentment. For example, saying, "Your voice really gets on my nerves" is not helpful feedback.

5. (a) *Timely,* (b) *Late*
Feedback is most effective when it is given as soon as possible after the occurrence. Of course, "as soon as possible" must be considered in light of your state of mind and with deference to the feeling of the individual to whom you wish to give the feedback. It is not a good idea to give feedback when you are angry, when it might embarrass the receiver, or when the receiver is particularly vulnerable.

6. (a) *Effect,* (b) *Analyze*

Effective feedback focuses on the effect the behavior has on you. Analyzing the reasons for an individual's behavior is beyond the boundary of feedback; it belongs in a psychologist's office. It is most helpful to assume that the target of our feedback had good intentions.

7. (a) *Positive and negative,* (b) *Negative only*

Effective feedback can be both positive and negative. Both are important. Yet there is a tendency to think of feedback in only negative terms. People are more likely to take negative feedback seriously if they believe that their positive behavior is also observed and acknowledged. People are also more likely to believe the positive feedback you give them if they know you are being honest with them in general; sometimes being honest involves negative feedback. The ideal is to find a balance between the two. This does *not* mean that every time you give someone negative feedback you must also strain to find something positive to say. It *does* mean that over time there should be a balance. During a structured feedback situation, such as performance appraisal, there should be a balance during the session.

8. (a) *Help,* (b) *Punish*

Before you give feedback you should be honest with yourself about your motivation. As much as we would all like to deny it, we are human with human emotions and weaknesses. Remember, feedback is not a demand to change, nor should it ever be done to punish, win against, or dominate the other person. You should only give feedback if you can honestly tell yourself that your motivation is to help the other person or strengthen your relationship.

Section 2: Receiving Feedback

1. (a) *Elicit,* (b) *Wait*

Because people may not always be willing to take the risk to tell you about how your behavior is affecting them, you may get this valuable information only if you ask. This does not mean that you should ask everyone you meet about how they feel about you. It does mean that, when you have a question about how a behavior has been received—the more specific the better—you should take the chance and ask.

2. (a) *Listen,* (b) *Wander*

To be effective, feedback must be heard and understood. For this to happen it is important that you concentrate on what is being said to you. This may take some effort. Our minds tend to wander, and it is common to spend the time trying to formulate an appropriate response. Listening is the stage where communication most commonly breaks down. Therefore, when someone is giving you feedback—whether you think he or she is right or wrong—listen carefully and concentrate on understanding what is being said.

3. (a) *Check,* (b) *Assume*

When you receive feedback, make sure that what you understand is what the giver means. We all hear things through a variety of different filters, which can distort meaning and cause misunderstanding. To avoid this, rephrase the feedback and ask the person giving you feedback whether that is what was meant.

4. (a) *Clarify,* (b) *Justify*

One of the most common errors people make when receiving feedback is justifying, explaining, or defending their behavior. This is counterproductive. In the first place, your reasons are really irrelevant. What you should be interested in is the effect your behavior is having on the other person: your motivation will not change that effect. In the second place, justifying, explaining, and defending often makes people reluctant to give you feedback in the future because they may feel that they are wasting their time. What you should do is ask questions to maximize your understanding. These questions may involve the clarification of points that are not clear to you or a request for specific examples. If you ask these questions, it is important not to be challenging or defensive. For example, it is a good idea to say, "It would help me understand what you mean if you could give me an example." It is not helpful to say, "I don't think I do that. Give me a specific time when I did what you are talking about."

5. (a) *Ask others,* (b) *Discount*

At times you will receive feedback that is inconsistent with your perceptions of your behavior. When this happens, it is easy to discount what you have heard. However, we are often the worst judge of the effects of our behavior on others. Rather than just automatically discounting incongruous feedback, you should elicit additional feedback from others. This is an especially good time to actively seek feedback.

Action Plan I

Part 1: Self-Assessment

Strength (a): Giving	Weakness (b): Giving
Descriptive	Evaluative
Feeling evoked	Do it differently
Specific	General
Controllable	Uncontrollable
Timely	Late
Effect	Analyze
Positive and negative	Negative only
Help	Punish
Strength (a): Receiving	Weakness (b): Receiving
Elicit	Wait
Listen	Wander
Check	Assume
Clarify	Justify
Ask others	Discount

Part II: Performance Appraisal Role-Play

Directions: In Part II you will have the opportunity to practice giving and receiving feedback in a typical organizational situation—the performance appraisal. You will be playing two roles. In one you will provide feedback; in the other you will receive feedback.

Choose someone else in the class as a partner. This should be someone with whom you feel relatively comfortable but need not be someone you know well.

With your partner, decide who will be the first to give and receive feedback. Whoever gives feedback first will play the role of Patrick/Patricia (Pat) Simmons. The person receiving feedback will play the role of Alexander/Alexandra (Alex) Thompson.

Both of you should read the General Information section. The individual portraying Pat Simmons should also read the role description entitled "Role of Pat Simmons: Alex Thompson Performance Appraisal." The individual portraying Alex Thompson should read the role description entitled "Role of Alex Thompson." You may elaborate on these roles as much as you like. For example, you may want to make up specific examples of behavior. Note: Do not read any roles that are not yours.

You will have 20 minutes to complete the performance appraisal. When you finish, you should fill out the Performance Appraisal Role-Play Feedback Form. On this form you will indicate how effectively your partner in the role-play gave or received feedback. That is, the person who portrayed Simmons should evaluate how effectively the person who portrayed Thompson received feedback. The person who portrayed Thompson should evaluate how effectively the person who portrayed Simmons gave feedback. You should evaluate your partner on the dimensions presented in the feedback guidelines. The code words are provided on the form, but if you have any questions refer to the guidelines. For each dimension about which you have information, indicate the behavior and its effect on you. For example, for *Justify* the *Behavior* could be "tried to blame production department for late delivery" and the *Impact on You* could be "felt like you can't handle responsibility." You may not have information about all of the dimensions.

When you have completed the Performance Appraisal Role-Play Feedback Form, switch roles for the next 20-minute performance appraisal. The person who played Pat Simmons will play Samuel/Samantha (Sam) Reynolds and should read that role description. The person who played Alex Thompson will be playing Pat Simmons and should read the description entitled "Role of Pat Simmons: Sam Reynolds' Performance Appraisal."

When you finish the performance appraisal, complete the Performance Appraisal Role-Play Feedback Form.

Performance Appraisal Role-Play Feedback Form
Giving Feedback

	Behavior	*Impact on You*
Descriptive		
Evaluative		
Feeling evoked		
Do it differently		
Specific		
General		
Controllable		
Uncontrollable		
Effect		
Analyze		
Positive and negative		
Negative only		
Help		
Punish		

Performance Appraisal Role-Play Feedback Form
Receiving Feedback

	Behavior	*Impact on You*
Elicit		
Wait		
Listen		
Wander		
Check		
Assume		
Clarify		
Justify		

GENERAL INFORMATION

Plastimold, Inc. is a major force in the packaging industry. They are currently the largest manufacturer of plastic containers in the United States. Plastimold employs 3,500 employees at one location in New England. Last year they had $175 million in sales.

The Industrial Plastics division produces disposal and storage containers for the chemical industry, holding tanks, and other components for the automotive industry, and specialized shipping and product handling containers for the aerospace industry.

The Consumer Plastics division, which is almost twice as large as the Industrial division, produces plastic containers for a range of consumer products, including food products, toiletries, pharmaceuticals, soaps, detergents, cleansers, soft drinks, alcoholic beverages, and motor oil. See Figure 1 for Plastimold's organizational chart.

FIGURE 1
Organization Chart, Plastimold, Inc.

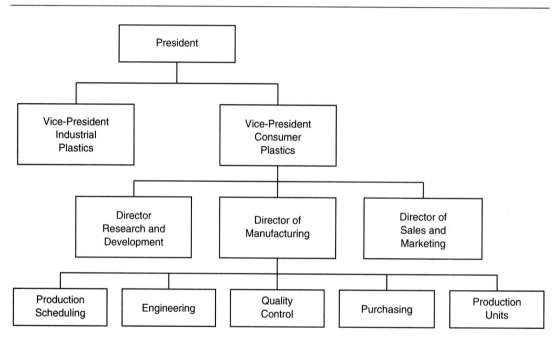

Pat Simmons is the head of the engineering department. This department is responsible for the product and tool design. They also "troubleshoot" all production problems. Five section chiefs report directly to Simmons (see Figure 2). Simmons is about to give a yearly performance appraisal to two of the section chiefs, Alex Thompson and Sam Reynolds. Both section chiefs are senior engineers whose duties are both technical and supervisory. Six draftsmen and one junior engineer report directly to each of them.

Alex Thompson has a degree in mechanical engineering from an Ivy League university and has twelve years of experience in the industry. Alex was hired by Plastimold three years ago.

FIGURE 2
Organization Chart, Department of Engineering

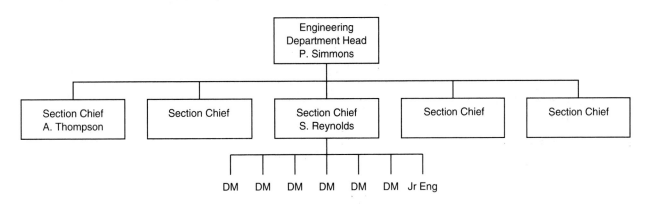

Sam Reynolds has been with Plastimold for twenty-one years. He/she started out as a draftsman and received his/her degree in mechanical engineering by attending school at night. Sam was promoted to section chief four years ago.

Role of Pat Simmons:
Alex Thompson Performance Appraisal

You are about to meet Alex Thompson. You are very pleased with Alex's technical performance. He/she has the most productive section in the department. The designs Alex's section produces are top-drawer. Production rarely finds any problems with them, and as a result Alex spends less time than any other section head troubleshooting design problems in the production units. In fact, you have been giving Alex's section the overflow that the other sections haven't been able to complete. On occasion you have even asked Alex to consult with other section heads who were having technical problems.

In spite of this you are concerned about Alex's relationship with his/her subordinates and the other section heads as well as his/her attitude toward you.

Alex seems to go through draftsmen like water. The section has almost twice the turnover of any other section, and the Personnel Department is having trouble replacing all of the draftsmen who have quit. You have received some complaints about Alex's management style. You think that this might be related to the low morale and high turnover that seem to characterize the section.

According to the interviews Personnel conducted with the draftsmen who quit, Alex is always on their backs. He/she doesn't trust them to do anything on their own and is constantly checking and criticizing their work. As one departing draftsman put it, "Alex was always on me, every line I drew. Plus, I could do a thousand things exactly right and then make one small inconsequential mistake, and you'd think I had just bombed the plant. I just can't stand being treated like an incompetent fool anymore." Another draftsman said, "Alex is constantly pressuring us to do more, get more done, do it better. We all work very hard, but Alex either doesn't realize that or doesn't care. Nothing we do is ever good enough."

Alex's fellow section chiefs are also displeased by his/her behavior. They say Alex is arrogant and acts like he/she is the only one who knows how to do the job.

You are also becoming increasingly uncomfortable with Alex's attitude toward you. Sometimes you wonder who the boss is. Alex frequently usurps your authority and ignores your directives.

Role of Alex Thompson

You feel pretty good about your upcoming performance appraisal. Your section is the most productive in the consumer engineering department. You rarely have to spend time correcting problems once your designs are in production. You know the same cannot be said for the other section heads. You can't figure out why they don't fire some of them. It seems to you they spend as much time fixing their mistakes as they do designing products. Pat often has to have you go pull their fat out of the fire. They aren't even grateful for all your effort. In fact they act resentful, as if you were intruding or something, rather than helping them out of a tight spot.

You don't know what Pat expects from you and you resent all the extra work he/she heaps on you. You feel you're being punished for being the most productive department. Every time you get a little ahead Pat dumps someone else's work on you. Sometimes you feel like you're doing everyone else's work in addition to your own. Plus, Pat often doesn't know as much as you do about the technical end of the job, and you're often forced to do his/her work as well as your own and the rest of the section chiefs'.

You also feel as though you're doing such a good job against incredible odds. The draftsmen that the Personnel Department sends you are not as qualified as they should be. You feel as though you spend all your time redoing their designs. You've often said that you might as well do it yourself. Not only that, but they are an unreliable bunch. By the time you get them broken in to your way of doing things, they up and leave for another job. People just aren't as reliable as they used to be.

Role of Pat Simmons:
Sam Reynolds' Performance Appraisal

You are about to meet with Sam Reynolds. Sam has a great relationship with his/her subordinates and the other section heads. You also find Sam easy to work with. He/she is always eager to comply with your wishes and supports your goals for the department.

Sam's section has the lowest turnover in the department. The draftsmen and junior engineers who work for Sam are always singing his/her praises. They say that they like the way Sam delegates responsibility to them. It makes them feel like he/she trusts them. Sam's style seems to be to coach and guide rather than tightly control. Sam also wants his/her people to get ahead. He/she has even encouraged two of the draftsmen who report to him/her to go back to school for their engineering degrees.

Sam's section appears to work like a team. Whenever you go into his/her section, you see people talking together and trying to help each other out. You've never seen any real conflict in Sam's section; there's always a nice relaxed atmosphere. Sam really seems to have a talent for keeping things running smoothly.

However, you have some questions about Sam's technical performance. He/she has the least productive section in the department. Sam spends too much of his/her time in the production units trying to iron out problems with his/her section's designs. In the past year you have had to give another section head work that Sam should have been able to complete.

You feel that Sam may not be supervising his/her staff closely enough. Too many mistakes are getting by him/her. You also wonder if Sam may not be carrying this relaxed atmosphere a little too far. Sometimes it seems like Sam's section spends as much time talking as working.

Sam also spends a lot of time talking with the other section heads and the people in production. It is not uncommon for you to find him/her standing around one of the production units talking with one of his/her old cronies. Maybe Sam's not spending enough time on the nuts and bolts.

Role of Sam Reynolds

You feel pretty confident about your upcoming performance appraisal. Your section is working well together and morale is high. You have a good relationship with Pat as well as your subordinates, the other section heads, and the people in production. In fact, just last week you were able to save the department about two weeks in down time because of the relationship that you've established with the production department.

Some of the other section heads don't seem to understand the importance of maintaining a good relationship with the other parts of the company. You've been around long enough to know that the way you get things done around here is through the people you know, not the things you know.

It's not that you don't know your job; you do. Your designs are innovative and creative. Because of this you sometimes have to spend a little extra time in the production units ironing out difficulties. Your designs are not just stock drawings reworked for a different job. Sometimes that takes a little extra time but you think it's worth it. One of the reasons that you can take those kinds of risks is that you have such a good relationship with the people in production.

You remember what it was like to be a draftsman. They're a pretty creative bunch and you try to let them have the room to exercise their talents. Often they have come up with ideas that saved the company a lot of money and resulted in a better product. You believe that your section is a team and should operate that way. You believe in involving your subordinates in all of the decisions that affect them. You are always open to suggestions, and you give people the opportunity to make mistakes. You figure that is the only way that they will learn.

You have a good relationship with the other section heads. You've helped them out with your contacts in the production units and they've helped you out when you had problems. All in all everyone gets along pretty well.

Part III: Feedback

Directions: In Part III you will give your partner feedback about how effectively he/she gave and received feedback in Part II and you will receive feedback from your partner. Using the Performance Appraisal Role-Play Feedback Form, spend ten minutes giving your partner the feedback that you have noted. You will then switch and your partner will give you feedback.

Be sure to observe the guidelines for effective feedback when you are giving and receiving feedback. A helpful way to phrase your feedback is to say, for example, "When you tried to blame production for the late delivery, it made me feel as though you can't handle the responsibility I've given you."

If there is anything about which you specifically want feedback, such as any potential weaknesses you identified in Part I, you should share them with your partner at this time. However, your partner is not limited to these areas.

While your partner is giving you feedback, make notes of your strengths and weaknesses on Action Plan II. The code words are provided for your convenience. One useful way to keep track of the feedback you are receiving is to circle the code word involved and make a note of the example in the space provided.

Action Plan II

Part III: Performance Appraisal Role-Play Feedback

Strength (a): Giving	*Weakness (b): Giving*
Descriptive	Evaluative
Feeling evoked	Do it differently
Specific	General
Controllable	Uncontrollable
Effect	Analyze
Positive and negative	Negative only
Help	Punish
Strength (a): Receiving	*Weakness (b): Receiving*
Elicit	Wait
Listen	Wander
Check	Assume
Clarify	Justify

Part IV: Action Plan III

Directions:

1. Compare your self-assessment with the feedback you received in Part III.

2. Define areas of agreement and disagreement for both giving and receiving feedback.

3. Indicate this information in your action plan in the space provided.

4. Determine the areas about which you want additional feedback. This need not be limited only to those areas about which there was disagreement.

5. Identify the person or persons from whom you intend to elicit this additional feedback.

Action Plan III

Giving Feedback:	
Parts I & III Agree: Strength	Where Can I Get Additional Information?
Parts I & III Agree: Weakness	Where Can I Get Additional Information?
Parts I & III Disagree	Where Can I Get Additional Information?
Receiving Feedback:	
Parts I & III Agree: Strength	Where Can I Get Additional Information?
Parts I & III Agree: Weakness	Where Can I Get Additional Information?
Parts I & III Disagree	Where Can I Get Additional Information?

DISCUSSION QUESTIONS

1. How much agreement was there between Part I and Part III? Where do you plan to get additional information about those skills for which there was disagreement?

2. What was the most difficult guideline for effective feedback for you to put into practice? Why?

3. Which of your relationships (subordinate, superior, peer) could benefit most from the increased use of effective feedback? Why?

REFERENCE

C. R. Mill. "Feedback: The Art of Giving and Receiving Help." In L. Porter and C. R. Mill (eds.), *The Reading Book for Human Relations Training*. NTL Institute, 1976.

CHAPTER 4

Leadership and Decision Making

INTRODUCTION

How would you describe an effective leader? There are as many perspectives as there are answers to this deceptively simple question. Few people really understand what leadership is. Although we recognize strong leaders when we see them in action, modeling those same behaviors is difficult to practice. Few valid prescriptions for effective leadership exist.

Historically, research in this area first linked leadership to individual traits, assuming that one central "leadership personality profile" would emerge. When this approach was unsuccessful, leader behaviors were examined to determine which styles were most effective. Contingency approaches then focused on the situational conditions the leader faces in an attempt to match styles to unique situational determinants. Currently, perspectives on leadership identify the critical skills that strong leaders demonstrate in an effort to further specify this phenomenon.

Despite all the research in this area, there is only limited agreement on what leadership really is. Most authors would agree that leadership involves making decisions. A leader is someone who is able to size up a situation quickly, define a direction to pursue, and mobilize subordinates' energies toward the achievement of a particular goal. In other words, leaders make decisions for others to follow.

READINGS

The three articles in this chapter illustrate different aspects of leadership and the decision-making process. The first article, "Two Decades of Research on Participation: Beyond Buzz Words and Management Fads," by Victor H. Vroom, discusses the dilemmas of participation in leadership decisions. Professor Vroom examines this dilemma carefully, presenting five styles of leadership based on how autocratic—or how consultative—a leader should act under different conditions. He offers a revised decision tree to help managers determine when subordinate participation in decision making is recommended.

The second article, "Leadership: Good, Better, Best," by Bernard M. Bass, identifies the necessary behaviors and characteristics for effective leadership. In this article, Bass describes the differences between transactional and transformational leadership. Bass argues that transformational leaders capture the fragile essence of effective leadership by inspiring others, by showing consideration toward subordinates, and by providing intellectual stimulation. Transactional leaders set up contingent reinforcement practices that specify the limits of their relationship with subordinates. Bass further identifies the characteristics of charismatic leaders, maintaining that charisma is what separates an ordinary leader from an effective one.

The third article, "Leadership: The Art of Empowering Others," by Jay A. Conger, illustrates exactly how effective leaders operate. Conger suggests that effective leaders empower subordinates in a variety of ways: by expressing confidence, by rewarding and encouraging employees, and by fostering initiative and responsibility. He shows the reader through examples of the strategies actual leaders use on how to accomplish these aims. Conger offers the notion that the process of empowerment should be accomplished in several stages and discusses how this can be done.

Because the study of leadership is so complex and intensive, we could not present readings that address each and every dimension of effective leadership. Rather, we chose to focus on those models that were actionable and realistic in their use.

EXERCISES AND CASES

The first exercise, "Leadership and Decision Making: Applying the Vroom Model," allows you to determine the range of participative behavior that should be used in different leadership situations. In this exercise, you will have an opportunity to use the updated Vroom and Jago decision tree to determine the appropriate leadership style for management problems. By understanding the conditions under which a leader should adopt participatory behaviors, compared with the conditions under which a leader should make decisions alone, you will be better able to assess this dimension in your own leadership practice.

The second exercise, a case entitled, "The Man Who Killed Braniff," analyzes the downfall of one corporate executive as a result of his management practices. The case describes the leadership style of Harding Lawrence, and the role his style played in the demise of Braniff airlines. This case best illustrates how *not* to manage or lead. By understanding what went wrong in this case, you will be able to determine what *not* to do when presented with a leadership dilemma.

The third exercise, "Leadership Empowerment Styles," is offered to help you determine your style of leadership. How do you react to subordinates? Are you overly friendly? Come on a bit too strong? Adopt an authoritarian posture? Or manage them with care and consideration? This exercise will help you model empowering behaviors as a future leader.

MEMO

The memo assignment for this chapter, *"Practicing Effective Leadership"* (located at the back of the book), asks you to consider leaders you have known. Which leaders have been effective managers? To what extent were they transformational? Which leaders, in your opinion, failed miserably? How can you learn from their mistakes? This memo assignment helps you develop an action plan to improve your leadership skills.

By the time you finish this chapter, you will have a better understanding of effective leadership practices in organizations. You will also have gained experience in determining the range of participative behavior required for effective management practice. In addition, you will have had the opportunity to reflect on your own leadership style and learn how you can empower others as a future leader.

Two Decades of Research on Participation: Beyond Buzz Words And Management Fads

Victor H. Vroom

Management may be an ancient practice, yet fads and fashions abound in our attempts to systemize the management process. Twenty years of research has enabled the author to make considerable progress in "separating the bedrock from the hucksterism." In the process, he has discovered truths that may surprise even the most experienced manager.

Management has been described as an ancient practice but a new academic discipline. It has been more than six thousand years since the Egyptians faced the monumental task of constructing the pyramids, a task that would be monumental even by today's standards. However, efforts to construct and test theories about management are relatively recent undertakings that have occurred largely within the last century. It is perhaps reflective of the "newness" of intellectual traditions surrounding management that some would argue that the term theory is far too dignified to convey the spirit of the fads and fashions that characterize many of our current attempts to systematize the management process. The task of separating the bedrock from the hucksterism appears, at times, to be like searching for the proverbial needle in the haystack.

One of the perennial debates in the managerial literature concerns the appropriateness or effectiveness of participative management. The scientific management of Frederick Winslow Taylor, which dominated management thought in the early part of this century and which viewed workers as inherently lazy and incapable of exercising judgment and discretion, seems gradually to have given way to a view of management that stresses human capability and the need to move from control to commitment. The "buzz words" of contemporary management include empowerment, self-managing work teams, and total quality management. For the time being, participative management is the "victor," in theory if not always in practice. We must ask, however, whether the current focus on worker involvement is the final answer or merely another perturbation of the ever swinging pendulum.

Reprinted from *Yale Management,* Spring 1993 by permission from Victor H. Vroom, © Victor H. Vroom. Tables 1 and 2 and Figure 1 reprinted by permission from Victor H. Vroom and Arthur G. Jago, © Victor H. Vroom and Arthur G. Jago, 1987.

The relative effectiveness of various forms and degrees of participation in decision making is a subject that we have been studying at Yale for almost two decades. We are convinced that "the bedrock" lies in a situational view of participation, i.e., that the most appropriate degree of participation must depend on the circumstances surrounding the participative act. Expressed in this simple way, our assertion approaches a truism. To be testable and meaningful, we must specify the nature of this situational dependency.

MATCHING THE DECISION PROCESS WITH THE SITUATIONAL DEMANDS

Let us begin with an elemental situation that will provide the foundation for our analysis. We assume that a manager is confronted with a problem or decision that falls within his or her area of freedom and the resolution of which has effects on a group of other persons. (We shall refer to this group as "direct reports," although the usefulness of the analysis that follows is not dependent on any particular hierarchical relationship between the manager and group.)

Table 1 shows a set of five decision processes, each varying in the degree to which the group has an opportunity to participate in the decision-making process.

Using the terminology of Table 1, one can ask both normative and descriptive questions. The normative questions are "should" questions. If we define our goal as maximizing the likely effectiveness of the manager's choice, our task is to define the circumstances under which each alternative would be preferred. The decision process is the independent variable and components of decision effectiveness become dependent variables.

Descriptive questions are "would" questions. The decision processes are dependent variables and characteristics of the manager and his or her situation become independent variables. From a descriptive standpoint, one can ask how decision processes vary with such factors as culture, the nature of the organization, and the gender of the manager.

For twenty years, I have been working with associates in the development of a normative model of the participative process. The latest version of this model was developed in collaboration with Professor Arthur Jago of the University of Houston. The Vroom-

TABLE 1
Decision Processes

The way in which a manager reaches a decision affects the degree to which his/her direct reports have the opportunity to participate in that decision (adapted from Vroom and Jago, 1988).

AI   You reach a decision alone, employing whatever facts you have at hand.

AII   You reach a decision alone, but first seek some specific data from those who report to you. You are not obliged to tell them about the nature of the situation you face. You seek only relevant facts from them—not their advice or counsel.

CI   You consult one-on-one with those who report to you, describing the problem to each and asking for the person's advice and recommendations. However, the final decision is yours alone.

CII   You consult with those who report to you in a meeting (or portion thereof) devoted to the situation. You receive their advice and recommendations in this meeting, but the task of resolving any differences of opinions and of choosing one or more options is yours alone.

GII   You devote a meeting (or portion thereof) to a discussion of the situation and identification and consideration of possible decisions. Avoiding voting, the group attempts to concur on a decision. You coordinate the meeting, facilitate the dialogue, protect minority viewpoints, and make sure all important factors are considered. Above all, you take care to ensure that your ideas are not given any greater weight than those of others simply because of your position.

Jago model makes use of the decision processes shown in Table 1 and seeks to provide guidance in matching the process with situational demands. This model is driven by a set of four equations which purport to model what is known about the effects of participation on four conceptually and empirically separable outcomes of the participation process. These outcomes are: 1) the *quality* of decisions made; 2) the amount of *commitment* to decisions; 3) the length of *time* required to make the decisions; and 4) the amount of growth or *development* of the group or team. The evidence is abundant that the decision process used affects each of these outcomes. Thus, the degree to which one involves one's direct reports in the making of a decision will have consequences for the quality of the decision as well as one's commitment to it, the time required to make it, and the team's subsequent learning.

    The evidence is also supportive of a situational view of each of these four relationships. Sometimes consensus-seeking impairs decision quality; sometimes consensus-seeking increases it. In general, increasing participation results in a greater degree of commitment and greater development, while consuming a greater amount of time. However, there are circumstances under which one's direct reports would commit equally to an autocratically made decision and circumstances under which consensus-seeking would not be expected to increase the value of the human resources in the teams (and might even damage the team's ability to function collaboratively in the future). Finally, the effects of participation on time, while seemingly invariant in direction, will vary in magnitude from one situation to another. While groups take longer to make decisions, the degree to which they do so will depend on such factors as the amount of conflict surrounding the issue and the degree to which the problem is unstructured.

    In addition, we argue that the importance of each of these four decision outcomes—quality, commitment, time, and group development—will vary from one situation to another. In some situations the analytical dimension is nonexistent, i.e., decision quality is not an issue. In other situations decision quality is paramount. Similarly, the importance of commitment, time, and development may vary from one decision problem to another.

    Table 2 lists the situational factors in the Vroom-Jago model. Each is expressed in the form of a question that pertains both to the decision problem that is faced and the social context within which that problem is embedded.

    The answers to four of the questions (QR, CR, MT, and MD) provide weights for the four decision outcomes by establishing upper bounds for the values of each outcome. Answers to the remaining eight questions are used in one or more of the equations to predict the relative amounts of each outcome that can be expected to be achieved by each decision process. All questions except TC and GD are answered on five-point scales.

TABLE 2
Situational Factors in the Vroom-Jago Model

Following are the key factors affecting the decision process.

QR: Quality Requirement How important is the technical quality of this decision?

CR: Commitment Requirement How important is it that those who report to you are committed to the decision?

LI: Leader Information Do you have the knowledge, or is it readily available in on-hand manuals or documents, to reach a sound decision?

ST: Problem Structure Is the problem well structured?

CP: Commitment Probability Are you confident that those who report to you would commit themselves to a decision that you would reach alone?

GC: Goal Congruence Do those who report to you share the organizational goals to be attained in solving this problem?

CO: Subordinate Conflict Are those who report to you likely to be in disagreement over the nature of the problem or over the alternatives that each might wish or recommend?

SI: Subordinate Information Do those who report to you collectively have the knowledge to reach a technically sound solution?

TC: Time Constraint Does a critically severe time constraint limit your ability to involve subordinates?

GD: Geographical Dispersion Are the costs involved in bringing together geographically dispersed subordinates prohibitive?

MT: Motivation-Time How important is it to you to minimize the time it takes to make the decision?

MD: Motivation-Development How important is it to you to maximize the opportunities for subordinate development?

(Adapted from Vroom and Jago, 1988)

USING THE MODEL:
TWO APPROACHES FOR MANAGERS

Managers interested in studying the intricacies of these equations may do so (see Vroom and Jago, p. 231). However, solving four equations for each of five decision processes and summing the twenty integers into the five values deemed to be reflective of the relative effectiveness of the five decision processes can be a very time-consuming process. As a practical matter, the Vroom-Jago model is best used on a personal computer. Jago's programming skill has produced an expert system that is called MPO (Managing Participation in Organizations). The program requires only 256K of memory and runs on any IBM-compatible computer. MPO runs in either novice or experienced user mode, and managers who have used it describe the program as very user friendly. To use MPO, a manager is asked to think of a specific decision problem with which he or she is faced and then to answer the 12 questions in Table 2. (Help screens are provided with each question to aid novice users in reaching a common understanding both of each question and of the alternative levels of response to it.) When all questions have been answered, the screen indicates the model's choice of a decision process as well as the optimal choice were each of the four underlying criteria considered alone.

On request, additional information is available about the problem and the tradeoffs that it poses among the four decision outcomes. For example, bar graphs depicting the predicted success of each process are available, along with sensitivity of the model's recommendation to the relative importance placed on short-range considerations (e.g., time) and longer range consequences (e.g., development).

MPO has been extremely useful both as a classroom teaching device and as a managerial tool. Twice each year, I offer a three- to four-day course on leadership and decision-making for executives who come from all parts of the country and sometimes, all parts of the world. A central focus of the course has been the "what and when" of the effective use of groups for decision making. MPO is used in the classroom to analyze cases furnished by participants. Additionally, the MPO system is given to participants at the conclusion of the course as a reminder of many of the more important contingencies involved in selecting the most effective decision process.

I also use MPO in a graduate course entitled Managerial Leadership, which I teach each year for a mixed set of students from the Schools of Management, Law, Forestry, Epidemiology and Health, and Drama. Students are given a copy of MPO on a floppy disk and are asked to use it in the analysis of several cases from their own experience. Each student writes a paper comparing the model's prescription with their behavior and discusses the implications of the differences.

While the Vroom-Jago model is too new to have been subject to much validation, the data that is available is very supportive of both its usability and validity. It doesn't consider all relevant situational factors and is certainly no guarantee of successful decisions, however it does appear to be a useful and important step toward effective decision making. Furthermore, the model helps to put the current focus on empowerment and participation in a useful perspective that includes both its costs and benefits.

In addition to the computer-based method for using the Vroom-Jago model, we have developed a decision tree version. The decision tree representation of the equations requires three simplifying assumptions. First, we must assume that there are no "shades of grey." The decision tree can be used only when the status of situational factors is clear cut, and only when yes/no answers exist. A second useful (although not absolutely necessary) assumption is that there are no critically severe time constraints and that subordinates are not geographically dispersed. This assumption restricts the applicability of the model by eliminating its use in some clearly defined but relatively infrequent situations.

The final simplifying assumption is that the importance of time and development is known and fixed. A set of 25 different and relatively simple decision trees can be drawn corresponding to the combinations of 5 values of MT and 5 values of MD. To illustrate, in Figure 1 we depict what we call the time-driven decision tree, representing the case where MT −5 and MD −1, i.e., time is very important and development is unimportant.

To use a decision tree, a manager selects a problem that is within his or her area of freedom and, in addition, has potential effects on an identifiable group of others, namely the direct reports. The tree is entered from the extreme left at "State the Problem," and the question asked pertains to attribute QR (How important is the technical quality of the decision?). The manager's answer ("High" or "Low") leads to a node signifying the next question. The process continues until an endpoint is encountered designating the recommended process.

The reader should be reminded that the particular decision tree shown in Figure 1 places no value on the long-range outcome of team development. Accordingly, it is the most autocratic of the decision trees that might have been depicted.

Before leaving the discussion of normative issues, I would like to describe an extension of the model to cover individual problems, namely those decision problems that affect not an entire group or team but rather a single other person such as a single direct report. Where the team is not involved, use of processes such as CII and GII appears inadvisable. These processes unilaterally bring together an entire group to discuss or decide an issue pertinent to only one person. In some instances these processes may constitute an invasion of privacy; in others they could be a waste of time.

There are, however, two other processes that we have labeled GI (joint decision making) and DI (delegation) that are potentially applicable. GI involves an attempt to reach consensus (through negotiation or problem solving) between the manager and the affected other. DI is more applicable in the case where the affected other is in a subordinate role. This process involves delegating or empowering the subordinate to make the decision. We have developed models to include appropriate choices of decision processes on individual problems. MPO contains these models and, in addition, there are decision tree versions to cover the kinds of special cases discussed earlier.

AUTOCRATIC OR PARTICIPATIVE MANAGEMENT:
THE SITUATION DETERMINES THE STYLE

So far in this discussion, we have been concerned with the normative issues related to what forms and degrees of participation are likely to be most effective in different situations. We have also conducted research on the descriptive question of the circumstances when managers do, in fact, involve their direct reports in decision making. While we have used several different research methods in studying this question, most of what follows is based on one method, called a problem set—a set of 30 or 54 cases each depicting a manager faced with a decision problem. The cases are

FIGURE 1
Time-Driven Decision Tree—Group Problems

QR	Quality Requirement:	How important is the technical quality of this decision?
CR	Commitment Requirement:	How important is subordinate commitment to the decision?
LI	Leaders Information:	Do you have sufficient information to make a high-quality decision?
ST	Problem Structure:	Is the problem well structured?
CP	Commitment Probability:	If you were to make the decision by yourself, is it reasonably certain that your subordinate(s) would be committed to the decision?
GC	Goal Congruence:	Do subordinates share the organizational goals to be attained in solving this problem?
SC	Subordinate Conflict:	Is conflict among subordinates over preferred solutions likely?
SI	Subordinate Information:	Do subordinates have sufficient information to make a high-quality decision?

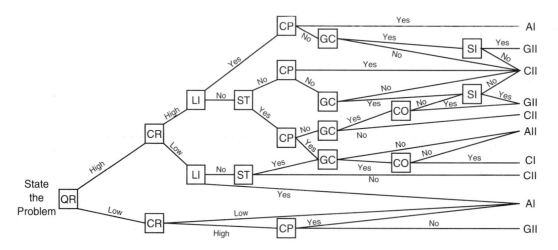

carefully constructed so that each situational factor (Table 2) is varied independently of other factors. In training programs, managers spend several hours working with the cases, putting themselves in the position of the manager in each case and indicating what they would do in that position. Most data has been collected in conjunction with management development programs in which each manager ultimately receives an individual computer-based analysis of his or her choices showing how they compare with one another and how they compare with the model.

One of the most robust findings from this line of investigation has been the weakening of support for the popular notion that the decision to involve others in decision making is directly controlled by a generalized personality trait. The tempting categorization of people as autocratic or participative or as varying in amount of a trait with these terms as anchors does not do justice to the data. Approximately 10 percent of the variance in behavior on standardized cases can be explained by the trait concept.

In fact, it is more meaningful to talk about autocratic or participative situations than autocratic or participative individuals since about three times as much variance is explicable by situational factors than by a general disposition to behave participatively or autocratically.

A participative situation is likely to have the following elements:

❑ The problem or decision is important to the organization.

❑ The manager is not an expert in the area of the problem, and his/her direct reports are experts.

❑ The problem is unstructured, thereby requiring creativity and ingenuity.

❑ The direct reports will be involved in the execution of the solution to the problem, and their commitment will be beneficial to their effectiveness in that role.

❑ The nature of the relationship between the manager and direct reports makes their commitment to his/her own solution unlikely.

❑ Direct reports would be unlikely to disagree about which solution would be most effective.

As these elements are removed one by one from the situation, behavior of the typical manager becomes progressively more autocratic. I do not wish to imply that managers' behavior can be understood as some linear combination of situational factors. Both managers and the normative model behave configurally, i.e., they respond to particular combinations (or patterns) among factors. This concept can be illustrated by a simple interaction that is built into the normative model. The model responds to conflict or disagreement among team members by recommending more participative processes (such as CII and GII) when there is a shared goal but recommends less participation in the absence of a shared goal. Thus, conflict and goal congruence are treated together, with the joint pattern of these variables dictating behavior. While both the model and managers show evidence of configurality, the model makes more use of pattern combinations, particularly more complex combinations, than do managers.

So far we have talked about *typical* managers and have implicitly assumed that all managers respond similarly to situational factors. In fact, there are marked individual differences—in both direction and magnitude—in how managers deal with each of the situational factors listed above. We estimate that about 20 percent of the variance in participative behavior can be thought of as differences in how managers interpret and respond to particular situational factors. For example, while most managers are more participative on more important decisions, one fifth are likely to involve others more on insignificant "cosmetic" issues. In the same vein, while most managers are conflict averse, i.e., respond to conflict or disagreement among others by using more autocratic methods, a minority of about 10–15 percent show exactly the opposite tendency (which we term "conflict confronting").

Both our normative and our descriptive work points to the importance of viewing the act of involving others in decision making *in relation to the situation.* Normatively, participation cannot be specified as either functional or dysfunctional without respect to the situation. Descriptively, the meaning and perceived consequences of participative decision making vary markedly with the situation in which the participation is embedded.

There are some purposes, however, for which it is illuminating to aggregate across a set of situations and talk about how the managers behave in these situations. When we do this, we are holding situations constant and ignoring variability among them. For example, we have asked whether there is any evidence of a change in the use of participative methods over the roughly two decades in which we have been collecting data. Holding situations constant by means of the kind of standardized set of situations that we discussed earlier, we find a sharp increase in the incidence of participative methods over this period. We believe that this increase reflects real differences in the culture of organizations brought about by changes in the labor force and the complexities of the environments in which organizations operate.

We have also done research on differences in participation across levels in the organizational hierarchy. Once again, we have held situations constant by employing a large number of standard decision situations. The evidence points to a higher incidence of participative practices as one ascends the organizational hierarchy.

Among the many other findings that we have examined in this vein are gender differences. By comparing the responses of female managers with a matched group of males from the same organizations, we have found women to be more participative than their male counterparts. This difference between men and women is consistent with differences in the pressures that each group encounters in carrying out its responsibilities. Our research suggests that when a manager is perceived as participative, the reactions of close associates generally are positive and are unaffected by whether the manager is male or female. However, women who are perceived to be autocratic tend to elicit much more negative reactions from others than do men who are perceived to be autocratic. Authoritarian behavior on the part of men may be viewed as a sign of decisiveness, but the same behavior on the part of women may be seen as inappropriate and violating the cultural stereotype of feminine behavior.

Early in our research program, we discovered great interest among managers in the program's findings. With few modifications, our data collection procedures could be reconfigured into a leadership development program. My earliest thoughts on this subject were described in an article I wrote called "Can Leaders Learn How to Lead?" (Vroom 1976). The concept was later elaborated in the Vroom and Jago work (Chapter 13). Integral to our approach has been the use of computerized analyses of managers' behavior on sets of standardized cases to help each manager become aware of *his or her* model of participation and of its similarity to or differences from the Vroom-Jago model. The goal of training is not to "program" managers to behave like the model but rather to develop a greater awareness of alternatives and to help managers make more informed judgments about the consequences of those alternatives.

Most managers have been making decisions for such a long period of time that the processes can become automatic or habituated. Habits reduce the need to make choices and enable one to act quickly. We don't have to think when we brush our teeth or tie our shoes. However, habits have another property that can be troublesome. At best, they reflect the learning environment at the time the habit was formed. If the environment remains constant, they are likely to continue to be effective. But if the environment changes markedly, habit patterns have to be re-evaluated.

Managers do not live in an unchanging world. They change jobs, change organizations, move from one country to another, or move from public sector to private or vice versa. Such changes bring with them new challenges, new opportunities, and new situational demands on leadership and management style. Old approaches need to be re-thought and new habits substituted for old.

While mobility requires change, it is by no means the only cause of change. Deregulation, global markets, and new tax laws have brought massive changes in the way in which corporations must be structured and managed. Managerial leadership no longer means maintaining the status quo. Old habits must be discarded if one is to respond to today's challenges and opportunities.

To meet these challenges, managers must have the capability to be both participative and autocratic, and to know when to employ each. They must be capable of identifying situational demands and of selecting or designing appropriate ways of dealing with them. Finally, they must have the skills necessary to implement their choices.

Our experience in working with managers over the last fifteen years suggests that training focused on models of participation—both descriptive and normative—builds these critical components of leadership.

REFERENCES

Vroom, V. H. "Can Leaders Learn How to Lead?" *Organizational Dynamics,* 1976, 4, pp. 17–28.

Vroom, V. H. and Jago, A. G. *The New Leadership: Managing Participation in Organizations.* Englewood Cliffs, NJ: Prentice Hall, 1988.

Leadership: Good, Better, Best

Bernard M. Bass

What does Lee Iacocca have that many other executives lack? Charisma. What would have happened to Chrysler without him? It probably would have gone bankrupt. Here are two more questions: How much does business and industry encourage the emergence of leaders like Iacocca? And how much effort has organizational psychology put into research on charismatic leadership? The answers are that business and industry have usually discouraged charismatic leadership and that, for the most part, organizational psychology has ignored the subject. It has been customary to see leadership as a method of getting subordinates to meet job requirements by handing out rewards or punishments.

Take a look at Barry Bargainer. Barry considers himself to be a good leader. He meets with subordinates to clarify expectations—what is required of them and what they can expect in return. As long as they meet his expectations, Barry doesn't bother them.

Cynthia Changer is a different kind of leader. When facing a crisis, Cynthia inspires her team's involvement and participation in a "mission." She solidifies it with simple words and images and keeps reminding her staff about it. She has frequent one-to-one chats with each of her employees at his or her work station. She is a consultant, coach, teacher, and mother figure.

Barry Bargainer, a transactional leader, may inspire a reasonable degree of involvement, loyalty, commitment, and performance from his subordinates. But Cynthia Changer, using a transformational approach, can do much more.

The first part of this article contrasts transactional and transformational leadership styles and the results that are obtained when managers select each approach. The second section reports on surveys of personnel in the military and in industry and examines factors in both approaches to leadership, as they emerged from the survey results. Transformational leadership is presented as a way to augment transactional approaches to management, since it is often more effective in achieving higher levels of improvement and change among employees.

A NEW PARADIGM

For half a century, leadership research has been devoted to studying the effects of democratic and autocratic approaches. Much investigative time has gone into the question of who should decide—the leader or the led. Equally important to research has been the distinction between task orientation and relations orientation. Still another issue has been the need of the leader to "initiate structure" for subordinates and to be considerate of them. At the same time, increasing attention has been paid to the ability to promote change in individuals, groups, and organizations.

The need to promote change and deal with resistance to it has, in turn, put an emphasis on democratic, participative, relations-oriented, and considerate leadership. Contingent rewards have been stressed in training and research with somewhat limited results.

In the past, we have mostly considered how to marginally improve and maintain the quantity or quality of performance, how to substitute one goal for another, how to shift attention from one action to another, how to reduce resistance to particular actions, or how to implement decisions. But higher-order changes are also possible. Increases in effort and the rate at which a group's speed and accuracy improve can sometimes be accelerated. Such higher-order changes also may involve larger shifts in attitudes, beliefs, values, and needs. Quantum leaps in performance may result when a group is roused out of its despair by a leader with innovative or revolutionary ideas and a vision of future responsibilities. Leaders may help bring about a radical shift in attention. The context may be changed by leaders. They may change what the followers see as figure and what they see as ground or raise the level of maturity of their needs and wants. For example, followers' concerns may be elevated from their need for recognition and achievement.

The lower order of improvement—changes in degree or marginal improvement—can be seen as the result of leadership that is an exchange process: a *transaction* in which followers' needs are met if their performance measures up to their explicit or implicit contracts with their leader. But higher-order improvement calls for *transformational* leadership. There is a great deal of difference between the two types of leadership.

TRANSACTIONAL LEADERSHIP IN ACTION

Transactional leaders like Barry Bargainer recognize what actions subordinates must take to achieve outcomes. Transactional leaders clarify these role and task requirements for their subordinates so that they are confident in exerting necessary efforts. Transactional leaders also recognize subordinates' needs and wants and clarify how they will be satisfied if necessary efforts are made. (See Exhibit 1.) This approach is currently stressed in leadership training, and it is good as far as it goes; however, the transactional approach has numerous shortcomings.

First, even after training, managers do not fully utilize transactional leadership. Time pressures, poor appraisal methods, doubts about the efficacy of positive reinforcement, leader and subordinate discomfort with the method, and lack of management skills are all partly responsible. How reinforcements are scheduled, how timely they are, and how variable or consistent they are all mediate the degree of their influence.

Some leaders, practicing management by exception, intervene only when things go wrong. In this instance, the manager's discomfort about giving negative feedback is even more self-defeating. When supervisors attribute poor performance to lack of ability, they tend to "pull their punches" by distorting feedback so that it is more positive than it should be.

Another common problem occurs when supervisors say and actually believe they are giving feedback to their subordinates, who feel they are not receiving it. For example, Barry Bargainer may

Reprinted with permission of The Free Press, a Division of Macmillan, Inc., from *Leadership and Performance Beyond Expectations* by Bernard M. Bass, as it appeared in *Organizational Dynamics,* Vol. 13(3), Winter 1985 issue. Copyright © 1985 by The Free Press.

EXHIBIT 1
Transactional Leadership (L = Leader; F = Follower).

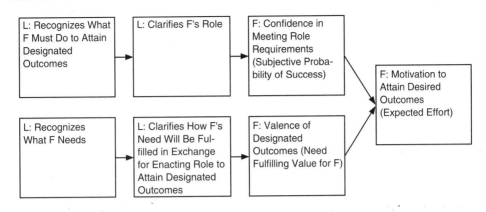

meet with his group of subordinates to complain that things are not going well. Barry thinks he is giving negative feedback while his subordinates only hear Barry grumbling about conditions. Barry may give Henry a pat on the back for a job he thinks has been done well. Henry may feel that he knows he did a good job, and it was condescending for Barry to mention it.

People differ considerably in their preference for external reinforcement or self-reinforcement. Task-oriented and experienced subordinates generally are likely to be self-reinforcing. They may say: "If I have done something well, I know it without other people telling me so," and "As long as I think I have done something well, I am not too concerned about what other people think I have done."

Subordinates and supervisors attach differing importance to various kinds of feedback. Many subordinates attach more importance than do supervisors to their own success or failure with particular tasks, and to their own comparisons with the work of others. Subordinates are also likely to attach more importance than do supervisors to co-workers' comments about their work. Supervisors tend to put the most weight on their own comments to their subordinates, and to recommendations for rewards they, as supervisors, can make, such as raises, promotions, and more interesting assignments.

Transactional leadership often fails because the leaders lack the reputation for being able to deliver rewards. Transactional leaders who fulfill the self-interested expectations of their subordinates gain and maintain the reputation for being able to deliver pay, promotions, and recognition. Those that fail to deliver lose their reputation and are not considered to be effective leaders.

Transactional leadership may be abandoned by managers when noncontingent rewards (employees are treated well, regardless of performance) will work just as well to boost performance. For example, in a large, nonprofit organization, a study by Phillip Podsakoff et al. showed that contingent rewards (those given only if performance warrants them) did contribute to employee performance, but noncontingent rewards were correlated almost as strongly with performance as contingent rewards.

Noncontingent rewards may provide a secure situation in which employees' self-reinforcement serves as a consequence for good performance (for example, IBM's straight salaries for all employees). An employee's feeling of obligation to the organization for providing noncontingent rewards fuels his or her effort to perform at least adequately. The Japanese experience is exemplary; in the top third of such Japanese firms as Toyota, Sony, and Mitsubishi, employees and the companies feel a mutual sense of lifetime obligation. Being a good family member does not bring immediate pay raises and promotions, but overall family success will bring year-end bonuses. Ultimately, opportunities to advance to a higher level and salary will depend on overall meritorious performance.

When the contingent reinforcement used is aversive (reinforcement that recipients prefer to avoid), the success of the transactional leader usually plummets. In the same not-for-profit organization studied by Podsakoff et al., neither contingent reprimand, disapproval, nor punishment had any effect on performance or overall employee satisfaction. The same results have been observed in other organizations. Contingent approval and disapproval by results-oriented leaders did improve subordinates' understanding of what was expected of them but failed to have much effect on motivation or performance. In general, reprimand may be useful in highlighting what not to do, but usually it does not contribute to positive motivation, particularly when subordinates are expected to be innovative and creative.

Even when it is based solely on rewards, transactional leadership can have unintended consequences. When expounding on the principles of leadership, Vice Admiral James B. Stockdale argued that people do not like to be programmed:

> . . . You cannot persuade (people) to act in their own self-interest all of the time. A good leader appreciates contrariness.
>
> . . . some men all of the time and all of the men some of the time knowingly will do what is clearly to their disadvantage if only because they do not like to be suffocated by carrot-and-stick coercion. I will not be a piano key. I will not bow to the tyranny of reason.

In working subtly against transactional leadership, employees may take short-cuts to complete the exchange of reward for compliance. For instance, quality may suffer if the leader does not monitor it as closely as he or she does the quantity of output. The employee may begin to react defensively rather than adequately; in some cases, reaction formation, withdrawal, hostility, or "game playing" may result.

THE ALTERNATIVE: ADD TRANSFORMATIONAL LEADERSHIP TO THE MANAGER-EMPLOYEE RELATIONSHIP

James McGregor Burns, the biographer of Franklin D. Roosevelt and of John F. Kennedy, was the first to contrast transactional with transformational leadership. The transformational leader motivates us to do more than we originally expected to do. Such a transformation can be achieved in the following ways:

1. Raising our level of consciousness about the importance and value of designated outcomes and ways of reaching these outcomes.

2. Getting us to transcend our own self-interests for the sake of the team, organization, or larger polity.

3. Raising our need level on Abraham Maslow's hierarchy from, say, the need for security to the need for recognition, or expanding our portfolio of needs by, for example, adding the need for self-actualization to the need for recognition.

Cynthia Changer is a transformational leader; Barry Bargainer is not. Exhibit 2 is a model of transformational leadership that starts with a current level of effort based on a follower's current level of confidence and desire for designated outcomes. A transactional leader contributes to such confidence and desire by clarifying what performance is required and how needs will be satisfied as a consequence. The transformational leader induces additional effort by directly increasing the follower's confidence as well as by elevating the level of outcomes through expanding his or her transcendental interests and level or breadth of needs in Maslow's hierarchy.

The need for more transformational leaders in business and industry was illustrated in an in-depth interview survey of a representative national sample of 845 working Americans. The survey found that while most employees liked and respected their managers, they felt their managers really didn't know how to motivate employees to do their best. Although 70% endorsed the work ethic, only 23% said they were working as hard as they could in their jobs. Only 9% agreed that their performance was motivated by transaction; most reported that there actually was little connection between how much they earned and the level of effort they put into the job.

REPORT ON A STUDY OF TRANSFORMATIONAL LEADERSHIP

I set out to find evidence of transformational leadership and its effects at various levels in industrial and military organizations, *not just at the top.*

I defined transformational leadership for 70 senior executives. Then, I asked them to describe in detail a transformational leader whom they had encountered at any time during their career. All respondents claimed to have known at least one such person. Most cited a former immediate supervisor or higher-level manager in the organization. A few mentioned family members, consultants, or counselors.

This transformational leader induced respondents to work ridiculous hours *and to do more than they ever expected to do.* Respon-

EXHIBIT 2
Transformational Leadership (L = Leader; F = Follower).

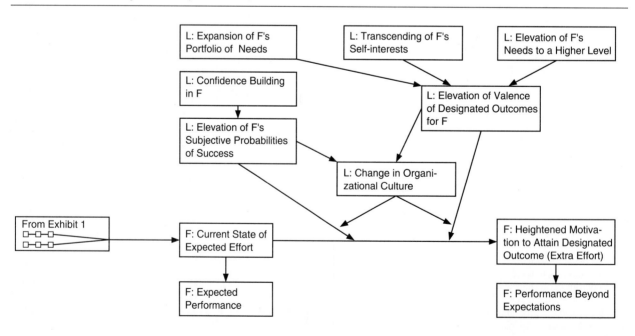

dents reported that they aimed to satisfy the transformational leader's expectations and to give the leader all the support asked of them. They wanted to emulate the leader. The transformational leader increased their awareness of and promoted a higher quality of performance and greater innovativeness. Such a leader convinced followers to extend themselves and to develop themselves further. Total commitment to and belief in the organization emerged as consequences of belief in the leader and heightened self-confidence.

Many respondents (all were male) indicated that the transformational leader they could identify in their own careers was like a benevolent father who remained friendly and treated the respondent as an equal despite the leader's greater knowledge and experience. The leader provided a model of integrity and fairness and also set clear and high standards of performance. He encouraged followers with advice, help, support, recognition, and openness. He gave followers a sense of confidence in his intellect, yet was a good listener. He gave followers autonomy and encouraged their self-development. He was willing to share his greater knowledge and expertise with them. Yet he could be formal and firm and would reprimand followers when necessary. Most respondents, however, were inclined to see the transforming leader as informal and accessible. Such a leader could be counted on to stand up for his subordinates. Along with the heightened and changed motivation and awareness, frequent reactions of followers to the transforming leader included trust, strong liking, admiration, loyalty, and respect.

In conducting a second survey, I used the descriptions from the first to create a questionnaire of 73 behavioral items. Responses to each item were on a five-point frequency scale. A total of 176 senior U.S. Army officers completed the questionnaire describing the behavior of their immediate superiors. Five factors emerged from a statistical factor analysis of the data. Two dealt with transactional leadership, the exchange relationship between superior and subordinate: contingent reward, by which subordinates earned benefits for compliance with the leader's clarification of the paths toward goals, and management by exception, by which the leader gave negative feedback for failure to meet agreed-upon standards. Three of the factors dealt with transformational leadership—the broadening and elevating of goals and of subordinates' confidence in their ability to go beyond expectations. These factors were (1) charismatic leadership (leaders aroused enthusiasm, faith, loyalty, and pride and trust in themselves and their aims); (2) individualized consideration (leaders maintained a developmental and individualistic orientation toward subordinates); and (3) intellectual stimulation (leaders enhanced the problem-solving capabilities of their associates). An interesting sidelight was that more transformational leadership was observed (by respondents) in combat units than in support units.

As expected, the three transformational factors were more highly correlated with perceived unit effectiveness than were the two transactional factors. Parallel results were obtained for subordinates' satisfaction with their leader. Charismatic, considerate, and intellectually stimulating leaders were far more satisfying to work for than were those who merely practiced the transactions of contingent reinforcement. I obtained similar results from a survey of 256 business managers, 23 educational administrators, and 45 professionals. Moreover, in these latter samples, respondents reported that they made greater efforts when leaders were charismatic, individualizing, and intellectually stimulating. Contingent reward was also fairly predictive of extra effort, but management by exception was counterproductive. Further analysis of the data by my colleague, David Waldman, supported the model shown in Exhibit 2. The analysis demonstrated that when a leader displayed transformational abilities and engaged in transactional relationships, extra effort made by subordinates was above and beyond what could be attributed to transactional factors alone.

TRANSACTIONAL FACTORS: CONTINGENT REINFORCEMENT AND MANAGEMENT-BY-EXCEPTION

According to our questionnaire surveys, positive and aversive contingent reinforcement are the two ways managers in organized settings engage in transactional leadership to influence employee performance. Ordinarily, contingent reward takes two forms: praise for work well done and recommendations for pay increases, bonuses, and promotion. In addition, this kind of reward can take the form of commendations for effort or public recognition and honors for outstanding service.

Contingent punishment can take several forms as a reaction to a deviation from norms—when, for example, production falls below agreed-upon standards or quality falls below acceptable levels. The manager may merely call attention to the derivation. Being told of one's failure to meet standards may be sufficient punishment to change behavior. Being told why one has failed can be helpful, particularly to the inexperienced or inexpert subordinate, especially if the negative feedback is coupled with further clarification about what kind of performance is expected. While other penalties—such as fines, suspensions without pay, loss of leader support, or discharge—may be imposed, these are less frequently used and are less likely to promote effectiveness.

When the manager, for one reason or another, chooses to intervene only when failures, breakdowns, and deviations occur, he or she is practicing management by exception. The rationale of those who use this practice is, "If it ain't broke, don't fix it!" The research studies I have completed with military officers, business executives, professionals, and educational administrators generally indicate that as a steady diet, management by exception can be counterproductive. But contingent rewards yield a fairly good return in terms of subordinate effort and performance. Nevertheless, in the aggregate, there will be additional payoff when the transformational factors appear in a leader's portfolio.

Charismatic and Inspirational Leadership

Charisma is not exclusively the province of world-class leaders or a few generals or admirals. It is to be found to some degree in industrial and military leaders throughout organizations. Furthermore, charisma is the most important component in the larger concept of transformational leadership. In my study I found that many followers described their military or industrial leader as someone who made everyone enthusiastic about assignments, who inspired loyalty to the organization, who commanded respect from everyone, who had a special gift of seeing what was really important, and who had a sense of mission that excited responses. Followers had complete faith in the leaders with charisma, felt proud to be associated with them, and trusted their capacity to overcome any obstacle. Charismatic leaders served as symbols of success and accomplishment for their followers.

Charisma is one of the elements separating the ordinary manager from the true leader in organizational settings. The leader attracts intense feelings of love (and sometimes hatred) from his or her subordinates. They want to identify with the leader. Although feelings about ordinary managers are bland, relations are smoother and steadier. Like most intimate relationships, the relations between the charismatic leader and his or her followers tend to be more turbulent.

There may be a scarcity of charismatic leaders in business and industry because managers lack the necessary skills. On the other hand, managers who have the skills may not recognize opportunity or may be unwilling to risk what is required to stand out so visibly among their peers. More charismatic leaders potentially exist in organizational settings; furthermore, they may be necessary to an organization's success.

The ability to inspire—arouse emotions, animate, enliven, or even exalt—is an important aspect of charisma. Inspirational leadership involves the arousal and heightening of motivation among followers. Followers can be inspired by a cold, calculating, intellectual discourse, the brilliance of a breakthrough, or the beauty of an argument. Yet it is the followers' emotions that ultimately have been aroused. Followers may hold an intellectual genius in awe and reverence, but the inspirational influence on them is emotional.

Consider the specific leadership behaviors Gary Yukl used to illustrate what he meant by inspirational leadership:

> My supervisor held a meeting to talk about how vital the new contract is for the company and said he was confident we could handle it if we all did our part. My boss told us we were the best design group he had ever worked with and he was sure that this new product was going to break every sales record in the company.

The inspiring supervisor was not dispassionate. The supervisor talked about how *vital* the new contract was to the company. He said he was *confident* in his people. He told them they were the *best* group he had *ever* worked with. He was sure the product would *break every record.*

In summary, as a consequence of his or her self-confidence, absence of inner conflict, self-determination, and requisite abilities, a leader will be held in high esteem by followers, particularly in times of trouble. He or she can generally inspire them by emotional support and appeals that will transform their level of motivation beyond original expectations. Such a leader can sometimes also inspire followers by means of intellectual stimulation. The charismatic leader can do one or the other, or both.

Individualized Consideration

The transformational leader has a developmental orientation toward followers. He evaluates followers' potential both to perform their present job and to hold future positions of greater responsibility. The leader sets examples and assigns tasks on an individual basis to followers to help significantly alter their abilities and motivations as well as to satisfy immediate organizational needs.

Delegating challenging work and increasing subordinate responsibilities are particularly useful approaches to individualized development. As General Omar Bradley pointed out, there is no better way to develop leadership than to give an individual a job involving responsibility and let him work it out. A survey of 208 chief executives and senior officers by Charles Margerison reported that important career influences on them before age 35 included being "stretched" by immediate bosses and being given leadership experience, overall responsibility for important tasks, and wide experience in many functions.

The transformational leader will consciously or unconsciously serve as a role model for subordinates. For example, in the Margerison survey, the executives attributed their own successful development as managers to having had early on in their careers managers who were models.

Managerial training supports the idea that managers profit from role models. What may be different in what I propose, however, is that the transformational leader emphasizes *individualism.* Personal influence and the one-to-one superior-subordinate relationship is of primary importance to the development of leaders. An organizational culture of individualism, even of elitism, should be encouraged; an organization should focus attention on identifying prospective leaders among subordinates.

Individualized attention is viewed as especially important by the new military commander of a unit. The commander is expected to learn the names of all those in the units at least two levels below his and to become familiar with their jobs. *Military leaders need to avoid treating all subordinates alike.* They must discover what best motivates each individual soldier or sailor and how to employ him most effectively. They must be generous in the use of their time. But as General Eugene Meyer notes, the leaders' interest must be genuine.

Individualized consideration implies that seniors maintain face-to-face contact or at least frequent telephone contact with juniors. The Intel Corporation accepted the fact that recently graduated engineers are more up to date on the latest advances in technology than are experienced executives of greater power and status in the firm. Therefore, the firm has consciously encouraged frequent contact and open communication between the recent college graduates and the senior executives through leveling arrangements. Senior executives and junior professionals are all housed in small, unpretentious, accessible offices that share common facilities. The organization stresses that influence is based on knowledge rather than power. In other well-managed firms, "walk-around management" promotes individual contact and communication between those low and high in the hierarchy.

In another study of a high-tech company, Rudi Klauss and Bernard Bass found that project engineers were most influenced by and gained most of their information relevant to decision making from informal contact and individual discussion rather than from written documentation. This company did not believe that the aggregated data from management information systems were the most important inputs for decision making. Rather, two-thirds to three-quarters of the total work time of managers was spent in oral communication. It was the immediate, timely tidbits of gossip, speculation, opinion, and relevant facts that was most influential, not generalized reports reviewing conditions over a recent period of time. Individualized attention of superior to subordinate provided this opportunity for inputs of current and timely information.

Managers are most likely to make face-to-face contact with colleagues at their same organizational level (or by telephone for such colleagues at a distance physically). For superiors and subordinates, written memos are more frequently used. Yet regular, face-to-face debriefing sessions to disseminate important information from superior to subordinate will provide a better basis for organizational decision making and make the superior better equipped to deal with the erratic flow of work and demands on his or her time and the speed that decision making often requires. Unfortunately, unless personal contact becomes a matter of policy (such as walk-around management), communications from superior to subordinate are more likely to be on paper—or now, no doubt, increasingly on computer—rather than face-to-face.

Individualized consideration is reflected when a manager keeps each employee fully informed about what is happening and why—preferably in a two-way conversation rather than a written memo. Employees come to feel that they are on the inside of developments and do not remain bystanders. Sudden changes of plan are less likely to surprise them. If the interaction is two-way, employees have the opportunity to ask questions to clarify understanding. At the same time, managers learn first-hand their subordinates' concerns.

Individualized consideration is also demonstrated when the senior executive or professional takes time to serve as mentor for the junior executive or professional. A mentor is a trusted counselor who accepts a guiding role in the development of a younger or less experienced member of the organization. The mentor uses his or her greater knowledge, experience, and status to help develop his or her protégé and not simply to pull the protégé up the organizational ladder on the mentor's coattails. This relationship is different from one in which a manager is supportive or provides advice when asked for it. Compared with the formal, distant relationship most often seen between a high-level executive and a junior somewhere down the line, the mentor is paternalistic or maternalistic and perhaps is a role model for the junior person.

A follow-up of 122 recently promoted people in business indicated that two-thirds had had mentors. This popularity of mentoring in business, government, and industry reflects the current interest on the part of both individuals and organizations in the career development of the individual employee.

Intellectual Stimulation

The statement, "These ideas have forced me to rethink some of my own ideas, which I had never questioned before," sums up the kind of intellectual stimulation that a transformational leader can provide. Intellectual stimulation can lead to other comments like, "She enables me to think about old problems in new ways," or "He provides me with new ways of looking at things that used to be a puzzle for me."

Intellectual stimulation arouses in followers the awareness of problems and how they may be solved. It promotes the hygiene of logic that is compelling and convincing. It stirs the imagination and generates thoughts and insights. It is not the call to immediate action aroused by emotional stimulation. This intellectual stimulation is seen in a discrete leap in the followers' conceptualization, comprehension, and discernment of the nature of the problems they face and their solutions.

Executives should and can play a role as transforming leaders to the degree that they articulate what they discern, comprehend, visualize, and conceptualize to their colleagues and followers. They should articulate what they see as the opportunities and threats facing their organization (or unit within it) and the organization's strengths, weaknesses, and comparative advantages. Leadership in complex organizations must include the ability to manage the problem-solving process in such a way that important problems are identified and solutions of high quality are found and carried out with the full commitment of organization members.

The intellectual component may be obscured by surface considerations. Accused of making snap decisions, General George Patton commented: "I've been studying the art of war for 40-odd years . . . [A] surgeon who decides in the course of an operation to change its objective is not making a snap decision but one based on knowledge, experience, and training. So am I."

The importance of a leader's technical expertise and intellectual power, particularly in high-performing systems, often is ignored in comparison with the attention paid to his or her interpersonal competence. Where would Polaroid be without Edwin Land? What kind of corporation would Occidental Petroleum be without Armand Hammer?

In this intellectual sphere, we see systematic differences between transformational and transactional leaders. The transformational leader may be less willing to accept the status quo and more likely to seek new ways of doing things while taking maximum advantage of opportunities. Transactional managers will focus on what can clearly work, will keep time constraints in mind, and will do what seems to be the most efficient and free of risk.

What may intellectually separate the two kinds of leaders is that transformational leaders are likely to be more proactive than reactive in their thinking, more creative, novel, and innovative in their ideas, and less inhibited in their ideational search for solutions. Transactional leaders may be equally bright, but their focus is on how best to keep running the system for which they are responsible; they react to problems generated by observed deviances and modify conditions as needed while remaining ever mindful of organizational constraints.

TRANSFORMATIONAL LEADERSHIP: BENEVOLENT OR MALEVOLENT?

Charismatic leadership, individual consideration, and intellectual stimulation have been clearly seen in the moving and shaking that took place between 1982 and 1984 in a number of firms, such as General Electric, Campbell Soup, and Coca Cola. In each instance, the transformation could be attributed to a newly appointed chief. These transformational leaders were responsible for iconoclastic changes of image, increased organizational flexibility, and an upsurge of new products and new approaches. In each case, the transformational leadership of John F. Welch, Jr. of General Electric, Gordon McGovern of Campbell Soup, and Roberto Goizueta of Coco Cola paid off in invigoration and revitalization of their firms and an acceleration in business success.

Clearly, heads may be broken, feelings hurt, and anxieties raised with the advent of transformational leaders such as Welch, McGovern, or Goizueta. "Business as usual" is no longer tolerated. Such transformations may be moral or immoral.

For James Burns, transformational leadership is moral if it deals with true needs and is based on informed choice. The moral transformational leader is one who is guided by such universal ethical principles as respect for human dignity and equal rights. The leadership mobilizes and directs support for "more general and comprehensive values that express followers' more fundamental and enduring needs" (*Leadership,* Harper, 1978). Moral leadership helps followers to see the real conflict between competing values, the inconsistencies between espoused values and behavior, the need for realignments in values, and the need for changes in behavior or transformations of institutions. Burns argued that if the need levels elevated by transformational leaders were not authentic, then the leadership was immoral.

The well-being of organizational life will be better served in the long run by moral leadership. That is, transformations that result in the fulfillment of real needs will prove to be more beneficial to the organization than transformations that deal with manufactured needs and group delusions. Organizational leaders should subscribe to a code of ethics that is accepted by their society and their profession.

The ethical transformational leader aims toward and succeeds in promoting changes in a firm—changes that strengthen firm viability, increase satisfaction of owners, managers, employees, and customers, and increase the value of the firm's products. But transformational leaders can be immoral if they create changes based on false images that cater to the fantasies of constituencies. Firms can be driven into the ground by such leaders. A transformational leader can lull employees and shareholders alike with false hopes and expectations while he or she is preparing to depart in a golden parachute after selling out the company's interests.

Whether transformational or transactional leadership will take hold within an organization will depend to some extent on what is happening or has happened outside of it. Welch, McGovern, and Goizueta all came into power to transform firms that were in danger of failing to keep pace with changes in the marketplace. Transformational leadership is more likely to emerge in times of distress and rapid change.

The personalities of followers will affect a leader's ability to be transformational. Charisma is a two-way process. A leader is seen as charismatic if he or she has followers who imbue him or her with extraordinary value and personal power. This is more easily done when subordinates have highly dependent personalities. On the other hand, subordinates who pride themselves on their own rationality, skepticism, independence, and concern for rules of law and precedent are less likely to be influenced by a charismatic leader or the leader who tries to use emotional inspiration. Subordinates who are egalitarian, self-confident, and high in status are likely to resist charismatic leaders.

WHICH KIND OF LEADERSHIP SHOULD MANAGERS USE?

Managers need to appreciate what kind of leadership is expected of them. Current leadership training and management development emphasize transactional leadership, which is good as far as it goes, but clearly has its limits. Transactional leaders will let their subordinates know what is expected of them and what they can hope to receive in exchange for fulfilling expectations. Clarification makes subordinates confident that they can fulfill expectations and achieve mutually valued outcomes. But subordinates' confidence and the value they place on potential outcomes can be further increased, through transformational leadership. Leadership, in other words, can become an inspiration to make extraordinary efforts.

Charismatic leadership is central to the transformational leadership process. Charismatic leaders have great referent power and influence. Followers want to identify with them and to emulate them. Followers develop intense feelings about them, and above all have trust and confidence in them. Transformational leaders may arouse their followers emotionally and inspire them to extra effort and greater accomplishment. As subordinates become competent with the mainly transformational leader's encouragement and support, contingent reinforcement may be abandoned in favor of self-reinforcement.

Clearly, there are situations in which the transformational approach may not be appropriate. At the same time, organizations need to draw more on the resources of charismatic leaders, who often can induce followers to aspire to and maintain much higher levels of productivity than they would have reached if they had been operating only through the transactional process.

Leadership:
The Art of Empowering Others

Jay A. Conger

"One ought to be both feared and loved, but as it is difficult for the two to go together, it is much safer to be feared than loved . . . for love is held by a chain of obligation which, men being selfish, is broken whenever it serves their purpose; but fear is maintained by a dread of punishment which never fails."

The Prince, Niccolo Machiavelli

In his handbook, *The Prince,* Machiavelli assures his readers—some being aspiring leaders, no doubt—that only by carefully

amassing power and building a fearsome respect could one become a great leader. While the shadowy court life of 16th-century Italy demanded such treachery to ensure one's power, it seems hard to imagine Machiavelli's advice today as anything but a historical curiosity. Yet, interestingly, much of the management literature has focused on the strategies and tactics that managers can use to increase their own power and influence.[1] As such, a Machiavellian quality often pervades the literature, encouraging managers to ensure that their power base is strong and growing. At the same time

Reprinted with permission from the *Academy of Management Executive,* 1989, Vol. 3(1), pp. 17–24.

1. See, for example, J. P. Kotter, *Power in Management,* New York: AMACOM, 1979, and J. Pfeffer, *Power in Organizations,* Marshfield, MA: Pitman, 1981.

a small but increasing number of management theorists have begun to explore the idea that organizational effectiveness also depends on the sharing of power—that the distribution of power is more important than the hoarding of power.[2]

While the idea of making others feel more powerful contradicts the stereotype of the all-powerful executive, research suggests that the traditional ways of explaining a leader's influence may not be entirely correct. For example, recent leadership studies argue that the practice of empowering—or instilling a sense of power—is at the root of organizational effectiveness, especially during times of transition and transformation.[3] In addition, studies of power and control within organizations indicate that the more productive forms of organizational power increase with superiors' sharing of power and responsibility with subordinates.[4] And while there is an increasing awareness of this need for more empowering leadership, we have only recently started to see documentation about the actual practices that leaders employ to effectively build a sense of power among organizational members as well as the context most suited for empowerment practices.[5]

In this article, I will explore these practices further by drawing upon a recent study of senior executives who proved themselves highly effective leaders. They were selected by a panel of professors at the Harvard Business School and management consultants who were well acquainted with them and their companies. The study included eight chief executive officers and executive vice-presidents of *Fortune* 500 companies and successful entrepreneurial firms, representing industries as diverse as telecommunications, office automation, retail banking, beverages, packaged foods, and management consulting. In each case, these individuals were responsible for either the creation of highly successful companies or for performing what were described as remarkable turnarounds. During my study of these executives, I conducted extensive interviews, observed them on the job, read company and other documents, and talked with their colleagues and subordinates. While the study focused on the broader issue of leadership styles, intensive interviews with these executives and their subordinates revealed that

many were characterized as empowering leaders. Their actions were perceived as building confidence and restoring a sense of personal power and self-efficacy during difficult organizational transitions. From this study, I identified certain organizational contexts of powerlessness and management practices derived to remedy them.

In this article I will also illustrate several of these practices through a series of vignettes. While the reader may recognize some of the basic ideas behind these practices (such as providing greater opportunities for initiative), it is often the creative manner in which the leader deploys the particular practice that distinguishes them. The reader will discover how they have been carefully tailored to fit the context at hand. I might add, however, that these practices represent just a few of the broad repertoire of actions that leaders can take to make an empowering difference in their organizations.

A WORD ABOUT EMPOWERMENT

We can think of empowerment as the act of strengthening an individual's beliefs in his or her sense of effectiveness. In essence, then, empowerment is not simply a set of external actions; it is a process of changing the internal beliefs of people.[6] We know from psychology that individuals believe themselves powerful when they feel they can adequately cope with environmental demands—that is, situations, events, and people they confront. They feel powerless when they are unable to cope with these demands. Any management practice that increases an individual's sense of self-determination will tend to make that individual feel more powerful. The theory behind these ideas can be traced to the work of Alfred Bandura, who conceptualized the notion of self-efficacy beliefs and their role in an individual's sense of personal power in the world.[7]

From his research in psychology, Bandura identified four means of providing empowering information to others: (1) through positive emotional support during experiences associated with stress and anxiety, (2) through words of encouragement and positive persuasion, (3) by observing others' effectiveness—in other words, having models of success with whom people identified—and (4) by actually experiencing the mastering of a task with success (the most effective source). Each of these sources of empowerment was used by the study executives and will be identified in the practice examples, as will other sources identified by organizational researchers.

Several Empowering Management Practices

Before describing the actual practices, it is important to first draw attention to an underlying attitude of the study participants. These empowering leaders shared a strong underlying belief in their subordinates' abilities. It is essentially the Theory Y argument;[8] if you believe in people's abilities, they will come to believe in them. All the executives in the study believed that their subordi-

2. See P. Block, *The Empowered Manager,* San Francisco: Jossey-Bass, 1987; W. W. Burke, "Leadership as Empowering Others," in S. Srivastva (Ed.), *Executive Power,* San Francisco: Jossey-Bass, 1986, pp. 51–77; and R. M. Kanter, *The Change Masters,* New York: Simon & Schuster, 1983.

3. W. Bennis and B. Nanus, *Leaders,* New York: Harper & Row, 1985; and R. M. Kanter, "Power Failure in Management Circuits," *Harvard Business Review,* July–August 1979, pp. 65–75.

4. See Kanter, Footnote 3; and A. S. Tannenbaum, *Control in Organizations,* New York: McGraw-Hill, 1968.

5. See J. A. Conger and R. N. Kanungo, "The Empowerment Process: Integrating Theory and Practice," *Academy of Management Review,* July 1988; and R. J. House, "Power and Personality in Complex Organizations," in L. L. Cummings and B. M. Staw (Eds.), *Research in Organizational Behavior: An Annual Review of Critical Essays and Reviews,* Vol. 10, Greenwich, CT: JAI Press, 1988. The author is grateful to Rabindra N. Kanungo for insights and help in conceptualizing the empowerment process.

6. See Conger and Kanungo, Footnote 5.

7. A. Bandura, "Self-Efficiency: Toward a Unifying Theory of Behavioral Change," *Psychological Review,* 1977, 84(2), pp. 191–215.

8. D. McGregor, *The Human Side of Enterprise,* New York: McGraw-Hill, 1960.

nates were capable of managing their current situations. They did not employ wholesale firings as a means of transforming their organizations. Rather, they retained the majority of their staff and moved those who could not perform up to standard to positions where they could. The essential lesson is that an assessment of staff skills is imperative before embarking on a program of empowerment. This basic belief in employees' abilities underlies the following examples of management practices designed to empower. We will begin with the practice of providing positive emotional support.

1. *The Squirt-gun Shootouts: Providing a Positive Emotional Atmosphere.* An empowering practice that emerged from the study was that of providing positive emotional support, especially through play or drama. For example, every few months, several executives would stage dramatic "up sessions" to sustain the motivation and excitement of their staff. They would host an afternoon-long, or a one- or two-day event devoted solely to confidence building. The event would open with an uplifting speech about the future, followed by a special, inspirational speaker. At these events there would often be films meant to build excitement or confidence—for example, a film depicting a mountain climber ascending a difficult peak. The message being conveyed is that this person is finding satisfaction in the work he or she does at an extraordinary level of competence. There would also be rewards for exceptional achievements. These sessions acted as ceremonies to enhance the personal status and identity of employees and revive the common feelings that binded them together.[9]

An element of play appears to be especially liberating in situations of great stress and demoralization. In the study's examples, play allowed for the venting of frustrations and in turn permitted individuals to regain a sense of control by stepping back from their pressures for a moment. As Bandura suggests, the positive emotional support provided by something like play alleviates, to some extent, concerns about personal efficacy.[10]

For example, one of the subjects of the study, Bill Jackson, was appointed the head of a troubled division. Demand had outstripped the division's ability to maintain adequate inventories, and product quality had slipped. Jackson's predecessors were authoritarian managers, and subordinates were demoralized as well as paranoid about keeping their jobs. As one told me, "You never knew who would be shot next." Jackson felt that he had to break the tension in a way that would allow his staff to regain their sense of control and power. He wanted to remove the stiffness and paranoia and turn what subordinates perceived as an impossible task into something more fun and manageable.

So, I was told, at the end of his first staff meeting, Jackson quietly pulled out a squirt-gun and blasted one of his managers with water. At first, there was a moment of stunned silence, and then suddenly the room was flooded with laughter. He remarked with a smile, "You gotta have fun in this business. It's not worth having

your stomach in ulcers." This began a month of squirt-gun fights between Jackson and his managers.

The end result? A senior manager's comment is representative: "He wanted people to feel comfortable, to feel in control. He used waterguns to do that. It was a game. It took the stiffness out of the business, allowed people to play in a safe environment—as the boss says, 'to have fun'." This play restored rapport and morale. But Jackson also knew when to stop. A senior manager told me, "We haven't used waterguns in nine months. It has served its purpose. . . . . The waterfights were like being accepted into a club. Once it achieved its purpose, it would have been overdone."

Interview after interview with subordinates confirmed the effectiveness of the squirt-gun incident. It had been experienced as an empowering ritual. In most contexts, this behavior would have been abusive. Why did it work? Because it is a management practice that fit the needs of subordinates at the appropriate time.

The executive's staff consisted largely of young men, "rough and ready" individuals who could be described as fun-loving and playful. They were accustomed to an informal atmosphere and operated in a very down-to-earth style. Jackson's predecessor, on the other hand, had been stiff and formal.

Jackson preferred to manage more informally. He wanted to convey, quickly and powerfully, his intentions of managing in a style distinct from his predecessor's. He was concerned, however, that his size—he is a very tall, energetic, barrel-chested man—as well as his extensive background in manufacturing would be perceived as intimidating by his young staff and increase their reluctance to assume initiative and control. Through the squirt-gun fights, however, he was able to (1) relieve a high level of tension and restore some sense of control, (2) emphasize the importance of having fun in an otherwise trying work environment, and (3) direct subordinates' concerns away from his skills and other qualities that intimidated them. It was an effective management practice because he understood the context. In another setting, it might have been counter-productive.

2. *The "I Make a Difference Club": Rewarding and Encouraging in Visible and Personal Ways.* The majority of executives in the study rewarded the achievements of their staffs by expressing personal praise and rewarding in highly visible and confidence-building ways. They believed that people appreciated recognition of their hard work and success. Rewards of high incentive value were particularly important, especially those of personal recognition from the leader. As Rosabeth Kanter notes, a sense of power comes ". . . when one has relatively close contact with sponsors (higher-level people who confer approval, prestige, or backing)."[11] Combined with words of praise and positive encouragement, such experiences become important sources of empowerment.

The executives in the study took several approaches to rewards. To reward exceptional performance, one executive established the "I Make a Difference Club." Each year, he selects two or three staff members to be recognized for their excellence on the job. It is a very exclusive club, and only the executive knows the eligibility rules, which are based on outstanding performance. Inductees are invited to dinner in New York City but are not told

9. See J. M. Beyer and H. M. Trice, "How an Organization Reveals Its Culture," *Organizational Dynamics,* Spring 1987, pp. 4–25.

10. A. Bandura, *Social Foundations of Thought and Action: A Cognitive View,* Englewood Cliffs, NJ: Prentice-Hall, 1986.

11. See Kanter, Footnote 3, p. 153.

beforehand that they are about to join the "I Make a Difference Club." They arrive and meet with other staff members whom they believe are there for a staff dinner. During dinner, everyone is asked to speak about what is going on in his or her part of the company. The old-timers speak first, followed by the inductees (who are still unaware of their coming induction). Only after they have given their speeches are they informed that they have just joined the club. As one manager said, "It's one of the most wonderful moments in life."

This executive and others also make extensive use of personal letters to individuals thanking them for their efforts and projects. A typical letter might read, "Fred, I would personally like to thank you for your contribution to _____, and I want you to know that I appreciate it." Lunches and dinners are hosted for special task accomplishments.

Public recognition is also employed as a means of rewarding. As one subordinate commented about his boss,

> "He will make sure that people know that so and so did an excellent job on something. He's superb on giving people credit. If the person has done an exceptional job on a task or project, he will be given the opportunity to present his or her findings all the way to the board. Six months later, you'll get a call from a friend and learn that he has dropped your name in a speech that you did well. It makes you want to do it again."

I found that the investment in rewards and recognition made by many of these executives is unusually high, consuming a significant portion of their otherwise busy day. Yet the payoff appeared high. In interviews, subordinates described these rewards as having an empowering impact on them.

To understand why some of these rewards proved to be so successful, one must understand their organizational contexts. In some cases, the organizations studied were quite large, if not enormous. The size of these organizations did little to develop in employees a sense of an "I"—let alone an "I" that makes a difference. It was easy for organization members to feel lost in the hierarchy and for their achievements to be invisible, for recognition not to be received for personal contributions. The study's executives countered this tendency by institutionalizing a reward system that provided visibility and recognition—for example, the "I Make a Difference Club," presentations to the Board, and names dropped in speeches. Suddenly, you as a member of a large organization stood out—you were special.

Outstanding performance from each of the executives' perspectives was also something of a necessity. All the executives had demanding goals to achieve. As such, they had to tend to subordinates' sense of importance and contribution. They had to structure reward systems that would keep people "pumped up"—that would ensure that their confidence and commitment would not be eroded by the pressures placed on them.

3. *"Praising the Troops": Expressing Confidence.* The empowering leaders in the study spent significant amounts of time expressing their confidence in subordinates' abilities. Moreover, they expressed their confidence throughout each day—in speeches, in meetings, and casually in office hallways. Bandura comments that "people who are persuaded verbally that they possess the capabilities to master given tasks are likely to mobilize greater sustained

effort than if they harbor self-doubts and dwell on personal deficiencies when difficulties arise." [12]

A quote from Irwin Federman, CEO of Monolithic Memories, a highly successful high-tech company, captures the essence and power of a management practice that builds on this process:

> "If you think about it, we love others not for who they are, but for how they make us feel. In order to willingly accept the direction of another individual, it must make you feel good to do so. . . . If you believe what I'm saying, you cannot help but come to the conclusion that those you have followed passionately, gladly, zealously—have made you feel like somebody. . . . This business of making another person feel good in the unspectacular course of his daily comings and goings is, in my view, the very essence of leadership." [13]

This proactive attitude is exemplified by Bob Jensen. Bob assumed control of his bank's retail operations after a reorganization that transferred away the division's responsibility for large corporate clients. Demoralized by a perceived loss in status and responsibility, branch managers were soon asking, "Where's our recognition?" Bob, however, developed an inspiring strategic vision to transform the operation. He then spent much of his time championing his strategy and expressing his confidence in employees' ability to carry it out. Most impressive was his personal canvass of some 175 retail branches.

As he explained,

> "I saw that the branch system was very down, morale was low. They felt like they'd lost a lot of their power. There were serious problems and a lot of staff were just hiding. What I saw was that we really wanted to create a small community for each branch where customers would feel known. To do that, I needed to create an attitude change. I saw that the attitudes of the branch staff were a reflection of the branch manager. The approach then was a manageable job—now I had to focus on only 250 people, the branch managers, rather than the 3,000 staff employees out there. I knew I had to change their mentality from being lost in a bureaucracy to feeling like the president of their own bank. I had to convince them they were special—that they had the power to transform the organization. . . . All I did was talk it up. I was up every night. In one morning, I hit 17 branches. My goal was to sell a new attitude. To encourage people to 'pump iron.' I'd say, 'Hi, how's business?', encourage them. I'd arrange tours of the branches for the chairman on down. I just spent a lot of time talking to these people—explaining that they were the ones who could transform the organization."

It was an important tactic—one that made the branch managers feel special and important. It was all countercultural. As one executive told me, "Bob would go out into the field to visit the operations, which was very unusual for senior people in this indus-

---

12. See Bandura, Footnote 10, p. 154.

13. W. Bennis and B. Nanus, *Leaders,* New York: Harper & Row, pp. 64–65.

try." His visits heightened the specialness that branch managers felt. In addition, Bob modeled self-confidence and personal success—an important tactic to build a sense of personal effectiveness among subordinates.[14]

I also watched Jack Eaton, president of a regional telephone company, praise his employees in large corporate gatherings, in executive council meetings, and in casual encounters. He explained his philosophy:

> "I have a fundamental belief and trust in the ability and conscientiousness of others. I have a lot of good people. You can turn them loose, let them feel good about their accomplishments. . . . You ought to recognize accomplishment as well as build confidence. I generally do it in small ways. If someone is doing well, it's important to express your confidence to that person—especially among his peers. I tend to do it personally. I try to be genuine. I don't throw around a lot of b.s."

This practice proved especially important during the transition of the regional phone companies away from the parent organization.

4. "President of My Own Bank": Fostering Initiative and Responsibility. Discretion is a critical power component of any job.[15] By simply fostering greater initiative and responsibility in subordinates' tasks, a leader can empower organizational members. Bob Jensen, the bank executive, is an excellent example of how one leader created opportunities for greater initiative despite the confines of his subordinates' positions. He transformed what had been a highly constricted branch manager's job into a branch "president" concept. The idea was simple—every manager was made to feel like the president of his own community bank, and not just in title. Goals, compensation, and responsibilities were all changed to foster this attitude. Existing measurement systems were completely restructured. The value-of-funds-generated had been the principal yardstick—something over which branch managers had only very limited control because of interest rate fluctuations. Managers were now evaluated on what they could control—that is, deposits. Before, branch managers had rotated every couple of years. Now they stayed put. "If I'm moving around, then I'm not the president of my own bank, so we didn't move them anymore," Jensen explained. He also decentralized responsibilities that had resided higher in the hierarchy—allowing the branch manager to hire, give money to charities, and so on. In addition, a new ad agency was hired to mark the occasion, and TV ads were made showing the branch managers being in charge, rendering personal services themselves. The branch managers even thought up the ad lines.

What Jensen did so skillfully was recognize that his existing managers had the talent and energy to turn their operations around successfully, but that their sense of power was missing. He recognized their pride had been hurt and that he needed to restore a sense of ownership and self-importance. He had to convince his managers through increased authority that they were no longer "pawns" of the system—that they were indeed "presidents" of their own banks.

Another example—this one demonstrating a more informal delegation of initiative—was quite surprising. The setting was a highly successful and rapidly growing computer firm, and the study participant was the vice-president of manufacturing. The vice-president had recently been hired away from another firm and was in the process of revamping manufacturing. During the process, he discovered that his company's costs on its terminal video monitors were quite high. However, he wanted his staff to discover the problem for themselves and to "own" the solution. So one day, he placed behind his desk a black-and-white Sony TV with a placard on top saying $69.95. Next to it he placed a stripped-down version of the company's monitor with a placard of $125.95. Both placards reflected the actual costs of the two products. He never said a word. But during the day as staff and department managers entered their boss's office, they couldn't help but notice the two sets. They quickly got the message that their monitor was costing twice as much as a finished TV set. Within a month, the manufacturing team had lowered the monitor's costs by 40%.

My first impression on hearing this story was that, as a subordinate, I would be hard pressed not to get the point and, more important, I would wonder why the boss was not more direct. Ironically, the boss appears to be hitting subordinates over the head with the problem. Out of context, then, this example hardly seems to make others feel more competent and powerful. Yet staff described themselves as "turned on" and motivated by this behavior. Why, I wondered? A little history will illustrate the effectiveness of this action.

The vice-president's predecessor had been a highly dictatorial individual. He tightly controlled his staff's actions and stifled any sense of discretion. Implicitly, his behavior said to subordinates, "You have no ideas of your own." He fired freely, leaving staff to feel that they had little choice in whether to accept his orders or not. By his actions, he essentially transformed his managers into powerless order-takers.

When the new vice-president arrived, he found a group of demoralized subordinates whom he felt were nonetheless quite talented. To restore initiative, he began to demonstrate the seriousness of his intentions in highly visible and symbolic ways. For example, rather than tell his subordinates what to do, he started by seeding ideas and suggestions in humorous and indirect ways. The TV monitor is only one of many examples. Through these actions, he was able eventually to restore a sense of initiative and personal competence to his staff. While these examples are illustrative of effective changes in job design, managers contemplating job enrichment would be well advised to consult the existing literature and research before undertaking major projects.[16]

5. Early Victories: Building on Success. Many of the executives in the study reported that they often introduced organizational change through pilot or otherwise small and manageable projects. They designed these projects to ensure early success for their organizations. For example, instead of introducing a new sales structure nationwide, they would institute the change in one region; a new technology would have a pilot introduction at a single plant rather than systemwide. Subordinates described these early suc-

---

14. See Bandura, Footnote 10.

15. See Kanter, Footnote 3.

16. See J. R. Hackman, "The Design of Work in the 1980s," *Organizational Dynamics,* Summer 1978, pp. 3–17.

cess experiences as strongly reinforcing their sense of power and efficacy. As Mike Beer argues:

> "In order for change to spread throughout an organization and become a permanent fixture, it appears that early successes are needed. . . . When individuals, groups, and whole organizations feel more competent than they did before the change, this increased sense of competence reinforces the new behavior and solidifies learning associated with change."[17]

An individual's sense of mastery through actual experience is the most effective means of increasing self-efficacy.[18] When subordinates are given more complex and difficult tasks, they are presented with opportunities to test their competence. Initial success experiences will make them feel more capable and, in turn, empowered. Structuring organizational changes to ensure initial successes builds on this principle.

CONTEXTS OF POWERLESSNESS

The need to empower organizational members becomes more important in certain contexts. Thus, it is important to identify conditions within organizations that might foster a sense of powerlessness. Certain circumstances, for instance, appear to lower feelings of self-efficacy. In these cases, subordinates typically perceive themselves as lacking control over their immediate situation (e.g., a major reorganization threatens to displace responsibility and involves limited or no subordinate participation),[19] or lacking the required capability, resources, or discretion needed to accomplish a task (e.g., the development of new and difficult-to-learn skills for the introduction of a new technological process).[20] In either case, these experiences maximize feelings of inadequacy and lower self-confidence. They, in turn, appear to lessen motivation and effectiveness.

Exhibit 1 identifies the more common organizational factors that affect these self-efficacy or personal power beliefs and contribute to feelings of powerlessness. They include organizational factors, supervisory styles, reward systems, and job design.

For example, during a major organizational change, goals may change—often dramatically—to respond to the organization's new direction. Rules may no longer be clearly defined as the firm seeks new guidelines for action. Responsibilities may be dramatically altered. Power alliances may shift, leaving parts of the organization with a perceived loss of power or increasing political activity.

17. M. Beer, *Organizational Change and Development,* Santa Monica, CA: Goodyear, 1980, p. 64.

18. See Bandura, Footnote 10.

19. F. M. Rothbaum, J. R. Weisz, and S. S. Snyder, "Changing the World and Changing Self: A Two Process Model of Perceived Control," *Journal of Personality and Social Psychology,* 1982, 42, pp. 5–37; and L. Y. Abramson, J. Garber, and M. E. P. Seligman, "Learned Helplessness in Humans: An Attributional Analysis," in J. Garber and M. E. P. Seligman (Eds.), *Human Helplessness: Theory and Applications,* New York: Academic Press, 1980, pp. 3–34.

20. See Kanter, Footnote 2.

EXHIBIT 1
Context Factors Leading to Potential State of Powerlessness

Organizational Factors:

❐ Significant organizational changes/transitions
❐ Start-up ventures
❐ Excessive, competitive pressures
❐ Impersonal bureaucratic climate
❐ Poor communications and limited network-forming systems
❐ Highly centralized organizational resources

Supervisory Style:

❐ Authoritarian (high control)
❐ Negativism (emphasis on failures)
❐ Lack of reason for actions/consequences

Reward Systems:

❐ Noncontingency (arbitrary reward allocations)
❐ Low incentive value of rewards
❐ Lack of competence-based rewards
❐ Lack of innovation-based rewards

Job Design:

❐ Lack of role clarity
❐ Lack of training and technical support
❐ Unrealistic goals
❐ Lack of appropriate authority/discretion
❐ Low task variety
❐ Limited participation in programs, meetings, and decisions that have a direct impact on job performance
❐ Lack of appropriate/necessary resources
❐ Lack of network-forming opportunities
❐ Highly established work routines
❐ Too many rules and guidelines
❐ Low advancement opportunities
❐ Lack of meaningful goals/tasks
❐ Limited contact with senior management

Source: Adapted from J. A. Conger and R. N. Kanungo, "The Empowerment Process: Integrating Theory and Practice," *Academy of Management Review,* July 1988.

Certain functional areas, divisions, or acquired companies may experience disenfranchisement as their responsibilities are felt to be diminished or made subordinate to others. As a result, employees' sense of competence may be seriously challenged as they face having to accept and acquire new responsibilities, skills, and management practices as well as deal with the uncertainty of their future.

In new venture situations, uncertainty often appears around the ultimate success of the company's strategy. A major role for leaders is to build an inspiring picture of the firm's future and convince organizational members of their ability to achieve that future. Yet, market lead times are often long, and tangible results may be slow in coming. Long work hours with few immediate rewards can diminish confidence. Frustration can build, and questions about the organization's future can arise. In addition, the start-up's success and responses to growth can mean constant change in responsibility, pushing managers into responsibilities where they have had little prior experience; thus, failure may be experienced initially as new responsibilities are learned. Entrepreneurial executives may be reluctant to relinquish their control as expansion continues.

Bureaucratic environments are especially conducive to creating conditions of powerlessness. As Peter Block points out, bureaucracy encourages dependency and submission because of its top-down contract between the organization and employees.[21] Rules, routines, and traditions define what can and cannot be done, allowing little room for initiative and discretion to develop. Employees' behavior is often guided by rules over which they have no say and which may no longer be effective, given the present-day context.

From the standpoint of supervision, authoritarian management styles can strip away subordinates' discretion and, in turn, a sense of power. Under an authoritarian manager, subordinates inevitably come to believe that they have little control—that they and their careers are subject to the whims or demands of their boss. The problem becomes acute when capable subordinates begin to attribute their powerlessness to internal factors, such as their own personal competence, rather than to external factors, such as the nature of the boss's temperament.

Rewards are another critical area for empowerment. Organizations that do not provide valued rewards or simply do not reward employees for initiative, competence, and innovation are creating conditions of powerlessness. Finally, jobs with little meaningful challenge, or jobs where the task is unclear, conflicting, or excessively demanding can lower employees' sense of self-efficacy.

IMPLICATIONS FOR MANAGERS

Managers can think of the empowerment process as involving several stages.[22] Managers might want to begin by identifying for themselves whether any of the organizational problems and characteristics described in this article are present in their own firms. In addition, managers assuming new responsibilities should conduct an organizational diagnosis that clearly identifies their current situation, and possible problems and their causes. Attention should be aimed at understanding the recent history of the organization. Important questions to ask would be: What was my predecessor's supervisory style? Has there been a recent organizational change that negatively affected my subordinates? How is my operation perceived by the rest of the corporation? Is there a sense of disenfranchisement? Am I planning to change significantly the outlook of this operation that would challenge traditional ways of doing things? How are people rewarded? Are jobs designed to be motivating?

Once conditions contributing to feelings of powerlessness are identified, the managerial practices identified in this article and in the management literature can be used to provide self-efficacy information to subordinates. This information in turn can result in an empowering experience for subordinates and may ultimately lead to greater initiative, motivation, and persistence.

However, in applying these practices, it is imperative that managers tailor their actions to fit the context at hand. For example, in the case of an authoritarian predecessor, you are more likely to need praise and confidence-building measures and greater opportunities for job discretion. With demanding organizational goals and tasks, the practices of confidence building and active rewarding, an element of play, and a supportive environment are perhaps most appropriate. The specific character of each practice must necessarily vary somewhat to fit your particular situation. For instance, what makes many of the previous examples so important is that the executives responded with practices that organizational members

---

21. See Block, Footnote 2.

22. See Conger and Kanungo, Footnote 5.

EXHIBIT 2
Stages of the Empowerment Process

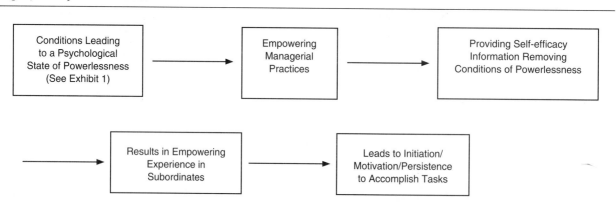

Source: Adapted from J. A. Conger and R. N. Kanungo, "The Empowerment Process: Integrating Theory and Practice," *Academy of Management Review,* July 1988.

could relate to or that fit their character—for instance, the television and squirt-gun examples. Unfortunately, much of today's popular management literature provides managers with tools to manage their subordinates, yet few highlight the importance of matching the practice to the appropriate context. Empowering is not a pill; it is not simply a technique, as many workshops and articles would lead us to believe. Rather, to be truly effective it requires an understanding of subordinates and one's organizational context.

Finally, although it is not as apparent in the examples themselves, each of the study executives set challenging and appealing goals for their organizations. This is a necessary component of effective and empowering leadership. If goals are not perceived as appealing, it is difficult to empower managers in a larger sense. As Warren Bennis and Burt Nanus argue: "Great leaders often inspire their followers to high levels of achievement by showing them how their work contributes to worthwhile ends. It is an emotional appeal to some of the most fundamental needs—the need to be important, to make a difference, to feel useful, to be part of a successful and worthwhile enterprise."[23] Such goals go hand in hand with empowering management practices. They were and are an integral part of the empowerment process I observed in the companies I studied.

A WORD OF CAUTION

In closing, it is important to add a note of caution. First of all, empowerment is not the complete or always the appropriate answer to building the confidence of managers. It can lead to overconfidence. A false sense of confidence in positive outcomes may lead employees and organizations to persist in what may, in actuality, prove to be tactical errors. Thus, a system of checks and balances is needed. Managers must constantly test reality and be alert to signs of "group think."

Some managers may be incapable of empowering others. Their own insecurities may prevent them from instilling a sense of power in subordinates. This is ironic, since often these are the individuals who need to develop such skills. Yet, as Kanter argues, "Only those leaders who feel secure about their own power outward . . . can see empowering subordinates as a gain rather than a loss."[24]

Certain situations may not warrant empowerment. For example, there are contexts where opportunities for greater initiative or responsibility simply do not exist and, in some cases, subordinates may be unwilling or unable to assume greater ownership or responsibility. As Lyman Porter, Edward Lawler, and Richard Hack point out, research "strongly suggests that only workers with reasonably high strength of desire for higher-order need satisfaction . . . will respond positively and productively to the opportunities present in jobs which are high in meaning, autonomy, complexity, and feedback."[25] Others may not have the requisite experience or knowledge to succeed. And those given more than they are capable of handling may fail. The end result will be the opposite of what you are seeking—a sense of powerlessness. It is imperative that managers assess as accurately as possible their subordinates' capabilities before undertaking difficult goals and empowering them to achieve.

Second, certain of the empowerment practices described in this article are not appropriate for all situations. For example, managers of subordinates who require structure and direction are likely to find the example of the manager "seeding" ideas with the television set an ineffective practice. In the case of a pressing deadline or crisis, such seeding is inappropriate, given its longer time horizons.

When staging playful or unconventional events, the context must be considered quite carefully. What signals are you sending about yourself and your management philosophy? Like rewards, these events can be used to excess and lose their meaning. It is imperative to determine the appropriateness and receptivity of such practices. You may inadvertently mock or insult subordinates, peers, or superiors.

In terms of expressing confidence and rewarding, both must be done sincerely and not to excess. Praising for nonaccomplishments can make rewards meaningless. Subordinates may suspect that the boss is simply flattering them into working harder.

In general, however, empowerment practices are an important tool for leaders in setting and achieving higher goals and in moving an organization past difficult transitions.[26] But remember that they do demand time, confidence, an element of creativity, and a sensitivity to one's context to be effective.

23. See Bennis and Nanus, Footnote 13, p. 155.

24. See Kanter, Footnote 3, p. 153.

25. L. W. Porter, E. E. Lawler, and J. R. Hackman, *Behavior in Organizations,* New York: McGraw-Hill, 1975, p. 306.

26. See N. M. Tichy and M. A. Devanna, *The Transformational Leader,* New York: John Wiley, 1986.

Exercise: Leadership and Decision Making: Applying the Vroom-Jago Model

PURPOSE

The purpose of this exercise is to help you become more aware of the conditions that lead to effective participation. By the time you finish this exercise, you will

1. Apply the Vroom-Jago model to different decision-making situations

2. Diagnose the conditions under which participative (GII), versus autocratic (AI, AII) and consultative (CI, CII), leadership styles should be employed

3. Understand how to determine leadership style decisions with your own group of subordinates

INTRODUCTION

Leadership and the decision-making process in management jobs are inexorably intertwined. Managers make decisions every day regarding problems that must be effectively handled. Some of those decisions may require the acceptance of subordinates for their successful implementation. Other decisions may have far reaching consequences. Depending on the type of decision to be made, managers must determine whether or not to employ a participative leadership style. Some decisions require subordinate participation; others do not.

Victor H. Vroom and Arthur Jago (1988) have developed a normative model of leadership and decision-making practices that describes the conditions under which leaders or managers should (1) engage in participative decision making with subordinates or (2) utilize a more autocratic or directive style. This exercise asks you to apply this theory to a variety of cases that illustrate a decision-making problem.

INSTRUCTIONS

1. Read the article by Vroom, "Two Decades of Research on Participation: Beyond Buzz Words and Management Fads."

2. Review the four case situations. Which leadership style do *you* think is best to employ in each situation? Use Table 1, "Decision Processes," presented in the article by Vroom, to make your determination.

This exercise was adapted by Victor H. Vroom from Lewicki, R. J., Bowen, D. D., Hall, D. T., and Hall, F. S. *Experiences in Management and Organizational Behavior, Third Edition,* "Choosing a Leadership Style: Applying the Vroom and Yetton Model" (New York: John Wiley and Sons, 1988). Cases I and III are reprinted from *Leadership and Decision Making,* by Victor H. Vroom and Phillip W. Yetton, by permission of the University of Pittsburgh Press. © 1973 by the University of Pittsburgh Press. Cases II and IV originally appeared in Vroom, V. H. and Jago, A. G. *The New Leadership: Managing Participation in Organizations,* pp. 41–43. Reprinted by permission of Prentice Hall, Englewood Cliffs, New Jersey.

3. Follow the decision tree presented in the article by Vroom.

4. In small groups of four to seven people, determine your answers to the four situations.

5. Report your answers when instructed to do so.

6. Participate in a class discussion.

CASE I

You are general foreman in charge of a large gang laying an oil pipeline. It is now necessary to estimate your expected rate of progress in order to schedule material deliveries to the next field site.

You know the nature of the terrain you will be traveling and have the historical data needed to compute the mean and variance in the rate of speed over that type of terrain. Given these two variables, it is a simple matter to calculate the earliest and latest times at which materials and support facilities will be needed at the next site. It is important that your estimate be reasonably accurate. Underestimates result in idle foremen and workers, and an overestimate results in tying up materials for a period of time before they are to be used.

Progress has been good, and your five foremen and other members of the gang stand to receive substantial bonuses if the project is completed ahead of schedule.

CASE II

You have recently been appointed manager of a new plant, which is presently under construction. Your team of five department heads has been selected, and they are now working with you in selecting their own staff, purchasing equipment, and generally anticipating the problems that are likely to arise when you move into the plant in three months.

Yesterday you received from the architect a final set of plans for the building, and for the first time you examined the parking facilities that are available. There is a large lot across the road from the plant intended primarily for hourly workers and lower-level supervisory personnel. In addition, there are seven spaces immediately adjacent to the administrative offices, intended for visitor and reserved parking. Company policy requires that a minimum of three spaces be made available for visitor parking, leaving you only four spaces to allocate among yourself and your five department heads. There is no way of increasing the total number of spaces without changing the structure of the building.

Up to now there have been no obvious status differences among your team, which has worked together very well in the planning phase of the operation. To be sure, there are salary differences, with your administrative, manufacturing, and engineering managers receiving slightly more than the quality-control and industrial-relations managers. Each has recently been promoted to the new position and expects reserved parking privileges as a consequence of the new status. From past experience you know that people feel strongly about things that would be indicative of their status. So far you and your subordinates have been working together as a team, and you are reluctant to do anything that might jeopardize this relationship.

CASE III

You are the head of a staff unit reporting to the vice-president of finance. He has asked you to provide a report on the firm's current portfolio to include recommendations for changes in the selection criteria currently employed. Doubts have been raised about the efficiency of the existing system in the current market conditions, and there is considerable dissatisfaction with prevailing rates of return.

You plan to write the report, but at the moment you are quite perplexed about the approach to take. Your own specialty is the bond market, and it is clear to you that a detailed knowledge of the equity market, which you lack, would greatly enhance the value of the report. Fortunately, four members of your staff are specialists in different segments of the equity market. Together, they possess a vast amount of knowledge about the intricacies of investment. However, they seldom agree on the best way to achieve anything when it comes to the stock market. Although they are obviously conscientious as well as knowledgeable, they have major differences when it comes to investment philosophy and strategy.

You have six weeks before the report is due. You have already begun to familiarize yourself with the firm's current portfolio and have been provided by management with a specific set of constraints that any portfolio must satisfy. Your immediate problem is to come up with some alternatives to the firm's present practices and select the most promising for detailed analysis in your report.

CASE IV

You are the manufacturing manager in a large electronics plant. The company's management has always been searching for ways of increasing efficiency. They have recently installed new machines and put in a new, simplified work system, but to the surprise of everyone, including yourself, the expected increase in productivity was not realized. In fact, production has begun to drop, quality has fallen off, and the number of employee separations has risen.

You do not believe that there is anything wrong with the machines. You have had reports from other companies that are using them, and the reports confirm this opinion. You have also had representatives from the firm that built the machines go over them, and they report that the machines are operating at peak efficiency.

You suspect that some parts of the new work system may be responsible for the change, but this view is not widely shared among your immediate subordinates, who are four first-level supervisors, each in charge of a section, and your supply manager. The drop in production has been variously attributed to poor training of the operators, lack of an adequate system of financial incentives, and poor morale. Clearly this is an issue about which there is considerable depth of feeling within individuals and potential disagreement among your subordinates.

This morning you received a phone call from your division manager. He had just received your production figures for the last six months and was calling to express his concern. He indicated that the problem was yours to solve in any way that you thought best, but that he would like to know within a week what steps you planned to take.

You share your division manager's concern with the falling productivity and know that your people are also concerned. The problem is to decide what steps to take to rectify the situation.

DISCUSSION QUESTIONS

1. Where does your preferred strategy fall on the leadership and decision-making continuum: autocratic, consultative, or participative?

2. Which "errors" do you commonly make in your leadership decisions: quality, acceptance, or time?

3. What factors may account for differences in how people diagnose leadership situations?

4. How useful is this theory in making decisions on how to lead your group of subordinates in actual leadership situations?

REFERENCE

Vroom, V. H. and Jago, A. G. *The New Leadership: Managing Participation in Organizations,* Englewood Cliffs, NJ: Prentice Hall, 1988.

Case: The Man Who Killed Braniff

PURPOSE

The "Man Who Killed Braniff" describes the impact Harding Lawrence had on Braniff Airlines as its chief executive. By the time you finish this case assignment you will

1. Understand the impact a leader's style can have on an organization

2. Use the theories of leadership and decision making presented in this chapter to understand events that affected the survival of a major organization

3. Determine the effect that a different style of leadership and decision making would have had on the survival of Braniff Airlines

INTRODUCTION

This case presents the facts behind a major news story. It describes the leadership and decision-making style of Harding Lawrence and the role that style played in the "death" of Braniff Airlines. Keep the articles in this chapter—Vroom and Jago (1988), Bass (1983), and Conger (1989)—in mind as you read and analyze the case.

INSTRUCTIONS

1. Read "The Man Who Killed Braniff."

2. Analyze the case using the theories of leadership and decision making presented in this chapter.

3. Participate in a class discussion.

The Man Who Killed Braniff

Byron Harris

It was a gray June morning in 1979. Under the taupe concrete spars and crossbars of the Braniff International terminal at the Dallas-Fort Worth Regional Airport (DFW), hundreds of people had gathered on the apron of the runway. It was a bizarre corporate festivity, a combination diplomatic ceremony and high school halftime. A band played. Twenty ticket agents in designer uniforms had been pressed into service as flag bearers. They carried 12-foot poles with foreign flags and marched in choreographed patterns. Their faces wore a variety of expressions, from amusement to lock-jawed company loyalty to irritation at being forced to participate in the spectacle.

The occasion was the inauguration of Braniff air service from DFW to the European continent. After speeches by local dignitaries, the stars of the show, three Boeing 747 jets, were introduced. They flew over the field a few hundred feet off the ground, circling back over the crowd again and again. A rented film crew recorded the pageantry, and all retired to the terminal.

In a VIP lounge, champagne flowed and strudel was served. An accordion player mingled with the crowd. Harding Lawrence, the Braniff chief executive, moved serenely among the guests, nodding here, touching an elbow there. It was his special day. His planes would now fly not only to London but also to Frankfurt, Paris, Brussels, and Amsterdam. So calm was Lawrence that, uncharacteristically, he was talking to the press. He even admitted that there was a cloud on Braniff's horizon. "The problem we have, of course, is the price of petroleum products," he said to a television reporter. "Jet fuel is about 55¢ a gallon, and that's awfully expensive." The reporter was accustomed to the airline industry's cries of concern over fuel prices. What he wasn't used to came at the end of the interview when Lawrence nodded benignly and said, "God bless you."

It takes a man with a special kind of self-image to bestow a blessing on a reporter after an interview. But Lawrence had always been extraordinary—he stood out as a showman even in a business where executives were known for their flamboyance. He was the spitting image of a captain of industry: gray hair, bushy salt-and-pepper eyebrows, a gravelly voice that exuded self-confidence. Lawrence *was* his airline, and vice versa. When he took it over in 1965, Braniff was an obscure regional carrier that had barely entered the jet age. Lawrence immediately expanded the jet fleet. He bought routes to South America from Pan American Grace Airways. He

painted his planes exotic colors, dressed his stewardesses in uniforms designed by Pucci, and then had them actually take off parts of those outfits after the planes were airborne, in what was promoted as the "air strip." Lawrence's Braniff was flashy and au courant, and it made money. In 1974, the airline earned an 18.2% return on equity, the best in the industry. By 1978, it had become the nation's seventh largest carrier, with a 19.6% return on equity, double the industry average.

But just as the airline's fortunes had risen on the wings of Lawrence's vision, so they fell. By the end of 1980, when Lawrence was forced out, Braniff was losing nearly $6 million a week, consumed by the very flair that had propelled it to greatness. Less than 16 months later the airline went out of business, bankrupted by monstrous debt and a skittish public. Texas was obsessed with the drama of those last months—the acrimonious fare wars, the desperate selling off of routes, the celebrity ad campaigns, all the financial gymnastics that sustained the illusion that the company was still salvageable. For a while, the day-to-day headlines even obscured the truth: that Braniff's demise was a certainty long before Lawrence Harding left, as much a certainty as that his genius was the seed of its success and his ego the seed of its destruction.

A ONE-MAN AIR SHOW

The identification of an airline with one man was not unique to Braniff and Harding Lawrence, although they may have been its most extreme embodiment. It was a historical part of the airline industry. TWA, originally Transcontinental Air Transport, hired Charles Lindbergh to survey its early routes and called itself the Lindbergh Line. Juan Trippe started Pan Am as a mail carrier after failing to establish a passenger line on Long Island with nine used Navy biplanes. The airline grew in a large part because of Trippe's extraordinary skill at securing foreign routes. Eastern carved its identity under the tutelage of Eddie Rickenbacker, the top U.S. flying ace in World War I, who was referred to by Eastern's employees simply as "the captain." Continental was founded by a young pilot named Robert Six in 1934. He borrowed $90,000 from his father-in-law and converted a small Western mailcarrier into a passenger airline. Six, who is 6′ 4″ tall, built his airline on the strength of his personality and his physical presence. He was the only one of the early pioneers still in the business when he retired this spring. His chief assistant until 1965 was Harding Lawrence.

Both Lawrence's genius and his ego were honed in the adolescence of the airline industry. He was born in 1920 in Perkins, Oklahoma. During World War II, he helped run an Army Air Force pilot training school in Terrell, east of Dallas. He hired on with Pioneer Airlines after the war, working at Houston's Hobby Field in the hangar next to that of another rising star: Lamar Muse of Trans-Texas Airways. Muse, who went on to pilot Southwest Airlines and Muse Air, remembers Lawrence vividly. "He was convinced he was a brilliant man," says Muse. "He was very smart and very astute." Lawrence stayed with Pioneer after it merged with Continental, ascending rapidly through the ranks to the number two spot under Robert Six. When Braniff, which had toddled along on the fringes of the industry for 37 years, went looking for a president in 1965, it looked to Continental.

From the day of Lawrence's arrival, Braniff was a one-man show. He was a master salesman, a persuader, above all a consummate actor who, according to staff members, often appeared to be rendering his own thespian interpretation of what an executive ought to be. Sometimes he would test his persuasive powers just to see how far he could go with them; at the height of his form he could talk people into believing things they knew to be untrue. Dave Stamey, a former Braniff vice-president, tells a story similar to those told by others who worked for Lawrence. "He could sit here in this chair, look out the window, and convince you it was raining, even though the sun was shining," Stamey says. "He'd say it was climatic aberration, or that it was a seasonal variation, or that the angle of the sun was refracting the light, making the rain invisible. Even though all your experience told you it wasn't raining, when you went outside you'd put your raincoat on."

Sometimes, say the executives who worked closely with him over the years, Lawrence didn't seem to know where the actor stopped and the real person began. But the real person had acumen as well as charm. Revenue passenger miles, available seat miles, break-even load factors, all these data were in his brain, evolving into a matrix of facts and figures that reflected the airline's health from day to day. In addition to being an "operations guy," he was a big thinker, a maestro of creative marketing. He was a brilliant man, his executives say, a brilliant man whose skills were rewarded. After three years as president, he became chairman of Braniff Airways in 1968 and chairman and chief executive officer to its parent company, Braniff International, in 1973.

That noteworthy year was marred only by Lawrence's pleading guilty to making illegal contributions to Richard Nixon's reelection campaign, a $40,000 indiscretion made in Braniff's name for which he was fined $1,000. The $40,000 was a fraction of a slush fund that Braniff used principally to pay kickbacks to travel agents in South America. The Civil Aeronautics Board, which investigated and even made noises about taking away some of Braniff's routes, described the fund as holding more than $641,000; Lawrence described it as less than $1 million. Whatever the amount, the CAB backed down in 1976, letting Braniff off with a $300,000 fine. In those days it seemed that nothing could keep Lawrence from leaving the airline in triumph at retirement age. No one foresaw the economic turns that would prove Braniff's mortal enemies. But the airline's biggest enemy had been there all along. It was Harding Lawrence himself.

THE TERROR OF FLIGHT 6

Lawrence the enemy won notoriety on Braniff's Flight 6, an early-evening run from DFW to La Guardia. Lawrence's wife Mary Wells, lived in New York City, where she ran her advertising agency, Wells, Rich, Greene, so he spent his workdays in Dallas and com-muted to New York for weekends. Flight 6 was a Boeing 727. Lawrence always sat in seat 6B of first class. He demanded it. If another passenger had somehow been assigned to 6B, that passenger would have to be coaxed out of his seat by the ticket agent—and God help the agent for making the oversight in the first place.

Hell hath no fury like the wrath Lawrence could unleash on an employee who did not meet his standards. After all, he *was* the airline. A slip in the airline's service was a personal insult to him. His tantrums on Flight 6 are legend. On one flight a stewardess served him an entire selection of condiments with his meal instead of asking him which ones he preferred. He slammed his fist into the plate splattering food on the surrounding seats of the first-class cabin. "Don't you *ever* assume what I want!" he screamed.

Another time he arrived at the plane in what the flight attendant describes as a state of inebriation. Shortly after takeoff he began yelling orders and shouting profanity, she says. As the flight progressed he became more intoxicated, continued to swear, and threatened the whole crew with dismissal. He broke a wine glass over his dinner tray. He charged that the attendants had used the wrong plates for dessert. Gradually, other passengers began leaving the cabin for the quieter coach section. The tirade continued: he complained repeatedly that the attendants were mixing his drink wrong. He was drinking Scotch on the rocks.

"On several occasions flight attendants came to me in tears, fearful of losing their jobs," says Ed Clements, former director of flight attendant services at Braniff. "I was sickened by what he was doing to the employees." Clements says few of the incidents were reported in writing because the women were afraid they'd suffer reprisals. And he says Lawrence abused his flight privileges as well as the cabin crews. On transatlantic flights, Clements says, Lawrence would commonly block the first two rows on one side of the coach section in addition to taking his two complimentary seats in first class. This was so he and his wife could lie down and sleep on their way to London. The practice often left six passengers in Dallas, for the planes to London regularly flew full.

The transatlantic flights were not without incident either. On one flight Lawrence dumped a trayful of food onto a stewardess's lap because it had gotten cold while he was away from his seat. On another he overturned a champagne bucket that was being used to store fruit. On a third he threw a dinner roll at a flight attendant. Stories about these displays spread rapidly through the employee ranks. By the late 1970s Lawrence's appearance on an aircraft was likely to arouse two emotions in the crew: fear and hatred. Workers went to great lengths to prevent a tantrum. Row six in first class would be made spotless before Lawrence's arrival: even windows on his aisle would be washed. Flight attendants would study their service manuals before takeoff. The rest of the plane might be a mess, coach service might suffer, but Lawrence's service would be up to par.

Inevitably, perhaps, dissatisfied employees meant dissatisfied customers. Marketing surveys showed that Braniff was not popular with many of the people who flew on it. While an ostentatious, entrepreneurial customer was attracted to the airline's first-class service, many of the passengers who flew in coach chose Braniff because there was no other airline that flew at the time of day they had to travel. Although Braniff was Dallas's hometown airline, it did not enjoy great goodwill there. Says Hal Salfen, a Braniff vice-president from 1971 to 1973, "People hated Braniff. That's absolutely true. The employees had the attitude that they were doing you a favor to get you on the plane."

THURSDAY, BLOODY THURSDAY

If Lawrence was a terror in the air, he cut just as wide a swath through his executives on the ground. Thursdays were dreaded by vice-presidents, for on Thursday the big boss held his top-level staff meeting. The executives grouped around a large table, Lawrence at the head. The focus of attention would shift from man to man (no more than two women were ever listed among the corporate officers) as each gave a report on his department. The process would go smoothly for the first few reports, then a snag would develop. A computer was down, say, or traffic had been slower than expected over the previous weekend. Suddenly the bearer of bad tidings would find himself stopped in midsentence.

"Why is the computer down?" Lawrence would ask. Then, "Why didn't you fix it?" Then, "When will it be fixed?" or "Why didn't you tell me this sooner?" Then, "How will this affect projected revenue?" The volume would rise as the questions went on, until the unlucky executive found Lawrence standing beside him, yelling, "I pay you a good salary and I expect you to do your job! Why don't you do it?" Leaning forward, Lawrence would stop with his bushy eyebrows just inches from the malefactor's face, his eyes, which sometimes appeared to be solid brown, devoid of pupils, boring in. And finally would come the growled question, "Why don't you get *on the team?*"

When the meeting ended, recalls one staff member, the victim would have to be "shoveled into his seat and wheeled down the hall." In some cases the sufferer would have invited the explosion by falling down on his job. But often the outbursts were simply a chance for the chief to flex his muscles—Lawrence had to have his sacrificial lamb every Thursday. For the top-level staff, the lesson of these episodes had little to do with Braniff's computer problems, traffic projections, or other facets of running the company. Smart executives simply learned not to give Lawrence bad news.

Thursdays evolved their own ritual, in which details such as where one sat became urgent matters of self-preservation. No one wanted to be "downwind" of an executive who was to be sacrificed: some of the invective might splatter. Early on a Thursday, the phone lines at Braniff headquarters would begin to buzz as executives asked each other the question: who is going to give Harding bad news today? Shortly before the meeting was to begin, a decorous scramble for chairs ensued—after the lamb had selected his seat.

A few stubborn souls would brave the machine-gun fire and persist in the delivery of a report even if its contents were unfavorable. One of these was Ed Acker, president of the airline under Lawrence from 1970 to 1975 and now chairman of Pan Am, who was widely known for his ability to handle the big boss. "Nobody gave Harding bad news," he says, "because nobody *wanted* to give him bad news." The point recurs in other descriptions of the Lawrence regime. Many of his executives were weak, untrained as managers, selected haphazardly from the airline's ranks by Lawrence himself. Appointed to their positions through his magnanimity, they were reluctant to displease him. In addition, they were often unsure of their own abilities. Their insecurity, combined with Lawrence's natural tendency toward management by intimidation, created a climate that was at best paralytic.

"They started out as strong customers," says Neal Robinson, a veteran of the Lawrence years, now executive vice-president of U.S. Telephone. "They were very serious about themselves and their jobs. But the constant pounding from Harding over the years sapped them of the will to fight."

The result was a group that could carry out decisions once they were made but generally deferred to Lawrence on policymaking, no matter how flawed the policies he made might be. By the late 1970s the company's managerial structure resembled a pyramid with an illusory base, the chief executive floating above an ineffectual management corps. Braniff lacked what management analysts call infrastructure, the network of people who transmit information and make decisions, giving the company internal direction. The big boss didn't get all the information he needed, and his ego often prevented him from trusting what his subordinates did tell him. He flew the airline by the seat of his pants. For a while, though, it was quite an air show. The 1978 balance sheet showed a profit of $45.2 million, the company's largest ever.

Much of Braniff's success, however, was as attributable to good fortune as to shrewdness. Between 1973 and 1975, for example, many airlines were laboring to pay for widebodied jets—DC-10s, L-1011s and 747s—that were flying nearly empty or were mothballed because passenger traffic had not grown as fast as they had expected. (There are still more than 100 747s and DC-10s for sale on the world market.) Braniff was widely congratulated in the press for having sagaciously decided not to buy the big jets, for taking the conservative road when others took chances. But the truth is that when other airlines were ordering those planes in 1969 and 1970, Braniff didn't have the money to buy them. "It was sheer-ass luck," says one former vice-president. And by the end of 1978, record profits notwithstanding, that luck was running out.

FLYING TOO HIGH

That year was a watershed for the entire industry. On October 24, the Airline Deregulation Act became law. Over a short period of time, it started phasing out regulation of routes and fares, the two elements that had shaped the industry since its beginning. Airlines had been rigidly regulated by the Civil Aeronautics Board since 1938. Until deregulation, the CAB decided where individual airlines would be allowed to fly by awarding route authorities. These pearls were parceled out after hearings and deliberations that often took years. Airlines vying for routes had to present detailed arguments as to why they, and not their competitors, should be allowed to fly from one city to another. This protracted process conditioned executives like Lawrence to think of routes as commodities of immense value. In a world where routes were scarce, they must be procured and protected at any cost.

The CAB's first move in implementing deregulation was to open dormant routes—those for which authority had been granted but which were not being flown—on a first-come, first-served basis. The airlines dispatched representatives to the CAB in Washington to snap up these windfalls. Press accounts of the event describe lawyers in pin-striped suits queued up all day, briefcases in hand, outside the CAB office. At night they would turn over their places to paid stand-ins who bedded down in sleeping bags on the sidewalks.

The frenzy was prompted partly by the airlines' uncertainty as to how far deregulation would go. Braniff, which had decided to seize every route it could get its hands on, applied for more than 300 of them in one day. The airline had nowhere near the resources to fly all those routes; the strategy was to take the most suitable ones and incorporate them into the existing system, to establish Braniff's presence in new markets before the CAB changed its mind and went back to parceling out routes the old way. The flaw in the strategy was fundamental. The reason the routes were dormant was that other carriers had found them unprofitable. That didn't dissuade Lawrence, however. He insisted that routes that had failed for other carriers would work for Braniff if properly integrated into the system.

To Lawrence, the decision transcended considerations of short-term profit and loss; it was a matter of survival. He foresaw the deregulated industry as one with a few large airlines and several small ones, but few middle-sized competitors. And in this he may have been right. For Braniff, Lawrence believed, it was grow or be eaten, so he made the airline bigger. On December 15, 1978, Braniff began service on 32 routes to 16 new cities. It was now making runs such as Memphis to Orlando, Kansas City to Philadelphia—flights that other airlines had found they couldn't make money on. Meanwhile, most carriers were either expanding cautiously or waiting to see how deregulation developed. "Lawrence was off on a trip that boggled the minds of most people in this business," says Morten Beyer, president of Avmark, a Washington-based aviation consulting firm. "From a business standpoint he was off his rocker. You should dominate the markets you're in, but the Braniff expansion was helter-skelter. They did not support their DFW operations. If they had done that, they might have succeeded."

Lawrence's empire building was approved by a board of directors that had for years been a rubber stamp for his proposals. Company records indicate that the board members may have regarded their positions as honors rather than duties. In 1978 six of the eleven outside directors of the company—those who were not Braniff officers—attended less than 75% of the board's meetings and committee meetings. But if the board seemed to lack diligence in reviewing Lawrence's plans, it was not acting any differently from most airline boards of the day. Moreover, Lawrence's past success was a convincing reason to let him have his way.

His way took money. New stations had to be opened, personnel to be moved to new cities, new employees to be hired. A new Boeing 727 cost $12 million, a 747 more than $45 million. According to the 1978 annual report, Braniff planned to spend $925.2 million on 41 new aircraft through 1981. Some experts say that to service the new routes properly, the company would have had to spend even more than that on planes, well over $1 billion. Airline analysts stress that a route is in essence a business in itself. Although part of a larger system, it must be conceived, executed, staffed, advertised and sold as a trip between two cities. By the end of 1978 Braniff was on the verge of adding four cities in Europe and four in the Pacific on top of the 16 new cities in the U.S. It was starting 24 new businesses in less than 12 months.

That the board acquiesced in this decision is no less surprising than that the company was able to borrow money to do it. Even though Braniff had earned $45.2 million in 1978, it still had long-term debt and lease obligations of $423 million, and its current liabilities exceeded its assets by $14 million. In the short term, Braniff was $14 million in the hole. The proposed spending spree meant that the company's debt-to-equity ratio would climb astronomically. Still, in 1978 Lawrence was able to secure credit from Boeing and $100 million in insurance company and bank loans.

How did he do it? It was the Lawrence charm, the acting skill, and the ability to persuade, aided considerably by the past record of success. "He had them mesmerized," says one insider, "and he had himself convinced he could do it too." At age 58, he wanted to establish Braniff as a worldwide airline before he retired. The plans were going forward: applications were filed to fly to a dozen additional destinations in Latin America and to Bahrain in the Middle East, Peking, Shanghai, Canton, Bangkok, Djakarta, and New Delhi. With just a few more links, Braniff would girdle the globe!

FORT LAWRENCE

Meanwhile, back in Dallas, another of Lawrence's dreams was consuming more than $70 million. Lawrence conceived Braniff Place, on the outskirts of DFW, as the gemstone of the airline. Not only would it house the company's world headquarters—its executive offices and training facilities—but when completed in 1978 it would also be a 113-room hotel for Braniff employees. It would include an employee recreation center with a nine-hole, par-three golf course, a swimming pool, saunas, and tennis and hand-ball courts.

The complex was as unconventional as Lawrence himself. The design was Mediterranean: four brilliant white terraced buildings, flanked by raised earthen shoulders, set beside a man-made lake. A sunken parking lot was rimmed with blue tile and centered around a fountain. The buildings made a glittering monument to Lawrence, but they looked better than they functioned. Lawrence had selected a California firm as the architect and a Texas company as the interior designer. He insisted on overseeing the minutest construction details himself. Communication between the three was cumbersome; hundreds of change orders were necessary. The complex was funded in 1976 with $35 million in DFW Airport bonds, but in 1978 Braniff had to go back for more bonds totaling $36 million to cover cost overruns and equipment.

Executive offices were to have gardens on the terraces outside their windows, so French doors were installed to open onto the gardens, but then the garden plan was scrapped. The doors leaked air, creating drafts strong enough to blow papers off desks. Some of them eventually had to be welded shut. Many of the desks, which were custom designed, had to be repaired shortly after installation. The office and hotel wings each had courtyards with imported Italian marble benches and olive trees flown in from California. Two of the trees were so big they had to be lifted in with cranes. The landscapers had neglected to note, however, that North Texas winters are too cold for olive trees. The trees died.

Every office had stark white walls enlivened only by a work from Braniff's collection of 54 paintings by Alexander Calder (whom Lawrence also commissioned to decorate two of the airline's jets). No personal artifacts or mementos were allowed. Each desk held two phones, one a normal telephone, the other an intercom that allowed any executive, including Lawrence, to speak directly into any office, even if the phone was not taken off the hook. Frequently, a vice-president would be in the middle of a meeting in his office when Lawrence's voice would interrupt. The executive could shut the device off, but only at the risk of enraging Lawrence. Some referred to the instruments as Gestapo phones and to the office complex as Fort Lawrence.

The back section of the top floor in the executive wing was Harding Lawrence's apartment, which he rented from the company for $1,775 a month. Furnished and decorated at airline expense, it was a sumptuous exercise in white and off-white. Paintings from Lawrence's private collection hung on the walls. In the living room, a neon sculpture adorned a glass coffee table, a large antique bird-cage occupied one corner, a polar bear rug lay in front of the fireplace. All these objects belonged to the airline. With a restaurant-size kitchen, the living room, a sitting room, two bedrooms, two and a half baths done in Italian marble, and a small swimming pool on the terrace out back, the apartment was well worth what the big boss paid for it.

Lawrence lived in his suite alone. He had a full-time personal valet and a housekeeper. They were provided at company expense, and most employees knew it. They saw the valet pick up Lawrence's rawhide luggage when he flew on the airline. (A special handler made sure his luggage was always last on and first off the plane and was carried to him directly at the baggage claim, which tended to draw the interest of the other passengers.)

There were other fringe benefits that the employees knew less about: a three-story house in London and a villa in Mexico. The latter was maintained at a cost, according to Braniff's 1978 proxy statement, of $92,000 a year. (That would rise to $172,000 a year in 1980.) Like top executives of many corporations, Lawrence also had a stock option plan. It gave him thousands of shares of company stock at a fixed value, which he could sell back to the company at the market price. If the market price increased, he could make a lot of money. In 1977 Lawrence exercised options on more than 78,000 shares, netting $236,000. In 1978 he sold another 200,000 shares, netting $1.4 million. He also received $871,794 in "salaries, fees, directors' fees, commissions, bonuses, and incentive compensation" during those two years.

THE STORM GATHERS

Even in those flush days, however, there was serious trouble in paradise. In December 1978 a high-ranking financial officer told Lawrence privately that Braniff's prospects for survival were nil. The airline was at the height of its expansion, and Lawrence was ginning out copious projections on the profits the coming months would bring. But he had already committed himself to spend so much on new planes and new routes that Braniff wasn't going to be able to bring in enough money to pay its bills. When the executive spoke to him, however, Lawrence insisted that everything would work out just as he predicted, that the executive "just didn't know about airlines." As the months passed and profits evaporated, the big boss talked to the man less and less.

Fuel costs, which represented about one fourth of the carrier's operating expenses, were fast becoming a critical drain on profits. They rose from 40¢ a gallon in 1978 to 62¢ in 1979, making the delicate economics of expansion more delicate still. Many of Braniff's new domestic routes were "add-ons" to old ones. Service to Milwaukee, for example, could be added because the airline had a plane in Chicago late in the evening. A 727 could be flown from there to Milwaukee less than half full without losing money. If more than half the seats could be filled, the flight would turn a profit. But as the price of fuel rose, the break-even load factor, the number of passengers needed to make the flight pay for itself, also rose. Soon the flight might have to be two-thirds full to be profitable, and who wants to go from Chicago to Milwaukee in the late evening? Not that many people, the airline found.

On international flights, where the operating costs were multiplied over vast distances, the stage was set for huge losses. Some of the bolder executives advised Lawrence to delay inaugurating Braniff's new foreign routes, but the expansion moved on. In June 1979 came the four European cities. A month later, four destinations in the Pacific—Seoul, Hong Kong, Singapore, and Guam—were added over the protests of those who warned Lawrence that price cutting among nationally owned airlines in the

Pacific is vicious and the volume of travelers small. Who wants to go to Seoul, South Korea, regardless of the time of day? Not that many people, the airline found.

At the same time all this was happening, the CAB was unexpectedly speeding up deregulation instead of slowing it. Route access was loosened even further. The franchise to fly from one city to another, that valuable commodity that in past had been so difficult to acquire, had almost no value at all. The analysis of each route's cost and yield potential, which previously had been performed as part of the CAB route certification process, was no longer routine. The agency that had acted as a restraint to overzealous airlines was no longer a barrier to them. Decisions had to be based on economics, not chauvinism.

Airlines that made their decisions on the basis of economics have little sympathy with the course Braniff took. At the March 1982 stockholders' meeting of Continental Airlines in Los Angeles, Frank Lorenzo, president of Continental's parent company, Texas Air, which also owns Texas International Airlines, took pains to distinguish Continental from Braniff. "It's important to note that Continental took a fundamentally different approach to deregulation than the management of Braniff took," Lorenzo said. "The management of Braniff had a basic belief that deregulation was an opportunity to become more aggressive; Continental looked upon deregulation as a time of extreme caution. Time will tell who was right."

GOING DOWN

In fact, time had already told. In late 1979 Lawrence began receiving news that might have shaken the confidence of another executive. His new routes, particularly those in the Pacific, were losing millions a month. The company's total operating expenses were 92% higher than they had been two years earlier. Braniff lost $9.8 million in the third quarter. But chauvinism won out over economics: the jumbo jets kept flying.

As costs rose, fares were falling. On June 1, 1979, the very same day that Braniff was serving strudel to the Dallas-Fort Worth city fathers, Texas International trotted out a brass band in its DFW terminal to inaugurate service to New Orleans. It was selling round-trip tickets for 35¢ that day, as a promotion, and would soon be selling one-way "peanuts fare" tickets for $35. A ticket to New Orleans on Braniff cost twice as much. Price was now a selling point in a business where it never had been before. To compete on price, airlines would have to trim profits, and Braniff's profits were already nonexistent.

By the end of 1979 the company had lost $44.3 million. In the first quarter of 1980 its losses exceeded $21 million. Lawrence's tirades at staff meetings continued. The big boss seemed unable to fully admit to himself the severity of Braniff's illness. He dispatched two executives to Los Angeles to inquire about the possibility of purchasing Continental—which at that time was an independent company. They returned with the answer that no, it was Continental that wanted to buy Braniff.

The big boss lived at Braniff Place, needing only to step through a door in his living room to be in the Braniff boardroom, and yet another door to be in his office. Employees called Lawrence's sanctuary the Howard Hughes suite because they rarely saw him outside of it. He was occasionally spied padding about the halls of the headquarters building late at night in his stocking feet, but he was cut off from the outside world. He never had to leave Fort Lawrence even to go to the 7-11 to buy a quart of milk or a newspaper. His valet did that.

His insularity was only compounded by his dealings with upper management. Occasionally an executive working late in the evening would be summoned to Lawrence's flat to thrash out one problem or another with the big boss. But Lawrence usually did most of the talking, sometimes until the early hours of the morning, pacing back and forth, drink in hand, in the all-white living room. One did not speak unless spoken to or voice an opinion unless asked; it was so much easier to find ways of agreeing with Lawrence than to tell him the truth.

As 1980 progressed, however, the truth became inescapable. The red ink was a hemorrhage—second-quarter losses were more than $48 million. The Pacific routes were consuming millions every month. Fuel prices were still headed upward. The economy edged into a recession, eroding the base of potential customers. And inflation continued to bloat expenses. Eventually, even Lawrence was compelled to acknowledge the need to cut costs. A labor relations expert was hired to help negotiate pay concessions with employee groups. Braniff was forced to do something it had never done much of: talk to its employees. On two occasions Lawrence was persuaded to attend the meetings to stress the urgency of Braniff's predicament. The very prospect sent ripples through the rank and file. Here was the man who threw food at his workers asking them to do him a favor. At the first gathering with the flight attendants, the big boss had the temerity to arrive in his chauffeur-driven Mercedes. "There was," says an executive who attended, "a broad-based feeling of contempt for Harding."

THE FINAL DAYS

With his airline in a nose dive, Lawrence became even more unpredictable. He singled out certain executives for early-morning phone calls. Awakened at 3 A.M., they would have to endure harangues about their "mistakes." The big boss was frustrated: at himself, at events, at the staff of incompetents who had let him down. Still, most employees stayed loyal; they felt a need to help the firm through its bad times. Moreover, after years of being told they were incompetent, many had come to believe it. "He had them believing they were so dumb they couldn't get a job anywhere else," says one who lived through this period. Two executives regularly sat in their offices and wept. Another concocted a series of business trips that kept him away from headquarters continuously; by staying away, he avoided the misery of the disintegration.

Lawrence sequestered himself in his apartment, which became known as the bunker. "He was out of touch with reality," says one vice-president. "He said we were gonna line up this loan and that loan, but he was dreaming. The numbers he talked about were much different from what was really happening. The airline was falling apart, but people were still running around trying to figure out how to deal with Harding. He had us moving armies we didn't have."

The employees who dealt with the public every day only heard rumors of this disintegration. But they had been whipsawed by the airline's growth and contraction. They had seen their ranks swell from 11,500 in 1977 to 15,200 in 1979 and then shrink back to 11,500 the very next year as the airline finally pared its unsuccessful routes. Never among the best-trained personnel in the industry, they tended to take their long-festering frustration with management out on the ticket buyers. At the same time, the company was in the midst of a "We Better Be Better" advertising campaign that in the eyes of Sam Coats, who later became senior vice-president for marketing, conveyed a sense of arrogance. It was as if all the company's difficulties—its financial problems, its management style, its public image—were converging at once to seal its destruction.

Lawrence met with financial reporters in August, during Braniff's last profitable quarter, to convince them of the airline's good health. "Braniff is a financially sound company," he said. "Braniff is not a company that is in financial trouble." But even he seemed to know the end was near. "My board, my stockholders, and all those people, I have a responsibility to them," he said, "I will be here as long as they require my service." He gave his home phone number to reporters, urging them to call him at any time with their questions. Indeed, it was not unusual for reporters to receive calls from Lawrence during this period—calls accusing them of biased reporting.

In the last quarter of 1980 the airline lost $77 million. In December the board of directors, at the mandate of the lenders, had no choice but to call for Lawrence's resignation. With a pension of $306,969 guaranteed for each year of the rest of his life, the big boss resigned without putting up a fight. (Now that Braniff is bankrupt, he may get less.) Quietly, on the night of December 30, 1980, Lawrence climbed the outside stairs of a Braniff gate at DFW, avoiding reporters waiting for him inside the terminal. He was boarding a jet for Mexico, for what he has since described as retirement. He keeps an office at his wife's advertising agency in New York, but there employees say he is traveling and unavailable for interviews.

AMONG THE RUINS

John Casey, vice-chairman under Lawrence, was promoted to fill the big boss's shoes. He succeeded in lessening the flow of red ink somewhat in 1981, but to reverse the airline's fortunes, he decided, new talent was needed. In September, Casey hired Howard Putnam as president for finance. Both men were lured away from Southwest Airlines, which had been the wunderkind of the industry in the '70s, compiling the highest profit margin of any U.S. airline. Even with their impressive credentials, Putnam and Guthrie would need a huge chunk of luck to succeed at Braniff: the airline had a demoralized work force, a degenerating public image, debts totaling well over $700 million, and creditors growling at the door. But Putnam was known for being tough, unpretentious, and unorthodox, and Guthrie had a reputation for financial expertise.

So it was with some optimism that the two of them drove out to the Braniff offices in Putnam's Oldsmobile last fall. Neither had ever seen Braniff Place before, and as they drove across the treeless grassland north of the airport, it loomed up in all its sparkling white glory. It was entirely different from Southwest's spartan offices in a converted airline terminal at Love Field. As they drew closer, they could see 28 flagpoles, which had been placed at the entrance to the complex at Harding Lawrence's direction. Originally there had been only two, but Lawrence had ordered the number increased as the airline expanded, so that the flag of every Braniff nation would fly above his office. Now, with the routes dropped to save money, the poles were empty. "My God," said Putnam, gazing at them, "they look just like masts of a sunken ship."

DISCUSSION QUESTIONS

1. What was Lawrence's leadership style? What effect did his leadership style have on Braniff Airlines? Did Lawrence exhibit any of the charismatic qualities described in the reading by Bass (1983)? Discuss these questions.

2. How did Lawrence make decisions? What effect did this have on Braniff Airlines?

3. What was it about Lawrence's leadership and decision-making style that caused the demise of Braniff Airlines?

4. Would a different leadership and decision-making style have led to a different outcome for Braniff? How? What should Lawrence have done?

Exercise: Leadership Empowerment

PURPOSE

The purpose of this exercise is to provide you with an opportunity to explore your management style. By the time you finish this exercise, you will

1. Identify your empowerment style

2. Observe different management styles in action

3. Determine ways in which you can become an effective motivator of people

INTRODUCTION

Managing others effectively involves learning how to motivate subordinates to perform the tasks associated with their jobs. How you do so defines your style, or approach, to managing others. If you have had more than one boss in your work life, you know that there are as many different styles of management as there are people. Defining your style is one of the most essential tasks of becoming a new manager.

But learning how to become an effective leader is a complex problem. For years debates have raged over whether good leaders are made or born to the task. The readings in this chapter provide good insights into this age-old dilemma. Whether or not you believe that leaders are made or born, there are particular skills that effective leaders exercise in their management styles that allow their subordinates to name them as effective leaders.

Originally titled, the "Motivational Styles Inventory," this exercise was developed by John Veiga of the University of Connecticut. Used with permission of the author. The idea for Part II of this exercise was originally presented by J. Veiga and J. Yanouzas at the Eastern Academy of Management Convention, Boston, 1987.

One of those skills involves empowering others. The term, empowerment, refers to creating a climate in which subordinates feel creatively responsible for their own work, skilled to accomplish their tasks, and ideally free of obstacles and barriers that might get in the way. Providing an empowering climate requires that a number of conditions be put in place for you to empower others. One of those conditions is that you exercise an empowering rather than a controlling style of management.

This exercise is designed to help you identify your particular style of leadership. Most people exercise friendly or controlling styles. Few understand how to empower others. This exercise will offer you insights into how you can alter your style so that your efforts at managing others can be made more empowering—and therefore more rewarding—for you and for those you manage.

This is a two-part exercise. In Part I, you will complete a questionnaire that determines your likely leadership empowerment style. In Part II, you will participate in a group observation in which others will provide you with feedback about your motivational approach to subordinates.

INSTRUCTIONS

Part I

1. Complete the Leadership Empowerment Styles Questionnaire.

2. Score your results as indicated.

3. Decide if you agree with your score. Does your profile accurately describe you?

Part II

1. Form groups of four to six. Each person will demonstrate how they manage others by coaching the remaining members of the group to complete a simple production task defined in Part II.

2. On the worksheet provided, select a production task.

3. When it is your turn to be the manager, select two members of your group to serve as your subordinates for the production task you have chosen.

4. While the remaining group members serve as observers, show your "subordinates" how to complete the task you have selected.

5. Listen to the feedback offered by other group members concerning your motivational style. To what extent does it match your questionnaire results?

6. Observe other group members until each group member has had a chance to "empower" subordinates in your group.

7. Participate in a class discussion.

Part I: Leadership Empowerment Styles Questionnaire

Directions: Each question consists of an incomplete sentence and three possible phrases that complete the sentence. Read each set of phrases and then distribute a *total* of 10 points to those phrases that best characterize your management style or belief. For example, if phrase "a" is the only one which is characteristic of you, then give that response the full 10 points. If, however, phrase "b" is also somewhat like you, then you might distribute 7 points to phrase "a" and 3 points to phrase "b," for a total of 10 points. You might also believe that all three phrases fit you to some extent so that you might distribute 3 points to "a," 3 points to "b," and 4 points to "c," for a total of 10 points. *Remember, you must distribute the full 10 points—no more, no less.* Place the points in the column marked "Your Rating."

	Your Rating	Scoring		
		EC	CC	FC
1. In establishing performance goals for others, I				
a. trust my people to set their own pace	_____			_____
b. try to encourage goals that challenge and stretch	_____	_____		
c. leave little doubt about what I expect	_____		_____	
2. When people come to me with personal problems, I				
a. try to act like a sounding board, let them grapple with the problem, then help them explore alternatives	_____	_____		
b. try to fix things if I can; otherwise I stay out of such problems	_____		_____	
c. try to act like a good friend	_____			_____
3. In making work assignments, I				
a. ask people what their preferences are and strive for a good match	_____			_____
b. rely on my own judgment and then tell the individuals involved what's expected	_____		_____	
c. try to get people to experiment with new areas and provide the necessary support while they learn	_____	_____		
4. When discipline is necessary, I				
a. try to make sure the person realizes that it's nothing personal	_____		_____	
b. try to encourage the individual to develop ways to avoid the need for future disciplinary action	_____			_____
c. let the individual know how disappointed I am and what I will and will not tolerate in the future	_____		_____	
5. The work climate I seek to create emphasizes				
a. stimulating excitement and enthusiasm toward achieving goals	_____	_____		
b. warmth and support	_____	_____		
c. that people won't be asked to do more than I can do	_____		_____	

	Your Rating	Scoring		
		EC	CC	FC

6. In developing employee potential, I
   a. provide encouragement and help people remove barriers to experimentation ____ ____
   b. try to create a friendly and supportive climate ____ ____
   c. think you have to be realistic and accept that some people can't be developed further ____ ____

7. I believe a good manager should promote values that
   a. emphasize caring and trust among subordinates ____ ____
   b. serve to make others stronger both individually and collectively ____ ____
   c. place organizational goals ahead of any individual's needs or desires ____ ____

8. When I discuss work assignments with subordinates I
   a. make sure that they understand how their part fits into the picture ____ ____
   b. try to be sensitive to their feelings and deal with their concerns ____ ____
   c. try to be as detailed as I can, so that there won't be any excuses for not doing what I've told them ____ ____

9. As a manager, I strive to
   a. set the example for everyone to follow ____ ____
   b. contribute to the organization by helping my subordinates gain a sense of purpose and personal power ____ ____
   c. be valued by others as someone who can be counted on for support and understanding ____ ____

10. As a manager I
    a. want people to like me ____ ____
    b. get overzealous and end up running over some people ____ ____
    c. try to create enthusiasm for high performance goals ____ ____

11. A good leader
    a. maintains tight control and follows up regularly on subordinates ____ ____
    b. seeks to help others feel in control and powerful ____ ____
    c. promotes harmony and trust among subordinates ____ ____

12. As a leader, I
    a. seek my followers' loyalty ____ ____
    b. seek my followers' friendship and understanding ____ ____
    c. seek to help my followers to do the best they can ____ ____

13. Performance evaluations should
    a. not damage the person's self-esteem in any way ____ ____
    b. make clear what the person must do ____ ____
    c. get the individual to take personal responsibility for achieving some small step toward improvement ____ ____

	Your Rating	EC	CC	FC

14. When delegating, a manager should

	Your Rating	EC	CC	FC
a. follow up regularly to ensure the individual is staying on track	_____		_____	
b. try to ensure, whenever possible, that the individuals develop and grow from the experience	_____	_____		
c. try to make sure no one feels manipulated into simply doing more work	_____			_____

15. When subordinates fail to deliver after I have discussed with them the need to do better, I am inclined to

	Your Rating	EC	CC	FC
a. ignore it, if possible, assuming that they already feel bad and will try even harder the next time	_____			_____
b. call them on it immediately and demand an explanation	_____		_____	
c. see what we can learn from the failure so as to minimize its happening again	_____	_____		

Column totals

[ ] A   [ ] B   [ ] C

Scoring

Directions: Transpose each rating directly across to the A, B, or C column marked next to each rating. Then total your ratings for each of the three columns. The bar chart below can be developed into a profile of your motivational style. To do so, shade in the area in each bar to correspond with each of your column totals. For example, if your total for column A is 38 then you would shade in the area up to 38 on that bar. (You will have to approximate the location of your score if it is not printed on the bar.) The percentiles along the left column provide you with a way to compare yourself to other managers who have completed the inventory. For example, a score of 42 on Column A means that about 80 percent of all managers score *lower* than you on this dimension and about 20 percent score *higher* than you.

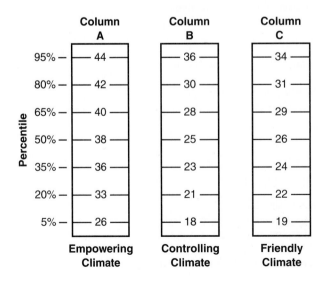

Percentile	Column A	Column B	Column C
95%	44	36	34
80%	42	30	31
65%	40	28	29
50%	38	25	26
35%	36	23	24
20%	33	21	22
5%	26	18	19
	Empowering Climate	Controlling Climate	Friendly Climate

Scoring

Directions: Transpose your ratings *directly across* to the space provided under one of the three columns marked **EC, CC,** or **FC** in the scoring area. Then total your ratings down each of the three columns for all 15 questions. The bar chart below can be developed into a profile of your motivational style. To do so, shade in the area in each bar to correspond with each of your column totals. For example, if your total for Column **EC** is 93, then you would shade in the area up to 93 on that bar. (You will have to approximate the location of your score if it is not printed on the bar.) The percentiles along the left column provide you with a way to compare yourself to other managers who have completed the inventory. For example, a score of 93 on Column **EC** means that about 80 percent of all managers score *lower* than you on this dimension and about 20 percent score *higher* than you.

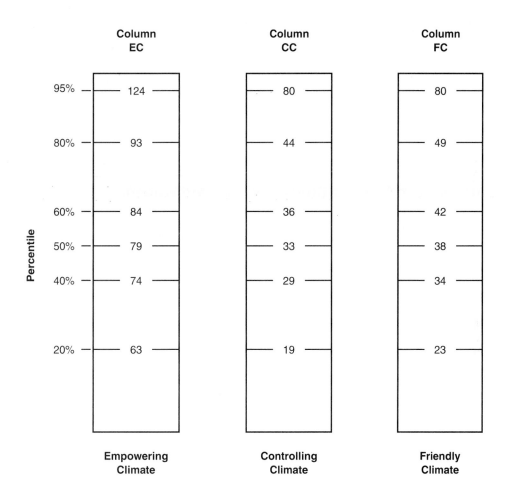

Interpretation: Managers vary widely on the kind of motivational climate their actions tend to create. However, generally these actions contribute to one of three climates: (1) a climate that tends to empower people—measured by *Column EC;* (2) a controlling climate that tends to create "pawns"—measured by *Column CC;* and (3) a climate that tends to emphasize friendly relations—measured by *Column FC.* The higher your score on each of these dimensions, the greater the tendency for your management practices and beliefs to create the climate described. On the next page is a more complete description of each of these climates.

EC Empowering Climate: A climate that empowers people so that they feel in control of their surroundings, they feel personally energized, they feel they can have impact on their environment, and they feel uplifted and more powerful.

CC Controlling Climate: A climate that tends to create pawnish behavior in subordinates; that is, people who do not feel in control, who feel constrained by rules and procedures, who feel they have little control over their organizational fate, and who expect the boss to tell them what to do and when to do it.

FC Friendly Climate: A climate that tends to emphasize friendly and harmonious relations between superior and subordinate over achievement of high performance goals.

Of course, the major question is "Which climate is the most effective?" Research on employee motivation suggests that the *Empowering Climate* is the one that managers should strive to create whenever possible. Clearly, the extent to which your actions work against creating such a climate—and thereby produce a more controlling or friendly climate—the less effective you are likely to be in motivating and developing others.

Moreover, while having a friendly climate is often desirable, such a climate can be dysfunctional if a manager places greater emphasis on being liked than on helping subordinates to do their best. Hence, the ideal motivational profile would be a high score on the empowering climate (80th percentile and above), a low score on the controlling climate (20th percentile or below), and a low to moderate score (40th percentile or below) on the friendly climate.

Part II: Leadership Empowerment Style Observation

Directions: Select one of the six tasks described below. Then select two members of your group to serve as your "subordinates." Your job is to motivate these subordinates to successfully perform the task you have chosen in the way in which you think it should be accomplished. The remaining group members will serve as observers. It will be the observer's duty to provide feedback to each "manager" about his or her leadership style. Remember to record your observations on the Observation Sheet provided.

Tasks

In the manager role, you will need to manage your subordinates to do one of the following tasks:

1. Drawing concentric circles on the board.
2. Building a house of cards.
3. Creating paper airplanes.
4. Measuring the dimensions of desks and chairs.
5. Drawing a picture of a horse.
6. Creating notepads out of scratch paper.

How to Use the Observation Sheet

In observing each manager's style, does the manager

Empowering

❒ Energize subordinates to create their own style, be creative and innovative in completing tasks?

❒ Allow subordinates to feel that they are in control of the task, rather than being controlled by the manager?

❑ Encourage subordinates to grow and develop from the learning that takes place by performing the tasks?

Controlling

❑ Force subordinates to conform to the manager's rules and regulations?

❑ Cause subordinates to feel they are not in control of the task?

❑ Encourage the reliance of subordinates on the manager's every direction, rule, and deadline in completing the task?

Friendly

❑ Suggest that the manager wants to be liked and accepted by subordinates?

❑ Imply that the manager is more concerned with employee morale than performance?

❑ Encourage the pursuit of friendly cooperation to the exclusion of emphasizing standards, goals, and deadlines?

Observation Sheet

Manager 1: _____

Most likely style: _____

Evidence: _____

_____

_____

_____

_____

Manager 2: _____

Most likely style: _____

Evidence: _____

_____

_____

_____

_____

Manager 3: _____

Most likely style: _____

Evidence: _____

_____

_____

_____

_____

Manager 4: _____

Most likely style: _____

Evidence: _____

_____

_____

_____

_____

Observation Sheet (cont.)

Manager 5: _____

Most likely style: _____

Evidence: _____

_____

_____

_____

_____

Manager 6: _____

Most likely style: _____

Evidence: _____

_____

_____

_____

_____

DISCUSSION QUESTIONS

1. To what extent did your questionnaire results match the feedback given by group members about your leadership style?

2. If differences exist, which results do you think represent a truer picture of yourself as a leader? Why or why not?

3. What is the leadership style of your boss (or professor)? What behaviors have you observed in your boss (or professor) that lead you to this conclusion?

CHAPTER 5

Power and Politics

INTRODUCTION

Power is endemic to organizational life. Most of us are aware of those who have it—and those who don't. But the dynamics that underlie the use of power are most mysterious. To be effective as managers, we need to understand how to use power productively. As you will see, the productive use of power is vital for managerial success.

Power and politics are different aspects of the same process. While power results from your position, politics represents the tactics employees use to manipulate power in organizational settings. Sometimes these tactics can be used to assume greater power or to lessen another's. For this reason power and politics often carry an adverse connotation. The negative side of power is most clearly epitomized by people who use power to aggrandize themselves at the expense of greater organizational goals. When this occurs, the misuses of power that result from political game playing may interfere with the organization's overall productivity.

But there is a positive side to power. Power can be used as both a tool and a resource, a means and an end. As Rosabeth Kanter says, power is the ability to get things done. Those in power are able to marshal their resources in a way that helps them achieve their goals. They are able to be effective in their jobs and earn the respect of others. Having power as a resource can help you gain support, information, supplies—everything and anything that is needed to be productive in your job. Without sufficient productive power, you will be unable to be effective as a manager.

READINGS

The first article, "Patterns of Managerial Influence: Shotgun Managers, Tacticians, and Bystanders," by David Kipnis, Stuart M. Schmidt, Chris Swaffin-Smith, and Ian Wilkinson, illustrates the strategies managers use to influence others. The authors identified three profiles of influence: shotgun managers, who are inexperienced and overdo their influence attempts; tacticians, who use reasoned influence strategies to get the job done; and bystander managers, who underuse opportunities for influencing others. Managers also may use different tactics for dealing with subordinates rather than superiors and peers.

In "Power Failure in Management Circuits," Rosabeth Moss Kanter suggests that power is not as much a function of the individual as the position. She argues that certain situational factors, such as visibility, centrality, and a variety of task assignments, enhance position power, while the lack of these factors diminishes one's power. Power, she maintains, is not directly related to authority. Even upper-level executives can be rendered powerless when the lines of information, supply, and support are no longer effective in their jobs. Sharing power, rather than hoarding it, may help managers eliminate the sources of powerlessness and improve overall organizational effectiveness.

The third article, by Gerald R. Salancik and Jeffrey Pfeffer, "Who Gets Power and How They Hold Onto It: A Strategic Contingency Model of Power," explains departmental sources of power. These authors studied the differences among departmental resource allocations and attributed power in a university setting. They found, surprisingly, that departmental power is a function of how dependent the organization as a whole is on a department's ability to deal with critical problems affecting that organization. When a department is considered critical to the overall functioning of the organization, resource allocation monies flow to that department to enhance its effectiveness. But, once in power, such departments will do whatever it takes to distort reality to maintain their power. In short, the powerful get more, while the weak remain powerless. Salancik and Pfeffer show how these dynamics work in organizational settings using several examples to support their arguments.

EXERCISES AND CASES

The exercises provide an opportunity for you to understand and use power productively and effectively. The first exercise, "Dependency Situations," helps you determine how you might react to situations in which you might be required to exercise influence. Understanding the relationship of power to dependence will help you choose an empowerment style in situations in which you are dependent on others to achieve a particular goal.

The case, "Jennifer Carson at the Science Museum," offers an intriguing description of a politically difficult job situation. Jennifer Carson is hired at the Science Museum with no clear job description. The case details how she accomplishes her goals in a politically charged situation in which her peers are not comfortable with her presence and her boss is resentful of her relationship with higher-ups.

A third exercise, "Power Lab," explores intergroup power relationships. A simulated group situation is created to allow you to experience how it feels to be in control, powerless, or caught in the middle. This exercise tests your myths and assumptions about power dynamics in organizational settings, and helps you determine how it feels to wield power—or lose it—as a manager.

MEMO

The memo assignment for this chapter, *Power and Dependence Analysis* (located at the back of the book), asks you to consider the structural and interpersonal sources of power that affect you personally in your job. Where do you stand in the political network of your department? How does your department fit into the political network of your organization? What strategies, if any, can be used to empower yourself, given the constraints of your position and your department? What are the structural sources of power that are contributing—or not contributing—to your current job?

By the time you finish this chapter, you will have a better understanding of power dynamics in organizational settings. You will also have an opportunity to assess your own empowerment profile and your reactions to authority. Finally, you will appreciate the impact of power in your organization and how politics affects you personally in your job.

Patterns of Managerial Influence: Shotgun Managers, Tacticians, and Bystanders

David Kipnis

Stuart M. Schmidt

Chris Swaffin-Smith

Ian Wilkinson

"I urged a client to complain to my boss about the need for more personnel to assist me at the client's site. . . ."

"I had all the facts and figures ready before I made my suggestion. . . ."

"I told my assistant that he was the most capable person to perform the work and that I knew he would produce a professional product. . . ."

"After presenting my superior with a checklist as to why I felt myself worthy of a promotion, I was turned down. But upon appeal to the vice-president, I was promoted. . . ."

The exercise of influence is a fundamental activity in organizations. The above examples, taken from interviews, illustrate some of the ways in which managers carry out this activity on a daily basis. These are not particularly subtle, Machiavellian, or statesmanlike examples of influence tactics. Nevertheless, they do represent typical forms of influence used in organizations. At the outset, we note that most managers do not exercise influence for the sheer joy of changing other people's behavior. For the most part there are logical reasons underlying their attempts to influence people. Sometimes influence is used for such personal reasons as securing personal benefits or better work assignments. Most often, however, it is used in the course of performing organizational roles that require influencing others—for example, to encourage others to perform effectively, to promote new ideas, or to introduce new work procedures. Frequently a combination of personal and organizational reasons underlie the exercise of influence.

In previous research we empirically identified seven influence strategies that managers use to get their way in their organi-

zations. The purpose of this article is to describe the findings of a three-nation study of how managers use these seven influence strategies. First we will describe these influence strategies and the frequency with which they are used by managers to influence superiors and subordinates. Then we will examine the factors that determine the choice of influence strategies. This will give some insight into why managers choose certain strategies rather than others. Finally, we will describe how managers rely on different "mixes" of these seven strategies. Here a distinction is made between the "raging bull," a manager who uses all possible means of influence—and the "timid soul" who seemingly never tries to convince others. Basically we want to explain why managers use different influence strategies.

PREVIOUS STUDIES OF INFLUENCE

Despite the fact that the essence of managerial work is the exercise of influence, there is a paucity of systematic research on the ways in which managers attempt to change the behavior of others. For example, Henry Mintzberg's classic analysis of managerial work describes the range of activities performed by managers but does not describe the influence tactics that managers use. Yet it is our belief that the "how" of managerial work—that is, how managers exercise influence and their choice of various influence strategies—is of profound importance to managers and to students of organizational behavior.

We began our studies by reviewing management books and articles dealing with the subject of managerial power and influence. Generally, this material relies on scattered interviews, anecdotes, subjective impressions, and armchair theorizing. A large body of work focuses on influencing one's subordinates. These "leadership" studies represent the best-documented materials on these subjects. Articles that describe the well-known scale to measure a manager's use of consideration and initiating structure or the use of "management by objectives" are examples of researched approaches to the ways in which managers use influence with their subordinates.

Less empirically based approaches to managerial influence stem from a particular theory of social power. For example, one finds frequent reference to the well-known theory of John R. P. French, Jr. and Bertram Raven that proposes bases of power that include rewards, coercion, legitimate power, referent power, and expertise. The problem here, we have found, is that this theoretical approach does not help us identify all the strategies actually used by managers—that is, mangers use strategies not mentioned by French and Raven—coalitions, for example. Furthermore, other writers describe a number of influence strategies that are based simply on their perception of effective management action. Such observations are not grounded in either theory or empirical research.

The most confusing discussions about influence are found in articles that deal with influencing superiors in an organization. Generally, this literature relies on books and anecdotes of writers ranging from Machiavelli to Michael Korda, many of which focus on impression management, manipulation, deceit, and various ploys and dirty tricks designed to overcome the resistance of others. Needless to say, there is little research to suggest that these upward influence strategies are effective.

In general, the advice contained in writings on managerial influence is frequently contradictory—with some advocating assertiveness, others suggesting stealth, and still others advising the use of rationality to influence others. One wonders if they can all be right. Further, many of the tactics, if used consistently, could well have dysfunctional consequences for organizations, for the individuals who are the targets of influence and, possibly, for the users themselves. It doesn't take much imagination to visualize the effect upon an organization of executives whose influence tactics consist of ingratiation, deceit, and avoidance of anything that might cause offense.

MEASURING MANAGERIAL USE OF INFLUENCE

With these thoughts in mind we decided to study managerial use of influence as it is actually practiced. Further, rather than rely on an intensive case-history approach in which the activities of only six or seven managers are studied, we decided to gather information from many managers. This approach allowed us to sample a greater range of managerial experiences. Our work began by asking managers to describe actual incidents in which they attempted to change the behavior of subordinates, peers, or superiors. These descriptions were then used to construct questionnaires that contained the many different influence tactics described by the managers. Next different groups of managers answered the questionnaire in terms of how frequently they used each tactic to influence others. On the basis of a series of factor analyses of this information we found that seven dimensions of influence represented the wide variety of tactics initially described by managers. The dimensions or strategies of influence that we identified are as follows:

Reason. This strategy involves the use of facts and data to support the development of a logical argument.

Friendliness. This strategy involves the use of impression management, flattery, and the creation of goodwill.

Coalition. This strategy involves the mobilization of other people in the organization.

Bargaining. This strategy involves the use of negotiation through the exchange of benefits or favors.

Assertiveness. This strategy involves the use of a direct and forceful approach.

Higher authority. This strategy involves gaining the support of higher levels in the organization to back up requests.

Sanctions. This strategy involves the use of organizationally derived rewards and punishments.

By describing the actual behavior that managers use in achieving their objectives and by defining what these influence strategies are, we gain a way to examine influence in more detail. Instead of simply getting answers from managers on how often they exercise influence as part of their work, we're able to consider the particular strategies they rely upon to influence others. For example, do they rely mainly on assertiveness, higher authority, reason, or perhaps a combination of strategies? From our research, we developed a new scale, *The Profile of Organizational Influence Strategies* (POIS), to measure the use of these seven influence strategies. One form of the POIS measures how frequently managers use each strategy to influence their superiors. A second form measures the use of influence directed toward co-workers, and a third toward subordinates.

THREE-NATION STUDY OF MANAGERIAL INFLUENCE STYLES

Managers from many firms in England, Australia, and the United States were surveyed using the POIS to measure the ways in which they try to influence their superiors and their subordinates. In addition, all managers completed a supplemental questionnaire describing their work as well as their attitudes toward their work. These managers were attending developmental sessions in their respective countries. In total, 360 first- and second-line managers participated in the international comparison. Of these, 113 were from the United States, 126 were from Australia, and 121 were from England.

WHAT ARE THE MOST POPULAR STRATEGIES?

We make no claims that the samples in this study are necessarily representative of managers in the three countries. However, we found essentially no difference among countries in how managers exercised influence. In all three countries, the frequency with which managers used the various influence strategies was virtually identical. When seeking to influence their superiors, managers reported that they relied most often on reason, followed by coalitions, and then by friendliness. Going over the "boss's head" or resorting to higher authority was used least often to influence superiors.

The rank order of preferred strategies was somewhat different when influencing subordinates. Once again managers reported that the most frequently used strategy was reason. Interestingly, however, the second most popular strategy was assertiveness. While perhaps not surprising, this finding confirms the common

FIGURE 1

Most-to-Least Popular Strategies Used in All Countries.

	*When Managers Influenced Superiors**	*When Managers Influenced Subordinates*
Most	Reason	Reason
Popular	Coalition	Assertiveness
to	Friendliness	Friendliness
Least	Bargaining	Coalition
Popular	Assertiveness	Bargaining
	Higher Authority	Higher Authority Sanctions

*The strategy of sanctions is omitted in the scale that measures upward influence.

belief that managers can assert themselves aggressively when they demand compliance from their subordinates, but not when they are seeking compliance with their requests from their superiors. These findings appear in Figure 1.

WHAT AFFECTS THE CHOICE OF TACTICS?

Having identified seven influence strategies and devised a way of measuring the frequency with which they are used, we considered whether there are any special circumstances that determine a manager's choice of a particular strategy. As social scientists we doubted that the choices are simply random or based on managerial predilections. Rather, we expected that various organizational, personal, and situational factors might combine to determine a manager's influence style.

We have already indicated that there were no differences in influence styles among managers in the three English-speaking countries. We found, however, that three variables did affect the selection of influence strategies: the manager's relative power, the manager's objectives for wanting to use influence, and the manager's expectation of the target person's willingness to comply.

The Manager's Power

Power enters into the selection of strategies in two ways. First, managers who control resources that are valued by others, or who are perceived to be in positions of dominance, use a greater variety of influence strategies than those with less power. Second, managers with power use assertiveness with greater frequency than those with less power.

Variety of Influence Strategies

Perhaps the most striking illustration of the variety of influence strategies used by managers with power can be found by examining how they influence superiors and subordinates. In all countries, managers use the following four strategies more frequently to influence subordinates than superiors: assertiveness, friendliness, bargaining, and higher authority. Only reason was used more frequently to influence superiors. While this finding is perhaps not too surprising, it indicates that managers apply greater pressure on subordinates to comply because they potentially have a greater

range of strategies available. Thus if one strategy fails, managers maintain steady pressure on subordinates through the use of an alternative strategy.

Another example of this relationship between power and variety of influence strategies is found by comparing the approaches of managers who direct units of varying technological complexity. The sociologist Charles Perrow has pointed out that managers who supervise complex technology are relatively more powerful than those who supervise more routine activities, because other units depend on their expertise to solve important organizational problems. In comparison, managers who direct routine kinds of work are generally taken for granted because the contributions of their units tend to be of less consequence. Consistent with this reasoning, we found that managers who directed nonroutine technologies used a greater variety of strategies when trying to influence their superiors. In particular, they frequently used reason, assertiveness, and higher authority.

Assertiveness

In addition to using a greater variety of influence strategies, managers with power are more likely to invoke stronger influence strategies—for example, assertiveness. While this relationship makes sense, its pervasiveness requires comment. It is found with increasing regularity both in organizations and in general social relations. For example, assertiveness is reported in studies of primate colonies; children trying to influence younger children, peers, and adults; and the internal operations of business organizations. In all instances, those with greater power (or resources) use more directive tactics to influence others. We speculate that there is an "Iron Law of Power" that holds that the greater the discrepancy in power between the influencer and the target, the greater the probability that more directive influence strategies will be used.

This does not necessarily mean that powerful managers use assertiveness as their first strategy. Given a choice, most managers initially seek to exert influence through the use of simple requests and reason. Assertiveness is used when the target of influence refuses or appears reluctant to comply with the request. When such resistance is encountered, managers with power tend to use more directive strategies. Typically they shift from using simple requests to insisting that their demands be met. In contrast, managers without power are more likely to stop trying to influence when they encounter resistance. This is because they feel the costs associated with assertiveness are unacceptable. They may be unwilling, for example, to provoke the ill-will of the target.

The Manager's Objectives

Our findings also show that managers vary their strategies in relation to their objectives. When managers seek benefits from a superior, they often rely on the use of soft words, impression management, and the promotion of pleasant relationships—that is, tactics encompassed by the strategy of friendliness. In comparison, managers attempting to persuade their superiors to accept new ideas usually rely on the use of data, explanations, and logical arguments—that is, tactics encompassed by the strategy of reason. In addition, such managers are likely to use assertiveness to gain organizational objectives, but not personal objectives.

Similarly, this matching of strategies to objectives holds true when managers influence their subordinates. For example, they use reason to sell ideas to subordinates and friendliness to obtain favors. As a general rule, the more reasons managers have for exercising influence, the greater the variety of strategies they will use. Only the most inflexible of managers can be expected to rely rigidly on a single strategy, say assertiveness, to achieve both personal and organizational objectives. It may be appropriate to "insist" that one's boss pay more attention to cost overruns; it is less appropriate to "insist" on time off for a game of golf.

The Manager's Expectations of Success

Managers also vary strategies according to how successful they expect to be in influencing the target. When past experience indicates a high probability of success, managers use simple requests to gain compliance. In contrast, where success is less predictable, managers are more tempted to use assertiveness and sanctions to achieve objectives.

Managers in comparable positions may differ with regard to their expectations for success in exercising influence. This difference in expectations may occur for many reasons. Thus, for example, social psychologists report that the more dissimilar people are in terms of attitudes, race, and sex, the less cooperative they will be with one another. Given these lowered expectations, it is not surprising that there are frequent complaints that managers use more directive tactics with minorities. This behavior may not be the result of malicious prejudice, but the mistaken notion that the target will not comply with simple requests. Hence, managers feel the need to use harsher and more directive tactics with those who are different in these dimensions.

A summary of how managers use the three popular influence strategies discussed above appears in the box on page 185.

PROFILES OF MANAGERS WHO USE DIFFERENT MIXES OF INFLUENCE STRATEGIES

Do managers vary the mix of influence strategies that they typically use? That is, do some managers use only the same one or two strategies all of the time, while others use all seven? To answer this question, we used the statistical technique of cluster analysis on the POIS to determine patterns of managerial influence in each of the three countries. Cluster analysis is an analytical technique used to develop subgroups of individuals who are similar to each other. The findings revealed that managers in all three countries fall into three groupings, referred to as "shotgun" managers, "tactician" managers, and "bystander" managers.

Shotgun Managers

Shotgun managers used all seven strategies from reason to sanctions with above-average frequency to influence others. Shotgun managers, then, attempt to get their way by using the full range of influence strategies. This seems to mean that they want a great deal from others, and as a result they must keep on trying out different strategies.

To test this possibility, data from shotgun managers were further analyzed. Our analysis indicated that shotgun managers reported having many unfulfilled objectives in terms of being able to sell their ideas, obtaining personal benefits, or getting others to work more effectively. In addition, in each country they were the ones with the least organizational experience. In summary, shotgun managers are inexperienced and probably ambitious, and they have great expectations. To this end, they openly attempt to obtain what they want through the indiscriminate use of influence strategies.

Use of Influence Strategies

Assertiveness is frequently used when:

- ❏ Objectives are to benefit the organization.
- ❏ Expectations for success are *low*.
- ❏ Organizational power is *high*.

Reason is frequently used when:

- ❏ Objectives are to benefit the organization.
- ❏ Expectations for success are *high*.
- ❏ Organizational power is *high*.

Friendliness is frequently used when:

- ❏ Objectives are to benefit the person.
- ❏ Expectations for success are *low*.
- ❏ Organizational power is *low*.

Tactician Managers

Tactician managers relied heavily on reason to influence others, but they had at least average scores on the other strategies. Tacticians, then, get their way by using facts and data in logical arguments. The image portrayed here is that of rational organizational managers, exercising influencing in a deliberate manner.

Statistical analysis revealed several organizational and personal characteristics that distinguish tacticians from other managers. Perhaps most important is that they have power in their organizations. This was shown in several ways. First, tacticians managed work units that did technologically complex work. Their employees were skilled, and the work they managed required considerable planning before it could be carried out. As we pointed out earlier, managers of "high-tech" units should have power in their organizations. Our study confirmed that this is so. Tacticians stated that they had considerable influence over such matters as setting budgets, influencing company policy, and dealing with personnel matters. In general, they expressed satisfaction with their ability to perform their work.

In sum, our impression is that tacticians are flexible in their use of influence, find their organizational objectives generally met, and rate themselves as effective in carrying out their tasks. At the same time they occupy positions of power on the basis of their skills and knowledge, which allows them to influence others by relying mainly on the strategy of reason.

Bystander Managers

This group had below-average scores on all seven influence strategies. They exercised little influence in their organizations, despite the fact that they occupy managerial roles. There are two possible explanations for their inactivity. One is that bystanders occupy such powerful positions in their organizations that others continually anticipate their needs; hence they do not have to exercise influence because they get their way without effort. The other possible explanation for their inactivity is that they lack power in their organizations, and therefore they feel it is futile to even try to influence others.

The results of our analysis support the second explanation. Bystanders are managers who direct units carrying out routine work. They also supervise the greatest number of subordinates—another indication of routinization. Given this kind of work, it is not surprising that they perceive themselves as having little organizational power as signified by their inability to influence budget, personnel, and/or company policy. Further, in each country those in this group have been in the same job for the longest time. In sum, our impression is that bystanders are managers marking time in mundane jobs, who see themselves as helpless because they have little or no organizational impact. This interpretation is consistent with what social psychologists have described as "learned helplessness." This condition is produced by having little personal control over important life events. The result of this lack of control is that individuals stop wanting and stop trying. This was true of our bystander managers. They have stopped influencing others and, more important, they no longer try to influence others in their organizations, either to obtain personal benefits or to achieve organizational objectives. Not surprisingly, as a group, they express the least satisfaction with their abilities to do their work effectively. Figure 2 summarizes the three types of managers.

IMPLICATIONS

Several implications both for individual managers and for organizations arise from this research. As we said at the beginning of this article, the exercise of influence is a fundamental activity of managers. All managers say they influence others as part of their work. Yet our findings show that the kinds of influence managers use varies systematically with their objectives, their control of resources or power, and their expectations about the willingness of others to comply. Although climate, or culture, was not examined in our research, it seems likely that the choice of influence strategies will also vary with this aspect of the organization. Even a cursory reading of the management literature shows that some organizational cultures encourage the use of friendliness and ingratiation, while others encourage reason, and still others rely on sanctions and assertiveness.

Thus managers are frequently unable to select the most appropriate influence strategy because they are constrained by their lack of power, their objectives, and the organizational climate. However, managers also choose the wrong strategies because of habit,

FIGURE 2
Types of Managers by Use of Influence.

Type of Manager	Manager's Behavioral Mode
Shotgun	High on all seven influence strategies. Unfulfilled on objectives. Inexperienced in job.
Tactician	High on the use of *reason* (average use of other strategies). Successful in achieving own objectives. High on organizational power. Satisfied.
Bystander	Low on all seven influence strategies. Low on organizational power. Seeking few organizational or personal objectives. Dissatisfied.

lack of forethought, or incorrect assessment of the target's willingness to comply. We are convinced that a manager's ability to choose the most appropriate influence strategy can be improved by training and self-examination. It is our experience that effective managers are flexible and are able to identify and use the most appropriate strategy in a given situation. The tactician profile best exemplifies this approach. Such managers use the whole spectrum of influence strategies to a moderate extent, but they rely most on reason, a strategy that appears to have the greatest utility in organizational life.

The question for managers to consider is how satisfied they are with the way influence is used in their organization. By influence, we mean not only strategies directed toward subordinates, but also those directed toward co-workers and superiors. In organizations whose culture does not encourage vigorous expression of ideas upward, managers may become apathetic and lapse into a bystander pattern. Such an organization may be easy to control; however, we suspect that pressure for innovation and change would also be at a minimum. In the past, such questions have been ignored when organizations were evaluated. Our research has shown that now issues involving the exercise of influence in organizations can be rigorously addressed. One implication is that managers can learn a variety of influence strategies rather than rely on the traditional strategy of exercising power as a function of position.

SELECTED BIBLIOGRAPHY

A widely cited approach for understanding power is that of John R. P. French, Jr. and Bertram Raven in their article, "The Bases of Social Power," in *Studies in Social Power* (University of Michigan Press, 1959). This influential article describes how people respond to influence attempts when they are based on such resources as the ability to reward or punish. Another view of power is provided in the book by David Kipnis, *The Powerholders* (University of Chicago Press, 1976). This book examines the ways in which people use power both in organizational settings and in their personal lives.

For the reader who would like to gain greater familiarity with the development of the Profile of Organizational Influence Strategies (POIS), this information is provided in an article coauthored by the present writers, "Intraorganizational Influence Tactics: Explorations in Getting One's Way" (*Journal of Applied Psychology,* Fall 1980). Copies of the POIS can be obtained from University Associates (8517 Production Avenue, P.O. Box 6240, San Diego, California 92126).

A thought-provoking and intensive analysis of the day-to-day activities of managers is given in Henry Mintzberg's book, *The Nature of Managerial Work* (Prentice-Hall, 1980). Here the reader is provided with rich descriptions of the activities of a small group of managers. In an earlier article entitled, "A Framework for the Comparative Analysis of Organizations" (*American Sociological Review,* Spring 1967), Charles Perrow analyzed the effect of technology on the exercise of influence within organizations. Perrow argues that power in an organization is, in part, derived from a manager's ability to solve important organizational problems. Technology aids the manager in this regard by helping to reduce uncertainty. Perrow's approach to understanding organizations stresses the ways in which technology guides the development of social relations.

ACKNOWLEDGEMENTS

We wish to thank Pat Insley for her invaluable technical assistance. We also wish to thank the Manufacturers' Association of Delaware Valley for their assistance in gathering data. This research was supported in part by a small grant from Temple University.

Power Failure in Management Circuits

Rosabeth Moss Kanter

Power is America's last dirty word. It is easier to talk about money—and much easier to talk about sex—than it is to talk about power. People who have it deny it; people who want it do not want to appear to hunger for it; and people who engage in its machinations do so secretly.

Yet, because it turns out to be a critical element in effective managerial behavior, power should come out from undercover. Having searched for years for those styles or skills that would identify capable organization leaders, many analysts, like myself, are rejecting individual traits or situational appropriateness as key and finding the sources of a leader's real power.

Access to resources and information and the ability to act quickly make it possible to accomplish more and to pass on more resources and information to subordinates. For this reason, people tend to prefer bosses with "clout." When employees perceive their manager as influential upward and outward, their status is enhanced by association and they generally have high morale and feel less critical or resistant to their boss.[1] More powerful leaders are also more likely to delegate (they are too busy to do it all themselves), to reward talent, and to build a team that places subordinates in significant positions.

Powerlessness, in contrast, tends to breed bossiness rather than true leadership. In large organizations, at least, it is powerlessness that often creates ineffective, desultory management and petty, dictatorial, rules-minded managerial styles. Accountability without power—responsibility for results without the resources to get them—creates frustration and failure. People who see themselves as weak and powerless and find their subordinates resisting or discounting them tend to use more punishing forms of influence. If organizational power can "ennoble," then, recent research shows, organizational powerlessness can (with apologies to Lord Acton) "corrupt."[2]

So perhaps power, in the organization at least, does not deserve such a bad reputation. Rather than connoting only dominance, control, and oppression, *power* can mean efficacy and capacity—something managers and executives need to move the organization toward its goals. Power in organizations is analogous in simple terms to physical power: it is the ability to mobilize resources (human and material) to get things done. The true sign of power, then, is accomplishment—not fear, terror, or tyranny. Where the power is "on," the system can be productive; where the power is "off," the system bogs down.

But saying that people need power to be effective in organizations does not tell us where it comes from or why some people, in some jobs, systematically seem to have more of it than others. In this article I want to show that to discover the sources of productive power, we have to look not at the *person*—as conventional classifications of effective managers and employees do—but at the *position* the person occupies in the organization.

WHERE DOES POWER COME FROM?

The effectiveness that power brings evolves from two kinds of capacities: first, access to the resources, information, and support necessary to carry out a task; and, second, ability to get cooperation in doing what is necessary. (*Exhibit I* identifies some symbols of an individual manager's power.)

Reprinted by permission of *Harvard Business Review,* "Power Failure in Management Circuits" by Rosabeth Moss Kanter, 57(4). Copyright © 1979 by the President and Fellows of Harvard College; all rights reserved.

1. Donald C. Pelz, "Influence: A Key to Effective Leadership in the First-Line Supervisor," *Personnel,* November 1952, p. 209.

2. See my book, *Men and Women of the Corporation* (New York: Basic Books, 1977), pp. 164–205; and David Kipnis, *The Powerholders* (Chicago: University of Chicago Press, 1976).

EXHIBIT I
Some Common Symbols of a Manager's Organizational Power
(Influence Upward and Outward).

To what extent a manager can—

Intercede favorably on behalf of someone in trouble with the organization

Get a desirable placement for a talented subordinate

Get approval for expenditures beyond the budget

Get above-average salary increases for subordinates

Get items on the agenda at policy meetings

Get fast access to top decision makers

Get regular, frequent access to top decision makers

Get early information about decisions and policy shifts.

Both capacities derive not so much from a leader's style and skill as from his or her location in the formal and informal systems of the organization—in both job definition and connection to other important people in the company. Even the ability to get cooperation from subordinates is strongly defined by the manager's clout outward. People are more responsive to bosses who look as if they can get more for them from the organization.

We can regard the uniquely organizational sources of power as consisting of three "lines":

1. *Lines of supply.* Influence outward, over the environment, means that managers have the capacity to bring in the things that their own organizational domain needs—materials, money, resources to distribute as rewards, and perhaps even prestige.

2. *Lines of information.* To be effective, managers need to be "in the know" in both the formal and the informal sense.

3. *Lines of support.* In a formal framework, a manager's job parameters need to allow for nonordinary action, for a show of discretion or exercise of judgment. Thus managers need to know that they can assume innovative, risk-taking activities without having to go through the stifling multi-layered approval process. And, informally, managers need the backing of other important figures in the organization whose tacit approval becomes another resource they bring to their own work unit as well as a sign of the manager's being "in."

Note that productive power has to do with *connections* with other parts of a system. Such systemic aspects of power derive from two sources—job activities and political alliances:

1. Power is most easily accumulated when one has a job that is designed and located to allow *discretion* (nonroutinized action permitting flexible, adaptive, and creative contributions), *recognition* (visibility and notice), and *relevance* (being central to pressing organizational problems).

2. Power also comes when one has relatively close contact with *sponsors* (higher-level people who confer approval, prestige, or backing), *peer networks* (circles of acquaintanceship that provide reputation and information, the grapevine often being faster than formal communication channels), and *subordinates* (who can be developed to relieve managers of some of their burdens and to represent the manager's point of view).

When managers are in powerful situations, it is easier for them to accomplish more. Because the tools are there, they are likely to be highly motivated and, in turn, to be able to motivate subordinates. Their activities are more likely to be on target and to net them successes. They can flexibly interpret or shape policy to meet the needs of particular areas, emergent situations, or sudden environmental shifts. They gain the respect and cooperation that attributed power brings. Subordinates' talents are resources rather than threats. And, because powerful managers have so many lines of connection and thus are oriented outward, they tend to let go of control downward, developing more independently functioning lieutenants.

The powerless live in a different world. Lacking the supplies, information, or support to make things happen easily, they may turn instead to the ultimate weapon of those who lack productive power—oppressive power: holding others back and punishing with whatever threats they can muster.

Exhibit II summarizes some of the major ways in which variables in the organization and in job design contribute to either power or powerlessness.

POSITIONS OF POWERLESSNESS

Understanding what it takes to have power and recognizing the classic behavior of the powerless can immediately help managers make sense out of a number of familiar organizational problems that are usually attributed to inadequate people:

❏ The ineffectiveness of first-line supervisors.

❏ The petty interest protection and conservatism of staff professionals.

❏ The crises of leadership at the top.

Instead of blaming the individuals involved in organizational problems, let us look at the positions people occupy. Of course, power or powerlessness in a position may not be all of the problem. Sometimes incapable people *are* at fault and need to be retrained or replaced. (See the copy on page 194 for a discussion of another special case, women.) But where patterns emerge, where the troubles associated with some units persist, organizational power failures could be the reason. Then, as Volvo President Pehr

EXHIBIT II

Ways Organizational Factors Contribute to Power or Powerlessness.

Factors	Generates Power When Factor Is	Generates Powerlessness When Factor Is
Rules inherent in the job	few	many
Predecessors in the job	few	many
Established routines	few	many
Task variety	high	low
Rewards for reliability/predictability	few	many
Rewards for unusual performance/innovation	many	few
Flexibility around use of people	high	low
Approvals needed for nonroutine decisions	few	many
Physical location	central	distant
Publicity about job activities	high	low
Relation of tasks to current problem areas	central	peripheral
Focus of tasks	outside work unit	inside work unit
Interpersonal contact in the job	high	low
Contact with senior officials	high	low
Participation in programs, conferences, meetings	high	low
Participation in problem-solving task forces	high	low
Advancement prospects of subordinates	high	low

Gyllenhammar concludes, we should treat the powerless not as "villains" causing headaches for everyone else but as "victims."[3]

First-Line Supervisors

Because an employee's most important work relationship is with his or her supervisor, when many of them talk about "the company," they mean their immediate boss. Thus a supervisor's behavior is an important determinant of the average employee's relationship to work and is in itself a critical link in the production chain.

Yet I know of no U.S. corporate management entirely satisfied with the performance of its supervisors. Most see them as supervising too closely and not training their people. In one manufacturing company where direct laborers were asked on a survey how they learned their job, on a list of seven possibilities "from my supervisor" ranked next to last. (Only company training programs ranked worse.) Also, it is said that supervisors do not translate company policies into practice—for instance, that they do not carry

out the right of every employee to frequent performance reviews or to career counseling.

In court cases charging race or sex discrimination, first-line supervisors are frequently cited as the "discriminating official."[4] And, in studies of innovative work redesign and quality of work life projects, they often appear as the implied villains; they are the ones who are said to undermine the program or interfere with its effectiveness. In short, they are often seen as "not sufficiently managerial."

The problem affects white-collar as well as blue-collar supervisors. In one large government agency, supervisors in field offices were seen as the source of problems concerning morale and the flow of information to and from headquarters. "Their attitudes are negative," said a senior official. "They turn people against the agency; they put down senior management. They build themselves up by always complaining about headquarters, but prevent their staff from getting any information directly. We can't afford to have such attitudes communicated to field staff."

3. Pehr G. Gyllenhammar, *People at Work* (Reading, Mass.: Addison-Wesley, 1977), p. 133.

4. William E. Fulmer, "Supervisory Selection: The Acid Test of Affirmative Action," *Personnel,* November-December 1976, p. 40.

Is the problem that supervisors need more management training programs or that incompetent people are invariably attracted to the job? Neither explanation suffices. A large part of the problem lies in the position itself—one that almost universally creates powerlessness.

First-line supervisors are "people in the middle," and that has been seen as the source of many of their problems.[5] But by recognizing that first-line supervisors are caught between higher management and workers, we only begin to skim the surface of the problem. There is practically no other organizational category as subject to powerlessness.

First, these supervisors may be at a virtual dead end in their careers. Even in companies where the job used to be a stepping stone to higher-level management jobs, it is now common practice to bring in MBAs from the outside for those positions. Thus moving from the ranks of direct labor into supervision may mean, essentially, getting "stuck" rather than moving upward. Because employees do not perceive supervisors as eventually joining the leadership circles of the organization, they may see them as lacking the high-level contacts needed to have clout. Indeed, sometimes turnover among supervisors is so high that workers feel they can outwait—and outwit—any boss.

Second, although they lack clout, with little in the way of support from above, supervisors are forced to administer programs or explain policies that they have no hand in shaping. In one company, as part of a new personnel program supervisors were required to conduct counseling interviews with employees. But supervisors were not trained to do this and were given no incentives to get involved. Counseling was just another obligation. Then managers suddenly encouraged the workers to bypass their supervisors or to put pressure on them. The personnel staff brought them together and told them to demand such interviews as a basic right. If supervisors had not felt powerless before, they did after that squeeze from below, engineered from above.

The people they supervise can also make life hard for them in numerous ways. This often happens when a supervisor has himself or herself risen up from the ranks. Peers that have not made it are resentful or derisive of their former colleague, whom they now see as trying to lord it over them. Often it is easy for workers to break rules and let a lot of things slip.

Yet first-line supervisors are frequently judged according to rules and regulations while being limited by other regulations in what disciplinary actions they can take. They often lack the resources to influence or reward people; after all, workers are guaranteed their pay and benefits by someone other than their supervisors. Supervisors cannot easily control events; rather, they must react to them.

In one factory, for instance, supervisors complained that performance of their job was out of their control: they could fill production quotas only if they had the supplies, but they had no way to influence the people controlling supplies.

The lack of support for many first-line managers, particularly in large organizations, was made dramatically clear in another company. When asked if contact with executives higher in the organization who had the potential for offering support, information, and alliances diminished their own feelings of career vulnerability and the number of headaches they experienced on the job, supervisors in five out of seven work units responded positively. For them *contact* was indeed related to a greater feeling of acceptance at work and membership in the organization.

But in the two other work units where there was greater contact, people perceived more, not less, career vulnerability. Further investigation showed that supervisors in these business units got attention only when they were in trouble. Otherwise, no one bothered to talk to them. To these particular supervisors, hearing from a higher-level manager was a sign not of recognition or potential support but of danger.

It is not surprising, then, that supervisors frequently manifest symptoms of powerlessness: overly close supervision, rules-mindedness, and a tendency to do the job themselves rather than to train their people (since job skills may be one of the few remaining things they feel good about). Perhaps this is why they sometimes stand as roadblocks between their subordinates and the higher reaches of the company.

Staff Professionals

Also working under conditions that can lead to organizational powerlessness are the staff specialists. As advisers behind the scenes, staff people must sell their programs and bargain for resources, but unless they get themselves entrenched in organizational power networks, they have little in the way of favors to exchange. They are seen as useful adjuncts to the primary tasks of the organization but inessential in a day-to-day operating sense. This disenfranchisement occurs particularly when staff jobs consist of easily routinized administrative functions which are out of the mainstream of the currently relevant areas and involve little innovative decision making.

Furthermore, in some organizations, unless they have had previous line experience, staff people tend to be limited in the number of jobs into which they can move. Specialists' ladders are often very short, and professionals are just as likely to get "stuck" in such jobs as people are in less prestigious clerical or factory positions.

Staff people, unlike those who are being groomed for important line positions, may be hired because of a special expertise or particular background. But management rarely pays any attention to developing them into more general organizational resources. Lacking growth prospects themselves and working alone or in very small teams, they are not in a position to develop others or pass on power to them. They miss out on an important way that power can be accumulated.

Sometimes staff specialists, such as house counsel or organization development people, find their work being farmed out to consultants. Management considers them fine for the routine work, but the minute the activities involve risk or something problematic, they bring in outside experts. This treatment says something not only about their expertise but also about the status of their function. Since the company can always hire talent on a temporary basis, it is unclear that the management really needs to have or considers important its own staff for these functions.

And, because staff professionals are often seen as adjuncts to primary tasks, their effectiveness and therefore their contribution

---

5. See my chapter (coauthor, Barry A. Stein), "Life in the Middle: Getting In, Getting Up, and Getting Along," in *Life in Organizations,* eds. Rosabeth M. Kanter and Barry A. Stein (New York: Basic Books, 1979).

to the organization are often hard to measure. Thus visibility and recognition, as well as risk taking and relevance, may be denied to people in staff jobs.

Staff people tend to act out their powerlessness by becoming turf-minded. They create islands within the organization. They set themselves up as the only ones who can control professional standards and judge their own work. They create sometimes false distinctions between themselves as experts (no one else could possibly do what they do) and lay people, and this continues to keep them out of the mainstream.

One form such distinctions take is a combination of disdain when line managers attempt to act in areas the professionals think are their preserve and of subtle refusal to support the managers' efforts. Or staff groups battle with each other for control of new "problem areas," with the result that no one really handles the issue at all. To cope with their essential powerlessness, staff groups may try to elevate their own status and draw boundaries between themselves and others.

When staff jobs are treated as final resting places for people who have reached their level of competence in the organization—a good shelf on which to dump managers who are too old to go anywhere but too young to retire—then staff groups can also become pockets of conservatism, resistant to change. Their own exclusion from the risk-taking action may make them resist *anyone's* innovative proposals. In the past, personnel departments, for example, have sometimes been the last in their organization to know about innovations in human resource development or to be interested in applying them.

Top Executives

Despite the great resources and responsibilities concentrated at the top of an organization, leaders can be powerless for reasons that are not very different from those that affect staff and supervisors: lack of supplies, information, and support.

We have faith in leaders because of their ability to make things happen in the larger world, to create possibilities for everyone else, and to attract resources to the organization. These are their supplies. But influence outward—the source of much credibility downward—can diminish as environments change, setting terms and conditions out of the control of the leaders. Regardless of top management's grand plans for the organization, the environment presses. At the very least, things going on outside the organization can deflect a leader's attention and drain energy. And, more detrimental, decisions made elsewhere can have severe consequences for the organization and affect top management's sense of power and thus its operating style inside.

In the go-go years of the mid-1960s, for example, nearly every corporation officer or university president could look—and therefore feel—successful. Visible success gave leaders a great deal of credibility inside the organization, which in turn gave them the power to put new things in motion.

In the past few years, the environment has been strikingly different and the capacity of many organization leaders to do anything about it has been severely limited. New "players" have flexed their power muscles: the Arab oil bloc, government regulators, and congressional investigating committees. And managing economic decline is quite different from managing growth. It is no accident that when top leaders personally feel out of control, the control function in corporations grows.

As powerlessness in lower levels of organizations can manifest itself in overly routinized jobs where performance measures are oriented to rules and absence of change, so it can at upper levels as well. Routine work often drives out nonroutine work. Accomplishment becomes a question of nailing down details. Short-term results provide immediate gratifications and satisfy stockholders or other constituencies with limited interests.

It takes a powerful leader to be willing to risk short-term deprivations in order to bring about desired long-term outcomes. Much as first-line supervisors are tempted to focus on daily adherence to rules, leaders are tempted to focus on short-term fluctuations and lose sight of long-term objectives. The dynamics of such a situation are self-reinforcing. The more the long-term goals go unattended, the more a leader feels powerless and the greater the scramble to prove that he or she is in control of daily events at least. The more he is involved in the organization as a short-term Mr. Fix-it, the more out of control of long-term objectives he is, and the more ultimately powerless he is likely to be.

Credibility for top executives often comes from doing the extraordinary: exercising discretion, creating, inventing, planning, and acting in nonroutine ways. But since routine problems look easier and more manageable, require less change and consent on the part of anyone else, and lend themselves to instant solutions that can make any leader look good temporarily, leaders may avoid the risky by taking over what their subordinates should be doing. Ultimately, a leader may succeed in getting all the trivial problems dumped on his or her desk. This can establish expectations even for leaders attempting more challenging tasks. When Warren Bennis was president of the University of Cincinnati, a professor called him when the heat was down in a classroom. In writing about this incident, Bennis commented, "I suppose he expected me to grab a wrench and fix it."[6]

People at the top need to insulate themselves from the routine operations of the organization in order to develop and exercise power. But this very insulation can lead to another source of powerlessness—lack of information. In one multinational corporation, top executives who are sealed off in a large, distant office, flattered and virtually babied by aides, are frustrated by their distance from the real action.[7]

At the top, the concern for secrecy and privacy is mixed with real loneliness. In one bank, organization members were so accustomed to never seeing the top leaders that when a new senior vice president went to the branch offices to look around, they had suspicion, even fear, about his intentions.

Thus leaders who are cut out of an organization's information networks understand neither what is really going on at lower levels nor that their own isolation may be having negative effects. All too often top executives design "beneficial" new employee programs or declare a new humanitarian policy (e.g., "Participatory management is now our style") only to find the policy ignored or mistrusted because it is perceived as coming from uncaring bosses.

The information gap has more serious consequences when executives are so insulated from the rest of the organization or from

---

6. Warren Bennis, *The Unconscious Conspiracy: Why Leaders Can't Lead* (New York: AMACOM, 1976).

7. See my chapter, "How the Top Is Different," in *Life in Organizations*.

other decision makers that, as Nixon so dramatically did, they fail to see their own impending downfall. Such insulation is partly a matter of organizational position and, in some cases, of executive style.

For example, leaders may create closed inner circles consisting of "doppelgängers," people just like themselves, who are their principal sources of organizational information and tell them only what they want to know. The reasons for the distortions are varied: key aides want to relieve the leader of burdens, they think just like the leader, they want to protect their own positions of power, or the familiar "kill the messenger" syndrome makes people close to top executives reluctant to be the bearers of bad news.

Finally, just as supervisors and lower-level managers need their supporters in order to be and feel powerful, so do top executives. But for them sponsorship may not be so much a matter of individual endorsement as an issue of support by larger sources of legitimacy in the society. For top executives the problem is not to fit in among peers; rather, the question is whether the public at large and other organization members perceive a common interest which they see the executives as promoting.

If, however, public sources of support are withdrawn and leaders are open to public attack or if inside constituencies fragment and employees see their interests better aligned with pressure groups than with organizational leadership, then powerlessness begins to set in.

When common purpose is lost, the system's own politics may reduce the capacity of those at the top to act. Just as managing decline seems to create a much more passive and reactive stance than managing growth, so does mediating among conflicting interests. When what is happening outside and inside their organizations is out of their control, many of the people at the top turn into decline managers and dispute mediators. Neither is a particularly empowering role.

Thus when top executives lose their own lines of supply, lines of information, and lines of support, they too suffer from a kind of powerlessness. The temptation for them then is to pull in every shred of power they can and to decrease the power available to other people to act. Innovation loses out in favor of control. Limits rather than targets are set. Financial goals are met by reducing "overhead" (people) rather than by giving people the tools and discretion to increase their own productive capacity. Dictatorial statements come down from the top, spreading the mentality of powerlessness farther until the whole organization becomes sluggish and people concentrate on protecting what they have rather than on producing what they can.

When everyone is playing "king of the mountain," guarding his or her turf jealously, then king of the mountain becomes the only game in town.

TO EXPAND POWER, SHARE IT

In no case am I saying that people in the three hierarchical levels described are always powerless, but they are susceptible to common conditions that can contribute to powerlessness. *Exhibit III* summarizes the most common symptoms of powerlessness for each level and some typical sources of that behavior.

I am also distinguishing the tremendous concentration of economic and political power in large corporations themselves from the powerlessness that can beset individuals even in the highest positions in such organizations. What grows with organizational position in hierarchical levels is not necessarily the power to accomplish—productive power—but the power to punish, to prevent, to

EXHIBIT III

Common Symptoms and Sources of Powerlessness for Three Key Organizational Positions.

Position	Symptoms	Sources
First-line supervisors	Close, rules-minded supervision	Routine, rules-minded jobs with little control over lines of supply
	Tendency to do things oneself, blocking of subordinates' development and information	Limited lines of information
	Resistant, underproducing subordinates	Limited advancement or involvement prospects for oneself/subordinates
Staff professionals	Turf protection, information control	Routine tasks seen as peripheral to "real tasks" of line organization
	Retreat into professionalism	Blocked careers
	Conservative resistance to change	Easy replacement by outside experts
Top executives	Focus on internal cutting, short-term results, "punishing"	Uncontrollable lines of supply because of environmental changes
	Dictatorial top-down communications	Limited or blocked lines of information about lower levels of organization
	Retreat to comfort of like-minded lieutenants	Diminished lines of support because of challenges to legitimacy (e.g., from the public or special interest groups)

sell off, to reduce, to fire, all without appropriate concern for consequences. It is that kind of power—oppressive power—that we often say corrupts.

The absence of ways to prevent individual and social harm causes the polity to feel it must surround people in power with constraints, regulations, and laws that limit the arbitrary use of their authority. But if oppressive power corrupts, then so does the absence of productive power. In large organizations, powerlessness can be a bigger problem than power.

David C. McClelland makes a similar distinction between oppressive and productive power:

"The negative . . . face of power is characterized by the dominance-submission mode: if I win, you lose. . . . It leads to simple and direct means of feeling powerful [such as being aggressive]. It does not often lead to effective social leadership for the reason that such a person tends to treat other people as pawns. People who feel they are pawns tend to be passive and useless to the leader who gets his satisfaction from dominating them. Slaves are the most inefficient form of labor ever devised by man. If a leader wants to have far-reaching influence, he must make his followers feel powerful and able to accomplish things on their own. . . . Even the most dictatorial leader does not succeed if he has not instilled in at least some of his followers a sense of power and the strength to pursue the goals he has set."[8]

Organizational power can grow, in part, by being shared. We do not yet know enough about new organizational forms to say whether productive power is infinitely expandable or where we reach the point of diminishing returns. But we do know that sharing power is different from giving or throwing it away. Delegation does not mean abdication.

Some basic lessons could be translated from the field of economics to the realm of organizations and management. Capital investment in plants and equipment is not the only key to productivity. The productive capacity of nations, like organizations, grows if the skill base is upgraded. People with the tools, information, and support to make more informed decisions and act more quickly can often accomplish more. By empowering others, a leader does not decrease his power; instead he may increase it—especially if the whole organization performs better.

This analysis leads to some counterintuitive conclusions. In a certain tautological sense, the principal problem of the powerless is that they lack power. Powerless people are usually the last ones to whom anyone wants to entrust more power, for fear of its dissipation or abuse. But those people are precisely the ones who might benefit most from an injection of power and whose behavior is likely to change as new options open up to them.

Also, if the powerless bosses could be encouraged to share some of the power they do have, their power would grow. Yet, of course, only those leaders who feel secure about their own power outward—their lines of supply, information, and support—can see empowering subordinates as a gain rather than a loss. The two sides of power (getting it and giving it) are closely connected.

There are important lessons here for both subordinates and those who want to change organizations, whether executives or change agents. Instead of resisting or criticizing a powerless boss,

which only increases the boss's feeling of powerlessness and need to control, subordinates instead might concentrate on helping the boss become more powerful. Managers might make pockets of ineffectiveness in the organization more productive not by training or replacing individuals but by structural solutions such as opening supply and support lines.

Similarly, organizational change agents who want a new program or policy to succeed should make sure that the change itself does not render any other level of the organization powerless. In making changes, it is wise to make sure that the key people in the level or two directly above and in neighboring functions are sufficiently involved, informed, and taken into account, so that the program can be used to build their own sense of power also. If such involvement is impossible, then it is better to move these people out of the territory altogether than to leave behind a group from whom some power has been removed and who might resist and undercut the program.

In part, of course, spreading power means educating people to this new definition of it. But words alone will not make the difference; managers will need the real experience of a new way of managing.

Here is how the associate director of a large corporate professional department phrased the lessons that he learned in the transition to a team-oriented, participatory, power-sharing management process:

"Get in the habit of involving your own managers in decision making and approvals. But don't abdicate! Tell them what you want and where you're coming from. Don't go for a one-boss grass roots 'democracy.' Make the management hierarchy work for you in participation. . . .

"Hang in there, baby, and don't give up. Try not to 'revert' just because everything seems to go sour on a particular day. Open up—talk to people and tell them how you feel. They'll want to get you back on track and will do things to make that happen—because they don't really want to go back to the way it was. . . . Subordinates will push you to 'act more like a boss,' but their interest is usually more in seeing someone else brought to heel than getting bossed themselves."

Naturally, people need to have power before they can learn to share it. Exhorting managers to change their leadership styles is rarely useful by itself. In one large plant of a major electronics company, first-line production supervisors were the source of numerous complaints from managers who saw them as major roadblocks to overall plant productivity and as insufficiently skilled supervisors. So the plant personnel staff undertook two pilot programs to increase the supervisors' effectiveness. The first program was based on a traditional competency and training model aimed at teaching the specific skills of successful supervisors. The second program, in contrast, was designed to empower the supervisors by directly affecting their flexibility, access to resources, connections with higher-level officials, and control over working conditions.

After an initial gathering of data from supervisors and their subordinates, the personnel staff held meetings where all the supervisors were given tools for developing action plans for sharing the data with their people and collaborating on solutions to perceived problems. But then, in a departure from common practice in this organization, task forces of supervisors were formed to develop new systems for handling job and career issues common to them and their people. These task forces were given budgets, consultants, representation on a plantwide project steering committee alongside managers at much higher levels, and wide latitude in defining the

8. David C. McClelland, *Power: The Inner Experience* (New York: Irvington Publishers, 1975), p. 263. Quoted by permission.

nature and scope of the changes they wished to make. In short, lines of supply, information, and support were opened to them.

As the task forces progressed in their activities, it became clear to the plant management that the hoped-for changes in supervisory effectiveness were taking place much more rapidly through these structural changes in power than through conventional management training; so the conventional training was dropped. Not only did the pilot groups design useful new procedures for the plant, astonishing senior management in several cases with their knowledge and capabilities, but also, significantly, they learned to manage their own people better.

Several groups decided to involve shop-floor workers in their task forces; they could now see from their own experience the benefits of involving subordinates in solving job-related problems. Other supervisors began to experiment with ways to implement "participatory management" by giving subordinates more control and influence without relinquishing their own authority.

Soon the "problem supervisors" in the "most troubled plant in the company" were getting the highest possible performance ratings and were considered models for direct production management. The sharing of organizational power from the top made possible the productive use of power below.

One might wonder why more organizations do not adopt such empowering strategies. There are standard answers: that giving up control is threatening to people who have fought for every shred of it; that people do not want to share power with those they look down on; that managers fear losing their own place and special privileges in the system; that "predictability" often rates higher than "flexibility" as an organizational value; and so forth.

But I would also put skepticism about employee abilities high on the list. Many modern bureaucratic systems are designed to minimize dependence on individual intelligence by making routine as many decisions as possible. So it often comes as a genuine surprise to top executives that people doing the more routine jobs could, indeed, make sophisticated decisions or use resources entrusted to them in intelligent ways.

In the same electronics company just mentioned, at the end of a quarter the pilot supervisory task forces were asked to report results and plans to senior management in order to have their new budget requests approved. The task forces made sure they were well prepared, and the high-level executives were duly impressed. In fact, they were so impressed that they kept interrupting the presentations with compliments, remarking that the supervisors could easily be doing sophisticated personnel work.

At first the supervisors were flattered. Such praise from upper management could only be taken well. But when the first glow wore off, several of them became very angry. They saw the excessive praise as patronizing and insulting. "Didn't they think we could think? Didn't they imagine we were capable of doing this kind of work?" one asked. "They must have seen us as just a bunch of animals. No wonder they gave us such limited jobs."

As far as these supervisors were concerned, their abilities had always been there, in latent form perhaps, but still there. They as individuals had not changed—just their organizational power.

Women Managers Experience Special Power Failures

The traditional problems of women in management are illustrative of how formal and informal practices can combine to engender powerlessness. Historically, women in management have found their opportunities in more routine, low-profile jobs. In staff positions, where they serve in support capacities to line managers but have no line responsibilities of their own, or in supervisory jobs managing "stuck" subordinates, they are not in a position either to take the kinds of risks that build credibility or to develop their own team by pushing bright subordinates.

Such jobs, which have few favors to trade, tend to keep women out of the mainstream of the organization. This lack of clout, coupled with the greater difficulty anyone who is "different" has in getting into the information and support networks, has meant that merely by organizational situation women in management have been more likely than men to be rendered structurally powerless. This is one reason those women who have achieved power have often had family connections that put them in the mainstream of the organization's social circles.

A disproportionate number of women managers are found among first-line supervisors or staff professionals; and they, like men in those circumstances, are likely to be organizationally powerless. But the behavior of other managers can contribute to the powerlessness of women in management in a number of less obvious ways.

One way other managers can make a woman powerless is by patronizingly overprotecting her: putting her in "a safe job," not giving her enough to do to prove herself, and not suggesting her for high-risk, visible assignments. This protectiveness is sometimes born of "good" intentions to give her every chance to succeed (why stack the deck against her?). Out of managerial concerns, out of awareness that a woman may be up against situations that men simply do not have to face, some very well-meaning managers protect their female managers ("It's a jungle, so why send her into it?").

Overprotectiveness can also mask a manager's fear of association with a woman should she fail. One senior bank official at a level below vice president told me about his concerns with respect to a high-performing, financially experienced woman reporting to him. Despite *his* overwhelmingly positive work experiences with her, he was still afraid to recommend her for other assignments because he felt it was a personal risk. "What if other managers are not as accepting of women as I am?" he asked. "I know I'd be sticking my neck out; they would take her more because of my endorsement than her qualifications. And what if she doesn't make it? My judgment will be on the line."

Overprotection is relatively benign compared with rendering a person powerless by providing obvious signs of lack of managerial support. For example, allowing someone supposedly in authority to be bypassed easily means that no one else has to take him or her seriously. If a woman's immediate supervisor or other managers listen willingly to criticism of her and show they are concerned every time a negative comment comes up and that they assume she must be at fault, then they are helping to undercut her. If managers let other people know that they have concerns about this person or that they are testing her to see how she does, then they are inviting other people to look for signs of inadequacy or failure.

Furthermore, people assume they can afford to bypass women because they "must be uninformed" or "don't know the ropes." Even though women may be respected for their competence or expertise, they are not necessarily seen as being informed beyond the technical requirements of the job. There may be a grain of historical truth in this. Many women come to senior management positions as "outsiders" rather than up through the usual channels.

Also, because until very recently men have not felt comfortable seeing women as businesspeople (business clubs have traditionally excluded women), they have tended to seek each other out for informal socializing. Anyone, male or female, seen as organizationally naive and lacking sources of "inside dope" will find his or her own lines of information limited.

Finally, even when women are able to achieve some power on their own, they have not necessarily been able to translate such personal credibility into an organizational power base. To create a network of supporters out of individual clout requires that a person pass on and share power, that subordinates and peers be empowered by virtue of their connection with that person. Traditionally, neither men nor women have seen women as capable of sponsoring others, even though they may be capable of achieving and succeeding on their own. Women have been viewed as the *recipients* of sponsorship rather than as the sponsors themselves.

(As more women prove themselves in organizations and think more self-consciously about bringing along young people, this situation may change. However, I still hear many more questions from women managers about how they can benefit from mentors, sponsors, or peer networks than about how they themselves can start to pass on favors and make use of their own resources to benefit others.)

Viewing managers in terms of power and powerlessness helps explain two familiar stereotypes about women and leadership in organizations: that no one wants a woman boss (although studies show that anyone who has ever had a woman boss is likely to have had a positive experience), and that the reason no one wants a woman boss is that women are "too controlling, rules-minded, and petty."

The first stereotype simply makes clear that power is important to leadership. Underneath the preference for men is the assumption that, given the current distribution of people in organizational leadership positions, men are more likely than women to be in positions to achieve power and, therefore, to share their power with others. Similarly, the "bossy woman boss" stereotype is a perfect picture of powerlessness. All of those traits are just as characteristic of men who are powerless, but women are slightly more likely, because of circumstances I have mentioned, to find themselves powerless than are men. Women with power in the organization are just as effective—and preferred—as men.

Recent interviews conducted with about 600 bank managers show that, when a woman exhibits the petty traits of powerlessness, people assume that she does so "because she is a woman." A striking difference is that, when a man engages in the same behavior, people assume the behavior is a matter of his own individual style and characteristics and do not conclude that it reflects on the suitability of men for management.

Who Gets Power and How They Hold Onto It:
A Strategic Contingency Model of Power

Gerald R. Salancik

Jeffrey Pfeffer

Power is held by many people to be a dirty word or, as Warren Bennis has said, "It is the organization's last dirty secret."

This article will argue that traditional "political" power, far from being a dirty business, is, in its most naked form, one of the few mechanisms available for aligning an organization with its own reality. However, institutionalized forms of power—what we prefer to call the cleaner forms of power: authority, legitimization, centralized control, regulations, and the more modern "management information systems"—tend to buffer the organization from reality and obscure the demands of its environment. Most great states and institutions declined, not because they played politics, but because they failed to accommodate to the political realities they faced.

Reprinted, by permission of the publishers, from *Organizational Dynamics,* Winter 1977. Copyright © 1977, American Management Association, New York. All rights reserved.

Political processes, rather than being mechanisms for unfair and unjust allocations and appointments, tend toward the realistic resolution of conflicts among interests. And power, while it eludes definition, is easy enough to recognize by its consequences—the ability of those who possess power to bring about the outcomes they desire.

The model of power we advance is an elaboration of what has been called strategic-contingency theory, a view that sees power as something that accrues to organizational subunits (individuals, departments) that cope with critical organizational problems. Power is used by subunits, indeed, used by all who have it, to enhance their own survival through control of scarce critical resources, through the placement of allies in key positions, and through the definition of organizational problems and policies. Because of the processes by which power develops and is used, organizations become both more aligned and more misaligned with their environments. This contradiction is the most interesting aspect of organizational power, and one that makes administration one of the most precarious of occupations.

WHAT IS ORGANIZATIONAL POWER?

You can walk into most organizations and ask without fear of being misunderstood, "Which are the powerful groups or people in this organization?" Although many organizational informants may be *unwilling* to tell you, it is unlikely they will be *unable* to tell you. Most people do not require explicit definitions to know what power is.

Power is simply the ability to get things done the way one wants them to be done. For a manager who wants an increased budget to launch a project that he thinks is important, his power is measured by his ability to get that budget. For an executive vice-president who wants to be chairman, his power is evidenced by his advancement toward his goal.

People in organizations not only know what you are talking about when you ask who is influential but they are likely to agree with one another to an amazing extent. Recently, we had a chance to observe this in a regional office of an insurance company. The office had 21 department managers; we asked ten of these managers to rank all 21 according to the influence each one had in the organization. Despite the fact that ranking 21 things is a difficult task, the managers sat down and began arranging the names of their colleagues and themselves in a column. Only one person bothered to ask, "What do you mean by influence?" When told "power," he responded, "Oh," and went on. We compared the rankings of all ten managers and found virtually no disagreement among them in the managers ranked among the top five or the bottom five. Differences in the rankings came from department heads claiming more influence for themselves than their colleagues attributed to them.

Such agreement on those who have influence, and those who do not, was not unique to this insurance company. So far we have studied over 20 very different organizations—universities, research firms, factories, banks, retailers, to name a few. In each one we found individuals able to rate themselves and their peers on a scale of influence or power. We have done this both for specific decisions and for general impact on organizational policies. Their agreement was unusually high, which suggests that distributions of influence exist well enough in everyone's mind to be referred to with ease—and we assume with accuracy.

WHERE DOES ORGANIZATIONAL POWER COME FROM?

Earlier we stated that power helps organizations become aligned with their realities. This hopeful prospect follows from what we have dubbed the strategic-contingencies theory of organizational power. Briefly, those subunits most able to cope with the organization's critical problems and uncertainties acquire power. In its simplest form, the strategic-contingencies theory implies that when an organization faces a number of lawsuits that threaten its existence, the legal department will gain power and influence over organizational decisions. Somehow other organizational interest groups will recognize its critical importance and confer upon it a status and power never before enjoyed. This influence may extend beyond handling legal matters and into decisions about product design, advertising production, and so on. Such extensions undoubtedly would be accompanied by appropriate, or acceptable, verbal justifications. In time, the head of the legal department may become the head of the corporation, just as in times past the vice-president for marketing had become the president when market shares were

a worrisome problem and, before him, the chief engineer, who had made the production line run as smooth as silk.

Stated in this way, the strategic-contingencies theory of power paints an appealing picture of power. To the extent that power is determined by the critical uncertainties and problems facing the organization and, in turn, influences decisions in the organization, the organization is aligned with the realities it faces. In short, power facilitates the organization's adaptation to its environment—or its problems.

We can cite many illustrations of how influence derives from a subunit's ability to deal with critical contingencies. Michael Crozier described a French cigarette factory in which the maintenance engineers had a considerable say in the plantwide operation. After some probing he discovered that the group possessed the solution to one of the major problems faced by the company, that of trouble-shooting the elaborate, expensive, and irascible automated machines that kept breaking down and dumbfounding everyone else. It was the one problem that the plant manager could in no way control.

The production workers, while troublesome from time to time, created no insurmountable problems; the manager could reasonably predict their absenteeism or replace them when necessary. Production scheduling was something he could deal with since, by watching inventories and sales, the demand for cigarettes was known long in advance. Changes in demand could be accommodated by slowing down or speeding up the line. Supplies of tobacco and paper were also easily dealt with through stockpiles and advance orders.

The one thing that management could neither control nor accommodate to, however, was the seemingly happenstance breakdowns. And the foremen couldn't instruct the workers what to do when emergencies developed since the maintenance department kept its records of problems and solutions locked up in a cabinet or in its members' heads. The breakdowns were, in truth, a critical source of uncertainty for the organization, and the maintenance engineers were the only ones who could cope with the problem.

The engineers' strategic role in coping with breakdowns afforded them a considerable say on plant decisions. Schedules and production quotas were set in consultation with them. And the plant manager, while formally their boss, accepted their decisions about personnel in their operation. His submission was to his credit, for without their cooperation he would have had an even more difficult time in running the plant.

Ignoring Critical Consequences

In this cigarette factory, sharing influence with the maintenance workers reflected the plant manager's awareness of the critical contingencies. However, when organizational members are not aware of the critical contingencies they face, and do not share influence accordingly, the failure to do so can create havoc. In one case, an insurance company's regional office was having problems with the performance of one of its departments, the coding department. From the outside, the department looked like a disaster area. The clerks who worked in it were somewhat dissatisfied; their supervisor paid little attention to them, and they resented the hard work. Several other departments were critical of this manager, claiming that she was inconsistent in meeting deadlines. The person most critical was the claims manager. He resented having to wait for work that was handled by her department, claiming that it held up his claims adjusters. Having heard the rumors about dissatisfaction among her subordinates, he attributed the situation to poor supervision. He was second in command in the office and therefore took up the issue with her immediate boss, the head of administrative services. They consulted with the personnel manager and the three of them concluded that the manager needed leadership training to improve her relations with her subordinates. The coding manager objected, saying it was a waste of time, but agreed to go along with the training and also agreed to give more priority to the claims department's work. Within a week after the training, the results showed that her workers were happier but that the performance of her department had decreased, save for the people serving the claims department.

About this time, we began, quite independently, a study of influence in this organization. We asked the administrative services director to draw up flow charts of how the work of one department moved on to the next department. In the course of the interview, we noticed that the coding department began or interceded in the work flow of most of the other departments and casually mentioned to him, "The coding manager must be very influential." He said "No, not really. Why would you think so?" Before we could reply he recounted the story of her leadership training and the fact that things were worse. We then told him that it seemed obvious that the coding department would be influential from the fact that all the other departments depended on it. It was also clear why productivity had fallen. The coding manager took the training seriously and began spending more time raising her workers' spirits than she did worrying about the problems of all the departments that depended on her. Giving priority to the claims area only exaggerated the problem, for their work was getting done at the expense of the work of the other departments. Eventually the company hired a few more clerks to relieve the pressure in the coding department and performance returned to a more satisfactory level.

Originally we got involved with this insurance company to examine how the influence of each manager evolved from his or her department's handling of critical organizational contingencies. We reasoned that one of the most important contingencies faced by all profit-making organizations was that of generating income. Thus we expected managers would be influential to the extent to which they contributed to this function. Such was the case. The underwriting managers, who wrote the policies that committed the premiums, were the most influential; the claims managers, who kept a lid on the funds flowing out, were a close second. Least influential were the managers of functions unrelated to revenue, such as mailroom and payroll managers. And contrary to what the administrative services managers believed, the third most powerful department head (out of 21) was the woman in charge of the coding function, which consisted of rating, recording, and keeping track of the codes of all policy applications and contracts. Her peers attributed more influence to her than could have been inferred from her place on the organization chart. And it was not surprising, since they all depended on her department. The coding department's records, their accuracy and the speed with which they could be retrieved, affected virtually every other operating department in the insurance office. The underwriters depended on them in getting the contracts straight; the typing department depended on them in preparing the formal contract document; the claims department depended on them in adjusting claims; and accounting depended on them for billing. Unfortunately, the "bosses" were not aware of these dependencies, for unlike the cigarette factory, there were no massive breakdowns that made them obvious, while the coding manager,

who was a hard-working but quiet person, did little to announce her importance.

The cases of this plant and office illustrate nicely a basic point about the source of power in organizations. The basis for power in an organization derives from the ability of a person or subunit to take or not take actions that are desired by others. The coding manager was seen as influential by those who depended on her department, but not by the people at the top. The engineers were influential because of their role in keeping the plant operating. The two cases differ in these respects: The coding supervisor's source of power was not as widely recognized as that of the maintenance engineers, and she did not use her source of power to influence decisions; the maintenance engineers did. Whether power is used to influence anything is a separate issue. We should not confuse this issue with the fact that power derives from a social situation in which one person has a capacity to do something and another person does not, but wants it done.

POWER SHARING IN ORGANIZATIONS

Power is shared in organizations; and it is shared out of necessity more than out of concern for principles of organizational development or participatory democracy. Power is shared because no one person controls all the desired activities in the organization. While the factory owner may hire people to operate his noisy machines, once hired they have some control over the use of the machinery. And thus they have power over him in the same way he has power over them. Who has more power over whom is a mooter point than that of recognizing the inherent nature of organizing as a sharing of power.

Let's expand on the concept that power derives from the activities desired in an organization. A major way of managing influence in organizations is through the designation of activities. In a bank we studied, we saw this principle in action. This bank was planning to install a computer system for routine credit evaluation. The bank, rather progressive-minded, was concerned that the change would have adverse effects on employees and therefore surveyed their attitudes.

The principal opposition to the new system came, interestingly, not from the employees who performed the routine credit checks, some of whom would be relocated because of the change, but from the manager of the credit department. His reason was quite simple. The manager's primary function was to give official approval to the applications, catch any employee mistakes before giving approval, and arbitrate any difficulties the clerks had in deciding what to do. As a consequence of his role, others in the organization, including his superiors, subordinates, and colleagues, attributed considerable importance to him. He, in turn, for example, could point to the low proportion of credit approvals, compared with other financial institutions, that resulted in bad debts. Now, to his mind, a wretched machine threatened to transfer his role to a computer programmer, a man who knew nothing of finance and who, in addition, had ten years less seniority. The credit manager eventually quit for a position at a smaller firm with lower pay, but one in which he would have more influence than his redefined job would have left him with.

Because power derives from activities rather than individuals, an individual's or subgroup's power is never absolute and derives ultimately from the context of the situation. The amount of power an individual has at any one time depends, not only on the activities he or she controls, but also on the existence of other persons or means by which the activities can be achieved and on those who determine what ends are desired and, hence, on what activities are desired and critical for the organization. One's own power always depends on other people for these two reasons. Other people, or groups or organizations, can determine the definition of what is a critical contingency for the organization and can also undercut the uniqueness of the individual's personal contribution to the critical contingencies of the organization.

Perhaps one can best appreciate how situationally dependent power is by examining how it is distributed. In most societies, power organizes around scarce and critical resources. Rarely does power organize around abundant resources. In the United States, a person doesn't become powerful because he or she can drive a car. There are simply too many others who can drive with equal facility. In certain villages in Mexico, on the other hand, a person with a car is accredited with enormous social status and plays a key role in the community. In addition to scarcity, power is also limited by the need for one's capacity in a social system. While a racer's ability to drive a car around a 90° turn at 80 mph may be sparsely distributed in a society, it is not likely to lend the driver much power in the society. The ability simply does not play a central role in the activities of the society.

The fact that power revolves around scarce and critical activities, of course, makes the control and organization of those activities a major battleground in struggles for power. Even relatively abundant or trivial resources can become the bases for power if one can organize and control their allocation and the definition of what is critical. Many occupational and professional groups attempt to do just this in modern economies. Lawyers organize themselves into associations, regulate the entrance requirements for novitiates, and then get laws passed specifying situations that require the services of an attorney. Workers had little power in the conduct of industrial affairs until they organized themselves into closed and controlled systems. In recent years, women and blacks have tried to define themselves as important and critical to the social system, using law to reify their status.

In organizations there are obviously opportunities for defining certain activities as more critical than others. Indeed, the growth of managerial thinking to include defining organizational objectives and goals has done much to foster these opportunities. One sure way to liquidate the power of groups in the organization is to define the need for their services out of existence. David Halberstam presents a description of how just such a thing happened to the group of correspondents that evolved around Edward R. Murrow, the brilliant journalist, interviewer, and war correspondent of CBS News. A close friend of CBS chairman and controlling stockholder William S. Paley, Murrow, and the news department he directed, were endowed with freedom to do what they felt was right. He used it to create some of the best documentaries and commentaries ever seen on television. Unfortunately, television became too large, too powerful, and too suspect in the eyes of the federal government that licensed it. It thus became, or at least the top executives believed it had become, too dangerous to have in-depth, probing commentary on the news. Crisp, dry, uneditorializing headliners were considered safer. Murrow was out and Walter Cronkite was in.

The power to define what is critical in an organization is no small power. Moreover, it is the key to understanding why organizations are either aligned with their environments or misaligned. If an organization defines certain activities as critical when in fact they are not critical, given the flow of resources coming into the organization, it is not likely to survive, at least in its present form.

Most organizations manage to evolve a distribution of power and influence that is aligned with the critical realities they face in the environment. The environment, in turn, includes both the internal environment, the shifting situational contexts in which particular decisions get made, and the external environment that it can hope to influence but is unlikely to control.

THE CRITICAL CONTINGENCIES

The critical contingencies facing most organizations derive from the environmental context within which they operate. This determines the available needed resources and thus determines the problems to be dealt with. That power organizes around handling these problems suggests an important mechanism by which organizations keep in tune with their external environments. The strategic-contingencies model implies that subunits that contribute to the critical resources of the organization will gain influence in the organization. Their influence presumably is then used to bend the organization's activities to the contingencies that determine its resources. This idea may strike one as obvious. But its obviousness in no way diminishes its importance. Indeed, despite its obviousness, it escapes the notice of many organizational analysts and managers, who all too frequently think of the organization in terms of a descending pyramid, in which all the departments in one tier hold equal power and status. This presumption denies the reality that departments differ in the contributions they are believed to make to the overall organization's resources, as well as to the fact that some are more equal than others.

Because of the importance of this idea to organizational effectiveness, we decided to examine it carefully in a large midwestern university. A university offers an excellent site for studying power. It is composed of departments with nominally equal power and is administered by a central executive structure much like other bureaucracies. However, at the same time it is a situation in which the departments have clearly defined identities and face diverse external environments. Each department has its own bodies of knowledge, its own institutions, its own sources of prestige and resources. Because the departments operate in different external environments, they are likely to contribute differentially to the resources of the overall organization. Thus a physics department with close ties to NASA may contribute substantially to the funds of the university; and a history department with a renowned historian in residence may contribute to the intellectual credibility or prestige of the whole university. Such variations permit one to examine how these various contributions lead to obtaining power within the university.

We analyzed the influence of 29 university departments throughout an 18-month period in their history. Our chief interest was to determine whether departments that brought more critical resources to the university would be more powerful than departments that contributed fewer or less critical resources.

To identify the critical resources each department contributed, the heads of all departments were interviewed about the importance of seven different resources to the university's success. The seven included undergraduate students (the factor determining size of the state allocations by the university), national prestige, administrative expertise, and so on. The most critical resource was found to be contract and grant monies received by a department's faculty for research or consulting services. At this university, contract and grants contributed somewhat less than 50 percent of the overall budget, with the remainder primarily coming from state appropriations. The importance attributed to contract and grant monies, and the rather minor importance of undergraduate students, was not surprising for this particular university. The university was a major center for graduate education; many of its departments ranked in the top ten of their respective fields. Grant and contract monies were the primary source of discretionary funding available for maintaining these programs of graduate education, and hence for maintaining the university's prestige. The prestige of the university itself was critical both in recruiting able students and attracting top-notch faculty.

From university records it was determined what relative contributions each of the 29 departments made to the various needs of the university (national prestige, outside grants, teaching). Thus, for instance, one department may have contributed to the university by teaching 7 percent of the instructional units, bringing in 2 percent of the outside contracts and grants, and having a national ranking of 20. Another department, on the other hand, may have taught 1 percent of the instructional units, contributed 12 percent to the grants, and be ranked the third best department in its field within the country.

The question was: Do these different contributions determine the relative power of the departments within the university? Power was measured in several ways; but regardless of how measured, the answer was "Yes." Those three resources together accounted for about 70 percent of the variance in subunit power in the university.

But the most important predictor of departmental power was the department's contribution to the contracts and grants of the university. Sixty percent of the variance in power was due to this one factor, suggesting that the power of departments derived primarily from the dollars they provided for graduate education, the activity believed to be the most important for the organization.

THE IMPACT OF ORGANIZATIONAL POWER ON DECISION MAKING

The measure of power we used in studying this university was an analysis of the responses of the department heads we interviewed. While such perceptions of power might be of interest in their own right, they contribute little to our understanding of how the distribution of power might serve to align an organization with its critical realities. For this we must look at how power actually influences the decisions and policies of organizations.

While it is perhaps not absolutely valid, we can generally gauge the relative importance of a department of an organization by the size of the budget allocated to it relative to other departments. Clearly it is of importance to the administrators of those departments whether they get squeezed in a budget crunch or are given more funds to strike out after new opportunities. And it should also be clear that when those decisions are made and one department can go ahead and try new approaches while another must cut back on the old, then the deployment of the resources of the organization in meeting its problems is most directly affected.

Thus our study of the university led us to ask the following question: Does power lead to influence in the organization? To answer this question, we found it useful first to ask another one, namely: Why should department heads try to influence organizational decisions to favor their own departments to the exclusion of other departments? While this second question may seem a bit

naive to anyone who has witnessed the political realities of organizations, we posed it in a context of research on organizations that sees power as an illegitimate threat to the neater rational authority of modern bureaucracies. In this context, decisions are not believed to be made because of the dirty business of politics but because of the overall goals and purposes of the organization. In a university, one reasonable basis for decision making is the teaching workload of departments and the demands that follow from that workload. We would expect, therefore, that departments with heavy student demands for courses would be able to obtain funds for teaching. Another reasonable basis for decision making is quality. We would expect, for that reason, that departments with esteemed reputations would be able to obtain funds both because their quality suggests they might use such funds effectively and because such funds would allow them to maintain their quality. A rational model of bureaucracy intimates, then, that the organizational decisions taken would favor those who perform the stated purposes of the organizations—teaching undergraduates and training professional and scientific talent—well.

The problem with rational models of decision making, however, is that what is rational to one person may strike another as irrational. For most departments, resources are a question of survival. While teaching undergraduates may seem to be a major goal for some members of the university, developing knowledge may seem so to others; and to still others, advising governments and other institutions about policies may seem to be the crucial business. Everyone has his own idea of the proper priorities in a just world. Thus goals rather than being clearly defined and universally agreed upon are blurred and contested throughout the organization. If such is the case, then the decisions taken on behalf of the organization as a whole are likely to reflect the goals of those who prevail in political contests, namely, those with power in the organization.

Will organizational decisions always reflect the distribution of power in the organization? Probably not. Using power for influence requires a certain expenditure of effort, time, and resources. Prudent and judicious persons are not likely to use their power needlessly or wastefully. And it is likely that power will be used to influence organizational decisions primarily under circumstances that both require and favor its use. We have examined three conditions that are likely to affect the use of power in organizations: scarcity, criticality, and uncertainty. The first suggests that subunits will try to exert influence when the resources of the organization are scarce. If there is an abundance of resources, then a particular department or a particular individual has little need to attempt influence. With little effort, he can get all he wants anyway.

The second condition, criticality, suggests that a subunit will attempt to influence decisions to obtain resources that are critical to its own survival and activities. Criticality implies that one would not waste effort, or risk being labeled obstinate, by fighting over trivial decisions affecting one's operations.

An office manager would probably balk less about a threatened cutback in copying machine usage than about a reduction in typing staff. An advertising department head would probably worry less about losing his lettering artist than his illustrator. Criticality is difficult to define because what is critical depends on people's beliefs about what is critical. Such beliefs may or may not be based on experience and knowledge and may or may not be agreed upon by all. Scarcity, for instance, may itself affect conceptions of criticality. When slack resources drop off, cutbacks have to be made—those "hard decisions," as congressmen and resplendent administrators like to call them. Managers then find themselves scrapping projects they once held dear.

The third condition that we believe affects the uses of power is uncertainty: When individuals do not agree about what the organization should do or how to do it, power and other social processes will affect decisions. The reason for this is simply that, if there are no clear-cut criteria available for resolving conflicts of interest, then the only means for resolution is some form of social process, including power, status, social ties, or some arbitrary process like flipping a coin or drawing straws. Under conditions of uncertainty, the powerful manager can argue his case on any grounds and usually win it. Since there is no real consensus, other contestants are not likely to develop counter arguments or amass sufficient opposition. Moreover, because of his power and their need for access to the resources he controls, they are more likely to defer to his arguments.

Although the evidence is slight, we have found that power will influence the allocations of scarce and critical resources. In the analysis of power in the university, for instance, one of the most critical resources needed by departments is the general budget. First granted by the state legislature, the general budget is later allocated to individual departments by the university administration in response to requests from the department heads. Our analysis of the factors that contribute to a department getting more or less of this budget indicated that subunit power was the major predictor, overriding such factors as student demand for courses, national reputations of departments, or even the size of a department's faculty. Moreover, other research has shown that when the general budget has been cut back or held below previous uninflated levels, leading to monies becoming more scarce, budget allocations mirror departmental powers even more closely.

Student enrollment and faculty size, of course, do themselves relate to budget allocations, as we would expect since they determine a department's need for resources, or at least offer visible testimony of needs. But departments are not always able to get what they need by the mere fact of needing them. In one analysis it was found that high-power departments were able to obtain budget without regard to their teaching loads and, in some cases, actually in inverse relation to their teaching loads. In contrast, low-power departments could get increases in budget only when they could justify the increases by a recent growth in teaching load, and then only when it was far in excess of norms for other departments.

General budget is only one form of resource that is allocated to departments. There are others such as special grants for student fellowships or faculty research. These are critical to departments because they affect the ability to attract other resources, such as outstanding faculty or students. We examined how power influenced the allocations of four resources department heads had described as critical and scarce.

When the four resources were arrayed from the most to the least critical and scarce, we found that the departmental power best predicted the allocations of the most critical and scarce resources. In other words, the analysis of how power influences organizational allocations leads to this conclusion: Those subunits most likely to survive in times of strife are those that are more critical to the organization. Their importance to the organization gives them power to influence resource allocations that enhance their own survival.

HOW EXTERNAL ENVIRONMENT IMPACTS EXECUTIVE SELECTION

Power not only influences the survival of key groups in an organization, it also influences the selection of individuals to key leadership positions, and by such a process further aligns the organization with its environmental context.

We can illustrate this with a recent study of the selection and tenure of chief administrators in 57 hospitals in Illinois. We assumed that since the critical problems facing the organization would enhance the power of certain groups at the expense of others, then the leaders to emerge should be those most relevant to the context of the hospitals. To assess this we asked each chief administrator about his professional background and how long he had been in office. The replies were then related to the hospitals' funding, ownership, and competitive conditions for patients and staff.

One aspect of a hospital's context is the source of its budget. Some hospitals, for instance, are run much like other businesses. They sell bed space, patient care, and treatment services. They charge fees sufficient both to cover their costs and to provide capital for expansion. The main source of both their operating and capital funds is patient billings. Increasingly, patient billings are paid for, not by patients, but by private insurance companies. Insurers like Blue Cross dominate and represent a potent interest group outside a hospital's control but critical to its income. The insurance companies, in order to limit their own costs, attempt to hold down the fees allowable to hospitals, which they do effectively from their positions on state rate boards. The squeeze on hospitals that results from fees increasing slowly while costs climb rapidly more and more demands the talents of cost accountants or people trained in the technical expertise of hospital administration.

By contrast, other hospitals operate more like social service institutions, either as government healthcare units (Bellevue Hospital in New York City and Cook County Hospital in Chicago, for example) or as charitable institutions. These hospitals obtain a large proportion of their operating and capital funds, not from privately insured patients, but from government subsidies or private donations. Such institutions rather than requiring the talents of a technically efficient administrator are likely to require the savvy of someone who is well integrated into the social and political power structure of the community.

Not surprisingly, the characteristics of administrators predictably reflect the funding context of the hospitals with which they are associated. Those hospitals with larger proportions of their budget obtained from private insurance companies were most likely to have administrators with backgrounds in accounting and least likely to have administrators whose professions were business or medicine. In contrast, those hospitals with larger proportions of their budget derived from private donations and local governments were most likely to have administrators with business or professional backgrounds and least likely to have accountants. The same held for formal training in hospital management. Professional hospital administrators could easily be found in hospitals drawing their incomes from private insurance and rarely in hospitals dependent on donations or legislative appropriations.

As with the selection of administrators, the context of organizations has also been found to affect the removal of executives. The environment, as a source of organizational problems, can make it more or less difficult for executives to demonstrate their value to the organization. In the hospital we studied, long-term administrators came from hospitals with few problems. They enjoyed amicable and stable relations with their local business and social communities and suffered little competition for funding and staff. The small city hospital director who attended civic and Elks meetings while running the only hospital within a 100-mile radius, for example, had little difficulty holding on to his job. Turnover was highest in hospitals with the most problems, a phenomenon similar to that observed in a study of industrial organizations in which turnover was highest among executives in industries with competitive environments and unstable market conditions. The interesting thing is that instability characterized the industries rather than the individual firms in them. The troublesome conditions in the individual firms were attributed, or rather misattributed, to the executives themselves.

It takes more than problems, however, to terminate a manager's leadership. The problems themselves must be relevant and critical. This is clear from the way in which an administrator's tenure is affected by the status of the hospital's operating budget. Naively we might assume that all administrators would need to show a surplus. Not necessarily so. Again, we must distinguish between those hospitals that depend on private donations for funds and those that do not. Whether an endowed budget shows a surplus or deficit is less important than the hospital's relations with benefactors. On the other hand, with a budget dependent on patient billing, a surplus is almost essential; monies for new equipment or expansion must be drawn from it, and without them quality care becomes more difficult and patients scarcer. An administrator's tenure reflected just these considerations. For those hospitals dependent upon private donations, the length of an administrator's term depended not at all on the status of the operating budget but was fairly predictable from the hospital's relations with the business community. On the other hand, in hospitals dependent on the operating budget for capital financing, the greater the deficit the shorter was the tenure of the hospital's principal administrators.

CHANGING CONTINGENCIES
AND ERODING POWER BASES

The critical contingencies facing the organization may change. When they do, it is reasonable to expect that the power of individuals and subgroups will change in turn. At times the shift can be swift and shattering, as it was recently for powerholders in New York City. A few years ago it was believed that David Rockefeller was one of the ten most powerful people in the city, as tallied by *New York* magazine, which annually sniffs out power for the delectation of its readers. But that was before it was revealed that the city was in financial trouble, before Rockefeller's Chase Manhattan Bank lost some of its own financial luster, and before brother Nelson lost some of his political influence in Washington. Obviously David Rockefeller was no longer as well positioned to help bail the city out. Another loser was an attorney with considerable personal connections to the political and religious leaders of the city. His talents were no longer in much demand. The persons with more influence were the bankers and union pension fund executors who fed money to the city; community leaders who represent blacks and Spanish-Americans, in contrast, witnessed the erosion of their power bases.

One implication of the idea that power shifts with changes in organizational environments is that the dominant coalition will tend to be that group that is most appropriate for the organization's environment, as also will the leaders of an organization. One can observe this historically in the top executives of industrial firms in the United States. Up until the early 1950s, many top corporations were headed by former production line managers or engineers who gained prominence because of their abilities to cope with the problems of production. Their success, however, only spelled their demise. As production became routinized and mechanized, the problem of most firms became one of selling all those goods they so efficiently produced. Marketing executives were more frequently found in corporate boardrooms. Success outdid itself again, for keeping markets and production steady and stable requires the kind of control that can only come from acquiring competitors and suppliers or the invention of more and more appealing products—ventures that typically require enormous amounts of capital. During the 1960s, financial executives assumed the seats of power. And they, too, will give way to others. Edging over the horizon are legal experts, as regulation and antitrust suits are becoming more and more frequent in the 1970s, suits that had their beginnings in the success of the expansion generated by prior executives. The more distant future, which is likely to be dominated by multinational corporations, may see former secretaries of state and their minions increasingly serving as corporate figureheads.

THE NONADAPTIVE CONSEQUENCES
OF ADAPTATION

From what we have said thus far about power aligning the organization with its own realities, an intelligent person might react with a resounding ho-hum, for it all seems too obvious: Those with the ability to get the job done are given the job to do.

However, there are two aspects of power that make it more useful for understanding organizations and their effectiveness. First, the "job" to be done has a way of expanding itself until it becomes less and less clear what the job is. Napoleon began by doing a job for France in the war with Austria and ended up Emperor, convincing many that only he could keep the peace. Hitler began by promising an end to Germany's troubling postwar depression and ended up convincing more people than is comfortable to remember that he was destined to be the savior of the world. In short, power is a capacity for influence that extends far beyond the original bases that created it. Second, power tends to take on institutionalized forms that enable it to endure well beyond its usefulness to an organization.

There is an important contradiction in what we have observed about organizational power. On the one hand we have said that power derives from the contingencies facing an organization and that when those contingencies change so do the bases for power. On the other hand we have asserted that subunits will tend to use their power to influence organizational decisions in their own favor, particularly when their own survival is threatened by the scarcity of critical resources. The first statement implies that an organization will tend to be aligned with its environment since power will tend to bring to key positions those with capabilities relevant to the context. The second implies that those in power will not give up their positions so easily; they will pursue policies that guarantee their continued domination. In short, change and stability operate through the same mechanism, and, as a result, the organization will never be completely in phase with its environment or its needs.

The study of hospital administrators illustrates how leadership can be out of phase with reality. We argued that privately funded hospitals needed trained technical administrators more so than did hospitals funded by donations. The need as we perceived it was matched in most hospitals, but by no means in all. Some organizations did not conform with our predictions. These deviations imply that some administrators were able to maintain their positions independent of their suitability for those positions. By dividing administrators into those with long and short terms of office, one finds that the characteristics of longer-termed administrators were virtually unrelated to the hospital's context. The shorter-termed chiefs on the other hand had characteristics more appropriate for the hospital's problems. For a hospital to have a recently appointed head implies that the previous administrator had been unable to endure by institutionalizing himself.

One obvious feature of hospitals that allowed some administrators to enjoy a long tenure was a hospital's ownership. Administrators were less entrenched when their hospitals were affiliated with and dependent upon larger organizations, such as governments or churches. Private hospitals offered more secure positions for administrators. Like private corporations, they tend to have more diffused ownership, leaving the administrator unopposed as he institutionalizes his reign. Thus he endures, sometimes at the expense of the performance of the organization. Other research has demonstrated that corporations with diffuse ownership have poorer earnings than those in which the control of the manager is checked by a dominant shareholder. Firms that overload their boardrooms with more insiders than are appropriate for their context have also been found to be less profitable.

A word of caution is required about our judgment of "appropriateness." When we argue some capabilities are more appropriate for one context than another, we do so from the perspective of an outsider and on the basis of reasonable assumptions as to the problems the organization will face and the capabilities they will need. The fact that we have been able to predict the distribution of influence and the characteristics of leaders suggests that our reasoning is not incorrect. However, we do not think that all organizations follow the same pattern. The fact that we have not been able to predict outcomes with 100 percent accuracy indicates they do not.

MISTAKING CRITICAL CONTINGENCIES

One thing that allows subunits to retain their power is their ability to name their functions as critical to the organization when they may not be. Consider again our discussion of power in the university. One might wonder why the most critical tasks were defined as graduate education and scholarly research, the effect of which was to lend power to those who brought in grants and contracts. Why not something else? The reason is that the more powerful departments argued for those criteria and won their case, partly because they were more powerful.

In another analysis of this university, we found that all departments advocate self-serving criteria for budget allocation. Thus a department with large undergraduate enrollments argued that enrollments should determine budget allocations, a department with a strong national reputation saw prestige as the most reasonable basis for distributing funds, and so on. We further found that advocating such self-serving criteria actually benefited a department's budget allotments but, also, it paid off more for departments that were already powerful.

Organizational needs are consistent with a current distribution of power also because of a human tendency to categorize problems in familiar ways. An accountant sees problems with organizational performance as cost accountancy problems or inventory flow problems. A sales manager sees them as problems with markets, promotional strategies, or just unaggressive salespeople. But what is the truth? Since it does not automatically announce itself, it is likely that those with prior credibility, or those with power, will be favored as the enlightened. This bias, while not intentionally self-serving, further concentrates power among those who already possess it, independent of changes in the organization's context.

INSTITUTIONALIZING POWER

A third reason for expecting organizational contingencies to be defined in familiar ways is that the current holders of power can structure the organization in ways that institutionalize themselves. By institutionalization we mean the establishment of relatively permanent structures and policies that favor the influence of a particular subunit. While in power, a dominant coalition has the ability to institute constitutions, rules, procedures, and information systems that limit the potential power of others while continuing their own.

The key to institutionalizing power always is to create a device that legitimates one's own authority and diminishes the legitimacy of others. When the "Divine Right of Kings" was envisioned centuries ago it was to provide an unquestionable foundation for the supremacy of royal authority. There is generally a need to root the exercise of authority in some higher power. Modern leaders are no less affected by this need. Richard Nixon, with the aid of John Dean, reified the concept of executive privilege, which meant in effect that what the President wished not to be discussed need not be discussed.

In its simpler form, institutionalization is achieved by designating positions or roles for organizational activities. The creation of a new post legitimizes a function and forces organization members to orient to it. By designating how this new post relates to older, more established posts, moreover, one can structure an organization to enhance the importance of the function in the organization. Equally, one can diminish the importance of traditional functions. This is what happened in the end with the insurance company we mentioned that was having trouble with its coding department. As the situation unfolded, the claims director continued to feel dissatisfied about the dependency of his functions on the coding manager. Thus he instituted a reorganization that resulted in two coding departments. In so doing, of course, he placed activities that affected his department under his direct control, presumably to make the operation more effective. Similarly, consumer-product firms enhance the power of marketing by setting up a coordinating role to interface production and marketing functions and then appoint a marketing manager to fill the role.

The structures created by dominant powers sooner or later become fixed and unquestioned features of the organization. Eventually, this can be devastating. It is said that the battle of Jena in 1806 was lost by Frederick the Great, who died in 1786. Though the great Prussian leader had no direct hand in the disaster, his imprint on the army was so thorough, so embedded in its skeletal underpinnings, that the organization was inappropriate for others to lead in different times.

Another important source of institutionalized power lies in the ability to structure information systems. Setting up committees to investigate particular organizational issues and having them report only to particular individuals or groups, facilitates their awareness of problems by members of those groups while limiting the awareness of problems by the members of other groups. Obviously, those who have information are in a better position to interpret the problems of an organization, regardless of how realistically they may, in fact, do so.

Still another way to institutionalize power is to distribute rewards and resources. The dominant group may quiet competing interest groups with small favors and rewards. The credit for this artful form of co-optation belongs to Louis XIV. To avoid usurpation of his power by the nobles of France and the Fronde that had so troubled his father's reign, he built the palace at Versailles to occupy them with hunting and gossip. Awed, the courtiers basked in the reflected glories of the "Sun King" and the overwhelming setting he had created for his court.

At this point, we have not systematically studied the institutionalization of power. But we suspect it is an important condition that mediates between the environment of the organization and the capabilities of the organization for dealing with that environment. The more institutionalized power is within an organization, the more likely an organization will be out of phase with the realities it faces. President Richard Nixon's structuring of his White House is one of the better documented illustrations. If we go back to newspaper and magazine descriptions of how he organized his office from the beginning in 1968, most of what occurred subsequently follows almost as an afterthought. Decisions flowed through virtually only the small White House staff; rewards, small presidential favors of recognition, and perquisites were distributed by this staff to the loyal; and information from the outside world—the press, Congress, the people on the streets—was filtered by the staff and passed along only if initialed "bh." Thus it was not surprising that when Nixon met war protestors in the early dawn, the only thing he could think to talk about was the latest football game, so insulated had he become from their grief and anger.

One of the more interesting implications of institutionalized power is that executive turnover among the executives who have structured the organizations is likely to be a rare event that occurs only under the most pressing crisis. If a dominant coalition is able to structure the organization and interpret the meaning of ambiguous events like declining sales and profits or lawsuits, then the "real" problems to emerge will easily be incorporated into traditional molds of thinking and acting. If opposition is designed out of the organization, the interpretations will go unquestioned. Conditions will remain stable until a crisis develops, so overwhelming and visible that even the most adroit rhetorician would be silenced.

IMPLICATIONS FOR THE MANAGEMENT OF POWER IN ORGANIZATIONS

While we could derive numerous implications from this discussion of power, our selection would have to depend largely on whether one wanted to increase one's power, decrease the power of others, or merely maintain one's position. More important, the real implications depend on the particulars of an organizational situation. To understand power in an organization one must begin by looking outside it—into the environment—for those groups that mediate the organization's outcome but are not themselves within its control.

Instead of ending with homilies, we will end with a reversal of where we began. Power, rather than being the dirty business it is often made out to be, is probably one of the few mechanisms for reality testing in organizations. And the cleaner forms of power, the institutional forms, rather than having the virtues they are often credited with, can lead the organization to become out of touch. The real trick to managing power in organizations is to ensure somehow that leaders cannot be unaware of the realities of their environments and cannot avoid changing to deal with those realities. That, however, would be like designing the "self-liquidating organization," an unlikely event since anyone capable of designing such an instrument would be obviously in control of the liquidations.

Management would do well to devote more attention to determining the critical contingencies of their environments. For if you conclude, as we do, that the environment sets most of the structure influencing organizational outcomes and problems, and that power derives from the organization's activities that deal with those contingencies, then it is the environment that needs managing, not power. The first step is to construct an accurate model of the environment, a process that is quite difficult for most organizations. We have recently started a project to aid administrators in systematically understanding their environments. From this experience, we have learned that the most critical blockage to perceiving an organization's reality accurately is a failure to incorporate those with the relevant expertise into the process. Most organizations have the requisite experts on hand but they are positioned so that they can be comfortably ignored.

One conclusion you can, and probably should, derive from our discussion is that power—because of the way it develops and the way it is used—will always result in the organization suboptimizing its performance. However, to this grim absolute, we add a comforting caveat: If any criteria other than power were the basis for determining an organization's decisions, the results would be even worse.

Exercise: Dependency Situations

PURPOSE

The purpose of this exercise is to help you understand how to cope with situations in which you must empower yourself. By the time you complete this exercise you will

1. Diagnose your empowerment strategy profile

2. Understand a set of conditions that cause managers to become powerless in their jobs

3. Develop an action plan to help you recognize and deal with similar situations

INTRODUCTION

How managers exercise influence to gain power in organizations is a hotly debated topic. Less studied is how managers empower themselves from positions of powerlessness. Managers frequently are dependent on a variety of individuals in their jobs for information, support, or supplies. When you are dependent on someone else, you are powerless until your request is honored. In fact, many argue that power is the inverse of dependence (Emerson, 1962).

Studying how you might react in situations in which you are dependent on others provides an opportunity to analyze the influence tactics you may use to empower yourself. This exercise has that objective. The first part will provide an opportunity for you to assess your empowerment strategy profile. The second part will ask you to reflect upon current and similar dependency situations in your job and to develop strategies to overcome your powerlessness.

INSTRUCTIONS

Part I

1. Complete the questionnaire on dependency situations as directed by your instructor.

2. Score your results to determine your typical empowerment strategy profile.

3. Read the enclosed reading insert, "Empowerment Strategies and Dependency Situations."

4. Participate in a classroom tabulation of the class results (if directed to do so by your instructor).

This exercise was developed by Lisa A. Mainiero and was presented at the Eastern Academy of Management, Philadelphia, PA, 1987. Ideas for the exercise are adapted from the article by Lisa A. Mainiero, "Coping with Powerlessness: The Relationship of Gender and Job Dependency to Empowerment Strategy Usage," *Administrative Science Quarterly,* 1986, Vol. 31(4), 633–653.

Part II

1. Reflect upon a recent situation in which you found yourself dependent on someone (a co-worker, teacher, boss, roommate, or someone). On a separate piece of paper, briefly describe the situation and the strategies used.

2. Answer the questions that apply to Part II on the Empowerment Strategy Profile. Then determine an action plan to help you meet your goals.

3. In a group, share your experiences with others. You may want to reflect upon your questionnaire score to determine whether or not your questionnaire results are consistent with how you behave in actual situations.

4. Participate in a class discussion.

Empowerment Strategies and Dependency Situations

Managers frequently find themselves dependent upon their bosses for career support, dependent upon subordinates to get their job tasks done on time, and dependent upon peers to provide the information or resources that is needed. The problem is, when you are dependent on someone else, that individual has power over you. Power has little to do with formal line authority. Instead, research suggests it has everything to do with the dependency of others derived from that formal line authority.

Dependency creates a power imbalance. When managers find themselves dependent, they are rendered vulnerable and powerless. Under such conditions, it is necessary to employ empowerment strategies to restore the balance of power. By taking action to empower themselves, managers are able to gain control over the situation once more. In this way, they are able to be effective and productive in their jobs.

Which strategies, therefore, might an individual employ to restore the balance of power when dependent? There are a multitude of available strategies. The use of particular strategies will depend on the situation at hand and the choices made by the manager.

For the purposes of this exercise, six typical strategies have been chosen:

1. *Assertion:* Describing the reasons for being dependent and requesting help from the high-power target.

2. *Ingratiation:* Offering concessions or favors to the high-power target to achieve what is desired.

3. *Alternatives:* Searching for an alternative person or route to obtain what is needed.

4. *Coalition Formation:* Joining with at least one other individual or set of individuals to put pressure on the target to achieve the goal.

5. *Coercion:* Using threats to put pressure on the high-power target.

6. *Acquiescence:* Accepting the situation and giving into the demands of the high-power target.

The types of strategies you use may be influenced by the target of the situation. Kipnis, Schmidt, Swaffin-Smith, and Wilkinson (1984) argue that the exercise of influence is a fundamental activity for all managers, and they have researched the pattern of responses that managers use with superiors and subordinates. They found that managers they used:

- ❏ Reasoning/assertive tactics first.
- ❏ Then coalition formation.
- ❏ Friendliness/ingratiation.
- ❏ Bargaining/alternatives.
- ❏ Further assertive tactics.
- ❏ Appeals to higher authorities.

For subordinates:

- ❏ Reasoning and assertive tactics first.
- ❏ Then friendliness/ingratiation.
- ❏ Coalition formation.
- ❏ Bargaining/alternatives.
- ❏ Appeals to higher authorities.
- ❏ Finally coercion/sanctions.[1]

Kipnis, Schmidt, Swaffin-Smith, and Wilkinson (1984) further identified three categories of managers based on their study of influence attempts:

- ❏ "Shotgun" managers were high on the use of all six influence strategies across the board.
- ❏ "Tactician" managers were high on the use of reason/assertion more so than the other strategies.
- ❏ "Bystander" managers were low on the use of influence strategies across the board.

Managers categorized as tacticians were found to be the highest on organizational power, were most successful in achieving their own objectives, and most satisfied in their jobs.

Shotgun managers generally were inexperienced on the job; bystander managers were the most dissatisfied.

Which of the strategies best describes your actions and responses? What is your empowerment strategy profile?

---

1. The titles Kipnis et al. (1984) use in their research are slightly different from the titles of the strategies used in this exercise. For this reason the (/) slash bar is used in the insert to describe conceptually similar strategies between the terms used in the exercise versus those employed in the research study. For further clarification, see Kipnis et al., "Patterns of Managerial Influence: Shotgun Managers, Tacticians, and Bystanders," *Organizational Dynamics,* Winter 1984, 58–67.

Part I: The Dependency Situation Questionnaire

Directions: The following cases represent problematic situations that require employees to be dependent on others for information, resources, or support. Please read each case carefully and indicate which strategies you might employ if you were faced with the situation described.

Rank the strategies described below. Indicate a (1) for the strategy you would use first, a (2) for the strategy you would use second, a (3) for the strategy you would use third in the situation, and so on until you reach (6), the last strategy you would attempt. If you would *never* attempt a particular strategy in the hypothetical situation described, leave a blank space to indicate your lack of usage of that strategy. Please read each description carefully before you complete your rankings.

Situation #1. You have been serving in your present job for over three years, and you have recently decided that it is time for a change. A position in another department, for which you are qualified, has become available, and you would very much like to take the position. The new job would provide you with additional visibility and recognition, since you would have the chance to work on a "hot" new project. Last week you went to your boss to discuss the possibility of a transfer, but your boss seemed unwilling to let you move at the present time. It is true that you are currently working on a project that needs your special expertise, but it could be handled in a short period (if you did some overtime). The other department needs to fill the position quickly, and the manager of the department would very much like to hire you for the job. You are dependent on your boss to release you from your present position; you need the support of your boss.

If you were in this situation, what would you do? How would you handle the situation?

a. _____ Ask the manager of the new department to discuss the situation with your boss on your behalf.

b. _____ Discuss the situation with your boss, explaining your reasons for wanting the job transfer.

c. _____ Try to do your boss a favor by putting in a few weeks' overtime on the special project so you could ask for your release a second time.

d. _____ Find another way to obtain the transfer by bypassing bureaucratic channels and asking higher-ups to grant your release.

e. _____ Put pressure on your boss by threatening to leave the company unless he or she supports your transfer.

f. _____ Accept the situation, decide that it is not the right time, wait for the next opportunity, and hope for the best.

Situation #2. You have been working on a project for a few months that requires you to interact with members of another department to gain the information that you need. In particular, you need information from a peer in the other department who has the necessary expertise to help you solve some of the problems on the project. This individual has a tendency to put off your requests for information because he or she has a great deal of work of his or her own to accomplish. You are dependent on this individual because he or she is the only person who has the necessary information readily available to help you do your work. A deadline for your project is approaching fast, and you really need your colleague to give you some critical information in the next few days.

If you were involved in this situation, what would you do? How would you handle the situation?

a. _____ Put pressure on this individual by threatening to go to his or her boss if help is not forthcoming.

b. _____ Try to do this individual a favor early in the week so that he or she will be more willing to do the work you need when you ask him or her later in the week.

c. _____ Discuss the situation with this individual, letting him or her know how important the information is to you and the fast-approaching deadline.

d. _____ Try to find another individual in the same department who may be able to provide some of the information.

e. _____ Accept the situation, wait for the next opportunity, face up to the situation with your boss, and hope for the best.

f. _____ Ask your peers in the department to support your cause by discussing your situation with this individual at the next opportunity.

Situation #3. Your boss has just been handed the assignment of heading up a task force on a coveted project, and you want very much to become a member of the task force. Your boss will be making selections of candidates for the task force shortly, and you very much would like to get on the list. It is a project in which you have a great deal of interest, and your background and qualifications show that you have expertise that may be helpful in assessing the project. You are dependent on your boss to get on the task force, for your boss is the only person who will be making the selection decisions.

If you were involved in this situation, what would you do? How would you handle the situation?

a. _____ Discuss your desire to become a member of the task force with your boss, highlighting your qualifications and interest.

b. _____ Do your boss a favor by finishing some extra work ahead of time to put you in the right position to discuss the task force assignment.

c. _____ Put pressure on your boss by threatening to leave the company if you can't get on the task force.

d. _____ Ask another manager who has been supporting your career to support your cause in a meeting with your boss.

e. _____ Find another way to get on the task force by accessing valuable information the task force members will need. This way, regardless of whether or not you are selected, they will need you to be part of the task force.

f. _____ Accept the situation, wait it out, and hope for the best.

Situation #4. To complete a special project, you need to use a piece of equipment in another department. Your manager had told you that you have permission to use the equipment at any time, but every time you try to use the equipment, someone else is on the machine. You are dependent upon your peers in the other department to let you use the machine, for you are not a direct member of their group. A deadline is fast approaching, and your career hinges on meeting that deadline.

If you were involved in this situation, what strategy would you use? How would you handle the situation?

a. _____ Discuss the situation with your peers, explaining why you must use the equipment in short order.

b. _____ Put pressure on your peers by threatening to go to their boss.

c. _____ Find another way to use the equipment by working overtime and using it at night and in the early morning hours.

d. _____ Accept the situation, wait it out, and hope for the best.

e. _____ Do your peers a favor by helping them with something they need; then ask them to help you.

f. _____ Ask your boss to talk to the manager of the department to ensure that you have sufficient time to use the equipment.

Situation #5. You are a manager of a group of production workers, and your boss has just given you a deadline that must be met by the end of the month. Lately, a subset of your group of subordinates has been working more slowly than usual, and they are taking longer coffee breaks and lunches. You have not mentioned anything to them about this issue, because they are generally a good group of workers characterized by a strong sense of camaraderie and friendship. However, you are dependent upon them to work steadily until the end of the month in order to meet the deadline set by your boss. You feel this may be a test set by your boss to determine whether or not you should be promoted to the next level.

If you were involved in this situation, what would you do? How would you handle the situation?

a. _____ Discuss the deadline with your total group of subordinates, highlighting its importance and necessity.

b. _____ Ask some of your other subordinates (not members of the problematic group) to do some voluntary overtime work.

c. _____ Put pressure on your problematic group of subordinates by threatening that, if they don't shape up, there will be some repercussions by the end of the month.

d. _____ Ask your other subordinates to outline your need to make the deadline to the problematic group.

e. _____ Do your problematic group of subordinates a favor by saying that you won't report their recent behavior if they will work to capacity until the end of the month.

f. _____ Accept the situation, decide you don't want to rock the boat, and hope for the best.

Situation #6. You are the manager of a staff engineering group involved in several active projects. A conflict in your schedule for next week requires you to be in New York for a meeting, and you also are scheduled to meet with another client in Boston at the same time. Neither meeting can be rescheduled to a different day, and your boss has requested your participation at the Boston meeting. The only subordinate who is capable of representing you at the New York meeting has been traveling a lot lately and does not want to go. You are dependent upon her to represent you since she is the only one with the expertise from your group to serve the New York customer.

If you were involved in this situation, how would you handle the situation? What would you do?

a. _____ Discuss with your subordinate your need to have her represent you at the New York meeting.

b. _____ Do your subordinate a favor by giving her a few days off to compensate her upon returning.

c. _____ Find another less qualified subordinate from your group to attend the New York meeting.

d. _____ Ask other subordinates in your group to impress upon her how important it is that she attend the New York meeting regardless of her concerns.

e. _____ Put pressure on your subordinate by saying that if she doesn't attend the meeting, there will be repercussions later.

f. _____ Accept the situation, talk to your boss about the meeting conflicts, and hope for the best.

Situation #7. Your department is a field function designed to provide crisis support on out-of-the-ordinary service problems. The members of your department are highly skilled and have trained for many years to develop the qualifications needed to provide second-tier support. Over the weekend a new equipment installation will take place that might potentially fail and require the crisis support of your team. The three employees whom you wish to assign the weekend work just completed a lengthy service request and are looking forward to taking the weekend off. In addition, one of the three members is supposed to be attending a wedding this weekend and another has nonrefundable airplane tickets to Florida. You are dependent on these three members to agree to the additional weekend assignment, as you believe and your boss agrees that these three individuals are the most qualified for the job and should be placed on call.

If you were involved in the situation described, what would you do? How would you handle the situation?

a. _____ Accept the situation, assume that things will work themselves out, and hope for the best.

b. _____ Discuss the situation with your employees, stressing the importance of the assignment.

c. _____ Do your employees a favor by promising that if they work overtime this one time, you will provide them with additional time off at a later date.

d. _____ Find another way to get around the situation by assigning other members who might be less qualified to the team and hope for the best.

e. _____ Ask your boss to intercede in the situation by discussing with your employees the importance of the weekend assignment and his reasons why they should be placed on call.

f. _____ Put pressure on your employees by telling them that their first responsibility is to their work and unless they work overtime they can expect no raises at year's end.

Situation #8.   You have been arguing for months that you need to hire two additional people to support the amount of work that currently is being expected of your department. Due to a downsizing that took place in your division a year ago, your department was left understaffed and overworked. Your employees are finding it difficult to handle the stress of the increased workload and recently have begun to complain. Your boss, however, is trying to "toe the line" and maintain control over the headcount of the departments for which she is responsible. Over the past week, two people from another division became available and have indicated their interest in transferring to your department. You are dependent on your boss to give her approval to negotiate the transfer quickly or else this opportunity will be lost.

If you were involved in the situation described, what would you do? How would you handle the situation?

a. _____ Promise your boss that by adding two to your headcount now, you will make changes in your headcount by year's end so it will not adversely affect her departmental quotas.

b. _____ Find another way around the situation by arranging the transfers without your boss's prior approval. Then tell your boss about the opportunity and the need to move quickly.

c. _____ Ask the manager of the department arranging the transfers to discuss the situation with your boss and to recommend the transfers.

d. _____ Accept the situation, assume things will work themselves out, and hope for the best.

e. _____ Discuss the situation with your boss, underscoring the importance of this new opportunity to arrange a quick transfer.

f. _____ Put pressure on your boss by stating that unless these people are moved to your department quickly, departmental performance will suffer and you will have no choice but to request a transfer on your own.

Situation #9.   Because your boss has been dissatisfied with the work of one of your colleagues on an important project, she has reassigned the project to you. You have been instructed to work with your colleague to gather the necessary information and prepare a project report by the end of the month. However, your colleague, upset about the reassignment, has not been forthcoming in providing information to you concerning the project. You are dependent on this colleague to provide you with the information as you will be unable to make the deadline at the end of the month unless he cooperates.

If you were involved in the situation described, what would you do? How would you handle the situation?

a. _____ Find another way around the situation by enlisting the help of the people who work for this colleague to provide the information you need.

b. _____ Ask another colleague to intercede with this individual to impress upon him the need for teamwork against a deadline.

c. _____ Put pressure on this individual that unless he cooperates, you will have no choice but to tell the boss.

d. _____ Accept the situation, assume things will work themselves out, and hope for the best.

e. _____ Discuss the situation with this colleague, and impress upon him the need for cooperation as a team.

f. _____ Do your colleague a favor by stating that if he cooperates, you will intercede on his behalf with your boss.

Situation #10. For months you have been carefully building to a sale with an important customer. This customer will be on site in two days and has requested a tour of the plant. You assigned one of your employees the task of escorting this important customer that day. However, this employee came to your office this morning complaining that he did not want to perform this "Mickey Mouse" assignment. He felt that his time could be better spent working on other projects that had been assigned, which he was now bringing to a close. You recognize that this employee is working on a number of projects, but you believe that he is the most knowledgeable to answer questions about the plant and therefore want him to serve as the escort. You are dependent on him to do a good job as an escort without demotivating him.

If you were involved in the situation described, what would you do? How would you handle the situation?

a. _____ Ask one of your most trusted subordinates to privately discuss the situation with this employee and to impress upon him the importance of the customer's visit.

b. _____ Put pressure on this employee by threatening the loss of his job unless he takes the customer on the plant tour.

c. _____ Accept the situation, assume things will work themselves out, and hope for the best.

d. _____ Discuss the situation with this employee, explaining the importance of this on-site customer visit.

e. _____ Do your employee a favor by promising him that if he takes the customer on tour, you will provide him with uninterrupted time for the next several weeks so that he can complete his favorite projects without interference.

f. _____ Find another way to get around the situation by asking another less qualified employee to escort the customer around the plant.

Situation #11. The people who work under you are hardworking and deserving of promotion. However, they lack the necessary educational qualifications to make the grade to the next level. Recently you proposed a new "technical advancement ladder" that will circumvent educational qualifications for promotion and reward individual contributors for good work. However, your boss has been reluctant to support the new system as he views this as a major shift in emphasis for career development at your firm. Without your boss's support, you will be unable to promote your people under the standard system. You are dependent on your boss for his support if this project is to move forward.

If you were involved in the situation described, what would you do? How would you handle the situation?

a. _____ Discuss the situation with your boss, impressing on him the need for a new promotional system.

b. _____ Negotiate with your boss that if he will support the new system, you will ensure that increased work quotas are achieved by year's end.

c. _____ Find another way around the situation by enlisting the support of other managers at your boss's level.

d. _____ Ask another manager with whom you have contact at the next level to discuss the situation with your boss.

e. _____ Put pressure on your boss by threatening that unless he supports the new system, you will be unable to ensure that your employees will remain in the department in the long term.

f. _____ Accept the situation, assume things will work themselves out, and hope for the best.

Situation #12. A new installation of computer equipment is about to take place, and you are responsible for the installation. You must make arrangements with members of the support team to do the prep work required to aid the installation process. You are acquainted with the manager of the support team, and you have heard from the grapevine that he can be difficult to deal with on projects like this one. You sent two memos to enlist his cooperation, but he has not answered your requests for help. You are dependent on him to provide support because if he does not cooperate soon, the entire installation project will be backlogged. Peers already are complaining that the installation is late as they want their upgraded equipment as soon as possible.

If you were involved in the situation described, what would you do? How would you handle the situation?

a. _____ Negotiate with this manager, telling him that if he accelerates your request for support, you will provide him with information he needs about a different project.

b. _____ Find another way around the situation by enlisting the help of another department to provide site preparation support.

c. _____ Ask a colleague whom you know well to intercede on your behalf with this manager.

d. _____ Put pressure on this manager by sending him another memo documenting the situation and stating that unless a reply is sent immediately, you will have no choice but to accelerate the situation to the next level.

e. _____ Accept the situation, assume things will work themselves out, and hope for the best.

f. _____ Discuss the situation with this manager, imploring him to do the site preparation as soon as possible.

Situation #13. You are the manager of a group of highly skilled computer programmers. One of your subordinates is considered the "star" performer of the computer group in the company. This subordinate developed the company's premier software a year ago and has contributed a great deal to software development in the company. Recently, however, this individual has not been concentrating on his work. He took a number of days off lately to spend time on his new boat, and upon returning to the office he spent more time on the phone talking to the marina than doing work. You promised your boss that you would have the new software package delivered by the next divisional meeting, and that meeting will occur next month. You are dependent on this subordinate for the technical development of the software; no one else in the company shares this individual's level of expertise.

If you were involved in the situation described above, how would you handle the situation? What would you do?

a. _____ Try to do this employee a favor by promising him that if he concentrates his efforts on software development over the next few weeks, you'll grant him additional time off for his boat later.

b. _____ Find another employee to assist your "star" performer so that when he loses concentration, someone else can continue the work.

c. _____ Have your boss meet with the employee while you are present so both of you can discuss the urgency of the software development and the need to work together as a team.

d. _____ Threaten to fire this employee unless he concentrates his mind on the software development task.

e. _____ Accept the situation, decide that you can only push a computer genius so far, and hope for the best.

f. _____ Discuss the situation with this employee, explaining the urgency of the software development.

Situation #14. You like your job and would prefer to continue working for your firm, but you have just built a new house and are in desperate need of a raise. Your spouse has encouraged you to request a raise from your boss. You have heard from one of your peers that your boss is disinclined to offer any additional raises this year as a proposed restructuring is about to take place and budgetary allocations for salaries are about to be thrown out of whack. In fact, your colleague told you that with this news, job security for the entire department may be in jeopardy. Your yearly performance review is about to take place. You are dependent on your boss to provide support for your request with higher-ups, and, further, you need his assurances that your position will remain viable even after the restructuring.

If you were involved in the situation described, what would you do? How would you handle the situation?

a. _____ Discuss the situation with your boss, imploring him for a raise at this time.

b. _____ Do your boss a favor by proposing to help with the restructuring. This way, your boss will feel compelled not only to retain your job but also to give you a raise when the time comes.

c. _____ Find another way around the situation by sending out your resume to determine what other offers might be available.

d. _____ Ask your mentor to discuss your personal finances with your boss to encourage his support of your raise.

e. _____ Put pressure on your boss by threatening to leave the firm unless you get a raise and assurances about your future job security.

f. _____ Accept the situation, assume that you will retain your job despite restructuring, and hope for the best concerning your raise.

Situation #15. You want to take all four of your vacation weeks together this year, but your boss has a policy that at least two of the managers at your level must remain in the office at all times. Two of your colleagues also want to take their vacation weeks at the same time you planned, and their weeks will overlap the month that you wish to take off. This will compromise your boss's policy. Unless your colleagues are willing to compromise, you are unlikely to be able to take your vacation time all at once. This would be unfortunate as you already have put down a deposit on a rental cottage for the month and have paid your nonrefundable airline reservations in advance. You are dependent on your colleagues to compromise their vacation times if your vacation is to take place as planned.

If you were involved in the situation described, what would you do? How would you handle the situation?

a. _____ Ask your colleagues to discuss the situation with your boss to get him to overturn his vacation policy this year.

b. _____ Put pressure on your colleagues that unless they help you out with your scheduling problem, you will be unable to help them in the future.

c. _____ Accept the situation, assume that things will work themselves out, and hope for the best.

d. _____ Discuss the situation with your colleagues, stating that your airline tickets are nonrefundable.

e. _____ Find another way around the situation by identifying someone who could take your place during the overlap weeks.

f. _____ Negotiate with your peers that if they reschedule their vacation weeks this year, you will accommodate their wishes next year.

Scoring Key: Dependency Situation Questionnaire

Part I: Primary Strategy Style

Directions: Write in your rankings in accordance with the order of the situation items listed below for each strategy. Total the number of points per strategy. Your *lowest* score is your primary strategy style.

Assertion	Ingratiation	Alternatives
Case 1. b _____	1. c _____	1. d _____
Case 2. c _____	2. b _____	2. d _____
Case 3. a _____	3. b _____	3. e _____
Case 4. a _____	4. e _____	4. c _____
Case 5. a _____	5. e _____	5. b _____
Case 6. a _____	6. b _____	6. c _____
Case 7. b _____	7. c _____	7. d _____
Case 8. e _____	8. a _____	8. b _____
Case 9. e _____	9. f _____	9. a _____
Case 10. d _____	10. e _____	10. f _____
Case 11. a _____	11. b _____	11. c _____
Case 12. f _____	12. a _____	12. b _____
Case 13. f _____	13. a _____	13. b _____
Case 14. a _____	14. b _____	14. c _____
Case 15. d _____	15. e _____	15. f _____
total: _____	total: _____	total: _____

Coalition Formation	Coercion	Acquiescence
Case 1. a _____	1. e _____	1. f _____
Case 2. f _____	2. a _____	2. e _____
Case 3. d _____	3. c _____	3. f _____
Case 4. f _____	4. b _____	4. d _____
Case 5. d _____	5. c _____	5. f _____
Case 6. d _____	6. e _____	6. f _____
Case 7. e _____	7. f _____	7. a _____
Case 8. c _____	8. f _____	8. d _____
Case 9. b _____	9. c _____	9. d _____
Case 10. a _____	10. b _____	10. c _____

Case 11. d _____   11. e _____   11. f _____

Case 12. c _____   12. d _____   12. e _____

Case 13. c _____   13. d _____   13. e _____

Case 14. d _____   14. e _____   14. f _____

Case 15. a _____   15. b _____   15. c _____

   total: _____   total: _____   total: _____

Primary strategy style (lowest score) = _____ .

Strategy Diagram Directions:

Diagram your strategies over time on the graph below. For each situation, which strategy did you use first, second, third, to last? To graphically display your results:

Use a single line (_____) for situations that involve a *superior* target (Cases 1, 3, 8, 11, 14)

Use a dotted line (. . . . .) for situations that involve a *peer* target (Cases 2, 4, 9, 12, 15)

Use a dashed line (- - - - -) for situations that involve a *subordinate* target (Cases 5, 6, 7, 10, 13)

Empowerment Profile: Strategy Usage Over Time

Acquiescence

Coercion

Coalitions

Alternatives

Ingratiation

Assertion

First   Second   Third   Fourth   Fifth   Sixth

Strategies

Part II: Actual Dependency Situations

Directions:

I. Reflect upon two recent situations in which you found yourself dependent. Using the worksheets on the following two pages, describe each of these situations, including the target of the situation (whether a boss, subordinate, or peer), and the actions you took in the situation to overcome your dependency on that individual.

II. What are the implications of your profile? How do you behave in actual dependency situations?

a. Are you a Shotgun Manager, using a multitude of strategies; a Tactician, employing primarily assertive strategies; or a Bystander, low on influence attempts in general?

b. How does your strategy profile differ depending upon the target of the situation (superior/boss, subordinate, peer/colleague)?

c. Which strategies did you *omit* using in the situation? Are there other strategies that you could be using (but have chosen not to) in your relationships with superiors, subordinates, and peers upon whom you are dependent?

Dependency Situation Worksheet

Summary of the Situation: _____

_____

_____

_____

_____

_____

_____

_____

_____

_____

_____

_____

_____

_____

_____

_____

_____

_____

_____

_____

_____

Primary Target in the Situation
(Superior, Subordinate, or Peer): _____

Actions Taken in the Situation: _____

_____

_____

_____

_____

_____

_____

_____

Dependency Situation Worksheet

Summary of the Situation: _____

_____

_____

_____

_____

_____

_____

_____

_____

_____

_____

_____

_____

_____

_____

_____

_____

_____

_____

Primary Target in the Situation
(Superior, Subordinate, or Peer): _____

Actions Taken in the Situation: _____

_____

_____

_____

_____

_____

_____

_____

III. Develop an action plan that describes how you will handle future dependency situations at work. Identify two dependency situations that you anticipate will cause you to employ empowerment strategies in the future, and focus your action plan on dealing with these situations.

Dependency Situation Action Plan

Anticipated Situation	Target of the Situation	Recommended Actions	Estimated Probability of Success	Contingency Plan
Situation #1: _____ _____ _____ _____ _____ _____ _____ _____	Circle one: Boss Peer Subordinate	First Choice Strategy— Second Choice Strategy— Third Choice Strategy—	_____ _____ _____	_____ _____ _____ _____ _____ _____ _____
Situation #2: _____ _____ _____ _____ _____ _____ _____	Circle one: Boss Peer Subordinate	First Choice Strategy— Second Choice Strategy— Third Choice Strategy—	_____ _____ _____	_____ _____ _____ _____ _____ _____

Dependency Situation Decision Tree

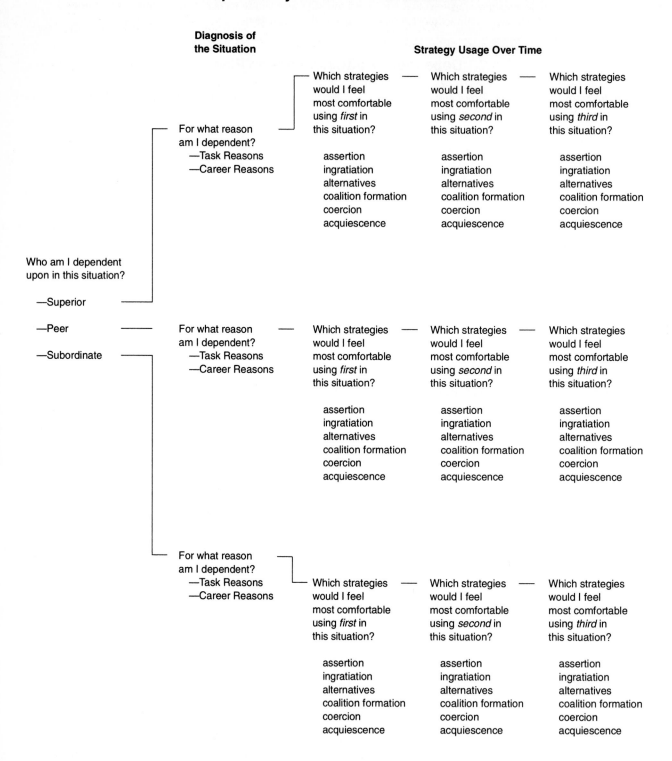

DISCUSSION QUESTIONS

1. What is your empowerment strategy profile? To what extent did your questionnaire results model your actions in "real life"?

2. Which strategies were more commonly used for superior relationships? Peer relationships? Subordinate relationships? What does this say about the use of formal authority (or lack thereof) and the kinds of strategies you should employ in work relationships?

3. Under what conditions are stronger, more definitive strategies preferable? More subtle ones?

REFERENCES

R. E. Emerson. "Power-Dependence Relations." *American Sociological Review,* 1962, *27,* 33–41.

J. P. Kotter. 1977, "Power, Dependence, and Effective Management." *Harvard Business Review,* 1977, *55,* 125–136.

L. A. Mainiero. "Coping with Powerlessness: The Relationship of Gender and Job Dependency to Empowerment Strategy Usage." *Administrative Science Quarterly,* 1986, Vol. 31(4), 633–653.

Case: Jennifer Carson at the Science Museum

PURPOSE

The purpose of this case is to provide you with an understanding of power and political dynamics at work. By the time you complete this case, you will

1. Identify how empowerment strategies can be used effectively

2. Understand situations in which power failures erupt

3. Determine how to cope with the politics of an ambiguous job situation

INTRODUCTION

The Jennifer Carson case illustrates the politics of an ambiguous job situation and the difficulties associated with creating productive change. In this case, Jennifer Carson is placed in the tenuous position of developing relationships with peers who resent her presence. It is her responsibility to serve as a project manager, but she cannot do so without the support and help of her peers. Complicating this situation is the relationship Jennifer has with her boss's boss, Robert Allston, and his management style.

INSTRUCTIONS

1. Read all three articles in the chapter as preparation for this case.

2. Read the Jennifer Carson case.

3. Answer the Discussion Questions that conclude the exercise.

4. Participate in a class discussion.

JENNIFER CARSON
AT THE SCIENCE MUSEUM (A)

Jennifer Carson joined the staff of the Science Museum in Boston in July 1986, one year after receiving her MBA at the age of 43. Although she had applied for a job managing all of the museum's revenue-generating activities, Carson was offered a newly-created position as head of exhibitions and special events. This opportunity had materialized during the course of her interviews with the director of the museum, Robert Allston.

Dr. Allston viewed Jennifer Carson as one who could use project management principles to coordinate and produce the elaborate special exhibitions with which the museum was increasingly involved. Since museum departments did not currently function on a project basis, Dr. Allston's idea signalled an organizational change for the museum, and he was very enthusiastic about adding a professional manager to his staff. Once at the museum, however, Jennifer found that the professional staff was highly resistant to working with someone who had neither a science or a museum background. Further, she had been hired without the knowledge and in the absence of the man who would be her immediate superior, the associate director in charge of education and visitor services. Jennifer would find that his behavior toward her was openly hostile.

Jennifer considered offering her resignation to the director, but by December felt that she had developed an acceptable working relationship with her boss, and that she was building considerable credibility with the other four associate directors. Her staff was increased and she was given major budget responsibility. In addition Jennifer received a promotion from unit to section manager.

In the following paragraphs Jennifer Carson describes how she established herself and a new department within the Science Museum organization.

Personal Background

Jennifer Carson briefly described her career and her family life:

My first job was with the Peace Corps in Nepal in 1962, after I graduated from Katherine Gibbs. I was married overseas and worked for the UN for a while. Then I had my

first child and worked for five years while my husband went through the seminary. I had two additional children and was at home for nine years.

When her youngest child started school, Jennifer was asked to manage a fabric business, which she was able to reorganize and make profitable. She later took a full-time job with a company that was starting up a program to teach English in Saudi Arabia; Jennifer successfully managed the project, including the hiring of overseas personnel. The president of the company subsequently offered to assist her if she decided to return to school.

As an entering MBA student, Jennifer was concerned about her age, her lack of an undergraduate degree, and about having been out of school for twenty-five years. Although the course work was difficult and the hour-long commute exhausting, she managed, and as she says now, "In a large class you build on each other's strengths."

During the time she was at business school, the health of her former boss began to deteriorate, and when she graduated Jennifer was asked to take on a major role in the firm's management. Six months later a decision was made to cease operations.

The Science Museum

In early 1986, Jennifer Carson began an intense job-search process. "I approached it very much as they tell you to," she recalls. "Send out résumés, call people you know, follow every lead, and talk to every human being you possibly can."

An executive recruiter sent Jennifer to the Science Museum, where she was interviewed by the director, Robert Allston. Dr. Allston was known in museum circles as the man who had developed a relatively small and conservatively run science museum into the foremost institution of its kind in the world. As Jennifer described it, Boston's Science Museum was "a sleepy, non-profit institution that was being cranked into the 20th century with a speed that would make most non-profit institutions look like they were standing still."

The museum served a metropolitan area with a high density of universities, hospitals, and high technology firms unlike any other in the U.S. and was able to draw on an extensive array of resources for its programs, exhibits, and professional staff. During Dr. Allston's tenure, the museum's Board of Trustees had grown in stature; among Boston's business and professional leaders the Science Museum ranked with the Boston Symphony and the Museum of Fine Arts as a desirable philanthropic affiliation. In 1987, the trustees included chief executives from Boston's largest banks, insurance companies, and technology firms, as well as prominent doctors, lawyers, and educators. Between 1982 and 1987, the oper-

This case was prepared by Jeanne Stanton for the Institute for Case Development and Research, Graduate School of Management, Simmons College, Boston, MA 02215. Copyright © 1989 by the President and Trustees of Simmons College. Revised 1991. Used with permission.

ating budget increased from $2 million to $16 million, and the staff grew to 400 from less than one hundred. From 1985 to 1986, annual attendance at the museum rose from 800,000 to 1.2 million, and the Development Office raised $18 million. A new wing was added to the museum and many innovative projects and exhibits were introduced.

Jennifer Carson was initially interviewed for a job overseeing revenue areas such as the shop and parking garage, but as they talked Allston became extremely enthusiastic about using her to direct special exhibits, as well as all of the special events that went on within the museum. Large-scale "theme" exhibitions, which drew upon the professional resources of a number of museum departments, were an area of increasing interest for Allston, and he perceived a need to have a permanent staff member who would coordinate and monitor the production of these exhibitions.

As a minister's wife, Jennifer was not enthusiastic about working for a non-profit institution; nonetheless, the job had several advantages. Although the proposed salary was barely adequate, she would have 23 vacation days annually—in addition to holidays—and the museum was prepared to send her to several museum management programs. Then there was the institution itself: "For me there were ethical considerations," Jennifer said. "The Science Museum was a place I could stand behind 100%."

Jennifer acknowledged that the prospect of working for Robert Allston was also very appealing:

> What I learned at my first interview was that Robert had come in after a man who had been there forty years. Robert Allston is a creative, innovative force.
>
> He is not a manager. He is a ball of fire, he is driven, and he has more ideas than you can imagine. So he knew he needed people who could manage at a time of transition.

Jennifer talked about how her job description developed:

> What Robert needed was someone to manage the big theme exhibitions, which come to us from other countries, other institutions, and so require extensive transport and installation arrangements, but which also require a unified marketing and promotional effort. An example would be the India exhibit which was here during the summer of 1987. Like the earlier China exhibit, this kind of project is different in both size and scope. Not only are there the artifacts which must be catalogued and displayed, but there are special events, educational programs, tie-ins with other areas of the museum. These are expensive exhibits to mount, and so we must have sufficient publicity to ensure that the admissions meet expectations. The museum is 80% self-supporting, which means that most of our operating funds come from admissions, the store, the restaurants, and parking. And corporate donations are based on traffic, because they want the visibility. So it is essential that the museum both attract visitors and provide them with a pleasant experience.
>
> What I was hired to do is project management. I was to bring the efforts of all the different departments into a cohesive whole, so that from the visitor's point of view an exhibition would come across as a total picture. Marketing should not oversell a modest exhibit, or if an exhibit was to be spectacular, we should have proportionate education programs. The reality would then meet the visitors' expectations.

The Science Museum, which also housed a planetarium, was located on the Charles River between Boston and Cambridge. Physical facilities included a parking garage that could accommodate 1000 cars, three restaurants, and a substantial gift shop. The Omni Theater, opened in March 1987, featured one of the world's first large-format film projection and sound systems, housed in a domed structure four stories high.

The Science Museum was organized into five divisions, each under the aegis of an associate director. (See Exhibit 1 for an outline of the organization.) The divisions were further divided into sections and units. There had been a good deal of restructuring and turnover at the associate director level prior to Jennifer's joining the Museum; as of early 1988, only two associate directors had been at the museum longer than Jennifer had.

Existing Policies and Practices

Despite the enthusiastic sponsorship of Robert Allston, Jennifer Carson experienced a period of extreme difficulty in forging a working relationship with the museum's associate directors, including her own boss, a man she did not meet until she had been at the museum for six weeks. Jennifer described the beginning of her career at the museum as follows:

> The museum was not ready for me. It is a very complex institution that found itself stretched in many ways, with systems not able to handle all of the demands. I was thrust into the middle of a difficult transition, and I had no idea what the politics were and what the hidden agenda might be.

Jennifer also discovered that, as inspiring and energizing as he was, Robert Allston proved to be something of a problem as a manager. Dr. Allston had a habit of acting on his ideas without consulting others. This often meant that he hired people and inserted them into the organization regardless of qualifications. He also recruited staff members to work on new projects without consulting their superiors. Jennifer explained how this impulsiveness with respect to hiring had affected her own situation:

> The director had a tendency to hire people because he liked something about them. Sometimes he was right and sometimes he was wrong. I had an MBA but no museum experience, and the first reaction of the museum body was, why was she hired? I knew that right away. I knew that I had to prove myself to the other 300 or 400 people here.

Jennifer described Allston's mode of operating as follows:

> He was an M.D. who had a tenured seat at Harvard, and he had come to the museum five years earlier. He had wonderful vision, tremendous dynamism. He was the kind of person you are willing to give so much for. But I could see that there were drawbacks. He pulled people out of departments and gave them authority that they shouldn't have had. He created tensions between people.
>
> My own boss had no idea I had been hired and was very upset. Why was an MBA hired, for a job that didn't exist, and why was he stuck with me? I had been hired for a job Robert developed in his imagination. Every time something new came up, Robert would say, "Why don't we let Jennifer

do that?" Within a month of my being at the museum his five associate directors were off the wall. They didn't know what my job was, and neither did I.

Jennifer explained her initial perception of the working environment as follows:

> People were very territorial. They very much owned their jobs. They take great personal and professional pride in what they do. So putting a non-museum person in charge of major projects was not well-received.
>
> What I had to do, because my job was so undefined, was to find out who in the museum would play with me at all. There were a few that saw that maybe I could lighten their load, but the majority saw me as a pain in the neck. Project management had never existed in the museum before, and it is an approach that requires the support of everybody.
>
> The director told people about the change to project management, but that didn't mean anything because they had no experience with it. They were sure that it would be more trouble than it was worth. What I had to do was teach people how budgeting was done, how my job worked, that I wasn't making decisions for them but needed their decisions to do my job. I continually reinforced that they were the ones that had the responsibility.

She described how she approached her job initially:

> There was one exhibit on the floor and one in planning, and those people began to report to me. I decided I would listen to them and learn from them, rather than assume I had anything to offer at this point. My management style is very hands-off. I tried to be extremely supportive of the two people who were doing the project, letting them make the decisions and tell me what they were doing. I put in my time on that exhibit, making very sure that I knew what was happening so I could learn how these things worked, but I tried not to be interfering.
>
> In the meantime we were developing a number of exhibits, including one on Robotics, and I had to start working on it because it was my project. I had hired a staff member to work on it. When I hired people I told them, "One of the most important jobs you have here is diplomacy. We're a new department and no one quite trusts us yet." We set up meetings of the teams on each project and we sent people notes and follow-up notes. People began to see that if they needed to know something about a project we were the people to ask.
>
> I also was fighting a battle in the budget area. People would decide whether or not they would contribute anything out of their department budget, and I wanted the budgets viewed as total project budgets. Then, if a cut has to be made it is made on the total project, instead of cutting a piece of it out. There had been a lot of turnover in the finance area—there have been four people since I have been here, and I have had to sell the concept to each one.

As her role developed Jennifer was charged with managing the opening festivities for all major exhibitions. She devised a system for classifying exhibitions according to scope and type and set up a committee of top-level managers to oversee planning of large-scale exhibitions, thus ensuring that the associate directors were involved in all major projects.

The Associate Director of Education and Visitor Services

The most difficult problem for Jennifer proved to be her relationship with her immediate supervisor, Frank Lassiter. Frank had been hired as associate director of her department in April of 1986, but he did not begin work at the museum until mid-July. When he arrived he found that Jennifer, an MBA without any science background, had been hired, and he was furious; he proceeded to treat her in a manner which prompted her to think about leaving. Jennifer described this period as follows:

> In mid-summer I started reporting to a new associate director who, had he been there when I was interviewed, never would have hired me. He was a lawyer by training, and he was difficult—at best—to deal with. He was all over my case about everything. The first couple of meetings with him unnerved me. Every time I tried to talk with him he would cut me off and tell me what was on his mind. It was impossible to get through to him. After six weeks I was ready to hand in my resignation.
>
> I knew we were having trouble communicating but I also knew that he wasn't going to do anything about it. I finally decided that I would try asking him to tell me about himself.
>
> He handed me his résumé. I said, No, Frank, I want to know what you do in your spare time. What you like to eat. Where do you go on the weekends? It seemed to break the ice. He began to open up, although he still didn't care who I was. He was convinced that I was a misfit, so I had to find a way to show him that I was going to be an asset to him. I had to figure out what he wanted to prove, because he was so argumentative about everything. He was so defensive and anxious he couldn't deal with the rest of us. But then he had just arrived, too.

Jennifer soon realized that she was at a disadvantage with Frank because she had a direct line to the top:

> Of course Robert and I had already developed a strong rapport, and now Frank, my new boss, had to deal with this triangular relationship. But I had to be able to work with Frank in such a way that he wasn't going to mess me up. I had to develop a relationship with him in order to make him feel that I supported and worked for him, when at the same time I was constantly being called into the director's office. When he first saw me coming out of the director's office he snapped at me. "What were you in there for? Never go in there without telling me!" He was very threatened by my direct contact with the director. So I was careful to keep him informed about everything I did. I kept him in touch on what I was doing, where I was going, and what projects I was working on. But it was very difficult. Who was I really reporting to?

Despite her difficulty with Frank, Jennifer learned that at least one associate director had discovered that her "interference" had resulted in several well-executed projects, which had reflected well on the professional staff without costing them an undue amount of effort. As Jennifer explained later, "What he said was that I had taken on many things that other people weren't prepared to do, and as a result I had justifiably acquired a lot of power and influence at the museum. It frequently happens here that people are willing to take on a project but not really the responsibility for executing it."

As an example, Jennifer cited the previous year's Washburn Awards Dinner, the first major project to be her total responsibility:

> This was an important assignment. It was the first project I did as an employee here and it is also their largest fund-raising dinner. The dinner was scheduled for October.
>
> I hired an assistant and the two of us worked on this project all by ourselves. I had told her, "This project must be flawless." Robert Allston is the kind of person who can always find something that isn't quite right. He is wonderful at congratulating you, but he will always add, "Next time let us make sure that we do the following."
>
> I interviewed the woman who had done it the year before. I got to know a woman who worked here who had done a lot of these kinds of projects. I had to be sure that everything that could possibly go wrong was addressed beforehand.
>
> The food, the audio-visual presentation, hosting special guests, the written materials—everyone on the Board of Trustees has an idea of how these things should be done. Who sits at what table, what happens when—these events only work if they are good from the point of view of the people who pay for them. So I listened a lot and figured out what was important to each and every one of them. I would say, "All right, and what else is on your mind?"
>
> One of the concerns was the upstairs bathroom, which would be used extensively by people before going into dinner. It had to be kept clean. The handling of people—this building is not set up for functions, and we had to figure out the easiest way to get people from one floor to another. We had to be able to get a feeling for what the event would be like from the point of view of the guests. This is what I harp on with my staff: how do you make a visit here a pleasant experience for a visitor? Our viewpoint here can become very inverted.
>
> At the end of the evening Robert Allston came to me and said, "This is the first event that we have done at the museum that has been perfect."

EXHIBIT 1
List of Museum Divisions, Sections, and Units, 1985–86

President and Director
Robert L. Allston

Assistant to the President
Executive Secretary
Deputy Director
Special Assistant to the President

Administration and Finance Division
Associate Director and Division Head

Museum Purchasing
Employee Services
Data Processing

Physical Plant and Technical Services Section
Electronics and Technical Services
Garage and Security

Operations Section
Museum Store
Group Sales and Telemarketing
Function Sales

Education and Visitor Services Division
Frank Lassiter, Associate Director and Division Head

Education Section
Discovery Spaces
Library

Public Services Section
Admissions
Volunteer Services

Interpretation and Training

Special Events and Exhibitions Coordination:
Jennifer Carson, Head

Educational Technology Section
ComputerPlace
Science Resource Center
Special Program Services

Exhibits Division
Associate Director and Division Head

Traveling Exhibits

Theaters and Marketing Division
Associate Director and Division Head

Omni Theater
Planetarium Section
Marketing Section
Publications

Resources Division
Associate Director and Division Head

Development Section
Development
Corporate Membership
Membership

Other Development Services
Governmental Grants and Support
Special Events and Traveling Exhibits

Jennifer added that her success in managing the Awards Dinner did not further her credibility with anyone but Allston. In order to gain the trust and cooperation of the other professionals, Jennifer spent much of her time visiting the departments, asking questions, and reassuring people that she was there to work with them. In Jennifer's words,

> I knew that I couldn't get raises or promotions or anything if I didn't get the associate directors' support. I need those five people to view me as credible and as a person worth working with. I knew that it would be very, very dangerous to just hook my star to the director.
>
> I got acquainted with people, learned what they did, and was very up front about my lack of a science background. I would say, what I am good at is management. What you are good at is the content of this exhibit. I'm good at making sure it works and you know what it needs to have to have value. I tried to get them to view my department's contribution as another layer, and not to take away from what they were contributing.

The Process of Developing an Exhibition

The 1988 Ramesses II exhibition would be representative of the new "blockbuster" approach favored by Allston. The project would engage the resources of the entire museum and would be promoted on a scale to entice the interest, and hopefully attendance, of a significant segment of the Northeastern population. A promotional brochure published by the museum communicated the importance of the exhibit as follows:

> "Since much of our knowledge of Ramesses II and his time comes to us through the science of archaeology, the Boston Science Museum is honored to host the only Northeast United States appearance of the Ramesses the Great exhibition.
>
> This largest and most varied assembling of treasures from Egypt's Golden Age ever brought to the United States offers a dual opportunity that may come only once in a lifetime. First, a journey back over 3000 years to the time of Ramesses the Great and the New Kingdom to examine the priceless evidence and artifacts of Egyptian accomplishments. And second, the chance to explore the methods and analyses that led archaeologists to their discoveries."

The exhibition was set to open in late April 1988 and was preceded by a massive publicity effort, including numerous articles and advertisements in Boston-area publications and billboards featuring the Ramesses coffin with the slogan, "Grand opening April 30." An article in the May 14 *Boston Ledger* described the week of special events leading up to the opening of the exhibit, which included a champagne and caviar reception for Queen Farida, the former queen of Egypt:

> "A full week of festivities royally welcomed Egypt's most famous pharaoh, Ramesses the Great, to the banks of Boston's Nile—the Charles River. Before the show's public unveiling, Science Museum volunteers and staffers braced themselves for a series of private receptions, dinners, and exhibit tours to fête Fidelity and Sheraton corporate spon-

sors, museum trustees and VIPs, and an unexpectedly huge press contingent. To top off the excitement, the museum even planned one big final fundraising bash of their own."

Numerous additional exhibits within the museum were planned to support and expand on the Ramesses material. There were to be lectures and a film series, as well as several museum-sponsored trips to Egypt scheduled to coincide with the exhibition.

Jennifer explained that the current Ramesses II exhibition was not typical, in that most projects were not as elaborate and did not require so much involvement from senior management. She described the usual process as follows:

> In many cases ideas originate with Robert. He will hear about something marvelous and go after it. There is a process whereby exhibit proposals go to the exhibit department, then to a committee, and then up to Robert. But often Robert will say, "I want this exhibit," and whether or not everyone agrees, it comes here.
>
> With Ramesses I felt that I needed control of the budget. Each department had a part of a $6 million budget and they were unwilling to let it be seen as part of a whole. There was a lot of in-fighting. It was finally decided that Robert would head up the project and that I would work with him directly on it. But without control of their budget, I could not make any of the other department directors do anything.

Jennifer described the usual process of developing an exhibition as follows:

1. Brainstorming—Jennifer and all involved department heads would talk about what the exhibit as visualized would need in terms of total programming, what Jennifer called "a pool of intentions."

2. All costs of the exhibit would be determined.

3. Jennifer's department would develop a budget and make a recommendation based on what the departments each projected as their part of the exhibit.

4. A project budget was developed and Jennifer communicated to each of the departments what their budget was, in return for what they were expected to contribute to that particular exhibit.

5. Jennifer would periodically report back to individual departments on their performance with respect to the budget.

Jennifer added that because she did not have the "final clout," departments could spend their allotment for the Ramesses exhibition however they wished. "If the associate director didn't back me up there would be nothing I could do about it," she explained. "I didn't have that final control, and no one wanted to relinquish that much power—the budget for Ramesses was $6 million."

For the Ramesses exhibit, Jennifer and the project managers met with the associate directors every week. But even on smaller projects she made it a point to involve management from other departments as soon and as often as possible. She explained that this was necessary in order to ensure that the promotion and educational programs all were directed at the same target audience:

> One of the ways we get people to buy into a unified concept is to bring all of the departments together at the very

early stages and say, "This is kind of what the exhibit is going to look like and this is the kind of scope we are planning. The marketing effort will be pretty extensive. We may need to add some programming. So you come back and tell us what you think."

When I actually go into a department to get something, it may be because that department is out of sync with the others. For example, marketing uses numbers in ways that can be very deceptive. The Kenya exhibit has 250 artifacts and the Ramesses exhibit 72, but Kenya is taking 400 square feet and the Ramesses II exhibit is being housed in the entire museum. So using the number in promotion pieces is very deceptive, because with Kenya there are a lot of little things, like combs and pieces of paper. Finally we were able to get them to see that it was not good to oversell.

The Situation in January 1988

After eighteen months at the Science Museum, Jennifer Carson felt that she had achieved a measure of acceptance. She had increased her own staff to thirteen people. She was currently managing $8.5 million worth of projects. She had been promoted from unit to section head, and, since there were few other women managers at her level, she found that other women in the museum had begun to come to her for counseling.

There continued to be a good deal of turnover among associate directors. Jennifer rationalized the stability of her own department as follows:

> My department was created by a man who understood the need for it. He understood that to make the museum a world-class one they would have to do more theme exhibitions and that they would have to be managed well to achieve maximum effect. He has an awareness of what is happening in the museum industry, that we are competing with other "leisure" activities, and that we have to be very effective in competing for that time. My department was his solution to how to manage a continual flow of new things, to keep the audience enticed and coming back.

Jennifer believed that she and Frank Lassiter had finally developed a good working relationship, as she realized when he told her one day that, "It's amazing that we think so much alike!" Jennifer commented, "Part of it was his own anxiety about adapting to a new environment. He is very outspoken and he was having problems with almost everyone." Further,

> He is very clear-thinking, but he takes in information in certain ways and he shuts down very quickly if he isn't getting it that way.
> Over time he built a bit better relationship with the director himself, and as our own relationship became stronger he became more comfortable. I was always on budget, always kept him informed, always produced the visual aids he needed, gave him graphs and support material that made him feel he had a grasp on what I was doing. I gave him things that he would then take to Robert. Now he very rarely interferes with what I do.
> We work extremely well together now. I don't think it's because he likes me any better. It's because I have proven

to be his most valuable staff member. He knows he can depend on me. But it took a long time.

JENNIFER CARSON (B)

On December 10, 1987, Robert Allston, director of the Science Museum, died suddenly. As his brilliant leadership of one of Boston's major institutions came to an abrupt end, Jennifer Carson and the rest of the Museum of Science staff were left both saddened and disoriented. In late January 1988, Jennifer described how the death of the director had affected her own position at the museum:

> The evening before he died I had met with him unexpectedly. I was working late, we had a meeting scheduled the next day, and he called me into his office and told me that he was going to make me an acting associate director. I was going to be put in charge of a new, branch museum in another city, a project in which he was extremely interested. He told me, "You have remarkable talents in administration and management, and although you are weak in science and education, you are the best person I have to send on this project."
> The next morning he was dead. I was no longer an acting associate director. The project was going to be put on hold. I was devastated—at my loss of a friend and of a person with whom I had worked closely. Then, the interim director and the board chairman became very, very anxious about the Ramesses exhibit. It was the biggest thing on our plate for the year, and the man who was responsible for it was gone.

Jennifer continued working on the Ramesses exhibit, which was slated to open on April 30, although, in her words, "The board put me through hoops doing presentations. They were scared. I knew we could do the job, but they needed to know that we could do the job."

A larger question for Jennifer was whether or not her position, and her future, would be assured at the museum. She felt that she "got along well" with the interim director, but that as a 32-year veteran of IBM he was not a risk-taker, and he definitely was not a strong supporter of women as managers. Jennifer assessed her situation as follows:

> I am not concerned about keeping this job. I believe that three of the associate directors completely support this department. It takes a load off of them and brings a consistent level of professionalism to every exhibit.
> The issue for me is whether I can go from here to somewhere else. This museum is on the cutting edge of science museums all over the world, and it takes a kind of energy and entrepreneurial disposition to run it. I came here because I believed in the vision of the director and because it was not your typical staid, non-profit institution. I'll only stay if it remains that kind of dynamic place.

During the following months, Jennifer began interviewing for positions outside the museum. Events had developed that convinced her of the need to change jobs. The interim director appeared to be permanent. More to the point, her relationship with her boss, Frank Lassiter, had deteriorated. According to Jennifer, resentment built up over her closeness with Robert Allston had manifested itself in Frank's treating her in an authoritarian, dictatorial manner:

> After Roger died I began to find out how angry Frank had been about my relationship with the director. He turned on me. He thought I had been given too much freedom. Everything I do now has to have his approval. I write everything for him, and he presents it. I no longer speak for myself.

Although the Ramesses exhibit opened smoothly and was extremely successful, and Jennifer was offered a new job at the museum, she did not feel that there was sufficient support for her efforts to make it worth her while to continue. She summarized her reasons for deciding to leave as follows:

> The current acting director is likely to be here much longer than I thought. I was told directly that he does not believe that women belong in senior management.
> The Ramesses exhibit was budgeted to make $.5 million based on 600,000 attendance. We had over 700,000 and made $3 million. I got no credit or recognition. The financial statements do not attribute the increase in revenue to the exhibition.
> I have been offered a new position, which is very subtle acknowledgment that I am valued as an employee. It is as section head for operations, which means I would manage admissions, group sales, the stores, telemarketing— all revenue-producing activities except the restaurants, which are subcontracted. What they call "ancillary services." I would have many more people reporting to me, but it is still a lateral move.
> I feel it is the interim director's way of saying that they want me and that there is a place for me. But there would be no growth. Within the context of the museum I would be moving into an area which is regarded as a necessary evil. I would have to move to another museum to move up.
> I want the opportunity to help something grow. I want to be a member of senior management. And so I believe that at age 47 I must work somewhere for five years and establish myself.

In August 1988, Jennifer accepted a job offer managing the financial, development, and "business" operations of a four-year-old non-profit service and training organization. She would be working on an equal basis with the three directors who had started the company. She described the rationale for this move as follows:

> My next job will be working as part of senior management with three people who know very little about finance or business management. They view me as a savior. This new situation appeals to me for the following reasons:
> I am supportive of their mission; there is potential for growth; there is the challenge of an entrepreneurial venture; I can develop credibility as a senior manager; I will have a voice in policy-making and a chance to speak on behalf of the firm.

Jennifer concluded by saying that she would have done better to have entered the museum as a specialist, since "manager" was still an unfamiliar, and unpalatable, term there, and as such she had been viewed with skepticism:

> One of my main strengths is being able to see how all the pieces fit together. I have always thought of myself as a generalist. Being a general manager means that I know and understand finance, marketing communications. But if you tell someone you are a general manager, they say, what's that? Is it that you're not good at anything, or that you are sort of good at everything?
> The understanding of what goes on between people is far more important than understanding basic business skills—which are easier to learn. You can learn accounting. It is harder to learn effective communications, how to listen, to hear what people are saying, to negotiate. It requires being able to step out of yourself, not to be threatened, to realize that it might not work out the way you wanted it. It is so much easier to make a decision and do something than it is to get other people to work together.

DISCUSSION QUESTIONS

1. Which empowerment strategies did Jennifer Carson use effectively? Which other strategies did she choose not to use? Why or why not?

2. Jennifer Carson's dilemmas stemmed from her ambiguous job situation, the fact that she had no museum experience, and the special rapport she shared with her boss's boss. What suggestions can you offer to cope with the tricky politics of such real-life situations?

3. Upon reading the (B) case, do you feel Jennifer Carson managed the situation effectively after all?

Exercise: Power Lab

PURPOSE

The purpose of this exercise is to help you understand groups within organizations' power dynamics that occur among authority. By the time you finish this exercise you will

1. Experience intergroup power dynamics first-hand.

2. Understand the intersection of resource allocation decisions and power dynamics across departments and groups within an organization.

3. Explore different perspectives on power and authority.

INTRODUCTION

As discussed in the Salancik and Pfeffer article, power can have a significant effect on organizational functioning. Those in power can alter the resource allocations to remain in power, while those who lack power remain powerless. Upper management holds the most power by virtue of the authority present in their management positions. Those at the lower levels must fight for recognition and resources, and those at the middle management level often are caught between both groups.

In this exercise, you will participate in a three-tiered intergroup simulation that is designed to simulate the power dynamics among these three groups. Some of you will experience what it is like to be Tops, controlling the resources of the organization. Others will serve as Bottoms, serving the most menial tasks of the organization. Still others will experience a liaison role as Middles, negotiating between both groups.

INSTRUCTIONS

1. Prior to this exercise, read the article by Salancik and Pfeffer, "Who Gets Power and How They Hold Onto It: A Strategic Contingency Model of Power."

2. Your instructor will ask you to bring a one-dollar bill to class for the purpose of this exercise. Turn in your one-dollar bill to the instructor upon entering the class.

3. At the start of class, you will be assigned to serve as a participant in one of the three groups: Tops, Middles, and Bottoms. Read the Power Lab Description and Rules that follow.

4. Begin the simulation. Complete the tasks that you are assigned.

5. Participate in a class discussion. Your instructor will request that you elect a representative from your group to speak for your group about your feelings and attitudes throughout the exercise.

6. Summarize and wrap up.

This exercise is adapted from a version entitled, "A Simple But Powerful Simulation" that appeared in Dorothea Hai's book, *Organizational Behavior: Experiences and Cases* (New York: West Publishers, 1986). This exercise originally appeared in an article by Lee Bolman and Terence Deal in *Exchange,* Vol. 4(3), 38–42. Teaching notes have also been adapted from these sources. All have been used with permission of the publishers.

POWER LAB DESCRIPTION AND RULES

In this simulation, there are three groups with the following responsibilities:

1. *The Top Group:* Responsible for the overall effectiveness and learning from the simulation, as well as for determining resource allocation decisions.

2. *The Middle Group:* Responsible for assisting the Tops in providing for the overall welfare of the organization, and for serving as a liaison between the Tops and Middles.

3. *The Bottom Group:* Responsible for the identification of the organization's resources, and for producing the goods and services for the organization.

The rules for the simulation are as follows:

1. The Bottoms will produce the goods for the organization, namely the construction of rectangular buildings out of index cards, staples, and tape as provided by your instructor.

2. The Middles will supervise the construction of the rectangular buildings.

3. The Tops will determine the design of the buildings and are free to reject any buildings they deem unfit for sale.

4. The Tops retain all the money. They may determine what portion can be doled out to the Middles for the procurement of additional supplies and resources and the Bottoms as payment for their labor.

5. Members of the Top Group are free to enter the space of either of the other groups and to communicate whatever they wish, whenever they wish. Members of the Middle Group may enter the space of the lower group whenever they wish but must request permission to enter the Top Group's space (a request the Top Group may refuse). Members of the Bottom Group may not disturb the Top Group in any way unless specifically invited by the Tops to do so. The Bottom Group does have the right to knock on the door of the Middle Group and request permission to communicate with them (though that permission may be refused).

6. The Bottoms must remain in their assigned space unless told to do otherwise.

DISCUSSION QUESTIONS

1. How did you feel as a member of your particular group? How would you expect the members of the other groups to feel during the simulation?

2. Did your feelings grow stronger or weaker throughout the simulation?

3. Were you satisfied with the amount of power you were allocated?

4. Did you attempt to exercise or gain more power (or reduce and share your power) during the exercise?

5. What parallels can be drawn between this exercise and real-life organizational situations?

REFERENCE

Barry Oshry. *Power and Position.* Boston: Power Systems, 1979.

CHAPTER 6
Group Dynamics

INTRODUCTION

Working in groups is an increasingly popular practice in corporate settings. Many managers, however, find working in groups to be a frustrating experience. This negative reaction to team management is a result of diverse factors. For example, groups take longer than individuals to make decisions. Groups can also fall prey to destructive conflict that can distort the simplicity of the decision-making process. Further, groups sometimes go off on a tangent that can lead to unrealistic and poorly implemented policies.

However, working in groups need not be a negative experience. When effectively managed, groups can make higher-quality decisions that are more widely accepted. Groups also facilitate communication among disparate parties so that all sides of an issue can be fully understood. And the group morale that arises from an effectively managed team can be a most satisfying experience. The challenge for managers is to understand the dynamics that contribute to effective group decision making so they can create the proper conditions for excellent team management.

The subject of group behavior is a vast and considerably complicated topic. We cannot possibly do justice to the topic in this chapter alone. The readings we have included highlight particular aspects of group dynamics that we thought would be most instructive for future managers.

READINGS

The first article, Norman R. F. Maier's "Assets and Liabilities in Group Problem Solving: The Need for an Integrative Function," focuses on some of the benefits and problems associated with group decision-making processes. Maier outlines the advantages and disadvantages of group problem solving. For example, one well-known advantage of group decision making is the opportunity to generate more alternatives. An equally well-known disadvantage is pressure for social conformity, which can decrease the breadth of alternatives presented. After reading this article, you will be better able to discern the conditions under which a group decision may be warranted versus the conditions under which it should be avoided.

The second reading, "Groupthink," by Irving L. Janis, is considered a classic by many. "Groupthink" is a term that describes a mind-set to which some groups fall victim as they make decisions of consequence. Janis uses examples of policy formulation in the Kennedy and Johnson administrations, such as the Bay of Pigs fiasco and the Vietnam War, to illustrate how groupthink evolves. When groups believe they are invulnerable, righteous, and inherently moral, they override self-censorship to create an illusion of assumed consensus. When this occurs, groups usually make poor decisions. They are unable to complete a thorough survey of alternatives. Often, such groups take risks that are out of proportion to the problems at hand. Groups that fall victim to groupthink take on a life of their own, and the quality of their decisions can suffer as a consequence.

The third article, "The Development and Enforcement of Group Norms," by Daniel C. Feldman, examines the concept of group norms. A norm is a standard of behavior that evolves spontaneously from social interaction. This article illustrates why group norms are enforced and how they develop. Because group norms play a large role in determining whether a group will be productive or not, author Feldman suggests that understanding group norms is essential to management practice. Critical events in the group's history, explicit statements from supervisors, and the primacy effect all may contribute to group norm development. He offers several examples pertinent to management practice to illustrate his assertions.

EXERCISES AND CASES

The first exercise in the chapter, "Group Decision Making and Effectiveness," gives you the opportunity to determine the effectiveness of group versus individual decisions. You will complete a survival exercise individually and in a group. Then you will be asked to reflect upon the decision-making process that occurred in your group. Were the decisions based on consensus or majority rule? How was the disagreement handled? Did the group fall victim to groupthink? These and other issues are the focus of this exercise.

The case, "The NASA/Challenger Incident," asks you to apply groupthink concepts to an analysis of the Challenger space shuttle disaster. Many of us were surprised when the Rogers Commission issued its report on the Challenger crash. They highlighted ineffective decision-making processes and poor communication as two of the many causes of the crash. Groupthink may have been a part of the problem. After reading this case, you will have an opportunity to debate the issues and determine whether or not groupthink was at fault.

Sometimes norms are most easily identifiable when a group member violates them. The third exercise, "Norms and Deviance," asks you to identify norms in groups in which you currently participate. Determining who may have violated a norm, and/or whom in the group may serve as its "deviant" (that is, deviant from group norms), often is instructive to illustrate the overall health of the group. Effective and ineffective approaches to group deviance are highlighted in this exercise.

MEMO

The memo assignment, *"Assessing Your Team"* (located at the back of the book), asks you to reflect upon a group of which you are currently a member—a task force, your department, or any intact group. The questions presented in the assignment direct you to analyze the dynamics within your group or department. After you have completed this analysis, you will develop a plan for improvement. By understanding group dynamics in a real-life situation, you will be able to apply the concepts and skills from this chapter to increase the likelihood of working cooperatively as an effective team.

By the time you finish this chapter, you will have a greater understanding of group dynamics and decision-making processes. Group norms and their relationship to productivity will become more apparent to you than ever before. You will also learn how to monitor, cope with, and intervene to improve decision-making practices and team relations.

Assets and Liabilities in Group Problem Solving: The Need for an Integrative Function

Norman R. F. Maier

A number of investigations have raised the question of whether group problem solving is superior, inferior, or equal to individual problem solving. Evidence can be cited in support of each position so that the answer to this question remains ambiguous. Rather than pursue this generalized approach to the question, it seems more fruitful to explore the forces that influence problem solving under the two conditions (see reviews by Hoffman, 1965; Kelley & Thibaut, 1954). It is hoped that a better recognition of these forces will permit clarification of the varied dimensions of the problem solving process, especially in groups.

The forces operating in such groups include some that are assets, some that are liabilities, and some that can be either assets or liabilities, depending upon the skills of the members, especially those of the discussion leader. Let us examine these three sets of forces.

GROUP ASSETS

Greater Sum Total of Knowledge and Information

There is more information in a group than in any of its members. Thus problems that require the utilization of knowledge should give groups an advantage over individuals. Even if one member of the group (e.g., the leader) knows much more than anyone else, the limited unique knowledge of lesser-informed individuals could serve to fill in some gaps in knowledge. For example, a skilled machinist might contribute to an engineer's problem solv-

ing and an ordinary workman might supply information on how a new machine might be received by workers.

Greater Number of Approaches to a Problem

It has been shown that individuals get into ruts in their thinking (Duncker, 1945; Maier, 1930; Wertheimer, 1959). Many obstacles stand in the way of achieving a goal, and a solution must circumvent these. The individual is handicapped in that he tends to persist in his approach and thus fails to find another approach that might solve the problem in a simpler manner. Individuals in a group have the same failing, but the approaches in which they are persisting may be different. For example, one researcher may try to prevent the spread of a disease by making man immune to the germ, another by finding and destroying the carrier of the germ, and still another by altering the environment so as to kill the germ before it reaches man. There is no way of determining which approach will best achieve the desired goal, but undue persistence in any one will stifle new discoveries. Since group members do not have identical approaches, each can contribute by knocking others out of ruts in thinking.

Participation in Problem Solving Increases Acceptance

Many problems require solutions that depend upon the support of others to be effective. Insofar as group problem solving permits participation and influence, it follows that more individuals accept solutions when a group solves the problem than when one person solves it. When one individual solves a problem he still has the task of persuading others. It follows, therefore, that when groups solve such problems, a greater number of persons accept and feel

From *Psychological Review,* 1967, Vol. 74(4), pp. 239–249. Copyright © 1967 by the American Psychological Association. Reprinted by permission of the publisher and author.

responsible for making the solution work. A low-quality solution that has good acceptance can be more effective than a higher-quality solution that lacks acceptance.

Better Comprehension of the Decision

Decisions made by an individual, which are to be carried out by others, must be communicated from the decision-maker to the decision-executors. Thus individual problem solving often requires an additional stage—that of relaying the decision reached. Failures in this communication process detract from the merits of the decision and can even cause its failure or create a problem of greater magnitude than the initial problem that was solved. Many organizational problems can be traced to inadequate communication of decisions made by superiors and transmitted to subordinates, who have the task of implementing the decision.

The chances for communication failures are greatly reduced when the individuals who must work together in executing the decision have participated in making it. They not only understand the solution because they saw it develop, but they are also aware of the several other alternatives that were considered and the reasons why they were discarded. The common assumption that decisions supplied by superiors are arbitrarily reached therefore disappears. A full knowledge of goals, obstacles, alternatives, and factual information is essential to communication, and this communication is maximized when the total problem-solving process is shared.

GROUP LIABILITIES

Social Pressure

Social pressure is a major force making for conformity. The desire to be a good group member and to be accepted tends to silence disagreement and favors consensus. Majority opinions tend to be accepted regardless of whether or not their objective quality is logically and scientifically sound. Problems requiring solutions based upon facts, regardless of feelings and wishes, can suffer in group problem-solving situations.

It has been shown (Maier & Solem, 1952) that minority opinions in leaderless groups have little influence on the solution reached, even when these opinions are the correct ones. Reaching agreement in a group often is confused with finding the right answer, and it is for this reason that the dimensions of a decision's acceptance and its objective quality must be distinguished (Maier, 1963).

Valence of Solutions

When leaderless groups (made up of three or four persons) engage in problem solving, they propose a variety of solutions. Each solution may receive both critical and supportive comments, as well as descriptive and explorative comments from other participants. If the number of negative and positive comments for each solution are algebraically summed, each may be given a *valence index* (Hoffman & Maier, 1964). The first solution that receives a positive valence value of 15 tends to be adopted to the satisfaction of all participants about 85% of the time, regardless of its quality. Higher quality solutions introduced after the critical value for one of the solutions has been reached have little chance of achieving real consideration. Once some degree of consensus is reached, the jelling process seems to proceed rather rapidly.

The critical valence value of 15 appears not to be greatly altered by the nature of the problem or the exact size of the group. Rather, it seems to designate a turning point between the idea-getting process and the decision-making process (idea evaluation). A solution's valence index is not a measure of the number of persons supporting the solution, since a vocal minority can build up a solution's valence by actively pushing it. In this sense, valence becomes an influence in addition to social pressure in determining an outcome.

Since a solution's valence is independent of its objective quality, this group factor becomes an important liability in group problem solving, even when the value of a decision depends upon objective criteria (facts and logic). It becomes a means whereby skilled manipulators can have more influence over the group process than their proportion of membership deserves.

Individual Domination

In most leaderless groups a dominant individual emerges and captures more than his share of influence on the outcome. He can achieve this end through a greater degree of participation (valence), persuasive ability, or stubborn persistence (fatiguing the opposition). None of these factors is related to problem-solving ability, so that the best problem solver in the group may not have the influence to upgrade the quality of the group's solution (which he would have had if left to solve the problem by himself).

Hoffman and Maier (1967) found that the mere fact of appointing a leader causes this person to dominate a discussion. Thus, regardless of his problem-solving ability a leader tends to exert a major influence on the outcome of a discussion.

Conflicting Secondary Goal: Winning the Argument

When groups are confronted with a problem, the initial goal is to obtain a solution. However, the appearance of several alternatives causes individuals to have preferences and once these emerge the desire to support a position is created. Converting those with neutral viewpoints and refuting those with opposed viewpoints now enters into the problem-solving process. More and more the goal becomes that of winning the decision rather than finding the best solution. This new goal is unrelated to the quality of the problem's solution and therefore can result in lowering the quality of the decision (Hoffman & Maier, 1966).

FACTORS THAT SERVE AS ASSETS OR LIABILITIES, DEPENDING LARGELY UPON THE SKILL OF THE DISCUSSION LEADER

Disagreement

The fact that discussion may lead to disagreement can serve either to create hard feelings among members or lead to a resolution of conflict and hence to an innovative solution (Hoffman, 1961; Hoffman, Harburg, and Maier, 1962; Hoffman & Maier, 1961; Maier, 1958, 1963; Maier & Hoffman, 1965). The first of these outcomes of disagreement is a liability, especially with regard to the acceptance of solutions; while the second is an asset, particularly where innovation is desired. A leader can treat disagreement as undesirable and thereby reduce the probability of both hard feelings and innovation, or he can maximize disagreement and risk hard feelings in his attempts to achieve innovation. The skill of a leader requires his ability to create a climate for disagreement which will permit innovation without risking hard feelings. The leader's perception of disagreement is one of the critical factors in this skill area (Maier & Hoffman, 1965). Others involve permissiveness (Maier, 1953), delaying the reaching of a solution (Maier & Hoffman, 1960b; Maier & Solem, 1962), techniques for processing information and opinions (Maier, 1963; Maier & Hoffman, 1960a; Maier & Maier, 1957), and techniques for separating idea-getting from idea-evaluation (Maier, 1960, 1963; Osborn, 1953).

Conflicting Interests Versus Mutual Interests

Disagreement in discussion may take many forms. Often participants disagree with one another with regard to solutions, but when issues are explored one finds that these conflicting solutions are designed to solve different problems. Before one can rightly expect agreement on a solution, there should be agreement on the nature of the problem. Even before this, there should be agreement on the goal, as well as on the various obstacles that prevent the goal from being reached. Once distinctions are made between goals, obstacles, and solutions (which represent ways of overcoming obstacles), one finds increased opportunities for cooperative problem solving and less conflict (Hoffman & Maier, 1959; Maier, 1960, 1963; Maier & Solem, 1962; Solem, 1965).

Often there is also disagreement regarding whether the objective of a solution is to achieve quality or acceptance (Maier & Hoffman, 1964b), and frequently a stated problem reveals a complex of separate problems, each having separate solutions so that a search for a single solution is impossible (Maier, 1963). Communications often are inadequate because the discussion is not synchronized and each person is engaged in discussing a different aspect. Organizing discussion to synchronize the exploration of different aspects of the problem and to follow a systematic procedure increases solution quality (Maier & Hoffman, 1960a; Maier & Maier, 1957). The leadership function of influencing discussion procedure is quite distinct from the function of evaluating or contributing ideas (Maier, 1950, 1953).

When the discussion leader aids in the separation of the several aspects of the problem-solving process and delays the solution-mindedness of the group (Maier, 1958, 1963; Maier & Solem, 1962), both solution quality and acceptance improve; when he hinders or fails to facilitate the isolation of these varied processes, he risks a deterioration in the group process (Solem, 1965). His skill thus determines whether a discussion drifts toward conflicting interests or whether mutual interests are located. Cooperative problem solving can only occur after the mutual interests have been established and it is surprising how often they can be found when the discussion leader makes this his task (Maier, 1952, 1963; Maier & Hayes, 1962).

Risk Taking

Groups are more willing than individuals to reach decisions involving risks (Wallach & Kogan, 1965; Wallach, Kogan, & Bem, 1962). Taking risks is a factor in acceptance of change, but change may either represent a gain or a loss. The best guard against the latter outcome seems to be primarily a matter of a decision's quality.

In a group situation this depends upon the leader's skill in utilizing the factors that represent group assets and avoiding those that make for liabilities.

Time Requirements

In general, more time is required for a group to reach a decision than for a single individual to reach one. Insofar as some problems require quick decisions, individual decisions are favored. In other situations acceptance and quality are requirements, but excessive time without sufficient returns also represent a loss. On the other hand, discussion can resolve conflicts, whereas reaching consensus has limited value (Wallach & Kogan, 1965). The practice of hastening a meeting can prevent full discussion, but failure to move a discussion forward can lead to boredom and fatigue-type solutions, in which members agree merely to get out of the meeting. The effective utilization of discussion time (a delicate balance between permissiveness and control on the part of the leader), therefore, is needed to make the time factor an asset rather than a liability. Unskilled leaders tend to be too concerned with reaching a solution and therefore terminate a discussion before the group potential is achieved (Maier & Hoffman, 1960b).

Who Changes

In reaching consensus or agreement, some members of a group must change. Persuasive forces do not operate in individual problem solving in the same way they operate in a group situation; hence, the changing of someone's mind is not an issue. In group situations, however, who changes can be an asset or a liability. If persons with the most constructive views are induced to change the end-product suffers; whereas if persons with the least constructive points of view change the end-product is upgraded. The leader can upgrade the quality of a decision because his position permits him to protect the person with a minority view and increase his opportunity to influence the majority position. This protection is a constructive factor because a minority viewpoint influences only when facts favor it (Maier, 1950, 1952; Maier & Solem, 1952).

The leader also plays a constructive role insofar as he can facilitate communications and thereby reduce misunderstandings (Maier, 1952; Solem, 1965). The leader has an adverse effect on the end-product when he suppresses minority views by holding a contrary position and when he uses his office to promote his own views (Maier & Hoffman, 1960b, 1962; Maier & Solem, 1952). In many problem-solving discussions the untrained leader plays a dominant role in influencing the outcome, and when he is more resistant to changing his views than are the other participants, the quality of the outcome tends to be lowered. This negative leader-influence was demonstrated by experiments in which untrained leaders were asked to obtain a second solution to a problem after they had obtained their first one (Maier & Hoffman, 1960a). It was found that the second solution tended to be superior to the first. Since the dominant individual had influenced the first solution, he had won his point and therefore ceased to dominate the subsequent discussion which led to the second solution. Acceptance of a solution also increases as the leader sees disagreement as idea-producing rather than as a source of difficulty or trouble (Maier & Hoffman, 1965). Leaders who see some of their participants as trouble-makers obtain fewer innovative solutions and gain less acceptance of decisions made than leaders who see disagreeing members as persons with ideas.

THE LEADER'S ROLE
FOR INTEGRATED GROUPS

Two Differing Types of Group Process

In observing group problem solving under various conditions it is rather easy to distinguish between cooperative problem-solving activity and persuasion or selling approaches. Problem-solving activity includes searching, trying out ideas on one another, listening to understand rather than to refute, making relatively short speeches, and reacting to differences in opinion as stimulating. The general pattern is one of rather complete participation, involvement, and interest. Persuasion activity includes the selling of opinions already formed, defending a position held, either not listening at all or listening in order to be able to refute, talking dominated by a few members, unfavorable reactions to disagreement, and a lack of involvement of some members. During problem solving the behavior observed seems to be that of members interacting as segments of a group. The interaction pattern is not between certain individual members, but with the group as a whole. Sometimes it is difficult to determine who should be credited with an idea. "It just developed," is a response often used to describe the solution reached. In contrast, discussions involving selling or persuasive behavior seem to consist of a series of interpersonal interactions with each individual retaining his identity. Such groups do not function as integrated units but as separate individuals, each with an agenda. In one situation the solution is unknown and is sought; in the other, several solutions exist and conflict occurs because commitments have been made.

The Starfish Analogy

The analysis of these two group processes suggests an analogy with the behavior of the rays of a starfish under two conditions; one with the nerve ring intact, the other with the nerve ring sectioned (Hamilton, 1922; Moore, 1924; Moore & Duodoroff, 1939; Schneirla & Maier, 1940). In the intact condition, locomotion and righting behavior reveal that the behavior of each ray is not merely a function of local stimulation. Locomotion and righting behavior reveal a degree of coordination and interdependence that is centrally controlled. However, when the nerve ring is sectioned, the behavior of one ray still can influence others, but internal coordination is lacking. For example, if one ray is stimulated, it may step forward, thereby exerting pressure on the sides of the other four rays. In response to these external pressures (tactile stimulation), these rays show stepping responses on the stimulated side so that locomotion successfully occurs without the aid of neural coordination. Thus integrated behavior can occur on the basis of external control. If, however, stimulation is applied to opposite rays, the specimen may be "locked" for a time, and in some species the conflicting locomotions may divide the animal, thus destroying it (Crozier, 1920; Moore & Duodoroff, 1939).

Each of the rays of the starfish can show stepping responses even when sectioned and removed from the animal. Thus each may be regarded as an individual. In a starfish with a sectioned nerve ring the five rays become members of a group. They can successfully work together for locomotion purposes by being controlled by the dominant ray. Thus if uniformity of action is desired, the group

of five rays can sometimes be more effective than the individual ray in moving the group toward a source of stimulation. However, if "locking" or the division of the organism occurs, the group action becomes less effective than individual action. External control, through the influence of a dominant ray, therefore can lead to adaptive behavior for the starfish as a whole, but it can also result in a conflict that destroys the organism. Something more than external influence is needed.

In the animal with an intact nerve ring, the function of the rays is coordinated by the nerve ring. With this type of internal organization the group is always superior to that of the individual actions. When the rays function as a part of an organized unit, rather than as a group that is physically together, they become a higher type of organization—a single intact organism. This is accomplished by the nerve ring, which in itself does not do the behaving. Rather, it receives and processes the data which the rays relay to it. Through this central organization, the responses of the rays become part of a larger pattern so that together they constitute a single coordinated total response rather than a group of individual responses.

The Leader as the Group's
Central Nervous System

If we now examine what goes on in a discussion group we find that members can problem-solve as individuals, they can influence others by external pushes and pulls, or they can function as a group with varying degrees of unity. In order for the latter function to be maximized, however, something must be introduced to serve the function of the nerve ring. In our conceptualization of group problem solving and group decision (Maier, 1963), we see this as the function of the leader. Thus the leader does not serve as a dominant ray and produce the solution. Rather, his function is to receive information, facilitate communications between the individuals, relay messages, and integrate the incoming responses so that a single unified response occurs.

Solutions that are the product of good group discussions often come as surprises to discussion leaders. One of these is unexpected generosity. If there is a weak member, this member is given less to do, in much the same way as an organism adapts to an injured limb and alters the function of other limbs to keep locomotion on course. Experimental evidence supports the point that group decisions award special consideration to needy members of groups (Hoffman & Maier, 1959). Group decisions in industrial groups often give smaller assignments to the less gifted (Maier, 1952). A leader could not effectually impose such differential treatment on group members without being charged with discriminatory practices.

Another unique aspect of group discussion is the way fairness is resolved. In a simulated problem of how to introduce a new truck into a group of drivers, the typical group solution involves a trading of trucks so that several or all members stand to profit. If the leader makes the decision the number of persons who profit is often confined to one (Maier & Hoffman, 1962; Maier & Zerfoss, 1952). In industrial practice, supervisors assign a new truck to an individual member of a crew after careful evaluation of needs. This practice results in dissatisfaction, with the charge of *unfair* being leveled at him. Despite these repeated attempts to do justice, supervisors in the telephone industry never hit upon the notion of a general reallocation of trucks, a solution that crews invariably reach when the decision is theirs to make.

In experiments involving the introduction of change, the use of group discussion tends to lead to decisions that resolve differences (Maier, 1952, 1953; Maier & Hoffman, 1961, 1964a, 1964b). Such decisions tend to be different from decisions reached by individuals because of the very fact that disagreement is common in group problem solving and rare in individual problem solving. The process of resolving difference in a constructive setting causes the exploration of additional areas and leads to solutions that are integrative rather than compromises.

Finally, group solutions tend to be tailored to fit the interests and personalities of the participants; thus group solutions to problems involving fairness, fears, face-saving, etc., tend to vary from one group to another. An outsider cannot process these variables because they are not subject to logical treatment.

If we think of the leader as serving a function in the group different from that of its membership, we might be able to create a group that can function as an intact organism. For a leader, such functions as rejecting or promoting ideas according to his personal needs are out of bounds. He must be receptive to information contributed, accept contributions without evaluating them (posting contributions on a chalkboard to keep them alive), summarize information to facilitate integration, stimulate exploratory behavior, create awareness of problems of one member by others, and detect when the group is ready to resolve differences and agree to a unified solution.

Since higher organisms have more than a nerve ring and can store information, a leader might appropriately supply information, but according to our model of a leader's role, he must clearly distinguish between supplying information and promoting a solution. If his knowledge indicates the desirability of a particular solution, sharing this knowledge might lead the group to find this solution, but the solution should be the group's discovery. A leader's contributions do not receive the same treatment as those of a member of the group. Whether he likes it or not, his position is different. According to our conception of the leader's contribution to discussion, his role not only differs in influence, but gives him an entirely different function. He is to serve much as the nerve ring in the starfish and to further refine this function so as to make it a higher type of nerve ring.

This model of a leader's role in group process has served as a guide for many of our studies in group problem solving. It is not our claim that this will lead to the best possible group function under all conditions. In sharing it we hope to indicate the nature of our guidelines in exploring group leadership as a function quite different and apart from group membership. Thus the model serves as a stimulant for research problems and as a guide for our analyses of leadership skills and principles.

CONCLUSIONS

On the basis of our analysis, it follows that the comparison of the merits of group versus individual problem solving depends on the nature of the problem, the goal to be achieved (high quality solution, highly accepted solution, effective communication and understanding of the solution, innovation, a quickly reached solution, or satisfaction), and the skill of the discussion leader. If liabilities inherent in groups are avoided, assets capitalized upon, and conditions that can serve either favorable or unfavorable outcomes are effectively used, it follows that groups have a potential which in many instances can exceed that of a superior individual functioning alone, even with respect to creativity.

This goal was nicely stated by Thibaut and Kelley (1961) when they

> wonder whether it may not be possible for a rather small, intimate group to establish a problem solving process that capitalizes upon the total pool of information and provides for great interstimulation of ideas without any loss of innovative creativity due to social restraints [p. 268].

In order to accomplish this high level of achievement, however, a leader is needed who plays a role quite different from that of the members. His role is analogous to that of the nerve ring of the starfish which permits the rays to execute a unified response. If the leader can contribute the integrative requirement, group problem solving may emerge as a unique type of group function. This type of approach to group processes places the leader in a particular role in which he must cease to contribute, avoid evaluation, and refrain from thinking about solutions or group *products.* Instead he must concentrate on the group *process,* listen in order to understand rather than to appraise or refute, assume responsibility for accurate communication between members, be sensitive to unexpressed feelings, protect minority points of view, keep the discussion moving, and develop skills in summarizing.

REFERENCES

Crozier, W. J. Notes on some problems of adaptation. *Biological Bulletin,* 1920, 39, 116–129.

Duncker, K. On problem solving. *Psychological Monographs,* 1945, 58 (5, Whole No. 270).

Hamilton, W. F. Coordination in the starfish. III. The righting reaction as a phase of locomotion (righting and locomotion). *Journal of Comparative Psychology,* 1922, 2, 81–94.

Hoffman, L. R. Conditions for creative problem solving. *Journal of Psychology,* 1961, 52, 429–444.

Hoffman, L. R. Group problem solving. In L. Berkowitz (Ed.), *Advances in experimental social psychology,* Vol. 2. New York: Academic Press, 1965, pp. 99–132.

Hoffman, L. R., Harburg, E., & Maier, N. R. F. Differences and disagreement as factors in creative group problem solving. *Journal of Abnormal and Social Psychology,* 1962, 64, 206–214.

Hoffman, L. R., & Maier, N. R. F. The use of group decision to resolve a problem of fairness. *Personnel Psychology,* 1959, 12, 545–559.

Hoffman, L. R., & Maier, N. R. F. Quality and acceptance of problem solutions by members of homogeneous and heterogeneous groups. *Journal of Abnormal and Social Psychology,* 1961, 62, 401–407.

Hoffman, L. R., & Maier, N. R. F. Valence in the adoption of solutions by problem-solving groups: Concept, method, and results. *Journal of Abnormal and Social Psychology,* 1964, 69, 264–271.

Hoffman, L. R., & Maier, N. R. F. Valence in the adoption of solutions by problem-solving groups: II. Quality and acceptance as goals of leaders and members. Unpublished manuscript, 1967. (Mimeo)

Kelley, H. H., & Thibaut, J. W. Experimental studies of group problem solving and process. In G. Lindzey (Ed.), *Handbook of social psychology.* Cambridge, Mass.: Addison Wesley, 1954, pp. 735–785.

Maier, N. R. F. Reasoning in humans. I. On direction. *Journal of Comparative Psychology,* 1930, 10, 115–143.

Maier, N. R. F. The quality of group decisions as influenced by the discussion leader. *Human Relations,* 1950, 3, 155–174.

Maier, N. R. F. *Principles of human relations.* New York: Wiley, 1952.

Maier, N. R. F. An experimental test of the effect of training on discussion leadership. *Human Relations,* 1953, 6, 161–173.

Maier, N. R. F. *The appraisal interview.* New York: Wiley, 1958.

Maier, N. R. F. Screening solutions to upgrade quality: A new approach to problem solving under conditions of uncertainty. *Journal of Psychology,* 1960, 49, 217–231.

Maier, N. R. F. *Problem solving discussions and conferences: Leadership methods and skills.* New York: McGraw-Hill, 1963.

Maier, N. R. F., & Hayes, J. J. *Creative management.* New York: Wiley, 1962.

Maier, N. R. F., & Hoffman, L. R. Using trained "developmental" discussion leaders to improve further the quality of group decisions. *Journal of Applied Psychology,* 1960, 44, 247–251. (a)

Maier, N. R. F., & Hoffman, L. R. Quality of first and second solutions in group problem solving. *Journal of Applied Psychology,* 1960, 44, 278–283. (b)

Maier, N. R. F., & Hoffman, L. R. Organization and creative problem solving. *Journal of Applied Psychology,* 1961, 45, 277–280.

Maier, N. R. F., & Hoffman, L. R. Group decision in England and the United States. *Personnel Psychology,* 1962, 15, 75–87.

Maier, N. R. F., & Hoffman, L. R. Financial incentives and group decision in motivating change. *Journal of Social Psychology,* 1964, 64, 369–378. (a)

Maier, N. R. F., & Hoffman, L. R. Types of problems confronting managers. *Personnel Psychology,* 1964, 17, 261–269. (b)

Maier, N. R. F., & Hoffman, L. R. Acceptance and quality of solutions as related to leaders' attitudes toward disagreement in group

problem solving. *Journal of Applied Behavioral Science,* 1965, 1, 373–386.

Maier, N. R. F., & Maier, R. A. An experimental test of the effects of "developmental" vs. "free" discussions on the quality of group decisions. *Journal of Applied Psychology,* 1957, 41, 320–323.

Maier, N. R. F., & Solem, A. R. The contribution of a discussion leader to the quality of group thinking: The effective use of minority opinions. *Human Relations,* 1952, 5, 277–288.

Maier, N. R. F., & Solem, A. R. Improving solutions by turning choice situations into problems. *Personnel Psychology,* 1962, 15, 151–157.

Maier, N. R. F., & Zerfoss, L. F. MRP: A technique for training large groups of supervisors and its potential use in social research. *Human Relations,* 1952, 5, 177–186.

Moore, A. R. The nervous mechanism of coordination in the crinoid *Antedon rosaceus. Journal of Genetic Psychology,* 1924, 6, 281–288.

Moore, A. R., & Duodoroff, M. Injury recovery and function in an aganglionic central nervous system. *Journal of Comparative Psychology,* 1939, 28, 313–328.

Osborn, A. F. *Applied imagination.* New York: Scribner's, 1953.

Schneirla, T. C., & Maier, N. R. F. Concerning the status of the starfish. *Journal of Comparative Psychology,* 1940, 30, 103–110.

Solem, A. R. 1965: Almost anything I can do, we can do better. *Personnel Administration,* 1965, 28, 6–16.

Thibaut, J. W., & Kelley, H. H. *The social psychology of groups.* New York: Wiley, 1961.

Wallach, M. A., & Kogan, N. The roles of information, discussion and consensus in group risk taking. *Journal of Experimental and Social Psychology,* 1965, 1, 1–19.

Wallach, M. A., Kogan, N., & Bem, D. J. Group influence on individual risk taking. *Journal of Abnormal and Social Psychology,* 1962, 65, 75–86.

Wertheimer, M. *Productive thinking.* New York: Harper, 1959.

Groupthink

Irving L. Janis

"How could we have been so stupid?" President John F. Kennedy asked after he and a close group of advisers had blundered into the Bay of Pigs invasion. For the last two years I have been studying that question, as it applies not only to the Bay of Pigs decision-makers but also to those who led the United States into such other major fiascos as the failure to be prepared for the attack on Pearl Harbor, the Korean War stalemate and the escalation of the Vietnam War.

Stupidity certainly is not the explanation. The men who participated in making the Bay of Pigs decision, for instance, comprised one of the greatest arrays of intellectual talent in the history of American Government—Dean Rusk, Robert McNamara, Douglas Dillon, Robert Kennedy, McGeorge Bundy, Arthur Schlesinger Jr., Allen Dulles and others.

It also seemed to me that explanations were incomplete if they concentrated only on disturbances in the behavior of each individual within a decision-making body: temporary emotional states of elation, fear, or anger that reduce a man's mental efficiency, for example, or chronic blind spots arising from a man's social prejudices or idiosyncratic biases.

I preferred to broaden the picture by looking at the fiascos from the standpoint of group dynamics as it has been explored over the past three decades, first by the great social psychologist Kurt Lewin and later in many experimental situations by myself and other behavioral scientists. My conclusion after poring over hundreds of relevant documents—historical reports about formal group meetings and informal conversations among the members—is that the groups that committed the fiascos were victims of what I call "groupthink."

"GROUPY"

In each case study, I was surprised to discover the extent to which each group displayed the typical phenomena of social conformity that are regularly encountered in studies of group dynamics among ordinary citizens. For example, some of the phenomena appear to be completely in line with findings from social-psychological experiments showing that powerful social pressures are brought to bear by the members of a cohesive group whenever a dissident begins to voice his objections to a group consensus. Other phenomena are reminiscent of the shared illusions observed in encounter groups and friendship cliques when the members simultaneously reach a peak of "groupy" feelings.

Above all, there are numerous indications pointing to the development of group norms that bolster morale at the expense of critical thinking. One of the most common norms appears to be that of remaining loyal to the group by sticking with the policies to which the group has already committed itself, even when those policies are obviously working out badly and have unintended consequences that disturb the conscience of each member. This is one of the key characteristics of groupthink.

1984

I used the term groupthink as a quick and easy way to refer to the mode of thinking that persons engage in when *concurrence-seeking* becomes so dominant in a cohesive ingroup that it tends to override realistic appraisal of alternative courses of action. Groupthink is a term of the same order as the words in the newspeak vocabulary George Orwell used in his dismaying world of *1984*. In that context, groupthink takes on an invidious connotation. Exactly such a connotation is intended, since the term refers to a deterioration in mental efficiency, reality testing and moral judgments as a result of group pressures.

The symptoms of groupthink arise when the members of decision-making groups become motivated to avoid being too harsh in their judgments of their leaders' or their colleagues' ideas. They adopt a soft line of criticism, even in their own thinking. At their meetings, all the members are amiable and seek complete concurrence on every important issue, with no bickering or conflict to spoil the cozy, "we-feeling" atmosphere.

KILL

Paradoxically, soft-headed groups are often hard-hearted when it comes to dealing with outgroups or enemies. They find it relatively easy to resort to dehumanizing solutions—they will readily authorize bombing attacks that kill large numbers of civilians in the name of the noble cause of persuading an unfriendly government to negotiate at the peace table. They are unlikely to pursue the more difficult and controversial issues that arise when alternatives to a harsh military solution come up for discussion. Nor are they inclined to raise ethical issues that carry the implication that *this fine group of ours, with its humanitarianism and its high-minded principles, might be capable of adopting a course of action that is inhumane and immoral.*

NORMS

There is evidence from a number of social-psychological studies that as the members of a group feel more accepted by the others, which is a central feature of increased group cohesiveness, they display less overt conformity to group norms. Thus we would expect that the more cohesive a group becomes, the less the members will feel constrained to censor what they say out of fear of being socially punished for antagonizing the leader or any of their fellow members.

In contrast, the groupthink type of conformity tends to increase as group cohesiveness increases. Groupthink involves non-deliberate suppression of critical thoughts as a result of internalization of the group's norms, which is quite different from deliberate suppression on the basis of external threats of social punishment. The more cohesive the group, the greater the inner compulsion on the part of each member to avoid creating disunity, which inclines him to believe in the soundness of whatever proposals are promoted by the leader or by a majority of the group's members.

In a cohesive group, the danger is not so much that each individual will fail to reveal his objections to what the others propose but that he will think the proposal a good one, without attempting to carry out a careful scrutiny of the pros and cons of the alternatives. When groupthink becomes dominant, there also is considerable suppression of deviant thoughts, but it takes the form of each person's deciding that his misgivings are not relevant and should be set aside, that the benefit of the doubt regarding any lingering uncertainties should be given to the group consensus.

STRESS

I do not mean to imply that all cohesive groups necessarily suffer from groupthink. All ingroups may have a mild tendency toward groupthink, displaying one or another of the symptoms from time to time, but it need not be so dominant as to influence the quality of the group's final decision. Neither do I mean to imply that there is anything necessarily inefficient or harmful about group decisions in general. On the contrary, a group whose members have properly defined roles, with traditions concerning the procedures to follow in pursuing a critical inquiry, probably is capable of making better decisions than any individual group member working alone.

The problem is that the advantages of having decisions made by groups are often lost because of powerful psychological pressures that arise when the members work closely together, share the same set of values and, above all, face a crisis situation that puts everyone under intense stress.

The main principle of groupthink, which I offer in the spirit of Parkinson's Law, is this: *The more amiability and esprit de corps there is among the members of a policy-making ingroup, the greater the danger that independent critical thinking will be replaced by group-*

think, which is likely to result in irrational and dehumanizing actions directed against outgroups.

SYMPTOMS

In my studies of high-level governmental decision-makers, both civilian and military, I have found eight main symptoms of groupthink.

1. Invulnerability

Most or all of the members of the ingroup share an *illusion* of invulnerability that provides for them some degree of reassurance about obvious dangers and leads them to become over-optimistic and willing to take extraordinary risks. It also causes them to fail to respond to clear warnings of danger.

The Kennedy ingroup, which uncritically accepted the Central Intelligence Agency's disastrous Bay of Pigs plan, operated on the false assumption that they could keep secret the fact that the United States was responsible for the invasion of Cuba. Even after news of the plan began to leak out, their belief remained unshaken. They failed even to consider the danger that awaited them: a worldwide revulsion against the U.S.

A similar attitude appeared among the members of President Lyndon B. Johnson's ingroup, the "Tuesday Cabinet," which kept escalating the Vietnam War despite repeated setbacks and failures. "There was a belief," Bill Moyers commented after he resigned, "that if we indicated a willingness to use our power, they [the North Vietnamese] would get the message and back away from an all-out confrontation. . . . There was a confidence—it was never bragged about, it was just there—that when the chips were really down, the other people would fold."

A most poignant example of an illusion of invulnerability involves the ingroup around Admiral H. E. Kimmel, which failed to prepare for the possibility of a Japanese attack on Pearl Harbor despite repeated warnings. Informed by his intelligence chief that radio contact with Japanese aircraft carriers had been lost, Kimmel joked about it: "What, you don't know where the carriers are? Do you mean to say that they could be rounding Diamond Head (at Honolulu) and you wouldn't know it?" The carriers were in fact moving full-steam toward Kimmel's command post at the time. Laughing together about a danger signal, which labels it as a purely laughing matter, is a characteristic manifestation of groupthink.

2. Rationale

As we see, victims of groupthink ignore warnings; they also collectively construct rationalizations in order to discount warnings and other forms of negative feedback that, taken seriously, might lead the group members to reconsider their assumptions each time they recommit themselves to past decisions. Why did the Johnson ingroup avoid reconsidering its escalation policy when time and again the expectations on which they based their decisions turned out to be wrong? James C. Thompson Jr., a Harvard historian who spent five years as an observing participant in both the State Department and the White House, tells us that the policymakers avoided critical discussion of their prior decisions and continually invented new rationalizations so that they could sincerely recommit themselves to defeating the North Vietnamese.

In the fall of 1964, before the bombing of North Vietman began, some of the policymakers predicted that six weeks of air strikes would induce the North Vietnamese to seek peace talks. When someone asked, "What if they don't?" the answer was that another four weeks certainly would do the trick.

Later, after each setback, the ingroup agreed that by investing just a bit more effort (by stepping up the bomb tonnage a bit, for instance), their course of actions would prove to be right. *The Pentagon Papers* bear out these observations.

In *The Limits of Intervention,* Townsend Hoopes, who was acting Secretary of the Air Force under Johnson, says that Walt W. Rostow in particular showed a remarkable capacity for what has been called "instant rationalization." According to Hoopes, Rostow buttressed the group's optimism about being on the road to victory by culling selected scraps of evidence from news reports or, if necessary, by inventing "plausible" forecasts that had no basis in evidence at all.

Admiral Kimmel's group rationalized away their warnings, too. Right up to December 7, 1941, they convinced themselves that the Japanese would never dare attempt a full-scale surprise assault against Hawaii because Japan's leaders would realize that it would precipitate an all-out war which the United States would surely win. They made no attempt to look at the situation through the eyes of the Japanese leaders—another manifestation of groupthink.

3. Morality

Victims of groupthink believe unquestioningly in the inherent morality of their ingroup; this belief inclines the members to ignore the ethical or moral consequences of their decisions.

Evidence that this symptom is at work usually is of a negative kind—the things that are left unsaid in group meetings. At least two influential persons had doubts about the morality of the Bay of Pigs adventure. One of them, Arthur Schlesinger Jr., presented his strong objections in a memorandum to President Kennedy and Secretary of State Rusk but suppressed them when he attended meetings of the Kennedy team. The other, Senator J. William Fulbright, was not a member of the group, but the President invited him to express his misgivings in a speech to the policymakers. However, when Fulbright finished speaking the President moved on to other agenda items without asking for reactions of the group.

David Kraslow and Stuart H. Loory, in *The Secret Search for Peace in Vietnam,* report that during 1966 President Johnson's ingroup was concerned primarily with selecting bomb targets in North Vietnam. They based their selections on four factors—the military advantage, the risk to American aircraft and pilots, the danger of forcing other countries into the fighting, and the danger of heavy civilian casualties. At their regular Tuesday luncheons, they weighed these factors the way school teachers grade examination papers, averaging them out. Though evidence on this point is scant, I suspect that the group's ritualistic adherence to a standardized procedure induced the members to feel morally justified in their destructive way of dealing with the Vietnamese people—after all, the danger of heavy civilian casualties from U.S. air strikes was taken into account on their checklists.

4. Stereotypes

Victims of groupthink hold stereotyped views of the leaders of enemy groups: they are so evil that genuine attempts at negotiating differences with them are unwarranted, or they are too weak or too stupid to deal effectively with whatever attempts the ingroup makes to defeat their purposes, no matter how risky the attempts are.

Kennedy's groupthinkers believed that Premier Fidel Castro's air force was so ineffectual that obsolete B-26s could knock it out completely in a surprise attack before the invasion began. They also believed that Castro's army was so weak that a small Cuban-exile brigade could establish a well-protected beachhead at the Bay of Pigs. In addition, they believed that Castro was not smart enough to put down any possible internal uprisings in support of the exiles. They were wrong on all three assumptions. Though much of the blame was attributable to faulty intelligence, the point is that none of Kennedy's advisers even questioned the CIA planners about these assumptions.

The Johnson advisers' sloganistic thinking about "the Communist apparatus" that was "working all around the world" (as Dean Rusk put it) led them to overlook the powerful nationalistic strivings of the North Vietnamese government and its efforts to ward off Chinese domination. The crudest of all stereotypes used by Johnson's inner circle to justify their policies was the domino theory ("If we don't stop the Reds in South Vietnam, tomorrow they will be in Hawaii and next week they will be in San Francisco," Johnson once said). The group so firmly accepted this stereotype that it became almost impossible for any adviser to introduce a more sophisticated viewpoint.

In the documents on Pearl Harbor, it is clear to see that the Navy commanders stationed in Hawaii had a naive image of Japan as a midget that would not dare to strike a blow against a powerful giant.

5. Pressure

Victims of groupthink apply direct pressure to any individual who momentarily expresses doubts about any of the group's shared illusions or who questions the validity of the arguments supporting a policy alternative favored by the majority. This gambit reinforces the concurrence-seeking norm that loyal members are expected to maintain.

President Kennedy probably was more active than anyone else in raising skeptical questions during the Bay of Pigs meetings, and yet he seems to have encouraged the group's docile, uncritical acceptance of defective arguments in favor of the CIA's plan. At every meeting, he allowed the CIA representatives to dominate the discussion. He permitted them to give their immediate refutations in response to each tentative doubt that one of the others expressed, instead of asking whether anyone shared the doubt or wanted to pursue the implications of the new worrisome issue that had just been raised. And at the most crucial meeting, when he was calling on each member to give his vote for or against the plan, he did not call on Arthur Schlesinger, the one man there who was known by the President to have serious misgivings.

Historian Thomson informs us that whenever a member of Johnson's ingroup began to express doubts, the group used subtle social pressures to "domesticate" him. To start with, the dissenter was made to feel at home, provided that he lived up to two restrictions: 1) that he did not voice his doubts to outsiders, which would play into the hands of the opposition; and 2) that he kept his criticisms within the bounds of acceptable deviation, which meant not challenging any of the fundamental assumptions that went into the group's prior commitments. One such "domesticated dissenter" was Bill Moyers. When Moyers arrived at a meeting, Thomson tells

us, the President greeted him with, "Well, here comes Mr. Stop-the-Bombing."

6. Self-Censorship

Victims of groupthink avoid deviating from what appears to be group consensus; they keep silent about their misgivings and even minimize to themselves the importance of their doubts.

As we have seen, Schlesinger was not at all hesitant about presenting his strong objections to the Bay of Pigs plan in a memorandum to the President and the Secretary of State. But he became keenly aware of his tendency to suppress objections at the White House meetings. "In the months after the Bay of Pigs I bitterly reproached myself for having kept so silent during those crucial discussions in the cabinet room," Schlesinger writes in *A Thousand Days*. "I can only explain my failure to do more than raise a few timid questions by reporting that one's impulse to blow the whistle on this nonsense was simply undone by the circumstances of the discussion."

7. Unanimity

Victims of groupthink share an *illusion* of unanimity within the group concerning almost all judgments expressed by members who speak in favor of the majority view. This symptom results partly from the preceding one, whose effects are augmented by the false assumption that any individual who remains silent during any part of the discussion is in full accord with what the others are saying.

When a group of persons who respect each other's opinions arrives at a unanimous view, each member is likely to feel that the belief must be true. This reliance on consensual validation within the group tends to replace individual critical thinking and reality testing, unless there are clear-cut disagreements among the members. In contemplating a course of action such as the invasion of Cuba, it is painful for the members to confront disagreements within their group, particularly if it becomes apparent that there are widely divergent views about whether the preferred course of action is too risky to undertake at all. Such disagreements are likely to arouse anxieties about making a serious error. Once the sense of unanimity is shattered, the members no longer can feel complacently confident about the decision they are inclined to make. Each man must then face the annoying realization that there are troublesome uncertainties and he must diligently seek out the best information he can get in order to decide for himself exactly how serious the risks might be. This is one of the unpleasant consequences of being in a group of hardheaded, critical thinkers.

To avoid such an unpleasant state, the members often become inclined, without quite realizing it, to prevent latent disagreements from surfacing when they are about to initiate a risky course of action. The group leader and the members support each other in playing up the areas of convergence in their thinking, at the expense of fully exploring divergencies that might reveal unsettled issues.

"Our meetings took place in a curious atmosphere of assumed consensus," Schlesinger writes. His additional comments clearly show that, curiously, the consensus was an illusion—an illusion that could be maintained only because the major participants did not reveal their own reasoning or discuss their idiosyncratic assumptions and vague reservations. Evidence from several sources makes it clear that even the three principals—President

Kennedy, Rusk and McNamara—had widely differing assumptions about the invasion plan.

8. Mindguards

Victims of groupthink sometimes appoint themselves as mindguards to protect the leader and fellow members from adverse information that might break the complacency they shared about the effectiveness and morality of past decisions. At a large birthday party for his wife, Attorney General Robert F. Kennedy, who had been constantly informed about the Cuban invasion plan, took Schlesinger aside and asked him why he was opposed. Kennedy listened coldly and said, "You may be right or you may be wrong, but the President has made his mind up. Don't push it any further. Now is the time for everyone to help him all they can."

Rusk also functioned as a highly effective mindguard by failing to transmit to the group the strong objections of three "outsiders" who had learned of the invasion plan—Undersecretary of State Chester Bowles, USIA Director Edward R. Murrow, and Rusk's intelligence chief, Roger Hilsman. Had Rusk done so, their warnings might have reinforced Schlesinger's memorandum and jolted some of Kennedy's ingroup, if not the President himself, into reconsidering the decision.

PRODUCTS

When a group of executives frequently displays most or all of these interrelated symptoms, a detailed study of their deliberations is likely to reveal a number of immediate consequences. These consequences are, in effect, products of poor decision-making practices because they lead to inadequate solutions to the problems under discussion.

First, the group limits its discussions to a few alternative courses of action (often only two) without an initial survey of all the alternatives that might be worthy of consideration.

Second, the group fails to reexamine the course of action initially preferred by the majority after they learn of risks and drawbacks they had not considered originally.

Third, the members spend little or no time discussing whether there are nonobvious gains they may have overlooked or ways of reducing the seemingly prohibitive costs that made rejected alternatives appear undesirable to them.

Fourth, members make little or no attempt to obtain information from experts within their own organizations who might be able to supply more precise estimates of potential losses and gains.

Fifth, members show positive interest in facts and opinions that support their preferred policy; they tend to ignore facts and opinions that do not.

Sixth, members spend little time deliberating about how the chosen policy might be hindered by bureaucratic inertia, sabotaged by political opponents, or temporarily derailed by common accidents. Consequently, they fail to work out contingency plans to cope with foreseeable setbacks that could endanger the overall success of their chosen course.

SUPPORT

The search for an explanation of why groupthink occurs has led me through a quagmire of complicated theoretical issues in the murky area of human motivation. My belief, based on recent social psychological research, is that we can best understand the various symptoms of groupthink as a mutual effort among the group members to maintain self-esteem and emotional equanimity by providing social support to each other, especially at times when they share responsibility for making vital decisions.

Even when no important decision is pending, the typical administrator will begin to doubt the wisdom and morality of his past decisions each time he receives information about setbacks, particularly if the information is accompanied by negative feedback from prominent men who originally had been his supporters. It should not be surprising, therefore, to find that individual members strive to develop unanimity and esprit de corps that will help bolster each other's morale, to create an optimistic outlook about the success of pending decisions, and to reaffirm the positive value of past policies to which all of them are committed.

PRIDE

Shared illusions of invulnerability, for example, can reduce anxiety about taking risks. Rationalizations help members believe that the risks are really not so bad after all. The assumption of inherent morality helps the members to avoid feelings of shame or guilt. Negative stereotypes function as stress-reducing devices to enhance a sense of moral righteousness as well as pride in a lofty mission.

The mutual enhancement of self-esteem and morale may have functional value in enabling the members to maintain their capacity to take action, but it has maladaptive consequences insofar as concurrence-seeking tendencies interfere with critical, rational capacities and lead to serious errors of judgment.

While I have limited my study to decision-making bodies in Government, groupthink symptoms appear in business, industry and any other field where small, cohesive groups make the decisions. It is vital, then, for all sorts of people—and especially group leaders—to know what steps they can take to prevent groupthink.

REMEDIES

To counterpoint my case studies of the major fiascos, I have also investigated two highly successful group enterprises, the formulation of the Marshall Plan in the Truman Administration and the handling of the Cuban missile crisis by President Kennedy and his advisers. I have found it instructive to examine the steps Kennedy took to change his group's decision-making processes. These changes ensured that the mistakes made by his Bay of Pigs ingroup were not repeated by the missile-crisis ingroup, even though the membership of both groups was essentially the same.

The following recommendations for preventing groupthink incorporate many of the good practices I discovered to be characteristic of the Marshall Plan and missile-crisis groups:

1. The leader of a policy-forming group should assign the role of critical evaluator to each member, encouraging the group to give high priority to open airing of objections and doubts. This practice needs to be reinforced by the leader's acceptance of criticism of his own judgments in order to discourage members from soft-pedaling their disagreements and from allowing their striving for concurrence to inhibit critical thinking.

2. When the key members of a hierarchy assign a policy-planning mission to any group within their organization, they should

adopt an impartial stance instead of stating preferences and expectations at the beginning. This will encourage open inquiry and impartial probing of a wide range of policy alternatives.

3. The organization routinely should set up several outside policy-planning and evaluation groups to work on the same policy questions, each deliberating under a different leader. This can prevent the insulation of an ingroup.

4. At intervals before the group reaches a final consensus, the leader should require each member to discuss the group's deliberations with associates in his own unit of the organization—assuming that those associates can be trusted to adhere to the same security regulations that govern the policymakers—and then to report back their reactions to the group.

5. The group should invite one or more outside experts to each meeting on a staggered basis and encourage the experts to challenge the views of the core members.

6. At every general meeting of the group, whenever the agenda calls for an evaluation of policy alternatives, at least one member should play devil's advocate, functioning as a good lawyer in challenging the testimony of those who advocate the majority position.

7. Whenever the policy issue involves relations with a rival nation or organization, the group should devote a sizable block of time, perhaps an entire session, to a survey of all warning signals from the rivals and should write alternative scenarios on the rivals' intentions.

8. When the group is surveying policy alternatives for feasibility and effectiveness, it should from time to time divide into two or more subgroups to meet separately, under different chairmen, and then come back together to hammer out differences.

9. After reaching a preliminary consensus about what seems to be the best policy, the group should hold a "second-chance" meeting at which every member expresses as vividly as he can all his residual doubts, and rethinks the entire issue before making a definitive choice.

HOW

These recommendations have their disadvantages. To encourage the open airing of objections, for instance, might lead to prolonged and costly debates when a rapidly growing crisis requires immediate solution. It also could cause rejection, depression and anger. A leader's failure to set a norm might create cleavage between leader and members that could develop into a disruptive power struggle if the leader looks on the emerging consensus as anathema. Setting up outside evaluation groups might increase the risk of security leakage. Still, inventive executives who know their way around the organizational maze probably can figure out how to apply one or another of the prescriptions successfully, without harmful side effects.

They also could benefit from the advice of outside experts in the administrative and behavioral sciences. Though these experts have much to offer, they have had few chances to work on policy-making machinery within large organizations. As matters now stand, executives innovate only when they need new procedures to avoid repeating serious errors that have deflated their self-images.

In this era of atomic warheads, urban disorganization and ecocatastrophes, it seems to me that policymakers should collaborate with behavioral scientists and give top priority to preventing groupthink and its attendant fiascos.

The Development and Enforcement of Group Norms

Daniel C. Feldman

This paper examines why group norms are enforced and how group norms develop. It is argued here that groups are likely to bring under normative control only those behaviors that ensure group survival, increase the predictability of group members' behavior, avoid embarrassing interpersonal situations, or give expression to the group's central values. Group norms develop through explicit statements by supervisors or co-workers, critical events in the group's history, primacy, or carry-over behaviors from past situations.

Group norms are the informal rules that groups adopt to regulate and regularize group members' behavior. Although these norms are infrequently written down or openly discussed, they often

Reprinted by permission from the *Academy of Management Review,* 1984, Vol. 9, No. 1, 47–53.

have a powerful, and consistent, influence on group members' behavior (Hackman, 1976).

Most of the theoretical work on group norms has focused on identifying the types of group norms (March, 1954) or on describing their structural characteristics (Jackson, 1966). Empirically, most of the focus has been on examining the impact that norms have on other social phenomena. For example, Seashore (1954) and Schachter, Ellertson, McBride, and Gregory (1951) use the concept of group norms to discuss group cohesiveness; Trist and Bamforth (1951) and Whyte (1955a) use norms to examine production restriction; Janis (1972) and Longley and Pruitt (1980) use norms to illuminate group decision making; and Asch (1951) and Sherif (1936) use norms to examine conformity.

This paper focuses on two frequently overlooked aspects of the group norms literature. First, it examines *why* group norms are enforced. Why do groups desire conformity to these informal rules? Second, it examines *how* group norms develop. Why do some norms develop in one group but not in another? Much of what is known about group norms comes from post hoc examination of their impact on outcome variables; much less has been written about how these norms actually develop and why they regulate behavior so strongly.

Understanding how group norms develop and why they are enforced is important for two reasons. First, group norms can play a large role in determining whether the group will be productive or not. If the work group feels that management is supportive, group norms will develop that facilitate—in fact, enhance—group productivity. In contrast, if the work group feels that management is antagonistic, group norms that inhibit and impair group performance are much more likely to develop. Second, managers can play a major role in setting and changing group norms. They can use their influence to set task-facilitative norms; they can monitor whether the group's norms are functional; they can explicitly address counterproductive norms with subordinates. By understanding how norms develop and why norms are enforced, managers can better diagnose the underlying tensions and problems their groups are facing, and they can help the group develop more effective behavior patterns.

WHY NORMS ARE ENFORCED

As Shaw (1981) suggests, a group does not establish or enforce norms about every conceivable situation. Norms are formed and enforced only with respect to behaviors that have some significance for the group. The frequent distinction between task maintenance duties and social maintenance duties helps explain why groups bring selected behaviors under normative control.

Groups, like individuals, try to operate in such a way that they maximize their chances for task success and minimize their chances of task failure. First of all, a group will enforce norms that facilitate its very survival. It will try to protect itself from interference from groups external to the organization or harassment from groups internal to the organization. Second, the group will want to increase the predictability of group members' behaviors. Norms provide a basis for predicting the behavior of others, thus enabling group members to anticipate each other's actions and to prepare quick and appropriate responses (Shaw, 1981; Kiesler & Kiesler, 1970).

In addition, groups want to ensure the satisfaction of their members and prevent as much interpersonal discomfort as possible. Thus, groups also will enforce norms that help the group avoid embarrassing interpersonal problems. Certain topics of conversation might be sanctioned, and certain types of social interaction might be openly discouraged. Moreover, norms serve an expressive function for groups (Katz & Kahn, 1978). Enforcing group norms gives group members a chance to express what their central values are, and to clarify what is distinctive about the group and central to its identity (Hackman, 1976).

Each of these four conditions under which group norms are most likely to be enforced is discussed in more detail below.

(1) *Norms are likely to be enforced if they facilitate group survival.* A group will enforce norms that protect it from interference or harassment by members of other groups. For instance, a group might develop a norm not to discuss its salaries with members of other groups in the organization, so that attention will not be brought to pay inequities in its favor. Groups might also have norms about not discussing internal problems with members of other units. Such discussions might boomerang at a later date if other groups use the information to develop a better competitive strategy against the group.

Enforcing group norms also makes clear what the "boundaries" of the group are. As a result of observation of deviant behavior and the consequences that ensue, other group members are reminded of the *range* of behavior that is acceptable to the group (Dentler & Erikson, 1959). The norms about productivity that frequently develop among piecerate workers are illustrative here. By observing a series of incidents (a person produces 50 widgets and is praised; a person produces 60 widgets and receives sharp teasing; a person produces 70 widgets and is ostracized), group members learn the limits of the group's patience: "This far, and no further." The group is less likely to be "successful" (i.e., continue to sustain the low productivity expectations of management) if it allows its jobs to be reevaluated.

The literature on conformity and deviance is consistent with this observation. The group is more likely to reject the person who violates group norms when the deviant has not been a "good" group member previously (Hollander, 1958, 1964). Individuals can generate "idiosyncrasy credits" with other group members by contributing effectively to the attainment of group goals. Individuals expend these credits when they perform poorly or dysfunctionally at work. When a group member no longer has a positive "balance" of credits to draw on when he or she deviates, the group is much more likely to reject that deviant (Hollander, 1961).

Moreover, the group is more likely to reject the deviant when the group is failing in meeting its goals successfully. When the group is successful, it can afford to be charitable or tolerant towards deviant behavior. The group may disapprove, but it has some margin for error. When the group is faced with failure, the deviance is much more sharply punished. Any behavior that negatively influences the success of the group becomes much more salient and threatening to group members (Alvarez, 1968; Wiggins, Dill, & Schwartz, 1965).

(2) *Norms are likely to be enforced if they simplify, or make predictable, what behavior is expected of group members.* If each member of the group had to decide individually how to behave in each interaction, much time would be lost performing routine activities. Moreover, individuals would have more trouble predicting the behaviors of others and responding correctly. Norms enable group members to anticipate each other's actions and to prepare the most appropriate response in the most timely manner (Hackman, 1976; Shaw, 1981).

For instance, when attending group meetings in which proposals are presented and suggestions are requested, do the presenters really want feedback or are they simply going through the motions? Groups may develop norms that reduce this uncertainty and provide a clearer course of action, for example, make suggestions in small, informal meetings but not in large, formal meetings.

Another example comes from norms that regulate social behavior. For instance, when colleagues go out for lunch together, there can be some awkwardness about how to split the bill at the end of the meal. A group may develop a norm that gives some highly predictable or simple way of behaving, for example, split evenly, take turns picking up the tab, or pay for what each ordered.

Norms also may reinforce specific individual members' roles. A number of different roles might emerge in groups. These roles are simply expectations that are shared by group members regarding who is to carry out what types of activities under what circumstances (Bales & Slater, 1955). Although groups obviously create pressure toward uniformity among members, there also is a tendency for groups to create and maintain *diversity* among members (Hackman, 1976). For instance, a group might have one person whom others expect to break the tension when tempers become too hot. Another group member might be expected to keep track of what is going on in other parts of the organization. A third member might be expected to take care of the "creature" needs of the group—making the coffee, making dinner reservations, and so on. A fourth member might be expected by others to take notes, keep minutes, or maintain files.

None of these roles are *formal* duties, but they are activities that the group needs accomplished and has somehow parcelled out among members. If the role expectations are not met, some important jobs might not get done, or other group members might have to take on additional responsibilities. Moreover, such role assignments reduce individual members' ambiguities about what is expected specifically of them. It is important to note, though, that who takes what role in a group also is highly influenced by individuals' personal needs. The person with a high need for structure often wants to be in the note-taking role to control the structuring activity in the group; the person who breaks the tension might dislike conflict and uses the role to circumvent it.

(3) *Norms are likely to be enforced if they help the group avoid embarrassing interpersonal problems.* Goffman's work on "facework" gives some insight on this point. Goffman (1955) argues that each person in a group has a "face" he or she presents to other members of a group. This "face" is analogous to what one would call "self-image," the person's perceptions of himself or herself and how he or she would like to be seen by others. Groups want to insure that no one's self-image is damaged, called into question, or embarrassed. Consequently, the group will establish norms that discourage topics of conversation or situations in which face is too likely to be inadvertently broken. For instance, groups might develop norms about not discussing romantic involvements (so that differences in moral values do not become salient) or about not getting together socially in people's homes (so that differences in taste or income do not become salient).

A good illustration of Goffman's facework occurs in the classroom. There is always palpable tension in a room when either a class is totally unprepared to discuss a case or a professor is totally unprepared to lecture or lead the discussion. One part of the awkwardness stems from the inability of the other partner in the interaction to behave as he or she is prepared to or would like to behave. The professor cannot teach if the students are not prepared, and the students cannot learn if the professors are not teaching. Another part of the awkwardness, though, stems from self-images being called into question. Although faculty are aware that not all students are serious scholars, the situation is difficult to handle if the class as a group does not even show a pretense of wanting to learn. Although students are aware that many faculty are mainly interested in research and consulting, there is a problem if the professor does not even show a pretense of caring to teach. Norms almost always develop between professor and students about what level of preparation and interest is expected by the other because both parties want to avoid awkward confrontations.

(4) *Norms are likely to be enforced if they express the central values of the group and clarify what is distinctive about the group's identity.* Norms can provide the social justification for group activities to its members (Katz & Kahn, 1978). When the production group labels rate-busting deviant, it says: "We care more about maximizing group security than about individual profits." Group norms also convey what is distinctive about the group to outsiders. When an advertising agency labels unstylish clothes deviant, it says:

"We think of ourselves, personally and professionally, as trend-setters, and being fashionably dressed conveys that to our clients and our public."

One of the key expressive functions of group norms is to define and legitimate the power of the group itself over individual members (Katz & Kahn, 1978). When groups punish norm infraction, they reinforce in the minds of group members the authority of the group. Here, too, the literature on group deviance sheds some light on the issue at hand.

It has been noted frequently that the amount of deviance in a group is rather small (Erikson, 1966; Schur, 1965). The group uses norm enforcement to show the *strength* of the group. However, if a behavior becomes so widespread that it becomes impossible to control, then the labeling of the widespread behavior as deviance becomes problematic. It simply reminds members of the *weakness* of the group. At this point, the group will redefine what is deviant more narrowly, or it will define its job as that of keeping deviants *within bounds* rather than that of obliterating it altogether. For example, though drug use is and always has been illegal, the widespread use of drugs has led to changes in law enforcement over time. A greater distinction now is made between "hard" drugs and other controlled substances; less penalty is given to those apprehended with small amounts than large amounts; greater attention is focused on capturing large scale smugglers and traffickers than the occasional user. A group, unconsciously if not consciously, learns how much behavior it is capable of labeling deviant *and* punishing effectively.

Finally, this expressive function of group norms can be seen nicely in circumstances in which there is an inconsistency between what group members *say* is the group norm and how people actually *behave.* For instance, sometimes groups will engage in a lot of rhetoric about how much independence its managers are allowed and how much it values entrepreneurial effort; yet the harder data suggest that the more conservative, deferring, or dependent managers get rewarded. Such an inconsistency can reflect conflicts among the group's expressed values. First, the group can be ambivalent about independence; the group knows it needs to encourage more entrepreneurial efforts to flourish, but such efforts create competition and threaten the status quo. Second, the inconsistency can reveal major subgroup differences. Some people may value and encourage entrepreneurial behavior, but others do not—and the latter may control the group's rewards. Third, the inconsistency can reveal a source of the group's self-consciousness, a dichotomy between what the group is really like and how it would like to be perceived. The group may realize that it is too conservative, yet be unable or too frightened to address its problem. The expressed group norm allows the group members a chance to present a "face" to each other and to outsiders that is more socially desirable than reality.

HOW GROUP NORMS DEVELOP

Norms usually develop gradually and informally as group members learn what behaviors are necessary for the group to function more effectively. However, it also is possible for the norm development process to be short-cut by a critical event in the group or by conscious group decision (Hackman, 1976).

Most norms develop in one or more of the following four ways: explicit statements by supervisors or co-workers; critical events in the group's history; primacy; and carry-over behaviors from past situations.

(1) *Explicit statements by supervisors or co-workers.* Norms that facilitate group survival or task success often are set by the leader of the group or powerful members (Whyte, 1955b). For instance, a group leader might explicitly set norms about not drinking at lunch because subordinates who have been drinking are more likely to have problems dealing competently with clients and top management or they are more likely to have accidents at work. The group leader might also set norms about lateness, personal phone calls, and long coffee breaks if too much productivity is lost as a result of time away from the workplace.

Explicit statements by supervisors also can increase the predictability of group members' behavior. For instance, supervisors might have particular preferences for a way of analyzing problems or presenting reports. Strong norms will be set to ensure compliance with these preferences. Consequently, supervisors will have increased certainty about receiving work in the format requested, so they can plan accordingly; workers will have increased certainty about what is expected, so they will not have to outguess their boss or redo their projects.

Managers or important group members also can define the specific role expectations of individual group members. For instance, a supervisor or a co-worker might go up to a new recruit after a meeting to give the proverbial advice: "New recruits should be seen and not heard." The senior group member might be trying to prevent the new recruit from appearing brash or incompetent or from embarrassing other group members. Such interventions set specific role expectations for the new group member.

Norms that cater to supervisor preferences also are frequently established even if they are not objectively necessary to task accomplishment. For example, although organizational norms may be very democratic in terms of everybody calling each other by their first names, some managers have strong preferences about being called Mr., Ms., or Mrs. Although the form of address used in the work group does not influence group effectiveness, complying with the norm bears little cost to the group member, whereas noncompliance could cause daily friction with the supervisor. Such norms help group members avoid embarrassing interpersonal interactions with their managers.

Fourth, norms set explicitly by the supervisor frequently express the central values of the group. For instance, a dean can set very strong norms about faculty keeping office hours and being on campus daily. Such norms reaffirm to members of the academic community their teaching and service obligations, and they send signals to individuals outside the college about what is valued in faculty behavior or distinctive about the school. A dean also could set norms that allow faculty to consult or do executive development two or three days a week. Such norms, too, legitimate other types of faculty behavior and send signals to both insiders and outsiders about some central values of the college.

(2) *Critical events in the group's history.* At times there is a critical event in the group's history that established an important precedent. For instance, a group member might have discussed hiring plans with members of other units in the organization, and as a result new positions were lost or there was increased competition for good applicants. Such indiscretion can substantially hinder the survival and task success of the group; very likely the offender will be either formally censured or informally rebuked. As a result of such an incident, norms about secrecy might develop that will protect the group in similar situations in the future.

An example from Janis's *Victims of Groupthink* (1972) also illustrates this point nicely. One of President Kennedy's closest advisors, Arthur Schlesinger, Jr., had serious reservations about the Bay of Pigs invasion and presented his strong objections to the Bay of Pigs plan in a memorandum to Kennedy and Secretary of State Dean Rusk. However, Schlesinger was pressured by the President's brother, Attorney General Robert Kennedy, to keep his objections to himself. Remarked Robert Kennedy to Schlesinger: "You may be right or you may be wrong, but the President has made his mind up. Don't push it any further. Now is the time for everyone to help him all they can." Such critical events led group members to silence their views and set up group norms about the bounds of disagreeing with the president.

Sometimes group norms can be set by a conscious decision of a group after a particularly good or bad experience the group has had. To illustrate, a group might have had a particularly constructive meeting and be very pleased with how much it accomplished. Several people might say, "I think the reason we got so much accomplished today is that we met really early in the morning before the rest of the staff showed up and the phone started ringing. Let's try to continue to meet at 7:30 a.m." Others might agree, and the norm is set. On the other hand, if a group notices it accomplished way too little in a meeting, it might openly discuss setting norms to cut down on ineffective behavior (e.g., having an agenda, not interrupting others while they are talking). Such norms develop to facilitate task success and to reduce uncertainty about what is expected from each individual in the group.

Critical events also can identify awkward interpersonal situations that need to be avoided in the future. For instance, a divorce between two people working in the same group might have caused a lot of acrimony and hard feeling in a unit, not only between the husband and wife but also among various other group members who got involved in the marital problems. After the unpleasant divorce, a group might develop a norm about not hiring spouses to avoid having to deal with such interpersonal problems in the future.

Finally, critical events also can give rise to norms that express the central, or distinctive, values of the group. When a peer review panel finds a physician or lawyer guilty of malpractice or malfeasance, first it establishes (or reaffirms) the rights of professionals to evaluate and criticize the professional behavior of their colleagues. Moreover, it clarifies what behaviors are inconsistent with the group's self-image or its values. When a faculty committee votes on a candidate's tenure, it, too, asserts the legitimacy of influence of senior faculty over junior faculty. In addition, it sends (hopefully) clear messages to junior faculty about its values in terms of quality of research, teaching, and service. There are important "announcement effects" of peer reviews; internal group members carefully reexamine the group's values, and outsiders draw inferences about the character of the group from such critical decisions.

(3) *Primacy.* The first behavior pattern that emerges in a group often sets group expectations. If the first group meeting is marked by very formal interaction between supervisors and subordinates, then the group often expects future meetings to be conducted in the same way. Where people sit in meetings or rooms frequently is developed through primacy. People generally continue to sit in the same seats they sat in at their first meeting, even though those original seats are not assigned and people could change where they sit at every meeting. Most friendship groups of students develop their own "turf" in a lecture hall and are surprised/dismayed when an interloper takes "their" seats.

Norms that develop through primacy often do so to simplify, or make predictable, what behavior is expected of group members.

There may be very little task impact from where people sit in meetings or how formal interactions are. However, norms develop about such behaviors to make life much more routine and predictable. Every time a group member enters a room, he or she does not have to "decide" where to sit or how formally to behave. Moreover, he or she also is much more certain about how other group members will behave.

(4) *Carry-over behaviors from past situations.* Many group norms in organizations emerge because individual group members bring set expectations with them from other work groups in other organizations. Lawyers expect to behave towards clients in Organization I (e.g., confidentiality, setting fees) as they behave towards those in Organization II. Doctors expect to behave toward patients in Hospital I (e.g., "bedside manner," professional distance) as they behaved in Hospital II. Accountants expect to behave towards colleagues at Firm I (e.g., dress code, adherence to statutes) as they behaved towards those at Firm II. In fact much of what goes in professional schools is giving new members of the profession the same standards and norms of behavior that practitioners in the field hold.

Such carry-over of individual behaviors from past situations can increase the predictability of group members' behaviors in new settings and facilitate task accomplishment. For instance, students and professors bring with them fairly constant sets of expectations from class to class. As a result, students do not have to relearn continually their roles from class to class; they know, for instance, if they come in late to take a seat quietly at the back of the room without being told. Professors also do not have to relearn continually their roles; they know, for instance, not to mumble, scribble in small print on the blackboard, or be vague when making course assignments. In addition, presumably the most task-successful norms will be the ones carried over from organization to organization.

Moreover, such carry-over norms help avoid embarrassing interpersonal situations. Individuals are more likely to know which conversations and actions provoke annoyance, irritation, or embarrassment to their colleagues. Finally, when groups carry over norms from one organization to another, they also clarify what is distinctive about the occupational or professional role. When lawyers maintain strict rules of confidentiality, when doctors maintain a consistent professional distance with patients, when accountants present a very formal physical appearance, they all assert: "These are the standards we sustain *independent* of what we could 'get away with' in this organization. This is *our* self-concept."

SUMMARY

Norms generally are enforced only for behaviors that are viewed as important by most group members. Groups do not have the time or energy to regulate each and every action of individual members. Only those behaviors that ensure group survival, facilitate task accomplishment, contribute to group morale, or express the group's central values are likely to be brought under normative control. Norms that reflect these group needs will develop through explicit statements of supervisors, critical events in the group's history, primacy, or carry-over behaviors from past situations.

Empirical research on norm development and enforcement has substantially lagged descriptive and theoretical work. In large part, this may be due to the methodological problems of measuring norms and getting enough data points either across time or across groups. Until such time as empirical work progresses, however, the

usefulness of group norms as a predictive concept, rather than as a post hoc explanatory device, will be severely limited. Moreover, until it is known more concretely why norms develop and why they are strongly enforced, attempts to *change* group norms will remain haphazard and difficult to accomplish.

REFERENCES

Alvarez, R. Informal reactions to deviance in simulated work organizations: A laboratory experiment. *American Sociological Review,* 1968, 33, 895–912.

Asch, S. Effects of group pressure upon the modification and distortion of judgment. In H. H. Guetzkow (Ed.), *Groups, leadership, and men.* Pittsburgh: Carnegie, 1951, 117–190.

Bales, R. F., & Slater, P. E. Role differentiation in small groups. In T. Parsons, R. F. Bales, J. Olds, M. Zelditch, & P. E. Slater (Eds.), *Family, socialization, and interaction process.* Glencoe, Ill.: Free Press, 1955, 35–131.

Dentler, R. A., & Erikson, K. T. The functions of deviance in groups. *Social Problems,* 1959, 7, 98–107.

Erikson, K. T. *Wayward Puritans.* New York: Wiley, 1966.

Goffman, E. On face-work: An analysis of ritual elements in social interaction. *Psychiatry,* 1955, 18, 213–231.

Hackman, J. R. Group influences on individuals. In M. Dunnette (Ed.), *Handbook of industrial and organizational psychology.* Chicago: Rand McNally, 1976, 1455–1525.

Hollander, E. P. Conformity, status, and idiosyncrasy credit. *Psychological Review,* 1958, 65, 117–127.

Hollander, E. P. Some effects of perceived status on responses to innovative behavior. *Journal of Abnormal and Social Psychology,* 1961, 63, 247–250.

Hollander, E. P. *Leaders, groups, and influence.* New York: Oxford University Press, 1964.

Jackson, J. A conceptual and measurement model for norms and roles. *Pacific Sociological Review,* 1966, 9, 35–47.

Janis, I. *Victims of groupthink: A psychological study of foreign-policy decisions and fiascos.* New York: Houghton-Mifflin, 1972.

Katz, D., & Kahn, R. L. *The social psychology of organizations.* 2nd ed. New York: Wiley, 1978.

Kiesler, C. A., & Kiesler, S. B. *Conformity.* Reading, Mass.: Addison-Wesley, 1970.

Longley, J., & Pruitt, D. C. Groupthink: A critique of Janis' theory. In Ladd Wheeler (Ed.), *Review of personality and social psychology.* Beverly Hills: Sage, 1980, 74–93.

March, J. Group norms and the active minority. *American Sociological Review,* 1954, 19, 733–741.

Schachter, S., Ellertson, N., McBride, D., & Gregory, D. An experimental study of cohesiveness and productivity. *Human Relations,* 1951, 4, 229–238.

Schur, E. M. *Crimes without victims.* Englewood Cliffs, N.J.: Prentice-Hall, 1965.

Seashore, S. *Group cohesiveness in the industrial work group.* Ann Arbor: Institute for Social Research, University of Michigan, 1954.

Shaw, M. *Group dynamics.* 3rd ed. New York: Harper, 1936.

Trist, E. L., & Bamforth, K. W. Some social and psychological consequences of the longwall method of coal-getting. *Human Relations,* 1951, 4, 1–38.

Whyte, W. F. *Money and motivation.* New York: Harper, 1955a.

Whyte, W. F. *Street corner society.* Chicago: University of Chicago Press, 1955b.

Wiggins, J. A., Dill, F., & Schwartz, R. D. On status-liability. *Sociometry,* 1965, 28, 197–209.

Exercise: Wilderness Survival:
Group Decision Making and Effectiveness

PURPOSE

The purpose of this exercise is to help you better understand group process and group effectiveness. By the time you finish this exercise you will

1. Identify the pros and cons of group versus individual decision making

2. Experience a group decision-making situation

3. Practice diagnosing work group effectiveness

INTRODUCTION

Much of the work that takes place in organizations is done in groups. In fact, the more important a task, the more likely it is to be assigned to a group. There is a tendency to believe that groups make better decisions and are better at solving problems than individuals. However, the evidence on this subject is contradictory and seems to suggest that "it depends." Groups are more effective under some circumstances and individuals under others. There are assets and liabilities associated with both (Maier, 1967). Because so much important work is done in groups, it is necessary for group members to learn to minimize the liabilities and capitalize on the assets of group problem solving.

This two-part exercise is designed to give you the opportunity to work with a group to solve a problem and then reflect on that experience. In Part I you will have the opportunity to find out whether your group was able to minimize the liabilities and capitalize on the assets of group problem solving. In Part II you will evaluate the process that your group used to solve the problem.

―――――

Wilderness Survival is reprinted from J. William Pfeiffer and John E. Jones (eds.), *1976 Annual Handbook for Group Facilitators.* San Diego, CA: Pfeiffer and Company, 1976. Used with permission. The Group Effectiveness Checklist is based on the ideas presented in I. L. Janis, "Groupthink," *Psychology Today,* November 1971; N. R. F. Maier, "Assets and Liabilities in Group Problem Solving: The Need for an Integrative Function," *Psychological Review,* 1967, *74,* 239–249. The "Group Effectiveness Checklist" was added to this exercise by Cheryl L. Tromley.

INSTRUCTIONS

Part I

1. Read the directions and complete the Wilderness Survival Worksheet.

2. Form groups of five to seven people.

3. In groups, read the directions for and complete the Wilderness Survival Group Consensus Task.

4. Calculate your scores according to the directions in the Wilderness Survival Scoring Sheet.

5. Interpret your score.

6. Participate in a class discussion.

Part II

1. Read the directions and evaluate your group using the Group Effectiveness Checklist.

2. Fill out the Group Effectiveness Worksheet.

3. Meet in our group to discuss the worksheets.

4. Develop a plan for improving group effectiveness.

5. Participate in a class discussion.

Part I: Wilderness Survival Worksheet

Directions: Here are twelve questions concerning personal survival in a wilderness situation. Your first task is to *individually* select the best of the three alternatives given under each item. Try to imagine yourself in the situation depicted. Assume that you are alone and have a minimum of equipment, except where specified. The season is fall. The days are warm and dry, but the nights are cold.

After you have completed the task individually, you will again consider each question as a member of a small group. Both the individual and group solutions will later be compared with the "correct" answers provided by a group of naturalists who conduct classes in woodland survival.

	Your Answer	*Your Group's Answer*	*Expert Answer*
1. You have strayed from your party in trackless timber. You have no special signaling equipment. The best way to attempt to contact your friends is to a. Call for "help" loudly but in a low register b. Yell or scream as loudly as you can c. Whistle loudly and shrilly	_____	_____	_____
2. You are in "snake country." Your best action to avoid snakes is to a. Make a lot of noise with your feet b. Walk softly and quietly c. Travel at night	_____	_____	_____
3. You are hungry and lost in wild country. The best rule for determining which plants are safe to eat (those you do not recognize) is to a. Try anything you see the birds eat b. Eat anything except plants with bright red berries c. Put a bit of the plant on your lower lip for five minutes; if it seems all right, try a little more	_____	_____	_____
4. The day becomes dry and hot. You have a full canteen of water (about one liter) with you. You should a. Ration it—about a capful a day b. Not drink until you stop for the night, then drink what you think you need c. Drink as much as you think you need when you need it	_____	_____	_____
5. Your water is gone; you become very thirsty. You finally come to a dried-up watercourse. Your best chance of finding water is to a. Dig anywhere in the stream bed b. Dig up plant and tree roots near the bank c. Dig in the stream bed at the outside of a bend	_____	_____	_____

6. You decide to walk out of the wild country by following a series of ravines where a water supply is available. Night is coming on. The best place to make camp is
   a. Next to the water supply in the ravine
   b. High on a ridge
   c. Midway up the slope

7. Your flashlight glows dimly as you are about to make your way back to your campsite after a brief foraging trip. Darkness comes quickly in the woods and the surroundings seem unfamiliar. You should
   a. Head back at once, keeping the light on, hoping the light will glow enough for you to make out landmarks
   b. Put the batteries under your armpits to warm them, and then replace them in the flashlight
   c. Shine your light for a few seconds, try to get the scene in your mind, move out in the darkness, and repeat the process

8. An early snow confines you to your small tent. You doze with your small stove going. There is danger if the flame is
   a. Yellow
   b. Blue
   c. Red

9. You must ford a river that has a strong current, large rocks, and some white water. After carefully selecting your crossing spot, you should
   a. Leave your boots and pack on
   b. Take your boots and pack off
   c. Take off your pack but leave your boots on

10. In waist-deep water with a strong current, when crossing the stream, you should face
    a. Upstream
    b. Across the stream
    c. Downstream

11. You find yourself rimrocked; your only route is up. The way is mossy, slippery rock. You should try it
    a. Barefoot
    b. With boots on
    c. In stocking feet

	Your Answer	*Your Group's Answer*	*Expert Answer*

12. Unarmed and unsuspecting, you surprise a large bear prowling around your campsite. As the bear rears up about ten meters from you, you should
   a. Run
   b. Climb the nearest tree
   c. Freeze, but be ready to back away slowly
	_____	_____	_____

Individual Score	_____		

WILDERNESS SURVIVAL GROUP CONSENSUS TASK

Directions: You have just completed an individual solution to Wilderness Survival. Now your small group will decide on a group solution to the same dilemmas. A decision by consensus is difficult to attain, and not every decision may meet with everyone's unqualified approval. There should be, however, a general feeling of support from all members before a group decision is made. Do not change your individual answers, even if you change your mind in the group discussion.

Scoring Sheet

Directions:

1. As your instructor reads the experts' answers, record these in the Expert Answer column of the Wilderness Survival Worksheet.

2. Compare these "correct" answers with your individual answers and record the number of questions you answered correctly in the Individual Score space provided at the end of the Wilderness Survival Worksheet.

3. Compare the experts' answers with your group's answers, and record the number of questions the group answered correctly in the Group Score space provided on the chart below.

4. Compute your group's Average Individual Score by adding the Individual Scores of all group members and dividing by the number of members in your group. Record the result on the chart below.

5. Compute your Asset/Liability Score by subtracting the Average Individual Score from the Group Score, and record the result on the chart. If the result is positive, your group was more effective than if the individual group members had been working independently. In other words, the group capitalized on the "assets" of group problem solving. If the result is negative, your group did not capitalize on its assets but fell prey to the "liabilities" of group problem solving.

6. Poll your group to find the highest and lowest individual scores. Record this range on the chart below. If any of the group members scored higher than the group, that individual would have performed better working alone than with the group. That individual was also unable to adequately influence the group.

7. Select a spokesperson to report your (a) Range of Individual Scores, (b) Average Individual Score, (c) Group Score, and (d) Asset/Liability Score.

Scoring Chart

Range of Individual Scores	
Average Individual Score	
Group Score	
Asset/Liability Score	

Part II: Group Effectiveness Checklist

Directions: Reflect on your group experience. Carefully read each of the following statements and decide whether it is *Mostly True* or *Mostly False*. Put a check in the corresponding space beside each statement. If you do not have enough information to answer any of the questions, leave it blank. When you complete the checklist, fill out the Group Effectiveness Worksheet according to the directions.

Mostly   *Mostly*
True   *False*

_____   _____   1. We listened to each other and considered each other's opinions.

_____   _____   2. During the discussion, objective quality was more important than majority rule.

_____   _____   3. Disagreements led to a more innovative solution.

_____   _____   4. Members felt comfortable expressing their opinions.

_____   _____   5. Disagreements did not cause hard feelings.

_____   _____   6. We all felt that we were working toward a common goal.

_____   _____   7. No one dominated the conversation.

_____   _____   8. People listened to understand rather than to refute.

_____   _____   9. Members' efforts were acknowledged and rewarded.

_____   _____   10. We openly discussed how we were going to perform the task.

_____   _____   11. Finding the best solution was more important to people than winning the argument.

_____   _____   12. We analyzed the task before beginning to perform it.

_____   _____   13. Individuals freely shared their knowledge and information.

_____   _____   14. The group carried out a careful critical scrutiny of the pros and cons of the alternatives.

_____   _____   15. The group seriously considered minority viewpoints.

_____   _____   16. We surveyed all of the alternatives before deciding on a solution.

_____   _____   17. We spent time trying to look beyond the obvious.

_____   _____   18. The group tried to get everyone's input.

_____   _____   19. Group members showed positive interest in facts and opinions that did not support their ideas.

Group Effectiveness Worksheet

Directions: With your group, go over the questions on the checklist. The items that you checked as *Mostly True* are the things that your group did that contributed to its effective performance. The items that you checked as *Mostly False* are the things that your group did that got in the way of its effective performance. Under the *Mostly True* column, list all of the items that the entire group agreed were mostly true. Do the same thing for the *Mostly False* column. List the items on which the group did not agree in the *Differences* column. Discuss the items for which there was disagreement and try to come to a consensus decision. Write these items in the appropriate column (*Mostly True* or *Mostly False*).

Mostly True	Mostly False	Differences

Action Plan

Directions: As a group, review the *Mostly False* column of your Group Effectiveness Worksheet and decide on a plan for improvement.

Problem Areas	*Plan for Improvement*

DISCUSSION QUESTIONS

1. Does your diagnosis of your group's interaction process help explain how well you did on the Wilderness Survival Exercise? How?

2. What were some of the items from the Group Effectiveness Checklist that your group disagreed on? What were the reasons for the differences in perception?

3. Were there any problem areas for which you were unable to identify any improvement strategies? Why?

4. If your group did a similar exercise tomorrow, do you think you would be more effective? Why?

5. Do you plan to use what you have learned about group effectiveness the next time you are in a task group? What are some of the difficulties that you may face implementing your plan? How do you plan to overcome these difficulties?

REFERENCES

I. L. Janis. "Groupthink." *Psychology Today,* November 1971.

N. R. F. Maier. "Assets and Liabilities in Group Problem Solving: The Need for an Integrative Function." *Psychology Review,* 1967, *74,* 239–249.

Exercise: The NASA/Challenger Incident

PURPOSE

The purpose of this exercise is to provide you with an opportunity to analyze group-think dynamics as they affect group decision-making processes. By the time you finish this exercise, you will

1. Apply the concepts of groupthink to a recent news event

2. Identify the pressures that caused groupthink to occur in this situation

3. Determine the ways in which groupthink processes could be averted

INTRODUCTION

As Maier (1967) states, there are as many disadvantages as advantages in group decision making. One disadvantage is the phenomenon of groupthink, described by Irving Janis. Groupthink is a mindset that causes the group to misread the decision situation. Because of some of the disadvantages of group decision-making processes, poor judgments sometimes are made, often with far-reaching consequences. Managers need to be aware of the pressures that cause groupthink *and* the ways in which it can be averted.

The case of the NASA/Challenger disaster provides a fruitful ground from which to understand groupthink processes at work. The Rogers Commission, when it published its report on the NASA/Challenger disaster, indicated that much of what went wrong concerned NASA's "flawed" decision-making processes. Read this case to determine what you think.

INSTRUCTIONS

1. Read the articles by Irving Janis, "Groupthink," and by Maier, "Assets and Liabilities in Group Problem Solving," as preparation for this case.

2. Read the insert, "Anatomy of a Tragedy."

3. Complete the discussion questions at the end of the case.

4. Participate in a class discussion.

Anatomy of a Tragedy

Six days after the Challenger disaster, on Feb. 3, 1986, President Reagan appointed a commission and charged it with reviewing the accident's circumstances, determining its probable cause, and recommending measures toward preventing another such disaster. Known as the Rogers commission after its chairman, former Secretary of State William P. Rogers, it had 120 days to work.

On June 6, the commission announced its conclusion: The immediate physical cause of Challenger's destruction was "a failure in the joint between the two lower segments of the right Solid Rocket Motor," the report said. "The specific failure was the destruction of the seals that are intended to prevent hot gases from leaking through the joint during the propellant burn. . . ."

But contributing to the accident was, in the commission's now-famous words, the fact that "the decision to launch the Challenger was flawed." The report continued: "Those who made that decision were unaware of the recent history of problems concerning the O-rings and the joint and were unaware of the initial written recommendation of the contractor advising against the launch at temperatures below 53 degrees Fahrenheit and the continued opposition of the engineers at Thiokol after the management reversed its position." It faulted the management structure of both Thiokol and NASA for not allowing such information to flow to the people who needed to know it.

After the Rogers commission report was released, the U.S. House of Representatives' Committee on Science and Technology spent two months conducting its own hearings and reached its own conclusions in November 1986. Although the House committee agreed with several of the Rogers commission's conclusions, it also stated that "the fundamental problem was poor technical decision-making over a period of several years by top NASA and contractor personnel."

© 1987 IEEE. Reprinted, with permission, from *IEEE Spectrum*, Vol. 24 (2), February 1987, pp. 44–51.

The House committee pointed out that ". . . information on the flaws in the joint design and on the problem encountered in missions prior to 51-L was widely available and had been presented to all levels of Shuttle management." But the committee's report continued: "The NASA and Thiokol technical managers failed to understand or to fully accept the seriousness of the problem. There was no sense of urgency on their part to correct the design flaws in the SRB. No one suggested grounding the fleet. . . . Rather NASA chose to continue to fly with a flawed design and to follow a measured, 27-month corrective program," leading to a new type of joint proposed for later missions—the capture joint. The committee came to the conclusion that the problem surrounding the field-joint O-rings had been recognized soon enough for it to have been corrected, but that no correction was made, because "meeting flight schedules and cutting cost were given a higher priority than flight safety."

The findings both of the Rogers commission and of the House committee suggest a fundamental question that neither investigation addressed: just how could NASA—an organization with a reputation for ingenuity, good design, meticulous engineering, reliability, and safety—have found itself in a position where it repeatedly overlooked the obvious until disaster struck?

WHY WASN'T THE DESIGN FIXED?

Design of the joint was not changed, say Thiokol and NASA engineers and managers, because it was assumed the joint would behave like the similar joints on the Titan boosters. "In an overall sense," said Thiokol's Joe Kilminster last December, "the comfort zone, if you will, was expanded because of the fact that the shuttle joint was so similar to the Titan joint, and its many uses had shown successful operation. That's why a lot of—I guess 'faith' is the right word—was based on the fact that the Titan had had all these tests and successful experience."

Furthermore, Boisjoly pointed out: "The working troops—and I consider myself one of the working troops—had no knowledge of the thing being changed to a Criticality 1. So far as we were concerned, we had two seals that were redundant. . . . So either you believe that you fly, or you don't believe it and shut the program down."

WHY WASN'T EROSION SEEN AS A DANGER SIGN?

By 1985, erosion and blow-by had come to be accepted as normal—to the point where, in the Level I flight-readiness review for STS 51-L that analyzed the results of the preceding flight STS 61-C, NASA's Mulloy noted there were "no 61-C flight anomalies" and "no major problems or issues," in spite of the fact that there had been erosion or blow-by in three joints. Although some engineers were beginning to be alarmed about the frequency of the erosion—especially after an analysis of the results of STS 51-B in April 1985 disclosed that the secondary O-ring of a nozzle joint had been eroded as well as its primary—they received little support from NASA or Thiokol.

In July 1985, for example, Thiokol's unofficial task force was told to solve the O-ring erosion problems for both the short and long term. But in a memorandum of July 31, Boisjoly noted the group's "essential nonexistence" and asked that it be officially endorsed. He wrote that the consequences of not dealing with the seal problems "would be a catastrophe of the highest order—loss of human life."

By October, however, one task-force member was dismayed enough to write a note to Allan McDonald: "HELP! The seal task force is constantly being delayed by every possible means. . . . This is a red flag." And around the same time Boisjoly went to Kilminster and, as he now recalls, "pleaded for help." But remembering that meeting, Boisjoly said: "And quite frankly, when we were leaving the room he [Kilminster] said, 'Well, it was a good bullshit session anyway.' And that was the end of it." Boisjoly now says he didn't use exactly those words when describing, in his weekly activity report of Oct. 4, 1985, his problem in obtaining support from Kilminster. "But I had it in my notebook. I was really ticked because we were pleading for help and we couldn't get it. We were fighting all the major inertia in the plant, just like everybody else, and yet we were supposed to be this tiger team to get a very severe problem solved." Kilminster, Boisjoly now says, "just didn't basically understand the problem. We were trying to explain it to him, and he just wouldn't hear it. He felt, I guess, that we were crying wolf."

OPERATIONAL: AND THEN WHAT?

"There's just no way that I can understand in God's green earth that an airline could undertake with its normal procedures the operation of the space shuttle," said former Apollo astronaut Frank Borman, now vice-chairman of Texas Air Corp. in Las Cruces, N.M. "When NASA came out with the request for a proposal from airlines to run the shuttle like it was a [Boeing] 727, I called them and I told them they were crazy. The shuttle is an experimental vehicle, and will remain an experimental, highly sophisticated vehicle on the edge of technology."

In the early 1980s there was much discussion about whether it made sense for NASA, a research and development agency, to run what was already being viewed as a common carrier, and proposals were solicited from airlines for operating agreements. "NASA's highest priority is to make the Nation's Space Transportation System (STS) fully operational and cost-effective in providing routine access to space." So stated National Security Decision Directive 42, in 1982, and Directive 144, in 1984. The directives set as a goal "a flight schedule of up to 24 flights per year with margins for routine contingencies attendant with a flight-surge capability."

The goal of being operational also changed NASA's philosophy on crew safety, as is seen from a 1985 report produced by Rockwell International for NASA's Langley Research Center, in Hampton, Va., titled "Space Station Crew Safety Alternatives Study." Wrote the Rockwell authors: "It is interesting to trace the evolution of crew safety philosophy [from Apollo through shuttle] and to understand the reasons for this evolution. The emphasis has gone historically in two directions: (1) a tendency to go from escape and rescue measure (e.g., abort systems) toward obtaining inherent safety (i.e., reduce/eliminate threats); and (2) an increasing interest in saving not only the crew, but also the very valuable space systems. We expect these trends to continue as space operations mature and become more routine."

This emphasis on eliminating or controlling threats rather than escaping from them is consistent with airline mentality. "You don't put parachutes on airlines because the margin of safety is built into the machine," said Borman, for 17 years president of Eastern Airlines. But, he pointed out, "The 727 airplanes that we fly are proven vehicles with levels of safety and redundancy built in"—levels, he said, that the space shuttle comes nowhere near to. The way Borman sees it, the shuttle is "a hand-made piece of experimental gear."

Nevertheless, people both within and outside NASA began to treat the shuttle like an airplane, with an attendant psychological casualness about its mechanical safety. Harold Finger, formerly NASA's associate administrator for organization and management and now president of the U.S. Committee for Energy Awareness in Washington, D.C., said the NASA successes may have led to a lack of vigilance and high-level knowledge of potential danger.

WHY NO SECOND SOURCES?

Ever since the start of the shuttle program, other manufacturers had been after NASA to let them be second sources for the boosters, the largest market anywhere for solid-fuel rocket motors. Congress had also wanted a second source, for national security reasons, so that the shuttles would be available for military payloads in the event of a work stoppage or accident at Thiokol.

Obedient to the U.S. Competition in Contracting Act, NASA announced on Dec. 26, 1985—less than a month before Challenger's original launch date—a set of rules under which other manufacturers could bid to become a second source for the boosters. Although the bidding rules favored Thiokol in many ways, the announcement, Levin said, still threatened "a very fat contract. . . . Why did Thiokol management surrender on the night of Jan. 27? They didn't have to," he said—except for the fact that they were in the midst of negotiating the next production buy, and they were being threatened with a second source in connection with that buy. "Thus, keeping this customer happy was very important," Levin said.

THE NASA/CHALLENGER INCIDENT

NASA and Thiokol were aware of the likely impact of redesigning the booster joint from the ground up at least six months before Challenger's last flight. On July 23, 1985, NASA budget analyst Richard C. Cook sent a memorandum to his superior, Michael Mann. It was clear that the booster seal threatened flight safety, Cook wrote. If the cause of the problems required a major redesign, it "would lead to the suspension of Shuttle flights, redesign of the SRB [solid-fuel rocket booster], and scrapping of existing stockpiled hardware. The impact on the FY 1987–8 budget could be immense."

Within Thiokol, Boisjoly wrote in his weekly report of July 22, 1985, that the company needed to focus attention on the problem. Otherwise, "We stand in danger of having one of our competitors solve our problem via an unsolicited proposal. This thought is almost as horrifying as having flight failure before a solution is implemented to prevent O-ring erosion."

HOW DID NASA AND THIOKOL VIEW THE ODDS?

"No data conclusively showed that low temperatures would increase the risk," said NASA's Mulloy. "I agree with the House committee that continually taking that risk was bad engineering judgment, but that bad judgment started long before the teleconference that night of Jan. 27, and had the highest levels of NASA management participating in it."

Marshall propulsion engineer Ben Powers said that, at the time, "my understanding was that the [booster] motor was qualified [down] to 31° [F]." However, he recalled little surprise in finding that the Thiokol engineers were now stating that it should not be flown in conditions that cold. The Jan. 27 teleconference, he said, was the first time his attention had been directed to it. "The emphasis was not enough earlier on."

According to Thiokol's Kilminster, "All the tests that showed that the resiliency of the [primary] O-ring was lower at low temperature did not include the effects of pressure acting on it during the motor ignition pressure rise. This pressure acting on the O-ring tended to move it into a sealing position," he said. "We felt—based on all the test experience we had to that point, plus flight experience—that pressure caused the O-ring to operate as it was designed to operate, even in some of the static tests that were relatively cold—40° F."

Mulloy, in recalling his own reasoning about the launch conditions, said he argued: "We've been addressing this problem of O-ring erosion *every* launch. What is *different* this time? What was different was temperature. What is the effect of temperature? Our conclusion was that there is no correlation between low temperature and O-ring erosion—in fact, our worst erosion was at one of the highest temperatures.

"I concluded that we're taking a risk every time," Mulloy said. "We all signed up for that risk. And the conclusion was, there was *no* significant difference in risk from previous launches. We'd be taking essentially the same risk on Jan. 28 that we have been ever since we first saw O-ring erosion," he said.

The fact that data linking low temperature to increased O-ring problems were uncertain may have had an underappreciated role. "In the face of uncertainty, people's preferences take over," said Dennis Mileti, professor of sociology and director of Colorado State University's Hazards Assessments Laboratory at Fort Collins, Colo. The risk is denied, discounted, and the chance is taken. . . . "This is not unique. It's just like any of us getting on an airplane—we all

know that airplanes crash, but in our hearts we don't believe that the one we get on will crash."

Uncertainty over the effect of cold on the seal came about in several ways. There was no launch-commit criterion for the booster joint with regard to temperature. Also, Boisjoly later noted, there was "no graph plotting flights, with or without erosion as a function of temperature," that might have enabled the engineers to assess whether or not there was a correlation.

Moreover, there was, and continues to be, uncertainty over what temperatures have been specified in the design criteria for the entire shuttle. McDonald and Lund of Thiokol both now say that the only specification they knew of called for the booster to operate between 40 and 90° F—although even what those limits referred to was unclear: Did it apply to the ambient temperature or to the propellant's mean bulk temperature inside each booster? Thiokol engineers say they never knew of a "higher-level spec," set at Johnson Space Center that called for the entire shuttle system to function at ambient temperatures from 31 to 99° F.

Mulloy calls that uncertainty "nonsense." Thiokol wrote the end-item specifications, he said, with 40 to 90° set for the propellant's mean bulk temperature, 31 to 99° for the ambient temperature, 21° for the external tank-booster strut interface, and 25° for the joint between the booster's aft and aft-center sections—the joint that failed on Challenger. Nonetheless, everyone at NASA up to Jesse Moore seems to have assumed that because specifications did exist, the entire shuttle met them. There also seems to have been confusion over the establishment of launch-commit criteria, as well as over when the criteria could be waived.

No one either at Thiokol or at NASA knew for sure how the O-rings would respond to cold, said Mulloy. He pointed out that the Viton rubber O-rings had never been tested below 50° F, mainly because the material had been designed to withstand the heat of combustion gases rather than the chill of winter launches. The Viton was formulated to military specifications for use between –30 and +500° F, but NASA did no tests of its own to see whether the O-rings met those specifications.

Even opposition by several Thiokol engineers to sending up the shuttle in freezing weather was not, in itself, seen as sufficient reason to scrub the launch, because experience itself is an uncertain guide. "When I was working as [NASA's] deputy administrator, I don't think there was a single launch where there was some group of subsystem engineers that didn't get up and say 'Don't fly,' " said Hans Mark, now chancellor of the University of Texas system in Austin. "You always have arguments."

WHAT ROLE DID NASA'S SAFETY OFFICE PLAY?

The Rogers commission noted the absence of safety personnel in making the decision to launch Challenger. Arnold Aldrich told the commission of five distinct failures that contributed to the decision, four of them relating to safety, reliability, and quality assurance. There was, he said, a lack of problem-reporting requirements, and a failure to involve NASA's safety office in critical discussions.

Indeed, NASA's own corporate architecture contributed to those problems. Safety, reliability, and quality assurance was the responsibility of NASA's chief engineer, Milton Silveira, at headquarters in Washington. As NASA's hub, the headquarters directs the 16 field centers and facilities all over the country. According to the Rogers commission, one of Silveira's headquarters staff of 20 devoted one-quarter of his time to space-shuttle concerns; another spent only one-tenth of his time on flight-safety issues.

"In the early days of the space program we were so damned uncertain of what we were doing that we always got everybody's opinion," said Silveira. "We would ask for continual reviews, continual scrutiny by anybody we had respect for, to look at this thing and make sure we were doing it right. As we started to fly the shuttle again and again, I think the system developed false confidence in itself and didn't do the same thing."

WAS NASA OR THIOKOL PRESSURED TO LAUNCH?

The push was on for 15 launches in 1986 and 24 launches a year by 1990. "That can't help but influence the degree of risk that one would take," said Mulloy. "But to me that is a self-imposed thing. You make a commitment and you try your damnedest to meet it. It's probably self-imposed professional pride—doing what you, by God, said you were going to do."

But the House committee report stressed the likely result of such a punishing schedule: "The pressure on NASA to achieve planned flight rates was so pervasive that it undoubtedly adversely affected attitudes regarding safety. . . . Operating pressures were causing an increase in unsafe practices," such as shortcuts in established launch-preparation procedures to save time.

The very day of the disaster brought speculation about pressure from the White House to have Challenger launched in time for President Reagan's State of the Union message, scheduled for that evening. NASA officials told the Rogers commission, however, that there was no such outside pressure and after a short discussion, the commission concluded that "the decision to launch the Challenger was made solely by the appropriate NASA officials without any outside intervention or pressure."

"I don't have any personal first-hand knowledge about presidential pressure, but circumstances and events were suggestive of pressure from the White House," said Traficant in August. "Whether or not there was any direct intent to apply pressure to have [the shuttle] launched in a timely way to orchestrate it with the State of the Union message, I believe NASA *perceived* that these types of timetables are important."

Richard C. Cook, the former NASA budget analyst who wrote the memorandum of July 23, 1985, warning of the possible effects of the joint's design, believes there was political pressure. In a 137-page report Cook stated: "The reason NASA overruled contractor engineers and lost Challenger was because they wanted to get the shuttle into the air by the time of the President's State of the Union Message, which mentioned the teacher in space. I believe that without political motivation, the accident would not have happened," he stated, adding: "I believe that the reason the White House formed its Presidential commission was to cover that up . . . and that there is perjury by NASA officials in the commission hearings."

In support of Dennis Mileti's theory that in the face of uncertainty people opt for their preferences, Levin said: "None of these folks that decided to fly Challenger wanted those people to die. None of them in their hearts would acknowledge that they were doing something stupid, evil, or rotten. We're not talking about murderers. We're talking about people who took a desperately high risk with other people's money, other people's lives—hoping like hell that the good luck that had always attended NASA activities would hold."

WHY DIDN'T THEY TALK TO EACH OTHER?

The Rogers commission perceived a lack of communication between engineers doing technical work at Thiokol and the top NASA managers who made the launch decisions. This breakdown meant that no information flowed on known problems with the booster joint—not only during the decision to launch Challenger, but also during the entire design and development process.

Hans Mark, widely regarded for his insight and skill in technology management, has observed: "The only criticism that I have of the [Rogers commission] report is that they laid more blame on the lower-level engineers and less blame on the upper-level management than they should have. As with most of those commissions, the guys on the bottom took the rap. They quote [associate administrator for space flight Jesse] Moore and [administrator James] Beggs and a few others saying they didn't know about the O-ring problems, which I find awfully hard to believe. I mean, hell, I knew about it two years before the accident and even wrote a memo about it. I just find it very hard to believe."

Robert Boisjoly at Thiokol, Ben Powers at NASA, and other technical people assert they did as much as they felt they could to air their concerns about the joint, short of risking being fired. They saw themselves as loyal employees, believing in the chain of command. Boisjoly told the Rogers commission: "I must emphasize, I had my say, and I never take [away] any management right to take the input out of an engineer and then make a decision based upon that input, and I truly believe that. . . . So there was no point in me doing anything any further."

And Powers said in an interview: "You don't override your chain of command. My boss was there; I made my position known to him; he did not choose to pursue it. At that point it's up to him; he doesn't have to give me any reasons; he doesn't work for me; it's his prerogative." And at least two others, asked by the Rogers commission why they did not voice their concerns to someone other than their immediate superior, replied in virtually identical language: "That would not be my reporting channel."

Following the chain of command is regarded favorably by managers and organizational theorists. But Harold Finger of the Committee for Energy Awareness warned: "You must organize for multiple lines of communication. You cannot be in a situation of any nature where you are limited by the requirement for a single reportage. In my mind, that's exactly what happened in the shuttle accident. There was no deliberate built-in system of multiple communications. Therefore, when objections were registered to somebody at Marshall or Houston or Kennedy, and he determined it didn't have to go up, it didn't go up."

Furthermore, even if the lower-level managers do pass the technical staff's concerns up the chain, they may make crucial modifications. "The fact that people are in a hierarchy tends to amplify misperceptions," said William H. Starbuck, ITT professor of creative management at New York University's Graduate School of Business Administration. "A low-level person has a fear that something might happen and reports it to a higher level. As it goes up the hierarchy, information gets distorted, usually to reflect the interests of the bosses."

WHAT ABOUT NASA'S SUCCESS STORY?

It is human nature to believe that success breeds success, when in some situations success may lead directly to failure. One of those situations is when people in an organization feel they have a problem licked. Said NYU's Starbuck: "As a company goes along and is successful, it assumes that success is inevitable. NASA had a history of 25 years of doing the impossible.

"My speculation is that this history made NASA come to have two points of view," Starbuck said. "First, risks as presented by engineers are always overstated—the actual risk is much smaller than it appears. Second, there is something magical about this group of people at NASA that can somehow surmount these risks. I think they developed a feeling of invulnerability."

Otto Lerbinger, professor of communications at Boston University, characterized this feeling that nothing can go wrong as "the Titanic syndrome." On the Titanic, he said, everyone felt that safety had been taken care of. "They even felt they didn't need lifeboats for everyone because the ship was unsinkable." It was the kind of situation where Lerbinger would see complacency setting in. "People make convenient assumptions because they want to move on. They note risks involved, but forget their assumptions and forget the risks they originally recognized," he said.

Starbuck, Lerbinger and Colorado State University's Dennis Mileti all sense that such feelings of invulnerability can gradually lead an organization to take greater chances. Starbuck mentioned a cut in the number of NASA inspectors assigned to oversee contractor's work, and the decrease in the safety, reliability, and quality assurance staff, disproportionate to other NASA staff cuts over the 15-year shuttle program.

All three experts mentioned NASA's shaving safety margins to increase shuttle payloads. "You build a bridge and it works, and so you figure on the next one you can trim it," said Starbuck. "That exceeds expectations, so you trim a bit more on the next one, until you build one that collapses." With the shuttle, he said, increasing amounts of O-ring erosion came to be accepted as normal.

John Hodge, who recently retired as NASA's acting associate administrator for space stations, said: "The problem is everybody thinks of engineering as an exact science. I think one of the real problems that we've had at NASA is that the more successful we are, the more people believe it's an exact science—and it isn't. There's a great deal of trade-off on design, and a great deal of judgment involved in engineering, and there always will be."

WHAT LESSONS HAVE BEEN LEARNED?

For Lawrence Mulloy, there are two major lessons to be learned from Challenger. "The paramount lesson is to assure that a product one sets the specs for and procures is designed, qualified, and certified to actually meet the design requirements," he said. "The fact that the booster was to function in 31° F ambient temperatures was flat missed. Whether that caused the accident is academic, but the fact was that it was missed."

Second, said Mulloy, "Be very, very careful in using subscale tests and analytical techniques to justify continuing operations on a flight vehicle where the component is not operating as you designed it to operate. Be careful in rationalizing the acceptance of anomalies you didn't expect."

According to Boston University's Lerbinger, corporate cultures try to ignore the unpleasant, and this has to be counteracted by deliberately creating a culture that encourages people to bring up unpleasant information. "In a group trying to move ahead with a decision, you find that those people that have anything negative to say are unpopular," said Lerbinger. "So a manager deliberately has to *encourage* people taking the devil's advocate position. In a crisis situation, somebody has got to think about the possibility of something going wrong, and to use a worst-case scenario approach."

Erasmus Kloman, retired consultant for the National Academy of Public Administration in Washington, has written six management studies of NASA. "The way to minimize uncertainty is to have an environment where bad news can travel up," he said. "Where there's that, there's trust and confidence."

Time and again there is the tendency to kill the messenger bringing bad news, rather than punish the wrongdoers. This was pointed out by NYU's Starbuck as well as by Myron Peretz Glazer, professor of sociology at Smith College in Northampton, Mass.

After the Challenger disaster Robert Boisjoly found he was ostracized within Thiokol and no longer allowed to work with NASA. In July he was put on permanent leave. Allan McDonald was initially stripped of his staff; later Thiokol sent out a press release that he was in charge of redesigning the booster joint. "They made it sound as if Al was heading up the whole thing, but that's a bunch of baloney," said Boisjoly. "He got his old job back, period."

"That's a very normal story," said Starbuck. "It's very typical for a whistleblower to be punished by an organization." Lerbinger agreed, pointing out that objections to Thiokol's determination to launch would be seen as "organizational treason."

On the other hand, as far as Thiokol and NASA were concerned, "The price was not nearly as heavy as one would have expected," said Glazer. "If one looks at the costs involved and the risks people took, it was the most disastrous thing that could have happened, yet they walked away okay." Glazer pointed out that William Lucas retired, by no means in disgrace, as director of Marshall Space Flight Center, shortly after the Challenger disaster. Research by Glazer and Penina Migdal Glazer for a book on whistleblowers shows, Glazer said, that "People who hung tough with their organization managed to do very well. Hanging in there and not protesting is valued highly. They manage to survive because of their fundamental and correct belief that the organization will protect them."

In fact, Starbuck said, "Thiokol's management worries me even more than NASA's. It's Thiokol where one manager said to another, 'Take off your engineering hat and put on your management hat.' They are the ones who should have looked into the questions surrounding the O-ring."

When no penalty is foreseen for being careless or doing wrong, the very behavior that should be prevented is actually enforced. Thus penalties have to be clarified and exacted, said attorney Robert Levin. "One of the things that's clear to me is that engineers do not speak the same language as managers," he said. "And engineers as a group are not politically savvy. What I would very much like to come out of all this—legislatively or otherwise—is that the next time this kind of dispute comes up, one of these engineers can say 'Damn it! Look what it *cost* Thiokol.' Now you're talking the language those folks understand."

Levin pointed out that not only is Thiokol reluctant to pay the $10 million penalty to NASA stipulated in its contract in the event of such a disaster, but "Thiokol has received millions of dollars as a result of this disaster; they're getting paid for the redesign."

The fact that there are few real penalties to organizations that commit avoidable errors also concerns Boston University's Lerbinger. "It's almost political law," he said. "Public memory is short. That puts managers in a position where they can *ignore* safety unless there is some reinforcement that gets public opinion aroused again."

1. In your opinion, in what ways is the Challenger disaster a result of group-think processes operating at NASA? At Morton Thiokol?

2. What antecedent conditions led to groupthink in the NASA and Morton Thiokol decision situation?

3. Could groupthink have been averted using Janis's principles for overcoming groupthink?

4. Is the groupthink explanation too simplistic to explain the faulty decision-making processes that affected the launch decision? What other processes (communication difficulties, strategic priorities, and the like) were operating in this situation?

Exercise: Norms and Deviance

PURPOSE

The purpose of this exercise is to help you understand group norms and the strategies groups use to cope with violations of those norms. By the time you finish this exercise you will

1. Understand the importance of norms for group functioning

2. Identify the strategies that groups use to deal with members who violate their norms

3. Learn the implications of strategy choice for group effectiveness

INTRODUCTION

Among the most important characteristics of groups are norms, which are shared ideas about which behaviors are approved and disapproved. As indicated in the reading, "The Development and Enforcement of Group Norms," by Daniel C. Feldman, the patterns of norms that a group develops will influence the character, climate, and effectiveness of that group. However, norms also have the potential to interfere with group effectiveness. The reading by Irving Janis, "Groupthink," demonstrates how this can occur.

Of particular interest is what happens in a group when members reject group norms. *Deviance* is defined as a violation of a group norm. Group members do not always conform to group norms, and when they reject or react against group norms, it can disrupt the otherwise smooth functioning of the group. If, for example, a group member refuses to participate in group meetings in which his or her input is needed, the group can become paralyzed and cease functioning. However, deviance also can

---

This exercise was developed by Cheryl L. Tromley.

serve as a warning signal of potential or actual problems within a group. For example, Arthur Schlesinger in the "Groupthink" article held an alternative point of view that went against the shared norms of the policy-making group of which he was a member. If other group members had listened to his warnings, more effective group decisions may have been made.

It is important to understand under which conditions deviance can be productive versus dysfunctional for group functioning. It is also important to learn to identify the strategies that group members can use to respond to deviance and some of the consequences of those strategies. This exercise will give you the opportunity to begin this process.

INSTRUCTIONS

1. Assign students all three readings in this chapter as preparation for this exercise.

2. Read the directions and complete the Individual Worksheet.

3. Form groups of three to four people.

4. In groups, discuss the Group Discussion questions provided.

5. Appoint a spokesperson to report one of your most interesting examples to the class.

6. Participate in a class discussion.

Individual Worksheet

Directions: Think about a group of which you are now or have been a member. Think of a time when someone in the group (either you or someone else) did something that the group normally found unacceptable (that is, violated a group norm). On the following worksheet indicate (1) the norm that was violated, (2) the norm violation—what the deviant group member did, and (3) how the group responded. Think of as many different examples as you can. You may use examples from one group or from several groups.

Norm	Norm Violation	Group Response

Group Discussion

Directions: Take turns sharing one of the examples from your individual worksheets. For each of the examples discuss the following. At the conclusion of your discussion, decide which example you want to present to the class. Appoint a spokesperson to report this example.

1. Did the norm in question help or hinder group effectiveness? How?

2. Was the deviance a potential warning signal? If so, a warning of what?

3. Given the preceding analysis, was the group's response to deviance in the best interests of the group? Why or why not?

4. Would an alternative response have been more effective? If so,

❑ What response would you recommend? Why?

❑ How might the use of an alternative strategy have changed the outcome?

❑ What are potential positive and negative consequences of both the response the group actually used and the alternative you propose?

DISCUSSION QUESTIONS

1. What responses to deviance did your group identify?

2. Can you identify any patterns across your group's examples and/or those presented by the other groups?

3. Can you think of other responses that a group could make to deviance that were not discussed in your group? Why do you think they did not come out in the examples?

4. Could you use what you have learned in this exercise to help you introduce innovation into a group? How?

REFERENCE

D. C. Feldman. "The Development and Enforcement of Group Norms." *Academy of Management Review,* 1984, Vol. 9(1), 47–53.

CHAPTER 7

Intergroup Dynamics

INTRODUCTION

Intergroup dynamics is a term that refers to relationships between groups, or departments, within a system or organization. In discussing intergroups, we could be referring to the relationship between two departments, between labor and management, or among males and females within an organization, to give just a few examples. What makes the study of intergroups so interesting is that often these relationships are marked by tension. Because groups within organizations typically pursue different goals while coveting the same resources, intergroup behavior is commonly characterized by conflict. This conflict can have either positive or negative effects for the organization.

On the positive side, intergroup conflict can result in increased motivation through competition. Intergroup competition also can increase the cohesion within each group. This *binds* each group together as a solid motivational force, but it *blinds* the group to the realities of its own and the other group's performance. Thus, it creates a distortion of reality such that what *we* do is judged more positively than what *they* do. In its most extreme form, *they* become the symbol for everything that is wrong and bad and *we* become the image of everything that is right and good.

When competition escalates into destructive conflict, "winning" becomes more important than reaching the organization's goals. As a result, any performance gains for the organization may turn into losses for productivity. The group that loses the competition experiences a lowering of status, resources, and support. Group members stop communicating with one another, and departments become uncooperative. Learning how to recognize the conditions that contribute to intergroup conflict and developing skills to deal with them effectively is an important ingredient in managerial success.

READINGS

In the first reading, "Managing Conflict Among Groups," L. Dave Brown cogently explores the basics of intergroup conflict and argues for the importance of effectively managing it in organizations. He presents the notion that there can be too little or too much conflict and neither of these situations is optimally effective. Rather he feels that managers should strive for a balance rather than assuming that conflict is always destructive. He presents a practical model for diagnosing symptoms of conflict and examines several varieties of intergroup conflict that are typical of organizations: functional differences, power differences, and societal differences.

The second reading, "Experiments in Group Conflict," by Muzafer Sherif is a report of a classic series of experiments that form the basis of much of what we know today about intergroup conflict. These experiments, which took place at a camp for boys, explored the development and subsequent remediation of intergroup conflict. Sherif discovered that a superordinate goal—a goal shared by both groups that can override minor concerns—can reduce intergroup conflict and force groups to work together. Applying the lesson to organizations, we can conclude that the more possible it is to develop widely accepted organizational goals, the more likely diverse groups will be willing to cooperate for the good of the total organization.

In the third reading of the chapter, "An Intergroup Perspective on Individual Behavior," Kenwyn K. Smith argues that much of individual behavior can be explained by intergroup processes. Through a series of three case studies he supports his assertion that intergroup processes affect individual behavior by (1) influencing our perceptions of the world and how we construct our sense of reality, (2) helping us define our individual identities, and (3) contributing to the emergence of leadership behaviors.

EXERCISES AND CASES

The first exercise, "Hilarity Greeting Card Company," will help you understand the consequences and causes of intergroup conflict. You will have the opportunity to experience the dynamics of intergroup conflict in a simulated organizational setting and identify ways to reduce excessive conflict. This is a very powerful exercise that dramatically illustrates what can happen when the potential for intergroup competition exists.

The second exercise, "Labor Relations and Intergroup Conflict," is an opportunity for you to experience intergroup dynamic-labor negotiations. A labor negotiation is an example of power differences identified by Brown in his article, "Managing Conflict Among Groups." During the exercise you will be a member of a team negotiating a simulated labor contract. This is an occasion for you to explore the problems and opportunities inherent in this type of negotiation.

The final exercise, "Battle of the Sexes Confrontation," provides an opportunity for you to explore an intergroup dynamic of which we are all part—male or female. During this exercise you will explore your feelings about the opposite sex, develop an understanding of how these feelings influence your relationships, and generate a plan for improving male-female relationships at work. You may be surprised with the stereotypes about male and female behavior that are generated by this exercise. However, it is when stereotypes are covert that they are the most dangerous. It is only through the process of accepting, understanding, and wrestling to submission our stereotypical beliefs that they lose the power to influence our behavior. This exercise forces this issue.

MEMO

The memo assignment for this chapter, *"Handling Interdepartmental Conflicts"* (located at the back of the book), asks you to analyze the relationship between your department and the departments with which you interact frequently and to develop a plan for improvement. This memo is an opportunity for you to apply the concepts from this chapter to a situation with which you are familiar to increase the likelihood of the cooperative pursuit of organizational goals.

By the time you finish this chapter, you will be able to identify and diagnose the intergroup dynamics that may be affecting the relationship among departments and groups in your organization. You will also have an idea of how to intervene to improve intergroup conflict. In addition, you will understand how your intergroup memberships may affect your behavior.

Managing Conflict Among Groups

L. Dave Brown

Conflict among groups is extremely common in organizations, although it often goes unrecognized. Managing conflict among groups is a crucial skill for those who would lead modern organizations. To illustrate:

Maintenance workers brought in to repair a production facility criticize production workers for overworking the machinery and neglecting routine maintenance tasks. The production workers countercharge that the last maintenance work was improperly done and caused the present breakdown. The argument results in little cooperation between the two groups to repair the breakdown, and the resulting delays and misunderstandings ultimately inflate organization-wide production costs.

A large manufacturing concern has unsuccessful negotiations with a small independent union, culminating in a bitter strike characterized by fights, bombings, and sabotage. The angry workers, aware that the independent union has too few resources to back a protracted battle with management, vote in a powerful international union for the next round of negotiations. Management prepares for an even worse strike, but comparatively peaceful and productive negotiations ensue.

Top management of a large bank in a racially mixed urban area commits the organization to system-wide integration. Recruiters find several superbly qualified young black managers, after a long and highly competitive search, to join

L. Dave Brown, "Managing Conflict Among Groups," in *Organizational Psychology: Readings on Human Behavior in Organizations*, D. A. Kolb, I. M. Rubin, and I. N. McIntyre (eds.), 4th ed. © 1984, pp. 254–255. Reprinted by permission of Prentice Hall, Englewood Cliffs, New Jersey.

the bank's prestigious but all-white trust division and yet, subsequently, several leave the organization. Since virtually all the managers in the trust division are explicitly willing to integrate, top management is mystified by the total failure of the integration effort.

These cases are all examples of conflict or potential conflict among organizational groups that influence the performance and goal attainment of the organization as a whole. The cases differ in two important ways.

First, the extent to which the potential conflict among group is *overt* varies across cases: conflict is all too obvious in the labor-management situation; it is subtle but still evident in the production-maintenance relations; it is never explicit in the attempt to integrate the bank's trust division. It is clear that *too much* conflict can be destructive, and much attention has been paid to strategies and tactics for reducing escalated conflict. Much less attention has been paid to situations in which organizational performance suffers because of *too little* conflict, or strategies and tactics for making potential conflicts more overt.

Second, the cases also differ in the *defining characteristics* of the parties: the production and maintenance groups are functionally defined; the distribution of power is critical to the labor and management conflict; the society's history of race relations is important to the black-white relations in the bank. Although there has been much examination of organizational conflict among groups defined by function, there has been comparatively little attention to organizational conflicts among groups defined by *power differences* (e.g., headquarters-branch relations, some labor-management relations) or by *societal history* (e.g., religious group relations, black-white relations, male-female relations).

It is increasingly clear that effective management of modern organizations calls for dealing with various forms of intergroup conflict: too little as well as too much conflict, and history-based and power-based as well as function-based conflicts. This paper offers a framework for understanding conflict among groups in the next section, and suggests strategies and tactics for diagnosing and managing different conflict situations.

CONFLICT AND INTERGROUP RELATIONS

Conflict: Too Much or Too Little?

Conflict is a form of interaction among parties that differ in interests, perceptions, and preferences. Overt conflict involves adversarial interaction that ranges from mild disagreements through various degrees of fighting. But it is also possible for parties with substantial differences to act as if those differences did not exist, and so keep potential conflict from becoming overt.

It is only too clear that it is possible to have *too much* conflict between or among groups. Too much conflict produces strong negative feelings, blindness to interdependencies, and uncontrolled escalation of aggressive action and counteraction. The obvious costs of uncontrolled conflict have sparked a good deal of interest in strategies for conflict reduction and resolution.

It is less obvious (but increasingly clear) that it is possible to have *too little* conflict. Complex and novel decisions, for example, may require pulling together perspectives and information from many different groups. If group representatives are unwilling to present and argue for their perspectives, the resulting decision may not take into account all the available information. The Bay of Pigs disaster during the Kennedy Administration may have been a consequence of too little conflict in the National Security Council, where critical information possessed by representatives of different agencies was suppressed to preserve harmonious relations among them (Janis, 1972).

In short, moderate levels of conflict—in which differences are recognized and extensively argued—are often associated with high levels of energy and involvement, high degrees of information exchange, and better decisions (Robbins, 1974). Managers should be concerned, in this view, with achieving levels of conflict that are *appropriate* to the task before them, rather than concerned about preventing or resolving immediately all intergroup disagreements.

Conflict Among Groups

Conflict in organizations takes many forms. A disagreement between two individuals, for example, may be related to their personal differences, their job definitions, their group memberships, or all three. One of the most common ways that managers misunderstand organizational conflict, for example, is to attribute difficulties to "personality" factors, when it is, in fact, rooted in group memberships and organizational structure. Attributing conflict between production and maintenance workers to their personalities, for example, implies that the conflict can be reduced by replacing the individuals. But if the conflict is, in fact, related to the differing goals of the two groups, *any* individual will be under pressure to fight with members of the other group, regardless of their personal preferences. Replacing individuals in such situations without taking account of intergroup differences will *not* improve relations.

Groups are defined in organizations for a variety of reasons. Most organizations are differentiated horizontally, for example, into functional departments or product divisions for task purposes. Most organizations also are differentiated vertically into levels or into headquarters and plant groups. Many organizations also incorporate in some degree group definitions significant in the larger society, such as racial and religious distinctions.

A good deal of attention has been paid to the relations among groups of relatively equal power, such as functional departments in organizations. Much less is known about effective management of relations between groups of unequal power or those having different societal histories. But many of the most perplexing intergroup conflicts in organizations include all three elements—functional differences, power differences, and historical differences. Effective management of the differences between a white executive from marketing and a black hourly worker from production is difficult indeed, because so many issues are likely to contribute to the problem.

Intergroup relations, left to themselves, tend to have a regenerative, self-fulfilling quality that makes them extremely susceptible to rapid escalation. The dynamics of escalating conflict, for example, have impacts within and between the groups involved. *Within* a group (i.e., within the small circles in Figure 1), conflict with another group tends to increase cohesion and conformity to group norms (Sherif, 1966; Coser, 1956) and to encourage a world view that favors "us" over "them" (Janis, 1972; Deutsch, 1973). Simultaneously, *between*-groups (i.e., the relations between the circles in Figure 1) conflict promotes negative stereotyping and distrust (Sherif, 1966), increased emphasis on differences (Deutsch, 1973), decreased communications (Sherif, 1966) and increased distortion of communications that do take place (Blake and Mouton, 1961). The *combination* of negative stereotypes, distrust, internal militance, and aggressive action creates a vicious cycle: "defensive" aggression by one group validates suspicion and "defensive" counter-aggression by the other, and the conflict escalates (Deutsch, 1973) unless it is counteracted by external factors. A less well understood pattern, in which positive stereotypes, trust, and cooperative action generate a benevolent cycle of increasing cooperation, may also exist (Deutsch, 1973).

To return to one of the initial examples, both the maintenance concern with keeping the machines clean and the production concern with maximizing output were organizationally desirable. But those concerns promoted a negative maintenance stereotype of production ("too lazy to clean machines") and a production stereotype of maintenance ("want us to polish the machine, not use it") that encouraged them to fight. Part A of Figure 1 illustrates the overt but not escalated conflict between the parties.

Introducing power differences into intergroup relations further suppresses communications among the groups. The low-power group is vulnerable, and so must censor communication—such as dissatisfaction—that might elicit retaliation from the high-power group. In consequence, the high-power group remains ignorant of information considered sensitive by the low-power group. The long-term consequences of this mutually reinforcing fear and ignorance can be either escalating oppression—a peculiarly destructive form of too little conflict—or sporadic eruptions of intense and unexpected fighting (Brown, 1978).

The fight between the small independent union and the large corporation described at the outset illustrates the potential for outbursts of violent conflict when the parties are separated by large differences in power. The small union felt unable to influence the corporation at the bargaining table, and so used violence and guerrilla tactics to express its frustration and to influence management without exposing the union to retaliation. Part B of Figure 1 illustrates the positions of the parties and the quality of their conflict.

FIGURE 1
Varieties of Intergroup Conflict.

A. Functional Differences:
Maintenance and Production

M = Maintenance
P = Production
←——→ = Overt Conflict

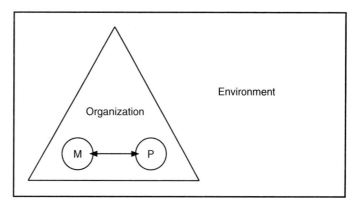

B. Power Differences:
Management and Labor

Mt = Management
L = Labor
←——→ = Escalated Conflict

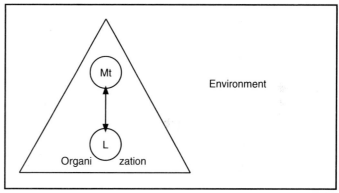

C. Societal Differences:
Black and White Managers

W = Whites
B = Blacks
←--→ = Convert Conflict

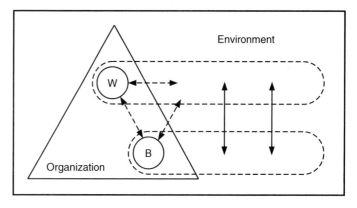

Conflicts among groups that involve societal differences may be even more complicated. Differences rooted in societal history are likely to be expressed in a network of mutually reinforcing social mechanisms—political, economic, geographic, educational—that serve to *institutionalize* the differences. Societal differences do not necessarily imply power differences between the groups, but very frequently the effect of institutionalization is to enshrine the dominance of one party over another. Relations among such groups within organizations are strongly influenced by the larger society.

Organizational tensions may be the result of environmental developments that the organization cannot control. In addition, differences associated with histories of discrimination or oppression may involve strong feelings and entrenched stereotypes that can lead to explosive conflict. Societal differences in organizations call for careful management that permits enough overt conflict so the differences are understood, but not so much that they are exacerbated.

The failure to integrate the trust division illustrates the problem of managing institutionalized racism. The black recruits had all the technical skills for success, but they could not join the all-white clubs or buy a house in the all-white suburbs where their colleagues lived, played, and learned the social ropes of the trust business. Nor could they challenge top-level decisions to keep them away from the oldest (and richest) clients ("who might be racist and so take their business elsewhere"). But the failure to face the potential conflicts—among members of the organization and between the organization and its clients—in essence made it impossible for the black managers to become full members. This situation is diagrammed in Part C of Figure 1.

Diagnosing the Conflict

Diagnosis is a crucially important and often-neglected phase of conflict management. Since conflict problems are often not recognized until after they have become acute, the need for immediate relief may be intense. But intervention in a poorly understood situation is not likely to produce instant successes. On the contrary, it may make the situation worse.

The manager of the conflict should at the outset answer three questions about the situation:

1. At what level or levels is the conflict rooted (e.g., personal, interpersonal, intergroup, etc.)?

2. What role does s/he play in the relations among the parties?

3. What is a desirable state of relations among the parties?

A conflict may be the result of an individual, an interpersonal relationship, an intergroup relationship, or a combination of the three. If the manager understands the contributions of different levels, s/he can respond appropriately. It is generally worthwhile to examine the conflict from *each* of these perspectives early in the diagnosis.

The position of the manager vis-a-vis the parties is also important. Managers who are themselves parties to the dispute are likely to be biased, and almost certainly will be perceived by their opponents as biased. Actual bias requires that the manager be suspicious of his/her own perceptions and strive to empathize with the other party; perceived bias may limit the manager's ability to intervene credibly with the other party until the perception is dealt with. Conflict managers who are organizationally superior to the parties may not be biased in favor of either, but they are likely to have poor access to information about the conflict. For such persons special effort to understand the parties' positions may be necessary. Third parties that are respected and seen as neutral by both sides are in perhaps the best position to intervene, but they are a rare luxury for most situations. In any case, awareness of one's position vis-a-vis the parties can help the manager avoid pitfalls.

Finally, a conflict manager needs to develop a sense of what is too much and what is too little conflict among the parties—when is intervention merited, and should it increase or decrease the level of conflict? Relations among groups may be diagnosed in terms of attitudes, behavior, and structure, and each of those categories has characteristic patterns associated with too much and too little conflict.

Attitudes include the orientations of groups and group members to their own and other groups—the extent to which they are aware of group interdependencies, the sophistication of group representatives about intergroup relations, and the quality of feelings and stereotypes within groups. Too much conflict is characterized by blindness to interdependencies, naiveté about the dynamics and costs of conflict, and strong negative feelings and stereotypes. Too little conflict, in contrast, is marked by blindness to conflicts of interests, naiveté about the dynamics and costs of collusion, and little awareness of group differences.

Behaviors include the ways in which groups and their members act—the levels of cohesion and conformity within groups, the action strategies of group representatives, the extent to which interaction between the groups is marked by escalating conflict or cooperation. Too much conflict often involves monolithically conforming groups, rigidly competitive action strategies, and escalating aggression among the groups. Too little conflict is associated with undefined or fragmented groups, unswervingly cooperative action strategies, and collusive harmony and agreement in place of examination of differences.

Structures are underlying factors that influence interaction in the long term—the larger systems in which parties are embedded, structural mechanisms that connect the parties, group boundaries and long-term interests, and regulatory contexts that influence interaction. Too much conflict is promoted by undefined or differentiated larger systems, lack of integrative mechanisms that link the groups, clearly defined and conflicting group interests and identities, and few rules or regulations to limit conflict. Too little conflict is encouraged by a shared larger system that suppresses conflict, no mechanisms to promote examination of differences, vague definitions of conflicting group interests and identities, and regulations that discourage overt conflict.

These diagnostic categories and the earmarks of too much and too little conflict are summarized in Table 1. Attitudinal, behavioral, and structural aspects of intergroup relations tend to interact with and support one another. The result is a tendency to escalate either the conflict or the collusion until some external force exerts a moderating effect. Thus, intergroup relations are volatile and capable of rapid escalatory cycles, but they also offer a variety of leverage points at which their self-fulfilling cycles may be interrupted by perceptive managers.

Intervention

Intervention to promote constructive conflict may involve *reducing* conflict in relations with too much or *inducing* conflict in relations with too little. In both cases, intervention involves efforts to disrupt a cyclical process produced by the interaction of attitudes, behavior, and structure. Interventions may start with any aspect of the groups' interaction, although long-term change will probably involve effects in all of them. More work has been done on the problem of reducing conflict than on inducing it—but conflict-reduction strategies often have the seeds of conflict induction within them.

Changing *attitudes* involves influencing the ways in which the parties construe events. Thus *altering group perceptions of their differences or similarities* may influence their interaction. Sherif (1966), for example, reports reduction in intergroup conflicts as a consequence of introducing superordinate goals that both groups desired but whose achievement required cooperation; emphasizing interdependencies may reduce escalated conflict. On the other hand, inducing conflict may require deemphasizing interdependencies and emphasizing conflicts of interest. Attitudes may also be changed by *changing the parties' understanding of their relations.* Increased understanding of the dynamics of intergroup conflict and

TABLE 1
Diagnosing Conflict Among Groups.

Area of Concern	General Issue	Symptoms of Too Much Conflict	Symptoms of Too Little Conflict
Attitudes	Awareness of similarities and differences	Blind to interdependence	Blind to conflicts of interest
	Sophistication about intergroup relations	Unaware of dynamics and costs of conflict	Unaware of dynamics and costs of collusion
	Feelings and perceptions of own and other group	Elaborated stereotypes favorable to own and unfavorable to other group	Lack of consciousness of own group and differences from other group
Behavior	Behavior within groups	High cohesion and conformity; high mobilization	Fragmentization; mobilization
	Conflict management style of groups	Overcompetitive style	Overcooperative style
	Behavior between groups	Aggressive, exploitative behavior; preemptive attack	Avoidance of conflict; appeasement
Structure	Nature of larger system	Separate or underdefined common larger system	Shared larger system that discourages conflict
	Regulatory context for interaction	Few rules to limit escalation	Many rules that stifle differences
	Relevant structural mechanisms	No inhibiting third parties available	No third parties to press differences
	Definition of groups and their goals	Impermeably bound groups obsessed with own interests	Unbounded groups aware of own interests

its costs, for example, may help participants reduce their unintentional contributions to escalation (e.g., Burton, 1969). By the same token, increased understanding may help parties control the development of collusion (Janis, 1972). *Feelings and stereotypes may also be changed* by appropriate interventions. Sharing discrepant perceptions of each other has helped depolarize negative stereotypes and reduce conflict in a number of intergroup conflicts (e.g., Blake, Shepard, and Mouton, 1964), and consciousness raising to clarify self and other perceptions may help to increase conflict in situations where there is too little. Attitude-change interventions, in short, operate on the ways in which the parties understand and interpret the relations among the groups.

Changing *behaviors* requires modifying ways in which group members act. *Altering within-group behavior,* for example, may have a substantial impact on the ways in which the groups deal with each other. When members of a highly cohesive group confront explicitly differences that exist *within* the group, their enthusiasm for fighting with outside groups may be reduced. Similarly, an internally fragmented group that becomes more cohesive may develop an increased appetite for conflict with other groups (Brown, 1977). A second behavior-changing strategy is to *train group representatives to manage conflict more effectively.* Where too much conflict exists, representatives can be trained in conflict-reduction strategies, such as cooperation induction (Deutsch, 1973) or problem solving (Filley, 1975). Where the problem is too little conflict, the parties might benefit from training in assertiveness or bargaining skills. A third alternative is to *monitor between-group behavior,* and so influence

escalations. Third parties trusted by both sides can control escalative tendencies or lend credibility to reduction initiatives by the parties that might otherwise be distrusted (Walton, 1969). Similarly, conflict induction may be an outcome of third-party "process consultation" that raises questions about collusion (Schein, 1969). Behavior-change strategies, in summary, focus on present activities as an influence on levels of conflict, and seek to move those actions into more constructive patterns.

Changing structures involves altering the underlying factors that influence long-term relations among groups. A common alternative is to *invoke larger system interventions.* Conflict between groups in the same larger system is often reduced through referring the question at issue to a higher hierarchical level (Galbraith, 1971). A similar press for conflict induction may be created when too little conflict results in lowered performance that catches the attention of higher levels. A related strategy for managing conflict is to *develop regulatory contexts* that specify appropriate behaviors. Such regulatory structures can limit conflict by imposing rules on potential fights, as collective bargaining legislation does on labor-management relations. Changes in regulatory structures can also loosen rules that stifle desirable conflict. A third strategy is the *development of new interface mechanisms* that mediate intergroup relations. Integrative roles and departments may help to reduce conflict among organizational departments (Galbraith, 1971), while the creation of ombudsmen or "devil's advocates" can help surface conflict that might otherwise not become explicit (Janis, 1972). Another possibility is *redefinition of group boundaries and goals,* so the nature of the parties themselves is reorganized. Redesigning organizations into a matrix structure, for example, in effect locates the conflicted interface within an individual to ensure that effective management efforts are made (Galbraith, 1971). Alternatively, too little conflict may call for clarifying group boundaries and goals so the differences among them become more apparent and more likely to produce conflict. Structural interventions typically demand heavier initial investments of time and energy, and they may take longer to bear fruit than attitudinal and behavioral interventions. But they are also more likely to produce long-term changes.

These strategies for intervention are summarized in Table 2. This sample of strategies is not exhaustive, but it is intended to be representative of interventions that have worked with groups that are relatively equal in power and whose differences are primarily related to the organization's task. The introduction of power differences and societal differences raises other issues.

Power Differences

Relations between high-power and low-power groups are worth special examination because of their potential for extremely negative outcomes. The poor communications that result from fear on the part of the low-power group and ignorance on the part of the high-power group can result in either extreme oppression (too little conflict) or unexpected explosions of violence (too much).

It is understandable that high-power groups prefer too little conflict to too much, and that low-power groups are anxious about the risks of provoking conflict with a more powerful adversary. But organizations that in the short run have too little conflict often have too much in the long term. Inattention to the problems of low-power groups requires that they adopt highly intrusive influence strategies in order to be heard (e.g., Swingle, 1967). So the comfort of avoiding conflict between high- and low-power groups may have high costs in the long run.

Managing conflict between high- and low-power groups requires dealing in some fashion with their power differences, since those differences drastically affect the flow of information and influence among the parties. A prerequisite to conflict management interventions may well be *evening the psychological odds,* so that both groups feel able to discuss the situation without too much risk. Evening the odds does not necessarily mean power equalization, but it does require trustworthy protection (to reduce the fear of low-power groups) and effective education (to reduce the ignorance of high-power groups). Given psychological equality, interventions related to attitudes, behavior, and structure that have already been discussed may be employed to promote constructive levels of conflict (e.g., Brown, 1977). It should be noted that for differently powerful groups the boundary between too much and too little conflict is easily crossed. Managers may find themselves oscillating rapidly between interventions to induce and interventions to reduce conflict between such groups.

To return once again to an initial example, the history of fighting and violence between the small union and the corporation led the latter's managers to expect even worse conflict when faced by the international union. But voting in the international in effect evened the odds between labor and management. Violent tactics considered necessary by the small union were not necessary for

TABLE 2
Intervening in Conflict Among Groups.

Area of Concern	General Issue	Strategies for Too Much Conflict	Strategies for Too Little Conflict
Attitudes	Clarify differences and similarities	Emphasize interdependencies	Emphasize conflict of interest
	Increased sophistication about intergroup relations	Clarify dynamics and costs of escalation	Clarify costs and dynamics of collusion
	Change feelings and perceptions	Share perceptions to depolarize stereotypes	Consciousness raising about group and others
Behavior	Modify within-group behavior	Increase expression of within-group differences	Increase within-group cohesion and consensus
	Train group representatives to be more effective	Expand skills to include cooperative strategies	Expand skills to include assertive, confrontive strategies
	Monitor between-group behavior	Third-party peacemaking	Third-party process consultation
Structure	Invoke larger system interventions	Refer to common hierarchy	Hierarchical pressure for better performance
	Develop regulatory contexts	Impose rules on interaction that limit conflict	Deemphasize rules that stifle conflict
	Create new interface mechanisms	Develop integrating roles of groups	Create "devil's advocates" or ombudsmen
	Redefine group boundaries and goals	Redesign organization to emphasize task	Clarify group boundaries and goals to increase differentiation

the international, and the regulatory structure of collective bargaining proved adequate to manage the conflict subsequently.

Societal Differences

Organizations are increasingly forced to grapple with societal differences. These differences are typically not entirely task-related; rather, they are a result of systematic discrimination in the larger society. Group members enter the organization with sets toward each other with which the organization must cope to achieve its goals. Societal differences are most problematic when they involve histories of exploitation (e.g., blacks by whites, women by men), and successful conflict management of such differences requires more than good intentions.

Managing societal differences in organizations may call for evening the odds, as in managing power differences, since societal differences so often include an element of power asymmetry. But coping with societal differences may also require more, since the effect of institutionalization is to ensure that the differences are preserved. *Invoking pressures from the environment* may be required even to get members of some groups into the organization at all. External forces such as federal pressure for "equal opportunity" and expanding educational opportunities for minorities can be used to press for more attention to societally based conflicts within organizations. Organizations may also develop *internal counterinstitutions* that act as checks and balances to systemic discrimination. A carefully designed and protected "communications group," which includes members from many groups and levels, can operate as an early warning system and as a respected third party for managing societal intergroup tensions in an organization (Alderfer, 1977).

The bank's failure to integrate the trust department turned largely on institutionalized racism. The decision to hire black managers was made partly in response to environmental pressure, and so overcame the initial barrier to letting blacks into the division at all. But once into the division, no mechanisms existed to press for overt discussion of differences. Without that discussion, no ways could be developed for the black managers to scale the insurmountable barriers facing them. The bank colluded with its supposedly racist clients by protecting them from contact with the new recruits. Although the first step—recruiting the black managers—was promising, trust division managers were unable to make the differences discussable or to develop the mechanisms required for effective management of the black-white differences in the division.

CONCLUSION

It may be helpful to the reader to summarize the major points of this argument and their implications. It has been argued that relations among groups in organizations can be characterized by too much or too little conflict, depending on their task, the nature of their differences, and the degree to which they are interdependent. This proposition suggests that *conflict managers should strive to maintain some appropriate level of conflict,* rather than automatically trying to reduce or resolve all disagreements. Effective management of intergroup conflict requires both understanding and appropriate action. Understanding intergroup conflict involves diagnosis of attitudes, behaviors, structures, and their interaction. *Effective intervention to increase or decrease conflict requires action to influence attitudes, behaviors, and structures grounded in accurate diagnosis.*

Power differences between groups promote fear and ignorance that result in reduced exchange of information between groups and the potential for either explosive outbursts of escalated conflict or escalating oppression. Evening the odds, at least in psychological terms, may be a prerequisite to effective intervention in such situations. *Managers must cope with fear, ignorance, and their consequences to effectively manage conflicts between unequally powerful groups.*

Societal differences institutionalized in the larger society may further complicate relations among groups in organizations by introducing environmental events and long histories of tension. Managing such differences may require invocation of environmental pressures and the development of counterinstitutions that help the organization deal with the effects of systemic discrimination in the larger society. *Environmental developments produce the seeds for organizational conflicts, but they also offer clues to their management.*

The importance of effective conflict management in organizations is increasing, and that development is symptomatic of global changes. We live in a rapidly shrinking, enormously heterogeneous, increasingly interdependent world. The number of interfaces at which conflict may occur is increasing astronomically, and so are the stakes of too much or too little conflict at those points. If we are to survive—let alone prosper—in our onrushing future, we desperately need skilled managers of conflict among groups.

REFERENCES

Alderfer, C. P. Improving Organizational Communications Through Long-Term Intergroup Intervention. *Journal of Applied Behavioral Science, 13,* 1977, 193–210.

Blake, R. R., and Mouton, J. S. Reactions to Intergroup Competition Under Win-Lose Conditions. *Management Science, 4,* 1961.

Blake, R. R., Shepard, H. A., and Mouton, J. S. *Managing Intergroup Conflict in Industry.* Ann Arbor, Mich.: Foundation for Research on Human Behavior, 1964.

Brown, L. D. Can Haves and Have-Nots Cooperate? Two Efforts to Bridge a Social Gap. *Journal of Applied Behavioral Science, 13,* 1977, 211–224.

Brown, L. D. Toward a Theory of Power and Intergroup Relations, in *Advances in Experiential Social Process,* edited by C. A. Cooper and C. P. Alderfer. London: Wiley, 1978.

Burton, J. W. *Conflict and Communication: The Use of Controlled Communication in International Relations.* London: Macmillan, 1969.

Coser, L. A. *The Functions of Social Conflict.* New York: Free Press, 1973.

Deutsch, M. *The Resolution of Conflict.* New Haven, Conn.: Yale University Press, 1973.

Filley, A. C. *Interpersonal Conflict Resolution.* Glenview, Ill.: Scott, Foresman, 1975.

Galbraith, J. R. *Designing Complex Organizations.* Reading, Mass.: Addison-Wesley, 1971.

Janis, I. *Victims of Groupthink.* Boston: Houghton-Mifflin, 1972.

Lawrence, P. R., and Lorsch, J. W. *Organization and Environment.* Boston: Harvard Business School, 1967.

Robbins, S. P. *Managing Organizational Conflict.* Englewood Cliffs, N.J.: Prentice Hall, 1974.

Experiments in Group Conflict

Muzafer Sherif

Conflict between groups—whether between boys' gangs, social classes, "races" or nations—has no simple cause, nor is mankind yet in sight of a cure. It is often rooted deep in personal, social, economic, religious and historical forces. Nevertheless it is possible to identify certain general factors which have a crucial influence on the attitude of any group toward others. Social scientists have long sought to bring these factors to light by studying what might be called the "natural history" of groups and group relations. Intergroup conflict and harmony is not a subject that lends itself easily to laboratory experiments. But in recent years there has been a beginning of attempts to investigate the problem under controlled yet lifelike conditions, and I shall report here the results of a program of experimental studies of groups which I started in 1948. Among the persons working with me were Marvin B. Sussman, Robert Huntington, O. J. Harvey, B. Jack White, William R. Hood and Carolyn W. Sherif. The experiments were conducted in 1949, 1953 and 1954; this article gives a composite of the findings.

We wanted to conduct our study with groups of the informal type, where group organization and attitudes would evolve naturally and spontaneously, without formal direction or external pressures. For this purpose we conceived that an isolated summer camp would make a good experimental setting, and that decision led us to choose as subjects boys about 11 or 12 years old, who would find camping natural and fascinating. Since our aim was to study the development of group relations among these boys under carefully controlled conditions, with as little interference as possible from personal neuroses, background influences or prior experiences, we selected normal boys of homogeneous background who did not know one another before they came to the camp.

They were picked by a long and thorough procedure. We interviewed each boy's family, teachers and school officials, studied his school and medical records, obtained his scores on personality tests and observed him in his classes and at play with his schoolmates. With all this information we were able to assure ourselves that the boys chosen were of like kind and background: all were healthy, socially well-adjusted, somewhat above average in intelligence and from stable, white, Protestant, middle-class homes.

None of the boys was aware that he was part of an experiment on group relations. The investigators appeared as a regular camp staff—camp directors, counselors and so on. The boys met one another for the first time in buses that took them to the camp, and so far as they knew it was a normal summer of camping. To keep the situation as lifelike as possible, we conducted all our experiments within the framework of regular camp activities and games. We set up projects which were so interesting and attractive that the boys plunged into them enthusiastically without suspecting that they might be test situations. Unobtrusively we made records of their behavior, even using "candid" cameras and microphones when feasible.

We began by observing how the boys became a coherent group. The first of our camps was conducted in the hills of northern Connecticut in the summer of 1949. When the boys arrived, they were all housed at first in one large bunkhouse. As was to be expected, they quickly formed particular friendships and chose buddies. We had deliberately put all the boys together in this expectation, because we wanted to see what would happen later after the boys were separated into different groups. Our object was to reduce the factor of personal attraction in the formation of groups. In a few days we divided the boys into two groups and put them in different cabins. Before doing so, we asked each boy informally who his best friends were, and then took pains to place the "best friends" in different groups so far as possible. (The pain of separation was assuaged by allowing each group to go at once on a hike and camp-out.)

As everyone knows, a group of strangers brought together in some common activity soon acquires an informal and spontaneous kind of organization. It comes to look upon some members as leaders, divides up duties, adopts unwritten norms of behavior, develops an *esprit de corps.* Our boys followed this pattern as they shared a series of experiences. In each group the boys pooled their efforts, organized duties and divided up tasks in work and play. Different individuals assumed different responsibilities. One boy excelled in cooking. Another led in athletics. Others, though not outstanding in any one skill, could be counted on to pitch in and do their level best in anything the group attempted. One or two seemed to disrupt activities, to start teasing at the wrong moment or offer useless suggestions. A few boys consistently had good suggestions and showed ability to coordinate the efforts of others in carrying them through. Within a few days one person had proved himself more resourceful and skillful than the rest. Thus, rather quickly, a leader and lieutenants emerged. Some boys sifted toward the bottom of the heap, while others jockeyed for higher positions.

We watched these developments closely and rated the boys' relative positions in the group, not only on the basis of our own observations but also by informal sounding of the boys' opinions as to who got things started, who got things done, who could be counted on to support group activities.

As the group became an organization, the boys coined nicknames. The big, blond, hardy leader of one group was dubbed "Baby Face" by his admiring followers. A boy with a rather long head became "Lemon Head." Each group developed its own jargon, special jokes, secrets and special ways of performing tasks. One group, after killing a snake near a place where it had gone to swim, named the place "Moccasin Creek" and thereafter preferred this swimming hole to any other, though there were better ones nearby.

Wayward members who failed to do things "right" or who did not contribute their bit to the common effort found themselves receiving the "silent treatment," ridicule or even threats. Each group selected symbols and a name, and they had these put on their caps and T-shirts. The 1954 camp was conducted in Oklahoma, near a famous hideaway of Jesse James called Robber's Cave. The two groups of boys at this camp named themselves the Rattlers and the Eagles.

Our conclusions on every phase of the study were based on a variety of observations, rather than on any single method. For

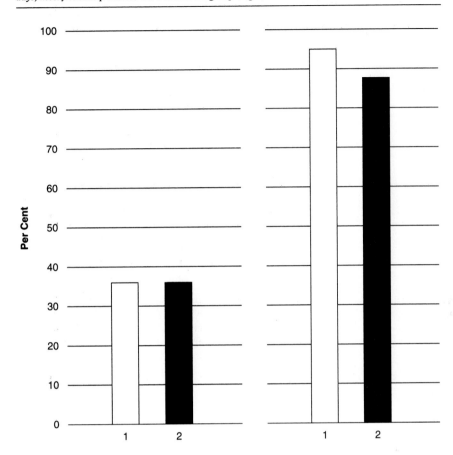

Friendship choices of campers for others in their own cabin are shown for Red Devils (white) and Bulldogs (black). At first a low percentage of friendships were in the cabin group (left). After five days, most friendship choices were within the group (right).

example, we devised a game to test the boys' evaluations of one another. Before an important baseball game, we set up a target board for the boys to throw at, on the pretense of making practice for the game more interesting. There were no marks on the front of the board for the boys to judge objectively how close the ball came to a bull's-eye, but, unknown to them, the board was wired to flashing lights behind so that an observer could see exactly where the ball hit. We found that the boys consistently overestimated the performances by the most highly regarded members of their group and underestimated the scores of those of low social standing.

The attitudes of group members were even more dramatically illustrated during a cook-out in the woods. The staff supplied the boys with unprepared food and let them cook it themselves. One boy promptly started to build a fire, asking for help in getting wood. Another attacked the raw hamburger to make patties. Others prepared a place to put buns, relishes and the like. Two mixed soft drinks from flavoring and sugar. One boy who stood around without helping was told by the others to "get to it." Shortly the fire was blazing and the cook had hamburgers sizzling. Two boys distributed them as rapidly as they became edible. Soon it was time for the

watermelon. A low-ranking member of the group took a knife and started toward the melon. Some of the boys protested. The most highly regarded boy in the group took over the knife, saying, "You guys who yell the loudest get yours last."

When the two groups in the camp had developed group organization and spirit, we proceeded to the experimental studies of intergroup relations. The groups had had no previous encounters; indeed, in the 1954 camp at Robber's Cave the two groups came in separate buses and were kept apart while each acquired a group feeling.

Our working hypothesis was that when two groups have conflicting aims—*i.e.,* when one can achieve its ends only at the expense of the other—their members will become hostile to each other even though the groups are composed of normal well-adjusted individuals. There is a corollary to this assumption which we shall consider later. To produce friction between the groups of boys we arranged a tournament of games: baseball, touch football, a tug-of-war, a treasure hunt and so on. The tournament started in a spirit of good sportsmanship. But as it progressed good feeling soon evaporated. The members of each group began to call their rivals

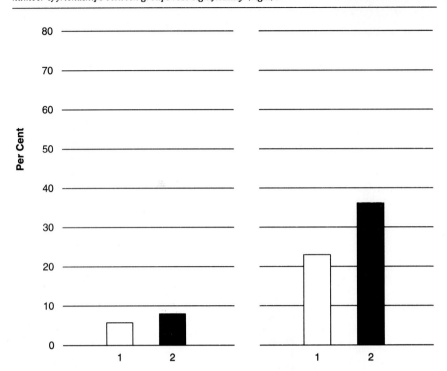

During conflict between the two groups in the Robber's Cave experiment there were few friendships between cabins (left). After cooperation toward common goals had restored good feelings, the number of friendships between groups rose significantly (right).

"stinkers," "sneaks" and "cheaters." They refused to have anything more to do with individuals in the opposing group. The boys in the 1949 camp turned against buddies whom they had chosen as "best friends" when they first arrived at the camp. A large proportion of the boys in each group gave negative ratings to all the boys in the other. The rival groups made threatening posters and planned raids, collecting secret hoards of green apples for ammunition. In the Robber's Cave camp the Eagles, after a defeat in a tournament game, burned a banner left behind by the Rattlers; the next morning the Rattlers seized the Eagles' flag when they arrived on the athletic field. From that time on name-calling, scuffles and raids were the rule of the day.

Within each group, of course, solidarity increased. There were changes: one group deposed its leader because he could not "take it" in the contests with the adversary; another group overnight made something of a hero of a big boy who had previously been regarded as a bully. But morale and cooperativeness within the group became stronger. It is noteworthy that this heightening of cooperativeness and generally democratic behavior did not carry over to the group's relations with other groups.

We now turned to the other side of the problem: How can two groups in conflict be brought into harmony? We first undertook to test the theory that pleasant social contacts between members of conflicting groups will reduce friction between them. In the 1954 camp we brought the hostile Rattlers and Eagles together for social

events: going to the movies, eating in the same dining room and so on. But far from reducing conflict, these situations only served as opportunities for the rival groups to berate and attack each other. In the dining-hall line they shoved each other aside, and the group that lost the contest for the head of the line shouted "Ladies first!" at the winner. They threw paper, food and vile names at each other at the tables. An Eagle bumped by a Rattler was admonished by his fellow Eagles to brush "the dirt" off his clothes.

We then returned to the corollary of our assumption about the creation of conflict. Just as competition generates friction, working in a common endeavor should promote harmony. It seemed to us, considering group relations in the everyday world, that where harmony between groups is established, the most decisive factor is the existence of "superordinate" goals which have a compelling appeal for both but which neither could achieve without the other. To test this hypothesis experimentally, we created a series of urgent, and natural, situations which challenged our boys.

One was a breakdown in the water supply. Water came to our camp in pipes from a tank about a mile away. We arranged to interrupt it and then called the boys together to inform them of the crisis. Both groups promptly volunteered to search the water line for the trouble. They worked together harmoniously, and before the end of the afternoon they had located and corrected the difficulty.

A similar opportunity offered itself when the boys requested a movie. We told them that the camp could not afford to rent one.

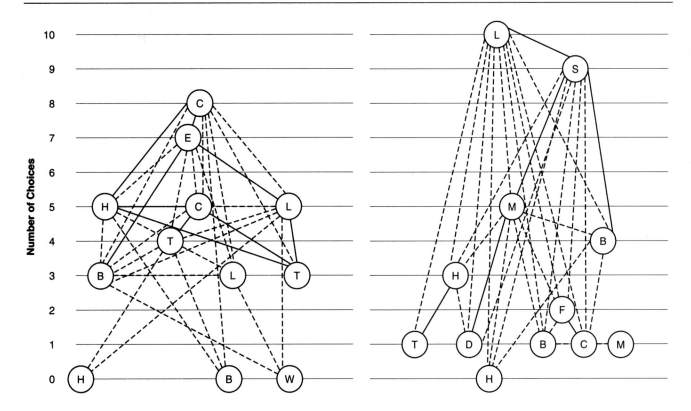

The two groups then got together, figured out how much each group would have to contribute, chose the film by a vote and enjoyed the showing together.

One day the two groups went on an outing at a lake some distance away. A large truck was to go to town for food. But when everyone was hungry and ready to eat, it developed that the truck would not start (we had taken care of that). The boys got a rope—the same rope they had used in their acrimonious tug-of-war—and pulled together to start the truck.

These joint efforts did not immediately dispel hostility. At first the groups returned to the old bickering and name-calling as soon as the job in hand was finished. But gradually the series of cooperative acts reduced friction and conflict. The members of the two groups began to feel more friendly to each other. For example, a Rattler whom the Eagles disliked for his sharp tongue and skill in defeating them because a "good egg." The boys stopped shoving in the meal line. They no longer called each other names, and sat together at the table. New friendships developed between individuals in the two groups.

In the end the groups were actively seeking opportunities to mingle, to entertain and "treat" each other. They decided to hold a joint campfire. They took turns presenting skits and songs. Members of both groups requested that they go home together on the same bus, rather than on the separate buses in which they had come. On the way the bus stopped for refreshments. One group still had five dollars which they had won as a prize in a contest. They decided to spend this sum on refreshments. On their own initiative they invited their former rivals to be their guests for malted milks.

Our interviews with the boys confirmed this change. From choosing their "best friends" almost exclusively in their own group, many of them shifted to listing boys in the other group as best friends [see chart on page 278.]. They were glad to have a second chance to rate boys in the other group, some of them remarking that they had changed their minds since the first rating made after the tournament. Indeed they had. The new ratings were largely favorable [see chart on page 280].

Efforts to reduce friction and prejudice between groups in our society have usually followed rather different methods. Much attention has been given to bringing members of hostile groups together socially, to communicating accurate and favorable information about one group to the other, and to bringing the leaders of groups together to enlist their influence. But as everyone knows, such measures sometimes reduce intergroup tensions and sometimes do not. Social contacts, as our experiments demonstrated, may only serve as occasions for intensifying conflict. Favorable information about a disliked group may be ignored or reinterpreted

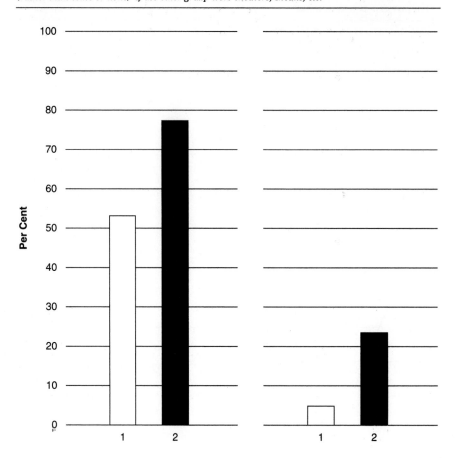

Negative ratings of each group by the other were common during the period of conflict (left) but decreased when harmony was restored (right). The graphs show the percent who thought that all (rather than some or none) of the other group were cheaters, sneaks, etc.

to fit stereotyped notions about the group. Leaders cannot act without regard for the prevailing temper in their own groups.

What our limited experiments have shown is that the possibilities for achieving harmony are greatly enhanced when groups are brought together to work toward common ends. Then favorable information about a disliked group is seen in a new light, and leaders are in a position to take bolder steps toward cooperation. In short, hostility gives way when groups pull together to achieve overriding goals which are real and compelling to all concerned.

An Intergroup Perspective on Individual Behavior

Kenwyn K. Smith

The history of psychology has been filled with attempts to understand the behavior of people either in terms of their personality, or as an interaction of individual and environmental characteristics (Lewin, 1947). In the latter case, the environment has been conceptualized at many levels, ranging from global influences of the culture at large to specific properties of the groups of which individuals are members. Although a great deal of attention has been given to group influences on individuals' beliefs, values, perceptions, and behaviors (Hackman, 1976), to date the impact on individuals of forces generated by relationships *between* groups has been largely unexplored.

Since there now exists an expanding body of knowledge about intergroup processes (Sherif, 1962; Rice, 1969; Levine & Campbell, 1972; Lorsch & Lawrence, 1972; Smith, 1974; Alderfer, 1977; Alderfer, Brown, Kaplan, & Smith, in press), our understanding of individual behavior can be significantly augmented by including this aspect of the social environment as a determinant of how people behave.

In this paper I explore the proposition that, when intergroup situations exist, *behavior can be viewed primarily as an enactment of the forces those intergroup processes generate.* This is not to claim that individual or group interpretations of the same behaviors have no validity. Rather, it is simply an assertion that if an analysis is made at an intergroup level, a substantial proportion of the variation in individual behavior is explainable in terms of the intergroup dynamics. In particular I propose that intergroup processes: (1) color profoundly our perceptions of the world, and may play a critical role in determining how we construct our personal sense of reality; (2) help define our individual identities; and (3) contribute significantly to the emergence of behavior patterns that we traditionally label as leadership.

Each of these assertions will be explored and illustrated by examining salient data from three very different social systems: (1) the experiences of a high school principal, and the way his personal sense of reality has been influenced by the various intergroup forces in his school system; (2) the development of the individual identity of a "village lunatic" in an experiential laboratory; and (3) the repeated changes of leadership behaviors in a group of survivors from an aircraft crash.

Reprinted with permission from the author from J. R. Hackman, E. E. Lawler III, and L. W. Porter (eds.), *Perspectives on Behavior in Organizations* (New York: McGraw-Hill Book Company, 1977). The concepts introduced in this article have been elaborated in greater depth in Kenwyn K. Smith, *Groups in Conflict: Prisons in Disguise* (Dubuque, Iowa: Kendall/Hunt, 1982) and Kenwyn K. Smith and David N. Berg, *Paradoxes of Group Life* (San Francisco: Jossey-Bass, 1987).

THE INTERGROUP AS A DETERMINER OF AN INDIVIDUAL'S PERCEPTIONS OF REALITY

It has long been recognized that people in different groups often perceive and understand the same event in radically different ways, particularly when there is an "ingroup" and an "outgroup." In such cases, one group usually will perceive an event in highly favorable terms, while the other sees the same event in an entirely derogatory manner. This phenomenon, referred to as "ethnocentrism" by Levine and Campbell (1972), is so powerful that group members may be unable to develop a view of reality that is independent of the group they belong to. The phenomenon becomes additionally potent when a person is caught in the context of multiple intergroups that involve interlocking sequences of events across time, and when the groups exist in a hierarchy of power relationships. Under these circumstances, the way one constructs his or her sense of reality may be almost completely determined by the interplay of intergroup processes.

Smith (1974) illustrates such a situation in his description of how Lewis Brook, principal of the high school in Ashgrove (New England), constructed his sense of what was taking place within the school system. Brook's perspectives changed dramatically from moment to moment, and these changes often were related directly to changes in his relative position in the power hierarchy of intergroup relationships.

For example, on one occasion Principal Brook was vociferously berating the superintendent, his superior, for something the superintendent had recently "done to" him. Lewis's recounting of the episode was cut short by a teacher who entered his office. Whereupon Lewis, without a moment's pause, responded to the teacher exactly as the superintendent had interacted with him. When confronted with this resounding obviousness, Lewis refused (or was unable) to see the similarity. When the two sets of events were dissected so that Lewis was caught by the brutal certitude of the similarities, he responded, "But it's different! I have reasons for treating the teacher that way." And when it was suggested that perhaps the superintendent had reasons for his treatment of the principal, Lewis, with more than a hint of impatience in his voice, retorted, "But mine were reasons; the superintendent's were merely rationalizations!"

This observation led me to formulate a theory of hierarchical intergroup relations in which the behavior of a person can be examined from the relative positions of upper, middle, and lower in the organizational structures in which he or she is embedded. Lewis Brook, as principal of the Ashgrove high school, had three assistant principals and a staff of one hundred teachers who served the educational needs of some 1,400 children in the ninth to twelfth grades. Relative to these two groups, the teachers and the students, Lewis was in an *upper* position. Superimposed on the school was an administrative and political hierarchy of a superintendent and an elected Board of Education. In relation to these two groups, Lewis was in a *lower* position. Finally, Lewis was in a *middle* position in the constellation of relationships between his subordinates (the teachers and students) and his superiors (the superintendent's office).

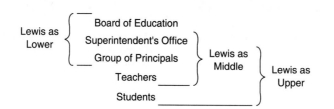

Brook's life as principal can be examined from each of these three relative positions in the hierarchical structure, as shown in Figure 2. In particular, it is possible to see how his perceptions of events were influenced by the position he happened to occupy at the time they took place.

Lewis as a Lower

When in a lower position, Brook regularly demonstrated a high degree of suspicion and excessive personal sensitivity. For example, on the day following each Board of Education meeting, Lewis would sit for long, anxious hours waiting for a call from the superintendent advising him of Board discussions that might be relevant to the life of his school. Usually no such call would come, and Lewis complained regularly and bitterly about how he was so faithfully ignored. But his protestation never triggered anything more than a retort from the superintendent that if anything relevant to his high school was discussed, he would be contacted within hours.

From the Board of Education's upper perspective, it was simple to conclude that if Lewis heard nothing it simply meant that the Board had not been debating anything relevant to his school's life. But from Lewis's lower perspective, hearing nothing did *not* mean that nothing was happening. Rather it meant "all hell is about to break loose," an inference that activated his "lower paranoia." Because Lewis assumed there was a conspiracy of silence, he would fantasize with meticulous dedication about all the possible things that could be "done to him," and would search for cues that might validate his worst suspicions. His failure to uncover a "plot" designed to undo him as principal was never interpreted by Lewis to mean that no such plot existed. Instead, he would conclude that his detection devices simply lacked the finesse required to detect what was happening in the "closed" ranks of the uppers.

Ironically, while Lewis was overcome with all this suspicion, reality for the Board of Education was that they were doing "nothing to anybody." In fact, they felt so paralyzed by their own stagnant inactivity that they would have been simultaneously dismayed and pleased to discover that someone, in his wildest imagination, was perceiving them as being in a state other than immobility. Ignorant of this alternative view, Lewis continued to construct a picture of the world about him that hung on trivial contingencies, but which for him was the pillar of his personal reality.

Brook's suspiciousness and oversensitivity when in a lower position can be seen as being a direct consequence of how people who feel powerless respond in intergroup exchanges with more powerful groups. Lower groups often develop strong protective devices and high cohesion to lessen their feelings of vulnerability. And one result of this response is that a lower group comes to define its essence in terms of this very cohesion and unity. In order to feed this sense of unity, members feel the need for the external threat to be continued. This creates a double bind: if the uppers cease to present a threat, that situation may be experienced by lowers as equally threatening, for it lessens the demand for their cohesion. This, in turn, recreates the sense of vulnerability of the lower group, because the *lack* of overt attack is a challenge to the very basis of unity on which group life is predicated. Either way it becomes imperative for members of the lower group to treat the uppers with suspicion. The bind reads as follows: "If they're getting at us, we've got to watch out. If they're not getting at us we've also got to watch out because they'll probably be getting at us in the long run by taking our unity away from us now by lessening the threat we feel." It is this process that ensures a lower group's paranoia and which, in my opinion, stirred Lewis Brook's intense feelings of sensitivity and suspiciousness when relating to his superiors.

Lewis as an Upper

Despite the disdain Lewis felt about his superiors' failure to consult him on matters in which he believed he had a basic right to participate, he reacted toward his own subordinate teachers and students with an equally elitist air. When in his upper position, Lewis always had a myriad of reasons why it was impossible to let the teachers participate fully in decisions that influenced their lives. The teachers felt these reasons were without substance, and they were perpetually distressed by the lack of confidence shown toward them by their principal, who demanded that approval be obtained for even the most trivial and routine of tasks.

When Lewis was in an upper position, he acted out the tendency of superior groups to see the behavior of subordinates in pessimistic terms—the very behaviors that he reacted to so negatively when he was a lower. As a member of the upper group, Lewis, like other uppers, tended to delegate responsibilities very willingly, but not the authority required to carry through on those responsibilities. This behavior of superiors guarantees that the actions of subordinate groups will not fulfill satisfactorily the expectations implied when the responsibilities are delegated. Although such shortcomings are caused largely by the uppers' withholding of necessary authority, they also are used by the superiors as justification for their original unwillingness to delegate authority. This phenomenon ensures a self-reinforcing and self-repeating set of perceptions, in that it heightens the likelihood that the subordinate groups will be seen as less competent than is desirable.

An insidious dimension of this phenomenon is that it enables upper groups to avoid taking full responsibility for their own behavior. In taking for themselves the role of designing organizational policy—but then delegating the implementation of that policy to the middle group—the uppers are able to build for themselves the perfect defense against failure. They can always conclude that their own policy was good but that the middles simply failed to implement it satisfactorily. Negative feedback can then be viewed merely as an indicator that subordinate groups are not as competent as is necessary. And, at the same time, the superiors can continue to avoid confronting their own expertise (or lack thereof) as uppers. Such a process locks upper groups into a way of viewing the world that ensures they will see the behavior of subordinates in increasingly depreciating terms.

Lewis Brook, as a member of an upper group, was caught by this intergroup dynamic as strongly as he was by the double binds of suspiciousness when he was located in a lower position.

Lewis as a Middle

When Brook was in a middle position, he was always espousing the need for "better communication" within the system. Despite this, he became caught in the trap of wanting to restrict information flow by making sure upper and lower groups communicated with each other only through him and his middle group. This situation is illustrated by the event described below.

Lewis was regularly embarrassed by learning about what was happening in his school for the first time from superiors who had been "leaked" information from below. Since he was an upper within the confines of the school itself, he often was unheeding to things teachers were trying to say to him. Therefore, they regularly felt the need to circumvent him in order to have their concerns attended to by the superintendent or the Board of Education. When teachers made attempts to contact the superintendent directly, Lewis became highly threatened and eventually decreed that no one could have access to the superintendent without first obtaining permission from one of the principals. By this action, Lewis clearly was working to preserve the centrality of his middle group's role as moderator of information flow.

Not to be daunted by this restriction on their liberties, the teachers found informal ways to gain access to the superintendent. The most frequently used device was to apply for study leave, even when not qualified for it. Such an application automatically led to an interview with the superintendent, which Lewis Brook allowed to occur without questioning his teachers. When ritualistically informed by the superintendent that they had not met the prerequisite conditions for study leave, the teachers willingly withdrew their applications and then confided the real reasons why they had sought an audience with him.

Lewis Brook never became aware of this practice, but he always felt distressed by the amount of information about his school of which the superintendent was aware. This distress only rein-

forced his dedication to make sure that teachers used his office alone as the means of communicating with the upper echelons of the system—an aspiration that he never realized.

To legitimize their own place in the system, middle groups need the uppers and lowers to be operating in a relatively polarized and noncommunicating fashion. Indeed, one of the ways for middle groups to be "confirmed" in the system is for them to become the central communication channel between the two extreme groups. This is possible primarily because both upper and lower groups use the withholding of information as a major strategy for dealing with each other. Upper groups limit information flow by using labels (such as "secret" or "in confidence") that designate who has legitimate access to what. For lowers, ground rules specifying what constitutes loyalty to the group determines what can be said to whom and under what circumstances, with the major concern being to minimize the vulnerability of the group.

If it were not for the rigid polarization of uppers and lowers, and their refusal to allow information to flow freely in the system, the middles might not be needed. But once the middle's role has become established as the communication link between upper and lower groups, the middles become very anxious to keep those polarized groups from talking frankly and openly. The middles become most threatened when the other two groups pass information to each other directly, or through any channel other than those the middles feel they have legitimized for the system. For this reason, the middles invest an inordinate amount of energy in defending the principle that all communication must pass through them. The net result of this dynamic is that middles will be constantly talking about the need to improve system-wide communication—while at the same time playing a vigorous role in restricting direct communication between other groups.

Summary

From the above account it is possible to recognize that intergroup processes cause groups at each of the three levels to become locked into a particular set of binds, and to create unique views of reality that are characteristic of those specific levels of the system. If these intergroup phenomena are conceded, it is predictable that an individual in a lower position will be supersensitive and suspicious of the activities of others. In an upper position, he or she will view the behavior of subordinates in a pessimistic light, and accordingly will delegate responsibility without the necessary authority. When in a middle position, the individual will espouse the need for greater communication, while acting to keep many communications restricted.

All these behaviors were exhibited by Lewis Brook in his role as Ashgrove's high school principal. It is easy to attribute these behaviors to Brook's unique personality. Yet, when viewed in the context of the intergroups operating in Brook's school system, it also becomes possible to understand how powerfully his own behavior and sense of reality were influenced by intergroup phenomena.

THE INTERGROUP AS A DETERMINANT OF INDIVIDUAL IDENTITY

Smith (1976) describes how intergroup interactions in a five-day power laboratory led to the creation of an identity for one individual that other members of the social system came to symbolize as "the village lunatic."

A power laboratory is an experiential, social, and psychological simulation designed for people interested in experiencing and learning about the dynamics of power and powerlessness. The laboratory is structured to create three classes of people: (1) the powerful "elite," who have access to and control over all the basic resources of the society, such as food, housing, money, and so forth; (2) the "ins," who have minimal control over some resources, at the discretion of the elites; and (3) the powerless "outs" who are totally deprived and have no control over any community resources. All conditions of living, such as standards of housing, quality of food, and so on, are differentiated to heighten "class" differences. For example, the outs live in a ghetto-like life style, while the elites live in comparatively leisurely luxury. On arrival at the laboratory all members are "born into" one of these three classes, without individual choice.

In the power laboratory described by Smith, the elite group of seven arrived half a day before the middles, and produced a plan which would enable them to keep their eliteness hidden. They decided to act as if they were regular, nonelite participants, while they actually would be quietly and powerfully pulling the strings of the social system like backstage puppeteers.

The plan ran into trouble, however, within hours of the arrival of the nine middles. The "birth" trauma of the middles was quite extreme: at induction, they had all their belonging (save one change of underwear) taken from them, an event that stirred their anger and their determination to discern "who did this to us." Anthony, one of the middles, had brought with him a tape recorder that he wanted to use for his learning and post-laboratory reflections. He was not allowed to keep the recorder, however, and his resentment about this heightened his sensitivity as to who was powerful and who was powerless in the system. It took him very little time to differentiate the elites from the nonelites—simply by observing the interactions that took place among various participants. In response to his awareness, Anthony tried to initiate a public debate intended to flush out the elite group. He was generally unsuccessful in this, partly because others lacked his acumen in discerning what was taking place, and partly because of the skill of the elite group in keeping their identity hidden.

After half a day all but two members of the elite group had tired of the charade and had made public their real status. This made the middle group angry, and Anthony became even more determined to end the elites' game of phantomness. But this did not occur. The most influential member of the upper group—Richard, a tall, strong, bearded, black man—did not identify himself as an elite and remained with the middles, continuing to manipulate them to do exactly as the elites ordained.

The successful smoking out of most of the elite group fanned Anthony's fires. He became consumed with his fixation to force all the elites to become visible, Richard included. That was not to be, because Richard was blessed with a resolve equal to Anthony's and the two became bitterly pitted against each other. Anthony's energies were focused entirely on Richard's eviction from the middle group, while Richard, with a simple indifference to these pressures, worked at massaging the middles into accepting obediently their role as servants of the elite.

Whenever Richard attempted to make an initiative, Anthony immediately attempted to frustrate it by accurately, though boringly, accusing him of being an elite spy, and arguing that the middles should do nothing until such time as all the elites had been ousted. Eventually Richard became symbolized as a force for *activity* while Anthony came to be seen as someone reinforcing *stagnation.* Richard skillfully presented himself as the champion of the middles' cause, and successfully led negotiations with the elites for return of some of their personal belongings. This success elevated Richard to the sole leadership role in the bourgeoisie and he accordingly dealt with Anthony's accusations by simply dismissing them as part of a personal vendetta against him as the middles' leader.

The middle group did very little in the first day and a half other than debate the spy issue, and this inactivity produced such intense frustration that some reached the point of being willing to do anything, including being led down any path by Richard, simply to escape the paralysis of their inertia. Whether or not he was a spy ceased to matter much.

Anthony recognized that his group had adopted the spirit of going along with anything that produced activity, yet he could not reconcile himself to the fact that almost everything Richard proposed served to make the middles into the elite's lackeys. Soon Anthony's fight was being stifled by others in his group who would audibly groan their protest over his persistent regurgitation of a theme they all wanted to ignore. To buffer himself against this visible hostility, Anthony began to preface his remarks with a statement designed to lessen his vulnerability. He could have said, "I know I'm the only person who is concerned about this issue," but that's not the way he phrased his protective remarks. Instead he would say, "I know you think this is just my problem, but . . ."

By articulating this "buffer" statement in this way, Anthony provided other middles with the opportunity they had been looking for. By simply agreeing, "Yes, Anthony, that's just *your* problem," they could quickly close him down and avoid the agony of further monotonous reiteration of the spy theme.

The symbolization processes began to develop at a fast pace, and very soon the middle group had made "Anthony's problem" the receptacle for all of their frustrations. (Of course, the middles would have experienced frustration having to do with their need to keep their relationships with both elites and outs functional, independent of Anthony's role. As middles, they found that whenever they acted in the possible interest of the elites, the outs would abuse them for having been co-opted. And whenever they responded to pressures from the outs, the elites would treat them punitively and leave them feeling alienated and alone. The reality was that no matter what they did—even if they did nothing—the middles would end up feeling uncomfortable.)

Since the middles had begun to believe that the cause of their discomfort was "Anthony's problem," they came to view that "problem" in more extreme form as their sense of impotence heightened. Eventually they settled on the belief that "he really must be crazy." To make matters worse, Anthony had been successful enough to convince many of the middles that the spy issue was critical, but this only reverberated back on him: given the way the group's "problem" had become symbolized and projected into Anthony, it made more sense to many members of the middle group to suspect that Anthony was the real spy rather than Richard.

When this possibility was raised in the group, Anthony recognized that his battle was lost. By then he was so much on the periphery of the group that he knew there was little chance of his finding a comfortable place in the middle group. He therefore began to search for an alternative role in the system. The alternatives were, of course, very limited. The doors of the elites clearly were closed to him. That left only the outs—who in fact welcomed him with open arms. For them, the possibility of someone becoming *downwardly* mobile had real strategic value in this particular society, and they quickly grasped at the opportunity Anthony's plight presented. In addition, the outs had developed a strong emotional support system. They sensed Anthony's pain, and willingly reached out to provide him a haven.

Anthony became so overwhelmed by the level of acceptance and warmth accorded him by the outs that he quickly concluded that this was where he wanted to see out his days in the society. Here he ran into a new problem. It had been their common pain, their collective fears and uncertainties, and their desperate need for each other in psychological survival tasks that had forged the group of outs into its particular shape. Nothing in Anthony's middle experience paralleled those forces, and there was no way to revise the "out history" to allow Anthony to be made a full partner in the "real" life of the group. At best, he could become only an adopted son.

Anthony needed acceptance by the outs so badly that he was willing to comply uncritically to any of the group's wishes. And here, Anthony's "way of being" changed dramatically. The overly perceptive characteristics he displayed in his bourgeois period now became clouded by an obsessional overconforming to the norms of the out group—a response which attempted to compensate for his sense of historical exclusion from the outs' world, and to pay an adequate price for his acceptance by them.

Another event added appreciably to the complexity of everyone's perceptions of Anthony's behavior. At the time of Anthony's migration to the outs, Richard (keen to keep tranquility disjointed) returned to the relative comfort of the elite group. However, still wishing to maximize deception, the elites continued the charade by refusing to acknowledge that Richard had been one of them all along. Instead they described his move as "upward mobility," provided to Richard because of his good leadership behavior and his service to the society.

The impact of the dual departures of Richard and Anthony from the middles left a powerful vacuum. The remaining middles started to experiment with new behaviors. Collectively (though only temporarily) they gained a new sense of vitality. This caused them to lay, even more vehemently than previously, total responsibility for their earlier stagnation at Anthony's feet. They attributed none of it to Richard. For his departure they grieved. For Anthony's, they celebrated.

The remaining history of this laboratory was filled with examples of how tension in the system—the byproduct of unhandled intergroup conflict—became attributed to Anthony's "craziness." No matter what discomforting event occurred, it was symbolized as being Anthony's fault.

Why?

My basic thesis is that once the society had created for Anthony alone a totally unique experience within the society, and once a chance was provided for his behavior to be seen as "crazy," the system gave him an identity that powerfully served the needs of the intergroup exchanges. The "village lunatic" identity provided a receptacle for the craziness of the whole system—the deceit, the multiple and conflicting senses of reality, the myriad of covert,

unarticulable processes, and so forth—which enabled the society at large to avoid having to confront its own pathology. In short, the social system had a vested interest in having Anthony become and remain crazy because it served admirably the continuation of the essential intergroup exchanges of the society at large.

And what became of Anthony himself?[1] Initially he was convinced his own perceptions were accurate. But across time, as others failed to see what was so obvious to him, he began to doubt his own sense of reality (even when he actually was perceiving correctly) and to wonder whether he was going mad. This eventually forced him to experience such discomfort that all of his energy became directed toward uncritically finding a place where he could feel support and acceptance. When the society transformed him into the "village lunatic," it created a form of madness aptly described by the poet Roethke, as mere "nobility of soul, at odds with circumstance."

One further question remains. What was it about Anthony as a person that caused him to become the lunatic? In my view, it was virtually accidental. The fact that he came originally with a tape recorder (and with a very high investment in being able to use it for his personal learning) meant that Anthony felt even more deprived than the others at induction time. This additional sense of deprivation heightened his activity to find out who the elites were much earlier than his fellow middles. Because he saw things differently than did the others, he started to become separated from the dominant sense of "reality" in the system. From there, the processes already described took off.

If Anthony had not come to this laboratory, would someone else have been made into a "lunatic" for the society's purposes? I suspect not. The forces which ended up focussing on him might well have been acted out in some other way—perhaps by creating another special identity for one individual, or by generating conditions of war between the groups, or even by the collapse of the society at large. The intergroup dynamics had to find *some* way to be acted out; the particular circumstances surrounding Anthony and his induction into the system were such that he became a convenient and useful vehicle for meeting that need.

The learning of overwhelming importance from this account is that often the personages or identities we take on may have very little to do with our own desires for ourselves, with our particular upbringings, or with our own values. Instead, they may, in fact, be mostly defined for us and forced upon us by external processes similar to those experienced by Anthony in the power laboratory.

THE INTERGROUP AS A DETERMINANT OF BEHAVIORS CHARACTERIZED AS LEADERSHIP

Perhaps one of the most gripping, passionate, and socially educative experiences ever recorded is the story of sixteen Uruguayan football players and their friends who not only survived an aircraft crash in the completely inaccessible heights of the Chilean

---

1. Anthony left the laboratory in good emotional health. During the critique phase of the experience, the staff of the laboratory spent a great deal of time with Anthony and others exploring how this "village lunatic" phenomenon had occurred.

Andes, but then existed for ten weeks in icy and desolate conditions with only the wrecked fuselage of the aircraft as their shelter and home (Read, 1974).

Of the original forty-three people on board, sixteen were killed in the crash or died in the next few days from injuries. Seventeen days later the surviving twenty-seven were further reduced to a group of nineteen by an avalanche of snow that buried alive almost the whole group, eight of whom could not be dug out before they froze to death. After the avalanche, the group of survivors (reduced later by another three deaths) kept alive for fifty more days before two of their number, under unbelievable conditions, climbed a cliff-faced mountain of ice to a height of 13,500 feet, and eventually stumbled across civilization and help.

The story is a deeply touching account of human relationships under the most extreme survival conditions. In order to stay alive, it was necessary for group members, despite the repugnancy of the idea, to eat the raw flesh of the dead. Much of the early life and struggles of these survivors revolved around the agonies of acknowledging and accepting this imperative. As dreams of rescue faded, and as the struggle together under intense conditions heightened, the earlier revulsions became translated into a very mystical and religious experience—to the extent that several of the boys, when they realized that their own deaths were imminent, asked their comrades to feel free to eat their bodies.

In the discussion that follows, I will explore the social system composed of the survivors, and show how behaviors that traditionally would be described as personal "leadership" can be understood in terms of the relationships between various groups that emerged within that system. Specifically, I will propose that who becomes focal in leadership activities (and what leadership behaviors are seen as appropriate) changes radically from situation to situation—largely as a function of changing intergroup dynamics.

Immediately after the crash, many of the survivors were bleeding and in desperate need of medical care. In this initial phase, during which group life was defined by the visibility of wounded bodies, the key survival task was seen as caring for the bleeding. Accordingly, two of the group, who had been medical students in the earliest phases of their training, were automatically elevated to dominant status. An intergroup structure emerged which delineated all survivors into one of three classes—the wounded, the potential workers, and the doctors. The medical students were given tremendous power, despite the fact that their skills and competence in the setting were minimal, especially given that they had no facilities or medical supplies. Others willingly subjected themselves to directives the students issued around appropriate work or treatment programs. The need for medical help was so intense that the differential status of the survivors enabled limited skill to become symbolized as expert competence, which, in turn, gave the "doctors" inordinate power to influence everyone else's behavior.

Within a day or so, new demands appeared. The acquisition of food and water, and the preservation of hygiene in the fuselage—which constituted the only shelter from subzero temperatures, blizzards, and thoroughly treacherous conditions—became critical. These demands required a group structure that was radically different from the one that had developed in the period immediately after the crash. In particular, it became important for someone to play an overall "social maintenance" role to give coherence to the whole system. The captain of the football team, who had been overshadowed in the first day by the medical students, was reelevated to his former position. Beneath him were two groups of approximately equal status: (1) the medical team of two "doctors" and a couple of helpers, and (2) a group that searched battered luggage for tidbits of food, and who made water by melting snow on metal sheets and bottling it in old soda bottles. At a still lower level, was a group of the younger boys who served as a clean-up crew to maintain livable internal social structures within the mountain-top society.

At the same time, the role of the "doctors" was further diminished. With virtually no medical supplies, their "special expertise" had been exhausted. The worst cases had died, and it was now clear to everyone that there was very little more that could be offered in the medical domain. The collapse of the medical team's function added to the power vacuum and increased the uncertainty about social relationships among group members.

Eventually another new social structure did emerge. It was defined primarily by each person's willingness or reluctance to eat human flesh. Those who did so early, and with a reasonable degree of spontaneity, were the ones who maintained the physical energy to persevere—and thereby to provide vitality for the endurance of the social system itself. Those who could not bring themselves to overcome their natural abhorrence to the idea became weak, and eventually degenerated into a new "poorer class." A third group struggled with the tensions of survival on the one hand, and their natural revulsion to the consumption of human flesh on the other. In so doing, members of this group came to formulate a new way of symbolizing the activity. They developed a very mystical and spiritual interpretation of their group experience, reinterpreting the eating of the flesh of the dead as being parallel to a religious communion in which they would consume the body and blood of Christ. This resymbolization of experience facilitated survival by helping everyone respond to the imperative that they eat the flesh of the dead, no matter how strongly the idea initially had repelled them.

During this period, the football captain moved further from his earlier position of prominence. This was, in part, because of his unwillingness to take the lead in eating human flesh. But, in addition, the captain lost credibility because his repeated assurances that rescue was imminent came increasingly to sound hollow.

When the survivors eventually heard on a transistor radio that all rescue operations had been called off, the energy in the system changed dramatically. Despair and outrage hit members like clenched fists, and produced radically different responses in different people. Parrado was ready to leave on an expedition immediately, while others were ready to resign themselves to the inevitability of death. Despair was heightened further a couple of days later when an avalanche of snow caused the death of eight more persons, including the football captain. Reluctantly, it was concluded that an expedition now offered the only hope for survival. And the internal social structure of the system went through yet another readjustment in response to this imperative.

Any social system can become subjected to crisis conditions which produce extreme pressures from outside, or from within. When this happens, members of the system must respond to these pressures or else risk long-term internal chaos. One common response is for clusters of people to form which eventually evolve into critical groups for the system. Moreover, the pressures that emerge from crisis experiences invariably demand that groups within the system relate to each other more intensely than had previously been the case. Even the composition of these groups will need to change. In the present case, the medical group was dominant initially, with others subservient to them. This structure was altered by the emergence of the football captain as the major mediator between several specialized work groups, and eventually by the emergence of an entirely new social structure defined in terms of members' willingness to consume human flesh.

When these changes are taking place in response to extreme pressures, it often is most unclear what should happen to produce a new form of stability in which both directionality and internal coherence are present. What an individual might do personally to provide leadership is unclear and speculative. Instead, each new set of stresses causes changes in group memberships or behaviors which, in turn, move the system toward some new equilibrium. As this happens, power, authority, critical resources, and ability to influence events become distributed differently than before. Only when the directionality and coherence of the system achieve a reasonable degree of stability is it possible to determine which behaviors actually moved the system in productive directions, or served to keep the various parts of the system integrated. Acts of leadership, then, are merely responses to the forces that emerge from the exchanges among groups within the system, and it would *not* be valid to construe them as reflecting a conscious intent to lead. If, in hindsight, an act appears to have been one of effective leadership, it may have been virtually accidental at the time it happened—and identifiable as leadership only in retrospect. This phenomenon is especially visible in the next phase of the survivors' experiences.

As preparations for the expedition went forward, all energies were dedicated to that task. Medical duties had slipped from any prominence, and the doctors simply took their place in the mainstream of the social structure. Four identifiable groups emerged as planning for the expedition proceeded. They were: (1) a collection of ten individuals who were designated as too weak to undertake any significant walking; (2) three first choices for the expedition, including one of the ex-doctors and Parrado, whose robust constitution and steely resolve to escape had helped buoy the energy of the fainthearted; (3) three cousins who were not fit for the expedition and who previously had not played significant roles in the system—but who had coalesced as a critical subgroup because of their strong support for each other in a common struggle (theirs, a blood relationship, was the only precrash grouping of friends that had not been fragmented by the ordeal); and (4) a trio of younger fellows who were potential expeditionaries—but who first had to be tested to prove their fitness.

Eventually a group of four was selected as the key expeditionaries. Once chosen, they became virtually a "warrior class" with extra rights and privileges. They were allowed to do anything that could be construed as bettering their physical condition. The whole group coddled them, both physically and psychologically, and everyone made sure that the only conversations within their earshot were optimistic in tone.

Read (1974) reports that the expeditionaries were *not* the leaders of the society. They were basically a class apart, linked to the rest of the system by a group of cousins, whose cohesion was the only force available to balance the unbelievable power that had been given to the expeditionaries. Because the cousins were the only ones able to keep the "warriors" in check (and thereby keep the system in equilibrium) they became the major locus of power within the remainder of the system. They virtually ruled from then on. The cousins controlled food allocation, determined who should do what work, and mediated when the "workers" (those who cut meat, prepared water, attended to hygiene, and so forth) felt that some of the sick were merely "malingering" and therefore should not be fed unless they also worked.

Beneath the cousins, a second echelon of three emerged. These individuals took roles equivalent to noncommissioned officers, receiving orders from above and giving them to those below. One of this trio, the second of the two doctors, became the "detective" in this phase of the society. He took upon himself the task of investigating misdemeanors and norm violations, and he flattered those more senior to him while bullying those more subservient.

It was several weeks before the expeditionaries departed. There were some valid reasons for the delay, but eventually everyone began to suspect that the ex-doctor was stalling and that he was using his expectant expeditionary status as a way of accruing privileges and minimizing work. At that point, his privileges were terminated. When one of the cousins volunteered to go in his place, the ex-doctor stirred himself and prepared for what proved to be a successful expedition: after a grueling ten-day trek, help was located and the remaining survivors were rescued.

One would have imagined that the ordeal was now over, but the system still had to face another extremely difficult event. Within a short time after the rescue, news leaked that the survivors had sustained themselves by consuming the flesh of the dead. This produced a strong reaction, especially among members of the press, who were poised to give world-wide publicity to this remarkable story. Religious figures, parents, and close friends were basically supportive during this period of new threat. But it soon became obvious that, if the survivors were ever to return to normal lives, it would be necessary for them to confront this issue together. So they called a press conference to tell their story.

The group debated at length as to who should explain the eating of human flesh. Several individuals felt they would be too emotional. It was eventually agreed that Delgado, who had been almost completely insignificant on the mountain top, should describe this aspect of their experience. His public presence and his eloquence—which of course had been of no value during the seventy-day ordeal—now came into its own, and he mediated brilliantly between the survivors, and the press, relatives, and other interested parties. His statement was a moving, passionate, religious, and emotional event, and through it he provided a way for everyone to resymbolize the meaning of the survival experience, thereby quelling criticism and laying to rest concerns over the consumption of the dead.

In this setting, Delgado's behavior, which to date had influenced nothing, was now seen by others as outstanding leadership. But did he lead? Or was it simply that his particular response to the tensions which intersected in his personhood in that situation touched the nerve fibers of the new sets of intergroup interactions, thereby triggering a new directionality and a wholesome coherence for the system?

CONCLUSION

The literature of organizational behavior is filled with concepts that help us understand the behavior of people in terms of their personal characteristics, or as a response to what takes place in the groups of which they are members. The material presented in this paper offers an alternative view: namely, that it is imperative to move beyond explanations that lie within people and within groups—and to include perspectives that derive from more global and systemic forces, including forces that derive from the dynamics of intergroups.

If, for example, the tools of personality theorists alone were applied to Lewis Brook in Ashgrove or to Anthony's identity struggle, we would obtain only a limited understanding of what affected their perceptions and their behaviors. Likewise, if we restricted our explorations of leadership among the aircraft survivors to traditional concepts that imply specific intentionality on the part of individuals (i.e., using notions such as participation, initiation of structure, socioemotional behavior, and so on), much of the essence of the leadership phenomena that developed on the mountain top would have been lost.

But how much relevance do the principles extracted from the materials presented in this paper have for understanding everyday experiences in everyday organizations? I submit, a great deal—and more than we usually realize or are comfortable acknowledging.

REFERENCES

Alderfer, C. P. Group and intergroup relations. In J. R. Hackman and J. L. Suttle (Eds.), *Improving life at work: Behavioral science approaches to organizational change.* Pacific Palisades, Calif.: Goodyear, 1977.

Alderfer, C. P., Brown, L. D., Kaplan, R. E., & Smith, K. K. *Group relations and organizational diagnosis.* London: Wiley, in press.

Hackman, J. R. Group influences on individuals in organizations. In M. D. Dunnette (Ed.), *Handbook of industrial and organizational psychology.* Chicago: Rand-McNally, 1976.

Levine, R. A., & Campbell, D. T. *Ethnocentrism.* New York: Wiley, 1972.

Lewin, K. Frontiers in group dynamics. *Human Relations,* 1947, 1, 5–41.

Likert, R. *New patterns of management.* New York: McGraw-Hill, 1964.

Lorsch, J. W., & Lawrence, P. R. *Managing group and intergroup relations.* Homewood, Ill.: Irwin, 1972.

Read, P. P. *Alive.* London: Pan Books, 1974.

Rice, A. K. Individual, group and intergroup processes. *Human Relations,* 1969, **22,** 565–585.

Sherif, M. (Ed.) *Intergroup relations and leadership.* New York: Wiley, 1962.

Smith, K. K. *Behavioral consequences of hierarchical structures.* Unpublished doctoral dissertation, Yale University, 1974.

Smith, K. K. The village lunatic. Unpublished manuscript, University of Melbourne, 1976.

Exercise: The Hilarity Greeting Card Company

PURPOSE

The purpose of this exercise is to help you understand how intergroup conflict occurs in organizations. By the time you finish his exercise you will

1. Understand some of the consequences and causes of interdepartmental conflicts

2. Experience the dynamics of interdepartmental conflict in a simulated organizational situation

3. Identify ways to reduce intergroup conflict in organizations

INTRODUCTION

One of the most common types of intergroup conflict in organizations is horizontal conflict. Horizontal conflict occurs among departments or groups laterally across the organization. When departmental goals are incompatible, when uncertainty abounds, or when resources are scarce, departments may generate conflict.

This exercise is an opportunity for you to gain increased awareness of the dynamics of intergroup conflict. One of the interesting aspects of intergroup conflict is that when we experience it we are often unaware of the dynamics of the situation.

This exercise originally was developed by Joel R. DeLuca of Coopers and Lybrand.

We tend to believe that we are right and the other group is wrong; that if they would only change their behavior everything would be fine. This exercise will help you understand how these dynamics occur and discover ways to improve such conflict situations.

INSTRUCTIONS

1. Your instructor will assign you a group as either a participant, an observer, or a judge.

2. Read the General Information.

3. Read the directions for the group to which you have been assigned.

4. Complete the exercise as instructed.

5. Participate in a class discussion.

General Information

The Hilarity Greeting Card Company (HGCC) makes a variety of humorous special occasion cards including get well cards and birthday cards. Each type of card is produced by a different department. The base salary for the creative employees of HGCC is $40,000. HGCC also has a generous incentive program through which employees can earn bonuses based on the performance of their department.

Incentive Program. The employees of the department with the highest quality output points, based on both the quantity and the "hilarity quotient" of their cards, receive quarterly bonuses as well as a yearly one.

❐ The quarterly bonus is 50 percent of the yearly base salary ($5,000) and is awarded to the employees of the department with the highest quality output points for that quarter.

❐ The yearly bonus is 100 percent of the yearly base salary ($40,000) and is awarded to the employees of the department with the highest quality output points for that year.

Thus, the minimum earnings for a creative employee of HGCC are $40,000 and the maximum earnings are $100,000 [$40,000 base salary + 4 ($5,000 quarterly bonus) + $40,000 yearly bonus].

Quality Output Points. The quality output points are determined by three judges who view the cards produced by each department every quarter.

❐ The judges rate each card on a scale of zero to ten for its hilarity quotient (zero = no humor, ten = broke your funny bone). These ratings are the quality points of each card.

❐ The quality points for each card produced by the department are added together for the total quality output for that quarter.

❐ Each department is also given an average-quality-per-card rating each quarter, which is found by dividing the total quality output by the number of cards produced.

❐ The yearly quality output is determined by adding the quality output of the four quarters together.

HGCC is about to start a new year. Read the directions for the group to which you have been assigned.

Judges

Directions: Your job is to rate the cards produced by each of the departments after every quarter and determine the quality output points for that department. Use the Judge's Evaluation Sheet to record your ratings. Complete one evaluation sheet for each department after each quarter as follows:

1. Where indicated, record your name, the department you are evaluating, and the quarter.

2. Review each department's cards for that quarter. For each card rate how funny you thought it was on a zero (no humor) to ten (broke your funny bone) scale.

3. Record your rating under Quality Points for each card.

4. Add up the Quality Points for the department and record the total in the Total Points space.

5. Divide the Total Points by the number of cards produced by that department for the Average-Quality-per-Card rating.

6. When you have finished your rating for the quarter, get together with the other two judges and average your Total Points. The department with the highest average Total Points receives the quarterly bonus of $5,000 per member.

7. Record the average Total Points (as determined by the average of all three judges' Total Points) for each department, as well as the department that received the quarterly bonus on the Team Performance Sheet posted on the blackboard.

8. At the end of the year, add up all of the average Total Points for each department to determine who will receive the yearly bonus.

Judge's Evaluation Sheet

Judge _____

Department _____

Quarter _____

	No Humor	*Broke Your Funny Bone*
	0 ——————— 10	
Card Number	*Quality Points*	
1	_____	
2	_____	
3	_____	
4	_____	
5	_____	
6	_____	
7	_____	
8	_____	
9	_____	
10	_____	
Total Points	_____	
Average Quality per Card	_____	

Product Departments

Directions: You are about to begin a new year at HGCC. Each quarter will last ten minutes. During that time your department should try to produce as many "hilarious" cards as possible. Your salary will depend on the quarterly and yearly bonuses you can earn. After each quarter of production, the cards created by your department will be evaluated based on the quantity you have produced and their hilarity quotient. You will receive a $5,000 bonus at the end of each quarter if your department receives the highest number of total points from the judges.

At the end of each quarter, as a team, fill out a Department Evaluation Sheet as follows:

1. Complete one Evaluation Sheet after each quarter.

2. Record your department name and the quarter you are evaluating where indicated.

3. As a team, come to a consensus decision on the average hilarity quotient of the cards your department produced during the quarter. Use the scale of zero (no humor) to ten (broke your funny bone).

4. As a team, come to a consensus decision on the average hilarity quotient of the cards the other department produced during the quarter. Use the scale of zero (no humor) to ten (broke your funny bone).

5. When you have completed this form, give it to an observer.

Department Evaluation Sheet

Department _____   *Quarter* _____

<table>
<tr><td></td><td align="center">*No
Humor*</td><td align="center">*Broke Your
Funny Bone*</td></tr>
<tr><td></td><td align="center">0 ——————— 10</td><td></td></tr>
</table>

1. Average hilarity quotient of
   your cards this quarter   _____

2. Average hilarity quotient of
   the other department's cards
   this quarter   _____

Observers

Directions: Your job is to observe the departments. Use the Observer Sheet to summarize your observations. You should be especially aware of how the departments interact, how they feel about their own department, how they feel about the other department, and the assumptions under which the departments seem to be operating. After each quarter the departments will fill out Department Evaluation Sheets, which they will give to one of the observers. Use these evaluations as data to support your observations.

Observer Sheet

1. *Major Work Processes*

   Team "A" _____

   _____

   Team "B" _____

   _____

2. *Views Toward Other Team*

   Team "A" _____

   _____

   Team "B" _____

   _____

3. *Views Toward Own Team*

   Team "A" _____

   _____

   Team "B" _____

   _____

4. *Implicit Assumptions Made*

   Team "A" _____

   _____

   Team "B" _____

   _____

DISCUSSION QUESTIONS

1. How did you feel about your department's cards versus the other department's cards?

2. Did the budget crunch change your feelings about the other team? How?

3. Was it easier to come to a decision with or without negotiating with the other team? Why? Were you thinking about the organization's goals or only the goals of your department when you made your decision?

4. What could HGCC have done to improve the relationship between you and the other department and to make you think more about the goals of the organization?

REFERENCE

D. L. Brown. "Managing Conflict Among Groups." In D. A. Kolb, I. M. Rubin, and I. N. McIntyre (eds.), *Organizational Psychology: Readings on Human Behavior in Organizations,* 4th ed. Englewood Cliffs, NJ: Prentice-Hall, 1984.

Exercise: Labor Relations and Intergroup Conflict

PURPOSE

The purpose of this exercise is to provide an opportunity for you to experience intergroup dynamics through a forced labor negotiation. By the time you finish this exercise you will

1. Determine an actual position for a labor negotiations dispute

2. Develop an understanding of intergroup dynamics as they affect labor negotiations

3. Identify ways to solve within-group conflict as well as between-group conflicts

INTRODUCTION

At some point in your career, you may find yourself in the middle of a labor negotiations dispute—either on the side of management or on the side of labor. Labor negotiations, by their very nature, are a good example of intergroup dynamics. Each

This exercise was revised by Bonita L. Betters-Reed and Judith A. Babcock, 1986, and again in 1992. Reprinted by permission from an original exercise by Arthur A. Whately and Nelson Lane Kelley in *Personnel Management in Action: Skill Building Experiences.* St. Paul: West, 1977. Copyright © 1977 by West Publishing Company. All rights reserved.

side must take a position, and each side must negotiate a final solution. Ideally, the solution achieved should be win-win.

In this exercise, you will have an opportunity to participate in a labor negotiations dispute. As a member of the negotiating team, you will need to identify a position and negotiate a solution. Your abilities to negotiate and solve the conflict will have a direct bearing upon the quality of the final solution.

INSTRUCTIONS

1. Your instructor will assign you to a negotiating team with four to six other members. Half of the groups will play the role of the union negotiators, while the other half will play the role of the management negotiators.

2. Read the P & M Manufacturing Company and Rules for Negotiations. All class members should study the Bargaining Issues and Table 1 on Labor–Management Agreements Among Competitors in the New England Area.

3. If playing the role of a union negotiator, read *only* the Negotiator's Role for TWA. If playing the role of a management negotiator, read *only* the Negotiator's Role for P & M.

4. Each team should meet separately to make the following decisions:
   a. Rank order the bargaining issues in terms of importance to the team.
   b. For each bargaining issue, determine three positions: the minimum for which you will settle, the maximum you will request, and a midpoint.
   c. Select a spokesperson and agree on a time-out signal.

5. Hold the negotiating session. If issues are not settled by the end of the session (25 minutes), a strike will be called.

6. Participate in a class discussion on the questions at the end of the exercise.

P & M MANUFACTURING COMPANY

P & M Manufacturing Company, located in Providence, Rhode Island, produces small toy cars for distribution and sales nationally. Employing about 300 manufacturing workers, it is much smaller than its competitors because P & M is not diversified in its operations. It has been able to meet its competition by emphasizing high production quality and personalized marketing techniques. It has the best reputation in the industry for quality.

In the early 1960s the employees at P & M were organized by the Toy Workers of America (TWA), and relations between the union and management have been very good. No time has ever been lost due to a work stoppage or strike. In the last year one of P & M's largest competitors dropped its market operation, which gave P & M a tremendous opportunity to increase its market share from 20 percent to 30 and perhaps 40 percent. Management is excited about the possibilities and wants to increase its production as soon as possible.

The current union contract expires in a week. Representatives from management and the union have been negotiating the new contract for several days, but no agreements have been reached.

Company Demographics

❏ In the past 10 years the male/female ratio has shifted from 80/20 to 50/50.

❏ Of all the workers, 20 percent are single; 80 percent are married or are heads of household (that is, usually divorced or widowed mothers; approximately 100 have preschool children). [A survey has shown that 50 percent of the absenteeism is related to baby-sitter problems. There is considerable sentiment among the workers (88 percent surveyed) favoring benefits to help pay for day care of preschool children of workers.]

❏ Thirty percent do not have a U.S. high school diploma (some are recent immigrants), 50 percent have finished high school, and 20 percent have had some college education.

Bargaining Issues*

1. Blue Cross and Blue Shield, Harvard Community Health Plan, or Ocean State Physician's Health Plan

   Past contract agreement:
   1991–1992: P&M paid full premiums for full family coverage

   Present bargaining positions:
   TWA: P&M should pay full cost, including vision and dental
   P&M: Employee should pay 10 percent of cost for individual coverage

	90% Individual	Full Individual	90% Family	Full Family	Full Family + Dental	Full Family Medical, Vision + Dental	
P&M							TWA
	−$459,000	−$390,000	−$108,900	0	$420,000	$600,000	

P&M Costs

$230/year		$360/year		

Employee Costs

2. Establishment of a third shift

   Past contract agreement:
   1991–1992: Third shift can be unilaterally established at any time with no allowances for difference in pay (150 on third shift, costs include wages + increase in Social Security)

   Present bargaining positions:
   TWA: $1.00 more per hour
   P&M: $.20 more per hour

Per Hour Increases

	$.20	$.40	$.60	$.80	$1.00	
P&M						TWA
	$67,080	$134,160	$202,800	$268,320	$336,960	

Costs

3. Wage Increases

   Past contract agreement:
   1991–1992: $8.25 per hour

   Present bargaining positions:
   TWA: $1.75 more per hour
   P&M: $.25 more per hour

Per Hour Increases

	$.25	$.37	$.50	$.75	$1.00	$1.25	$1.50	$1.75	
P&M									TWA
		$248,352		$503,568		$839,654		$1,928,160	
	$168,480		$335,712		$671,736		$1,007,760		

Costs

---

*These bargaining issues are conceptualized here in terms of "trading points." This approach is described in A. A. Sloane and F. Whitney, Labor Relations, 2nd ed. Englewood Cliffs, NJ: Prentice-Hall, 1972, pp. 194–195.

4. One additional employee per crew

Past contract agreement:
    1991–1992: 10 persons per crew (15 crews)

Present bargaining positions:
    TWA: One additional person at a cost of $22,632
    P&M: No increase

Increase Per Crew

P&M	0 person		1 person	TWA
	0		$339,480	

Costs

5. Vacation Benefits

Past contract agreement:
    1991–1992: One week for the first year, two weeks for all employees with two years of service

Present bargaining positions:
    TWA: Four weeks for 20 years of service
    P&M No change

P&M	2 weeks after 2 years	2 weeks after 1 year	4 weeks after 30 years	4 weeks after 25 years	4 weeks after 20 years	TWA
	0	$9,600	$12,800	$19,200	$32,000	

Costs

6. Child care (75 out of the 100 with preschool children would use child care benefits)

Past contract agreement:
    1991–1992: Not included in contract

Present bargaining positions:
    TWA: $250 per week
    P&M: $25 per week

P&M	$25/week	$50/week	$100/week	$175/week	$250/week	TWA
	$93,750	$187,500	$375,000	$626,250	$937,500	

7. Personal days (cumulative, unused days carried over)

Past contract agreement:
    1991–1992: One day

Present bargaining positions:
    TWA: Four days
    P&M: One day

P&M	1	2	3	4	TWA
	0	$21,960	$43,920	$65,880	

TABLE 1

Labor–Management Agreements Among Competitors in the New England Area.

	Competitor A (Boston)	Competitor B (Hartford)	Competitor C (Lowell)	Competitor D (Bangor)	Competitor E (Providence)
Company Contribution					
Medical	full medical + vision + dental	medical + dental	medical + dental	individual only	full family only
Third Shift Pay Differential	yes	no	yes	no	no
Hourly Wage Rate	$11.00	$8.75	$10.25	$8.25	$8.50
No. of Workers per Crew	10	10	10	11	10
Vacation Benefits	2 weeks after 1 year, 4 weeks after 15 years	2 weeks after 1 year, 4 weeks after 20 years	2 weeks after 1 year, 3 weeks after 20 years	2 weeks after 1 year	2 weeks after 2 years, 3 weeks after 20 years
Personal Days (Annual)	3	3	2	1	2
Child Care	250/week	100/week	50/week	no	25/week
Current Contract Expiration Date	12 months	9 months	15 months	1 month	3 months

Read only the role to which you have been assigned.

Negotiator's Role for P & M

You are the negotiator for P & M Manufacturing Company. The union demands for the new contract are viewed by you and the management as being extremely unrealistic. If the company meets the union demands at this time, the price of P & M's product will have to be increased and thus will prevent P & M from taking advantage of the opportunity to improve its market share brought about by a large competitor dropping out of the market. The union's stance is hard-nosed and you feel that, for the first time, a strike is a possibility. It has been estimated that a strike will cost P & M $100,000 per day in lost revenue.

Budgeting Information

Your financial vice president projects that with expansion and increased productivity you can afford $1.5 million in a union settlement without raising prices. If you settle for more than this, you will have to raise prices and are likely to lose market share as well as being unable to tap into the market share of the dropped competitor. (*Note:* Union negotiators do not have this information.)

Negotiator's Role for TWA

As the negotiator for the union in the current contract dispute with P & M Manufacturing Company, you are expected to take a hard position regarding the proposals your union has placed before management. The sentiment of the union membership is that P & M is on the verge of expansion and as a result has a very favorable chance of improving its profitability. The membership wants part of the action.

The union also feels that some personnel policies and practices of P & M lag behind those of its competitors. For example, since a third of the workers are mothers with preschool children, who are also heads of households, there is strong sentiment that the company should provide day care or funds for that purpose to be used for public or private day care centers. Also, since 80 percent of the workers are married or unmarried women who are heads of households (with children) and the company only pays medical insurance equivalent to 90 percent of the premium for individuals, many workers must pay extra to cover their families. These workers resent this extra cost. Employees feel so strongly about this issue that the possibility of a strike exists. A strike will cost the membership $25,000 per day in lost wages and benefits, including hospitalization.

You are to get as much for the union as you can.

Rules for Negotiations

1. One person on a team is to be designated as the team spokesperson. Only the spokesperson may talk during negotiations. During negotiations, the team may decide to designate another person as spokesperson. If so, the other team must be informed of the change.

2. Whenever a team member wishes a time-out for a team conference, that person signals the spokesperson who must initiate the time-out. Time-outs do not count toward the 25-minute deadline, but they must be restricted to 3 minutes each.

3. Any tactic is acceptable but keep in mind that time is important. If a contract is not approved in 25 minutes, a strike occurs—costing each side dearly.

4. During negotiations, record agreements that are reached on the form below:

Final Agreement

Medical _____

Third Shift Differential _____

Wage Increases _____

Enlarging Work Crew _____

Vacation Benefits _____

Personal Days _____

Child Care _____

5. Once an agreement on an issue is reached, it cannot be renegotiated. Issues may be linked together into a "package" but only if agreement has not been reached on the issues to be linked.

DISCUSSION QUESTIONS

1. Discuss the feelings and emotions of team members. How did those of you who were not the spokesperson feel? The spokesperson?

2. What approach to labor negotiations was most successful in terms of reaching an agreement? How did the goals of each side differ? Why?

3. Given that there was conflict between the two teams, was there also conflict within the teams? How was it resolved?

4. What preceding and current situational factors contribute positively to the resolution of conflict? What factors have a negative effect?

REFERENCE

A. A. Sloane and F. Whitney. *Labor Relations,* 2nd ed. Englewood Cliffs, NJ: Prentice-Hall, 1972, pp. 194–195.

Exercise: Battle of the Sexes Confrontation

PURPOSE

The purpose of this exercise is to explore and confront issues in gender relationships at work. By the time you finish this exercise you will

1. Diagnose the stereotypes that characterize men and women
2. Understand how your gender group is perceived
3. Develop action steps to improve gender relationships at work

INTRODUCTION

"I can't even flirt anymore because now I'll be accused of sexual harassment!" There exists a great deal of confusion today about how to relate to the opposite sex, both in personal as well as professional relationships. Many misunderstandings have emerged about what women expect from men and what men expect from women. Nowhere is this more crucial than in workplace relationships. Although many will agree that there has been great movement forward, covert stereotyping of gender roles still remains. This applies equally to men's expectations about women at work as it does to women's expectations about the behavior of men.

In this exercise, you will participate in an intergroup confrontation that will bring to the surface stereotypic attitudes and misperceptions men and women have about each other. You also will have an opportunity to explain what bothers you most about your work relationships with the opposite sex, and what you most respect and admire.

INSTRUCTIONS

1. As individuals, think about the following questions:
   a. In *personal* relationships, what really "bothers" you about members of the opposite sex?
   b. In *professional* relationships, what really "bothers" you about members of the opposite sex?
   c. What do you respect and admire about members of the opposite sex—in personal and professional relationships?
   d. What do you think members of the opposite sex group will say about you?

2. Form two groups: one of men, another of women. Discuss your responses to the preceding questions in your group.

3. Elect a spokesperson for your group and record your group's responses to these questions on sheets of paper that can be posted during an open class discussion.

This version of this exercise was developed by Lisa A. Mainiero.

4. Complete Part I of the Reaction Sheet.

5. Each group will present their items to the other group. When each group has received the other's perceptions, each group may request further clarification of the information posted by the other group. Clarification questions will be rotated so that each group has an equal opportunity to request additional information.

6. Members of each group will choose five items from the other group's list for further discussion.

7. Complete Part II of the Reaction Sheet.

8. Participate in a structured class discussion. The discussion will be rotated on an item-by-item basis until all 10 items identified by both groups are fully discussed.

9. Meet in small groups of four to six composed of equal numbers of men and women. In these groups you will
   a. Identify the ways in which men and women can work more productively together
   b. Determine the action steps needed so that men and women can improve workplace relationships

10. Record your action steps on sheets of paper. Post your results when your small group discussion is complete.

11. Discuss the action steps and identify common themes that characterize the discussion.

12. Complete Part III of the Reaction Sheet. Read the insert on "Intergroup Dynamics." Complete the general question at the end of the section.

13. Participate in a general class discussion.

Reaction Sheet

Directions: As you participate in this exercise, you will be asked to fill out this Reaction Sheet at different stages of the exercise. As instructed, place an X on the continua provided that describes your feelings and reactions.

Part I: How strongly do I agree at this moment with the perceptions of my group on male versus female issues?

Very strongly   Not at all

Part II: How strongly do I agree at this moment with the perceptions of my group on male versus female issues?

Very strongly   Not at all

Part III: How strongly do I agree at this moment with the perceptions of my group on male versus female issues?

Very strongly   Not at all

Intergroup Competition Dynamics

Directions: Read the following elements of intergroup competition and place an X on the scale provided to indicate the extent to which you believe that intergroup dynamics influenced your perceptions during this exercise.

1. Each group develops strong feelings of ingroup solidarity and righteousness of beliefs.

2. Each group stereotypes the outgroup in highly negative and extreme terms.

3. Extremist views are presented in the ingroup, as a means of protection against the outgroup.

4. Individuals with the extremist views become the leaders of each separate group.

5. Name-calling and taunts characterize communication between both groups as a means of competition.

6. The group that "wins" gains a stronger feeling of solidarity and self-worth and accepts collective responsibility for the win; the group that "loses" feels vanquished and breaks apart, blaming responsibility for the loss on individual group members.

To a great extent   Minimally if at all

DISCUSSION QUESTIONS

1. To what extent did your membership in a group influence your attitudes and feelings throughout the exercise?

2. At work, it is often difficult to assess the differences between sexual harassment and office romance. What prescriptions can you offer to separate the two?

3. What action steps can you personally take to improve relationships between men and women in the workplace?

CHAPTER 8

Organization Design, Evolution, and Culture

INTRODUCTION

Managers frequently ask how to design their organizations to achieve maximum effectiveness. Groups of similar jobs must be organized into departments, departments with similar functions must be organized into divisions, and the relationships between divisions and subsidiaries must be specified. Complicating these decisions is the fact that organizations are open systems that interact with, and depend on, their environment for survival.

Because an organization must continually interact with its environment, the most appropriate design will depend, to a large extent, on that environment. For example, it might be important for an organization to consider government regulation, economic conditions, competition, and availability of raw materials or customers. The specific elements that will be of interest to a particular firm will depend to a great degree on the strategic choices that organization has made. Those elements will, in turn, be complicated by the rate of evolutionary growth that the organization has experienced.

As the organization grows or the environment changes, the critical contingencies of the firm will also change. This, in turn, will influence the internal culture of the organization, which is typically defined as the set of shared assumptions, beliefs, norms, rules, and procedures that apply to all organizational members. Understanding an organization's culture and how it can be changed is an important aspect of organizational design. Design and culture are interdependent as both are shaped by the firm's external environment.

READINGS

The first reading, "What Is the Right Organization Structure? Decision Tree Analysis Provides the Answer," by Robert Duncan, presents a decision tree to help managers choose the right organizational structure. Duncan reviews the objectives of organizational design, which he sees as (1) facilitating the flow of information within the organization to reduce uncertainty in decision making and (2) achieving coordination between departments. He examines two of the predominant structures—functional and decentralized—and discusses the critical interaction between the design of an organization and its environment.

The second reading, "Evolution and Revolution as Organizations Grow," by Larry E. Greiner, describes the developmental phases that companies pass through as they develop into mature organizations. According to Greiner, an organization's design should match its stage of development as well as the demands of its environment. Thus, as an organization grows, its structure should change to keep pace with this development. He identifies five developmental phases: creativity, direction, delegation, coordination, and collaboration. Each of these phases is associated with a different management focus, organization structure, top management style, control system, and management reward system.

The third reading, "Implications of Corporate Culture: A Manager's Guide to Action," by Vijay Sathe, provides several insights into what corporate culture is and how it can be changed. The author argues that to effectively manage culture, we must first develop a better understanding of what it is. To this end he presents a framework for cultural diagnosis and examines the effect of culture on five behavioral processes: communication, cooperation, commitment, decision making, and implementation.

EXERCISES AND CASES

The exercises in this chapter are designed to help you become more aware of the challenges of organization design and evolution. The first exercise, "Small Business Design: The Case of a Start-up Publishing Firm," gives you the opportunity, as a group of consultants, to design a new organization. The business is plagued with problems, some of which relate to how the business has evolved as a start-up entrepreneurial venture. This exercise highlights the trade-offs associated with organizational design and the problems associated with entrepreneurial businesses.

"Fairfield Flyer Wagons" is an exercise that will help you understand the differences between pooled, sequential, and reciprocal technological interdependence. In Part I, you will become part of a production team manufacturing children's wagons under conditions of pooled interdependence. Interdepartmental communication is prohibited. In Part II, wagons are manufactured using a sequentially interdependent technology. Part III includes two conditions of reciprocal interdependence. Each part of this exercise emphasizes the increasing need for horizontal coordination as interdependence increases.

The case in this chapter, "Managing by Mystique," and its epilogue (located in the instructor's manual), provides several very interesting insights into the culture of a new business. The case discusses Tandem Computers in its early years and the influence of its founder, Jim Treybig, on Tandem's culture. Tandem is a very innovative firm with a number of alternative approaches to the way business is typically handled. But can Tandem sustain its innovative culture as the business grows? Read the epilogue and find out.

MEMO

The memo assignment for this chapter, *"Analyzing Your Organization's Design"* (located at the back of this book), gives you the opportunity to apply the theories and skills that you have learned in this chapter to your company. You are asked to diagnose the design of your organization by answering a series of questions concerning your firm's environment, current structure, and developmental stage. Using this information you will determine what—if any—changes should be made to the design of your organization.

By the time you finish this chapter you will have gained an appreciation for the critical role structure plays in organizational effectiveness. You will increase your skills at determining the most appropriate structure for an organization based on its environment, needs for integration, and developmental stage. You also will gain a better understanding of the role of corporate culture and its influence on individual behavior in organizations.

What Is the Right Organization Structure?
Decision Tree Analysis Provides the Answer

Robert Duncan

Organization design is a central problem for managers. What is the "best" structure for the organization? What are the criteria for selecting the "best" structure? What signals indicate that the organization's existing structure may not be appropriate to its tasks and its environment? This article discusses the purposes of organization structure and presents a decision tree analysis approach to help managers pick the right organization structure.

THE OBJECTIVES
OF ORGANIZATIONAL DESIGN

What is organization structure and what is it supposed to accomplish? Organization structure is more than boxes on a chart; it is a pattern of interactions and coordination that links the technology, tasks, and human components of the organization to ensure that the organization accomplishes its purpose.

An organization's structure has essentially two objectives: First, it facilitates the flow of information within the organization in order to reduce the uncertainty in decision making. The design of the organization should facilitate the collection of the information managers need for decision making. When managers experience a high degree of uncertainty—that is, when their information needs are great—the structure of the organization should not be so rigid as to inhibit managers from seeking new sources of information or developing new procedures or methods for doing their jobs. For example, in developing a new product, a manufacturing department may need to seek direct feedback from customers on how the new product is being accepted; the need to react quickly to customer

response makes waiting for this information to come through normal marketing and sales channels unacceptable.

The second objective of organization design is to achieve effective coordination—integration. The structure of the organization should integrate organizational behavior across the parts of the organization so it is coordinated. This is particularly important when the units in the organization are interdependent. As James Thompson had indicated, the level of interdependence can vary. In *pooled interdependence* the parts of the organization are independent and are linked together only in contributing something to the same overall organization. In many conglomerates, the divisions are really separate organizations linked only in that they contribute profits to the overall organization. Simple rules—procedures—can be developed to specify what the various units have to do. In *sequential interdependence,* however, there is an ordering of activities, that is, one organizational unit has to perform its function before the next unit can perform its. For example, in an automobile plant manufacturing has to produce the automobiles before quality control can inspect them. Now such organizations have to develop plans to coordinate activities; quality control needs to know when and how many cars to expect for inspection.

Reciprocal interdependence is the most complex type of organizational interdependence. Reciprocal interdependence is present when the outputs of Unit A become the inputs of Unit B and the outputs of B cycle back to become the inputs of Unit A. The relationship between the operations and maintenance in an airline is a good example of this type of interdependence. Operations produces "sick" airplanes that need repair by maintenance. Maintenance repairs these planes and the repaired planes become inputs to the operations division to be reassigned to routes. When reciprocal interdependence between organization units is present, a more complex type of coordination is required. This is coordination by feedback. Airline operations and maintenance must communicate with one another so each one will know when the planes will be coming to them so they can carry out their respective functions.

Organizational design, then, is the allocation of resources and people to a specified mission or purpose and the structuring of these resources to achieve the mission. Ideally, the organization is designed to fit its environment and to provide the information and coordination needed.

It is useful to think of organization structure from an information-processing view. The key characteristic of organizational structure is that it links the elements of the organization by providing the channels of communication through which information flows. My research has indicated that when organizational structure is formalized and centralized, information flows are restricted and, as a consequence, the organization is not able to gather and process the information it needs when faced with uncertainty. For example, when an organization's structure is highly centralized, decisions are made at the top and information tends to be filtered as it moves up the chain of command. When a decision involves a great deal of uncertainty, it is unlikely therefore that the few individuals at the top of the organization will have the information they require to make the best decision. So decentralization, that is, having more subordinates participate in the decision-making process, may generate the information needed to help reduce the uncertainty and thereby facilitate a better decision.

ALTERNATIVE ORGANIZATIONAL DESIGNS

The key question for the manager concerned with organization design is what are the different structures available to choose from. Contingency theories of organization have shown that there is no one best structure. However, organization theorists have been less clear in elaborating the decision process managers can follow in deciding which structure to implement.

In discussing organization design, organization theorists describe structure differently from the way managers responsible for organization design do. Organizational theorists describe structure as more or less formalized, centralized, specialized, or hierarchical. However, managers tend to think of organizational structure in terms of two general types, the *functional* and the *decentralized*. Most organizations today are either functional or decentralized or some modification or combination of these two general types. Therefore, if we are to develop a heuristic for helping managers make decisions about organization structure, we need to think of structures as functional or decentralized and not in terms of the more abstract dimensions of formalization, centralization, and so on, that organizational theorists tend to use.

ORGANIZATIONAL ENVIRONMENT AND DESIGN: A CRITICAL INTERACTION

In deciding on what kind of organization structure to use, managers need to first understand the characteristics of the environment they are in and the demands this environment makes on the organization in terms of information and coordination. Once the environment is understood, the manager can proceed with the design process.

FIGURE 1
Environmental Components List.

Internal Environment	External Envioronment
Organizational personnel component —Educational and technological background and skills —Previous technological and managerial skill —Individual member's involvement and commitment to attaining system's goals —Interpersonal behavior styles —Availability of manpower for utilization within the system	Customer component —Distributors of product or service —Actual users of product or service
	Suppliers component —New materials suppliers —Equipment suppliers —Product part suppliers —Labor supply
Organizational functional and staff units component —Technological characteristics of organizational units —Interdependence of organizational units in carrying out their objectives —Intraunit conflict among organizational functional and staff units	Competitor component —Competitors for suppliers —Competitors for customers
Organizational level component —Organizational objectives and goals —Integrative process integrating individuals and groups into contributing maximally to attaining organizational goals —Nature of the organization's product service	Sociopolitical component —Government regulatory control over the industry —Public political attitude toward industry and its particular product —Relationship with trade unions with jurisdiction in the organization
	Technological component —Meeting new technological requirements of own industry and related industries in production of product or service —Improving and developing new products by implementing new technological advances in the industry

The first step in designing an organization structure, therefore, is to identify the organization's environment. The task environment constitutes that part of the environment defined by managers as relevant or potentially relevant for organizational decision making. Figure 1 presents a list of environmental components managers might encounter. Clearly, no one organization would encounter all these components in decision making, but this is the master list from which organizational decision makers would identify the appropriate task environments. For example, a manager in a manufacturing division could "define an environment consisting of certain personnel, certain staff units and suppliers, and perhaps certain technological components." The usefulness of the list in Figure 1 is that it provides a guide for decision makers, alerting them to the elements in the environment they might consider in decision making.

Once managers have defined the task environment, the next step is to understand the state of that environment. What are its key characteristics? In describing organizational environments, we emphasize two dimensions: simple-complex and static-dynamic.

The simple-complex dimension of the environment focuses on whether the factors in the environment considered for decision making are few in number and similar or many in number and different. An example of a *simple* unit would be a lower-level production unit whose decisions are affected only by the parts department and materials department, on which it is dependent for supplies, and the marketing department, on which it is dependent for output. An example of a *complex* environment would be a programming and planning department. This group must consider a wide variety of environmental factors when making a decision. It may focus on the marketing and materials department, on customers, on suppliers, and so on. Thus this organizational unit has a much more heterogeneous group of environmental factors to deal with in decision making—its environment is more complex than that of the production unit.

The static-dynamic dimension of the environment is concerned with whether the factors of the environment remain the same over time or change. A *static* environment, for example, might be a production unit that has to deal with a marketing department whose requests for output remain the same and a materials department that is able to supply a steady rate of inputs to the production unit. However, if the marketing department were continually changing its requests and the materials department were inconsistent in its ability to supply parts, the production unit would be operating in a more *dynamic* environment.

Figure 2 provides a four-way classification of organizational environments and some examples of organizations in each of these environments. Complex-dynamic (Cell 4) environments are probably the most characteristic type today. These environments involve rapid change and create high uncertainty for managers. The proper organizational structure is critical in such environments if managers are to have the information necessary for decision making. Also, as organizations move into this turbulent environment, it may be necessary for them to modify their structures. For example, AT&T has moved from a functional organization to a decentralized structure organized around different markets to enable it to cope with more competition in the telephone market and in communications. This change in structure was in response to the need for more information and for a quicker response time to competitive moves.

FIGURE 2
Classification of Organizational Environments.

	Simple	Complex
Static	*Low Perceived Uncertainty* Small number of factors and components in the environment Factors and components are somewhat similar to one another Factors and components remain basically the same and are not changing *Example:* Soft drink industry 1	2 *Moderately Low Perceived Uncertainty* Large number of factors and components in the environment Factors and components are not similar to one another Factors and components remain basically the same *Example:* Food products
Dynamic	*Moderately High Perceived Uncertainty* 3 Small number of factors and components in the environment Factors and components are somewhat similar to one another Factors and components of the environment are in continual process of change *Example:* Fast food industry	4 *High Perceived Uncertainty* Large number of factors and components in the environment Factors and components are not similar to one another Factors and components of environment are in a continual process of change *Examples:* Commercial airline industry Telephone communications (AT&T)

FIGURE 3
Characteristics of the Functional Organization.

Organizational Functions	Accomplished in Functional Organization
Goals	Functional subgoal emphasis (projects lag)
Influence	Functional heads
Promotion	By special function
Budgeting	By function or department
Rewards	For special capability

Strengths	*Weaknesses*
1. Best in *stable* environment	1. Slow response time
2. Colleagueship ("home") for technical specialists	2. Bottlenecks caused by sequential tasks
3. Supports in-depth skill development	3. Decisions pile at top
4. Specialists freed from administrative/coordinating work	4. If multiproduct, product priority conflict
5. Simple decision/communication network excellent in small, limited-output organizations	5. Poor interunit coordination
	6. Stability paid for in less innovation
	7. Restricted view of whole

STRATEGIES FOR ORGANIZATIONAL DESIGN

Once the organization's environment has been diagnosed, what type of structure the organization should have becomes the key question.

Simple Design Strategy

When the organization's environment is relatively simple, that is, there are not many factors to consider in decision making, and stable, that is, neither the make-up of the environment nor the demands made by environmental components are changing, the information and coordination needs for the organization are low. In such circumstances, a *functional organization structure* is most appropriate.

A key characteristic of the functional organization is specialization by functional areas. Figure 3 presents a summary of this structure's strengths and weaknesses. The key strengths of the functional organization are that it supports in-depth skill development and a simple decision-communication network. However, when disputes or uncertainty arise among managers about a decision, they get pushed up the hierarchy to be resolved. A primary weakness of the functional organization, therefore, is that when the organization's environment becomes more dynamic and uncertainty tends to increase many decisions move to the top of the organization. Lower-level managers do not have the information required for decision making so they push decisions upward. Top-level managers become overloaded and are thus slow to respond to the environment.

Organizational Design Dilemma

The organizational designer faces a dilemma in such situations. Designs can be instituted that *reduce* the amount of information required for decision making. Decentralization is the principal strategy indicated. Or organizations can develop more lateral relations to *increase* the amount of information available for decision making.

A decentralized organization is possible whenever an organization's tasks are self-contained. Decentralized organizations are typically designed around products, projects, or markets. The decentralized healthcare organization in Figure 4 is organized around product areas (Medical and Dental) and market area (International). Each division has all the resources needed to perform its particular task. For example, Medical Products (Figure 4) has its own functional organization consisting of production, marketing, and R&D to carry out its mission. The information needed by Medical Product Division's managers is reduced because they have organized around a set of common medical products, and they don't have to worry about dental, pharmaceutical, or hospital support services or products.

In the decentralized organization, managers only have to worry about their own products or services; they have the resources to carry out these activities, and they don't have to compete for shared resources or schedule shared resources. There is also a full-time commitment to a particular product line. The decentralized structure is particularly effective when the organization's environment is very complex, that is, there are a large number of factors to be considered in decision making, and the environment can be segmented or broken down into product or market areas around which the organization can structure itself. For example, the health products organization (Figure 4) probably started out as a functional organization. However, as its product line increased, it undoubtedly became more difficult for one manufacturing unit to have the expertise to produce such a wide range of products efficiently and to handle the diversity of information needed to do it. It would also be difficult for one marketing unit to market such a diverse group of products; different kinds of information and skills would be required to sell the different products. Segmenting this complex environment into product areas facilitates increased specialization. As a result, divisional managers need less information than if they had to deal with all the products and services of the corporation.

Figure 5 summarizes the characteristics and the strengths and weaknesses of the decentralized organization. Decentralized organizations face several problems. For example, it is sometimes difficult to decide what resources are to be pooled in a corporate staff to be used to service the entire organization. If the divisions

FIGURE 4
Decentralized Organization.

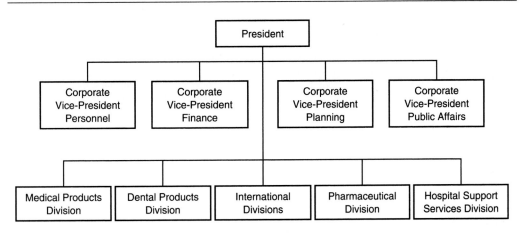

are very different from one another in terms of products, customers, technology, and so on, however, it becomes very difficult to staff a corporate services unit with the diverse knowledge needed to be able to help the divisions. A restricted approach to innovation is another problem decentralized organizations may encounter. Because each division is organized around a particular product or geographic area, each manager's attention is focused on his or her special area. As a result, their innovations focus on their particular specialties. Managers don't have the diverse information needed to produce radical innovations.

One major liability of decentralized organizations is their relative inability to provide integration-coordination among the divisions, even when their interdependence increases. When divisions are relatively autonomous and have only pooled interdependence, there is not much need for coordination. However, when uncertainty increases and the divisions have to work together because of increased either sequential or reciprocal interdependence between the units, decentralized organizations have no for-

mal mechanisms to coordinate and resolve the increased needs for information.

Since today's organizational environments are becoming more complex and interdependent, large decentralized corporations are finding that the need to integrate has increased for at least five reasons:

1. The increased level of regulation organizations face requires more and more coordination across divisions to be sure that all regulatory requirements are being met. For example, crackdowns by the SEC on illegal foreign payments and the increased liabilities of boards of directors have required organizations to have better control systems and information sources to enable their headquarters staff groups to know what's going on in the divisions. Affirmative action requirements have required that divisions share information on how they are doing and where possible pools of affirmative action candidates may be found.

FIGURE 5
Characteristics of the Decentralized Organization.

Organizational Functions	Accomplished in Decentralized Organization
Goals	Special product emphasis (technologies lag)
Influence	Product, project heads
Promotion	By product management
Budgeting	By product, project, program
Rewards	For integrative capability

Strengths	*Weaknesses*
1. Suited to fast change	1. Innovation/growth restricted to existing project areas
2. High product, project, or program visibility	2. Tough to allocate pooled resources (i.e., computer, lab)
3. Full-time task orientation (i.e., dollars, schedules, profits)	3. Shared functions hard to coordinate (i.e., purchasing)
4. Task responsibility, contact points clear to customers or clients	4. Deterioration of in-depth competence—hard to attract technical specialists
5. Processes multiple tasks in parallel, easy to cross functional lines	5. Possible internal task conflicts, priority conflicts
	6. May neglect high level of integration required in organization

2. Organizational environments are changing, and this can lead to a requirement of more coordination across divisions. New customer demands may require what were previously autonomous divisions to coordinate their activities. For example, if the International Group in the health products company mentioned earlier faces a demand to develop some new products for overseas, it may be necessary to provide a means by which the Medical Products and Pharmaceutical Divisions can work in a coordinated and integrated way with International to develop these new products.

3. Technological changes are placing more emphasis on increased interaction among divisions. More and more, computer systems and R&D services are being shared thus compelling the divisions to interact more with one another.

4. The cost of making "wrong" strategic decisions is increasing in terms of both sunk costs and losses because of failure to get market share. Since such "wrong" decisions sometimes result from a lack of contact between divisions, it emphasizes the need to have more coordination across divisions and more sharing of information. For example, AT&T has just recently begun to market telephone and support equipment to counter the completion of other suppliers of this equipment that have entered the market. To do this AT&T has organized around markets. It has also increased the opportunities for interaction among these market managers so they can share information, build on one another's expertise and competence, and ensure required coordination.

5. Scarce resources—for example, capital and raw materials—will require more interaction among divisions to set overall priorities. Is a university, for example, going to emphasize its undergraduate arts program or its professional schools? By setting up task forces of the deans of the schools, the university might be able to identify opportunities for new innovative programs that could benefit the entire organization. New programs in management of the arts—museums, orchestras, and so on—could draw on the expertise of the arts department and the business school and would not require a lot of new venture capital.

For a number of reasons, then, there is a need for increased coordination among divisions in decentralized organizations. Given the decentralized organization's weakness, organizational designers need to implement the second general design strategy, increasing the information flow to reduce uncertainty and facilitate coordination.

Lateral Relations: Increasing Information Available for Decision Making

Lateral relations is really a process that is overlaid on an existing functional or decentralized structure. Lateral relations as a process moves decision making down to where the problem is in the organization. It differs from decentralization in that no self-contained tasks are created.

Jay Galbraith has identified various types of lateral relations. *Direct contact,* for example, can be used by managers of diverse groups as a mechanism to coordinate their different activities. With direct contact, managers can meet informally to discuss their common problems. *Liaison roles* are a formal communication link between two units. Engineering liaison with the manufacturing department is an excellent example of the liaison role. The engineer

serving in the liaison role may be located in the production organization as a way of coordinating engineering and production activities.

When coordination between units becomes more complex, an *integrator role* may be established. Paul Lawrence and Jay Lorsch have indicated that the integrator role is particularly useful when organizational units that must be coordinated are differentiated from one another in terms of their structure, subgoals, time, orientation, and so on. In such situations, there is the possibility of conflict between the various units. For example, production, marketing, and R&D units in an organization may be highly differentiated from one another. Marketing, for example, is primarily concerned with having products to sell that are responsive to customer needs. R&D, on the other hand, may be concerned with developing innovative products that shape customer needs. Production, for its part, may want products to remain unchanged so that manufacturing setups don't have to be modified. Obviously there are differences among the three units in terms of their subgoals. The integrator role is instituted to coordinate and moderate such diverse orientations. The integrator could be a materials manager or a group executive whose additional function would be to coordinate and integrate the diverse units in ways that meet the organization's common objectives.

To be effective as an *integrator,* a manager needs to have certain characteristics. First, he needs wide contacts in the organization so that he possesses the relevant information about the different units he is attempting to integrate. Second, the integrator needs to understand and share, at least to a degree, the goals and orientations of the different groups. He cannot be seen as being a partisan of one particular group's perspective. Third, the integrator has to be rather broadly trained technically, so that he can talk the language of the different groups. By being able to demonstrate that he has some expertise in each area, he will be viewed as more credible by each group and will also be better able to facilitate information exchange between the units. The integrator can in effect become an interpreter of each group's position to the others. Fourth, the groups that the integrator is working with must trust him. Again, the integrator is trying to facilitate information flow and cooperation between the groups and thus the groups must believe that he is working toward a solution acceptable to all the groups. Fifth, the integrator needs to exert influence on the basis of his expertise rather than through formal power. The integrator can provide information and identify alternative courses of action for the different units as they attempt to coordinate their activities. The more he can get them to agree on solutions and courses of action rather than having to use his formal power, the more committed they will be to implementing the solution. Last, the integrator's conflict resolution skills are important. Because differentiation between the units exists, conflict and disagreement are inevitable. It is important, therefore, that confrontation is used as the conflict resolution style. By confrontation we mean that parties to the conflict identify the causes of conflict and are committed to adopting a problem-solving approach to finding a mutually acceptable solution to the conflict. The parties must also be committed, of course, to work to implement that solution.

When coordination involves working with six or seven different units, then task forces or teams can be established. Task forces involve a group of managers working together on the coordination problems of their diverse groups. For example, in a manufacturing organization, the marketing, production, R&D, finance, and engineering managers may meet twice a week (or more often

FIGURE 6
Characteristics of the Matrix Organization.

Organizational Functions	Accomplished in Matrix Organization
Goals	Emphasis on production/market
Influence	Matrix manager and functional heads
Promotion	By function or into matrix manager job
Budgeting	By matrix organization project
Rewards	By special functional skills and performance in matrix

Strengths	Weaknesses
1. Full-time focus of personnel on project of matrix	1. Costly to maintain personnel pool to staff matrix
2. Matrix manager is coordinator of functions for single project	2. Participants experience dual authority of matrix manager and functional area managers
3. Reduces information requirements as focus is on single product/market	3. Little interchange with functional groups outside the matrix so there may be duplication of effort, "reinvention of the wheel"
4. Masses specialized technical skills to the product/market	4. Participants in matrix need to have good interpersonal skills in order for it to work

when required) to discuss problems of coordination that they may be having that require their cooperation to solve. In this use a task force is a problem-solving group formed to facilitate coordination.

The matrix type of structure is the most complex form of lateral relations. The matrix is typically a formal structure in the organization; it is not a structure that is often added temporarily to an existing functional or decentralized structure. As Lawrence, Kolodny, and Davis have indicated in their article "The Human Side of the Matrix" (*Organizational Dynamics,* Summer 1977), there are certain key characteristics of a matrix structure. The most salient is that there is dual authority, that is, both the heads of the functions and the matrix manager have authority over those working in the matrix unit.

The matrix was initially developed in the aerospace industry where the organization had to be responsive to products/markets as well as technology. Because the matrix focuses on a specific product or market, it can generate the information and concentrate the resources needed to respond to changes in that product or market rapidly. The matrix is now being used in a variety of business, public, and health organizations. Figure 6 provides a summary of the characteristics and strengths and weaknesses of the matrix form of organization.

The matrix structure is particularly useful when an organization wants to focus resources on producing a particular product or service. The use of the matrix in the aerospace industry, for example, allowed these organizations to build manufacturing units to produce particular airplanes, thus allowing in-depth attention and specialization of skills.

Matrix organizations, however, are complicated to manage. Because both project managers and traditional functional area managers are involved in matrix organizations, personnel in the matrix have two bosses, and there is an inherent potential for conflict under such circumstances. As a result, the matrix form of lateral relations should only be used in those situations where an organization faces a unique problem in a particular market area or in the technological requirements of a product. When the information and technological requirements are such that a full-time focus on the market or product is needed, a matrix organization can be helpful. Citibank,

for example, has used a matrix structure in its international activity to concentrate on geographic areas. Boeing Commercial Airplane has used the matrix to focus resources on a particular product.

Lateral relations require a certain organizational design and special interpersonal skills if this process for reducing uncertainty by increasing the information available for improving coordination is going to be effective. From a design perspective, four factors are required:

1. The organization's reward structure must support and reward cooperative problem solving that leads to coordination and integration. Will a manager's performance appraisal, for example, reflect his or her participation in efforts to achieve coordination and integration? If the organization's reward does not recognize joint problem-solving efforts, then lateral relations will not be effective.

2. In assigning managers to participate in some form of lateral relations, it is important that they have responsibility for implementation. Line managers should be involved since they understand the problems more intimately than staff personnel and, more importantly, they are concerned about implementation. Staff members can be used, but line managers should be dominant since this will lead to more commitment on their part to implementing solutions that come out of lateral relations problem-solving efforts.

3. Participants must have the authority to commit their units to action. Managers who are participating in an effort to resolve problems of coordination must be able to indicate what particular action their units might take in trying to improve coordination. For example, in the manufacturing company task force example mentioned earlier, the marketing manager should be able to commit his group to increasing the lead time for providing information to production on deadlines for delivering new products to customers.

4. Lateral processes must be integrated into the vertical information flow. In the concern for increasing information exchange *across* the units in the organization there must be no loss of concern for vertical information exchange so that the top levels in the organization are aware of coordination efforts.

FIGURE 7
Organizational Design Decision Tree Heuristic.

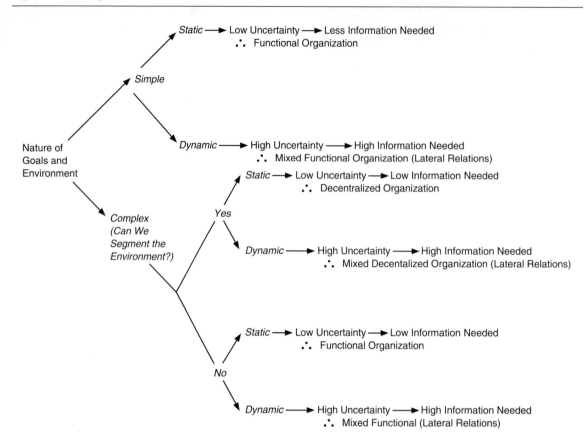

Certain skills are also required on the part of participants for lateral relations to work:

1. Individuals must deal with conflict effectively, in the sense of identifying the sources of conflict and then engaging in problem solving to reach a mutually acceptable solution to the conflict situation.

2. Participants need good interpersonal skills. They must be able to communicate effectively with one another and avoid making other participants defensive. The more they can learn to communicate with others in a descriptive, nonevaluative manner, the more open the communication process will be.

3. Participants in lateral relations need to understand that influence and power should be based on expertise rather than formal power. Because of the problem-solving nature of lateral relations, an individual's power and influence will change based on the particular problem at hand and the individual's ability to provide key information to solve the problem. At various times different members will have more influence because of their particular expertise.

Lateral relations, then, is a process that is overlaid onto the existing functional or decentralized organization structure. Lateral

relations requires various skills, so it is imperative that an organization never adopts this approach without training the people involved. Before implementing lateral relations, team building might be used to develop the interpersonal skills of the participating managers. These managers might spend time learning how to operate more effectively in groups, how to improve communication skills, and how to deal with conflict in a positive way so that it does not become disruptive to the organization.

The Organizational Design Decision Tree

We have discussed the different kinds of organization structure that managers can implement. We are now prepared to identify the decision-making process the manager can use in selecting the appropriate structure to "fit" the demands of the environment. Figure 7 presents a decision tree analysis for selecting either the functional or decentralized organization structure. This decision analysis also indicates when the existing functional or decentralized organization structure should be supplemented with some form of lateral relations in the form of a task force or team or a matrix. In general, an organization should use one of the simpler forms of lateral relations rather than the more complex and expensive matrix. In using this decision tree, there are a number of questions that the designer needs to ask.

The first question is whether the organization's environment is *simple,* that is, there are few factors to consider in the environment, or *complex,* that is, there are a number of different environmental factors to be considered in decision making. If the environment is defined as *simple,* the next question focuses on whether the environmental factors are *static,* that is, remain the same over time, or are *dynamic,* that is, change over time. If we define the environment as static, there is likely to be little uncertainty associated with decision making. In turn, information requirements for decision making are low. In this simple-static environment, the functional organization is most efficient. It can most quickly gather and process the information required to deal with this type of environment.

At this point the question might be raised, are there any organizational environments that are in fact both simple and static or is this a misperception on the part of the managers that oversimplifies the environment? There may be environments like this, but the key is that these environments may change, that is, they may become more dynamic as the marketplace changes, as resources become scarce, or the organization's domain is challenged. For example, the motor home/recreational vehicle industry was very successful in the early 1970s. Its market was relatively homogeneous (simple) and there was a constantly high demand (static) for its products. Then the oil embargo of 1973 hit, and the environment suddenly became dynamic. The industry had a very difficult time changing because it had done no contingency planning about "what would happen if" demand shifted, resources became scarce, and so

on. The important point is that an organization's environment may be simple and static today but change tomorrow. Managers should continually scan the environment and be sensitive to the fact that things can change and contingency planning may be useful.

If this simple environment is defined as dynamic, with some components in the environment changing, some uncertainty may be experienced by decision makers. Thus information needs will be greater than when the environment was static. Therefore, in this simple-dynamic environment the mixed functional organization with lateral relations is likely to be the most effective in gathering and processing the information required for decision making. Because the organization's environment is simple, the creation of self-contained units would not be efficient. It is more economical to have central functional areas responsible for all products and markets as these products and markets are relatively similar to one another. However, when uncertainty arises and there is need for more information, some form of lateral relations can be added, to the existing functional organization.

Figure 8 shows the functional organization of a manufacturing organization. The organization suddenly may face a problem with its principal product. Competitors may have developed an attractive replacement. As a result of this unique problem, the president of the firm may set up a task force chaired by the vice-president of sales to develop new products. The task force consists of members from manufacturing, sales, research, and engineering services. Its function, obviously, will be to develop and evaluate suggestions for new products.

If the organization's environment is defined by the managers as complex, that is, there are a large number of factors and

FIGURE 8
Functional Organization with Task Force.

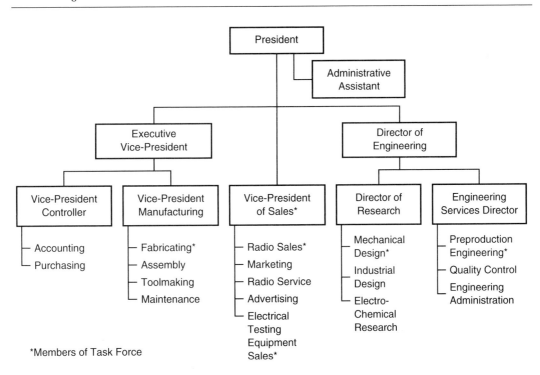

FIGURE 9
Decentralized Organization with Lateral Relations.

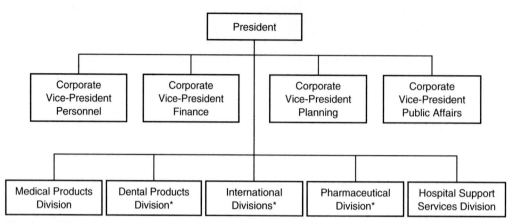

*Members of Task Force

components that need to be considered in decision making, the next question to ask is, can the organization *segment* its environment into geographic areas, market, or product areas? If the environment is defined as segmentable, then the next question focuses on whether the environment is static or dynamic. If the environment is defined as static, there is going to be low uncertainty and thus information needs for decision making are not going to be high. Thus, in the complex-segmentable-static environment, the decentralized organization is most appropriate, and the health products organization discussed earlier is a good example of this. The organization can break the environment apart in the sense that it can organize around products or markets, for example, and thus information, resources, and so forth, are only required to produce and market these more homogeneous outputs of the organization.

In the complex-segmentable-dynamic environment there is a change in the components of the environment and the demands they are making on the organization, or in fact the organization has to now consider different factors in the environment that it had not previously considered in decision making. Uncertainty and coordination needs may be higher. The result is that decision makers need more information to reduce uncertainty and provide information to facilitate coordination. The mixed decentralized organization with lateral relations is the appropriate structure here.

Figure 9 presents the design of a multidivision decentralized health products organization. Some form of lateral relations may be added to this structure to help generate more information. For example, the International Division may be attempting to develop new products but may be encountering problems, with the result that the entire organization, stimulated by the president's concern, may be experiencing uncertainty about how to proceed. In such a situation, a task force of the manager of the International Group and the Dental Group and the Pharmaceutical Group might work together in developing ideas for new products in the International Division. The lateral relations mechanism of the task force facilitates information exchange *across* the organization to reduce uncertainty and increase coordination of the efforts of the divisions that should be mutually supportive. By working together, in the task force, the

division managers will be exchanging information and will be gaining a better understanding of their common problems and how they need to work and coordinate with one another in order to solve these problems.

If the organization's complex environment is defined by managers as nonsegmentable, the functional organization will be appropriate because it is not possible to break the environment up into geographic or product/service areas.

In effect, there simply might be too much interdependence among environmental components, or the technology of the organization may be so interlinked, that it is not possible to create self-contained units organized around components of the environment.

A hospital is a good example of this organization type. The environment is clearly complex. There are numerous and diverse environmental components that have to be considered in decision making (for example, patients, regulatory groups, medical societies, third-party payers, and suppliers). In the complex-nonsegmentable-static environment, environmental components are rather constant in their demands. Thus here the functional organization is most appropriate.

However, the functional organization, through its very specific rules, procedures, and channels of communication, will likely be too slow in generating the required information. Therefore, some form of lateral relations may be added to the functional organization. Figure 10 presents an example of an aerospace functional organization that uses a matrix structure for its airplane and missile products divisions. The matrix structure provides in-depth concentration of personnel and resources on these different product areas, each of which has its own very unique information and technological requirements.

SYMPTOMS OF INAPPROPRIATE ORGANIZATIONAL STRUCTURE

The key question at this point is "So what?" What are the costs to an organization if it is using the wrong structure, given its

FIGURE 10
Functional Organization with Matrix

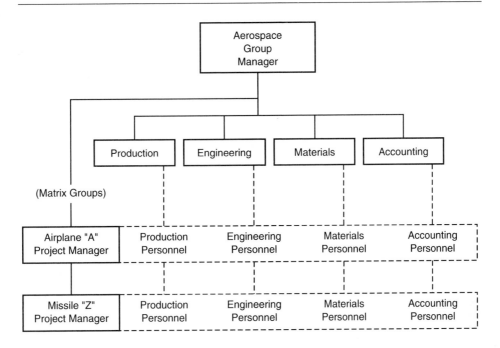

product/service and the environment in which it operates? In order to be effective, an organization needs to attain its goals and objectives, it needs to adapt to the environment, and last, it should be designed in such a way that its managers experience low role conflict and ambiguity.

Therefore, there are certain kinds of information the manager responsible for organizational design should be sensitive to in monitoring whether the appropriate structure is being used. While using the appropriate structure may have some direct impact on the organization's ability to attain its goals, its biggest impact will probably be on the adaptability of the organization and the role behavior of its managers.

Certain kinds of symptoms regarding ineffective adaptability may occur. For example:

❒ Organizational decision makers may not be able to anticipate problems before they occur. There may be a tendency in the organization to wait until problems occur and then react to them because the organization simply does not have enough information to develop contingency plans.

❒ Decision makers may err in trying to predict trends in their decision environment. Without proper coordination across divisions, the organization may lose control over the relationship between its internal functioning and its environment.

❒ The organization may not be able to get key information for decision making to the right place for effective decision making. For example, division managers from different product groups have information that quality and liability standards on their respective products are unrealistically high. However, because of decentralization and lack of effective coordination through some form of lateral

relations, this information may not get to the staff groups in the organization that are responsible for setting corporate policy in this area.

❒ The organization, having identified a problem vis-à-vis its environment, may simply not be able to take corrective action quickly enough.

Symptoms of poor fit between structure and environment may also show at the level of the individual in terms of some increase in either role conflict or role ambiguity. It is important, therefore, that the organization monitor the level of role conflict and role ambiguity among its managers and the resulting stress they experience so the system has a baseline for comparison. If there is a significant increase from this baseline in conflict and ambiguity and stress, then the organization may consider that the increase is a symptom of an organizational design problem. For example:

❒ Individuals may be experiencing increased role conflict. This may occur when the organization is implementing a functional organization in a dynamic environment. The environment may be changing and the individuals may be required to make quick responses to this changing environment. Having to wait for new policy changes to come down the hierarchy may delay the organization from responding appropriately. Decision makers at the top of the organization will also suffer from role conflict when the environment is changing rapidly. In the functional organization, when new situations occur they are referred to higher levels of the organization for decision and action. The result is that top-level decision makers become overloaded and the organization's response to the environment slows down. In a dynamic environment, the functional organization constrains the decision-making adaptation process.

❐ Individuals in the organization also may experience increased role ambiguity—they may be unclear as to what is expected of them in their roles. For example, role ambiguity is likely to occur when the decentralized organization is implemented without some effective use of lateral relations. Individuals may feel they don't have the information needed for decision making. Divisional managers may not know what the corporate staff's policy is on various issues, and corporate staff may have lost touch with the divisions.

These are the kinds of information managers should be aware of as indicators of dysfunctional organization design. These data can be collected in organizational diagnosis surveys that we have developed so that a more systemic monitoring of structure exists just as we monitor organizational climate. As fine tuning the organization's design to its environment becomes more critical, organizations will begin to monitor their organizational design more systematically.

SUMMARY

What are the advantages to managers in using the design decision tree? There appear to be several:

1. It provides a *broad framework* for identifying the key factors a manager should think about in considering an organiza-

tional design. For example: What is our environment? What different structural options do we have?

2. It forces the manager to *diagnose* the decision environment. What is our environment like? How stable is it? How complex is it? Is it possible to reduce complexity by segmenting the environment into product or geographical subgroups?

3. It causes managers to think about *how much interdependence* there is among segments of the organization. How dependent on one another are different parts of the organization in terms of technology, services, support, help in getting their tasks completed? The decision points in the heuristic forces managers to question themselves about what other parts of the organization they need to coordinate their activities with, and then to think about how to do it.

4. Once the organization is in either a functional or decentralized structure, the decision tree points out what can be done to meet *the increased needs for information* through the use of lateral relations. Lateral relations provide a mechanism for supplementing the existing structure to facilitate dealing with the organization's increased needs for information and coordination.

Managers in a variety of organizations have commented that the decision tree gives them "... a handle for thinking about organizational design so we can tinker with it, fine tune it and make it work better. We don't have to be coerced by structure. We now have a better feel for when certain structures should be used and for the specific steps we can take to make a given structure work."

Evolution and Revolution as Organizations Grow

Larry E. Greiner

A small research company chooses too complicated and formalized an organization structure for its young age and limited size. It flounders in rigidity and bureaucracy for several years and is finally acquired by a larger company.

Key executives of a retail store chain hold on to an organization structure long after it has served its purpose, because their power is derived from this structure. The company eventually goes into bankruptcy.

A large bank disciplines a "rebellious" manager who is blamed for current control problems, when the underlying cause is centralized procedures that are holding back expansion into new markets. Many younger managers subsequently leave the bank, competition moves in, and profits are still declining.

The problems of these companies, like those of many others, are rooted more in past decisions than in present events or outside market dynamics. Historical forces do indeed shape the future growth of organizations. Yet management, in its haste to grow, often overlooks such critical developmental questions as: Where has our organization been? Where is it now? And what do the answers to these questions mean for where we are going? Instead, its gaze is fixed outward toward the environment and the future—as if more precise market projections will provide a new organizational identity.

Companies fail to see that many clues to their future success lie within their own organizations and their evolving states of development. Moreover, the inability of management to understand its organization development problems can result in a company becoming "frozen" in its present stage of evolution or, ultimately, in failure, regardless of market opportunities.

My position in this article is that the future of an organization may be less determined by outside forces than it is by the organization's history. In stressing the force of history on an organization, I have drawn from the legacies of European psychologists (their thesis being that individual behavior is determined primarily by previous events and experiences, not by what lies ahead). Extending this analogy of individual development to the problems of organization development, I shall discuss a series of developmental phases through which growing companies tend to pass. But, first, let me provide two definitions:

1. The term *evolution* is used to describe prolonged periods of growth where no major upheaval occurs in organization practices.

2. The term *revolution* is used to describe those periods of substantial turmoil in organization life.

As a company progresses through developmental phases, each evolutionary period creates its own revolution. For instance, centralized practices eventually lead to demands for decentralization. Moreover, the nature of management's solution to each revolutionary period determines whether a company will move forward into its next stage of evolutionary growth. As I shall show later, there are at least five phases of organization development, each characterized by both an evolution and a revolution.

KEY FORCES IN DEVELOPMENT

During the past few years a small amount of research knowledge about the phases of organization development has been building. Some of this research is very quantitative, such as time-series analyses that reveal patterns of economic performance over time.[1] The majority of studies, however, are case-oriented and use company records and interviews to reconstruct a rich picture of corporate development.[2] Yet both types of research tend to be heavily empirical without attempting more generalized statements about the overall process of development.

A notable exception is the historical work of Alfred D. Chandler, Jr., in his book *Strategy and Structure*.[3] This study depicts four very broad and general phases in the lives of four large U.S. companies. It proposes that outside market opportunities determine a company's strategy, which in turn determines the company's organization structure. This thesis has a valid ring for the four companies examined by Chandler, largely because they developed in a time of explosive markets and technological advances. But more recent evidence suggests that organization structure may be less malleable than Chandler assumed; in fact, structure can play a critical role in influencing corporate strategy. It is this reverse emphasis on how organization structure affects future growth which is highlighted in the model presented in this article.

From an analysis of recent studies,[4] five key dimensions emerge as essential for building a model of organization development:

1. Age of the organization.
2. Size of the organization.
3. Stages of evolution.
4. Growth rate of the industry.

I shall describe each of these elements separately, but first note their combined effect as illustrated in *Exhibit I*. Note especially how each dimension influences the other over time; when all five elements begin to interact, a more complete and dynamic picture of organizational growth emerges.

After describing these dimensions and their interconnections, I shall discuss each evolutionary/revolutionary phase of development and show (a) how each stage of evolution breeds its own revolution, and (b) how management solutions to each revolution determine the next state of evolution.

Age of the Organization

The most obvious and essential dimension for any model of development is the life span of an organization (represented as the horizontal axis in *Exhibit I*). All historical studies gather data from various points in time and then make comparisons. From these observations, it is evident that the same organization practices are not maintained throughout a long time span. This makes a most basic point: management problems and principles are rooted in time. The concept of decentralization, for example, can have meaning for describing corporate practices at one time period but loses its descriptive power at another.

The passage of time also contributes to the institutionalization of managerial attitudes. As a result, employee behavior becomes not only more predictable but also more difficult to change when attitudes are outdated.

Size of the Organization

This dimension is depicted as the vertical axis in *Exhibit I*. A company's problems and solutions tend to change markedly as the number of employees and sales volume increase. Thus, time is not the only determinant of structure; in fact, organizations that do not grow in size can retain many of the same management issues and practices over lengthy periods. In addition to increased size,

1. See, for example, William H. Starbuck, "Organizational Metamorphosis," in *Promising Research Directions,* edited by R. W. Millman and M. P. Hottenstein (Tempe, Arizona, Academy of Management, 1968), p. 113.

2. See, for example, the *Grangesberg* case series, prepared by C. Roland Christensen and Bruce R. Scott, Case Clearing House, Harvard Business School.

3. *Strategy and Structure: Chapters in the History of the American Industrial Enterprise* (Cambridge, Massachusetts, The M.I.T. Press, 1962).

4. I have drawn on many sources for evidence: (a) numerous cases collected at the Harvard Business School; (b) *Organization Growth and Development,* edited by William H. Starbuck (Middlesex, England, Penguin Books, Ltd., 1971), where several studies are cited; and (c) articles published in journals, such as Lawrence E. Fouraker and John M. Stopford, "Organization Structure and the Multinational Strategy," *Administrative Science Quarterly,* Vol. 13, No. 1, 1968, p. 47; and Malcolm S. Salter, "Management Appraisal and Reward Systems," *Journal of Business Policy,* Vol. 1, No. 4, 1971.

however, problems of coordination and communication magnify, new functions emerge, levels in the management hierarchy multiply, and jobs become more interrelated.

Stages of Evolution

As both age and size increase, another phenomenon becomes evident: the prolonged growth that I have termed the evolutionary period. Most growing organizations do not expand for two years and then retreat for one year; rather, those that survive a crisis usually enjoy four to eight years of continuous growth without a major economic setback or severe internal disruption. The term evolution seems appropriate for describing these quieter periods because only modest adjustments appear necessary for maintaining growth under the same overall pattern of management.

Stages of Revolution

Smooth evolution is not inevitable; it cannot be assumed that organization growth is linear. *Fortune's* "500" list, for example, has had significant turnover during the last 50 years. Thus we find evidence from numerous case histories which reveals periods of substantial turbulence spaced between smoother periods of evolution.

I have termed these turbulent times the periods of revolution because they typically exhibit a serious upheaval of management practices. Traditional management practices, which were appropriate for a smaller size and earlier time, are brought under scrutiny by frustrated top managers and disillusioned lower-level managers. During such periods of crisis, a number of companies fail—those unable to abandon past practices and effect major organization changes are likely either to fold or to level off in their growth rates.

The critical task for management in each revolutionary period is to find a new set of organization practices that will become the basis for managing the next period of evolutionary growth. Interestingly enough, these new practices eventually sow their own seeds of decay and lead to another period of revolution. Companies therefore experience the irony of seeing a major solution in one time period become a major problem at a later date.

Growth Rate of the Industry

The speed at which an organization experiences phases of evolution and revolution is closely related to the market environment of its industry. For example, a company in a rapidly expanding market will have to add employees rapidly; hence, the need for new organization structures to accommodate large staff increases is accelerated. While evolutionary periods tend to be relatively short

EXHIBIT I
Model of Organization Development.

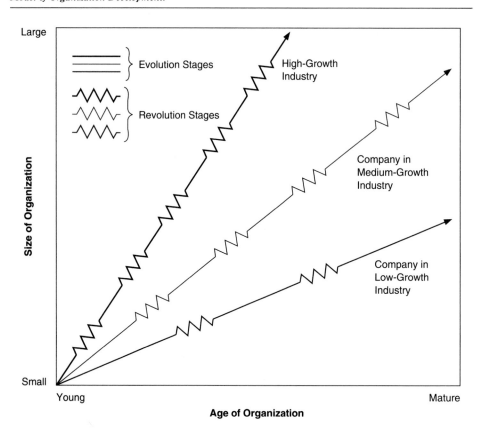

in fast-growing industries, much longer evolutionary periods occur in mature or slowly growing industries.

Evolution can also be prolonged, and revolutions delayed, when profits come easily. For instance, companies that make grievous errors in a rewarding industry can still look good on their profit and loss statements; thus they can avoid a change in management practices for a longer period. The aerospace industry in its infancy is an example. Yet revolutionary periods still occur, as one did in aerospace when profit opportunities began to dry up. Revolutions seem to be much more severe and difficult to resolve when the market environment is poor.

PHASES OF GROWTH

With the foregoing framework in mind, let us now examine in depth the five specific phases of evolution and revolution. As shown in *Exhibit II,* each evolutionary period is characterized by the dominant *management style* used to achieve growth, while each revolutionary period is characterized by the dominant *management*

problem that must be solved before growth can continue. The patterns presented in *Exhibit II* seem to be typical for companies in industries with moderate growth over a long time period; companies in faster growing industries tend to experience all five phases more rapidly, while those in slower growing industries encounter only two or three phases over many years.

It is important to note that *each phase is both an effect of the previous phase and a cause for the next phase.* For example, the evolutionary management style in Phase 3 of the exhibit is "delegation," which grows out of, and becomes the solution to, demands for greater "autonomy" in the preceding Phase 2 revolution. The style of delegation used in Phase 3, however, eventually provokes a major revolutionary crisis that is characterized by attempts to regain control over the diversity created through increased delegation.

The principal implication of each phase is that management actions are narrowly prescribed if growth is to occur. For example, a company experiencing an autonomy crisis in Phase 2 cannot return to directive management for a solution—it must adopt a new style of delegation in order to move ahead.

EXHIBIT II
The Five Phases of Growth.

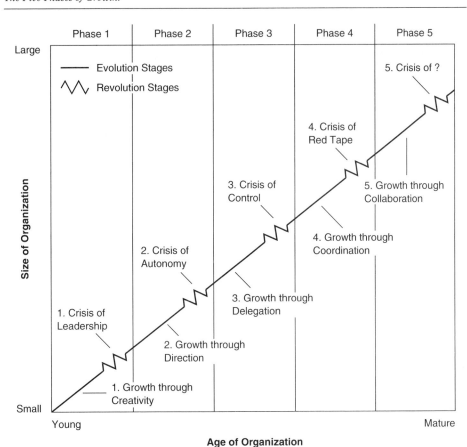

Phase 1: Creativity . . .

In the birth stage of an organization, the emphasis is on creating both a product and a market. Here are the characteristics of the period of creative evolution:

❑ The company's founders are usually technically or entrepreneurially oriented, and they disdain management activities; their physical and mental energies are absorbed entirely in making and selling a new product.

❑ Communication among employees is frequent and informal.

❑ Long hours of work are rewarded by modest salaries and the promise of ownership benefits.

❑ Control of activities comes from immediate marketplace feedback; the management acts as the customers react.

. . . & the leadership crisis: All of the foregoing individualistic and creative activities are essential for the company to get off the ground. But therein lies the problem. As the company grows, larger production runs require knowledge about the efficiencies of manufacturing. Increased numbers of employees cannot be managed exclusively through informal communication; new employees are not motivated by an intense dedication to the product or organization. Additional capital must be secured, and new accounting procedures are needed for financial control.

Thus the founders find themselves burdened with unwanted management responsibilities. So they long for the "good old days," still trying to act as they did in the past. And conflicts between the harried leaders grow more intense.

At this point a crisis of leadership occurs, which is the onset of the first revolution. Who is to lead the company out of confusion and solve the managerial problems confronting it? Quite obviously, a strong manager is needed who has the necessary knowledge and skill to introduce new business techniques. But this is easier said than done. The founders often hate to step aside even though they are probably temperamentally unsuited to be managers. So here is the first critical development choice—to locate and install a strong business manager who is acceptable to the founders and who can pull the organization together.

Phase 2: Direction . . .

Those companies that survive the first phase by installing a capable business manager usually embark on a period of sustained growth under able and directive leadership. Here are the characteristics of this evolutionary period:

❑ A functional organization structure is introduced to separate manufacturing from marketing activities, and job assignments become more specialized.

❑ Accounting systems for inventory and purchasing are introduced.

❑ Incentives, budgets, and work standards are adopted.

❑ Communication becomes more formal and impersonal as a hierarchy of titles and positions builds.

❑ The new manager and his key supervisors take most of the responsibility for instituting direction, while lower-level supervisors are treated more as functional specialists than as autonomous decision-making managers.

. . . & the autonomy crisis: Although the new directive techniques channel employee energy more efficiently into growth, they eventually become inappropriate for controlling a larger, more diverse and complex organization. Lower-level employees find themselves restricted by a cumbersome and centralized hierarchy. They have come to possess more direct knowledge about markets and machinery than do the leaders at the top; consequently, they feel torn between following procedures and taking initiative on their own.

Thus the second revolution is imminent as a crisis develops from demands for greater autonomy on the part of lower-level managers. The solution adopted by most companies is to move toward greater delegation. Yet it is difficult for managers who were previously successful at being directive to give up responsibility. Moreover, lower-level managers are not accustomed to making decisions for themselves. As a result, numerous companies flounder during this revolutionary period, adhering to centralized methods while lower-level employees grow more disenchanted and leave the organization.

Phase 3: Delegation . . .

The next era of growth evolves from the successful application of a decentralized organization structure. It exhibits these characteristics:

❑ Much greater responsibility is given to the managers of plants and market territories.

❑ Profit centers and bonuses are used to stimulate motivation.

❑ The top executives at headquarters restrain themselves to managing by exception, based on periodic reports from the field.

❑ Management often concentrates on making new acquisitions which can be lined up beside other decentralized units.

❑ Communication from the top is infrequent, usually by correspondence, telephone, or brief visits to field locations.

The delegation stage proves useful for gaining expansion through heightened motivation at lower levels. Decentralized managers with greater authority and incentive are able to penetrate larger markets, respond faster to customers, and develop new products.

. . . & the control crisis: A serious problem eventually evolves, however, as top executives sense that they are losing control over a highly diversified field operation. Autonomous field managers prefer to run their own shows without coordinating plans, money, technology, and manpower with the rest of the organization. Freedom breeds a parochial attitude.

Hence, the Phase 3 revolution is under way when top management seeks to regain control over the total company. Some top managements attempt a return to centralized management, which usually fails because of the vast scope of operations. Those companies that move ahead find a new solution in the use of special coordination techniques.

Phase 4: Coordination . . .

During this phase, the evolutionary period is characterized by the use of formal systems for achieving greater coordination and by top executives taking responsibility for the initiation and administration of these new systems. For example:

❐ Decentralized units are merged into product groups.

❐ Formal planning procedures are established and intensively reviewed.

❐ Numerous staff personnel are hired and located at headquarters to initiate companywide programs of control and review for line managers.

❐ Capital expenditures are carefully weighed and parceled out across the organization.

❐ Each product group is treated as an investment center where return on invested capital is an important criterion used in allocating funds.

❐ Certain technical functions, such as data processing, are centralized at headquarters, while daily operating decisions remain decentralized.

❐ Stock options and companywide profit sharing are used to encourage identity with the firm as a whole.

All of these new coordination systems prove useful for achieving growth through more efficient allocation of a company's limited resources. They prompt field managers to look beyond the needs of their local units. While these managers still have much decision-making responsibility, they learn to justify their actions more carefully to a "watchdog" audience at headquarters.

. . . & the red tape crisis: But a lack of confidence gradually builds between line and staff, and between headquarters and the field. The proliferation of systems and programs begins to exceed its utility; a red-tape crisis is created. Line managers, for example, increasingly resent heavy staff direction from those who are not familiar with local conditions. Staff people, on the other hand, complain about uncooperative and uninformed line managers. Together both groups criticize the bureaucratic paper system that has evolved. Procedures take precedence over problem solving, and innovation is dampened. In short, the organization has become too large and complex to be managed through formal programs and rigid systems. The Phase 4 revolution is underway.

Phase 5: Collaboration . . .

The last observable phase in previous studies emphasizes strong interpersonal collaboration in an attempt to overcome the red-tape crisis. Where Phase 4 was managed more through formal systems and procedures, Phase 5 emphasizes greater spontaneity in management action through teams and the skillful confrontation of interpersonal differences. Social control and self-discipline take over from formal control. This transition is especially difficult for those experts who created the old systems as well as for those line managers who relied on formal methods for answers.

The Phase 5 evolution, then, builds around a more flexible and behavioral approach to management. Here are its characteristics:

❐ The focus is on solving problems quickly through team action.

❐ Teams are combined across functions for task-group activity.

❐ Headquarters staff experts are reduced in number, reassigned, and combined in interdisciplinary teams to consult with, not to direct, field units.

❐ A matrix-type structure is frequently used to assemble the right teams for the appropriate problems.

❐ Previous formal systems are simplified and combined into single multipurpose systems.

❐ Conferences of key managers are held frequently to focus on major problem issues.

❐ Educational programs are utilized to train managers in behavioral skills for achieving better teamwork and conflict resolution.

❐ Real-time information systems are integrated into daily decision making.

❐ Economic rewards are geared more to team performance than to individual achievement.

❐ Experiments in new practices are encouraged throughout the organization.

. . . & the ? crisis: What will be the revolution in response to this stage of evolution? Many large U.S. companies are now in the Phase 5 evolutionary stage, so the answers are critical. While there is little clear evidence, I imagine the revolution will center around the "psychological saturation" of employees who grow emotionally and physically exhausted by the intensity of teamwork and the heavy pressure for innovative solutions.

My hunch is that the Phase 5 revolution will be solved through new structure and programs that allow employees to periodically rest, reflect, and revitalize themselves. We may even see companies with dual organization structures: a "habit" structure for getting the daily work done, and a "reflective" structure for stimulating perspective and personal enrichment. Employees could then move back and forth between the two structures as their energies are dissipated and refueled.

One European organization has implemented just such a structure. Five reflective groups have been established outside the regular structure for the purpose of continuously evaluating five task activities basic to the organization. They report directly to the managing director, although their reports are made public throughout the organization. Membership in each group includes all levels and functions, and employees are rotated through these groups on a six-month basis.

Other concrete examples now in practice include providing sabbaticals for employees, moving managers in and out of "hot spot" jobs, establishing a four-day workweek, assuring job security, building physical facilities for relaxation *during* the working day, making jobs more interchangeable, creating an extra team on the assembly line so that one team is always off for reeducation, and switching into longer vacations and more flexible working hours.

The Chinese practice of requiring executives to spend time periodically on lower-level jobs may also be worth a nonideological evaluation. For too long U.S. management has assumed that career progress should be equated with an upward path toward title, salary, and power. Could it be that some vice presidents of marketing might just long for, and even benefit from, temporary duty in the field sales organization?

IMPLICATIONS OF HISTORY

Let me now summarize some important implications for practicing managers. First, the main features of this discussion are depicted in *Exhibit III,* which shows the specific management actions that characterize each growth phase. These actions are also the solutions which ended each preceding revolutionary period.

In one sense, I hope that many readers will react to my model by calling it obvious and natural for depicting the growth of an organization. To me this type of reaction is a useful test of the model's validity.

But at a more reflective level I imagine some of these reactions are more hindsight than foresight. Those experienced managers who have been through a developmental sequence can empathize with it now, but how did they react when in the middle of a stage of evolution or revolution? They can probably recall the limits of their own developmental understanding at that time. Perhaps they resisted desirable changes or were even swept emotionally into a revolution without being able to propose constructive solutions. So let me offer some explicit guidelines for managers of growing organizations to keep in mind.

Know where you are in the developmental sequence.

Every organization and its component parts are at different stages of development. The task of top management is to be aware of these stages; otherwise, it may not recognize when the time for change has come, or it may act to impose the wrong solution.

Top leaders should be ready to work with the flow of the tide rather than against it; yet they should be cautious, since it is tempting to skip phases out of impatience. Each phase results in certain strengths and learning experiences in the organization that will be essential for success in subsequent phases. A child prodigy, for example, may be able to read like a teenager, but he cannot behave like one until he ages through a sequence of experiences.

I also doubt that managers can or should act to avoid revolutions. Rather, these periods of tension provide the pressure, ideas, and awareness that afford a platform for change and the introduction of new practices.

Recognize the limited range of solutions.

In each revolutionary stage it becomes evident that this stage can be ended only by certain specific solutions; moreover, these solutions are different from those which were applied to the problems of the preceding revolution. Too often it is tempting to choose solutions that were tried before, which makes it impossible for a new phase of growth to evolve.

Management must be prepared to dismantle current structures before the revolutionary stage becomes too turbulent. Top managers, realizing that their own managerial styles are no longer appropriate, may even have to take themselves out of leadership positions. A good Phase 2 manager facing Phase 3 might be wise to find another Phase 2 organization that better fits his talents, either outside the company or with one of its newer subsidiaries.

Finally, evolution is not an automatic affair; it is a contest for survival. To move ahead, companies must consciously introduce planned structure that not only are solutions to a current crisis but also are fitted to the *next* phase of growth. This requires considerable self-awareness on the part of top management, as well as great interpersonal skill in persuading other managers that change is needed.

Realize that solutions breed new problems.

Managers often fail to realize that organizational solutions create problems for the future (i.e., a decision to delegate eventually causes a problem of control). Historical actions are very much determinants of what happens to the company at a much later date.

An awareness of this effect should help managers to evaluate company problems with greater historical understanding instead of

EXHIBIT III
Organization Practices During Evolution in the Five Phases of Growth.

Category	PHASE 1	PHASE 2	PHASE 3	PHASE 4	PHASE 5
MANAGEMENT FOCUS	Make & Sell	Efficiency of operations	Expansion of market	Consolidation of organization	Problem solving & innovation
ORGANIZATION STRUCTURE	Informal	Centralized & functional	Decentralized & geographical	Line-staff & product groups	Matrix of teams
TOP MANAGEMENT STYLE	Individualistic & entrepreneurial	Directive	Delegative	Watchdog	Participative
CONTROL SYSTEM	Market results	Standards & cost centers	Reports & profit centers	Plans & Investment centers	Mutual goal setting
MANAGEMENT REWARD EMPHASIS	Ownership	Salary & merit increases	Individual bonus	Profit sharing & stock options	Team bonus

"pinning the blame" on a current development. Better yet managers should be in a position to *predict* future problems, and thereby to prepare solutions and coping strategies before a revolution gets out of hand.

A management that is aware of the problems ahead could well decide *not* to grow. Top managers may, for instance, prefer to retain the informal practices of a small company, knowing that this way of life is inherent in the organization's limited size, not in their congenial personalities. If they choose to grow, they may do themselves out of a job and a way of life they enjoy.

And what about the managements of very large organizations? Can they find new solutions for continued phases of evolution? Or are they reaching a stage where the government will act to break them up because they are too large?

Implications of Corporate Culture: A Manager's Guide to Action

Vijay Sathe

Corporate culture, which plays a subtle but pervasive role in organizational life, has important implications for managerial action. Consider these examples:

❏ Bob Drake accepted a lucrative, challenging job with a profitable company only to discover, six months later, that he could not operate successfully in a company whose managers shared such a deep faith in the virtues of cutthroat competition. He resigned.

❏ Doug Mills had innovative ideas for growing his business, but these went against the grain of his company's culture of risk-aversion. Doug was frustrated and demotivated, feeling that both he and the company were losing out.

❏ Matt Holt, whose company had been buffeted by shifting market forces, was convinced profitability would improve dramatically if a new shared commitment to technology could be created among the organization's key managers. Two years later, Matt felt he had been unsuccessful in this effort and wasn't sure what he could have done to accomplish his objective.

Although it is now generally agreed that corporate culture has a powerful impact on managers and their organizations, it is not equally clear why this is the case, and what can be done about it. For many people culture remains an elusive and fuzzy concept. Here I will attempt to show how the concept of culture can provide important insights for understanding and dealing appropriately with various managerial situations. Specifically, the following questions,

CONCLUDING NOTE

Clearly, there is still much to learn about processes of development in organizations. The phases outlined here are only five in number and are still only approximations. Researchers are just beginning to study the specific developmental problems of structure, control, rewards, and management style in different industries and in a variety of cultures.

One should not, however, wait for conclusive evidence before educating managers to think and act from a developmental perspective. The critical dimension of time has been missing for too long from our management theories and practices. The intriguing paradox is that by learning more about history we may do a better job in the future.

which will cover both basic concepts and their action implications, will be addressed:

Basic Concepts

1. What is corporate culture?

2. Why does culture have such a subtle but powerful influence on organizational life?

Implications for Action

1. What can be done to better anticipate and more effectively enter a new corporate culture, avoiding problems such as those encountered by Bob Drake?

2. How can one better operate within the existing corporate culture, and successfully deviate from it when necessary, to overcome obstacles such as those faced by Doug Mills?

3. How can managers influence change in the prevailing culture to realize gains such as those hoped for by Matt Holt?

BASIC CONCEPTS

What is culture? Unfortunately, there isn't one unanimously accepted definition. I will not go into all of the ways in which culture has been interpreted (one scholarly study in the field of anthropology, from which the concept derives, has listed 164 definitions), but I will illustrate the principal ways in which culture can be described.

One view of culture, preferred by the "cultural adaptationist" school in anthropology, is based on what is directly observable about the members of a community—that is, their patterns of behavior, speech, and use of material objects. Another view, favored by the "ideational school," looks at what is shared in community members' minds.

FIGURE 1
Framework for Diagnosing Culture.

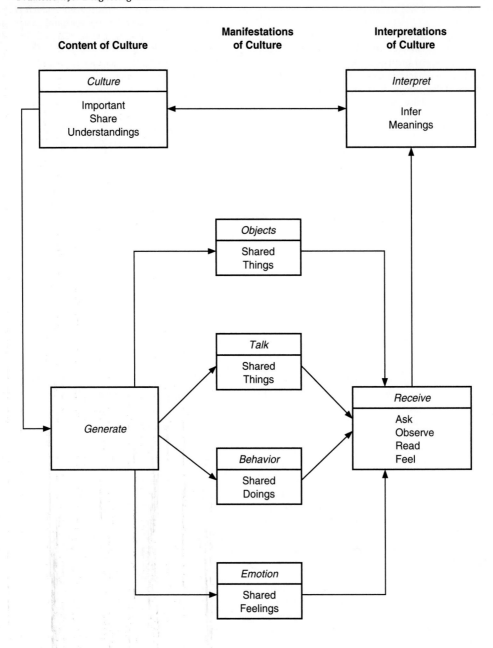

This is one reason the subject is confusing: Different people think of different slices of reality when they talk about culture. It is pointless to argue about which view is correct because, like other concepts, "culture" does not have some true and sacred meaning that is to be discovered. Each view has its place, depending on what one is interested in. I will argue that both perspectives on culture are important for managers, and that both views are interrelated but sufficiently distinct so that it is not analytically advantageous to combine them.

For the purposes of this article, the term *culture* will be used to denote the "ideational view"; the term *behavior* will refer to the "cultural adaptationist" view and both views will be considered simultaneously. Specifically, the following definition of culture will be adopted: *Culture is the set of important understandings (often unstated) that members of a community share in common.*

This definition limits the concept of culture to what is shared in the minds of community members; the phrase "often unstated" in the definition is crucial because members of a culture are frequently unaware of many of these mutual understandings. Thus the advantage of this definition of culture is that it forces us to pay attention to an important organizational reality that is otherwise easily missed because it is "invisible."

Diagnosing Culture

In order to decipher a culture, one cannot simply rely on what people say about it. Other evidence, both historical and current, must be taken into account to infer what the culture is. The example spelled out below illustrates one systematic procedure for doing this. It must be pointed out, however, that reading a culture is an interpretive, subjective activity. There are no exact answers, and two observers may come up with somewhat different descriptions of the same culture. The validity of the diagnosis must be judged by the utility of the insights it provides, not by its "correctness" as determined by some objective criteria.

A diagnostic framework for culture's important shared understandings is presented in Figure 1, and its use is illustrated with information on Company X in Figure 2. Each important shared understanding listed in Figure 2 is inferred from one or more shared things, shared sayings, shared doings, and shared feelings. One may come up with a somewhat different list, but the point is to distill from the "laundry list" of shared things, shared sayings, shared doings, and shared feelings (that is, from the *manifestations* of the culture) a much shorter list of important shared understandings (that is, the culture's content).

Beliefs and Values

In describing culture, we will talk about two principal types of shared understandings: beliefs and values. (A glossary of terms commonly used in discussing culture is provided in the box on page 333.) Beliefs are basic assumptions about the world and how it works. Because many facets of physical and social reality are difficult or impossible to experience personally or to verify, people rely on others they identify with and trust to help them decide what to believe and what not to believe. (One of these, for example, is: "Money is the most powerful motivator"—item 4 in Figure 2.)

FIGURE 2
Inferring Important Shared Understanding from Shared Things,
Shared Sayings, Shared Doings, and Shared Feelings (Company X).

Important Shared Understandings	*Shared Things*
1. Provide highly responsive, quality customer service (SS1, SS2, SD2, SD5).	ST1. Shirt sleeves.
	ST2. One-company town.
	ST3. Open offices.
2. Get things done well and quickly ("expediting") (SS1, SD1, SD4, SD5).	*Shared Sayings*
3. Operate informally (ST1, SS3, SD3, SD6).	SS1. "Get out there" to understand the customer. (Belief in travel)
4. Perceive company as part of the family (ST2, SD6, SF1, SF2, SF3).	SS2. "We cannot rely on systems" to meet customer needs. (Highly responsive customer service)
5. Encourage constructive disagreement (ST3, SD1).	SS3. "We don't stand on rank." (No parking privileges)
	Shared Doings
	SD1. Participate in lots of meetings.
	SD2. Make sure organization is detail-oriented to provide quality customer service.
	SD3. Engage in personal relationships and communications.
	SD4. Rally to meet customer needs in a crisis.
	SD5. Expedite jobs to deliver highly responsive service.
	SD6. Maintain close relationship with union.
	Shared Feelings
	SF1. The company is good to me.
	SF2. We like this place.
	SF3. We care about this company because it cares about us as individuals.

Like beliefs, values are also basic assumptions, but ones with an *ought to* implicit in them. The term *norms* is sometimes used interchangeably with *values,* but there is an important distinction. Although both have an *ought to* implicit in them, norms are more tactical and procedural than are values. Norms are standards of expected behavior, speech, and "presentation of self"—that is, being on time, disagreeing politely, dressing conservatively. Values, on the other hand, represent preferences for more ultimate end states—that is, striving to be no. 1, or avoiding debt at all costs (see items 1, 2, 3, and 5 in Figure 2).

Beliefs and values that have been held for a long time without being violated or challenged may become taken so much for granted that people are no longer aware of them. This is why organizational members frequently fail to realize what a profound influence culture has on them.

Corporate Culture or Cultures?

Although the term "corporate culture" is widely used in management circles, not everyone uses it in the same way. Some use the term to denote the culture of the corporation as a whole. Others use it to refer to the culture of any community within the corporate context. It is in this latter sense that the term will be used here—in other words, a work unit culture, a department culture, a division culture, and so forth. Each is viewed as a corporate culture in the sense that each refers to the culture of an organization within the corporate context. Depending on the circumstances, one or more of these organizational units and their cultures may have to be considered in addressing the problem at hand. For convenience of discussion, the term *culture* will be used here without reference to a particular organizational entity.

Let us now turn to the question of why culture has such a profound influence on organizational life.

Culture's Influence on Behavior

Culture is both an asset and a liability. It is an asset because shared beliefs ease and economize communications, and shared values generate higher levels of cooperation and commitment than is otherwise possible. This is highly efficient.

Efficiency, however, does not imply effectiveness. Efficiency is achieved when something is done with a minimum expenditure of resources (time, money, and so forth). The extent to which the something being done is the appropriate thing to do is a question of effectiveness. If culture guides behavior in inappropriate ways, we have efficiency but not effectiveness. Culture is a liability when the shared beliefs and values are not in keeping with the needs of the organization, its members, and its other constituencies.

To take a closer look at how culture affects behavior, let us examine five basic processes—communication, cooperation, commitment, decision making, and implementation—that lie at the heart of any organization. We will then be able to draw some generalizations about culture's influence on organizational behavior.

Communication

Miscommunication is common in organizations and in everyday life. Even two-person, face-to-face communication is fraught with dangers of misunderstanding the other person's meaning. Communication problems are even more complex when one orga-

nization member tries to communicate with someone in a different organizational unit or location, or when a corporate senior executive tries to reach "the masses."

Although culture does not do away with the basic difficulty, it reduces the dangers of miscommunication in two ways. First, there is no need to communicate items about which shared beliefs and values exist: Certain things go without saying. Second, such sharing provides guidelines and cues to help the receiver interpret messages.

The beliefs and values about what to communicate, and how openly to communicate, are crucial. In some organizations, the culture values open communications ("bad news is bad, but withholding it is worse"). In others, it doesn't. Withholding of information beyond that specifically asked for, secrecy, and outright distortion may prevail.

Cooperation

Assuming that communications are interpreted as intended, the question is: What will ensure that organizational members will act as intended by the communications? The answer seems obvious. Failure to do so could bring sanctions. But this merely begs the question, for it implies that organizational members are motivated to act only according to the "letter of the law," not necessarily in the "spirit of the law." The latter would mean true cooperation. The former could mean worse than no cooperation; it could mean subtle sabotage as illustrated by the "work-to-rule" tactic used by, for example, the air controllers, who have on occasion made their grievances known by following the rules too strictly (that is, more conservatively than demanded by the prevailing situation) to create bottlenecks and slowdowns at airports. The effect of adhering to the literal wording of a contract can be as devastating as an open violation of the contract—if not more so.

The point is that true cooperation cannot be "legislated." Management can resort to carefully worded employment contracts, spell out detailed expectations, and devise clever, complicated incentive schemes to reward just the right behavior. But such procedures, however well-thought-out, cannot anticipate all the contingencies that can conceivably arise. When one of these does, the organization is at the mercy of the employee to act in the "spirit of the law." Interpreting the spirit of the law is a problem of communication. Acting according to the spirit of the law is a question of intent, goodwill, and mutual trust. The degree of true cooperation is influenced by the shared beliefs and values in these areas.

Commitment

People feel a sense of commitment to an organization's objectives when they identify with those objectives and experience some emotional attachment to them. The shared beliefs and values that compose culture help generate such identification and attachment. In making decisions and taking actions, people who feel a sense of commitment automatically evaluate alternatives in terms of their impact on the organization.

Decision Making

Culture affects the decision-making process because shared beliefs and values give organizational members a consistent set of basic assumptions and preferences. This leads to a more efficient decision-making process, because there are fewer disagreements

GLOSSARY OF CULTURAL TERMS

The following terms are commonly used in describing culture. The items in parentheses refer to Company X, whose culture is diagnosed in the text. (See page 331 and Figures 1 and 2). The illustrative items can be found in Figure 2.

Beliefs. These are the basic assumptions concerning the world and how it works (see, for example, item 4).

Values. Like beliefs, values are also basic assumptions, but they have an "ought to" implicit in them (for example, items 1, 2, 3, and 5).

Identity. This includes the understandings that members share concerning who they are and what they stand for as a community (for example, item 4).

Image. This is the community's identity as understood by members of another community.

Attitudes. These are the set of understandings that members of a community share about a specific object or situation (for example, Company X's attitude about working relationships is that informality and confrontation are preferred—that is, items 3 and 5; and the attitude of Company X toward its customers is to do everything possible to provide superb service—that is, item 1).

Climate. This includes the understandings that members share about what it is like to work in the community. Climate surveys report aggregated perceptions on such dimensions as clarity (how well members understand goals and policies), responsibility (degree to which members feel personally responsible for their work), and teamwork (how well members believe they work together).

Pivotal Value. This is the most important corporate value (that is, item 1). All other corporate values "revolve around" the pivotal value.

Norms. These are the standards of expected behavior, speech, and "presentation of self" (for example, those items from the list of shared things, shared sayings, shared doings, and shared feelings in Figure 2 that imply such standards). Note the distinction between norms and values. Although both have an "ought to" implicit in them, norms are more tactical and procedural than are values.

Ideology. This is the dominant set of interrelated ideas that explain to members of a community why the important understandings they share "make sense." An ideology gives meaning to the content of a culture (for example, for Company X the ideology is: "Expediting behavior is valued because we believe it is critical to our competitive edge of highly responsive, quality customer service. Further, informal operation and constructive disagreement are encouraged because we believe these behaviors help bring about such service.")

---

about which premises should prevail. This does not mean that there is necessarily less overall conflict in a stronger culture than in a weaker one. That would depend on the shared beliefs and values about the role of conflict in organizational life. Where constructive dissent is a shared value, for instance, there would be greater conflict than where this is not a shared value—all other things being equal. All that is implied is that there are fewer areas of disagreement in a stronger culture because of the greater sharing of beliefs and values, and that this is efficient.

As pointed out earlier, however, efficiency does not imply effectiveness. If the shared beliefs and values are not in keeping with the needs of business, the organization, and its members, dysfunctional consequences will result.

Implementation

One of the difficulties commonly encountered when implementing organizational policy and decisions is this: What should be done when unforeseen difficulties arise? There are times when immediate action is called for in a more or less ambiguous situation where it is not possible to check with others concerning the appropriate response. Under these conditions, culture is a compass that helps point people in the right direction. Consider this situation:

> An important overseas customer was demanding immediate help from the company's local contact in connection with certain reciprocal arrangements involving a third party that did business with both the company and this customer. Such arrangements were not tolerated by the company. Despite the importance of the account, and the company's emphasis on customer service, the company's local contact declined this "urgent request."

In this case, two company values were in conflict: customer service and ethical sales practices. Although the customer was important, ethical corporate behavior was the company's pivotal value. ("Use every honorable means to satisfy the customer.") Culture provides such "guiding principles" that employees can rely on when close calls are to be made without consultation.

Strength of Culture

As we have seen, culture has a powerful influence on organizational behavior because the shared beliefs and values represent basic assumptions and preferences that guide such behavior. Further, the influence is subtle because many of these underlying premises have a taken-for-granted quality and tend to remain outside people's awareness. Thus the irony of culture (and the reason it can be so treacherous) is that, like the air people breathe, its powerful effects normally escape the attention of those it most affects.

However, not all cultures have an equally strong influence on behavior. The following conditions make a difference. First, cultures with more shared beliefs and values have a stronger influence on behavior because there are more basic assumptions guiding behavior. IBM, for example, has a "thick" culture with several deeply held beliefs and values (for example: respect for the individual, encouragement of constructive rebellion, an emphasis on doing what is right). "Thin" cultures have few such shared assumption, and thus a weaker influence on organizational life. Second, cultures whose beliefs and values are more widely shared have a more pervasive impact because a larger number of people are guided by them. At IBM, the values mentioned are very widely shared.

Finally, cultures whose beliefs and values are more clearly ordered (that is, where the relative importance of the various basic assumptions are well known) have a more profound effect on behavior because there is less ambiguity about which beliefs and values prevail when there is a conflict. IBMers know the pivotal importance of the values mentioned. Thicker, more widely shared, and more ordered cultures have a more profound influence on organizational behavior, and are therefore referred to as "stronger" cultures.

Why are some cultures stronger than others? The number of employees in the organization and their geographical dispersion are two important factors that make a difference. All other things being equal, smaller operations that are more localized facilitate the growth of a stronger culture because it is easier for shared beliefs and values to become widely shared. But larger organizations with worldwide operations can also have a strong culture, as IBM has, if there has been a continuity of strong leadership that has emphasized the same beliefs and values, and a relatively stable and long-tenured workforce. Under these conditions, there is time for a consistent set of beliefs and values to take hold and become widely shared and more clearly ordered.

To return to the illustration in Figure 2, Company X has several important beliefs and values that are widely shared and fairly well ordered. The pivotal value of highly responsive, quality customer service (item 1 in Figure 2) is tied directly to the value placed on expediting and informality (items 2 and 3), which in turn are supported by the belief in a family spirit (item 4). The value of constructive disagreement (item 5) is not as directly interconnected with the others. Thus Company X has a fairly strong culture because it has several widely shared and rather well-ordered beliefs and values.

Why does Company X have such a strong culture? History, leadership, organizational size, and the stability of its membership all have had an impact. Company X is a medium-size firm with low employee turnover. In its 60-year history, there have been only two generations of top management; the former chief executive officer and the former chief operating officer continue to serve as chairman of the board and chairman of the executive committee, respectively.

What we say about culture thus needs to be moderated by its strength. Stronger cultures produce more powerful effects than weaker cultures do. For convenience, I will not refer to this qualification during the rest of this discussion, but it is an important facet of culture to keep in mind.

IMPLICATIONS FOR ACTION

How does the view of culture developed here help managers deal more effectively with problems of the type mentioned at the beginning of this article? Let us begin with problems associated with entry into a new culture, which is typically accompanied by one or more surprises, rude awakenings, or painful revelations.

Culture Shock

Consider the following vignette from Bob Drake's experience:

The first unpleasant surprise for Bob came on his third day with the company when he heard two senior colleagues arguing "in public," cursing and shouting at each other. Within the next few weeks he realized this wasn't aberrant behavior in the company. He was also struck by the very long hours, the few group meetings, and the unusually high amount of rumor and gossip. Bob had previously worked for a company where more polite public behavior, shorter hours, more "team play," and more openness prevailed. He was disturbed, but reasoned: "It's too bad they operate this way, but I can live with that without becoming a part of it." The next shock was of higher voltage. After about two months with the company, Bob was called into his boss's office and told he was not being "tough enough." To "really contribute in this environment," he was told, he would have to "be more aggressive." Bob was upset, but tried to keep his cool. For one who prided himself on his managerial competence, the last thing he felt he needed was "advice on management style."

Bob decided he would redouble his efforts "to show these people what I can contribute." A large part of Bob's job involved dealings with peers in another department, and he decided to communicate his willingness and ability to contribute by putting in hours with them, and going out of his way to help them. What Bob experienced, however, was fierce internal competition, with such tactics as "memo battles," information withholding, and "end running" apparently condoned; appeals to various parties were of no avail. At the six months' performance review Bob's boss told him that he had failed to learn from the feedback given earlier. This was open competition, he was told, and he was not measuring up. Bob got an unsatisfactory rating and was given the option to resign. He did.

Such entry experiences are certainly not uncommon. What can the new manager do to handle these situations better? Presented first are some suggestions for one's recruitment phase, followed by guidelines for the period just after entry—during one's "liability of newness," to borrow a phrase that refers to a similarly treacherous period faced by new businesses.

Before making the decision to join, it is important to try to determine whether there are irreconcilable mismatches between the prospective corporate culture and one's personal beliefs and values. Needed are self-insight and culture-foresight. Constructive introspection and a willingness to learn from one's experience can facilitate the former; regarding the latter, it is best to anticipate that culture cannot be *fully* anticipated. However, everything that can be done should be done to explore major misfits before accepting a company's offer. It helps to approach encounters with the prospective culture in a spirit of adventure, with an inquisitive rather than an evaluative attitude, and to look and listen for underlying meanings. The common human tendency to rationalize, to inadequately test one's assumptions, and to confuse hopes with expectations must be avoided to the extent possible.

Bob Drake, for instance, might have profited by pursuing several early clues. Phrases such as these were used by company executives recruiting him: "We need people like you." "We play to win." "This is a rough place, but a fun place." "You will have to fight here to get your points across." Bob might have thought about, and perhaps asked: "Why *me*?" and "Whom are you playing *against*?" Given his background as a former star college basketball player, Bob thought that *team* play and a winning *team* were being alluded to. Apparently what was being communicated, however, was the importance of *internal individual* competition. Other probing by Bob might have included: "Why is it a *rough* place?" and "What do you mean you have to *fight* to get your point across?"

Whatever the assessment before entry, one or more culture shocks of greater or lesser intensity are typically experienced after joining any organization. To turn these episodes to one's advantage, they are best viewed as painful but timely invitations to learn the new culture, for they indicate that the novice has not as yet understood it. Bob reacted to these shocks with increased determination to overcome the hurdles encountered. Had equal attention been paid to their underlying significance, he might have realized that he had not really understood the ordering of two cultural values. While cooperation prevailed over competition where he had worked previously, it was just the reverse in his current company. Having grasped this, Bob might have been able to take appropriate action.

One might also look upon these early surprises, however unpleasant, as opportunities to better understand oneself. Like body fever, they are symptoms that all is not well and that additional investigation is needed. The self-insight that may result could spur personal growth. For instance, consideration of the following questions about one's perceived misfit with the prevailing culture may be appropriate: Am I resisting the culture because of implied new behaviors and skills that I'm afraid I won't be able to learn? Or is it that I'm afraid I won't be able to learn? Or is it that the beliefs and values embodied in the culture are basically incompatible with my own?

As the foregoing indicates, it is important to avoid irreconcilable mismatches, but it is usually neither possible nor necessarily desirable in the long run for either the individual or the organization to try to avoid culture/person misfits altogether. What is needed, therefore, is a way of thinking about them so as to facilitate both individual and organizational development. Such an approach is presented here.

Deviating from Culture

Figure 3, which is based on the distinction between culture and behavior emphasized earlier, derives from the fact that cultural beliefs and values are seldom completely shared—that is, not everyone believes and behaves as prescribed by the culture. The scheme can be viewed from either the individual or the organizational perspective, and the following questions are asked. First, to what extent does the individual behave as prescribed by the culture? The answer could range from "a great deal" (that is, behavior conformity) to "not at all" (that is, behavior nonconformity). Second, to what extent does the individual hold the beliefs and values of the culture? The answer could similarly vary from culture conformity to culture nonconformity. The answers to these two questions place an individual somewhere on the culture-prescribed behavior space shown in Figure 3. The four corners of the space are labeled *maverick, good soldier, adapter,* and *rebel*. These culture caricatures are intended to be memory and discussion aids for use in analysis; one should not fall into the trap of stereotyping flesh-and-blood people with these terms.

It is possible for one to be a misfit on the prescribed behavior dimension as well as on the culture dimension. However, such nonconformity requires sensitivity to resulting pressures, and the willingness and ability to overcome them. In general, the greater the distance from the "good soldier" corner, the greater the imagination, determination, and marshalling of personal and organizational resources needed to be effective.

Doug Mill's problems in the second vignette opening this article may now be more clearly understood. He had bought into most of the company's basic beliefs and values: business professionalism, social responsibility, and respect for the individual. One that he had not bought was risk-aversion. Since Doug was a near conformist on the prescribed behavior dimension, this placed him somewhere between good soldier and adapter in Figure 3. What he needed to do, if he wanted to implement the courage of his convictions, was to "go East" on this map.

Two basic strategies are available to successfully deviate from culture in this way: cultural insurance and self-insurance. The first calls for the support of powerful others—particularly those close to the good soldier corner. This spreads the risk of nonconformity among the culture's old faithful. It works because behavior deviance by culture conformists is more tolerated than is such nonconformity by others.

The second strategy—self-insurance—is to deviate from culture on the basis of one's own track record, personal power, and credibility within the system. Here one must cash in on one's existing resources and credit. Effective continued use of this strategy requires that one continue to replenish the pile of "chits" from which one draws each time one deviates. If this is done successfully over a period of time, one can acquire the reputation of "a nonconformist who gets away with murder around here"—an image that can enhance one's ability to buck the culture.

Culture Change vs. Behavior Change

Let us now turn to the question of culture change by taking a closer look at the problems faced by Matt Holt in the third vignette at the beginning of this article.

Buffeted by shifting market forces and management turnover, the corporate business strategy had lacked coher-

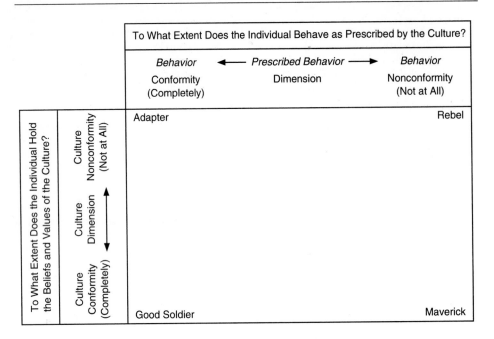

ent direction. Matt Holt's mandate was to take a longer-term view of the business and to create a technology-driven organization. Analysis conducted with the help of outside consultants indicated that a "cultural metamorphosis" was needed to accomplish this. A reorganization followed, including changes in the measurement and reward system to "encourage the required behavior."

Matt realized there would be a "wait-and-see" period while people tried to figure out "whether they really mean it." He knew that his "true intentions" would be judged on the basis of what he did, not just what he said. Accordingly, he tried to ensure that the management systems inspected and rewarded the required behavior, and he conducted his own affairs (that is, use of his time, visits, "pats on the back") to reinforce and support what the new formal systems were signalling.

Two years later, there had been some improvements. People appeared to be "doing the right things," allocating their time and resources as prescribed by the new systems. Missing, however, was the "missionary zeal"—the sense of excitement and commitment—that Matt had hoped to inject into the life of the company as people came to identify with and share his vision of the mission.

What happened here? This change was more carefully orchestrated than most. Particularly impressive was Matt's sensitivity to "By your actions shall ye be judged," and his resolve to "put his money where his mouth was." Put simply, the problem was that the important distinction between culture change and behavior change had not been recognized and addressed. The "cultural metamorphosis" was directed at changes in people's behavior patterns, and failed to pay

attention to their shared beliefs and values—that is, culture as defined in this article. Had this been done, results might have been different.

I am not arguing that managers should always strive to create culture change. There are times when only behavior change is appropriate or is all that is possible—for instance, when culture change would take too long or when only a temporary change in behavior is required to cope with a transient situation. However, be aware that behavior change without culture change requires constant monitoring of behavior to ensure compliance and the continued use of rewards and punishments to sustain it. Without such constant "payoff," the new behavior dies out. This is not the case, however, when behavior change is accompanied by culture change. Although more difficult to accomplish, such change is also more enduring because it is self-sustaining.

What I am saying, then, is that managers should assess what kind of change is needed and ensure that the methods they use are appropriate to the task. In the case just mentioned, Matt Holt was trying to inject a "missionary zeal" into the organization. This clearly required a change in shared beliefs and values—that is, a cultural change, not just the behavior change that his methods were directed at. Before turning to the question of how this can be done, let us pause to ask an important question that managers engaged in culture change will sooner or later confront.

Ethics of Culture Change

Do managers have any business trying to change people's beliefs and values? The following points may be made in addressing this issue. First, questions about changing people's beliefs and values are laden with emotion because they connote "brainwashing." Especially in the United States, born of the quest for religious and political freedom, any hint of this raises eyebrows as well as adrenalin levels. Second, such questions are personally threatening because a lot is at stake for the individual. One's beliefs and values are not a random assembly; changes in one or more of them require changes in related others. Such reorganization is painful and frequently resisted because the learning of new skills and behaviors is implied.

Finally, it is important to note that we are talking here about organization-related beliefs and values, not such private beliefs and values as religious or political ones. The problem is that the two sets are interrelated. Changes in one set most likely affect the other; more theoretical and empirical work is needed to better understand the interrelationship between people's organization-related beliefs and values and their private ones.

Despite these reservations, most people I have talked to have argued that, just as it is in the nature of the manager's job to influence organizational behavior in a responsible and professional manner, so it is his or her job to conscientiously shape organizational beliefs and values in the appropriate direction. I tend to agree and would now like to show how this can be done.

INFLUENCING CULTURE CHANGE

Managers interested in producing culture change must understand and intervene in each of the basic processes that cause culture to perpetuate itself (Figure 4). Let us consider each of them in turn.

Behavior

The process by which culture influences behavior was described earlier in this article, and it is consistent with the conventional wisdom—that is, that beliefs and values influence behavior. However, the opposite is also true. A considerable body of social science literature indicates that, under certain conditions to be discussed shortly, one of the most effective ways of changing people's beliefs and values is to first change their behavior. (The techniques for creating behavior change—Process 1, Figure 4—are well covered in the existing management literature and will not be dealt with here.)

Justifications of Behavior

Behavior change does not necessarily produce culture change, because of the intervening process of justification (Process 2, Figure 4). This is what happened in the case of Matt Holt. People were behaving as called for by the new formal systems, but they continued to share the old beliefs and values in common and "explained" their behavior to themselves by noting the external justifications for it—for example, "We are doing it because it is required of us." "We are doing it because of the incentives." There was behavior compliance, not culture commitment. In a very real sense, people in this case were behaving the way they were because they felt they had no real choice, not because they fundamentally believed in it or valued it.

FIGURE 4
How Culture Perpetuates Itself.

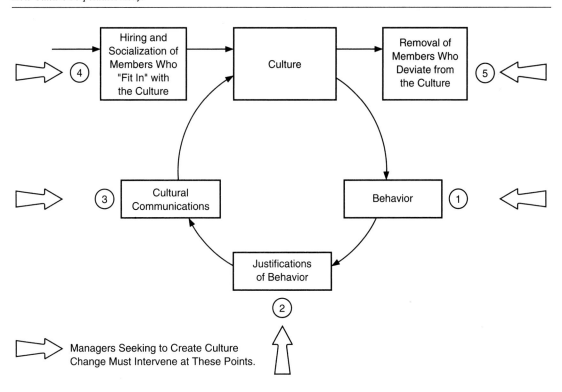

Thus managers seeking to produce culture change must work on two related fronts simultaneously. First, they must remove external justifications for the new behavior. This means, essentially, that they cannot place too great an emphasis on financial incentives and other extrinsic forms of motivation, but must rely instead on more intrinsic forms to motivate the new behavior—that is, getting people to see the inherent worth of what it is they are being asked to do. A combination of gentle incentives to engage in the new behavior and compelling persuasion is what is needed. Second, and closely related, managers engaged in culture change must communicate the new beliefs and values and get people to adopt them. Because both of these endeavors entail communications, let us now turn to this process.

Cultural Communications

Culture is communicated via both explicit and implicit forms (Process 3, Figure 4). The former include announcements, pronouncements, memos, and other explicit communications. The latter include rituals, ceremonies, stories, metaphors, heroes, logos, decor, dress, and other symbolic forms of communication. Both explicit and implicit communications must be relied on to nullify external justifications for the new behavior and persuade people to adopt new cultural beliefs and values.

If the new beliefs and values being communicated are already intrinsically appealing to the audience, the main problem is the communicator's credibility, as in much political campaign rhetoric ("I like what I am hearing, but is this what the communicator really believes?"). How can communications be made more credible? Given their nature, explicit communications about beliefs and values—"We believe people are our most important asset"—are likely to fall on deaf ears, or to be received as corporate propaganda, unless they are made credible by consistent action. Interestingly, research shows that communications are not only more memorable but also more believable—that is, credible—if more implicit forms are used, such as the telling of stories and anecdotes from company history or individual experience to make a point.

As one example, consider the ways in which T. J. Watson, Jr., tried to mold the IBM culture when he took over its leadership from his father. A case in point is his attempt to instill in the organization the virtues of constructive rebellion. One way in which he tried to do this was directly stating it as an important value in his speeches to company employees: "I just wish somebody would stick his head in my office and say (to me) 'you're wrong.' I would really like to hear that. I don't want yes-men around me." Reportedly, such pronouncements were met with skepticism, and as mere corporate propaganda, by many employees.

Much more credible were Watson's attempts to communicate this value by telling a variety of stories, including this one:

Early in 1961, in talking to our sales force, I attempted to size up the then new Kennedy Administration as I saw it. It was not a political talk. I urged no views on them. It was an optimistic assessment, nothing more. But at the close of the meeting, a number of salesmen came up front. They would listen to what I had to say about business, they said, but they didn't want to hear about the new Administration in a company meeting.

On my return to New York, I found a few letters in the same vein. Lay off, they seemed to say, you're stepping on our toes in something that's none of your business.

At first I was a bit annoyed at having been misunderstood. But when I thought about it, I was pleased, for they had made it quite clear they were no man's collar and they weren't at all hesitant to tell me so. From what I have read of organization men, that is not the way they are supposed to act.

Why are stories more credible? Essentially, it is their concreteness, as well as the fact that the moral of the story is not explicitly stated. Because the listener draws his or her own conclusions, he or she is more likely to believe them. The problem with such communications is that the moral inferred may be different from the one intended; however, for some stories the moral is less open to "misinterpretation."

What if the new beliefs and values being communicated are *not* intrinsically appealing to the audience? In this case, credible communications about the new beliefs and values result in their being believed to be true intentions rather than mere corporate propaganda (for example, "I think management is really serious about this."), but this doesn't mean the new values have been accepted as the audience's own. Without such acceptance the audience is aware of the important beliefs and values that are being communicated, but they don't internalize and share them.

If new beliefs and values are to be internalized and shared, communications about them must be not only emphatic and credible, but persuasive as well. Such "culture persuasion" cannot rely on statistics and other "facts" alone, for beliefs and values are not necessarily accepted and internalized on the basis of "hard evidence." Research and common observation indicate that it is no easy matter to get people to change their beliefs and values. When this key point is overlooked, and persuasion is based on a pile of facts alone, results are often disappointing. There are two basic approaches to effective culture persuasion: identification and "Try it, you'll like it."

Identification. This approach relies on the audience's identification with one or more persons who credibly communicate their attachment or conversion to the specific beliefs and values in question. Such a person could be the manager directing the culture change, or it could be anyone else whom the audience not only believes, but identifies with. Here is one example:

In a company with a long tradition of authoritarian management, a new CEO with a strong belief in participative management was having a great deal of difficulty getting managers to do more than "go through the motions." One of the senior executives from "the old school," who was widely respected and admired as a company "folk hero" who would never say or do anything he didn't really believe in, then began to come around. As word of his "conversion" spread informally, others began to change their beliefs. It got to the point that this "idol's" department became a model of the intended culture. The beliefs in participative management began to "seep" to the rest of the company and gradually became more widely shared.

Try It, You'll Like It. The following account of how this "folk hero" came to change his belief in participatory management in the first place indicates the second approach to effective culture persuasion:

He began to try the approach being advocated because he was a company loyalist who had an even stronger value: "I owe the new boss a fair shake." He was skeptical at first but then came a few fairly dramatic changes having to do with the improved morale of certain valued but difficult employees, changes that he attributed to the "new philosophy." Gradually, he changed his mind about the participative management. Advocacy followed, and eventually he became a "culture champion."

If people can be persuaded to "give it a fair chance," and they like the experience that they attribute to it, the new beliefs and values may become accepted and eventually internalized. As mentioned previously, such persuasion to try the new behavior must be based on gentle incentives—that is, it must not rely too heavily on financial and other extrinsic forms of motivation if it is to be effective at producing culture change. Otherwise the incentive will serve as external justification for the new behavior and will produce no changes in the prevailing beliefs and values. Both appeals and challenges can be tools in effective persuasion.

In the case just cited, the "folk hero" decided to "give it a try" because the appeal was to his higher value ("I owe the new boss a fair shake."). A more general form of this appeal is one that asks people to "give it a try" in more tentative, exploratory, and relatively nonthreatening ways. Another general form of appeal is one that draws on dormant beliefs and values that are part of the heritage of the people in question, but not part of their current tradition. For instance, this is one of the things AT&T management is currently doing to try to create a more marketing-driven organization. The appeal to engage in the new way of doing things is based on references to the company's heritage—for example, "This isn't new for us, we have done this before." In effect, the activation of dormant beliefs and values "gently induces" people and gives them the confidence "to give it a try."

Another way to get people to try the new behavior without heavy reliance on incentives is to challenge them to do so.

Hiring and Socializing Newcomers and Removing Deviants

A final set of processes that are important to consider if culture change is being attempted is (1) the hiring and socialization of newcomers to fit into the intended culture and (2) the "weeding out" and removal of existing members who do not (Processes 4 and 5, Figure 4).

First, as pointed out earlier, a "perfect" culture/person fit is not usually possible, or even desirable, as we shall presently see. However, it is important to avoid irreconcilable mismatches between the person being hired and the intended culture. Both the individual and the organization bear responsibility for ensuring this; suggestions from the individual's standpoint were made previously when discussing culture shock. From the organization's standpoint, one danger to guard against is the common human tendency to place undue emphasis on surface manifestations—such as dress, physical appearance, and background characteristics—in inferring another's beliefs and values. This can seriously undermine a reasoned determination based on all the evidence available.

Second, careful attention must be paid to the socialization process: how new members learn and are taught, the important corporate realities, including culture. It may be added that informal socialization is more effective than formal socialization programs perhaps because the spontaneity with which the latter takes place bestows on it somewhat greater credibility. Socialization does not end with the newcomer's having survived culture shock and the "liability of newness." It continues as members become more aware of the full scope of the culture and feel progressively more committed to it. Mentors play an important role in this continuing socialization.

Cultural Blindspots

Although it is difficult to make and usually takes longer to accomplish than behavior change, culture change can be made. Unfortunately, however, the need for such change often goes unrecognized—until it is too late. It typically takes new leadership to see the extent to which culture has become a liability, and the need to change it.

One way in which enlightened managers can avoid being blindsided by culture is to accommodate a certain degree of nonconformity in their organizations, especially in the case of individuals whose exceptional talents make them invaluable. People who believe and behave differently are difficult to deal with and retain, but they help keep others "honest" by demonstrating alternate ways of thinking and acting. Although this may cause some loss of cultural efficiency, it is an insurance against culture's becoming so firmly entrenched that people can no longer see its blindspots. Some important questions that organizational leaders must therefore ask are: What does the distribution of our membership look like on the culture-prescribed behavior space shown in Figure 3? Is it what it should be in light of our situation? How many people do we have close to the maverick, good soldier, adapter, and rebel corners? Are we losing capable and talented people who are close to one or more of these corners? Why?

Another way in which managers can help prevent a dysfunctional culture from perpetuating itself unheeded is to deviate from it themselves when necessary. How to do so was discussed earlier.

CONCLUSION

While its importance is generally accepted, culture remains an elusive and fuzzy concept for many people. I have tried to show how the approach to understanding culture developed here provides important insights for dealing with various managerial situations.

First, it is possible to see more clearly why culture has such a profound influence on organizational life. Shared beliefs and values represent important common assumptions that guide organizational thinking and action. Further, the influence is subtle, because people are not typically aware of their basic beliefs and values until those beliefs and values are violated or challenged.

Second, the distinction between culture nonconformity and behavior nonconformity can be examined and taken into account in entering and deviating from culture (Figure 3). Third, the dynamics in Figure 4 explain why culture's efficiency and durability are both an asset and a liability. The challenge for leaders is to harness culture's benefits while remaining alert to the dangers of perpetuating a culture that is out of tune with the needs of the business, the organization, and its members. Enlightened leadership can avoid cultural blindspots by accommodating selective nonconformity in their organizations, and by themselves deviating from culture when the situation calls for it.

Finally, the critical difference between culture change and behavior change can be recognized and addressed. It is possible to see why behavior change does not necessarily produce culture change and to determine what is needed to influence culture change, if this is deemed appropriate.

In sum, the approaches to understanding, entering, deviating from, and changing culture presented here can help enhance both organizational efficiency and organizational effectiveness.

SELECTED BIBLIOGRAPHY

A comprehensive review of the concept of culture, including 164 definitions, is contained in A. L. Kroeber and Clyde Kluckhohn's *Culture: A Critical Review of Concepts and Definitions* (Vintage Books, 1952).

The definition adopted in this article belongs to the "ideational" school, which views culture as a system of shared ideas, knowledge, and meanings. The rival school, the "cultural adaptationists," views culture as a system of socially transmitted behavior patterns that serve to relate human communities to their ecological settings. See Roger M. Keesing's "Theories of Culture" in *Annual Review of Anthropology* (1974).

Clifford Geertz's *The Interpretation of Cultures* (Basic Books, 1973) suggests that broad, all-encompassing definitions of culture, such as E. B. Taylor's original one that includes "knowledge, belief, art, law, morals, custom, and other capabilities and habits," obscure a good deal more than they reveal. Geertz argues that a narrower, more specialized definition is theoretically more powerful, a view that is consistent with the approach taken in this article.

The analytical benefits gained by separating culture from behavior are cogently articulated by Marc Swartz and David Jordan's *Culture: An Anthropological Perspective* (John Wiley, 1980).

The definitions of beliefs and values follow Milton Rokeach's *Beliefs, Attitudes, and Values* (Jossey-Bass, 1968) and Daryl J. Bem's *Beliefs, Attitudes, and Human Affairs* (Brooks/Cole, 1970). The definitions of identity and image in the glossary of cultural terms follow Renato Tagiuri's "Managing Corporate Identity: The Role of Top Management" (Harvard Business School Working Paper 82-68, March 1982) and the definition of ideology is consistent with George C. Lodge's *The New American Ideology* (Alfred A. Knopf, 1980).

An insightful analysis of culture shock and the socialization process is provided by Edgar H. Schein's "Organizational Socialization and the Profession of Management" (*Industrial Management Review,* Winter 1968). His *Career Dynamics* (Addison-Wesley, 1978) contains additional valuable information on this topic. John Van Maanen's "Breaking In: Socialization to Work" in Robert Dubin's (ed.) *Handbook of Work, Organization, and Society* (Rand McNally, 1976) is an excellent comprehensive review of the literature on entry into a new organization. See also Meryl Louis's "Surprise and Sense Making: What Newcomers Experience in Entering Unfamiliar Organizational Settings" (*Administrative Science Quarterly,* June 1980).

On culture/person misfits and the notion that some degree of misfit can ultimately benefit both the individual and the organization see Chris Argyris's *Personality and Organization* (Harper, 1957), and Edgar H. Schein's "Organizational Socialization and the Profession of Management," cited above.

Research linking type of communication with its perceived credibility is reported in Joanne Martin's "Stories and Scripts in Organizational Settings," in A. Hastorf and A. Isen's (eds.) *Cognitive Social Psychology* (Elsevier-North Holland Publishing Co., 1982). An early account which demonstrates that beliefs and values may continue to be held despite disconforming evidence is the classic study of a group of "doomsday prophets" by Leon Festinger, H. W. Riecken, and S. Shacter, *When Prophecy Fails* (The University of Minnesota Press, 1956). If people can point to external justifications for new behavior, changes in attitudes, beliefs, and values may not necessarily follow. See Daryl J. Bem's *Beliefs, Attitudes, and Human Affairs,* cited above, and Elliot Aronson's *The Social Animal,* Third Edition (W. H. Freeman, 1980).

The IBM stories in this article and their general analysis are from Joanne Martin and Melanie E. Powers's "Truth on Corporate Propaganda: The Value of a Good War Story," in L. Pondy, P. Frost, G. Morgan, and T. Dandridge, (eds.) *Organizational Symbolism* (JAI Press, 1983). The actual quotes are from R. Malik, *And tomorrow . . . the world? Inside IBM* (Mullington HD, 1975), and T. J. Watson, Jr.'s *A Business and Its Beliefs: The Ideas That Helped Build IBM* (McGraw-Hill, 1963).

Three excellent sources on the topic of organizational change are John P. Kotter and Leonard A. Schlesinger's "Choosing Strategies for Change" (*Harvard Business Review,* March-April 1979), Michael Beer's *Organization Change and Development* (Goodyear Publishing Co., 1980), and Edgar H. Schein's *Organizational Psychology* (Prentice-Hall, 1965, Third Edition, 1980).

ACKNOWLEDGMENT

The author wishes to thank Mark Rhodes, doctoral candidate in psychology and social relations at Harvard University, for suggesting the addition of "shared feelings" to the diagnostic framework in Figure 1.

Exercise: Small Business Design:
The Case of a Start-up Publishing Firm

PURPOSE

The purpose of this exercise is to provide you with the experience of designing a new organization. By the time you complete this exercise you will

1. Identify the differences between the product, functional, geographic, and matrix forms of organization

2. Determine an appropriate design for an emergent organization

3. Design job descriptions for the new functions in this organization

INTRODUCTION

The topic of organizational design is very complex, entailing many variables. The appropriate form of organization will depend on the size of the company, its environment, its product or services, its technological demands, its requirements for integration and differentiation, and its stage of growth.

Each of the *pure* forms of organzational design has its own advantages and disadvantages. Some of the pure forms (such as the product form of organization) enhance interdepartmental coordination but create redundancies and duplication of efforts. Others (such as the functional design) maintain efficiency but focus upon short rather than long-term horizons for product development. As indicated in the article by Duncan, the organizational environment and rate of change is another key factor that must be considered in determining organizational designs.

In this exercise you will have an opportunity to test these considerations while designing a new organization. In addition, you will also be developing job descriptions for the primary functions of the company.

INSTRUCTIONS

1. Read the readings in the chapter.

2. Read the case material on the Job-Getter Enterprise.

3. In small groups of four to six people, design an organizational structure for the Job-Getter Enterprise.

4. Draw an organizational chart depicting the reporting relationships of key players and departments.

5. Write job descriptions for the key positions in the Job-Getter Enterprise.

This exercise was developed by Lisa A. Mainiero. All names in the case are fictitious. This case was prepared as a basis for class discussion rather than to illustrate effective or ineffective approaches to management.

6. Choose a spokesperson from your group who will present your organizational design to the class.

7. Participate in a class discussion.

The Job-Getter Enterprise

The Job-Getter Enterprise is a start-up publishing firm. The publication produced by the firm, the "JOB GETTER," is a weekly magazine that publishes listings of available jobs in the area. The magazine is sold in local convenience stores, campus bookstores, and through vending machine newsracks, and it is distributed throughout northern California.

The business has been operating for three years and shows great promise. But the firm has yet to generate a regular profit. The founder, Martin Manicot, is convinced that his firm has grown to the point where he needs some help in redesigning his firm. He has asked you to serve as a team of consultants to help him redesign his organization. Here are some of the issues he wants you to consider.

THE ISSUES

Three key issues plague this entrepreneurial start-up:

1. Obtaining a variety of timely job listings is difficult. Job listings are advertised jobs that appear in the publication. If job listings are not timely, repeat sales for the magazine decline. Customers are unwilling to purchase the publication unless the job listings meet their needs, are timely, and are local.

2. Circulation and distribution remain a problem. Local distributors are not willing to carry an untested publication on their newsracks. Circulation has been low because the number of locations in which the new publication was sold were few. This is a problem because circulation is traditionally a key factor in attracting advertising for the publication.

3. The success of the publication depends on the number of advertisements sold. Full- and half-page advertisements account for the bulk of revenue. Advertisers include companies such as the local retail stores, employment placement agencies, food service firms, manufacturing firms, and others who have continuous needs for employment. However, advertisers are reluctant to purchase advertising space unless circulation is sufficiently widespread.

4. Turnover of sales personnel plagues the business. Manicot has continually hired salespeople to sell advertising space; once they realize the task is difficult, they leave for other jobs posted in the magazine. He has hired a number of college students part-time as salespeople; the continual drain of personnel out the door has taken considerable time away from Manicot's other duties as he spends most of his time training new salespeople and less of his time on increasing circulation.

It is the task of the new publication to identify and publish timely job listings, while simultaneously increasing circulation and distribution to attract competitive advertising space.

THE DEPARTMENTS AND FUNCTIONS

The key functions of the new enterprise are summarized as follows:

1. *Sales:* Selling job listings and advertising space

2. *Circulation and distribution:* Making the publication available in as many locations as possible; picking up and delivering the publication on a weekly basis

3. *Production:* Putting together the weekly job listings, advertising space, formatting and proofreading, and printing the magazines.

Sales encompasses two categories: (1) job listings, listed for free in the publication, and (2) advertising space, for companies who wish to advertise particular positions or continual employment needs. Job listings are gathered by telemarketing (calling local companies to determine if they want to list a job opening). Advertising space is sold through telemarketing and on-site sales visits. Typically, a company is contacted to determine if they would like to list available jobs for free. After the company receives a response from the publication (for example, twenty applicants say they saw the job listed in the magazine), that company is approached to see if they might like to purchase advertising space.

Circulation and distribution involve making the publication as widely available as possible. Currently approximately 700 outlets carry the magazine; there is potential for as many as 1,500 outlets or more. Owners of local convenience stores, college bookstores, grocery stores, and other likely locations must be visited regularly to obtain permission to distribute the magazine. Store owners receive a small percentage (10 percent) of every issue sold as an incentive. In addition, the publication is distributed through newsracks in urban areas. The magazine must be picked up and delivered to all these locations on a weekly basis so that timely information is distributed.

Production involves printing the magazine—typing the job listings, designing advertisements, and proofreading each issue. The issue is compiled by use of a graphics computer and then sent to a local print shop for presswork and binding.

THE JOBS AND THE PEOPLE

Currently seven people are employed in sales jobs. Salespeople have been hired on a part-time basis, with only the sales manager, Jennifer, and one other salesperson hired full-time. Full-time salespeople concentrate on on-site visitations for advertising sales; they are paid part salary ($100 per week) and part commission (25 percent of the advertising space sold). Part-time salespeople concentrate primarily on telemarketing sales; they are paid minimum wage on an hourly basis ($4.25 an hour) and receive a 10 percent commission. One employee, Greg, serves as the circulation manager. He is responsible for increasing circulation by improving the number of outlets that carry the publication. The circulation manager is a salaried position, paid $325 per week with no commission. Another employee has been hired on a full-time basis to supervise the drivers who distribute and pick up the publication. This individual is paid a single sum for the distribution and collection of each issue during the month. The drivers who distribute the publication are hired part-time; currently there are five drivers, paid on a hourly basis.

Two part-time secretaries are responsible for the production of the magazine. Their duties involve inputting the job listings, designing advertising space, and proofreading each issue. The production secretaries are paid on an hourly basis and are offered flextime hours to complete their job tasks.

THE PROBLEMS

Manicot has found that his current organization design is not working. The salespeople concentrate on telemarketing (which can be done easily from home) more than on-site visitations to sell advertising space. Advertising sales are much lower than projected. For those salespeople who have attempted on-site visits to sell advertising space, much of their activity has centered around locations close to their homes, rather than larger targeted sales areas. The geographic span includes a territory of over 200 miles, with the Monterey Bay area as one location, Sacramento and points east as another area, and San Francisco and the Silicon Valley–San Jose basin as a third. Manicot would like to expand into the Napa Valley area north of San Francisco as well, but he can't seem to get his salespeople to concentrate on that area.

The sales manager, Jennifer, complains that she cannot concentrate on sales, telemarketing, training new salespeople, and promotion all at the same time. She recognizes that in a small business it is often necessary to perform more than one task, but the combination of all four tasks is simply too much. As a result, her job performance suffers. Because her pay is directly tied to her sales, she spends most of her time selling rather than training or working on promotional activities.

The circulation manager, Greg, complains that his territory is too large for one individual. This is complicated by his other responsibilities, such as supervising Alfred, who oversees the truck drivers who distribute the publication. He says there is enough stress in his job battling major distributors who sell publications en masse to local stores. The geographic area for circulation is as dispersed as the sales territory. Additionally, he maintains he cannot sell the publication to new vendors until it is proven via circulation. Circulation will not be boosted until customers get to know the product, and are willing to purchase it on a repeat sales basis.

The distribution manager, Alfred, reports in only once every two weeks. He seems to want to do more than simple distribution and coordination of the drivers, but Manicot is unclear what that could be. Alfred is motivated, interested in earning more money, and a good co-worker. He has mentioned an interest in developing circulation or helping with sales from time to time, but as a part-time worker, it is unclear how much he really could contribute.

The production staff works primarily at home, and Manicot is displeased with the quality of their proofreading. Some of the listings were actually omitted in the last issue by mistake, causing delays in the timeliness of the information. Occasionally new advertisers have been omitted from the publication, causing delays in revenue.

Turnover has plagued the sales ranks. Four part-timers and one full-timer have left the company during the past three months. Over the past three years, Manicot has lost a circulation manager and two other members of his production staff. Although turnover is to be expected in a small business, each time someone leaves, a new person must be trained properly. New employees cannot work to full capacity until they have been on the job at least two full months. As a result, Manicot always seems to be running behind on his sales and circulation objectives.

Furthermore, Manicot is doing virtually everything himself—training new salespeople, performing on-site visits, proofreading the magazine, manning the phones, and obtaining new vendors for distribution. He feels he needs to create clear-cut jobs that specify the functions and responsibilities so that he can do what he really needs to do for the business—strategic planning and obtaining financing to capitalize the business. If he could get additional financing, he could afford to pay his personnel more competitively, hire more salespeople full-time, and reduce turnover.

At the moment, he is not paying benefits to his employees beyond what is required by the law. With additional financing, he could increase benefit coverage and attract more qualified personnel.

Manicot is convinced that his new enterprise will be a success if he can iron out these problems. Sales of the publication have been promising, and response is good. He has received a great deal of positive feedback on the publication from local customers, and he has investors ready to invest in the business provided that he cleans up some of his current organizational and staffing dilemmas.

Manicot has come to you to help him define and organize his enterprise. To increase sales, he needs to hire new people to fill as-yet-undefined positions because his organization is growing at a rapid rate. He is looking to you as a consultant to help him define his organization and determine the job descriptions for the functions of the new enterprise as it grows.

THE JOB-GETTER ENTERPRISE ORGANIZATIONAL CHART

Directions.

Part I:

Examine the current organizational chart for the Job-Getter Enterprise on the following pages. Working with members of your group, design an organizational chart that you feel is most appropriate to solve the problems of the Job-Getter Enterprise. Then draw the chart, complete with reporting relationships and functions that describe how you feel the Job-Getter Enterprise should be organized. *Be certain that your chart includes spaces for individual position responsibilities, similar to the one drawn for the current Job-Getter Enterprise organization.*

Current Organizational Chart: The Job-Getter Enterprise

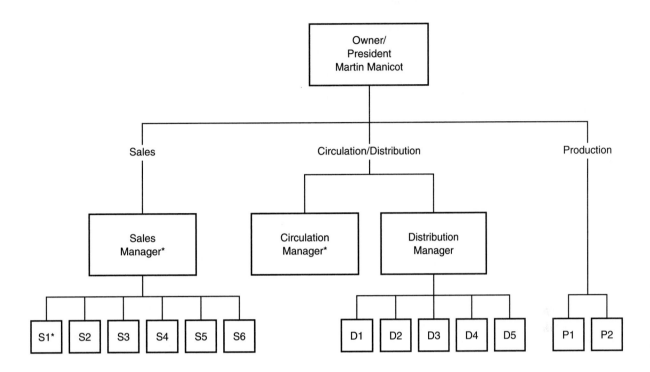

You may want to consider some of the following issues in your decisions regarding design.

Functional Design

Functional designs are the most common organizational structures. The functionally organized firm groups its activities into departments, and departments into divisions, based upon the commonality of function (for example, engineers serve together in engineering departments, salespeople in sales, and so on). The advantages of a functional organization include streamlined communication within departments and efficient use of resources. The disadvantages of this design include problems with coordination across departments or divisions and interdepartmental rivalry and conflict.

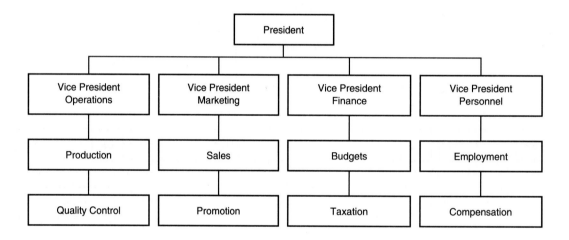

Product Design

Product design involves grouping activities according to the primary products produced by the firm. Each major product line is administered through a separate and semiautonomous division that includes specialists from every functional area. For example, the Soap division includes salespeople, marketing, personnel, a production staff, its own human resource and legal staff, a research and development unit, and finance and accounting specialists. The advantages of a product organization include increased coordination among functions and rapid responsiveness to customer needs. The disadvantages include a lack of clarity about functional area responsibilities and duplication of services across product lines in the organization.

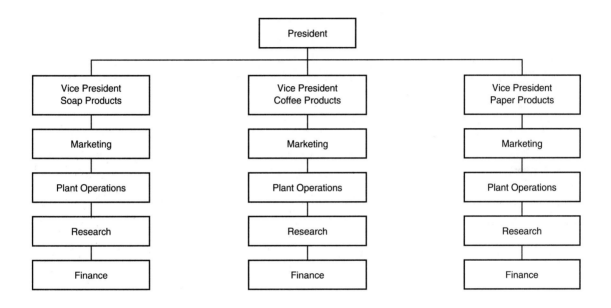

Geographic Design

Geographic or territorial designs require that activities be grouped according to the geographic territories served by the firm. It is especially appropriate for firms whose activities have become broadly dispersed. For example, firms using this design may have a northeast division, a southern division, a western division and a midwestern headquarters. The advantages of this design include easy adaptation to local circumstances and tailoring of product or service needs to local legal, political, and cultural differences. The disadvantages of this design include duplication of services and difficulties of control across local operations.

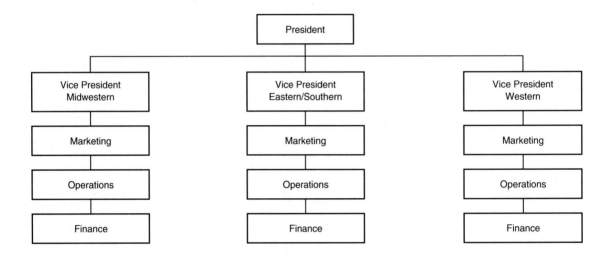

Customer Design

Customer designs are used when a firm's clients have very different needs. Rather than structuring activities around product lines, activities are grouped to serve different customer segments. For example, a manufacturer may group activities according to age groupings of customers. The advantages of this design include being responsive to customer needs, and performance can be tied directly to market segments. The disadvantages include difficulties in establishing uniform company-wide practices, and underutilization of resources.

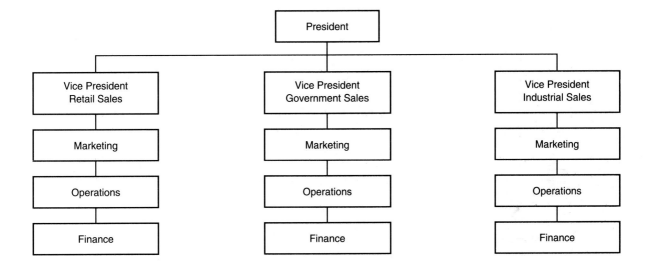

Matrix Organizations

Matrix organizations attempt to cross the product and functional approaches to departmentalization to get the best (and the worst) or both. Functional areas are overlaid on a grid across product lines in this design, so that employees belong simultaneously to two groups, a functional group and a product or project group. The advantages of this design are maximum use of resources, responsiveness to customer, product, or geographic needs, and increased communication and coordination among functions. The disadvantages include increased conflict, power struggles, and slower decision making.

Hybrid Organizations

Hybrid organizations utilize the elements of one organizational design in one area and another in a different area. They combine elements of several designs to best suit organizational needs. For example, a product form of organization may be used in one area and a geographic dispersion in another. The advantages to this design are responsiveness to customer needs and tailoring the organization. The disadvantages include duplication of resources and problems with coordination across units.

Part II:

Directions: After you have chosen and drawn your organization chart for the Job-Getter Enterprise, write out job descriptions for the key positions listed on your chart. Be certain to specify the job functions, reporting relationships, activities, and skill specifications to the extent possible.

Sample Job Description Format

Job Description:

Skill Requirements:

Specific Tasks:

Reporting Relationships:

Financial Information: The Job-Getter Enterprise

Revenue per month:

Approximately 4,000 issues sold at $1 per issue: @ .70 return*	$2,800
Approximately 10 full pages of advertising space sold per month at $350 per page (after commissions paid)	$3,500
Total Revenue	$6,300

Expenses per month:

Office expenses (including office rental, five telephone lines, supplies)	$2,000
Production costs per issue for printing (20,000 issues printed)	$1,400

Compensation Costs:

Sales: $100 per week plus 20% commission	$ 400
Telemarketing: Minimum wage ($4.25 per hour) plus 10% commission. Total $2,600 per month	$2,600
Circulation: $325 per week, no commission/ $1,400 per month	$1,400
Production: Minimum wage ($4.25 per hour)/ $200 per month	$ 200
Delivery: Minimum wage ($4.25 per hour)/ $1,100 per month	$1,110
Total month expenses:	$9,800
Net loss	($3,500)

Number of current locations: 800

------

*.30 cents goes to vendors

San Francisco Bay Area

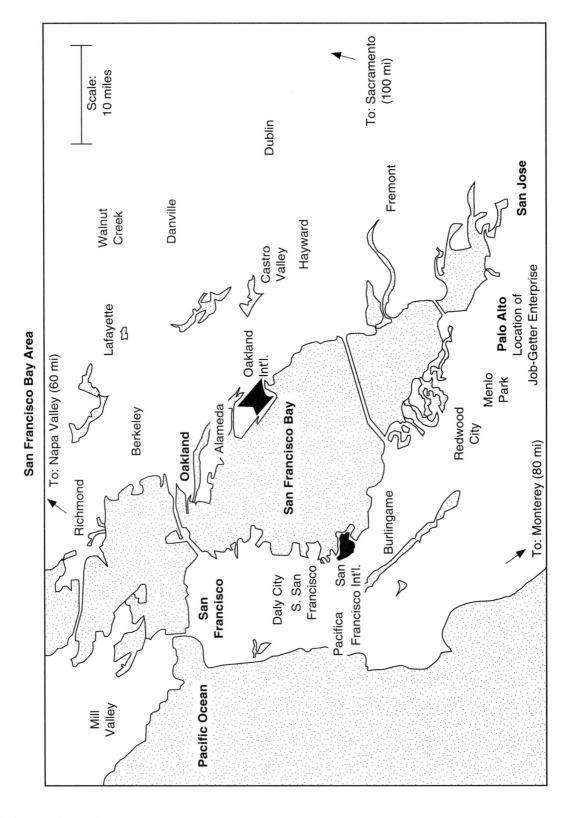

DISCUSSION QUESTIONS

1. Which organizational design did you choose for the Job-Getter Enterprise? What are the advantages and disadvantages of this design?

2. What state of evolution/revolution does the Job-Getter Enterprise represent in its current state of growth?

3. How would you characterize the environment of the Job-Getter Enterprise? Which variables did you consider in your design?

Exercise: Fairfield Flyer Wagons

PURPOSE

The purpose of this exercise is to explore the conditions under which pooled, sequential, and reciprocal interdependence best fit in designing organizational departments. By the time you finish this exercise, you will

1. Learn about the differences between pooled, sequential, and reciprocal interdependence

2. Experience what it is like to work under these conditions

3. Discuss the trade-offs associated with different types of interdependence in terms of communication and spatial relationships

INTRODUCTION

James Thompson (1967) has identified three levels of technological interdependence: pooled, sequential, and reciprocal. Under conditions of pooled interdependence departments work independently toward the organization's goals. They do not depend on each other to accomplish their tasks and very little interdepartmental coordination is needed.

Sequential interdependence involves a one-way production flow in which the output of one department becomes the input of another department and the output of that department becomes the input of the next department in an assembly-type sequence. Because these departments are dependent on each other, coordination between them is necessary for effective performance.

Under conditions of reciprocal interdependence, departments are highly dependent on one another. The production flow is two-way. The output of one department becomes the input of another department and the output of that department goes back to the first department as input. Departments exchange inputs in a reciprocal manner, and extensive interdepartmental coordination is needed. As tech-

This exercise was developed by Cheryl L. Tromley and was presented at the Eastern Academy of Management, Buffalo, NY, 1990.

nology becomes increasingly interdependent, the horizontal coordination mechanisms must become increasingly flexible and capable of carrying larger amounts of rich information.

This three-part exercise is designed to provide you with the opportunity to experience the three levels of technological interdependence. During the exercise you will become part of a company that manufactures children's wagons. You will experience the different demands for horizontal coordination that the pooled, sequential, and reciprocal interdependence create among departments in organizations.

INSTRUCTIONS:

Part I: Pooled Technological Interdependence

Directions: Students will manufacture wagon parts (wheels, long sides, short side, bottoms, and handles). These parts will be used during Part II.

1. Your instructor will pass out the necessary materials.
   Rulers
   Quarters
   Scissors
   Paper
   Pencils
   "Pooled Interdependence Template" (attached)
   IN/OUT labels (3 "OUT" for manufacturing departments; 1 "IN," 1 "OUT PASSED," and 1 "OUT REJECTED" for Quality Control). Pieces of paper with the above legends are sufficient.

2. Your instructor will arrange the room. Use extra chairs or desks for IN/OUT stations and attach IN/OUT labels with tape.

3. Your instructor will divide the class into the following four departments. Each will be provided with the materials specified below.
   a. Wheel Department: "Wheel Department Template" (attached), quarters, scissors, paper, pencils
   b. Sides Department: "Sides Department Template" (attached), rulers, scissors, paper, pencils
   c. Bottom and Handle Department: "Bottoms and Handle Department Template" (attached), rulers, scissors, paper, pencils
   d. Quality Control: All department templates, rulers

4. Appoint or have each department select a manager.

5. Review the following manufacturing procedures.

Wheel Department

Your job is to produce as many wheels as possible. Make sure that they are the right size (the diameter of a quarter) and do not waste materials. The department manager will distribute raw materials, collect the finished wheels, and deliver them to the "OUTPUT" table where they will be collected by the instructor for delivery to Quality Control.

Sides Department

Your job is to produce as many long and short sides as possible. Make sure that they are the right size (see your template) and do not waste materials. You should produce the same number of long and short sides. The department manager will collect the finished sides, separate them into long and short batches, and deliver them to the "OUTPUT" table where they will be collected by the instructor for delivery to Quality Control.

Bottom and Handle Department

Your job is to produce as many bottoms and handles as possible. Make sure that they are the right size (see your template) and do not waste materials. You should produce the same number of handles and bottoms. The department manager will collect the finished wheels and deliver them to the "OUTPUT" table where they will be collected by the instructor for delivery to Quality Control.

Quality Control

Check each part against the template. Put those that pass inspection on the "OUT PASSED" table and those that fail inspection on the "OUT REJECTED" table.

Communication *between* any of the departments is prohibited. Managers may communicate only with the people within their departments.

6. Have a 15-minute production run.

7. Participate in a brief discussion.
   a. Was there a need for communication between the manufacturing departments? If so, what kind? If not, why not?
   b. Was there a need for communication between the manufacturing departments and the Quality Control department? Why or why not?
   c. Did your physical/spatial relationship to any other department influence your ability to do your job? Why or why not?

Part II: Sequential Technological Interdependence

Directions: Students will assemble wagons from the parts manufactured during Part I. The technology will be sequentially interdependent.

1. Your instructor will pass out the necessary materials.
   Assembly Instructions (attached)
   Rulers
   Tape
   Pencils
   Wagon parts manufactured during Part I
   Sample finished wagon
   "IN/OUT" labels (as indicated on Suggested Room Layout)

2. Your instructor will rearrange the room according to the Suggested Room Layout.

3. Your instructor will divide the class into the following six departments and provide each with the materials specified below.

    a. Attach handle to bottom: Step 1 Assembly Instructions (attached), rulers, tape, pencils, handles and bottoms from Part I.

    b. Attach long sides to bottom: Step 2 Assembly Instructions, rulers, tape, pencils, long sides from Part I.

    c. Attach short sides: Step 3 Assembly Instructions, rulers, tape, pencils, short sides from Part I.

    d. Fold and tape sides together: Step 4 Assembly Instructions, tape.

    e. Attach wheels: Step 5 Assembly Instructions, rulers, tape, pencils, wheels from Part I.

    f. Quality control: All Assembly Instructions, sample finished wagon, rulers, "Quality Control Guidelines" (attached).

4. Appoint or have each department select a manager.

5. Go over production procedure. Each department should follow the Assembly Instructions provided.

6. Have a 15-minute production run.

7. Participate in a brief discussion.

    a. What difficulties did you have?

    b. Would your task have been easier or would you have been more productive if you could have communicated with the other departments? If so, which departments? What type of communication would have been the most effective? Would memos have helped?

    c. Did the spatial relationship between the departments help or hinder your ability to get your work done? How? How would it have affected your ability to get your work done if the departments with which you interacted were in different rooms? In a different order?

Part III: Reciprocal Technological Interdependence

Instructions: Participants will manufacture wagons under two conditions of reciprocal technological interdependence.

1. Your instructor will provide the necessary materials.
Assembly Instructions
Rulers
Tape
Pencils
Sample finished wagon
Paper clips
Paper cut into 11″ × 3⅝″ rectangles
"Reciprocal Drawing Template" (attached)
Scissors
Copies of "Interdepartmental Memos" (attached)
Quality Control Guidelines (attached)
"IN/OUT" labels (4 "IN," 4 "OUT")

2. Your instructor will rearrange the room according to Suggested Room Layout.

3. Your instructor will divide the class into the following departments and provide each with the materials specified below.

    a. Drawing: Paper cut into $11'' \times 3\frac{5}{8}''$ rectangles, pencils, rulers, quarters, "Reciprocal Drawing Template" (attached), copies of Interdepartmental Memo #1, paper clips

    b. Cutting: Scissors, pencils, copies of Interdepartmental Memo #2, paper clips

    c. Assembly: Tape, pencils, rulers, Step 1 through 5 Assembly Instructions (attached), copies of Interdepartmental Memo #3, paper clips

    d. Quality control: Rulers, sample completed wagon, pencils, Quality Control Guidelines (attached), copies of Interdepartmental Memos #4, #5, and #6, paper clips

Start assembly off with one handle and bottom per person and cutting with one set of long sides drawn per person.

4. Appoint or have each department appoint a manager.

5. Review the following manufacturing procedure:

Condition 1: You must follow all directions exactly. You are only permitted to communicate with other departments using the memos provided. Managers may only communicate with the workers within their own department. There is to be no discussion between departments. Your instructor will deliver any necessary memos, which should be placed on your "OUT" table for pick-up.

Drawing Department

Parts must be drawn according to the drawing template.

Step 1: Draw long sides on paper.
Step 2: Send to Cutting Department (put on "OUT" table).
Step 3: When paper returns from the Cutting Department (on "IN" table) draw handle and send back to Cutting Department.
Step 4: Repeat above for short sides, wheels, and bottom (in that order), sending the paper to the Cutting Department after each part is drawn (that is, after both short sides are drawn, after four wheels are drawn, after bottom is drawn).

You may work on several sheets of paper simultaneously, but you must follow the steps above in order. For example, from one sheet of raw material: draw two long sides, send to Cutting Department; draw one handle, send to Cutting Department; draw two short sides, send to Cutting Department; draw four wheels, send to Cutting Department; draw one bottom, send to Cutting Department.

If you receive requests from the Quality Control Department,
    1. Get more raw material (paper).
    2. Redraw the part specified on the "Redraw" memo.
    3. Send redrawn part to Cutting Department with a "Recut" memo completed and attached (attach memos with paper clips).
    4. Put remaining raw material aside for other rejected parts.

Cutting Department

Step 1: When you receive drawing from the Drawing Department cut out long sides.
Step 2: Send long sides to Assembly Department and paper back to Drawing Department.
Step 3: Repeat above for handle, short sides, wheels, and bottom, each time sending cut parts to Assembly and paper to Drawing.

You may work on different sheets simultaneously, but you must follow the steps above in order for each.

If you receive a "Recut" memo from the Drawing Department,
1. Recut part
2. Send recut part to Assembly Department with "Reassembly" memo completed and attached (attach memos with paper clips)

Assembly Department

Follow Assembly Instructions in the following order:

Step 1: Attach handle to bottom.
Step 2: Attach long sides to bottom.
Step 3: Attach short sides to bottom.
Step 4: Fold sides up and tape.
Step 5: Attach wheels to long sides.
Step 6: Send to Quality Control.

If you receive a rejected wagon from Quality Control,
1. Follow the directions on the attached memo. You will either have to reassemble the wagon or hold it until you receive a new part from the Cutting Department.
2. Send the reassembled wagon back to Quality Control with a "Reassembly" memo completed and attached (attach memos with paper clips).

Quality Control

Step 1: Check each wagon against the "Quality Control Guidelines" (attached).
Step 2: If the wagon meets specifications, send to shipping.
Step 3: If the wagon is assembled wrong return to Assembly Department with a "Reassemble" memo completed and attached (attach memos with paper clips).
Step 4: If wagon contains a part that is the wrong size,
1. Remove faulty part from wagon.
2. Send faulty part to Drawing Department with a "Redraw" memo completed and paper clipped to the faulty part.
3. Send remainder of wagon to Assembly Department with a "Hold" memo completed and paper clipped to the wagon.

6. Have a 15-minute production run.

7. Participate in a brief discussion.
   a. What difficulties did you have?
   b. Would your task have been easier or would you have been more productive if you could have communicated with the other departments? If so, which departments? What type of communication would have been most effective?
   c. Did the spatial relationship between departments help or hinder your ability to get your work done? What changes would you suggest?

8. *Condition 2:* Appoint a single "Plant Manager." Other managers become members of their department.

9. Take the next 20 minutes to decide what changes you would like to make. Use the previous discussion to guide your decisions. You may make changes within the following constraints:
   a. You must remain in the same functions—that is, you cannot change jobs.
   b. You must follow the same manufacturing procedure in the same order.

10. Participate in a 15-minute production run.

DISCUSSION QUESTIONS

1. Did the changes you made during Condition 2 improve your ability to do your job? How?

2. How did the need for interdepartmental coordination and communication change as the technology became more interdependent?

3. Did the spatial/physical relationship between departments become more important as technology became more interdependent? Why?

4. Can you diagnose any problems in a current or past job that might have resulted from a mismatch between technological interdependence and horizontal coordination?

REFERENCE

J. Thompson. *Organizations in Action.* New York: McGraw-Hill, 1967.

Case: Managing by Mystique

PURPOSE

The purpose of this case assignment is to diagnose a corporate culture. By the time you finish this case assignment you will

1. Diagnose a unique corporate culture
2. Determine the impact a founder can have on corporate culture
3. Understand the impact a corporate culture can have on employee behavior

INTRODUCTION

Organizational cultures comprise the shared values, beliefs, and assumptions that guide the behavior of the members of an organization. In the same way that people develop different personalities, corporations also create their own unique personalities, as reflected by the rites and rituals of daily company life. For example, in some firms, it may always be expected of you as an employee to attend meetings promptly, to never contradict your boss, and to avoid conflict. In other firms, advocating your own unique perspective to generate conflict may be not only encouraged but expected.

Tandem Computers, headquartered in the Silicon Valley area of California's technology belt, has a unique corporate culture. As you read this case, reflect upon what makes this particular company's culture unique, meaningful, and distinct from others.

INSTRUCTIONS

1. Read the case, "Managing by Mystique."

2. Read the Sathe reading, "Implications of Corporate Culture: A Manager's Guide to Action."

3. Diagnose the elements of this company's culture by completing the questions on the Corporate Cultures Worksheet in this exercise.

4. Participate in a class discussion.

Myron Magret, *Fortune,* June 28, 1982. © 1982, Time, Inc. All rights reserved. Used with permission. This case originally appeared in John F. Veiga and John N. Yanouzas. *The Dynamics of Organizational Theory: Gaining a Macro Perspective.* (2nd ed.) St. Paul, MN: West Publishing, 1984. The "Corporate Cultures Worksheet" was added to this version of the case by Lisa A. Mainiero.

Tandem Computers: Managing by Mystique

Myron Magret

It's 4:30 on Friday afternoon, and the weekly beer bust is in full swing at Tandem Computers' Cupertino, California, headquarters. Sun shines on the basketball court beyond the corporate patio and sparkles on the company swimming pool. Programmer A, bearded like a mountain man, is discussing stock options and tax-law changes while dancing in place to the secret music he hears in his own conversation. Earnest Programmer B, clinching his point about Silicon Valley culture by noting that the Programmer Bs have more married than single friends, turns to greet with a soulful kiss a convivial employee his visitor mistakes for Mrs. B.

Five hundred cheerfully bibulous souls, mostly young and casual-looking, are talking animatedly, glass in hand; and the same genial scene is being reenacted on a smaller scale at Tandem offices as far afield as Omaha or Kowloon. Every week 60 percent of the company drops in at the beer bust for an hour, joined sometimes by visiting customers or suppliers, who take away indelible memories. Says the representative of one satisfied user, a stately major bank, "When the president comes down in a cowboy hat and boots and swills beer—that's different!"

The fun's not confined to Fridays. Take the company's last Halloween costume party, which filled most of a gigantic warehouse. The merriment was heightened by the granting of a 100-share stock option to every employee. Another big event has left its mark, too, on a sunny, modest office belonging to the vice-president of software development, who's one of Tandem's phalanx of mid-thirtyish millionaires. With nondescript steel furniture and a humid display of potted plants, it's indistinguishable from any other Tandem executive's office, including the president's—except for the red satin sash on the wall, bearing the legend "Incredible Hunk," won a while ago by the vice-president himself. He and another Tandemite outshone thirty-odd gym-shorts-clad male opponents in a headquarters-wide beauty contest sponsored by the company's female employees.

GROWTH WITHOUT A HICCUP

Can this company be serious? Meteoric growth and surging profits say it is. Only 7½ years old and already a more than $300-million-a-year operation, it's one of the bright stars of the *Fortune* "Second 500" list and seems inexorably growing to "First 500" magnitude. This isn't only because its Nonstop II system—the computer that's never down—is an estimable machine, commanding a market only recently contested. As Ulric Weil, a Morgan Stanley security analyst, puts it, "No company could be as successful as Tandem is—without a hiccup—unless its management were gifted and kept its finger on the tiller."

Indeed, all the corporate high jinks play their part in an elaborate management scheme conceived largely by Tandem's founder-president, James G. Treybig (pronounced *Try*-big), a 41-year-old Texan whose hands-in-pockets slouch and untucked shirt-tail give him the incongruous air of a teenager hanging out on Main Street. Freewheeling theorizing comes naturally to Jimmy T., as Tandemites call him. Yet he's no idle daydreamer. Before he started Tandem he fleshed out his engineering BS and Stanford MBA with several years in sales and marketing at Texas Instruments and Hewlett-Packard and in venture capital at San Francisco's high-flying Kleiner Perkins Caufield & Byers partnership. He speaks, in his lovingly preserved Texas twang, from experience.

"Jim Treybig sometimes likes to shock people," says Samuel Wiegand, 50, Tandem's former marketing VP. The result, according to software-development VP Dennis McEvoy (the aforementioned Hunk), is that "a lot of people when they meet Jim for the first time think he's a bullshitter, just shuckin' and jivin'." Certainly getting to the heart of his management theory requires pushing through an exotic tangle of rhetoric about how the company represents "the convergence of capitalism and humanism" or how it tries to foster not just its employees but also their spouses and "spouse equivalents." What's more, Treybig (himself married and the father of three) is given to reducing complexity to a simplicity more elegant than true, as in his five cardinal points for running a company, beginning with the at least debatable assertion that "all people are good".

Is there anything in this provocative talk that other CEOs should be listening to? The answer comes down to yes, but. Behind the verbiage is a cluster of hard-headed policies, many of them familiar in high-tech companies, especially in the Bay Area, and some of them applicable to other businesses. But the swaggering tone also points to something in Tandem that's far out, even for California, and that every company wouldn't want.

Generous stock options aimed at riveting employees' attention on the business's success are nothing new in high-tech companies, though perhaps none has gone so far as Tandem, where *every* employee gets gift options. This can mean real money: Tandem's stock has risen steeply from the start, and each employee with the company since it went public in 1977 has drawn options theoretically worth almost $100,000. So raptly attentive to corporate performance have employees become that Tandem now posts the stock price three times a day on its work-station screens; formerly too many people were monopolizing the telex machines to find out. A forceful promotion-from-within policy, so diligently observed that three out of five new managers have risen from the ranks, similarly concentrates the mind.

Unrevolutionary too is Tandem's easy-going flexibility about working hours. As Michael Green, a company founder, puts it, "We don't want to pay people for attendance but for output." So time clocks are out, and managers often don't know just how long their subordinates toil, though indicators like the position of an employee's car in the democratically first-come, first-served parking lot speak volumes to the discerning. As for jogging trails, space for dance-exercise, and yoga classes, and periodic company-supplied weekend barbecues for employees working overtime—amenities like these are not unheard of in other companies.

Treybig argues that the swimming pool, to take one example, improves productivity by giving single parents an agreeable place to park their kids, thus enabling them to work on weekends. Perhaps so—if only because all such appurtenances help spark the so-called Hawthorne effect, an increase in productivity that appears to result from *any* new attention paid to employees' working conditions or amenities. Even the beer bust, in terms of the current fashion for fostering unstructured communication across an institution's vertical and horizontal boundaries, is arguably a productivity ploy.

THE TANDEM GOSPEL

Also hardly novel is soaking employees in an endless stream of company-boosting propaganda urging loyalty, hard work, self-esteem, and respect for co-workers. But Tandem's indoctrination effort goes so far beyond the ordinary as to make clear how radical a departure the company's managerial style, taken as a whole, really is. First, there's its sheer quantity—from orientation lectures and breakfasts, newsletters, and a glossy magazine that some Tandemites call "Propaganda Quarterly" to a fat tome (standard issue to all employees) called *Understanding Our Philosophy,* supplemented by a two-day course on its finer points. This is mandatory for all employees, notes James Katzman, a company founder, though mandatory is a taboo word, for it "goes against the culture." A lavish facility to house these so-called philosophy seminars and other programs is in the planning stage.

Then there's the content, in which conventional pieties, by their vehemence of expression, take on new meaning. For instance, here's "all employees should be treated with respect" rendered in Treybigese: "You never have the right at Tandem to screw a person or to mistreat them. It's not allowed. . . . No manager mistreats a human without a fear of their job." An aggrieved employee's ready access to anyone in the company gives this provision teeth: managers have been fired. Or take the idea that everyone in a company is essential to its success. In the Tandem ideology this platitude takes on a more egalitarian tinge than usual: Treybig dismisses with indulgent but characteristic sarcasm some German productivity experts who "had never danced with an assembly worker."

Yet the indoctrination goes further, for Tandem, in its "philosophy" book and seminars, takes pains to give each employee an understanding of the essence of the company's business and five-year plan. Folded into the philosophy book is a labyrinthine chart the size of a road map—it took two weeks of Treybig's time to draft—showing how a push on this spot of the complex system will have repercussions everywhere else. Several computers shipped late, for instance, can drop quarterly profits enough to lower the stock price, which makes raising capital more expensive, which leaves less money for research and incentives, which . . . You get the idea.

THE ONCE-A-MONTH MANAGER

Letting employees see the big picture and peek at strategic secrets boosts loyalty. "People really get a great kick out of being part of the team and trusted with the corporate jewels," as Jim Katzman says. But the deeper purpose is to lessen the need for management by pointing everybody in the right direction and explaining what's happening on all sides of him. "Most companies are overmanaged," Treybig believes. "Most people need less management than you think." Thus at Tandem, says marketing director Gerald Peterson, stating the company's fundamental managerial principle, "the controls are not a lot of reviews or meetings or reports, but rather the control is understanding the basic concept and philosophy." What this means in practice, says one software designer, is that "I speak to my manager about once a month—that's how often my manager manages me."

Not everyone can work this way, so hiring is crucial at Tandem. The philosophy, aiming to curb the all-too-human tendency of institutions to clog themselves with unthreatening mediocrities and yes-men, nags managers to choose smarter or more qualified people than themselves and not to "hire in their own image." Nor-

mally, only proved and experienced applicants get considered—which incidentally insures Tandem a steady flow of new ideas from other companies—and grueling interviews, sometimes twenty hours of them, put candidates through the wringer. Tandem's managers, not its essentially administrative personnel office, do all the hiring; prospective co-workers interview applicants too. "A manager will never hire somebody his people don't think is good," says a programmer. "Basically, he says will you work with this person, and you say yes or no." As a result, new employees are on their way to integration into the community even before their first day on the job.

Without question this system works. Tandem's productivity figures are among the highest in the industry; even shipping clerks don't seem just to go through the motions by rote. As to imbuing employees with zeal for the company's success—one satisfied customer speaks of a service technician who gladly gave out his home phone number, cheerfully took an emergency call at 2:30 in the morning, and turned up, toolbox in hand, at 6 A.M.

Yet this managerial style can't be applied indiscriminately to all businesses. What makes it work at Tandem is its close fit to that company's special circumstances. For instance, aiming everybody in the same direction and keeping supervision light makes sense in a company with one basic product and one clearly defined market, but it could spell chaos in a complex, diversified corporation. Lean management works well, too, in an operation with so many functions farmed out. Tandem buys most of its components from subcontractors and gets cleaned by a contract janitorial service. For all its talk about equality, the whole company is an elite, leaving the lowest functions to others.

What manufacturing Tandem does itself—in quiet, airy rooms more like labs than factories—is high-level assembly and massive testing. This requires skilled workers, self-disciplined and intelligent enough to dispense with a supervisor over each shoulder. Rare everywhere, such workers are especially hard to hire in Silicon Valley, where demand is so high that "assembly people and operators can literally walk across the street and find work the next day," as Gordon Campbell, president of neighboring Seeq Technology, puts it. Stoking employee loyalty with every conceivable amenity thus becomes a matter of urgency, particularly when sky-high Valley housing costs make an influx of new assembly workers most unlikely.

But the real competition is the battle for engineering talent among the Valley's high-tech companies, all constantly making passes at each other's technical staffs. "Once you have one of these guys," says Stanford computer-science Professor Edward Feigenbaum, "you don't want to lose him. You have to coddle these people." Hence the Tandem swimming pool (which competes with the health clubs and hot tubs of nearby companies), the six-week sabbaticals every four years that have sent Tandemites up the mountains of Nepal or into London's Cordon Bleu cooking school, and the stock options, some of them carefully calibrated to make leaving the company before four years very expensive. Such emoluments not only stay the footloose; they've also largely kept unions out of Silicon Valley.

"The most creative computer people are the semi-freakies," Feigenbaum notes, and—especially in the case of the software designers who breathe the soul into Tandem's machines—they need freedom and solitude to perform their occult art. After all, the continual refining and extending of the system's intelligence, not the bolting together of components, is the essence of Tandem's business and the key to its future. "When you have a good systems-development shop, things always look to the outside observer as if they're out of control—and to some extent they are," explains John Brodie, a software consultant who writes programs for some of Tandem's customers. "It's semi-channeled chaos." Tandem's loose, flexible style reflects this industry reality.

It reflects, too, the youth of its staff, many of whom went to college in the Sixties and early Seventies, when they were at least touched by the values of the counter-culture. "I used to call those development people down at Tandem pseudohippies," ex-VP Wiegand says with a chuckle, "but they were terribly hard workers." That statement sums up a tension common enough in people of that generation, especially in northern California, between the claims of openness, spontaneity, non-judgmental acceptance, brotherhood, freedom, and expressiveness on the one hand, and technical proficiency coupled with personal ambition on the other. Tandem, with its youthful style, beer-bust rap sessions, high-flown egalitarianism, engineering excellence, and hefty financial incentives, resolves that conflict.

Asked if this is the right way to run a company, one personnel officer, not quite 30, sounds the authentic Tandem tone: "It's progressive. It's ahead of the times. I don't know that it's right. I don't know what's right or wrong. I know that it's very unique. It sure feels right to me: it fits in with the way I like to see people treated."

Tandemites do have a way of growing vague when they try to make sense of the company mystique. Often enough, they are reduced to quoting *Understanding Our Philosophy* as if it were Chairman Mao's Little Red Book. "Some people might call it brainwashing," says corporate-materials VP Jerald Reaugh, "but I don't think it is. I don't think it's immoral or illegal." Treybig himself, half jokingly, makes a different analogy. "I know this sounds like religion or something," he says, adding, "It's almost like religion."

THE BOSS LIKES THAT NOISE

Certainly it resembles religion, at least of the sect or cult variety, in the premium it puts on inner dedication. As a programmer remarks, "I don't think someone who thought Tandem was just a job would work out, because Tandem expects commitment." Accordingly, ordeals like the prolonged interviews serve not just to hire good people but also to build loyalty by making employees feel tried and specially chosen by an exacting community. And such initiations boost dedication simply by being ordeals, for, in the economy of the emotions, people value what has cost them a lot.

All sects need a charismatic leader, and Tandem's is, of course, Treybig. "Jimmy gets almost like an evangelist when he talks about the basic people issues of running a company," says marketing director Peterson, and McEvoy allows that seeing Treybig address the Tandem staff in a huge tent in the parking lot brings unwelcome thoughts of religion to his mind. Venture capitalist Franklin "Pitch" Johnson, Jr., a Tandem director, describes the "muttering that builds up into a roar of approval" that greets Treybig at such events. "It's an acknowledgment that they believe in him and they support him," Johnson says. "Jimmy likes it when he stands up there and hears that noise—that Tandem noise—of approval." Says Yale management professor Rosabeth Moss Kanter of companies like these, "Their success makes it feel magical." Their employees, she says, feel that "we must be touched by some special gift."

Tandemites explain how all this has affected them by endless talk about how the company has helped them "grow." Like many Tandem values, this one, much emphasized in the corporate creed, is a little vague. "I can't describe it," says Richard Bixler, the company's engineering-operations manager, "but it feels pretty good. I feel like I'm accomplishing something with myself." Certainly the rich opportunities for promotion, learning, and initiative, added to the corporate culture's hold on the self-image of employees, gives them a sense of moving toward the full development of all their human potentialities. To convince employees that they are amply filling their innermost goals of self-realization as they advance the company's interest is almost a miraculous feat in itself. But the sense of self-realization Tandem's mystique produces may prove illusory, for the radiance of mystiques is, like the glow of moonshine, notoriously liable to fade.

It's on a less ineffable kind of growth—explosive corporate growth—that Tandem's system ultimately rests. This creates not only the big profits and lavish benefits, but also the acute need for new managers, rapid promotion, and the ability of employees to manage themselves that gives Tandemites their sense of personal growth and freedom. With nearly half the employees at the company for less than six months, hierarchies are not fully defined, roles are relatively unfixed, and there's potential power and opportunity for all.

"The haunting question," says Johnson, "is, if we have a hickey on our growth rate, will this fantastic morale we've built hold up?" He foresees no such blemish, but Tandem management is working to institutionalize and codify the magic. Such devices as those philosophy seminars are preparation for the fast-approaching day when the company is too big for Treybig to dance with every employee and the day, sometime after that, when the amazing growth inevitably starts to slow. Meanwhile Treybig, by announcing plans to expand a $300-million-a-year company with 3,000-odd employees into a $1-billion one with 11,000 employees over the next three years, has promised his next faith-inspiring wonder.

DISCUSSION QUESTIONS

1. To what extent do you believe that Tandem can maintain this particular culture over time?

2. Are loosely coupled corporate cultures a characteristic of young, growing organizations?

3. To what extent has the company's external environment influenced the development of this culture? How likely is it that a company operating in the staid Wall Street environment would develop a similar culture?

4. Which metanorms and values have the potential for being more dysfunctional than productive over time? Why? Explain.

REFERENCE

T. E. Deal, and A. A. Kennedy. "Strong Cultures: The New/Old Rule for Business Success." In *Corporate Cultures: The Rituals of Corporate Life*. Reading, MA: Addison-Wesley, 1982.

Corporate Cultures Worksheet

Directions: Diagnose the elements of this company's culture by answering the following questions:

1. What values and beliefs do employees espouse?

_____

_____

_____

2. Which metanorms or standards of behavior apply to all employees?

_____

_____

_____

3. What rites and rituals are expected behavior in which company employees must participate?

_____

_____

_____

4. Who are the heroes and what are the legends of the culture?

_____

_____

_____

5. What impact has the company founder had on the development of the culture?

_____

_____

_____

6. How would you describe this company's external environment?

_____

_____

_____

7. Is it likely this company will be able to maintain its culture over time as it grows and develops?

_____

_____

_____

CHAPTER 9

Careers and Stress

INTRODUCTION

Uppermost in the minds of young managers are such questions as "How can I get ahead in my job?" "What does it take to get promoted in this company?" Career development is one of the most intriguing subjects in any organizational behavior class. In fact, one of the primary reasons that many students decide to pursue a graduate degree is for career development purposes.

But planning a career is not an easy matter. Successful career planning requires that you set realistic goals, determine the strengths and weaknesses in your job performance, and develop skills that will make you marketable. The process of career planning requires that you answer three questions: (1) Who am I? (2) Where do I want to go? (3) How can I get there? To answer these questions, a careful self-assessment of your needs, interests, values, and abilities is in order.

Ironically, managing stress is a vital aspect of the career planning process, because career planning, stress, and burnout are very often interrelated. When we become stressed, we may experience job "burnout." The level of stress with which we must cope may lead us to look to other firms, jobs, or professions to provide new, and hopefully less stressful, challenges.

READINGS

The articles presented in this chapter encompass several key issues regarding career planning and stress management. "The Four Stages of Professional Careers—A New Look at Performance by Professionals," by Gene W. Dalton, Paul H. Thompson, and Raymond L. Price, describes four stages that characterize the careers of technical professionals. Contrary to other models of career development, the authors argue that not everyone passes through the same stages of development. Some people prefer an apprentice role. Others prefer to serve as mentors to others. Dalton, Thompson, and Price suggest that technical obsolescence is related not to age but to career stage growth.

The second article, by Douglas T. Hall and Judith Richter, "Career Gridlock: Baby Boomers Hit the Wall," offers an interesting perspective on the aging of the baby boom generation and its implications for career management. Streamlined corporate hierarchies have limited promotion possibilities for most of the baby boom generation. Career plateaus will affect many who aspire to top management. The authors suggest that while the number of ways of achieving promotional success is finite and shrinking, the number of ways of achieving psychological success is infinite. If the role of the middle manager is reconsidered, there may be ways to grow in place while fulfilling life and career aspirations.

The third reading, by Morely D. Glicken and Katherine Janka, "Executives Under Fire: The Burnout Syndrome," describes the causes and symptoms of burnout, which can be created by excessive stress on the job. This is most likely to occur in the earlier stages of career development, when stress around the choice of a career may be the greatest. Sometimes, burnout can be a symptom of the need for change—a new job, or perhaps even a new career. If left unmonitored, burnout can be incapacitating. It can negatively affect your motivation, your commitment to your job, and your productivity.

EXERCISES AND CASES

The case, "Jane Moore: An Executive Woman's Career Story," recounts the pressures and pitfalls experienced by executive women. The central figure in the case, Jane Moore, is being considered for the presidency of her company, Merey-Case, a fictitious pharmaceutical firm. This case represents a composite of three women interviewed by one of the authors of this book concerning career progression among executive women. The career path suggested by the case is, however, uniformly consistent among executive women who have made it to the top of their firms. Read the case to determine to what extent women's career paths follow the theoretical literature presented in this chapter.

The second exercise, "Career Anchors," helps you to identify the values that characterize you as a person, and the implications of such values for your career development. Career anchors define the motivational forces that may suggest a particular career direction. For example, some people may prefer to be technical experts while others are driven by job security. Your underlying values will influence the level of satisfaction you experience with your chosen career path. Take this questionnaire and discover what characterizes you best: (1) a manager, (2) a warrior involved in many different jobs, (3) an entrepreneur, (4) a technical expert, (5) an autonomous worker, or (6) a person driven by job and/or geographic security.

The third exercise, "The Burnout Questionnaire," will help you determine your potential for burnout in your current job. When you feel listless, uninterested in your job, and unable to get yourself motivated to accomplish your job tasks, you might be a candidate for burnout. Burnout has a way of sneaking up on us; too often, we do not notice that we are under chronic stress. If this is the case, it may be time for a job or career change.

MEMO

Finally, the memo assignment for this chapter, *"Career Prognosis"* (located at the back of the book), presents an opportunity for you to develop a career plan. To do so, a careful self-assessment will be needed. You will be asked to reflect upon your work history, your background, your skills and abilities, and your limitations. You will also be asked to define a realistic career goal. When this memo is completed, you will have a developmental plan in place to help you plan your future.

By the time you finish this chapter, you will have a better understanding of the stages and dilemmas faced in management careers. You also will learn about burnout and stress. As the chapter concludes, you will develop an action plan that may help you make choices about your future.

The Four Stages of Professional Careers—
A New Look at Performance by Professionals

Gene W. Dalton

Paul H. Thompson

Raymond L. Price

A person has to be able to change or he'll stagnate, but it is so hard to change in this organization. I'd like to move up or pursue a related career, but I'm cast in the role of radiochemist and I don't know how to move out of it. I have to go outside of work to get my rewards. [40-year-old engineer]

I really wonder what to do. I like technical work, but when I look at the specialists 15 years my senior still in those little cubbyholes, it scares me. I think I'll get a chance to try management, but if you let yourself get too far from your field, you're out on a limb with no way back if it doesn't work out. [28-year-old scientist]

I manage nearly three hundred professionals; and by all practical standards, I'm very successful. But I'm not satisfied. I feel it is time to make a change and try doing something new. However, it might mean that I wouldn't directly manage anyone anymore. I wonder what would happen to my career and my influence around here. [52-year-old manager]

These are some of the concerns we've heard expressed as we have talked with several hundred professionally trained employees over the past three years. These are the knowledge workers, the fastest growing part of our workforce, who at present constitute 32 percent of the workforce. (Blue collar workers are 33 percent of the workforce.) Their initial training was as engineers, scientists, accountants, MBAs, and so on, and they have spent their working lives as employees of large, complex organizations dependent in large part on their professional skills. Having done well in college and graduate school, they entered these organizations with high career expectations. They brought with them scarce and val-

ued skills, but few had any clear understanding of what forging a career in an organization is like. Few came with any understanding of the constantly changing activities, relationships, and emotional adjustments they would have to learn to manage if they were to remain highly valued contributors throughout their careers.

Perhaps it should come as no surprise, therefore, that we so often perceived a sense of frustration, bewilderment, even betrayal, as these people spoke about their careers. Any career guidance they may have received in college or graduate school was usually limited to helping them choose courses or majors. No one had given them an accurate preview of what life in a complex organization would be like.

Nor did many of them feel they had received much more help in career planning after they entered organizational life. A few talked about getting some valuable training or advice from a supervisor or a friend. But a large number expressed feelings that are captured best by a comment from a young financial analyst in a bank: "Nobody has helped me do any real career planning. I suspect it's because they're not sure of where they are going themselves."

We have in fact encountered uncertainty among managers of professional employees about how to guide the careers of their subordinates. From these managers we constantly heard comments such as these:

We bring in about a dozen of the best young people we can each year. Two years later, about eight are contributing. The rest are floundering and usually leave. I wish I could understand it. Those who floundered came with records as good as the others. [Laboratory Director]

We have some men in their 40s or 50s who are among our lowest performers. Their salaries are out of line with what we get from them, but they have been here so long we aren't likely to bring ourselves to fire them. We've told them to take courses to get current, but I can't see it's had any effect. What will we do with them for the next 15 or 20 years? [Chief Engineer]

CAREER MODELS

Those of us who study careers in organizations have found ourselves perplexed by the same questions. Several years ago we began examining the relationship between age and performance among engineers. In a study of 2,500 engineers in seven large organizations, we found a negative correlation after age 35 between age and performance rating. The older the engineer after the mid-30s, the lower his performance rating was likely to be.

But the message seemingly implied by these statistics was brought sharply into question when we examined our data more closely. Not all older engineers had low ratings. In fact, the top third of the engineers over 50 were almost as highly valued as the top third in any age group. Many engineers had remained highly valued contributors for the duration of their careers. But more of those in their 40s and 50s had low ratings than did younger engineers.

Why have some professionals remained high performers over the years while others have not? What have they done differently?

Existing Career Models

We have concluded that part of the confusion about careers has grown out of the career models we have all used, explicitly or implicitly. The first and most influential of these is of course the pyramidal model of organizations (and of careers), so graphically illustrated by most organizational charts. Authority, status, and pay all increase as the individual moves up the chart.

Implicit in this model is the concept that career development consists of moving as rapidly and as far up the pyramid as possible. As professionals first moved into industrial and governmental organizations, this was the sole career model they encountered. Many professionals with advanced degrees became prime candidates for management positions.

But there were also many who were dismayed to find that the ability and willingness to manage seemed almost the sole criteria for advancement, recognition, or reward in their organizations.

Similarly many organizations found that the pyramidal model failed to take important realities into account. Too often, they found themselves promoting a key technical specialist to a management position because it was the only way to reward him. More and more firms began to set up special new pay and promotion schemes such as the dual ladder for their professional employees in order to recognize the critical contributions they could make as individuals. In almost all those organizations, however, professionals began griping about the realities of the dual ladder:

> "Ours isn't a real dual ladder; it's been bastardized. It's been filled with ex-managers."
> "The men in the upper technical slots don't do real technical work. They prepare proposals and brochures."
> "The real rewards don't go to those on the technical ladder."

These criticisms have not subsided. Instead, they have persisted and indeed increased in recent years.

The Obsolescence Model

As the number of professionals with 20 and 25 years' experience grew, a new problem and a new model of professional careers began to emerge. The low performance ratings of many of these senior employees led to use of the metaphor of obsolescence. The picture projected by the metaphor was that of a rapidly changing technology in which the skills of the older professionals were rapidly outdated and in which recent graduates who had mastered the latest tools and techniques were at a premium.

Interestingly, the model carries with it an implied solution to the problem. When it is assumed that professionals become obsolete like machines, when we begin to talk as if a professional education has a half-life of so many years, like a uranium sample, the obvious solution is to update or reeducate professionals and to restore them to the state they were in when they came out of school—on top of the newest and most sophisticated techniques.

Millions of dollars have been spent on continuing education programs in companies and in universities. In addition, professional groups have pressed for legislation that requires continuing education as the price of continuing professional practice. For example, lawyers in Minnesota are required to take the equivalent of 15 course hours a year to avoid being placed on a restricted status. The Engineering Foundation of Ohio recently suggested a law requiring almost the same qualification of engineers. Accountants in several states face the possibility of having to return to the classroom in order to retain their professional status.

All this money and effort rests on a questionable model. It has not been demonstrated that courses improve performance. Our studies have in fact shown repeatedly that the high performers are no more likely to have taken continuing education courses than the low performers.

A NEW MODEL

If the high performers are not taking more courses than their peers, how *are* they different? What, if anything, are they doing differently? In what respects have their careers been different?

To answer these quetions, we interviewed 550 professionally trained employees: 155 scientists in four laboratories, 268 engineers in four organizations, 52 accountants in three firms, and 75 professors in three universities. We selected our subjects to give us representative samples of high- and low-rated performers. We began by simply asking them to describe their own careers and those of their fellow professionals. What, we asked them, characterized the high performers they knew? We coded their responses carefully and compared them with the way the high-rated and the low-rated performers described their own careers.

Our early analysis yielded only frustration. Each promising uniformity exhibited too many contradictions. Each new hypothesis failed to find support in the data. It was only when we began to look at the effects of time that a clear pattern began to emerge. High performers early in their careers were performing different functions from high performers at mid-career. And both these groups were different from high performers in late-career.

As we investigated further, it became increasingly clear that there are four distinct stages in a professionally trained employee's career. Each stage differs from the others in the tasks an individual is expected to perform well in that stage, in the types of relationships he engages in, and in the psychological adjustments he must make.

It was the individuals who were moving successfully through these stages who had received the high performance ratings. Conversely, individuals who had remained in the early stages were likely to be low-rated.

FIGURE 1
Four Career Stages.

	Stage I	*Stage II*	*Stage III*	*Stage IV*
Central activity	Helping Learning Following directions	Independent contributor	Training Interfacing	Shaping the direction of the organization
Primary relationship	Apprentice	Colleagues	Mentor	Sponsor
Major psychological issues	Dependence	Independence	Assuming responsibility for others	Exercising power

In Stage I, an individual works under the direction of others as an apprentice, helping and learning from one or more mentors.* In Stage II, he demonstrates his competence as an individual contributor. In Stage III, he broadens and acts as a mentor for others. Those in Stage IV provide direction for the organization. Figure 1 shows some of the central features of each stage. It is important to realize that while the stages can be thought of as distinct, there are elements in each stage that are present in each of the other stages, although in a different form. Our description of each stage focuses on the issues that clearly differentiate one stage from the next.

STAGE I

When a young professional joins an organization, he is immediately confronted with several challenges. He must learn to perform at least some of the organization's tasks competently. He needs to learn which elements of the work are critical and which activities require the greatest attention. He must learn how to get things done, using both formal and informal channels of communication. Finally, he must do this while he is being closely observed for indications of competence and future potential.

Because he lacks experience, and because others do not yet know how much they can rely on his judgment, he works under the fairly close supervision of a more experienced person. In other words, he must usually begin by helping someone else do the work for which no supervisor is responsible.

Activities

Much of the work in Stage I may involve fairly routine duties. One manager observed:

There is a lot of detailed work to be done between the time a project is conceived and its actual implementation. A new person is often stuck with many of these detailed tasks. I like a subordinate who recognizes that someone has to do the routine work and therefore doesn't complain about it all the time.

---

*We would like to acknowledge the helpfulness of the ideas of Daniel Levinson and his associates at Yale University. Their concept of the mentor helped us understand much of the phenomena we observed in this stage.

However, it is important for the person in this stage not to become completely bogged down in this detail work. He is also expected to show some initiative and be innovative in finding solutions to problems. So another manager commented:

I like a subordinate who has an aggressive attitude. He has to show initiative, be innovative, and be willing to take some risks. With an aggressive attitude, I can normally guide him in the direction in which he needs to go.

The differing views expressed by these managers illustrate the fact that it is often difficult to achieve the optimum balance in Stage I between willing acceptance of routine assignments and aggressive searching out of new and more challenging tasks.

Another characteristic of the work in this stage is that the individual customarily gets assignments that are part of a larger project or activity directed by a senior professional or a supervisor. Many young professionals find such a relationship frustrating. They are eager to have their own project or their own clients.

Such an attitude is understandable, but a person who tries to escape the subordinate relationship too quickly will miss out on an important aspect of career development. He will fail to learn what others have gained by experience. More important, if he undertakes sole responsibility for work he's not prepared to do, he may soon acquire a reputation for mediocre performance, which will be hard to overcome.

Relationships

As we have just indicated, the primary relationship in Stage I is that of being a subordinate. Our interviews suggest that the individual's skill in managing that relationship may be a critical factor in building an effective career. Ideally, in this stage he will work with a mentor who knows how to design a study, structure an audit, or analyze the critical risks involved in a loan. He works closely with the mentor, learning from observation and from trial and correction the approaches, the organizational savvy, and the judgment that no one has yet been able to incorporate into textbooks. He follows instructions and carries out detailed and sometimes boring work in exchange for the things he learns and the sponsorship of his mentor.

If he learns quickly and well at this stage, he will be given increasing responsibility. If he fails to do so, however, he may continue to do the routine work under close supervision as long as he remains with the organization. Tom Johnson's experience in a large research organization illustrates this point:

> In my first two years in the company I was unhappy with my job. I worked for a man that I disliked and did not respect. He provided very little assistance or guidance. As a result, I made little or no progress. Then I began to work with another engineer who could get things done; he protected me from the flack coming down from above. He provided a climate that I enjoyed and he was willing to go to bat for me. When he became a formal group leader, I insisted on being transferred into his group, where I became the informal leader. Later, he recommended me for a supervisory position.

Tom's experience points out some of the benefits of having a good mentor in the early stages of a career as well as some of the problems of having a poor one. The mentor knew the right people and could show Tom how the system worked—how to lay out a job, how to get computer funds, how to requisition necessary equipment and travel funds, how to negotiate faster delivery from suppliers, and so on. A mentor is also extremely helpful when anyone is learning the ropes in a complex organization.

A good mentor often becomes a model that the Stage I person can follow whenever he is unsure how to approach a problem. He instructs and provides the subordinate with a chance to try his hand, while making sure that he doesn't make important errors. These and other benefits suggest that finding a good mentor should be a key agenda item for any professional entering an organization. Providing him with the opportunity to find such a mentor is an equally important responsibility of higher-ups in the organization.

Psychological Issues

The psychological adjustments a person makes in Stage I are as critical as the way the activities are performed or the relationships that are developed. One of the major problems is adjusting to the dependence inherent in the role of subordinate. The people we interviewed said that in this stage a person "is expected to willingly accept supervision and direction . . ." and "is expected to exercise *directed* creativity and initiative."

Many professionals looked forward to completing their education so they could be free of the demands of their professors and find the independence they believed their profession provides. It is easy to understand their irritation when they find themselves forced once again into a dependent relationship. A physicist in a highly respected applied research laboratory described his feelings during his first year:

> My first year here was frustrating. I had a good record in graduate school. I was ready to go to work and make a contribution. But for a year, no one paid much attention to my suggestions. I almost left. It took me a year to realize that I didn't yet understand the complexity of the problems we were working on. Now I try to take enough time with new people to help them understand the dilemma of that first year.

Another difficult adjustment is learning to live with the never-ending routine work. A recent MBA described his frustrations in this area as follows:

> My job is very boring. All I'm doing is routine financial analysis. This work could be done by a high school graduate with a calculator. They didn't tell me in the MBA program that I'd be doing this routine work. We spent our time in the program discussing cases with important problems to be solved.

Many young professionals find themselves in a similar position, and it is a risky one. If they lose interest in the job and do sloppy work or lay down on the job, they may acquire a reputation that will compromise their future career development.

STAGE II

The primary theme in Stage II is independence. The individual who makes the transition into Stage II successfully does so by developing a reputation as a technically competent professional who can work independently to produce significant results. John, a young financial analyst, describes his transition into this stage:

> After about a year and a half with the company, I was capable of working on my own and therefore was placed in charge of monitoring the procurement accounts. Before this time, whenever a person from another department came in to ask a question, I had to consult with my supervisor before making a decision. When I was in charge of the accounts, this was no longer necessary.

Activities

Most professionals look forward to having their own project or area of responsibility. This does not mean that they are allowed to work completely on their own, because most projects must be coordinated with other projects and activities, but they are no longer closely supervised on the specific methods of getting the job done.

In this stage, a person is expected to hone his professional skills to a high level. One way to achieve this competence is to develop an area of specialization. The major career dilemma in this stage is how much to specialize. There is a great deal of discussion and dissension on this issue—with most people taking a strong stand in favor of their particular point of view. An article in *Business Week* (October 12, 1974) offers this advice to aspiring managers:

> Get experience in several fields—engineering, sales, manufacturing—right off, and be sure to get your ticket punched in finance early. If you're heading for the president's office, become a generalist fast. . . . Get out of your specialty fast, unless you decide that's all you ever want to do. This means rapid rejection of the notion that you are a professional engineer, lawyer, scientist, or anything but a manager.

Our data suggest that this advice could be misleading if a young professional interprets it to mean that he need never develop and demonstrate solid competence in some critical task of the organization. For in doing so, he will fail to establish a major building block to his career.

The environment in which most professionals operate is changing so rapidly that it is nearly impossible for any one individual to develop expertise in all areas of his field or profession. Therefore, it is often advisable to become a specialist, at least temporarily, and gain a reputation for competence within that specialty.

Using this strategy of focusing his energies in one area enables the individual to develop a sense of competence. In addition to increasing his self-esteem, the individual also tends to enhance his visibility in the organization. A person who has done outstanding work in one area is more likely than a jack-of-all-trades to gain visibility in a large organization.

There are two primary approaches to selecting an area of specialization. One strategy is to choose a content area in which to specialize, such as a CPA who is an expert on tax problems for banks, or a scientist who focuses on nondestructive testing, or a banker who concentrates on loans to utilities. The other is to develop a set of specialized skills and apply those skills in solving a variety of problems. People who are skillful in computer applications, statisticians, and those who are particularly effective in dealing with clients all fall into this category.

There are risks of specializing, of course, such as becoming pigeonholed in one area, or ending up in a specialty that's being phased out. But our research suggests that a carefully selected specialty in Stage II has usually formed the base for a productive and successful career. Failure to establish such a base is a risk few professionals can afford to take.

Relationships

In Stage II, peer relationships take on greater importance. A person at this stage continues to be someone's subordinate. But he comes to rely less on his supervisor or mentor for direction. This transition is not easy, involving as it does a change in attitude and behavior on the part of the supervisor as well as the individual himself.

Some supervisors are unable to make this switch, and the subordinate may need a transfer to accomplish the transition. Ray's experience as an electrical engineer with two supervisors illustrates this point.

> My first project engineer taught me a lot about basic engineering, but after a while I didn't need all the handholding and direction. So I was happy to be transferred to a new project. The new project engineer was a better manager. He helped me to expand my sphere of influence. He encouraged me to develop contacts with people in my field, both inside and outside the company. He showed me how to interact with these people as well as how to make presentations to management and customers. I also learned how to write papers while I worked with him, and several of my papers were published during that period.

Psychological Issues

It seems logical that everyone would want to move from dependence to independence; the transition should be easy. Far from it. By age 25 we have usually had a great deal of experience and indoctrination in being dependent, but little preparation for real independence. From the first grade to graduate school, to ensure a good grade the student has to find out what the teacher wants him to do and then do it. Similarly, on the first job the task is to find out what the boss wants done and then do it.

To move into Stage II, a professional needs to go beyond that dependence and begin to develop his own ideas on what is required in a given situation. He needs his own standards of performance. Some help in developing those standards is available from peers and

from professional standards, such as generally accepted accounting principles or engineering safety standards. Still, judgment is necessary in applying any professional standards.

Developing confidence in one's own judgment is a difficult but necessary process. One scientist's experience with this process may illustrate the point:

> I had been working with my mentor on research projects for three years before I developed the necessary confidence to submit a proposal on my own. But I found that my confidence was short-lived. I had been used to making decisions, but I had always checked them with my mentor; and he made the final decision, wrote the final draft, and so on. Now that I had my own project I lacked the confidence to make any of the important decisions. He was unavailable for about six months, and I was almost paralyzed during that period. I made very little progress on the project. Eventually I discovered that I could get the opinions of other people in the department and then make a decision using their input. It was a major discovery for me to find I didn't need a boss to approve my decisions.

This quotation came from a scientist, viewed by others as a very promising young man, who later became a successful professional.

Some people find Stage II uncomfortable and spend too little time in it to develop the skills that have to be acquired in this stage. This often happens when an individual takes on a supervisory position before he has had a chance to establish himself as a competent professional. Often the organization and the individual conspire in moving the person into a management position too soon.

The opportunity may be enticing, but it involves a high degree of risk. Time after time in our study, we encountered first-level managers who were not effective in their positions because they did not understand the technical aspects of the work they were supervising. This tended to undermine the manager's self-confidence as well as the confidence of his subordinates.

Our research indicates that doing well in Stage II is extremely important in the process of career development. Moreover, many people remain in Stage II throughout their careers, making substantial contributions to the organization and experiencing a high degree of professional satisfaction. However, the probability that they will continue to receive above-average ratings diminishes over time, if they do not move beyond this stage.

STAGE III

We have sometimes called Stage III the mentor stage because of the increased responsibility individuals in this stage begin to take for influencing, guiding, directing, and developing other people. It is usually persons in this stage who play the critical role in helping others move through Stage I.

A second characteristic of persons in Stage III is that they have broadened their interests and capabilities. The tendency to broaden comes about quite naturally for many professionals as part of the work process. One researcher who had been very specialized described his experience this way:

> When you are very close to the data, you are able to see the small differences. If you are observant and in a fruitful area, you soon have more ideas than you can possibly

pursue by yourself. You run the risk of eliminating some potentially good ideas unless you get others to help you.

From dealing with two or three clients, a bank lending officer or a public accountant may develop knowledge and skills that have applications throughout an entire industry. We have seen engineers learn or develop a new type of computer technique to solve a particular problem, for example, only to find that the approach has wide application to a range of problems facing the organization.

The third characteristic we observed of individuals in Stage III is that they deal with people outside the organization (or organization subunit) for the benefit of others inside. They obtain contracts, get budgets approved, secure critical and/or scarce resources or project funds, help others get salary increases, and so on. The reputation an individual has developed for results and solid achievement in Stage II is initially the keystone to this part of Stage III work.

Activities

We identified three roles played by those in Stage III: informal mentor, idea man, and manager. These are not mutually exclusive; one individual may play all three roles. The point that deserves emphasis here is that a person can carry out Stage III activities from more than one role base.

Informal Mentor. Often an individual begins to play the role of informal mentor as an outgrowth of his success in Stage II. He is asked to do more work because of his increased capabilities and contacts, which means that he needs more assistance. He begins to find others who can help do the detail work and develop his initial ideas. In doing this, he becomes a mentor for the people who assist him.

One informal technical mentor described his role in these words:

> Right now I find the sponsors for our work. I do the conceptual thinking, develop the project, and then get someone to support it. After I get the job, then I must supervise and collaborate with others who do most of the actual work.

He remained the force behind the project and also worked closely with those doing the detail work.

Idea Man. Some professionals are exceptionally innovative. Often this kind of individual becomes an idea man or consultant for a small group. Others come to him for suggestions on how to solve current problems. Sometimes he originates an idea and then discusses it with others, who may pursue it independent of his supervision. Either way, he is involved with and influences more than his own individual work. John Jensen, a 59-year-old scientist, described his work in this way:

> I sell ideas. I would describe myself as an innovative scientist. When I work on a problem, it starts to bug me. At some time, I will read something and apply it back to solve the original problem. Others often come to me with problems they cannot solve. Generally I can pull some information from my experience or reading and give them a direction to follow in solving the problems.

Manager. The most common role in Stage III and the one most easily understood is the formal role of manager or supervisor. Usually the management role for a Stage III person is not more than one or two levels in the organizational structure away from the work itself.

Professional competence usually continues to have some importance in the performance of the manager's work. Often the formal management role is given to a mentor who already has been informally performing many of the functions expected of a manager.

Transition to the formal role of manager is not dramatic. Bob Smith, a 37-year-old manager, described a fairly typical pattern of a professional moving into a Stage III management role:

> I gained knowledge of other programs and began to develop outside contacts. Finally, I discovered I could sell programs. With more programs coming in, I managed several long-term projects under time and money constraints. The business was expanding, and I was directing more and more technical people. Soon I became acting section manager and, after three months, the section manager.

Relationships

Probably the most central shift that occurs as a person moves into Stage III is the nature of his relationships. In Stage II he had to learn to take care of himself. In Stage III he has to learn to take care of others, to assume some form of responsibility for their work. When the mentor receives an assignment on which he needs the collaboration of others, he quickly learns the importance of tapping additional skills. To get even a small group of professionals working together effectively requires more than technical skills and an interesting problem. A scientist who had been doing a lot of independent work described the process:

> I wrote a successful proposal for basic research in energy. Now there are three other people working on the project. We are going full blast and having a ball. But there are new questions. I have always asked my boss to give me independence, and I gave him loyalty in return. Now I have to learn to do that with the people under me.

He finds that he needs interpersonal skills in setting objectives, delegating, supervising, and coordinating.

At this point he also has begun to accept the fact that he has to satisfy a number of people—multiple bosses. He experiences a shift in the relationship with those above him in the hierarchy. He now has responsibilities downward as well as upward, and he feels some of the tugs of the proverbial man in the middle. He must learn to cope with divided loyalties. If he is seen as only looking upward, he will find it hard to retain the loyalties of those working for him. At the same time, unless he has strong influence—and is perceived as having such influence—he will be ineffective at influencing the people he directs.

Psychological Issues

Moving into Stage III requires a number of internal changes as well. The individual must develop a sense of confidence in his own ability to produce results and to help others do the same. He needs to be able to build the confidence of junior people, not tear it down. If he is threatened by the success of his apprentices, he will not be able to provide them the guidance and freedom they need if they are to progress. There must be a delicate balance between directing them and providing them with the freedom to explore and to test their skills.

Second, he must be psychologically able and willing to take responsibility for someone else's output. As a mentor he assumes an obligation to both the apprentice and the customer. Implicitly he promises both parties that the output will be satisfactory.

Some competent people experience formal supervisory responsibility for others as confining and uncomfortable. Whenever this occurs, the question for the individual and his superiors is whether he can find a role in which he can still exert a broad influence without supervising others or whether he should move back into Stage II work.

Those in Stage III also often find themselves pulling away from technical work. The question is: How far? Some move fairly far away from it without ambivalence. Others, like Bill Rivers, make a great effort to stay close to their field. He describes both the feeling and the effort as follows:

> I assumed when I came here that being a good scientist was all that was necessary. Later I found that science was more than just research. You have to conceive, sell, and direct a program. I began to do all those things and found myself in management mainly because I didn't want to work for the other guys they were considering. I want to stay close to technical work and maybe move back into it. Because I know it is difficult to move out of management into technical work, I have stayed close to my field, written papers, and still consider myself to be a scientist.

Some, like Rivers, are able to meet these combined demands better than others, but the tension of keeping a foot in each camp is a problem for almost every professional at this stage of his career.

One further adjustment a person in this stage must make is learning to derive satisfaction out of seeing his apprentices move away from him, become independent, or take on new mentors. This can be a major source of gratification or of difficulty. Even though the mentor expects and looks forward to such eventual movement, differences in expectation about timing and methods may constitute a potential source of conflict and disappointment.

Not surprisingly, this adjustment seems to be harder for the Stage III individual without a formal supervisory position. The formal supervisory position carries certain psychological supports and a role clarity unavailable to those in less traditional roles. Counseling and dealing with the outside on behalf of others inside are part of the role definition of the supervisor. For the informal mentor, it is often less clear that these things are part of his job. On the other hand, the lack of an official boss–subordinate role often allows the nonsupervisor to enter into richer, more comfortable counseling relationships.

Along with conflicts, Stage III also brings long-term satisfaction. Challenges come from broadening the individual's thinking, increasing his knowledge by moving into new areas, or applying his skills to new problems. There is adequate social involvement, recognition from peers, and the satisfaction of helping junior professionals further their careers. Generally, the organizational rewards—both money and status—have reached a fairly satisfactory level. Some people find Stage III, with its combination of counseling, technical proximity, and recognition and rewards, viable and

satisfying until retirement. Some find that they are stagnating and are hard-pressed to keep up with younger competitors. Others move on to a new stage.

STAGE IV

Finally, as our study progressed it became clear that the careers of some individuals contain a definable fourth stage. The key characteristic that identified people in this stage was the influence they had in defining the direction of the organization or some major segment of it. Many of these Stage IV people occupied line management positions; others did not. But each had come, in his own way, to be a force in shaping the future of the organization.

A stereotype of organizations pictures this influence as being exercised by only one person—the chief executive officer. But this influence is in fact more widely distributed among key people than is commonly thought. They exercise this influence in a number of ways: negotiating and interfacing with the key parts of the environment; developing the new ideas, products, markets, or services that lead the organization into new areas of activity; or directing the resources of the organization toward specific goals.

Because these functions are so critical to the growth and survival of the organization, those who fulfill them are highly valued, and only those persons whose judgment and skill have been proved in the past are trusted to play these roles. Stage IV people have gained credibility by their demonstrated ability to read the environment accurately and respond appropriately.

Activities

The Stage IV people we encountered usually played at least one of three roles: manager, internal entrepreneur, idea innovator.

Upper-level managers are usually but not always in Stage IV of their careers, while a number of middle-level managers are making the transition to this stage. Unlike the Stage III supervisors, they are usually not involved in guiding Stage I people or even supervising people in Stage II. They are not close enough to the details of the daily work to perform in these roles. Instead, they formulate policy and initiate and approve broad programs.

One Stage IV manager described how he had changed his activities in order to work on directing his part of the organization as follows: "I have tried to develop my staff so that I could concentrate on where we are going instead of where we are at the moment. Consequently, things are running more smoothly, and I have more time to myself."

By no means are we implying that Stage IV managers spend all their time doing long-range planning. But the work they do and the decisions they make shape the direction of the organization, or at least a significant part of it.

There are others who, through their entrepreneurial activities within the organization, exercise an important influence on the direction of the firm. They are people with new ideas and a strong sense of the direction in which the organization should go. They bring resources, money, and people together in the furtherance of their ideas. One professional who seemed clearly in Stage IV described his work this way:

> I had an idea for a new product area and was getting very little support through the formal channels. So I talked to a couple of people on my level and convinced them it was

a good idea. We went ahead and did it. Today it is bringing in a significant part of our sales. Luckily, it worked out all right.

Entrepreneurs like this are often considered mavericks in their organizations. As long as they are successful at it, however, it is legitimate to be a maverick.

The third type, the idea innovator, seems distantly removed from the manager and the entrepreneur, but he has one thing in common with them—innovative ideas. The biggest opportunities, the most significant breakthroughs, probably most often originate with an individual contributor. He may puzzle over a problem or an idea for years before the solution finally presents itself. Such individuals may work quite closely with a manager or someone else to sell their ideas. Don Jones is an example of the technical or individual contributor. His department manager described him as follows:

> Don is one of the brightest people I know, but he doesn't like to talk. His knowledge of the field, however, is outstanding. He is talented, hardworking, and disciplined. He sets goals for himself on a technical project and achieves them. Every two or three years he has a new direction he wants the company to follow, and he is almost always right. He is not a salesman; he gets people like me to sell his ideas.

Often, the Stage IV individual contributor has also established a reputation outside the organization by his professional achievements and/or publications. This enhances his credibility inside the organization and may enable him to play a key role in recruiting and business development.

Relationships

One of the major ways in which those in Stage IV influence the direction of the organization is through the selection and development of key people. One of the managers we interviewed described this part of his work as follows:

> Since I first moved into management I have consistently tried to develop my staff. Just as others have sponsored me and made it possible for me to take their positions when they moved up, I have done the same.

There is of course a similarity between Stage III and IV in this respect. But there is also a difference. The individual in Stage IV is not concerned with getting new people started. Instead, he selects those who show promise of performing Stage IV activities in the future and grooms them. The focus is on opening up opportunities, assessing, and providing feedback rather than on teaching and instruction. He watches these people, notes their strengths and weaknesses, counsels them, and tries to guide each one into areas where he is most likely to be effective.

The development of key people is not restricted to Stage IV people in management roles but also forms a significant part of the work of Stage IV nonmanagers. The entrepreneurs and the idea men also tend to spend a considerable amount of time and energy in the development of key people and, interestingly, often not into their own mold. In one of the large laboratories we studied,

the director and two of the associates had been mentored by one senior scientist. He noted that he had suggested they move toward management because their greatest strengths seemed to be in that area. We frequently found that these nonmanagerial Stage IV people had played a major role in developing many of the most able managers.

Another characteristic of Stage IV people is that they are heavily involved in key relationships outside the organization. One of our Stage IV interviewees described himself as multiorganizational because he worked on so many external boards, committees, and associations. These outside contacts are critical not only because they bring into the organization current information about events and trends in the environment but also because they give the organization the visibility it needs to market its goods, services, and people. Senior partners in CPA firms, for example, are expected to be involved in professional associations and to have developed extensive relationships in the banking and legal communities.

We often found, particularly among nonmanagement Stage IV people, that writing and publication had been and continued to be a means of achieving visibility and contact. But extensive publication or extensive contact of any kind with the outside is no guarantee of Stage IV status inside the organization. Unless the publications or the outside relationships are structured and focused in areas of major concern to the organization, such activities are not likely to be viewed positively by others in the organization.

Psychological Issues

The psychological shifts a person must make to move successfully into Stage IV are even greater than the changes he must make in his activities and relationships. As we indicated, managers in Stage IV remove themselves from day-to-day operations and transactions. Even as a Stage III mentor it is possible to stay close enough to the operations to retain a sense of personal control. But that must be relinquished by managers moving into Stage IV. Nonmanager Stage IV people often stay closer to some aspects of operations, but they are also relentlessly pulled away. One of the essential psychological shifts in moving to Stage IV is to learn not to second-guess subordinates on operating decisions. It is necessary to learn to influence by means other than the direct supervision of ongoing work—through ideas, through personnel selection, through reviews, through resource allocation, and through changes in organizational design. The need for this mode of influence is even greater for nonmanagerial Stage IV people.

Another critical shift for those moving into Stage IV is a broadening of perspective and a lengthening of time horizons. These individuals must learn to think about the organization as a whole and act in terms of that framework. They must learn to think about the needs of the organization beyond the time period during which they will personally be affected, to think not about next month or next year but about the next five to ten years—or beyond.

Last, because the issues are critical, because they affect the lives of so many people, and because the decisions must be made on the basis of personal judgments, people in Stage IV must also become accustomed to using power. Even if the individual himself is not initially comfortable in the exercise of power, he will find himself forced to exercise power because so many others depend on him to fight for their programs. He also needs to be able to form alliances and to take strong positions without feeling permanent enmity toward those who differ with him.

QUESTIONS RAISED BY THE MODEL

Whenever we discuss this model with professionals and managers, a number of questions arise. One, for example, is whether our data predict that a person who skips a stage will be a failure. We can only answer that we have interviewed a number of successful people who said they did not experience Stage I and a few who said they did not go through Stage II. Some people replied that they did not have a mentor but learned "how the system works" and so on from their peers. In some cases a group of new people joined the organization at the same time, and they helped each other learn what they needed to know.

The preponderance of our interviews suggests, however, that this alternative strategy is usually not as effective as working with a competent mentor. The mentor is better equipped to help the new employee make the transition from the academic setting into a professional career.

Some people say the model implies that the only successful people are those who have progressed to Stage IV. That is not our position. People in all four stages make an important contribution to the organization. A number of people in each stage are necessary for organizational effectiveness. However, our research indicates that as people grow older they are less likely to be highly valued if they don't move beyond the early stages.

FIGURE 2

Relationship Between Stage and Performance Level for People over Age 40.

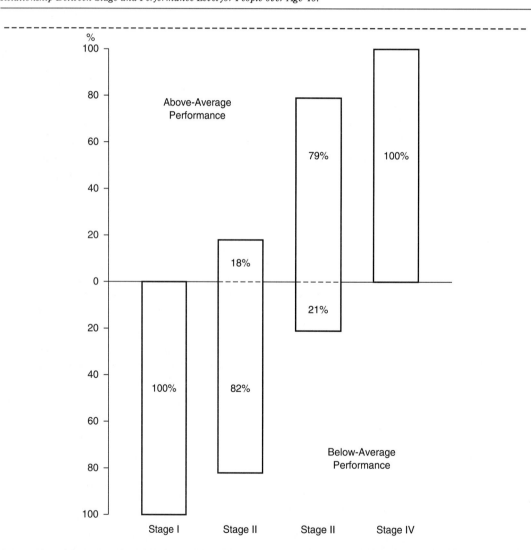

The data in Figure 2 provide an illustration of that point. We asked managers in two research and development organizations to classify the people in their departments in one or another of the four stages. Figure 2 contrasts stage and performance for all individuals over age 40. This figure suggests that only a small proportion of the people still in Stage II are rated as above-average performers. The implication is clear: To maintain a high performance rating throughout his career, an individual should seek to move at least to Stage III.

Another frequent question is, do people only move forward in these stages? If they do revert to an earlier stage, what is the likelihood of their being able to make the eventual transition to one of the later stages? That seems to depend on the climate of the organization. In some organizations, there seemed to be enough flexibility in both the formal and the informal systems to allow people to do some moving back and forth between stages. Even in these organizations, however, the thought of moving from Stage IV implied demotion, and people were reluctant to make such a transition. An example will illustrate the point.

At age 50, George Dunlap found himself in an uncomfortable position. He had been department manager of a group of 300 employees for eight years, and he realized the job was losing the challenge it had once had for him. He thought it unlikely that he would be promoted to the next step in the management hierarchy, and he felt that he might end up holding that position for the next 15 years. About that time he was given an opportunity to make a shift, which he describes as follows:

> I was asked to do a major study for the president that would require my full-time effort. I was reluctant to accept the assignment if it meant giving up my position as department manager because I didn't know where it would lead. I agreed that I would work on it full time for six months, but I would only take a temporary leave from my position as department manager. In order to do the study I had to go back and learn a lot about surveys, interviews, analyzing questionnaire data, and so on. After I finished the study, the president asked if I would take a position in which some of the things proposed in the report might be implemented. He invited me to become his assistant and work out of the office of the president. It sounded interesting, but I still had a lot of questions. There was the question of status. When I was head of a large department, I had secure status. I expected it to be difficult to assume a staff position with no one but a secretary reporting to me. It took time to adjust to the idea.
>
> After some extensive soul-searching, I decided to take the new position, and it has worked out very well. I enjoy my work, and I believe I'm having a major impact on the whole organization.

George accepted a position which, in our terms, temporarily moved him from Stage IV to a variety of Stage II activity in which he specializes in a new area of research. However, he made the transition successfully. He learned to exert considerable influence in his new role and clearly moved back into Stage IV, but in a different kind of work. This was done in a large laboratory where a precedent had been established by a former laboratory director who had made a similar move. In other organizations, we found less movement of this sort.

Some people have asked if the stages are merely another way to describe the management hierarchy. Stages III and IV are not

FIGURE 3

Percentage of People in Each Stage Holding Management and Nonmanagement Positions in Five R&D Organizations.

Stage	Individual Contributors (%)	Managers (%)	Total (%)
I	100.0	0.0	100
II	98.7	1.3	100
III	65.2	34.8	100
IV	25.9	74.1	100

limited to people in formal management positions in most organizations. Figure 3 shows the percentage of managers and individual contributors in each stage in five organizations. Figure 4 indicates the proportion of professionals and managers who were described by their superiors as being in each stage.

Upper-level managers described many nonmanagers as doing Stage III and IV work. We believe that any effective professional organization will have many nonmanagers in Stages III and IV. Professional organizations that are so rigidly structured that they provide no opportunities for Stages III and IV among nonmanagers are the poorer for it.

CONCLUSION

What is the value of this way of conceptualizing professional careers in organizations? What implications does it have for managing professional employees?

Edgar Schein pointed out in 1971 that "we do not have readily available concepts for describing the multitude of separate experiences that the individual encounters during the life of his organizational career." We experienced the need for such concepts in trying to wrestle with the problems of obsolescence and performance among professionally trained employees. To explain the differences we found in performance ratings, we especially needed a clearer picture of what Schein calls the organizational definition

FIGURE 4

Proportionate Distribution of Professionals and Managers in Each Stage Reported by Five R&D Organizations.

Stage	Proportionate Distribution of Professionals in Each Stage (%)
I	13.4
II	46.2
III	29.3
IV	11.1
	100.0

of a career—"the set of expectations held by individuals inside the organization which guide their decisions about who to move, when, how, and at what speed."

The concept of career stages has provided us with a way of describing that set of expectations. But it is important to note that these expectations were not necessarily a part of the formal organization. In fact, in the organizations we studied it was the informal and often unstated expectations about the critical activities and relationships a person should engage in at each stage that determined both formal and informal rewards. In our view, the study of an organization as a setting in which careers are lived provides both a fruitful lead and a new perspective for understanding organizations.

But our model of career stages has both pragmatic and theoretical implications for those who live in organizations as well as for those who manage them. Individuals need a longitudinal framework within which to form their own career decisions. Managers need a framework for predicting some of the long-term consequences of short-term career decisions. Managers in several organizations have found it useful to examine the stages of career development in their own organizations as a way of identifying the factors that block or facilitate movement between stages.

Performance Appraisal and Career Development

Too often performance appraisal interviews focus only on the past year or, at best, on plans for the forthcoming year. Rarely do a manager and a subordinate discuss careers, in the main because neither the manager nor the subordinate has a way to talk about career development in terms other than the prospects for promotion. The career stages model can be helpful in guiding such a discussion. A number of managers have found that just discussing the model with individuals helps them to think more clearly about their careers and begin to identify alternatives and strategies for development that they hadn't previously considered.

The concept of stages can help a person think more clearly not only about what he should be doing and learning in his present job but also about what he should do if he wants to advance to another stage. A person who has learned what he needs to do in Stage I can begin to demonstrate his ability to work independently, develop an expertise that others recognize, and begin to apply that expertise. A person in Stage II may begin to take a new employee under his wing, show him how the system works, teach him some of the finer technical points, and so on. The Stage I person who wants to progress in the organization could ask himself: "Am I reluctant to make decisions on my own?" A person aiming for Stage IV could ask himself whether he is able to think about the needs of the organization as a whole and not just about his own group.

Timing

We aren't saying that anyone can promote himself to Stage IV. We do say that people can begin to do the work of the next stage and thus facilitate the transition to that stage. However, timing is a significant issue. There is a fine line between trying to move too quickly into the next stage and staying in the present stage long enough to obtain a learning base sufficient for subsequent growth.

Too many people are so intent on getting into management that they don't establish the technical base they will need when they are called on to direct others.

Finally, and this is important, the individual must be responsible for deciding whether to stay in that organization. Sometimes an individual is capable of moving into Stage III or Stage IV activities and willing to do so, but the opportunities in the present organization are limited. On the other hand, failure to develop the skills and attitudes needed at the next stage could negate the effect of a change of organizations.

Manpower Planning

Although the primary responsibility for career management lies with the individual, the organization can do some things to facilitate career development. To become aware of the problem is the indispensable first step. Many managers are insensitive to the changing level of opportunities in their organizations. One company was having serious problems with turnover in its sales force. The company had grown rapidly for ten years, doubling sales every three years. Then growth leveled off to 5 percent a year. However, the district sales managers continued to recruit new salesmen with promises of promotion into management within 18 months and so on. When the promised promotions didn't materialize, the disillusioned salesmen left to go to work for the competition, usually within two or two and one-half years.

An awareness of this problem can come from an analysis of the demographic data. How many employees, engineers, accountants, and managers, for example, does the organization have in each stage? What are the prospects for expansion and for having new positions open up? What is the turnover in each group?

It is also important for managers to share data with their people. Recently 60 upper-level managers in a large organization were asked whether they thought they would be promoted at least one more time before retirement. Fully 80 percent said no, not because they felt they lacked ability but because they felt there were no opportunities. In fact, the organization was planning on having most of them assume higher-level responsibilities.

Dual Ladders

The concept of career stages could help to explain some of the confusion and disillusionment that have arisen around the dual ladder. In attempting to recognize the contributions a nonmanagerial professional can make to an organization, most dual ladder programs have dichotomized the technical and the managerial roles. Often the roles in the technical ladder are described in terms of the lone individual contributor—a super Stage II person.

As we noted earlier, organizations have other roles for their experienced and competent senior people to fill. Stage III people, whether or not they are in management, tend to deal with the outside, train and develop others, and provide direction for important projects or activities. A recognition of the similarities between the activities and relationships of Stage III managers and Stage III nonmanagers could help professionals to recognize that some experience in a management position may be a legitimate form of preparation for a senior technical role, just as a Stage III or IV nonmanager may make the best candidate for a formal management slot.

Job Assignments

All our research indicates that the job assignment is the single most important variable in career development. There are many ways in which this variable can be manipulated. A person who is seen as too narrow can be moved to a new project that forces him to apply his existing skills to new problems. Someone who is finding it difficult to become independent of his mentor can be transferred to a job that facilitates such a transition. A change of job assignment is no panacea, but it can be pivotal in helping people develop their careers.

Finally, organizations need to find ways of loosening their structures, rules, and procedures to make it possible for more people to move through the stages. In most organizations more people combine the ability and desire to do Stage III and IV work than are allowed to do so. Often there are policies or traditions that permit only certain people to deal with customers, suppliers, and so on or that make it difficult for individual contributors to serve as mentors. Some managers are unwilling, for example, to let senior employees serve as mentors to the newcomers in the organization.

Sometimes their fear is justified, but more often it prevents the formation of a very productive relationship.

Most organizations and most managers are both unsuccessful and uncreative in managing senior professionals. Organizations that learn to perform that task well will have a considerable competitive advantage.

Organizations need to be more creative in making it possible for people to move both ways through the stages without the fear of a clear or permanent loss of status or prestige. Often the individual and the organization are locked into motivating an unrewarding relationship. It needs to become much easier for people like George Dunlap to make the transition that he made. As more senior managers set the example of this type of transition, hopefully it will become a more acceptable career alternative.

Consciously or unconsciously we all carry in our heads models to help us think about careers in organizations. We have concluded that many of the models being used to make decisions that affect careers are misleading. In our view, the longitudinal concept of career stages can be helpful to both professionals and managers as they make decisions about their careers.

Career Gridlock:
Baby Boomers Hit the Wall*

Douglas T. Hall

Judith Richter

It would appear that the baby boomers have finally arrived. After enduring overcrowded public schools in the '50s and '60s, competing for admission and surviving mass education "megaversities" and the turmoil of war in the '60s and '70s, and then competing for jobs in recessions in the '70s and '80s, most are now in their 30s and comfortably established in careers. Now it's the employers' turn to adapt to the baby boom, as this group composes almost 55 percent of the United States labor force.[1] Indeed, in 1988, a well-publicized member of the baby boom generation was elected Vice President of the United States.

Have the baby boomers really "made it"? They happen to have "arrived" during a period of unprecedented restructuring of American industry, with widespread workforce reductions, streamlining, and reorganizations, all aimed at generating greater output from fewer people. Where have all the opportunities gone? How

should top management respond to the concerns of this large cluster of new arrivals at midcareer?

Consider the case of Mary Jackson (not her real name, as will be the case with the other baby boomers' names used). After competing with a large number of other bright college graduates 15 years ago, she was accepted into a training program at AT&T. She did outstanding technical work and struggled to get on the managerial track. Finally, after being turned down for a long-hoped-for promotion, she consulted a senior person for advice. He pointed out that the competition for management slots was becoming severe (the result of multiple workforce reductions at AT&T), that being turned down did not mean that she would never make it into management, and that she should be patient and wait for the next round of promotions.

Reconsidering her chances in light of the large number of candidates for the next round of promotions, Mary decided to step out of the race. She is now successfully running her own consulting firm. She also found that the exit from corporate life provides greater balance for marriage and family.

Unfortunately, the effort to stand out leads most baby boomers to feel that their work is taking up too much of their lives. A recent *Fortune* article called this group "the workaholic generation."[2] Work-family balance, which has been a visible management issue lately, is a major problem for members of the baby boom generation. Their attempts to restore balance, either by dropping out, cutting back to "mommy track" or "daddy track" involvement,

Douglas T. Hall (Boston University) and Judith Richter (Tel-Aviv University) "Career Gridlock: Baby Boomers Hit the Wall." Reprinted with permission from the *Academy of Management Executive,* 1990, Vol. 4 (3), 7–22.

*The authors gratefully acknowledge the helpful comments of Marcy Crary, Kathy Kram, and anonymous reviewers, as well as the support of the Human Resources Policy Institute of the Boston University School of Management and that of its Director, Fred Foulkes.

1. See Walter Kiechel III, "The Workaholic Generation," *Fortune,* April 10, 1989, 50–62.

2. *Ibid.*

or simply by continuing to operate at a higher level of conflict and stress, have become a major management "story" of the 1990s.

THE MISSING VIEW:
IMPACT OF THE BABY BOOM
ON MANAGERIAL CAREERS

Mary Jackson, Fred Revitch, and Brett Johnson are all members of the post-World War II baby boom generation, and they are dealing with issues of how to achieve fulfillment both at work and at home.

Significant media attention has been placed on the baby boom in recent years, even before the 1988 election campaign. *Time* announced in a cover story, "The Baby Boomers Turn 40" (May 19, 1986). The *Boston Globe* wondered about "Middle Managers With No Place To Go" (February 9, 1988). A movie was titled "Baby Boom," and then it became a television series. Several other series were targeted at baby boomers such as "thirtysomething" and "L.A. Law." As *The Wall Street Journal* put it in 1989, "Marketers have been in love with the baby boom for years now."[3]

Do the baby boomers look as distinctive in the workplace as they do in the marketplace? Should organizational career paths be redefined? This article examines these questions and attempts to determine the implications of the baby boom for the management of organizations.

A PROFILE OF THE BABY BOOMERS
AT WORK

What are the distinctive values and concerns which characterize people like Mary Jackson and the other baby boom employees? Based upon our own interviews, and other studies, we have identified the following profile of the baby boom:

1. A strong concern for basic values. Not only are there particular values which baby boomers tend to hold, but the issue of values *per se* is important to baby boomers. Whereas older generations may have been more concerned with achievements, success, status, or power for their own sake, baby boomers are more likely to question *why* they are seeking success and what the *personal meaning* of success is to them.

2. A sense of freedom to act on values. Baby boomers have a greater sense of freedom to act out their values than previous age groups. In a sense, this is the corporate extension of the 1960's campus rallying cry, "Do it." Now we see a generation of professional and managerial employees who, without making loud corporate protests, are more likely than their predecessors to behave in ways that are congruent with their values.

This quality of independence manifests itself in various ways: a computer specialist who would not even interview in one company because it did a lot of military contract work, the manager who turned down a promotion because it would require four days' travel each week and keep him away from his year-old son, and countless "whistle blowers" who report corporate fraud, at the expense of their careers. For example, Walker Williams, former head of human resources of Westin Hotels, estimates that when the telephone rings, and an employee is told, "We need you in Atlanta in 15 minutes, no questions, just go," half of the people will not go. He estimates that in a few years, 90 percent will say no.

Channeling humanistic values into a professional career is exemplified in the work of Susan McCrea. After completing her undergraduate degree, she wanted to "make health care more accessible to all people in the world." She wanted to influence domestic health care policy, so she took a job with the State of Minnesota as a state health planner. However, she left the public sector after concluding that health care policy didn't necessarily influence health care delivery systems. She went first to an HMO (health maintenance organization), and then became an independent marketing consultant to HMOs and nonprofit health organizations. She later earned an MBA in health care to increase her earning potential and to improve her professional credentials. She is now assistant to the president of a major Boston medical center, responsible for marketing and planning. She feels satisfied that she is able to influence organizational policies and practices in a way that is consistent with her social values.

3. A focus on self. Concern for values and consistency between values and behavior is related to a strong sense of self-awareness. Dr. Phyllis Horner, an internal personnel consultant at Ford Motor Company, reports that this group's definition of professionalism includes one's own determination of the source of one's self-concept. Finding one's work in life, then, becomes a way to find and express one's self-identity. Dr. Horner refers to this focus on self as a "healthy narcissism."

4. Need for autonomy and questioning authority. Implementing a self-concept and living out one's values require a certain level of freedom. Indeed, the need for freedom and the impatience with formal hierarchical authority is probably the most distinctive single feature of the baby boom group. Donald Kanter and Philip Mirvis, using a national probability sample of United States workers, found that only 22 percent reported trust in management, even though 70 percent are generally satisfied with their jobs, and 55 percent are satisfied with their job rewards (pay, promotion prospects, benefits, etc.). Although these data include workers of all ages, the authors cited the baby boomers' disillusionment as a major influence on workforce morale. When they sorted their data by age, they found a "relatively high level" of cynicism reported by the baby boomers. Kanter and Mirvis describe the importance of workers' age in this low trust of management:

> "These data suggest to us that a central problem in human resource management in 1985 is workers' response to authority in general. A young, hostile, cynical workforce that holds high opinions of itself . . . is not easy to manage, efficient, loyal, or (probably) very receptive to change."[4]

To be more positive, what qualities would baby boomers value in a leader? In a creative research design, William G. Dyer and Jeffrey H. Dyer conducted a survey of what they called the "M*A*S*H Generation" (1,000 people born in the late 1950s and early 1960s). The purpose was to identify the kinds of organizational

---

3. David Wessel, "One Sure Fact: Baby boomers Are Aging." *The Wall Street Journal,* January 3, 1989, B1.

4. Donald L. Kanter and Philip H. Mirvis, "Managing Jaundiced Workers," Working Paper, Boston University School of Management, 1985, 12. This work is also reported in D. L. Kanter and P. H. Mirvis, *The Cynical Americans,* (San Francisco: Jossey-Bass, 1989).

processes and conditions that people associated with the hospital organization in the TV show M*A*S*H, which was extremely popular among baby-boomers. Dyer and Dyer concluded that the show's Colonel Sherman Potter most clearly fits baby boomers' image of the effective boss:

> "He is the only one they identify as having the trait of leadership. Specifically, they want to work under a superior who treats subordinates with respect and is concerned about their welfare and tries to understand them. They list the important personal characteristics of the leader as being broadmindedness, competence, maturity, and fairness."[5]

5. Less concern with advancement. Related to the baby-boomers' questioning of authority is a weaker desire to become part of it. There appears to be less of a driving passion to move up the hierarchy among this group. For example, Ann Howard and James A. Wilson compared motivation profiles for two groups of AT&T managers, one hired in the 1950s and the other in the 1970s (baby boomers). In terms of intrinsic motivation to achieve and perform well on the job, there were no significant differences between the two groups. The big difference came in their desires for upward mobility, expressed in a variety of measures (e.g., a questionnaire measuring desires for upward mobility, needs for dominance, expectations for a higher position in the next five years). Although both groups wanted a challenging job and a middle manager's salary in the following five years, 54 percent of the 1950s sample indicated a desire to advance to a middle management position while only 34 percent of the 1970s cohort chose that outcome. Howard and Wilson concluded that, "By and large, the [1970s] recruits were inclined neither to push their way up the organization hierarchy nor to lead others. In short, the new managers weren't motivated to act like managers." Based on this AT&T research and his own interviews, Walter Kiechel concludes,

> "They don't like telling others what to do any more than they like being told. No respecters of hierarchy, they don't want to get to the top just because it's the top."[6]

These conclusions are supported by Miner and Smith's finding that the motivation to manage has declined among college students between 1960 and 1980.[7] Similarly, Driver reports a drop in what he calls "linear" (i.e., advancement) career motives for college students in the 1960s and early 1970s (although Driver finds that this trend has now reversed for the post-baby boom group).[8] Although challenging work and financial rewards are still very important to baby boomers, they may be less willing than other groups to assume higher-level managerial responsibilities to attain these rewards. (This may help explain the appeal to baby boomers of investment banking, real estate development, and entrepreneurship, activities in which financial rewards are high but organizational management responsibilities are relatively low.)

6. Crafting: In-place career development. Perhaps related to this lower need for advancement is the baby boomer's orientation to high quality in the current job. In this highly educated, highly principled group, utilizing one's potential (i.e., self-actualization) is not only an important need but a basic value. To perform poorly produces dissatisfaction and guilt.

An Opinion Research Corporation study found that by the late 1970s, concerns for self-fulfillment and personal growth had become pervasive in the work force as a result of the addition of the baby boomers.[9] As one person described his need for growth, "How do I keep myself growing even if my company isn't interested in that?" Walter Kiechel, who called boomers the workaholic generation, asks, "Why do they work so hard? Because they love it, they say, often using the words 'fun,' 'creative,' and 'stimulating' to describe the experience . . . Work is also where they perform, as an athlete performs, winning the applause of the crowd."[10]

This concern for craft in one's work shows up in the baby boomers' preference for professional work, as identified by Raelin (see Footnote 15). The critical motivation is the intrinsic reward which comes from crafting one's work, and doing a high-quality job in the service of a useful purpose.

7. Entrepreneurship. If the baby boomer values achievement and autonomy but does not want to submit to authority or exercise it, what career and organization design options are left open? One option is to become an entrepreneur. A study of 9,000 graduates of the Harvard Business School found that the peak age for entrepreneurship is in the early 30s (30 percent of the entrepreneurs studied start at this age). People in their early 30s represent the peak of the baby boom cohort.

Howard Stevenson of the Harvard Business School's entrepreneurship project sees entrepreneurship as a way of expressing the counter culture values of the 1960s and 1970s.[11] Warren Bennis views it as an expression of selfhood which is a major legacy of the

5. William G. Dyer and Jeffrey H. Dyer, "The M*A*S*H Generation: Implications for Future Organizational Values," *Organizational Dynamics,* Summer 1984, *13,* 78.

6. This research is reported in Ann Howard and James A. Wilson, "Leadership in a Declining Work Ethic," *California Management Review,* Summer 1982, Vol. XXIV, *4,* 33. See also Kiechel, *op. cit.,* 50.

7. See J. Miner and N. Smith, "Decline and Stabilization of Managerial Motivation over a 20-year Period," *Journal of Applied Psychology,* 1982, *67,* 297–305. More data on the lower levels of advancement motivation among baby boomers, compared to the previous generation, are reported in an excellent longitudinal AT&T study, Ann Howard and Douglas W. Bray, *Managerial Lives in Transition,* (New York, Guilford, 1988).

8. See Michael J. Driver, "Careers: A Review of Personal and Organizational Research," in C. L. Cooper and I. Robertson (Eds.), *International Review of Industrial Psychology 1988,* (London: John Wiley & Sons, Ltd., 1988), 245–277.

9. See M. R. Cooper, B. S. Morgan, P. M. Foley, and L. B. Kaplan, "Changing Employee Values: Deepening Discontent," *Harvard Business Review,* 1979, *57,* 117–125.

10. See Kiechel, *op cit.,* 51–52.

11. Howard Stevenson, "Entrepreneurship," presentation at Academy of Mangement Meeting, Boston, 1984.

1960s, and he predicts a major growth in self-employment over the next 10 years (10 percent of the United States working population is now self-employed). Bennis refers to this phenomenon as the "Big Chill" factor (named after the movie): if there is a hero, he or she is played by an entrepreneur.[12]

8. Concern for work/family balance: the total life perspective. The baby boom group is getting into parenting in a big way. Part of the concern for the self is an awareness of one's personal and family life. Even though work is important, as we have just said, there is a sense among baby boomers that "I work to live; I don't live to work."

The baby boom group has done well occupationally, despite the dire forecasts referred to earlier, and this work success may spill over into private life. Louise Russell found that, although crowded, the baby boom cohort has not suffered educationally because of its size. More of its members were educated than any previous generation, and more money was spent on education per student than ever before. Furthermore, despite the negative effects of their numbers, Russell concluded that baby boomers are still earning real income as high as, or higher than, any previous generation.[13]

Further evidence of the occupational success of this group is found in Joseph Raelin's analysis of what he calls "the 60's generation." Raelin uses census data to show that an unusually high proportion of the 60's generation's members are in professions. Similar findings were reported by Werner and Stillman and by Mills.[14]

There is a sense of costs and benefits of various life and career options (e.g., "Can I really have a truly satisfying career and a truly satisfactory parenting experience?"). There is an ability to make tradeoffs and establish balance between work and family concerns.

The fact that the baby boomer manager/professional cohort has a large proportion of women is a significant factor in this concern for family. We refer to this balanced, autonomous work life, in which the employee takes major responsibility, as the protean career. In the remaining sections, we consider how organizations can cope with these growing numbers of protean baby boomers.

---

12. Warren G. Bennis, "Leadership," presentation at Academy of Management, Boston, 1984. These ideas are elaborated in Bennis's book *Leaders* (co-authored with Burt Nanus), (New York: Harper & Row, 1985).

13. See Louise B. Russell, *The Baby Boom Generation and the Economy,* (Washington, DC: The Brookings Institute, 1982) 1. Another excellent source is Landon Jones, *Great Expectations: Americans and the Baby Boom Generation,* (New York: Ballantine Books, 1980).

14. See Joseph A. Raelin, "The '60s Kids in the Corporation: More than Just 'Daydream Believers,'" *The Academy of Management Executive,* February 1987, 21–30. The Mills survey is reported in D. Quinn Mills, *Not Like Our Parents,* (New York: William Morrow and Company, 1987). See also, Rex Werner and Deanne Stillman, *The Woodstock Census* (New York: Viking Press, 1979).

GUIDELINES: TOWARD MORE EFFECTIVE UTILIZATION OF BABY BOOM POTENTIAL

There seems to be great potential in the "problems" represented by the baby boom. They are exceptionally well-educated, value-driven, independent, and quality-oriented. In response to these qualities, what steps might management take to tap this potential? Let us detail some recommendations about how an organization might yield the maximum benefit from its baby boom managers and employees.

1. Concern for Values: Replace the "Promotion Culture" with a "Psychological Success" Culture. Since values are so important to the baby boomer, corporate cultures must be changed to accommodate these new career orientations. As Dave Cornett, a human resources consultant at DuPont said, "The continuous upward mobile employee is a thing of the past. The key for DuPont is to make the current position as rewarding and exciting as possible." In our work with organizations, we have repeatedly heard comments such as, "I personally would like to make a lateral move, but everyone else around here would see that as a mark of failure." Every organization has a career culture which acts as a powerful source of resistance to the changes we just recommended. How might these career cultures be modified to produce an organizational transformation?

Strategic human resource development has been advocated as a way to implement changes in how an organization nurtures its talent.[15] The culture of an organization is reinforced by forces at three levels: the top strategic level is translated into design through managerial systems and programs (the middle level), and put into action at the implementation (bottom) level.

Human resource policies that affect employees' personal growth (e.g., policies on promotion from within, cross-training and cross-functional moves, using key management jobs for developmental purposes, holding managers accountable for subordinate development, and a strong internal succession planning process) are key to human resource development.

We believe that the corporate career culture is changed by promoting dialogue on and establishing clear policies, endorsed and acted upon by top management, which promote more diverse and flexible forms of career growth. Time and energy should be directed at these basic development policies before work is put into managerial-level activities (such as training managers in new forms of career management) or implementation level changes (such as career workshops). While the latter activities are worthwhile, their effects are multiplied if supportive human resource policies are in place first.

---

15. See, for example, D. T. Hall, "Human Resource Development and Organizational Effectiveness," in C. J. Fombrun, N. M. Tichy, and M. A. Devanna, *Strategic Human Resource Development* (New York: John Wiley & Sons, 1984), 159–181; D. T. Hall, "Dilemmas in Linking Succession Planning to Individual Executive Learning," *Human Resource Planning,* 1986, *25,* 235–265; and D. T. Hall, and J. G. Goodale, *Human Resource Management: Strategy, Design, and Implementation* (Glenview, IL: Scott, Foresman, 1986).

More organizations *are* engaging in these new practices all the time. Companies, such as DuPont, IBM, and Johnson and Johnson, have committees or task forces on work/family issues, that raise awareness and create significant change in career management practices. DuPont's task force on career and family issues was made up of a cross-section of levels and job functions so that the total work force was represented. The task force met with groups of employees, identified key issues, commissioned a major employee survey, and recommended explicit policies and implementation strategies, that are currently being adopted. Conscious use of organizational development values and processes were important in the success of this process, according to Faith Wohl, co-chair of the task force.

2. Freedom to Act on Values: Support More Protean or Self-Directed Careers. Organizational careers must be reframed to reflect the notion that "up is not the only way," to use the words of author Beverly Kaye.[16] Career paths are becoming more differentiated and self-directed—i.e., more protean. As another part of the culture change process, these protean career paths should be more widely communicated and valued. Employees need to have the option of periodically changing direction, so they are not locked into one single, long-term, career plan. As Will Cookta, personnel director for Beringer Ingelheim Pharmaceuticals, put it, "We want our company to look at multiple options, not just up-or-out or up-or-you're-a-jerk. We need to crack the culture."

To tap the great diversity of the baby boom group in a leaner organization, there must be a range of career paths from which to choose: functional specialist (growth within a discipline), consultant, local generalist (rotational, lateral movement, while remaining in one location), fast-track or slow-track into management, project management, permanent part-timer, job specialist (career development within a specific job position), and multipath option (the freedom to move from one of the paths to another). These different career forms are already available in many organizations. However, they are often used on a case-by-case basis, without the realization that they represent the career preferences of large numbers of baby boomers and the needs of contemporary organizations. They need to be legitimized (or "blessed") by the culture as valued and respected careers.

How might we move toward these differentiated career paths to provide opportunities for more protean careers? The following approaches are being taken in some organizations:

❏ Articulate a policy that the career is the individual's responsibility. This is a radical departure for many organizations that take a more paternalistic approach to career development ("Trust us"). Ford Motor Company has made this change, and employees are assisted through training workshops in asserting more personal control over their careers.[17] It may mean supporting the employee in saying "no" to the company at times. The end result in giving the

employee more self-control, however, is often better choices and greater employee commitment to their own decisions.

❏ *Encourage the manager's self-assessment.* To crack the upward-mobility career culture, managers and executives require special attention. Managers need to become more self-aware and self-directed. A realistic self-assessment is important to a manager's self-directed career choices. Even in an era of widespread career planning, this self-assessment is still a relatively new activity in company-run management education programs. (It is more often done for lower-level employees.) Each person needs to take a good honest look at his or her own skills, interests, and values, compared to those required of fast-trackers. DuPont's Individual Career Management program (ICM), for example, helps employees assess their values, skills, and interests and then develop an action plan for work directions that express these personal preferences.

❏ *Promote early rotational (lateral) moves.* To give an employee a sense of the wide range of available career paths, there should be opportunities for lateral, cross-functional, moves early in the career. This prevents people from becoming stuck in a dead-end career path and makes rotational moves a realistic option later in the career. Periodic rotation creates a wide range of skills which can be used for general management or to produce a well-rounded specialist.

According to Goodyear career counselor Laura Bettinger, Goodyear employees submit applications for lateral moves, stating their skills, experience, and the position sought. Managers submit lists of openings and the human resource department serves as an internal placement broker. This lateral pool program has a positive reputation, and many people apply, creating competition for open slots.

❏ Discourage career planning; stress "work planning." While we have stressed the need for activities like self-assessment, we have not specifically recommended career planning. *Organizations should not encourage long-term career planning.*

In view of the volatile nature of today's organizational environments, it is difficult for both organizations and individuals to do effective long-term planning. What may be more realistic is to encourage people to assess their own values, interests, skills, and lifestyle needs in relation to various work options that are available.

The focus is on identifying the type of work the person would like to do over the next few years, without trying to worry about the rest of his or her career.

Self-assessment is different than setting a long-term plan for a career with a complete set of specific goals and stepping stones. Given the turbulence in the environments of today's organizations, the latter is unrealistic. Using solid, realistic self-understanding and skills the individual is empowered to recognize and use career opportunities as they arise. Shorter-term work plans, combined with a longer-term sense of personal direction, are required.

Indeed, a shorter-term focus fits well with that of most employers. As Joe Robinson, budget manager for First Union Corporation, said, "I've noticed in job interviews that nobody asks what you plan to be doing five to ten years from now. They only talk about one-year plans."

---

16. See Beverly Kaye, *Up Is Not the Only Way,* (Englewood Cliffs, NJ: Prentice-Hall, 1982).

17. This work was reported in Phyllis C. Horner, "Career Development in Traditional Manufacturing Organizations," Career Division Workshop presentation, Academy of Management Meetings, Boston, August 11, 1984.

□ Define career growth as the development and use of new skills and abilities. One concrete way to reinforce the notions of work planning and up-is-not-the-only-way is to communicate the idea that growth in the career is the development and use of new skills and abilities. For most people, and in particular for intrinsically-motivated, growth-oriented baby boom managers, the important experience in the career is learning and growing, not necessarily ascending the hierarchy, as mentioned earlier. However, top management must legitimize this concept and set a policy facilitating career-long growth. For example, Chrysler encourages employees to establish stretch goals for their current positions, an activity that is supported by a pay-for-performance program. These practices are combined with development of new learning through periodic job changes (e.g., rotational moves, in-place changes in responsibility).

3. Focus On the Self: Self-Development and Lifelong Learning in the Work Itself. Almost 30 years ago, Chris Argyris raised the issue of whether the needs of psychologically healthy individuals could be congruent with the goals of the employing organization.[18] Today, it seems clear that the answer is, yes, the *effective* organization can find ways to make human need satisfaction and organizational goal attainment compatible. The move to participative and team leadership practices in today's downsized and delayered organization is probably the most important change in management circles today, and it certainly fits well with the self-directed, authority-questioning values of the baby boom cohort.[19] This is the "silver lining" which can be seen in the wake of severe corporate cutbacks and restructuring.

John Morley, personnel manager at Kodak, described an example of this delayering, in which a vice president of operations moved up to replace an executive vice president who retired. However, there was no replacement for the vice president. This one move impacted ten levels in the company. While these changes do produce frustrations, they also result in greater spans of control and responsibility for lower-level managers and employees. To support this increased responsibility, managers are trained to coach and develop their employees. These in-place development activities are supported by a pay-for-performance program.

Creating small, autonomous work units, such as the small project team that developed IBM's personal computer, has great potential. Autonomous work teams, described in Tracy Kidder's *The Soul of a New Machine,* created a new computer at Data General.

Project engineers and managers (in their 20s and 30s, primarily) often would work late into the night and through the weekend, motivated by the "pinball theory": if you win the game, you get to play it again (i.e., you get another project, with greater significance and more resources). The rewards came from learning and solving complex problems, so that good performance demanded the development of new knowledge and skills.[20]

The autonomy and intrinsic challenges associated with these new leadership styles provides the employee with a greater opportunity for self-development. Another way to think of this is as in-place career development. The smart manager attempts to give employees freedom to generate their own solutions to work problems and to implement them in their own ways. Not only does this autonomy provide a way to tap employees' creativity and motivation most effectively, but it is often virtually demanded by the wider spans of control resulting from eliminating layers of management. Managers who try to supervise too closely soon realize that they are overworked to the point of burnout. Permitting greater employee freedom is congruent with the high-autonomy and self-related values of the baby-boom manager. More stress on life-long learning is a natural by-product of restructured, leaner organizations.

4. Concern for Autonomy: More Flexibility and Diversity. As organizations face the need for more flexible human resource policies, flexibility in employee work arrangements needs to be extended. This is especially important for women. A growing number of women and men in their mid-to-late-thirties are beginning to conclude that they cannot have it all (career, marriage, and family) and are opting for marriage and family. For women, this often happens after an attempt to resume working after the first baby is born. The realization comes that a) they have already proven to themselves that they can be successful in the career, b) life is short, and c) at this time in their life they would rather be home raising the family. At this point, many women are opting out of organizational careers. Our hunch is that in five to ten years, they will be back at a different form of work. For women to continue rising in the ranks of management, organizations are going to have to find even more flexible arrangements to accommodate them.[21]

How might this greater flexibility be attained? One method is to use more permanent part-time jobs. As organizations are forced to make part-time work available to recruit and retain qualified employees (especially working mothers), part-time work is becoming more common in professional and managerial positions. It has always been an option for hourly and clerical employees. Parental leaves, with a phased re-entry period, are becoming longer and more flexible. Flextime is also widespread and a boon to working parents. Similarly, "flexplace" (working in the home) is becoming more available thanks to computer technology and a more liberal

---

18. This idea was originally reported in Chris Argyris, *Personality and Organization,* (New York: Harper, 1957). It is now showing up in practice as a trend in organizational career programs. See, for example, Manuel London and Steven A. Stumpf, "Individual and Organizational Career Development in Changing Times," in Douglas T. Hall and Associates, *Career Development in Organizations,* (San Francisco: Jossey-Bass, 1985), 21–49, for more discussion of this guideline and the others which follow.

19. For more discussion on how cutting-edge organizations are designing their career systems to better match individual and corporate career needs, see Thomas Gutteridge, "Organizational Career Development Systems: The State of the Practice," in Douglas T. Hall and Associates, Footnote 18, 50–94.

20. See Tracy Kidder, *The Soul of A New Machine* (Boston: Little, Brown and Company, 1981).

21. See Felice N. Schwartz, "Management Women and the New Facts of Life," *Harvard Business Review,* 1989, *67,* 65–82; Douglas T. Hall and Judith Richter, "Balancing Work Life and Home Life: What Can Organizations Do to Help?" *Academy of Management Executive,* 1988, *2,* 213–223; and Douglas T. Hall, "Promoting Work/Family Balance: An Organization Change Approach," *Organizational Dynamics,* Winter 1990, 18, 5–18.

corporate culture. Baby boomers who are well established in their careers and are now part of management have more leverage to negotiate work arrangements. Given the choice of being flexible or losing a valued manager or professional, many organizations have opted for flexibility. This was the work/family balance track that Felice Schwartz recommended in her widely-quoted *Harvard Business Review* article, "Management, Women and the New Facts of Life."[22] However, if the organization has not been confronted by baby boom managers with this choice, this flexibility is not freely offered.)

Moving to part-time work has to be done carefully and on a job-by-job basis, as not all jobs are conducive to part-time schedules. One organizational inducement, however, is that part-time managers and professionals usually contribute full-time involvement.

Corporate timetables must be adjusted to let part-timers rise at a more gradual rate. In the Westin Hotel organization, for example, employees' needs and career preferences are included as part of the potential assessment process. The company uses different development strategies for employees who report they are geographically mobile and for those who are not. "When we know what they want to do, we won't try to sell the person on a move they don't want. In the past, managers could staff a position with exactly who they wanted. Now we will have to change the company's expectations," reported Walker Williams, former head of Westin's human resources.

5. Less Concern for Advancement: More Diversity in Career Paths. In contrast to earlier eras when people had to conform to the structure of the work place, the structure of assignments can be more responsive to people's needs. As industries become more competitive and new technologies widely available, the competitive edge is often obtained through the flexible use and development of people.

For example, a construction firm founded by two baby-boom Harvard graduates is rapidly acquiring a reputation for building individualized, high-quality, bright, airy, aesthetic, energy-efficient townhouses in the Cambridge area. (These townhouses are in great demand by their fellow baby boomers.) How do they maintain the quality of their work as the number of projects expands? They use fairly simple designs and simple, high-quality materials that are easy to install and are not labor-intensive. Since the Boston work force is so unpredictable, they adjust the structure of their designs to fit the capabilities of the available workforce resulting in a high level of quality.

Consulting is another way to retain a valued professional or manager in a more autonomous role. An employee who needs large blocks of time off can be hired on a retainer basis, and used for specific projects and problems. This keeps the employee involved and up to date so re-entering the organization on a basis if his or her personal situation changes is made easier.

Organization structures are also being made more flexible by *differentiated career paths*. Not everyone aspires to be president of the company. There are, of course, high potential young people who have senior executive aspirations, and they need to be moved across a variety of specialties, to learn the complete business. However, many other talented people aspire to be the best within their particular specialty:

---

22. See Schwartz, Footnote 21.

"Not everyone needs to be a high potential achiever. For many people, being the food and beverage director at the Plaza Hotel would be a lifelong fulfillment. We need to establish different disciplines (e.g., personnel, front office, maintenance) as *career objectives* and create specialized career paths within them." (Walker Williams, Westin Corporation)

Monsanto found that the focus on more specialized career paths fits well in a leaner organization with slower overall corporate growth. There is a need to invest more creativity and energy in specific businesses and plant locations. According to Charles Arnold:

"With less corporate mobility, there is a need to emphasize the employees' identification with their own unit or location. This does not mean that some employees will not be asked to move around the corporation, but it does mean that broad corporate career programs are being de-emphasized, and specialization is OK."

Local identification is a way to provide more freedom, and to nurture creativity and innovation with less bureaucracy, but within the context of a world-wide organization. It also places more stress on development within the current assignment.

Greater differentiation in career development paths means that development is being encouraged in the following directions:

❐ within the present job (in-place development)

❐ within the present function (or specialty or discipline)

❐ within the present geographic location (which could include cross-functional rotational moves within that location)

❐ across functions and locations (i.e., corporate mobility for high-potential employees)

Crafting: Reward Quality of Performance, Not Potential. In the management and professional ranks in most organizations, there is a tendency to pay for potential rather than performance. For example, if two people are both performing at the same level, and if one person is a 25 year old "high potential" manager and the other is 40 years old and seen as plateaued, the younger "hi-po" person usually gets larger salary increases, and the older manager feels unrewarded for his or her performance. The organization suffers a tremendous loss in motivation by linking pay to future promotions.

Many organizations, such as Eli Lilly, are now seeking ways to identify and reward performance excellence, regardless of the person's age or career stage. One-time cash awards can be given for outstanding achievements (and in some cases they can simply be honorific awards and still be effective). In addition to helping de-couple promotion and rewards, such excellence awards fit nicely with the baby boomer's appreciation of quality and craftsmanship.

7. Entrepreneurship: Encourage It in the Organization's Interest. We recommend two strategies for using baby boomers' entrepreneurial potential. The first, and preferable, route is to harness energy in the service of organizational change. When baby boom managers or professionals become restless and start thinking about starting up their own venture, find a "start up" activity for them in your own organization. This could be a project assignment (either full-time or part of the current job) to explore the creation of a new product, service, or process. The person would be responsible for gathering resources, forming coalitions with key supporters, and championing the idea. In Rosabeth Kanter's terms, he or she would be expected to be a "change master."

News columnist Ellen Goodman has commented on how much corporate vitality and renewal is lost when baby boom entrepreneurs (whom she calls "corporate misfits, blue-jeaned [people] in three-piece corporations") leave to start up their own ventures.

> "The new breed are among the liveliest most exciting business people I meet. I don't want to read failure into their personal success, but few are starting the next IBM. Few will become the employers of hundreds of thousands.
>
> And as they leave larger companies, those workplaces are diminished. They lose another agent for change. More to the point, as these entrepreneurs walk out the door, one by one, American corporations lose another source of ideas, of innovation, of energy.
>
> And sometimes, after I have heard these success stories, I wonder how many of their old colleagues and bosses ever realize the gap left by another "misfit" who dropped a pair of old floppy wing tips beside the exit door."[23]

As newly restructured organizations attempt to tap the commitment and involvement of all employees to produce "high-performance systems," the entrepreneurial spirit of baby boom employees is a perfect resource to tap more systematically.

A second strategy is to support baby boomers in exploring entrepreneurial activities outside the organization. Often, helping the individual gather realistic information on starting up one's own business, leads to a decision that the cost and risks are too high. For example, a computer professional in her early 30s was interested in starting a company to make and sell high-quality hand-sewn craft items. Her company, through a career exploration seminar, supported her in interviewing people who had started similar businesses. She also interviewed people in various parts of her own firm to get more realistic information about future career opportunities there. She concluded that even the most successful entrepreneurs in her area of interest were putting in longer hours than she was currently and making less money. At the same time, she found an opportunity to start up a new line of products in her current firm. (In a similar case, a 30 year old software manager who initially wanted to get into real estate development talked it over with his senior management, and they agreed to let him redesign his current job to include new venture activity, with a sizeable incentive compensation arrangement.)

But what if exploration had led these managers to leave rather than stay? We argue that it is in the company's interest to support a person in a decision to leave, if that would be the best fit for her or him. If managers feel coerced to stay, eventually their performance suffers, and they eventually have to leave anyway.

We also recommend that a company keep its door open to allow baby boomers to return if they ever become dissatisfied with

working on their own. Many firms, however, have a policy of not hiring ex-employees. To us, this seems self-punitive for the firm, since this strong performer would just go to work for the competition, if she were barred from rejoining her old employer.

Thus, our message is, fan this entrepreneurial spirit. Use it to help restructure and vitalize the organization, and support individuals in finding a good fit for their own form of entrepreneurship, either inside or outside the firm. Chances are, a good thorough search will lead them to stay and to use this energy on the organization's behalf.

8. Concern for Balance: More Organizational Sensitivity to the Employee's Home Life. While many organizations recognize that a manager's personal and family life affect work and career decisions, there is reluctance to do anything to assist with strains between work and family life. This arises out of a sincere desire not to intrude in the manager's personal life.

However, sometimes the organization already is intruding on the person's private life to a considerable extent (i.e., through disruptive relocations, demanding work schedules, job stress). There are ways to assist the manager in dealing with work-home conflicts in ways which maintain privacy and enhance autonomy and coping skills. A few possibilities are listed below.[24]

❐ Establishing corporate dialogue on work-family balance. The critical step is to make this a "discussable" topic in the organization and to establish mechanisms to work on it. The experiences of firms like DuPont and Stride Rite have shown that a representative task force or committee is effective in creating this dialogue.

❐ Management training sessions in managing the work-home interaction. One pharmaceutical company does this in a three hour seminar, using company cases and a sharing of managers' learnings about how best to deal with work-home conflicts. In this extremely popular seminar, managers consider both what they can do for themselves and to help subordinates.

❐ After-hours workshops for managers and spouses to share problems and solutions in specific family topics (e.g., coping with a move, the first child, adolescents).

❐ Including the spouse in discussions about an impending relocation.

❐ Job search assistance to a career spouse during a relocation. This is often done through informal personnel networks in the new location or by making the firm's outplacement consultants available to the spouse. What is critical is expanding the organization's sphere of perceived responsibility to include the spouse and family, as well as the employee.

❐ Including spouses in more social events or conferences to share the benefits of corporate life.

There are numerous ways the manager's private life could be insulated more from the stresses of the job. Older managers

---

23. Ellen Goodman, "Corporate Misfits," *Boston Globe,* November 1, 1988, 13.

24. For more discussion on work-home balance, see Hall and Richter, Footnote 21, and Hall, "Promoting Work/Family Balance," Footnote 21.

EXHIBIT I
Summary of Baby Boom Characteristics and Recommended Organizational Actions.

Profile of Baby Boom Characteristics	*Recommended Organizational Action*
1. Concern for basic values	1. a. Replace promotion culture with psychological success culture b. Examine, change corporate career criteria c. Focus on corporate ethics
2. Freedom to act on values	2. a. Support protean career paths b. More lateral mobility c. De-couple rewards and the linear career path
3. Focus on self	3. Build on-going development into the job through: • Self-development • Life-long learning
4. Need for Autonomy	4. More flexible careers
5. Less concern with advancement	5. More diversity in career paths. More change: • within present job • within present function • within present location • across function and locations
6. Crafting	6. Reward quality performance, not potential
7. Entrepreneurship	7. a. Create internal entrepreneurial assignments b. Encourage employee career exploration (internally and externally)
8. Concern for work/home balance	8. a. More organizational sensitivity to home life b. Training for managing the work-home interface c. Inclusion of spouse in career discussions d. Career assistance for employed spouse e. Flexible benefits to help meet family needs (e.g., child care, elder care, care for sick children) f. More flexible work arrangements

accept the intrusion of work into family life; baby boom managers do not.

Exhibit 1 summarizes these profile characteristics and provides recommendations. The need to provide support and opportunities for greater self-awareness and empowerment is the common thread running through the recommendations.

CONCLUSION

The basic career and personal values of the baby boom manager are congruent with today's changing management practices and philosophy—as long as we can recognize and be comfortable with the paradoxical idea that the more self-control the manager has over his or her career, the more control (in the form of information and predictability) the organization has as well. The dark side of the baby boom and the downsized organizations is that there are too many good people available for too few management slots. But the bright side is that a lot of good baby-boomers have their own sense of where they want to head with their protean careers. While the number of ways of achieving promotional (vertical) success is finite (and shrinking), the number of ways of

achieving psychological success is infinite. The more an organization can match its human resource management practices to this new protean career orientation, the more effective it will be in tapping the potential of the baby boom.

STUDY METHODOLOGY

We define career as a series of work-related experiences (events and the person's reactions to those events) which occur over the span of the person's work life. Note that this definition says nothing about advancement to a certain level, nothing about success as defined by salary or other external measures. In fact, surveys of work values in the contemporary work force indicate that the most important kind of success to most people is what we call *psychological success:* the achievement of those goals which the individual values most. To some people, psychological success might be measured in terms of professional competence, to others, family rewards, and to still others, fame and public recognition. To understand the career situation as it is perceived by members of the baby boom group in today's leaner organization, we need to consider their *values,* as well as career strategies.

Our information comes from the three sources. One source was research literature on the baby boom.[25] A second source is the numerous seminars and workshops, both for MBA students and corporate managers, on self-assessment and career planning which we have offered over the last 15 years. The participants in these seminars have been predominantly members of the baby boom cohort, and many of the issues raised have been related to career stage concerns of this group. Finally, although we did not intend for this to be an empirical article, we did interview 20 managers in the baby boom group and 25 human resource executives in companies noted for progressive human resource practices (e.g., Monsanto, DuPont, Westin, Kodak, Florida Power and Light, AT&T, Corning Glass) to obtain more in-depth examples of how individuals and organizations are being affected by this demographic phenomenon. While somewhat limited, our own data are useful for illustrative purposes, and they are consistent with trends in the research literature.

25. See, for example, the work of Raelin, Jones, Russell, Mills, and Werner & Stillman referred to in Notes 13 and 14. See also the work on student values in the 1960s reported in Douglas T. Hall, "Potential for Career Growth," *Personnel Administration,* May–June 1971, 18–30; Douglas T. Hall, "Humanizing Organizations: The Potential Impact of New People and Emerging Values Upon Organizations," in H. Meltzer and F. R. Wickert (eds.), *Humanizing Organizational Behavior* (Springfield, IL: Charles C. Thomas, 1976), 158–174; S. E. Seashore and T. Barnowe, "Collar Color Doesn't Count," *Psychology Today,* August 1972, 53–54, 80–82; L. D. Johnston, J. G. Backman, and P. M. O'Malley, "Monitoring the Future: Questionnaire Responses from the Nation's High School Seniors, 1979" (Ann Arbor, MI: Institute for Social Research, University of Michigan, 1979); D. Yankelovich, "Putting the New Work Ethic to Work," (New York: The Public Agenda Foundation, September 1983); P. Renwick, and E. E. Lawler III, "What You Really Want from Your Job," *Psychology Today,* May 1978, 53–58, 60, 65, 118; R. A. Easterlin, *Birth and Fortune: The Impact of Numbers on Human Welfare* (New York: Basic Books, 1980); "Americans Change," *Business Week,* February 20, 1978, 65–66; D. Quinn Mills, *Not Like Our Parents: A New Look at How the Baby Boom Generation Is Changing America,* (New York: William Morrow and Company, 1987); and Martin M. Greller and David M. Nee, *From Baby Boom to Baby Bust,* (Reading, MA: Addison-Wesley, 1989).

Executives Under Fire: The Burnout Syndrome

Morely D. Glicken

Katherine Janka

Worker burnout is suddenly a major concern in American industry and government. It may seem ironic at a time of layoffs, early retirement incentives, and other payroll cut measures, but the psychological condition of workers is a significant issue. Decreased productivity, shoddy work, high turnover, industrial sabotage, and high-level theft are compelling reasons to examine the causes and potential treatment of worker burnout. Because burnout at managerial levels is likely to affect workers at lower levels, this article considers burnout at the executive and managerial levels.

WHAT IS BURNOUT?

There is little agreement on the definition or the cause of burnout. Many researchers liken burnout to stress or see it as a reaction to job dissatisfaction or low morale. In our view, burnout is a unique adaptation to a variety of work-related and other factors, a clinically observable condition related to but often different from job dissatisfaction or stress.

Burnout, in our experience, is a type of existential crisis in which work is no longer a meaningful function. Burned-out workers may evidence high levels of apathy, depression, and lethargy—or they may not. The unifying factor is that such individuals no longer view their jobs as meaningful or important. Rather, work has become tedious, redundant, and insignificant. Whatever the cause, the act of work itself no longer satisfies the intrinsic needs of the executive. Burned-out executives feel either little enthusiasm for their work or an all-encompassing fatigue, which may show itself in the form of boredom, depression, and a powerful sense of alienation.

Burned-out executives may superficially appear to function adequately, but a careful look at their work-related behavior suggests that quality, quantity, creativity, enthusiasm, and true contribution to the organization are in jeopardy. Often, burned-out executives demonstrate a combination of the following predictable behaviors: a tendency to blame others in the organization for their burnout, to complain bitterly about aspects of work which in the past were not areas of concern, to miss work because of nonspecific and increasingly prevalent illness, to daydream or sleep on the job, to be the last to come to work and the first to leave, to bicker with coworkers or appear uncooperative, and to become increasingly isolated from others. Burned-out executives typically voice feelings that their present job does not seem suited to their needs and that outside pressures, such as financial need or parental manipulation, have forced them to work in fields unrelated to their real interests. It is not unusual for executives experiencing burnout to share with others fantasies about work in a totally different field or a desire to quit work and travel.

THE CAUSE OF BURNOUT

Executive burnout is a complex psycho-social state which may have a variety of causes. In our experience, it often stems from the following conditions.

Work Overstimulation

Overwork is commonly considered a major cause of burnout. We believe that overwork is seldom a cause of burnout if organization objectives are clear and a commitment to those objectives exists. However, when work takes place in a chaotic, unstable environment which encourages confusion about current duties and future directions, burnout is a likely result. Executives who feel that they are increasingly "putting out fires" are most likely to experience burnout as a result of overstimulation. Work as a reaction to crises, rather than a drive toward clear goals, often results in a sense of hopelessness, dejection, and immobilization.

Work Understimulation

When work continually fails to challenge and there seems little opportunity for future excitement, burnout is a distinct possibility. Executives frequently need a sense of challenge related to new problems and complex solutions. When work begins to lose its ability to stimulate and settles into a predictable routine, the probability of burnout is significantly increased.

Personal Problems

Times of extreme personal crisis and stress often affect an executive's productivity. It is not unusual for executives experiencing personal problems to feel less excitement about work than before or to experience the incapacitating emotional drain such personal problems may create. In fact, executives with a predisposition to burnout may be strongly affected by problems unrelated to work, having neither the internal mechanisms nor experience to resolve personal difficulties without spillover to the work place.

Job Mismatch

Often, executives choose jobs because of such extrinsic rewards as high salaries, status, and power, rewards which may initially heighten self-esteem. However, decisions to choose extrinsic rewards over intrinsic rewards frequently result in considerable unhappiness. Extrinsic rewards usually have limited ability to motivate executives and, in time, the lack of genuine gratification from work may lead to burnout. Other examples of mismatch are differences in personal and organizational values, in need and allowance for autonomy, and in need and allowance for use of special competencies.

Low Organizational Productivity

An executive may have excellent mental health work, satisfaction, and organizational commitment. If, however, the organization's objectives are not being met and the result is low productivity and reduced quality, burnout is possible. This is particularly the case when executives believe that they have limited ability to solve organizational problems and that outside factors, such as governmental regulations or labor strife, are primary reasons for low organizational achievement. Burnout may also occur in those organizations in which proper bureaucratic postures are more important than measurable productivity.

TREATMENT AND PREVENTION

Executive burnout can often be treated, and even prevented, within the organizational framework. In fact, it is the potential for remediation that distinguishes the burned-out executive from the "burned-up" executive. The burned-out individual is smoldering in place, riddled with stress and dissatisfaction and responding with an ever-intensifying loss of energy and interest. The burned-up individual has progressed to such a degree of lethargy and immobilization that he or she is generally destined for a radical event, such as mental or physical illness, sudden resignation, or involuntary termination.

Unfortunately, in the absence of either organizational assistance or individual competence for self-help, many executives facing burnout inaccurately diagnose themselves as burned up. They determine that it is too late to regenerate the vitality and enjoyment they once experienced in their work, but they stick with it for a while anyway, not so much in hope as in indecisiveness about the next step. While "hanging in there," they rarely attempt positive remedies. Instead they let the symptoms of burnout spill over to families and friends.

When this state becomes sufficiently intolerable, many executives call a halt by opting for a dramatic change just at the time when they may be least psychologically prepared to make reasoned personal decisions. The resultant actions include career change, early retirement, divorce, and geographic relocation, steps that often prove to be regrettable at worst and avoidable at best.

One thirty-six-year-old manager we spoke with had, a year earlier, dealt a radical blow to his own burnout symptoms. Plagued by stress on the job, financial worries, and personal problems, he submitted his resignation just as he was finally being considered for a promotion to a position he had always desired. He also sold his house, his car, and a small business he had owned on the side. After a year of travel and whittling away at savings, he stated, "I have had a lot of fun this year, but I still have no idea what I'll do when my money runs out—which will be soon. I don't really regret leaving, but I do fear that I may have to return to the same sort of job, lifestyle, and problems."

THE ORGANIZATION'S ROLE

For such individuals, early and deliberate attempts to search out causes and cures for burnout may provide more satisfactory solutions than those found in a traumatic downhill slide followed by radical change. While this argument is not meant to advocate the application of a band-aid when a tourniquet is needed, it does imply that organizations and individuals should seek ways to remedy burnout rather than simply respond to its symptoms. Without a considered effort to remedy burnout, organizations stand to lose top-level human resources, either by their departure or deficient performance, and individuals risk suffering continued stress and destructive coping mechanisms.

Two obvious areas in which organizations can take an active role in the fight against executive burnout are prevention and treatment. Preventative measures generally can be applied organization-wide, while treatment programs often must be tailored to each individual.

To prevent executive burnout and its negative impact on the organization and individuals, organizations can learn to recognize the potential for burnout before the fact. This requires an openness to critical self-examination and a resistance to rationalization of the sort that claims, "He just couldn't take the high performance standards we set around here anymore." The three elements that are crucial to the process of prevention are the recognition of early warning signals, the diagnosis of potential causes, and the development of prevention strategies.

EARLY WARNING AND DIAGNOSIS

While early indications of burnout may be confused, sporadic, and short-lived, clinical signs to be noted with concern include:

❐ periods of sustained lethargy or lack of consistent productivity;

❐ preoccupation with non-work related issues;

❐ a deep, if superficially considered, concern about the meaning of one's life;

❐ a tendency to feel that changing one's job and living arrangement may improve one's happiness on the job;

❐ a tendency to change jobs often without evidence of upward job mobility and increased responsibility;

❐ the indication that an executive is a loner but that isolation causes the executive acute discomfort;

❐ evidence that at crucial periods an executive may create situations which inhibit the possibility of personal success;

❐ failure to analyze future directions and a tendency to be directionless or claim that no direction is the best direction; and

❐ recent traumatic personal experiences such as the death of someone close, illness, or divorce.

The diagnostic element of prevention requires inquiry into the various factors of organizational life that may ultimately contribute to burnout. These may emanate from the organization and its policies and practices, from the nature of the work and the way in which it is accomplished, or from the personal characteristics of individual employees. It is likely, in fact, that all three of these areas harbor potential causes of burnout, especially in terms of possibilities for a mismatch between the individual, the work task, and the organizational structure and norms.

A diagnosis of the organization requires consideration of both the informal and formal interaction systems and how they are likely to agree with the values and needs of employees. A highly bureaucratic organization may be congruent with employees who have low growth needs and are satisfied with predictable and repetitive tasks. However, employees who are stimulated by more crea-

tive and complex tasks and the opportunity for growth may quickly burn out in such a setting.

Additional causes which may be generated by the organization itself are those which contribute to unstable work environments and career ambiguity. Organizations which undergo substantial internal change or financial uncertainty are likely to produce signs of burnout among executives who feel they are continually fighting against having the rug pulled out from under them. A major structural change, such as a shift from a purely hierarchical system to matrix management, leaves executives questioning their own competence and career futures.

For some individuals, especially those who have arrived at the executive suite by moving through the ranks, the nature of the work itself can cause burnout. Depending on an individual's personal orientation, the executive functions may produce a syndrome of overstimulation or understimulation. Such is the case with the successful scientist who is excited by laboratory research but later, as an executive, finds administrative tasks boring. Likewise, the overstimulation of seventy-hour work weeks, full calendars, travel, and major responsibilities creates awesome opportunities for burnout.

Any diagnosis of individuals largely concerns the fit between their personal characteristics and the characteristics of the job and the organization. It is important that some understanding of the type of people who comprise the executive ranks of an organization exist. Are they creative technicians or politically astute entrepreneurs? Are they professional managers or did they rise through the ranks? Do they enjoy change and challenge, or do they prefer stability and security? Are they stimulated by the work itself or by other factors, such as association with colleagues? Why are they working for this particular organization?

PREVENTION

The prevention strategies which may be undertaken by the organization include:

❐ seeking a fit between characteristics of the individual, complexity of the job, and type of organizational structure;

❐ developing programs which help individuals cope with the causes of stress that lead to burnout; and

❐ teaching and supporting self-diagnosis and individual adaptation strategies for addressing burnout symptoms.

Efforts to assure a fit of organization, task, and individual are the most elusive of these three categories. Generally, they must rely on individual and organizational awareness of the need for such a fit and the qualities that contribute to it. Such awareness can be supported by studies and surveys of executives themselves, the way their work is performed, and their perceptions of the organization.

Career development programs have been particularly useful in helping individuals assess their own capacities and needs, as well as the characteristics of jobs and values of the organization. Such programs need to be supported by organizational practices which reward the contributions of all highly competent professionals and do not reinforce the notion that executive ladder climbing is the sole sign of achievement. Experiments with dual career ladders, offering both technical and managerial rungs, provide some indication that organizations are seeking new strategies in this area, but they need to be carefully structured and monitored so that one ladder does not become a dumping ground for those who cannot make it on the other.

Additionally, organizations need to increase efforts to assure that the right person is selected for each job and to encourage change (without the stigma of retreat) when that does not occur. The use of assessment centers and rotational assignments allows companies to determine executive potential. However, they should be combined with candid feedback to individuals involved and efforts to encourage prospective executives to examine their own personal adaptability to the various functions required.

The organization must be flexible enough to accommodate various perspectives and values concerning executive work. For example, some executives may work twelve-hour days and never burn out, while others who are just as effective may need more time away from the office. Some may seek solitude, while others may thrive on conferences and negotiations with others. The organization that values and rewards only one type of executive may find it is contributing to the burnout of valuable resources. While job redesign efforts have centered on the functions of lower- and middle-level employees, they can be equally germane to enriching the work lives of top managers.

In a study of techniques used by workers to combat burnout, Christina Maslach found that sanctioned "time-outs" were "critically important for professionals."[1] Time-outs were defined as not merely short breaks, such as coffee breaks or rest periods, but opportunities in which the professional could choose other, less stressful work. Such findings indicate the usefulness of sabbaticals and mitigate against pay for accrued leave time which might discourage employees from taking vacations.

Company programs that help employees deal with stress-producing problems which affect work performance are growing in popularity but are generally utilized below the executive ranks. The employee assistance programs may be staffed by in-house counselors who help employees with legal, financial, family, alcohol, drug, and other problems, and who can guide employees to additional outside resources.

Top executives are typically reluctant to avail themselves of such programs, either because they do not want to admit that they have problems or because they do not want to identify with that segment of the work force comprising the major users of the programs. An alternative is to set apart special programs for executives, using a separate staff counselor or consultants and counselors from outside the organization. The probability of success of such a program can be greatly enhanced through initial orientation and training that breaks down reluctance to admit problems and through surveys of executives to determine what needs should be addressed by the program.

In the long run, it is the responsibility of each individual to recognize the signals of burnout and devise a personal strategy for dealing with his or her unique situation. Organizations, however, may help by providing information and education which help executives understand burnout and identify personal strategies to prevent it. Additionally, such support clearly signals that the organization is committed to assisting its top-level people and does not consider human needs a sign of failure.

We have found that programs which seek to assist burned-out workers, individually or in groups, work best when supported by consultation aimed at helping the organization develop positive support programs, such as career counseling, employee assistance programs, and educational strategies.

TREATMENT

In the process of treating a variety of workers who identified burnout symptoms as primary indicators of work-related pathology, we have developed an approach to treatment which suggests potential for counselors and therapists treating burnout. We call the approach Career Enhancement Therapy (CET). CET is designed to help burned-out workers achieve the following behavioral objectives:

❐ evaluate and understand the cause of burnout both at the obvious and the complex levels;

❐ determine changes, both personal and organizational, necessary to return to normal work-related functioning;

❐ develop sensitivity to the signs of burnout to help a worker cope more successfully with similar future episodes; and

❐ develop skills in discussing feelings and emotions which need to be processed with others so that burnout is less likely to occur in the future.

We have found that therapy is most effective when offered to a group of approximately twelve to fifteen executives. The approach, with its goal of helping executives design new strategies for coping with burnout, depends upon the ability of group members to develop a climate which encourages spontaneous and helpful interaction. It depends further upon the willingness of executives, who often lack introspection and self-awareness, to risk themselves by moving into a form of self and group evaluation which may be a unique and sometimes bewildering experience.

Our usual approach is to spend initial meetings with group members discussing the causes of burnout, techniques useful in changing burned-out behavior, and an explanation of the treatment used to help individuals in the group learn to change their behavior.

Burned-out executives are often unable to discuss the personal nature of their burnout and instead intellectualize or rationalize the causes. Our experience to date suggests that positive change generally does not occur until group members begin to look carefully at their own behavior, share it with others, establish awareness of the complexities of the behavior, and learn the often giddy and reinforcing skill of practicing new approaches to a problem initially recommended by others in the group. CET is very behavioral in the sense of attempting to establish new patterns of work-related behavior which may, in time, reduce or eliminate burnout. Sensitivity, insight, and awareness, while often important elements of treatment, are quite secondary to functional changes in behavior. Burned-out executives should, as a result of treatment, function at a more productive and less stressful level. They should be able to achieve prescribed goals which modify their painful behavior. If successful, treatment should lead to measurable improvements in an executive's work-related functioning.

After considerable experimentation, we found that CET is most effective when it is offered in a small group of twelve to fifteen

---

1. Christina Maslach, "Burn Out," *Human Behavior* (September 1976).

executives in a two-day, eight-hour-a-day treatment session. The initial two-day session is followed up by six monthly four hour group meetings to check on improvement and to offer the support and encouragement necessary for continued change.

Career Enhancement Therapy is, of course, not meant to be an intensive form of psychotherapy, and workers experiencing severe personal trauma, which may need a specific regimen of psychotherapy, are discouraged from group participation.

SUMMARY: OUT OF THE FRYING PAN?

The foregoing discussion has delineated individual and organizational roles in addressing the problem of executive burnout. The individual and the organization both have a stake in assuring the health, productivity, and satisfaction of top-level executives. When these factors are jeopardized by debilitating burnout, both share responsibility for positive action.

Case: Jane Moore: An Executive Woman's Career Story

PURPOSE

The purpose of this exercise is to provide you with an overview of an executive woman's career. By the time you finish this case you will

1. Understand the pressures and pitfalls in executive women's careers

2. Determine the extent to which the career stage literature models the progression of executive women

3. Consider whether an executive career is right for you

INTRODUCTION

Executives lead very busy and complicated lives. The stresses and pressures they face are enormous. The level of responsibility that executives carry in their jobs requires a consistent and unyielding level of dedication. This can be difficult for executive women, who may discover that the trade-offs they must make between their ambition and the quality of their personal lives are a sacrifice they may not have been fully prepared to make. This case concerns the pitfalls and trade-offs faced by executive women as they negotiate their way to the top.

INSTRUCTIONS

1. Read the articles in this chapter as preparation for this case.

2. Read the case, "Jane Moore: An Executive Woman's Career Story."

3. Participate in a class discussion.

This case was developed by Lisa A. Mainiero. The name and company used in the case are fictitious. This case was prepared as a basis for class discussion rather than to illustrate effective or ineffective approaches to management.

Jane Moore: An Executive Woman's Career Story

PROLOGUE

"Five o'clock. I should hear something by 5 o'clock," thought Jane Moore as she ran her carefullly polished fingernails across the papers on her desk. It had been a tense week for Jane as she knew a decision would be made today concerning whether she would be named to the chief executive officer position of the major pharmaceutical firm for which she worked. Jane sat back and reflected upon the events that had taken place in her career during the 22 years in which she had been with the company.

BACKGROUND

Jane Moore had graduated from Smith College in 1973 with a bachelor's degree in mathematics. She didn't know why exactly she had chosen to major in mathematics, but she was certain that she didn't want to spend her life reviewing artwork like so many of her friends who had majored in art history. Jane excelled in her studies and her professors urged her to consider graduate school. But Jane had other plans. She wanted to work at something "practical."

She didn't have a career plan in mind, but she assumed that she would end up working as an actuary for one of the insurance firms or as an analyst in the banking industry. She interviewed at a number of different insurance firms and banks, and one day, while waiting for a friend to finish her meeting with a professor, she attended an unexpected interview with Merey-Case pharmaceuticals. She was surprised by what she learned. Not only was Merey-Case offering a number of advantages that the other firms for which she had interviewed did not, but Merey-Case was actively recruiting women. She decided to give the firm a try.

JANE'S FIRST JOB

Her first job was as an economic analyst in the strategic planning department. All of the other employees in the department were men. She recalls her first impressions of that job:

> All the men in the department were engineers and it was the first time in my life that I experienced discrimination first-hand. Some of the guys could tell that I was serious, that I was a good worker, that I was there for a career and not just to get married. But others just weren't sure how to treat me and they joked around a lot. I didn't know how to treat them, either. From the guys, I heard about a training course that was considered very important if you were going to get anywhere in the company. I pleaded with my boss to get into the course and fortunately the person who was supposed to go became ill so at the last minute, without much consideration of whom they were sending, I got to attend. And it was a very eye-opening experience for me.

The course was an intensive three-month developmental experience for employees who are considered high potential. She was taught all the elements of the pharmaceutical business, from research to administration, as preparation for her future.

> Once I had that course behind me, I knew I could make it in this business. So when I returned to my job, I decided I wouldn't get sucked into their little childish games. I decided I wouldn't let them get to me. I worked at my desk during lunch, I handled all my assignments par excellence, I continually asked my boss for more. I was really frustrated with "grunt" work. I wanted more. And I didn't want to be typecast as just a woman so I felt I really had to prove myself.

SUPERVISING AND DEVELOPING EXPERTISE

Soon she was given a small group of employees (seven men and one woman) to supervise. Fortunately for her, the group to which she was assigned was granted a high-visibility project.

> My group didn't trust me at first, but I worked with them and showed them that I could be fair. I also showed them I could do the work right along with them. I listened to them and made changes in how the work was being done. One of the projects we were assigned had great significance for a sub-committee of the board concerning safety regulations and the interface with the community. We worked especially hard on that one. I worked weekends getting all the tasks on the project completed. Eventually we found an answer that satisfied everyone and that attracted the attention of the division manager whose neck was on the line with the project since he was doing the presentation to the board. He spent a lot of time with me, with us, so he came to know my work and support me.

This man became an early mentor for Jane. He recognized traits in Jane's character that reminded him of himself during his early years with the firm, and he bent over backward to introduce her to key managers at the firm.

> My mentor was very helpful to me. Although I think I would have still managed to be successful without his help, he gave me guidance and counsel that I never would have received otherwise at that stage in my career. He took the time to introduce me to higher-ups, to help me understand the culture of the firm. That kind of training at an early stage is invaluable.

GAINING LINE EXPERIENCE

Soon she was promoted again, this time to a line position that directly interfaced with one of the major pharmaceutical operating plants. She became known for her expertise in promoting safety issues, and the group that she supervised developed an entirely new set of safety procedures that was adopted by all the plants in the firm. Her work streamlined the chemical processing while enhancing safety, and improved productivity in the plants in which her pilot programs were run. She received considerable kudos for her work, and once again, caught the attention of upper management. In fact, she so impressed the plant manager with her abilities that he recommended her for his job when he was transferred to another area.

> Getting that plant job was a real coup for me. In that job they had never even seen a woman. I was working with machinery, with union employees, having full responsibility for a major operating plant. I had to earn their respect slowly and cautiously and eventually I won them over. I discovered things that were wrong that no one in the past ever had the courage to even ask about. In that job I was 29 years old and I was their boss. It was tough, but it was wonderful.

From that plant job she was promoted to headquarters where she ran a district responsible for human resource administration in the plants. She was disappointed by this turn of events.

> When they told me I was being promoted from the plant job to go to headquarters, I expected they would assign me a position with more meat. But instead they gave me this assignment. . . . I wasn't happy at all. Here I had just outperformed all the plant managers in my division, and where do I end up? Human resources? That's when I knew I had to fight because otherwise I would have been plateaued right then and there.

She asked her mentor to intervene on her behalf. Her mentor had risen to a general manager position at headquarters and his views were well respected throughout the executive ranks. He managed to get Jane a coveted position as an executive assistant to one of the corporate vice presidents.

> That job really was a significant assignment for me. In that position I learned so much about the company and how the executive level handles things. Things like managing politics and negotiating across divisions, and how career decisions are made. My boss and I really got along. It was like we had the same mind. . . . I was his right-hand person. By this point in my career I had figured out I was smarter than most of the men around me, and I used my intelligence to my advantage. I helped him out a lot by feeding him information, by doing his presentations for him, by doing lots of things that I knew I could do. He was so impressed with me that he didn't want me to leave. But fortunately for me, a position came up for which I was perfect and he knew it was in my best interest that he release me for the promotion.

This was Jane's division-level promotion. She was the second woman in the company who had reached the division level.

> At the division level, you know you have arrived. My first division-level job wasn't terribly challenging. It involved running a series of administrative groups. But I knew that they had plans for me so I finally was able to relax a little. Up until this point I was so career-driven I had not given any thought to getting married and raising a family. Only rarely did I get out because I was constantly taking work home on weekends. In fact, I found I preferred my work to most of the men I knew. Going out with them seemed like a waste of time because they did not understand my driving ambition. But then I met my

husband. He was the first man I had encountered who was willing to stand right by my side and support my career. I grabbed him as soon as he would let me.

JANE'S PERSONAL LIFE

They were married after a short courtship of six months. Jane's husband worked for a major New York law firm for which he frequently traveled on business. Jane's new position also involved a great deal of traveling.

> After we were first married, it seemed like we only saw each other in airports. He would be traveling to London, and I would be coming in from San Francisco, so we would arrange our flights so we could have dinner in a particular location. It probably looked glamorous to others that we had this high-flying life-style, but it took its toll on our marriage. Neither one of us wanted kids right away, but because I did not get married until 35, I kept hearing my biological clock ticking more and more loudly as time went on. Eventually I pressed my husband into a decision.

Jane and her husband soon discovered that they had fertility problems. Her desire to have a child grew as she endured test after test and three hospitalizations to improve her condition. She recounts this period of her life:

> I did not know what I wanted more—a successful career or a child. When I would become depressed about [not] having a child, I would throw myself into my work. When I became hopeful about having a child, I would take it easy with my career. It was a difficult period of constant ups and downs.

After Jane and her husband decided that further fertility testing would not improve their situation, Jane became rededicated to her career. Imagine her surprise when a year later, she found herself pregnant. Unfortunately, Jane lost the baby while traveling on assignment to Milwaukee. She reflects upon her situation:

> At the time I hadn't told anyone I was pregnant because I was so scared that something would happen. So I had no reason to refuse the Milwaukee assignment, not that I would have considered doing so or that it would have mattered anyway. My doctor assured me that it [the miscarriage] would have happened no matter what I had done. Still . . . I can't help feeling a tinge of sadness about my priorities at the time.

A NEW BEGINNING

Jane's marriage soured a year later and she and her husband mutually agreed to a divorce. Meanwhile Jane plunged back into her career.

> With all the tumult in my personal life, I found that my career was my one anchor, the foundation upon which my life was built. I found new motivation to take on projects, to do what others had not accomplished. I needed a challenge and I found one.

Jane assumed responsibility for a newly merged marketing and sales division within the pharmaceutical firm. This merger gave Jane considerable responsibility over the entire northeast sector, as well as nationwide plant management. She found herself negotiating a politically tricky assignment.

This assignment was difficult as it had been part of the company culture to go to marketing groups for certain kinds of answers and to deploy sales in a certain fashion. The culture of these groups also was quite strong . . . people wanted to keep on doing things the way they always had been done. But this is a new industry environment and we needed to develop more aggressive marketing strategies, to identify specific market niches, and so on. Others in the firm, especially those in the old vanguard who were running the place at the time, disagree. So I was in the uncomfortable position of shaking things up while also convincing my bosses that this was the right way to go. There was a point where I fell out of favor [with her bosses] because so much was happening in my division. They kept hearing complaints about my management style and about how I had restructured the orientation to be more market oriented rather than the comfortable geographic locations they previously served. Every day I heard complaints from someone about something. If I didn't believe in the changes I was making, I would have been demoralized. If I wasn't right, I would have lost my job. In time, my ideas were proven to be on target, and others respected me for toughing it out.

Soon after, she was promoted to general manager, plant operations, nationwide.

The promotion came at a time when I really needed some positive feedback about the five years I had just spent in very difficult circumstances. Getting this job was a real coup as it is considered a mainstream line capacity job where you are running the organization, practically speaking. I had all men reporting to me and they seemed okay about who I was and the directions I wanted to move toward. We developed into a coherent team. I visited all of the plants under my control and streamlined processing within each district. I modernized the plants with a reorientation of my capital budget, which now was in excess of $20 million. I also fired a lot of people and hand selected some of the best qualified candidates across the country to take key positions. With my marketing experience, I was able to make significant changes in how the plants were run. It was time for a change in how the plants operated, and I made sure that changes were made.

Fresh from her success as a general manager, she was moved to a position in charge of international operations.

The international assignment was a considerable challenge for me. I did not have much exposure to business in other countries, which is odd for someone with my career path. I should have had more international experience along the way. So I had to play catch-up at a very high level. I had to rely on my people for their understanding of how the work should get done. Even though I continually visited different countries on tour, I never could quite get the hands-on experience I wished I had earlier in my career.

Jane then was promoted to vice president, human resources. This move brought her back to the United States for an extended period of time.

> I wasn't pleased necessarily about being given the human resources slot. But on the one hand I had made it to the vice president level and that was an accomplishment no woman had previously achieved at that firm. So on the other hand I was delighted. I don't know to what extent my being female contributed to the board's decision to put me in this slot. I like to think I had become a proven producer who they thought could manage her way around any challenge, but I really don't know and I never will know the extent to which my gender played a role. As the token woman at the vice president level, I perform a lot of public relations work for the firm. I really like this job because it gets me out seeing how others in my industry do business. I serve on nationwide boards, I attend meetings in Washington, and I give many speeches to women's groups. I feel that is very important—helping others learn from you as a role model. I don't feel much like a role model sometimes, but I know that other young women see me in that light. So I play the role.

THE DECISION

Jane's assignment in human resources occurred at a time of a major union negotiation. Because of her plant experience, Jane was able to shepherd the negotiations expertly in a way that satisfied both management and the bargaining unit concerns. The union negotiations had placed Jane in a position of considerable visibility with the board, at the time that the current president of Merey-Case was due to retire. Jane considered her chances for the presidency in this way:

> The board . . . is very well acquainted with my accomplishments. One board member told me he thought I was the only executive he would trust with the presidency of this firm. But the others . . . I just don't know. And then the question becomes, "Do I really want to be president of this firm?" I would be the only female pharmaceutical chief executive officer in the country. I would be a groundbreaker. The responsibilities of such a position are huge. I have enough on my plate now. I don't know if I want to cross that barrier. I may be more comfortable being one of several women vice presidents across the country than the only female chief executive officer in my industry. If my marriage had gone in a different direction, I am relatively certain I would not have driven myself to this point. But now I don't know. If the position is offered to me I will take it. But this is one of those situations where you just don't know whether what is right for you careerwise is also right for you personally.

Just then, the phone buzzed. The board had made their decision. Jane's original mentor had been named the new chief executive officer of the pharmaceutical firm.

> "Whew!" thought Jane with a sigh of relief as she put down the telephone receiver. "I guess I didn't want the job quite as bad as I thought."

She immediately picked up the telephone and called her mentor to offer her congratulations.

DISCUSSION QUESTIONS

1. To what extent does the Dalton, Thompson, and Price (1977) model follow Jane Moore's career?

2. Is Jane Moore experiencing burnout? To what extent do you feel burnout may have influenced her feelings of relief at the conclusion of the case?

3. Should executives be prepared to make sacrifices in their personal lives for the sake of their careers? Why or why not?

Exercise: Career Anchors

PURPOSE

The purpose of this exercise is to help you determine the factors that influence your career decisions. By the time you finish this exercise you will

1. Diagnose your career anchors

2. Learn how these career anchors may influence your career decisions

3. Utilize the career anchors to determine a career plan for your future

INTRODUCTION

Just as there are motivating factors that influence life plans and career changes, there are also constraining factors that you may consider consciously or subconsciously when making career decisions. Career anchors, as the term implies, serve to help you guide, stabilize, and integrate your career. Identification—or recognition—of your career anchors can be useful in several ways. The concept can help you define job criteria and personal success factors. These anchors are defined as being achievement or values oriented. For example, some people need to see results (achievements) while others need to stay in one geographic area (values).

The anchors have been more specifically delineated by a number of authors such as Edgar Schein, C. Brooklyn Derr, and others as manager, technical expert, warrior, creative, security, and autonomy. Managers prefer to coordinate and control the activities of others. Technically driven people prefer to act as experts and use their knowledge as their career base. Warriors relish variety and troubleshooting problems. Creative people generate new ideas and become involved in new businesses. Security-driven people make career choices based on long-term needs. Autonomy-driven people insist on jobs that allow them to use flexible hours and make their own decisions.

This questionnaire was developed by C. Brooklyn Derr of Organizational Dynamics, Inc. 65 East 100 South, Alphine, UT 84004. Used with permission.

The purpose of this instrument is not to label you as a manager or warrior but rather to help you understand the comparative strengths that each of these areas exerts upon your career decisions.

INSTRUCTIONS

1. Complete the Career Anchors questionnaire.

2. Score your results according to the directions. Which is greater, your achievement or values orientation? Which career anchors best describe your career choices?

3. Read the insert, "Knowing Your Career Anchors," to interpret your results.

4. Participate in a class discussion.

Section I: Career Orientation

Directions: Career anchors may be based on achievement of accomplishment factors or the values one associates with his/her career. It is designed to help you compare the relative importance you place on these two criteria in your work environment.

Each item contains two statements. Choose one you feel more nearly identifies you. Darken all the symbols that parallel your choice.

If you choose (a) darken both squares.
If (b) is your choice darken all the triangles

Example I	1	2	3	4	5	6
1. (a) I like to be identified with a particular organization and the prestige that accompanies that organization.	□					□
(b) I do not want to be constrained by either an organization or the business world.		△		△	△	
1. (a) I prefer to work in a situation with at least a moderate amount of stress.	□	□			□	
(b) I prefer to work in a situation with little or no stress.			△	△		△
2. (a) I want to be part of an organization.	□					□
(b) I want to be independent.		△		△	△	
3. (a) Technical competence is a tool.	□	□		□	□	
(b) Technical competence is an end in itself.			△			
4. (a) I prefer to set a schedule and job description.			□			□
(b) I prefer flexible hours and to define my own job.		△		△	△	
5. (a) I like to be in a position to manage, control, or manipulate.	□				□	
(b) I like to be in a situation where I work independently or only with a cooperative group effort.			△	△		△
6. (a) I have difficulty separating work and personal life.	□	□			□	
(b) My personal life is distinctly different and isolated from work.			△	△		△
7. (a) Career decisions are based on opportunity or planning, not personal considerations.	□	□			□	
(b) Personal factors weigh heavily on career decisions.			△	△		△
8. (a) Ability and purpose, not values, determine decisions and career goals.	□	□	□			
(b) Values outweigh potential accomplishments in decisions.				△	△	△
9. (a) Short-term projects or special areas are more interesting than process.		□			□	
(b) Long-term goals, or the operational process, are more interesting than one-shot projects.	△		△	△		△
10. (a) Money is a measure of success.	□	□				
(b) Money is a basis for security.			△			△

Subtotals
Achievement Subtotal _____ —— —— —— —— —— ——
Values Subtotal _____

Section II: Career Anchors

Directions: This section is designed to help you more clearly identify your specific career anchor or anchors. It will help you define the degree to which you tend to be: Manager, Technician, Warrior, Security, Entrepreneur, or Autonomous.

Each item compares two modifiers, goals, or expectations. Choose the one that more accurately reflects you or your preferences. Darken the corresponding symbol. *Remember:* These are not weighty decisions. No personal evaluation of deep thought is needed. Mark the item you are first inclined to choose.

If you are a frustrated Edison, darken the square.
If you dream of Olympic Gold Medals, darken the triangle.

Example II

	1	2	3	4	5	6
1. (a) invent something.		□				
(b) set a world record.					△	

I can be described as:

	1	2	3	4	5	6
1. (a) an organizer.	□					
(b) a promoter.		△				
2. (a) an expert in my field.			□			
(b) my own person.				△		
3. (a) a team leader.	□					
(b) a team member.						△
4. (a) a risk taker.		□				
(b) a "rock."						△
5. (a) an "idea" person.		□				
(b) an independent thinker.				△		
6. (a) a detail-oriented person.			□			
(b) someone on the way up.	△					
7. (a) technically competent.			□			
(b) creative and innovative.		△				
8. (a) self-reliant, self-sufficient.				□		
(b) imaginative, broad-minded.		△				
9. (a) needing security.						□
(b) daring, exciting, and testing.					△	

A personal goal is to:

	1	2	3	4	5	6
10. (a) put myself to some ultimate test.					□	
(b) provide a secure and happy home for my family.						△
11. (a) attain a certain title or career position.	□					
(b) do my own thing, set my own rules.				△		
12. (a) attain a position of importance.	□					
(b) attain a secure position.						△

If my job phased out, I would seek to:

	1	2	3	4	5	6
13. (a) find another job within the company or in the same geographic location.						□
(b) try a new venture.		△				

I would rather:

	1	2	3	4	5	6
14. (a) stay in one career field. (b) move with the action.			□		△	
15. (a) lead a task force. (b) do my own thing.				△	□	
16. (a) work with ideas. (b) work with data.		□	△			
17. (a) not be in a competitive situation. (b) compete with myself and others. It's stimulating.			□		△	
18. (a) take a risk. (b) create something new.		△			□	
19. (a) excel in my field. (b) be considered dependable and loyal.			□			△

My career goals include:

	1	2	3	4	5	6
20. (a) working in one job content area. (b) staying with one company *or* in one location.			□			△
21. (a) setting an example for my team or task force. (b) not needing or depending on anyone else.				△	□	
22. (a) receiving increasingly challenging assignments in my own area of expertise. (b) pursuing my own life-style and setting my own goals.			□	△		

I need:

	1	2	3	4	5	6
23. (a) organizational visibility. (b) interesting work in my specialty.	□		△			
24. (a) affiliation and association. (b) privacy and personal space.				△		□
25. (a) recognition. (b) adventure.	□				△	

I prefer:

	1	2	3	4	5	6
26. (a) to create, or maintain, a good position in my organization. (b) to do my own thing. I would leave a job if I couldn't.	□			△		
27. (a) to manage or control my environment. (b) to find new ways to do things.	□	△				
28. (a) to know what is expected. (b) flexibility to do what I want.				△		□
29. (a) situations that require ideas, organizations, and risk. (b) situations that are daring, exciting, and have never been done.		□			△	
30. (a) managing people on a long-term basis. (b) managing people on a task force or project basis.	□				△	

Scoring

Directions: Total each column in Section II. Transfer these totals to the matching column below. Next transfer the totals from Section I to the lines indicated below. Add the two together. This total indicates the relative importance you place on each factor. The highest is your "prime" anchor, but the next two also influence your decisions.

	Column 1	*Column 2*	*Column 3*	*Column 4*	*Column 5*	*Column 6*
Section II Total	_____	_____	_____	_____	_____	_____
Section I Total	_____	_____	_____	_____	_____	_____
Total	_____	_____	_____	_____	_____	_____

Column 1: Manager
Column 2: Entrepreneur/creative
Column 3: Technical

Column 4: Autonomous/independent
Column 5: Warrior/adventurer
Column 6: Security

If your security total fell within the top three individual totals—or if you want to analyze your bent in this area—complete the following items. Circle either a or b indicating your choice in each item.

1. a. I want to try a variety of jobs.
   b. I want to live in a number of locations.

2. a. Extended family considerations influence career decisions.
   b. I only need to consider immediate family in my decisions.

3. a. I expect to work for one company, but have to have a variety of assignments during my career.
   b. The job may change, but I expect to "stay put" geographically.

4. a. If my job requires frequent transfers, I'll find a different one.
   b. Living with different sociological groups is a personal goal.

5. a. I'm comfortable with anyone.
   b. I enjoy being with my own group.

6. a. Climate and geography are important considerations in career decisions.
   b. The company can transfer me anywhere.

Total a's _____   Total b's _____

Your Geographic Security Orientation   Your Job Security Needs

Knowing Your Career Anchors

Used as a method of self-assessment, career anchors are the combination of motivating factors, ideas, interests, and constraints that guide, stabilize, and integrate career choices. The identification of one's career anchors can be useful in two ways. First, identifying your career anchors can help you understand yourself in terms of your interests, values, ideas, and constraints. Second, understanding your career anchors can help you to make better decisions about your future.

For example, some of us are *achievement oriented,* while others are *values oriented.* Individuals who are achievement oriented prioritize their goals ahead of their values and will pursue those goals as their top life priority. Individuals who are values oriented will carefully consider their priorities and values, considering only career goals that are consistent with their priorities, even if this means a less interesting or fulfilling career.

Career anchors describe the interacting forces that stabilize and influence one's career. The major career anchors can be defined as follows:

1. *Manager:* An integrating set of forces that describe an individual who chooses to influence, guide, and develop others

2. *Entrepreneur/Creativity:* An integrating set of forces that describe an individual who prefers to be creative, innovative, and challenged

3. *Technical:* An integrating set of forces that describe an individual who enjoys being an expert or specialist in a specific area of knowledge

4. *Autonomous:* An integrating set of forces that describe an individual who prefers remaining free from corporate constraints, flexible, and autonomous

5. *Warrior/Adventurer:* An integrating set of forces that describe an individual who craves variety in tasks and activities, prefers adventure, and enjoys serving as a corporate "troubleshooter."

6. *Security:* An integrating set of forces that describe an individual who is concerned about the future and wants to create a life-style or set of circumstances to assure his or her financial or geographic concerns.

Which of the preceding anchors describes you as an individual? How have your past decisions reflected these anchors? What do these anchors suggest for your future career decisions?

Directions: Diagram the strength of your career anchors on the following graph. Take the points from your scoring key and place them on the graph. What does this say about your career anchors profile? What profile do you have?

Manager	Warrior	Entrepreneur	Technical	Autonomy	Security

```
20  |
    |
    |
    |
15  |
    |
    |
    |
10  |
    |
    |
 5  |
    |
    |
    |_____
```

Manager	Warrior	Entrepreneur	Technical	Autonomy	Security

Career Anchors Profile

Which anchors best describe you? Are you better described by a single anchor or by a set of two or three anchors?

Manager _____ Warrior _____

Entrepreneur _____ Autonomy _____

Technical _____ Security _____

What values underlie your career anchors? _____

_____

_____

_____

What interests are suggested by your career anchors? _____

_____

_____

_____

Given this pattern of career anchors, what general career options make sense for your future? _____

_____

_____

_____

Which specific jobs can you name that will help you fulfill your needs? _____

_____

_____

_____

How can you achieve these goals? _____

_____

_____

_____

DISCUSSION QUESTIONS

1. Which career anchors best describe you? Are you best described by a solitary anchor or as a set of two or more anchors?

2. How closely do these anchors match your past career decisions?

3. What do these anchors suggest in terms of your future career decisions?

Exercise: The Burnout Questionnaire

PURPOSE

The purpose of this exercise is to help you better understand stress and burnout. By the time you finish this exercise you will

1. Identify the characteristics of your organization and job that could contribute to burnout

2. Determine whether or not your personal characteristics could predispose you to burnout

3. Develop strategies for controlling your level of stress and burnout

INTRODUCTION

Stress is the biological response of our bodies to physical or psychological demands from the environment. It is an inescapable part of organizational life, and, depending on its level, stress can have either positive or negative consequences. To be effective in our jobs we need enough stress to stay alert and challenged. Thus a certain level of stress is desirable. While there is no objective way to measure when stress is enough, we all know what it feels like when it becomes unbearable. Managers typically experience high levels of stress due to the nature of their jobs. When this stress becomes unremitting, burnout can be the result.

Stress and burnout are a combination of organizational, job, and personal characteristics. According to Freudenberger (1980), if you are experiencing a decline in enthusiasm, in your ability to function and care about others, combined with feelings of frustration, emptiness, and a lack of fulfillment, you may be a candidate for burnout. Understanding the characteristics of your job situation that may be particularly stressful and the personal characteristics that may predispose you to burnout can be the first step toward managing your stress.

INSTRUCTIONS

1. Review the article by Morely Glicken and Katherine Janka, "Executives Under Fire: The Burnout Syndrome."

2. Complete the Burnout Questionnaire.

3. Score the questionnaire and read the interpretation for your results.

4. Complete the worksheets provided.

5. Join a small group or find two people with whom you feel comfortable and develop strategies for improving the problem areas identified on your worksheets.

6. Participate in a class discussion.

This exercise was developed by Cheryl L. Tromley and was presented at the Eastern Academy of Management, Arlington, VA, 1988. The questionnaire in this exercise is based, in part, on the ideas presented in H. J. Freudenberger, *Burnout: The High Cost of Achievement* (New York: Anchor Press, 1980) and M. D. Glicken and K. Janka, "Executives Under Fire: The Burnout Syndrome." *California Management Review,* 1982, *24*(3), 67–82.

Burnout Questionnaire

Directions: The following questionnaire contains two sections: (1) a self-diagnosis of personal characteristics and (2) a diagnosis of your job situation. For both sections you should carefully read each of the statements and decide how strongly you agree or disagree with each according to the scale provided. Indicate your responses in the spaces provided beside the statements. When you complete the questionnaire, find the total for each section by adding up your answers. Put this score in the space provided at the end of each section. Be honest with yourself. Unless you decide otherwise, no one else will see your results.

1	2	3	4	5	6	7
Strongly Disagree	Disagree	Slightly Disagree	Neither Agree Nor Disagree	Slightly Agree	Agree	Strongly Agree

Section 1: Personal Characteristics

_____ 1. I tend to be impatient with other people's weaknesses and limitations.

_____ 2. I often try to do more than I could possibly accomplish.

_____ 3. I get upset if things don't go the way I planned; I have trouble rolling with the punches.

_____ 4. I have difficulty accepting my weaknesses and limitations.

_____ 5. I let my problems at work interfere with my personal life.

_____ 6. I feel very competitive toward my fellow workers.

_____ 7. I am unable to laugh at a joke about myself.

_____ 8. I often feel let down by people and situations.

_____ 9. I am impatient with activities; things just don't happen quickly enough.

_____ 10. I feel as though I am the only one who can do my job right.

_____ 11. I tend to distrust people's motives.

_____ 12. Sometimes I set up situations in which I cannot succeed.

_____ 13. I am very ambitious.

_____ 14. I need to continually generate excitement to keep from being bored.

_____ 15. When I make a mistake, I get very upset with myself.

_____ 16. I let my personal problems interfere with my work.

_____ 17. I have difficulty getting close to other people.

_____ 18. I expect too much of myself.

_____ 19. I have difficulty relaxing.

_____ 20. I rarely change my mind once I've taken a stand on something.

_____ 21. I feel that I am always under pressure to succeed.

_____ 22. I have difficulty accepting the differences among people.

_____ 23. I identify so closely with my work that, when something goes wrong in my work, I fall apart.

_____ 24. I am always worried about what others think of me.

_____ 25. I get very upset when other people make mistakes.

Section 1 Total _____

Section 2: Job/Organizational Characteristics

_____ 1. I am uncertain about my job duties and responsibilities.

_____ 2. Sometimes I don't have the resources I need to do my job.

_____ 3. My job requires skills that I haven't completely mastered.

_____ 4. There is a great deal of conflict in my company.

_____ 5. I don't have a say in the decisions that affect me.

_____ 6. No matter how hard I work in this job, I am not certain that I will get ahead.

_____ 7. I spend most of my time with other people in the course of doing my job (subordinates, peers, superiors, customers, clients).

_____ 8. I often feel a conflict between my family and the demands of my job.

_____ 9. There is a great deal of competition in my job.

_____ 10. I have more work in my job than anyone could reasonably do.

_____ 11. People in my workplace are unclear about their current duties and future directions.

_____ 12. I do not have enough time away from my job.

_____ 13. My job is predictable, repetitive, tedious, and boring.

_____ 14. I wish that I had more control over how I do my job.

_____ 15. The main reason I chose my job was salary, status, or power.

_____ 16. I don't understand how my work contributes to the goals of the organization.

_____ 17. People often make conflicting demands on me.

_____ 18. I usually can't take time out when I feel that I need it.

_____ 19. My job does not let me use my special skills or competencies.

_____ 20. I feel like I have no control over my productivity.

_____ 21. I seem to spend most of my time "putting out fires."

_____ 22. My workplace is often confusing and chaotic.

_____ 23. My values are not congruent with the values of the organization.

_____ 24. My company is financially unstable.

_____ 25. My job is not as creative as I want it to be.

Section 2 Total _____

Interpretation

Directions: Plot your Section Totals on the following graph and identify the sector (1–25) that your scores fall in. This is your Stress Profile. Find the Profile Interpretation that corresponds to your Stress Profile on the following pages.

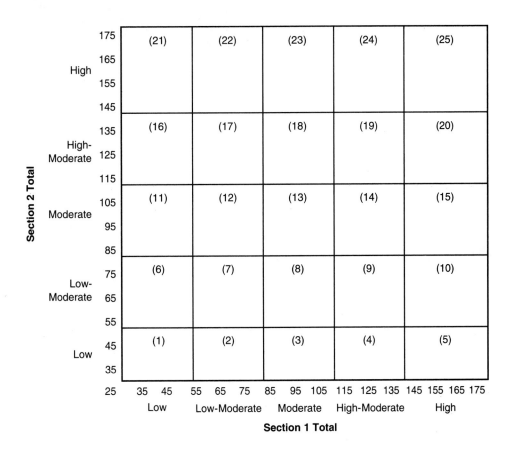

Stress Profile Interpretation

Personal Characteristics Section 1	Job/Organizational Characteristics Section 2	Profile Interpretation
1. Low 2. Low-Moderate	Low Low	You do not create unnecessary stress for yourself and your job situation is not stressful. You are in no danger of burnout at the present time..
3. Moderate	Low	Your job situation is not stressful but you create a moderate amount of unnecessary stress for yourself. You are probably not in danger of burnout at the present time. However, you should identify and monitor the areas where you create stress for yourself while you work on improving those areas.
4. High-Moderate 5. High	Low Low	Your job situation is not stressful, but you do create unnecessary stress for yourself. You could be a candidate for burnout, especially if your job situation becomes more stressful. You should concentrate on identifying the areas where you create stress for yourself and on finding possible ways to improve those areas.
6. Low 7. Low-Moderate	Low-Moderate Low-Moderate	You do not create unnecessary stress for yourself and your job situation is not overly stressful. You are in no danger of burnout at the present time.
8. Moderate	Low-Moderate	Your job situation is not very stressful but you create a moderate amount of unnecessary stress for yourself. You are probably not in danger of burnout at the present time. However, you should identify and monitor the areas where you create stress for yourself while you work on improving those areas.
9. High-Moderate 10. High	Low-Moderate Low-Moderate	Your job is not overly stressful, but you do create unnecessary stress for yourself. You could be a candidate for burnout, especially if your job situation becomes more stressful. You should identify the areas where you create stress for yourself and find ways to improve those areas.
11. Low 12. Low-Moderate	Moderate Moderate	You do not create unnecessary stress for yourself and your job is only moderately stressful. You are probably not in danger of burnout at the present time, but you should identify the characteristics of your job situation that are stressful and monitor them while you work on improving them.
13. Moderate	Moderate	You create a moderate amount of stress for yourself and your work situation is moderately stressful. You are probably in no immediate danger of burnout, but you should identify the areas where you create stress for yourself as well as the characteristics of your job situation that are stressful and monitor them closely while you work on improving them.
14. High-Moderate 15. High	Moderate Moderate	You create unnecessary stress for yourself and your job is moderately stressful. You should monitor it carefully. You could be a candidate for burnout. You should concentrate on identifying the areas where you create stress for yourself and find ways to improve those areas. You should also try to identify the characteristics of your job that are stressful and try to find ways to decrease the stress in your job situation. Your main emphasis should be on your personal characteristics.
16. Low 17. Low-Moderate	High-Moderate High-Moderate	You do not create unnecessary stress for yourself, but your job situation is quite stressful. You are probably in no immediate danger of burnout. But you should try to identify the characteristics of your job that are stressful and find ways to decrease those sources of stress to avoid trouble in the future.
18. Moderate	High-Moderate	You create a moderate amount of unnecessary stress for yourself and your job situation is quite stressful. You could be a candidate for burnout. You should identify the areas where you create stress for yourself, as well as the characteristics of your job situation that are stressful, and concentrate on finding ways to improve both your responses and the situation. Your main emphasis should be on your job situation.

Personal Characteristics Section 1	Job/Organizational Characteristics Section 2	Profile Interpretation
19. High-Moderate 20. High	High-Moderate High-Moderate	You create unnecessary stress for yourself and your job is quite stressful. You are a good candidate for burnout. You should identify the areas where you create stress for yourself, as well as the characteristics of your job situation that are stressful, and concentrate on finding ways to improve both your responses and the situation.
21. Low 22. Low-Moderate	High High	You do not create unnecessary stress for yourself, but your job situation is very stressful. You could be a candidate for burnout, especially if the stress continues without letup. You should identify the characteristics of your job situation that are stressful and concentrate on finding ways to improve the situation.
23. Moderate	High	You create a moderate amount of unnecessary stress for yourself and your job situation is very stressful. You could be a candidate for burnout. You should identify the areas where you create stress for yourself as well as the characteristics of your job situation that are stressful and concentrate on finding ways to improve both your responses and the situation. Your main emphasis should be on your job situation.
24. High-Moderate 25. High	High High	You are a serious candidate for burnout. You create unnecessary stress for yourself and your job situation is very stressful. You should identify the areas where you create stress for yourself, as well as the characteristics of your job situation that are stressful, and find ways to improve both your responses and the situation.

Filling Out the Worksheets

Directions: One way for you to identify where you create stress for yourself and where your job situation is stressful is to review your responses to the questionnaire. Go back through the questionnaire and identify all of the statements for which you answered 6 or 7. Enter these on the Worksheet under Problem Areas. There is one Worksheet for Section 1, Personal Characteristics, and one Worksheet for Section 2, Job/Organizational Characteristics. After you have recorded your Problem Areas, take a few minutes and think of some potential strategies for improvement. Your Personal Characteristics Improvement Strategies should include the steps you think would help you stop creating unnecessary stress for yourself. Your Job/Organizational Characteristics Improvement Strategies should include the steps you think would help you decrease the stress in your job situation or help you cope with it effectively. Record these Improvement Strategies on the Worksheet next to the corresponding Problem Area. Be as specific as you can.

Worksheet: Personal Characteristics

Problem Areas	Improvement Strategies

Worksheet: Job/Organizational Characteristics

Problem Areas	Improvement Strategies

Small Group Discussion

Directions: Find two people with whom you feel comfortable and spend the next 30 minutes helping each other complete the Worksheets. You will have 10 minutes to get input from the other two members of your group. The first person should select one of their problem areas for discussion. The other group members will serve as resources by suggesting ways of improving the problem area. You may discuss as many of your problem areas as you have time for. Make notes from the discussion on your Worksheets.

DISCUSSION QUESTIONS

1. What were some of the improvement strategies identified by your group?

2. Were there any problem areas for which you were unable to identify any improvement strategies? If so, why not?

3. How likely is it that people can change their personal characteristics to reduce the stress in their lives?

4. Do your scores agree with your feelings about yourself and your job? If not, why do you think they are different?

REFERENCES

H. J. Freudenberger. *Burn-Out: The High Cost of High Achievement.* Garden City, NY: Anchor Press, 1980.

M. D. Glicken, and K. Janka. "Executives Under Fire: The Burnout Syndrome." *California Management Review,* 1982, *24*(3), 67–72.

CHAPTER 10

Managing Diversity, Ethics, International Issues, and Corporate Social Responsibility

INTRODUCTION

The decade of the 1990s has brought about some long-awaited challenges in the field of management. One concerns the management of diversity within and across national boundaries. The increasing globalization of business, coupled with demographic changes in the workforce, has led corporate leaders to consider the management of cultural differences as a priority. As organizations cross national boundaries, they will become increasingly heterogeneous on dimensions such as gender, race, ethnicity and nationality. Managers in the nineties must know how to manage diversity effectively in order to manage successfully in the future.

In addition, improper junk bond dealings, poorly handled corporate takeovers, environmental chemical spills, and other misaligned ethical decisions highlighted by the media have led corporate leaders to rethink the issue of corporate social responsibility. In the past, too little thought has been given to the ethical parameters upon which corporate decisions have been made. In the quest for improved profits, many business decisions have been made that cast ethical considerations aside.

Managers in the next century will soon learn they must do more than simply manage. Managers in the year 2000 will weigh their responsibilities in terms of the impacts and consequences of their decisions on the local community, the larger society, and the environment as a whole. Managers in the year 2000 also will be prepared to manage a culturally diverse organization. As pressures for increasing globalization and ethical behavior continue, managers must learn new tools and ways of thinking to cope with the challenges that lie ahead.

READINGS

The first reading in this chapter, "The Multicultural Organization," by Taylor Cox, Jr., highlights the challenges faced in managing a culturally diverse enterprise. Professor Cox offers a model for managing diversity and suggests tools and techniques to assist managers in making the transition from traditional management to the new culturally diverse organization. He notes that potential benefits of diversity include improved decision making, creativity, and innovation; greater success in marketing to foreign and ethnic minority communities, and a better distribution of economic opportunity. Cultural mismanagement may lead to increased costs through higher turnover rates, interpersonal conflict, and communication breakdowns.

The second reading, "Changing Unethical Organizational Behavior," by Richard P. Nielsen, considers the merits of working with, or working against, unethical organizations. He characterizes this as (1) being an individual, which may require working against others and the organizations performing the unethical behaviors, and (2) being a part, by leading ethical organizational changes through working with others and the organization. He discusses whistle-blowing, the limits of intervention, and how one may lead an ethical change.

The third article presented in the chapter, "After Social Responsibility," by Paul H. Weaver, is a thought-provoking historical perspective on the purposes and aims of corporate social responsibility. He argues that corporate social responsibility, as it has been preached and practiced, is not an authentic business ethic, but propaganda. By embracing market-oriented, capitalist ideas of the business-society relationship, he suggests that executives may be more willing to discover areas of mutual interest that will enhance corporate social responsibility in the long term.

EXERCISES AND CASES

Three exercises are presented in this chapter to sharpen your skills in managing diversity and improving your knowledge of ethical considerations. The first exercise, "Four Cultures," offers an opportunity to consider diversity issues in organizations. Through visits with others who represent different cultures, you will experience what it is like to interact with others who may not share your norms of social interaction. Six cultural activities (such as nonverbal expressions and greetings) are included for your practice sessions.

"The Maquiladora Decision" is an exercise that crosses international boundaries and considerations of corporate social responsibility. In this exercise, you will play the role of a member of the top management group of a manufacturing company that must decide whether to open an assembly facility in Nogales, Mexico, just across the border from Arizona. You will need to weigh what is legal against what is ethical as you consider the merits of the decision. By the time you complete this exercise, you will have a better awareness of the utility of developing a code of ethics to guide your corporate behavior, and the differences between deontological and utilitarian perspectives in making ethical decisions.

The third exercise, "Vanatin—Group Decision Making and Ethics," forces you to consider the merits of corporate social responsibility in the context of an unethical, but profitable, decision. The case is constructed around a medical product, one that is considered by experts to be injurious to the health of consumers—even to the point of possibly causing death. The consequences must be evaluated against the potential economic losses to the firm, which may be substantial. This case will force you to consider the merits of corporate interests versus the public welfare as you weigh these decisions in a group context.

MEMO

The memo assignment, *"Managing Diversity"* (located at the end of the book), uses an approach of valuing differences rather than stereotyping other groups. Stereotyping can be destructive and may highlight aspects of potential conflict. In this memo, you will be asked to identify culturally diverse groups with whom you interact in your firm, or with whom you expect to interact within the next 10 years. You will then identify what contributions and values these groups may bring to your organization as your firm grows more diverse in the near future.

By the time you finish this chapter, you will have a sharper awareness of ethical practices in organizations, the role of corporate social responsibility, and decisions that cross international boundaries. You also will be more sensitive to issues of cultural diversity within organizations and their impacts on you as an individual and a manager of the future.

The Multicultural Organization

Taylor Cox, Jr.

As we begin the 1990s, a combination of workforce demographic trends and increasing globalization of business has placed the management of cultural differences on the agenda of most corporate leaders. Organizations' workforces will be increasingly heterogeneous on dimensions such as gender, race, ethnicity and nationality. Potential benefits of this diversity include better decision making, higher creativity and innovation, greater success in marketing to foreign and ethnic minority communities, and a better distribution of economic opportunity. Conversely, cultural differences can also increase costs through higher turnover rates, interpersonal conflict, and communication breakdowns.

To capitalize on the benefits and minimize the costs of worker diversity, organizations of the '90s must be quite different from the typical organization of the past. Specifically, consultants have advised organizations to become "multicultural."[1] The term refers to the degree to which an organization values cultural diversity and is willing to utilize and encourage it.[2]

Leaders are being charged to create the multicultural organization, but what does such an organization look like, and what are the specific ways in which it differs from the traditional organization? Further, what tools and techniques are available to assist organizations in making the transition from the old to the new?

This article addresses these questions. I have used an adaptation of the societal-integration model developed by Milton Gordon, as well as available information on the early experience of American organizations with managing diversity initiatives, to construct a model of the multicultural organization.

CONCEPTUAL FRAMEWORK

In his classic work on assimilation in the United States, Milton Gordon argued that there are seven dimensions along which the integration of persons from different ethnic backgrounds into a host society should be analyzed.[3] I use "integration" to mean the coming together and mixing of people from different cultural identity groups in one organization. A cultural identity group is a group of people who (on average) share certain values and norms distinct from those of other groups. Although the boundaries of these groups may be defined along many dimensions, I am primarily concerned with gender, race, ethnicity, and national origin. Gordon's seven dimensions are:

1. Form of acculturation
2. Degree of structural assimilation
3. Degree of intergroup marriage
4. Degree of prejudice
5. Degree of discrimination

Taylor Cox, Jr. (The University of Michigan) The Multicultural Organization. Reprinted with permission from the *Academy of Management Executive,* 1991, Vol. 5(2), pps. 34–47.

1. See, for example, Lennie Copeland, "Valuing Workplace Diversity," *Personnel Administrator,* November 1988; Badi Foster et al. "Workforce Diversity and Business," *Training and Development Journal,* April 1988, 38–42; and R. Roosevelt Thomas, "From Affirmative Action to Affirming Diversity," *Harvard Business Review,* Vol. 2, 1990, 107–117.

2. This definition has been suggested by Afsavch Nahavandi and Ali Malekzadeh, "Acculturation in Mergers and Acquisitions," *Academy of Management Review,* Vol. 13, 83.

3. In his book, *Assimilation in American Life* (New York; Oxford Press, 1964), Gordon uses the term assimilation rather than integration. However, because the term assimilation has been defined in so many different ways, and has come to have very unfavorable connotations in recent years for many minorities, I will employ the term integration here.

EXHIBIT 1

Conceptual Framework for Analysis of Organizational Capability
for Effective Integration of Culturally Diverse Personnel.

Dimension	Definition
1. Acculturation	Modes by which two groups adapt to each other and resolve cultural differences
2. Structural Integration	Cultural profiles of organization members including hiring, job-placement, and job status profiles
3. Informal Integration	Inclusion of minority-culture members in informal networks and activities outside of normal working hours
4. Cultural Bias	Prejudice and discrimination
5. Organizational Identification	Feelings of belonging, loyalty and commitment to the organization
6. Intergroup Conflict	Friction, tension and power struggles between cultural groups

6. Degree of identification with the dominant group of the host society

7. Degree of intergroup conflict (especially over the balance of power)

Although Gordon's interest was in societal-level integration, I believe his model can be easily and usefully adapted for analysis of cultural integration for organizations. Therefore, an adaptation of his seven-point framework is used here as a basis for describing organizational models for integrating culturally divergent groups. Exhibit 1 shows my proposed six-dimensional adaptation of the Gordon framework along with definitions of each term.

Acculturation is the method by which cultural differences between the dominant (host) culture and any minority culture groups are resolved or treated. There are several alternatives, the most prominent being: 1. a unilateral process by which minority culture members adopt the norms and values of the dominant group in the organization (*assimilation*); 2. a process by which both minority and majority culture members adopt some norms of the other group (*pluralism*); and 3. a situation where there is little adaptation on either side (*cultural separatism*).[4] Pluralism also means that minority culture members are encouraged to enact behaviors from their alternative culture as well as from the majority culture. They are therefore able to retain a sense of identity with their minority-culture group. Acculturation is concerned with the cultural (norms of behavior) aspect of integration of diverse groups, as opposed to simply their physical presence in the same location.

Structural integration refers to the presence of persons from different cultural groups in a single organization. Workforce profile data has typically been monitored under traditional equal opportunity and affirmative action guidelines. However, to get a proper understanding of structural integration it is important to look beyond organization-wide profile data, and examine cultural mix by function, level, and individual work group. This is because, it is commonplace in American companies for gaps of fifteen to thirty percentage points to exist between the proportion of minority members in the overall labor force of a firm, and their proportion at middle and higher levels of management.[5]

Even within levels of an organization, individual work groups may still be highly segregated. For example, a senior human resource manager for a Fortune 500 firm who is often cited as a leader in managing diversity efforts, recently told me that there are still many "white-male bastions" in his company. As an assistant vice-president with responsibility for equal opportunity, he indicated that breaking down this kind of segregation was a focal point of his current job.

The *informal integration* dimension recognizes that important work-related contacts are often made outside of normal working hours and in various social activities and organizations. This item looks at levels of inclusion of minority-culture members in lunch and dinner meetings, golf and other athletic outings, and social clubs frequented by organization leaders. It also addresses mentoring and other informal developmental relationships in organizations.

Cultural bias has two components. Prejudice refers to negative attitudes toward an organization member based on his/her culture group identity, and discrimination refers to observable adverse behavior for the same reason. Discrimination, in turn, may be either personal or institutional. The latter refers to ways that organizational culture and management practices may inadvertently disadvantage members of minority groups. An example is the adverse effect that emphasizing aggressiveness and self promotion has on many Asians. Many managers that I have talked to are sensitive to the fact that prejudice is a cognitive phenomenon and therefore much more difficult than discrimination for organization managers to change. Nevertheless, most acknowledge the importance of reducing prejudice for long range, sustained change.

---

4. These definitions are loosely based on J. W. Berry, 1983. "Acculturation: A Comparative Analysis of Alternative Forms," in R. J. Samuda and S. L. Woods: *Perspectives in Immigrant and Minority Education,* 1983, 66–77.

5. This conclusion is based on data from nearly 100 large organizations as cited in "Best Places for Blacks to Work," *Black Enterprise,* February 1986 and February 1989 and in Zeitz and Dusky, *Best Companies for Women,* 1988.

EXHIBIT 2
Organizational Types.

Dimension of Integration	Monolithic	Plural	Multicultural
Form of Acculturation	Assimilation	Assimilation	Pluralism
Degree of Structural Integration	Minimal	Partial	Full
Integration into Informal Org.	Virtually none	Limited	Full
Degree of Cultural Bias	Both prejudice and discrimination against minority-culture groups are prevalent	Progress on both prejudice and discrimination but both continue to exist especially institutional discrimination	Both prejudice and discrimination are eliminated
Levels of Organizational Identification*	Large majority-minority gap	Medium to large majority-minority gap	No majority-minority gap
Degree of Intergroup Conflict	Low	High	Low

*Defined as difference between organizational identification levels between minorities and majorities.

Prejudice may occur among minority-culture members as well as among dominant-culture members. Putting the debate over whether rates of prejudice differ for different groups aside, it must be emphasized that the practical impact of prejudice by majority-culture members is far greater than that of minority-culture members because of their far greater decision-making power (except under extraordinary conditions, such as those of South Africa).

Organizational identification refers to the extent to which a person personally identifies with, and tends to define himself or herself as a member in the employing organization. Levels of organizational identification have historically been lower in the United States than in other countries (notably Japan). Indications are that recent changes in organizational design (downsizing and de-layering) have reduced organizational identification even further. Although levels of organizational identification may be low in general in the U.S. workforce, we are concerned here with comparative levels of identification for members of different cultural identity groups.

Finally, *intergroup conflict* refers to levels of culture-group-based tension and interpersonal friction. Research on demographic heterogeneity among group members suggests that communication and cohesiveness may decline as members of groups become dissimilar.[6] Also, in the specific context of integrating minority-group members into organizations, concerns have been raised about backlash from white males who may feel threatened by these developments. It is therefore important to examine levels of intergroup conflict in diverse work groups.

TYPES OF ORGANIZATIONS

This six-factor framework will now be employed to characterize organizations in terms of stages of development on cultural diversity.[7] Three organization types will be discussed: the monolithic organization, the plural organization and the multicultural organization. The application of the six-factor conceptual framework to describe the three organization types appears in Exhibit 2.

Monolithic Organization

The most important single fact about the monolithic organization is that the amount of structural integration is minimal. The organization is highly homogeneous. In the United States, this commonly represents an organization characterized by substantial white male majorities in the overall employee population with few women and minority men in management jobs. In addition, these organizations feature extremely high levels of occupational segregation with women and racioethnic minority men (racially and/or culturally different from the majority) concentrated in low-status jobs such as secretary and maintenance. Thus, the distribution of persons from minority-cultural backgrounds is highly skewed on all three components of function, level, and work group.

To a large extent, the specifications on the frameworks' other five dimensions follow from the structural exclusion of people from different cultural backgrounds. Women, racioethnic minority men, and foreign nationals who do enter the organization must adopt the existing organizational norms, framed by the white male majority, as a matter of organizational survival.

Ethnocentrism and other prejudices cause little, if any, adoption of minority-culture norms by majority group members. Thus, a unilateral acculturation process prevails. The exclusionary practices of the dominant culture also

6. Examples of this research include Harry Triandis, "Some Determinants of Interpersonal Communication," *Human Relations,* Vol. 13, 1960, 279–287 and J. R. Lincoln and J. Miller, "Work and Friendship Ties in Organizations," *Administrative Science Quarterly,* Vol. 24, 1979, 181–199.

7. The concept of stages of development toward the multicultural organization has been suggested in an unpublished paper titled "Toward the Multicultural Organization" written by Dan Reigle and Jarrow Merenivitch of the Proctor and Gamble Company. I credit them with helping me to recognize the evolutionary nature of organizational responses to workforce diversity.

apply to informal activities. The severe limitations on career opportunities for minority-culture members create alienation, and thus the extent to which they identify with the organization can be expected to be low compared to the more fully enfranchised majority group.

One positive note is that intergroup conflict based on culture-group identity is minimized by the relative homogeneity of the workforce. Finally, because this organization type places little importance on the integration of cultural minority group members, discrimination, as well as prejudice, are prevalent.

While the white-male dominated organization is clearly the prototypical one for the monolithic organization, at least some of its characteristics are likely to occur in organizations where another identity group is dominant. Examples include minority-owned businesses, predominantly Black and predominantly Hispanic colleges, and foreign companies operating in the United States.

Aside from the rather obvious downside implications of the monolithic model in terms of under-utilization of human resources and social equality, the monolithic organization is not a realistic option for most large employers in the 1990s. To a significant degree, large U.S. organizations made a transition away from this model during the '60s and '70s. This transition was spurred by a number of societal forces, most notably the civil-rights and feminist movements, and the beginnings of changes in workforce demographics, especially in the incidence of career-oriented women. Many organizations responded to these forces by creating the plural organization.

Plural Organization

The plural organization differs from the monolithic organization in several important respects. In general, it has a more heterogeneous membership than the monolithic organization and takes steps to be more inclusive of persons from cultural backgrounds that differ from the dominant group. These steps include hiring and promotion policies that sometimes give preference to persons from minority-culture groups, manager training on equal opportunity issues (such as civil rights law, sexual harassment, and reducing prejudice), and audits of compensation systems to ensure against discrimination against minority group members. As a result, the plural organization achieves a much higher level of structural integration than the monolithic organization.

The problem of skewed integration across functions, levels, and work groups, typical in the monolithic organization, is also present in the plural organization. For example, in many large U.S. organizations racioethnic minorities now make up twenty percent or more of the total workforce. Examples include General Motors, Chrysler, Stroh Brewery, Phillip Morris, Coca-Cola, and Anheuser-Busch. However, the representations of non-whites in management in these same companies averages less than twelve percent.[8] A similar picture exists in work groups. For example, while more than twenty percent of the clerical and office staffs at General Motors are minorities, they represent only about twelve percent of technicians and thirteen percent of sales workers. Thus, the plural organization features partial structural integration.

Because of the greater structural integration and the efforts (cited previously) which brought it about, the plural organization is also characterized by some integration of minority-group members into the informal network, substantial reductions in discrimination, and some moderation of prejudicial attitudes. The improvement in employment opportunities should also create greater identification with the organization among minority-group members.

The plural organization represents a marked improvement over the monolithic organization in effective management of employees of different racioethnic, gender, and nationality backgrounds. The plural organization form has been prevalent in the U.S. since the late 1960s, and in my judgment, represents the typical large firm as we enter the 1990s. These organizations emphasize an affirmative action approach to managing diversity. During the 1980s increased evidence of resentment toward this approach among white males began to surface. They argue that such policies, in effect, discriminate against white males and therefore perpetuate the practice of using racioethnicity, nationality, or gender as a basis for making personnel decisions. In addition, they believe that it is not fair that contemporary whites be disadvantaged to compensate for management errors made in the past. This backlash effect, coupled with the increased number of minorities in the organization, often creates greater intergroup conflict in the plural organization than was present in the monolithic organization.

While the plural organization achieves a measure of structural integration, it continues the assimilation approach to acculturation which is characteristic of the monolithic organization. The failure to address cultural aspects of integration is a major shortcoming of the plural organization form, and is a major point distinguishing it from the multicultural organization.

The Multicultural Organization

In discussing cultural integration aspects of mergers and acquisitions, Sales and Mirvis argued that an organization which simply contains many different cultural groups is a plural organization, but considered to be multicultural only if the organization *values* this diversity.[9] The same labels and definitional distinction are applied here. The meaning of the distinction between *containing* diversity and *valuing* it follows from an understanding of the shortcomings of the plural organization as outlined previously. The multicultural organization has overcome these shortcomings. Referring again to Exhibit 2, we see that the multicultural organization is characterized by:

1. Pluralism
2. Full structural integration
3. Full integration of the informal networks
4. An absence of prejudice and discrimination
5. No gap in organizational identification based on cultural identity group
6. Low levels of intergroup conflict

---

8. See note 5.

9. A. L. Sales and P. H. Mirvis, "When Cultures Collide: Issues of Acquisitions," in J. R. Kimberly and R. E. Quinn, *Managing Organizational Transition*, 1984, 107–133.

I submit that while few, if any, organizations have achieved these features, it should be the model for organizations in the 1990s and beyond.

CREATING THE MULTICULTURAL ORGANIZATION

As I have discussed issues of managing diversity with senior managers from various industries during the past year, I have observed that their philosophical viewpoints cover all three of the organizational models of Exhibit 2. The few who are holding on to the monolithic model often cite geographic or size factors as isolating their organizations from the pressures of change.

Some even maintain that because American white males will continue to be the single largest gender/race identity group in the U.S. workforce for many years, the monolithic organization is still viable today. I think this view is misguided. By understanding the generic implications of managing diversity (that is, skill at managing work groups which include members who are culturally distinct from the organization's dominant group), it becomes clear that virtu-

ally all organizations need to improve capabilities to manage diverse workforces. Further, focusing too much attention on external pressures as impetus for change, misses the fact that gross under-utilization of human resources and failure to capitalize on the opportunities of workforce diversity, represent unaffordable economic costs.

Fortunately, the monolithic defenders, at least among middle and senior managers, seem to represent a minority view. Based on my observations, the majority of managers today are in plural organizations, and many are already convinced that the multicultural model is the way of the future. What these managers want to know is how to transform the plural organization into the multicultural organization. Although progress on such transformations is at an early stage, information on the tools that have been successfully used by pioneering American organizations to make this transformation is beginning to accumulate.

Exhibit 3 provides a list of tools that organizations have used to promote organization change toward a multicultural organization. The exhibit is organized to illustrate my analysis of which tools are most helpful for each of the six dimensions specified in Exhibit 1.

EXHIBIT 3
Creating the Multicultural Organization:
Tools for Organization Change.

Model Dimension	Tools
I. Pluralism *Objective/s:* —create a two-way socialization process —ensure influence of minority-culture perspectives on core organization norms and values	1. Managing/valuing diversity (MVD) training 2. New member orientation programs 3. Language training 4. Diversity in key committees 5. Explicit treatment of diversity in mission statements 6. Advisory groups to senior management 7. Create flexibility in norm systems
II. Full Structural Integration *Objective/s:* —no correlation between culture-group identity and job status	1. Education programs 2. Affirmative action programs 3. Targeted career development programs 4. Changes in manager performance appraisal and reward systems 5. HR policy and benefit changes
III. Integration in Informal Networks *Objective/s:* —eliminate barriers to entry and participation	1. Mentoring programs 2. Company sponsored social events
IV. Cultural Bias *Objective/s:* —eliminate discrimination —eliminate prejudice	1. Equal opportunity seminars 2. Focus groups 3. Bias reduction training 4. Research 5. Task forces
V. Organizational Identification —no correlation between identity group and levels of organization identification	1. All items from the other five dimensions apply here
VI. Intergroup Conflict *Objective/s:* —minimize interpersonal conflict based on group-identity —minimize backlash by dominant-group members	1. Survey feedback 2. Conflict management training 3. MVD training 4. Focus groups

Creating Pluralism

Exhibit 3 identifies seven specific tools for changing organizational acculturation from a unilateral process to a reciprocal one in which both minority-culture and majority-culture members are influential in creating the behavioral norms, values, and policies of the organization. Examples of each tool are given below.

Training and Orientation Programs. The most widely used tool among leading organizations is managing or valuing cultural diversity training. Two types of training are most popular: awareness and skill-building. The former introduces the topic of managing diversity and generally includes information on workforce demographics, the meaning of diversity, and exercises to get participants thinking about relevant issues and raising their own self-awareness. The skill-building training provides more specific information on cultural norms of different groups and how they may affect work behavior. Often, these two types of training are combined. Such training promotes reciprocal learning and acceptance between groups by improving understanding of the cultural mix in the organization.

Among the many companies who have made extensive use of such training are McDonnell Douglas, Hewlett Packard, and Ortho Pharmaceuticals. McDonnell Douglas has a program ("Woman-Wise and Business Savvy") focusing on gender differences in work-related behaviors. It uses same-gender group meetings and mixed-gender role-plays. At its manufacturing plant in San Diego, Hewlett Packard conducted training on cultural differences between American-Anglos and Mexicans, Indochinese, and Filipinos. Much of the content focused on cultural differences in communication styles. In one of the most thorough training efforts to date, Ortho Pharmaceuticals started its three-day training with small groups (ten to twelve) of senior managers and eventually trained managers at every level of the company.

Specific data on the effectiveness of these training efforts is hard to collect, but a study of seventy-five Canadian consultants found that people exposed to even the most rudimentary form of training on cultural diversity are significantly more likely to recognize the impact of cultural diversity on work behavior and to identify the potential advantages of cultural heterogeneity in organizations.[10]

In addition, anecdotal evidence from managers of many companies indicates that valuing and managing diversity training represents a crucial first step for organization change efforts.

New member orientation programs are basic in the hiring processes of many organizations. Some companies are developing special orientations as part of its managing diversity initiatives. Proctor and Gamble's "On Boarding" program, which features special components for women and minority hires and their managers, is one example.

Language training is important for companies hiring American Asians, Hispanics, and foreign nationals. To promote pluralism, it is helpful to offer second language training to Anglos as well as the minority-culture employees, and take other steps to communicate that languages other than English are valued. Leaders in this area include Esprit De Corp., Economy Color Card, and Pace Foods.

For many years, the women's clothier Esprit De Corp. has offered courses in Italian and Japanese. At Economy Color Card, work rules are printed in both Spanish and English. Pace Foods, where thirty-five percent of employees are Hispanic, goes a step further by printing company policies and also conducting staff meetings in Spanish and English. Motorola is a leader in the more traditional training for English as a second language where classes are conducted at company expense and on company time.

Insuring Minority-Group Input and Acceptance. The most direct and effective way to promote influence of minority-culture norms on organizational decision making is to achieve cultural diversity at all organization levels. However, an important supplemental method is through ensuring diversity on key committees. An example is the insistence of *USA Today* President Nancy Woodhull on having gender, racioethnic, educational, and geographic diversity represented in all daily news meetings. She attributes much of the company's success to this action.

Another technique is explicitly mentioning the importance of diversity to the organization in statements of mission and strategy. By doing this, organizations foster the mindset that increased diversity is an opportunity and not a problem. Examples of organizations that have done this are The University of Michigan and the Careers Division of the National Academy of Management. The latter group has fostered research addressing the impact of diversity on organizations by explicitly citing this as part of its interest.

Another way to increase the influence of minority-group members on organizational culture and policy is by providing specially composed minority advisory groups direct access to the most senior executives of the company. Organizations which have done this include Avon, Equitable Life Assurance, Intel, and U.S. West. At Equitable, committees of women, Blacks and Hispanics (called "Business Resource Groups") meet with the CEO to discuss important group issues and make recommendations on how the organizational environment might be improved. CEO John Carver often assigns a senior manager to be accountable for following up on the recommendations. U.S. West has a thirty-three member "Pluralism Council" which advises senior management on plans for improving the company's response to increased workforce diversity.

Finally, a more complex, but I believe potentially powerful, tool for promoting change toward pluralism is the development of flexible, highly tolerant climates that encourage diverse approaches to problems among all employees. Such an environment is useful to workers regardless of group identity, but is especially beneficial to people from nontraditional cultural backgrounds because their approaches to problems are more likely to be different from past norms. A company often cited for such a work environment is Hewlett Packard. Among the operating norms of the company which should promote pluralism are: 1. Encouragement of informality and unstructured work; 2. Flexible work schedules and loose supervision; 3. Setting objectives in broad terms with lots of individual employee discretion over how they are achieved; 4. A policy that researchers should spend at least ten percent of company time exploring personal ideas. I would suggest that item 4 be extended to all management and professional employees.

Creating Full Structural Integration

Education Efforts. The objective of creating an organization where there is no correlation between one's culture-identity group and one's job status implies that minority-group members are well

---

10. For details on this study see Nancy J. Adler, *International Dimensions of Organizational Behavior* (Kent Publishing Co., 1986), 77–83.

represented at all levels, in all functions, and in all work groups. Achievement of this goal requires that skill and education levels be evenly distributed. Education statistics indicate that the most serious problems occur with Blacks and Hispanics.[11]

A number of organizations have become more actively involved in various kinds of education programs. The Aetna Life Insurance Company is a leader. It has initiated a number of programs including jobs in exchange for customized education taught by community agencies and private schools, and its own in-house basic education programs. The company has created an Institute for Corporate Education with a full-time director. Other companies participating in various new education initiatives include Prim-America, Quaker Oats, Chase Manhattan Bank, Eastman Kodak, and Digital Equipment. In Minnesota, a project headed by Cray Research and General Mills allows businesses to create schools of its own design. I believe that business community involvement in joint efforts with educational institutions and community leaders to promote equal achievement in education is critical to the future competitiveness of U.S. business. Business leaders should insist that economic support be tied to substantive programs which are jointly planned and evaluated by corporate representatives and educators.

Affirmative Action. In my opinion, the mainstay of efforts to create full structural integration in the foreseeable future, will continue to be affirmative action programs. While most large organizations have some kind of program already, the efforts of Xerox and Pepsico are among the standouts.

The Xerox effort, called "The Balanced Workforce Strategy," is noteworthy for several reasons including: an especially fast timetable for moving minorities up; tracking representation by function and operating unit as well as by level; and national networks for minority-group members (supported by the company) to provide various types of career support. Recently published data indicating that Xerox is well ahead of both national and industry averages in moving minorities into management and professional jobs, suggests that these efforts have paid off (*Wall Street Journal,* November 5, 1989).

Two features of Pepsico's efforts which are somewhat unusual are the use of a "Black Managers Association" as a supplemental source of nominees for promotion to management jobs, and the practice of hiring qualified minorities directly into managerial and professional jobs.

Career Development. A number of companies including Mobil Oil, IBM, and McDonalds have also initiated special career

---

11. For example, see the book by William Julius Wilson which reviews data on educational achievement by Blacks and Hispanics in Chicago, *The Truly Disadvantaged: Inner City, the Underclass and Public Policy* (The University of Chicago Press, 1987). Among the facts cited is that less than half of all Blacks and Hispanics in inner city schools graduate within four years of high school enrollment and only four in ten of those who do graduate read at the eleventh grade level or above.

development efforts for minority personnel. IBM's long standing "Executive Resource System" is designed to identify and develop minority talent for senior management positions. McDonalds' "Black Career Development Program" provides career enhancement advice, and fast-track career paths for minorities. Company officials have stated that the program potentially cuts a fifteen year career path to regional manager by fifty percent.

Revamping Reward Systems. An absolutely essential tool for creating structural integration is to ensure that the organization's performance appraisal and reward systems reinforce the importance of effective diversity management. Companies that have taken steps in this direction include The Federal National Mortgage Association (Fannie Mae), Baxter Health Care, Amtrak, Exxon, Coca-Cola, and Merck. Fannie Mae, Baxter, Coca-Cola, and Merck all tie compensation to manager performance on diversity management efforts. At Amtrak, manager promotion and compensation are tied to performance on affirmative action objectives, and at Exxon, evaluations of division managers must include a review of career development plans for at least ten women and minority men employees.

For this tool to be effective, it needs to go beyond simply including effective management of diversity among the evaluation and reward criteria. Attention must also be given to the amount of weight given to this criterion compared to other dimensions of job performance. How performance is measured is also important. For example, in addition to work-group profile statistics, subordinate evaluations of managers might be useful. When coded by cultural group, differences in perceptions based on group identity can be noted and used in forming performance ratings on this dimension.

Benefits and Work Schedules. Structural integration of women, Hispanics, and Blacks is facilitated by changes in human resource policies and benefit plans that make it easier for employees to balance work and family role demands. Many companies have made such changes in areas like child care, work schedules, and parental leave. North Carolina National Bank, Arthur Anderson, Levi Strauss, and IBM are examples of companies that have gone farther than most. NCNB's "select time" project allows even officers and professionals in the company to work part-time for several years and still be considered for advancement. Arthur Anderson has taken a similar step by allowing part-time accountants to stay "on-track" for partnership promotions. Levi Strauss has one of the most comprehensive work-family programs in the country covering everything from paternity leave to part-time work with preservation of benefits. These companies are leaders in this area because attention is paid to the impact on advancement opportunities and fringe-benefits when employees take advantage of scheduling flexibility and longer leaves of absence. This kind of accommodation will make it easier to hire and retain both men and women in the '90s as parents struggle to balance work and home time demands. It is especially important for women, Hispanics, and Blacks because cultural traditions put great emphasis on family responsibilities. Organization change in this area will promote full structural integration by keeping more racioethnic minorities and white women in the pipeline.

Creating Integration in Informal Networks

Mentoring and Social Events. One tool for including minorities in the informal networks of organizations is company-initiated mentoring programs that target minorities. A recent research project in which a colleague and I surveyed 800 MBAs indicated that racioethnic minorities report significantly less access to mentors than whites. If company-specific research shows a similar pattern, this data can be used to justify and bolster support among majority-group employees for targeted mentoring programs. Examples of companies which have established such targeted mentoring programs are Chemical Bank and General Foods.

A second technique for facilitating informal network integration is company-sponsored social events. In planning such events, multiculturalism is fostered by selecting both activities and locations with a sensitivity to the diversity of the workforce.

Support Groups. In many companies, minority groups have formed their own professional associations and organizations to promote information exchange and social support. There is little question that these groups have provided emotional and career support for members who traditionally have not been welcomed in the majority's informal groups. A somewhat controversial issue is whether these groups hinder the objective of informal-network integration. Many believe that they harm integration by fostering a "we-versus-they" mentality and reducing incentives for minorities to seek inclusion in informal activities of majority-group members. Others deny these effects. I am not aware of any hard evidence on this point. There is a dilemma here in that integration in the informal networks is at best a long-term process and there is widespread skepticism among minorities as to its eventual achievement. Even if abolishing the minority-group associations would eventually promote full integration, the absence of a support network of any kind in the interim could be a devastating loss to minority-group members. Therefore, my conclusion is that these groups are more helpful than harmful to the overall multiculturalism effort.

Creating a Bias-Free Organization

Equal opportunity seminars, focus groups, bias-reduction training, research, and task forces are methods that organizations have found useful in reducing culture-group bias and discrimination. Unlike prejudice, discrimination is a behavior and therefore more amenable to direct control or influence by the organization. At the same time, the underlying cause of discrimination is prejudice. Ideally, efforts should have at least indirect effects on the thought processes and attitudes of organization members. All of the tools listed, with the possible exception of task forces, should reduce prejudice as well as discrimination.

Most plural organizations have used equal opportunity seminars for many years. These include sexual harassment workshops, training on civil rights legislation, and workshops on sexism and racism.

Focus Groups. More recently, organizations like Digital Equipment have used "focus groups" as an in-house, on-going mechanism to explicitly examine attitudes, beliefs, and feelings about culture-group differences and their effects on behavior at work. At Digital, the center piece of its "valuing differences" effort is the use of small groups (called Core Groups) to discuss four major objectives: 1. stripping away stereotypes; 2. examining underlying assumptions about outgroups; 3. building significant relationships with people one regards as different; 4. raising levels of personal empowerment. Digital's experience suggests that a breakthrough for many organizations will be achieved by the simple mechanism of bringing discussion about group differences out in the open.

Progress is made as people become more comfortable directly dealing with the issues.

Bias-Reduction Training. Another technique for reducing bias is through training specifically designed to create attitude change. An example is Northern Telecom's 16-hour program designed to help employees identify and begin to modify negative attitudes toward people from different cultural backgrounds. Eastman Kodak's training conference for its recruiters is designed to eliminate racism and sexism from the hiring process. This type of training often features exercises that expose stereotypes of various groups which are prevalent but rarely made explicit and may be subconscious. Many academics and consultants have also developed bias-reduction training. An example is the "Race Relations Competence Workshop," a program developed by Clay Alderfer and Robert Tucker of Yale University. They have found that participants completing the workshop have more positive attitudes toward Blacks and inter-race relations.

Leveraging Internal Research. A very powerful tool for reducing discrimination and (to a smaller extent) prejudice, is to conduct and act on internal research on employment experience by cultural group. Time Inc. conducts an annual evaluation of men and women in the same jobs to ensure comparable pay and equal treatment. A second example comes from a large utility company which discovered that minority managers were consistently underrepresented in lists submitted by line managers for bonus recommendations. As a result of the research, the company put pressure on the managers to increase the inclusion of minority managers. When that failed, the vice president of human resources announced that he would no longer approve the recommendations unless minorities were adequately represented. The keys to the organization change were, first obtaining the data identifying the problem and then acting on it. My experience suggests that this type of research-based approach is underutilized by organizations.

Task Forces. A final tool for creating bias-free organizations is to form task forces that monitor organizational policy and practices for evidence of unfairness. An example of what I consider to be a well-designed committee is the affirmative action committee used by Phillip Morris which is composed of senior managers and minority employees. This composition combines the power of senior executives with the insight into needed changes that the minority representatives can provide. Of course, minority culture-group members who are also senior managers are ideal but, unfortunately, such individuals are rare in most organizations.

Minimizing Intergroup Conflict

Experts on conflict management have noted that a certain amount of interpersonal conflict is inevitable and perhaps even healthy in organizations.[12] However, conflict becomes destructive when it is excessive, not well managed, or rooted in struggles for power rather than the differentiation of ideas. We are concerned here with these more destructive forms of conflict which may be

---

12. For example, see *Organization Behavior: Conflict in Organizations,* by Gregory Northcraft and Margaret Neale (The Dryden Press, 1990), 221.

present with diverse workforces due to language barriers, cultural clash, or resentment by majority-group members of what they may perceive as preferential, and unwarranted treatment of minority-group members.

Survey Feedback. Probably the most effective tool for avoiding intergroup conflict (especially the backlash form that often accompanies new initiatives targeting minority-groups of the organization) is the use of survey feedback. I will give three examples. As one of the most aggressive affirmative action companies of the past decade, Xerox has found that being very open with all employees about the specific features of the initiative as well as the reasons for it, was helpful in diffusing backlash by whites. This strategy is exemplified by the high profile which Chairman David Kearns has taken on the company's diversity efforts.

A second example is Proctor and Gamble's use of data on the average time needed for new hires of various culture groups to become fully integrated into the organization. They found that "join-up" time varied by race and gender with white males becoming acclimated most quickly, and black females taking the longest of any group. This research led to the development of their "on-boarding program" referred to earlier.

A final example is Corning Glass Works' strategy of fighting white-male resistance to change with data showing that promotion rates of their group was indeed much higher than that of other groups. This strategy has also been used by U.S. West which recently reported on a 1987 study showing that promotion rates for white men were seven times higher than white women and sixteen times higher than non-white women.

The beauty of this tool is that it provides the double benefit of a knowledge base for planning change, and leverage to win employee commitment to implement the needed changes.

Conflict-Resolution Training. A second tool for minimizing intergroup conflict is management training in conflict-resolution techniques. Conflict management experts can assist managers in learning and developing skill in applying alternative conflict management techniques such as mediation and superordinate goals. This is a general management skill which is made more crucial by the greater diversity of workforces in the '90s.

Finally, the managing and valuing diversity training and focus group tools discussed previously are also applicable here. AT&T is among the organizations which have explicitly identified stress and conflict reduction as central objectives of its training and focus group efforts.

CONCLUSION

Increased diversity presents challenges to business leaders who must maximize the opportunities that it presents while minimizing its costs. To accomplish this, organizations must be transformed from monolithic or plural organizations to a multicultural model. The multicultural organization is characterized by pluralism, full integration of minority-culture members both formally and informally, an absence of prejudice and discrimination, and low levels of intergroup conflict; all of which should reduce alienation and build organizational identity among minority group members. The organization that achieves these conditions will create an environment in which all members can contribute to their maximum potential, and in which the "value in diversity" can be fully realized.

Changing Unethical Organizational Behavior

Richard P. Nielsen

"To be, or not to be: that is the question:
Whether 'tis nobler in the mind to suffer
The slings and arrows of outrageous fortune,
Or to take arms against a sea of troubles,
And by opposing end them?"

William Shakespeare, *Hamlet*

What are the implications of Hamlet's question in the context of organizational ethics? What does it mean to be ethical in an organizational context? Should one suffer the slings and arrows of unethical organizational behavior? Should one try to take arms against unethical behaviors and by opposing, end them?

The consequences of addressing organizational ethics issues can be unpleasant. One can be punished or fired; one's career can suffer, or one can be disliked, considered an outsider. It may take courage to oppose unethical and lead ethical organizational behavior.

How can one address organizational ethics issues? Paul Tillich, in his book *The Courage to Be*, recognized, as Hamlet did, that dire consequences can result from standing up to and opposing unethical behavior. Tillich identified two approaches: *being* as an individual and *being* as a part of a group.[1]

In an organizational context, these two approaches can be interpreted as follows: (1) Being as an individual can mean intervening to end unethical organizational behaviors by working against others and the organizations performing the unethical behaviors;

Richard P. Nielsen (Boston College) "Changing Unethical Organizational Behavior." Reprinted with permission from the *Academy of Management Executive,* 1989, Vol. 3 (2), pp. 123–140.

1. Paul Tillich, *The Courage to Be.* New Haven, CT: Yale University Press, 1950.

and (2) being as a part can mean leading an ethical organizational change by working with others and the organization. These approaches are not mutually exclusive; rather, depending on the individual, the organization, the relationships, and the situation, one or both of these approaches may be appropriate for addressing ethical issues.

BEING AS AN INDIVIDUAL

According to Tillich, the courage to be as an individual is the courage to follow one's conscience and defy unethical and/or unreasonable authority. It can even mean staging a revolutionary attack on that authority. Such an act can entail great risk and require great courage. As Tillich explains, "The anxiety conquered in the courage to be . . . in the productive process is considerable, because the threat of being excluded from such a participation by unemployment or the loss of an economic basis is what, above all, fate means today. . . ."[2]

According to David Ewing, retired executive editor of the *Harvard Business Review,* this type of anxiety is not without foundation.

"There is very little protection in industry for employees who object to carrying out immoral, unethical or illegal orders from their superiors. If the employee doesn't like what he or she is asked to do, the remedy is to pack up and leave. This remedy seems to presuppose an ideal economy, where there is another company down the street with openings for jobs just like the one the employee left."[3]

How can one *be* as an individual, intervening against unethical organizational behavior? Intervention strategies an individual can use to change unethical behavior include: (1) secretly blowing the whistle within the organization; (2) quietly blowing the whistle, informing a responsible higher-level manager; (3) secretly threatening the offender with blowing the whistle; (4) secretly threatening a responsible manager with blowing the whistle outside the organization; (5) publicly threatening a responsible manager with blowing the whistle; (6) sabotaging the implementation of the unethical behavior; (7) quietly refraining from implementing an unethical order or policy; (8) publicly blowing the whistle within the organization; (9) conscientiously objecting to an unethical policy or refusing to implement the policy; (10) indicating uncertainty about or refusing to support a cover-up in the event that the individual and/or organization gets caught; (11) secretly blowing the whistle outside the organization; or (12) publicly blowing the whistle outside the organization. Cases of each strategy are considered below.

CASES

1. Secretly blowing the whistle within the organization. A purchasing manager for General Electric secretly wrote a letter to an upper-level manager about his boss, who was soliciting and accepting bribes from subcontractors. The boss was investigated and eventually fired. He was also sentenced to six months' imprisonment for taking $100,000 in bribes, in exchange for which he granted favorable treatment on defense contracts.[4]

2. Quietly blowing the whistle to a responsible higher-level manager. When Evelyn Grant was first hired by the company with which she is now a personnel manager, her job included administering a battery of tests that, in part, determined which employees were promoted to supervisory positions. Grant explained:

"There have been cases where people will do something wrong because they think they have no choice. Their boss tells them to do it, and so they do it, knowing it's wrong. They don't realize there are ways around the boss. . . . When I went over his [the chief psychologist's] data and analysis, I found errors in assumptions as well as actual errors of computation. . . . I had two choices: I could do nothing or I could report my findings to my supervisor. If I did nothing, the only persons probably hurt were the ones who 'failed' the test. To report my findings, on the other hand, could hurt several people, possibly myself."

She quietly spoke to her boss, who quietly arranged for a meeting to discuss the discrepancies with the chief psychologist. The chief psychologist did not show up for the meeting; however, the test battery was dropped.[5]

3. Secretly threatening the offender with blowing the whistle. A salesman for a Boston-area insurance company attended a weekly sales meeting during which the sales manager instructed the salespeople, both verbally and in writing, to use a sales technique that the salesman considered unethical. The salesman anonymously wrote the sales manager a letter threatening to send a copy of the unethical sales instructions to the Massachusetts insurance commissioner and the *Boston Globe* newspaper unless the sales manager retracted his instructions at the next sales meeting. The sales manager did retract the instructions. The salesman still works for the insurance company.[6]

4. Secretly threatening a responsible manager with blowing the whistle outside the organization. A recently hired manager with a San Francisco Real Estate Development Company found that the

---

2. See Footnote 1, page 159.

3. David Ewing, *Freedom Inside the Organization.* New York: McGraw-Hill, 1977.

4. The person blowing the whistle in this case wishes to remain anonymous. See also Elizabeth Neuffer, "GE Managers Sentenced for Bribery," *The Boston Globe,* July 26, 1988, p. 67.

5. Barbara Ley Toffler, *Tough Choices: Managers Talk Ethics.* New York: John Wiley, 1986, pp. 153–169.

6. Richard P. Nielsen, "What Can Managers Do About Unethical Management?" *Journal of Business Ethics,* 6, 1987, 153–161. See also Nielsen's "Limitations of Ethical Reasoning as an Action Strategy," *Journal of Business Ethics,* 7, 1988, pp. 725–733, and "Arendt's Action Philosophy and the Manager as Eichmann, Richard III, Faust or Institution Citizen," *California Management Review,* 26, 3, Spring 1984, pp. 191–201.

construction company his firm had contracted with was systematically not giving minorities opportunities to learn construction management. This new manager wrote an anonymous letter to a higher-level real estate manager threatening to blow the whistle to the press and local government about the contractor unless the company corrected the situation. The real estate manager intervened, and the contractor began to hire minorities for foremen-training positions.[7]

5. Publicly threatening a responsible manager with blowing the whistle. A woman in the business office of a large Boston-area university observed that one middle-level male manager was sexually harassing several women in the office. She tried to reason with the office manager to do something about the offensive behavior, but the manager would not do anything. She then told the manager and several other people in the office that if the manager did not do something about the behavior, she would blow the whistle to the personnel office. The manager then told the offender that if he did not stop the harassment, the personnel office would be brought in. He did stop the behavior, but he and several other employees refused to talk to the woman who initiated the actions. She eventually left the university.[8]

6. Sabotaging the implementation of the unethical behavior. A program manager for a Boston-area local social welfare organization was told by her superior to replace a significant percentage of her clients who received disability benefits with refugee Soviet Jews. She wanted to help both the refugees and her current clients; however, she thought it was unethical to drop current clients, in part because she believed such an action could result in unnecessary deaths. Previously, a person who had lost benefits because of what the program manager considered unethical "bumping" had committed suicide: He had not wanted to force his family to sell their home in order to pay for the medical care he needed and qualify for poverty programs. After her attempts to reason with her boss failed, she instituted a paperwork chain with a partially funded federal agency that prevented her own agency from dropping clients for nine months, after which time they would be eligible for a different funding program. Her old clients received benefits and the new refugees also received benefits. In discussions with her boss, she blamed the federal agency for making it impossible to drop people quickly. Her boss, a political appointee who did not understand the system, also blamed the federal agency office.[9]

7. Publicly blowing the whistle within the organization. John W. Young, the chief of NASA's astronaut office, wrote a 12-page internal memorandum to 97 people after the Challenger explosion that killed seven crew members. The memo listed a large number of safety-related problems that Young said had endangered crews since October 1984. According to Young, "If the management system is not big enough to stop the space shuttle program whenever necessary to make flight safety corrections, it will not survive and

neither will our three space shuttles or their flight crews." The memo was instrumental in the decision to broaden safety investigations throughout the total NASA system.[10]

8. Quietly refraining from implementing an unethical order/policy. Frank Ladwig was a top salesman and branch manager with a large computer company for more than 40 years. At times, he had trouble balancing his responsibilities. For instance, he was trained to sell solutions to customer problems, yet he had order and revenue quotas that sometimes made it difficult for him to concentrate on solving problems. He was responsible for signing and keeping important customers with annual revenues of between $250,000 and $500,000 and for aggressively and conscientiously representing new products that had required large R&D investments. He was required to sell the full line of products and services, and sometimes he had sales quotas for products that he believed were not a good match for the customer or appeared to perform marginally. Ladwig would quietly not sell those products, concentrating on selling the products he believed in. He would quietly explain the characteristics of the questionable products to his knowledgeable customers and get their reactions, rather than making an all-out sales effort. When he was asked by his sales manager why a certain product was not moving, he explained what the customers objected to and why. However, Ladwig thought that a salesman or manager with an average or poor performance record would have a difficult time getting away with this type of solution to an ethical dilemma.[11]

9. Conscientiously objecting to an unethical policy or refusing to implement it. Francis O'Brien was a research director for the pharmaceutical company Searle & Co. O'Brien conscientiously objected to what he believed were exaggerated claims for the Searle Copper 7 intrauterine contraceptive. When reasoning with upper-level management failed, O'Brien wrote them the following:

> "Their continued use, in my opinion, is both misleading and a thinly disguised attempt to make claims which are not FDA approved. . . . Because of personal reasons I do not consent to have my name used in any press release or in connection with any press release. In addition, I will not participate in any press conferences."

O'Brien left the company ten years later. Currently, several lawsuits are pending against Searle, charging that its IUD caused infection and sterility.[12]

10. Indicating uncertainty about or refusing to support a cover-up in the event that the individual and/or organization gets

---

7. The person involved wishes to remain anonymous.

8. The person involved wishes to remain anonymous.

9. See Footnote 6.

---

10. R. Reinhold, "Astronauts Chief Says NASA Risked Life for Schedule," *The New York Times,* 36, 1986, p. 1.

11. Personal conversation and letter with Frank Ladwig, 1986. See also Frank Ladwig and Associates' *Advanced Consultative Selling for Professionals.* Stonington, CT.

12. W. G. Glaberson, "Did Searle Lose Its Eyes to a Health Hazard?" *Business Week,* October 14, 1985, pp. 120–122.

caught. In the Boston office of Bear Stearns, four brokers informally work together as a group. One of the brokers had been successfully trading on insider information, and he invited the other three to do the same. One of the three told the others that such trading was not worth the risk of getting caught, and if an investigation ever occurred, he was not sure he would be able to participate in a cover-up. The other two brokers decided not to trade on the insider information, and the first broker stopped at least that type of insider trading.[13]

11. Secretly blowing the whistle outside the corporation. William Schwartzkopf of the Commonwealth Electric Company secretly and anonymously wrote a letter to the Justice Department alleging large-scale, long-time bid rigging among many of the largest U.S. electrical contractors. The secret letter accused the contractors of raising bids and conspiring to divide billions of dollars of contracts. Companies in the industry have already paid more than $20 million in fines to the government in part as a result of this letter, and they face millions of dollars more in losses when the victims sue.[14]

12. Publicly blowing the whistle outside the organization. A. Earnest Fitzgerald, a former high-level manager in the U.S. Air Force and Lockheed CEO, revealed to Congress and the press that the Air Force and Lockheed systematically practiced a strategy of underbidding in order to gain Air Force contracts for Lockheed, which then billed the Air Force and received payments for cost overruns on the contracts. Fitzgerald was fired for his trouble, but eventually received his job back. The underbidding/cost overruns, on at least the C-5/A cargo plane, were stopped.[15]

Limitations of Intervention

The intervention strategies described above can be very effective, but they also have some important limitations.

1. The individual can be wrong about the organization's actions. Lower-level employees commonly do not have as much or as good information about ethical situations and issues as higher-level managers. Similarly, they may not be as experienced as higher-level managers in dealing with specific ethical issues. The quality of experience and information an individual has can influence the quality of his or her ethical judgments. To the extent that this is true in any given situation, the use of intervention may or may not be warranted. In Case 9, for example, if Frank Ladwig had had limited computer experience, he could have been wrong about some of the products he thought would not produce the promised results.

---

13. The person involved wishes to remain anonymous.

14. Andy Pasztor, "Electrical Contractors Reel Under Charges That They Rigged Bids," *The Wall Street Journal,* November 29, 1985, pp. 1, 14.

15. A. Ernest Fitzgerald, *The High Priests of Waste.* New York: McGraw-Hill, 1977.

2. Relationships can be damaged. Suppose that instead of identifying with the individuals who want an organization to change its ethical behavior, we look at these situations from another perspective. How do we feel when we are forced to change our behavior? Further, how would we feel if we were forced by a subordinate to change, even though we thought that we had the position, quality of information, and/or quality of experience to make the correct decisions? Relationships would probably be, at the least, strained, particularly if we made an ethical decision and were nevertheless forced to change. If we are wrong, it may be that we do not recognize it at the time. If we know we are wrong, we still may not like being forced to change. However, it is possible that the individual forcing us to change may justify his or her behavior to us, and our relationship may actually be strengthened.

3. The organization can be hurt unnecessarily. If an individual is wrong in believing that the organization is unethical, the organization can be hurt unnecessarily by his or her actions. Even if the individual is right, the organization can still be unnecessarily hurt by intervention strategies.

4. Intervention strategies can encourage "might makes right" climates. If we want "wrong" people, who might be more powerful now or in the future than we are, to exercise self-restraint, then we may need to exercise self-restraint even when we are "right." A problem with using force is that the other side may use more powerful or effective force now or later. Many people have been punished for trying to act ethically both when they were right and when they were wrong. By using force, one may also contribute to the belief that the only way to get things done in a particular organization is through force. People who are wrong can and do use force, and win. Do we want to build an organization culture in which force plays an important role? Gandhi's response to "eye for an eye" was that if we all followed that principle, eventually everyone would be blind.

BEING AS A PART

While the intervention strategies discussed above can be very effective, they can also be destructive. Therefore, it may be appropriate to consider the advantages of leading an ethical change effort (being as a part) as well as intervening against unethical behaviors (being as an individual).

Tillich maintains that the courage to be as a part is the courage to affirm one's own being through participation with others. He writes,

> "The self affirms itself as participant in the power of a group, of a movement. . . . Self-affirmation within a group includes the courage to accept guilt and its consequences as public guilt, whether one is oneself responsible or whether somebody else is. It is a problem of the group which has to be expiated for the sake of the group, and the methods of punishment and satisfaction . . . are accepted by the individual. . . . In every human community, there are outstanding members, the bearers of the traditions and leaders of the future. They must have sufficient distance in order to judge and to change. They must take responsibility and ask questions. This unavoidably produces individual doubt and

personal guilt. Nevertheless, the predominant pattern is the courage to be a part in all members of the . . . group. . . . The difference between the genuine Stoic and the neocollectivist is that the latter is bound in the first place to the collective and in the second place to the universe, while the Stoic was first of all related to the universal Logos and secondly to possible human groups. . . . The democratic-conformist type of the courage to be as a part was in an outspoken way tied up with the idea of progress. The courage to be as a part in the progress of the group to which one belongs. . . ."[16]

Leading Ethical Change

A good cross-cultural conceptualization of leadership is offered by Yoshino and Lifson: "The essence of leadership is the influential increment over and above mechanical compliance with routine directives of the organization."[17] This definition permits comparisons between and facilitates an understanding of different leadership styles through its use of a single variable: created incremental performance. Of course, different types of leadership may be more or less effective in different types of situations; yet, it is helpful to understand the "essence" of leadership in its many different cultural forms as the creation of incremental change beyond the routine.

For example, Yoshino and Lifson compare generalizations (actually overgeneralizations) about Japanese and American leadership styles:

"In the United States, a leader is often thought of as one who blazes new trails, a virtuoso whose example inspires awe, respect, and emulation. If any individual characterizes this pattern, it is surely John Wayne, whose image reached epic proportions in his own lifetime as an embodiment of something uniquely American. A Japanese leader, rather than being an authority, is more of a communications channel, a mediator, a facilitator, and most of all, a symbol and embodiment of group unity. Consensus building is necessary in decision making, and this requires patience and an ability to use carefully cultivated relationships to get all to agree for the good of the unit. A John Wayne in this situation might succeed temporarily by virtue of charisma, but eventually the inability to build strong emotion-laden relationships and use these as a tool of motivation and consensus building would prove fatal."[18]

A charismatic, "John Wayne type" leader can inspire and/or frighten people into diverting from the routine. A consensus-building, Japanese-style leader can get people to agree to divert from the routine. In both cases, the leader creates incremental behavior change beyond the routine. How does leadership (being as a part) in its various cultural forms differ from the various intervention (being as an individual) strategies and cases discussed above? Some case data may be revealing.

Cases

1. Roger Boisjoly and the Challenger launch.[19] In January 1985, after the postflight hardware inspection of Flight 52C, Roger Boisjoly strongly suspected that unusually low temperatures had compromised the performance effectiveness of the O-ring seals on two field joints. Such a performance compromise could cause an explosion. In March 1985, laboratory tests confirmed that low temperatures did negatively affect the ability of the O-rings to perform this sealing function. In June 1985, the postflight inspection of Flight 51B revealed serious erosion of both primary and backup seals that, had it continued, could have caused an explosion.

These events convinced Boisjoly that a serious and very dangerous problem existed with the O-rings. Instead of acting as an individual against his supervisors and the organization, for example, by blowing the whistle to the press, he tried to lead a change to stop the launching of flights with unsafe O-rings. He worked with his immediate supervisor, the director of engineering, and the organization in leading this change. He wrote a draft of a memo to Bob Lund, vice-president of engineering, which he first showed and discussed with his immediate supervisor to "maintain good relationships." Boisjoly and others developed potential win-win solutions, such as investigating remedies to fix the O-rings and refraining from launching flights at too-low temperatures. He effectively established a team to study the matter, and participated in a teleconference with 130 technical experts.

On the day before the Challenger launch, Boisjoly and other team members were successful in leading company executives to reverse their tentative recommendation to launch because the overnight temperatures were predicted to be too low. The company recommendation was to launch only when temperatures were above 53 degrees. To this point, Boisjoly was very effective in leading a change toward what he and other engineering and management people believed was a safe and ethical decision.

However, according to testimony from Boisjoly and others to Congress, the top managers of Morton Thiokol, under pressure from NASA, reversed their earlier recommendation not to launch. The next day, Challenger was launched and exploded, causing the deaths of all the crew members. While Boisjoly was very effective in leading a change within his own organization, he was not able to counteract subsequent pressure from the customer, NASA.

2. Dan Phillips and Genco, Inc.[20] Dan Phillips was a paper products group division manager for Genco, whose upper-level management adopted a strategy whereby several mills, including the Elkhorn Mill, would either have to reduce costs or close down.

---

16. See Footnote 1, pp. 89, 93.

17. M. Y. Yoshino and T. B. Lifson, *The Invisible Link: Japan's Saga Shosha and the Organization of Trade.* Cambridge, MA: MIT Press, 1986.

18. See Footnote 17, p. 178.

19. Roger Boisjoly, address given at Massachusetts Institute of Technology on January 7, 1987. Reprinted in *Books and Religion,* March/April 1987, 3–4, 12–13. See also Caroline Whitbeck, "Moral Responsibility and the Working Engineer," *Books and Religion,* March/April 1987, 3, 22–23.

20. Personal conversation with Ray Bauer, Harvard Business School, 1975. See also R. Ackerman and Ray Bauer, *Corporate Social Responsiveness.* Reston, VA: Reston Publishing, 1976.

Phillips was concerned that cost cutting at Elkhorn would prevent the mill from meeting government pollution-control requirements, and that closing the mill could seriously hurt the local community. If he reduced costs, he would not meet pollution-control requirements; if he did not reduce costs, the mill would close and the community would suffer.

Phillips did not secretly or publicly blow the whistle, nor did he sabotage, conscientiously object, quietly refrain from implementing the plan, or quit; however, he did lead a change in the organization's ethical behavior. He asked research and development people in his division to investigate how the plant could both become more cost efficient and create less pollution. He then asked operations people in his division to estimate how long it would take to put such a new plant design on line, and how much it would cost. He asked cost accounting and financial people within his division to estimate when such a new operation would achieve a breakeven payback. Once he found a plan that would work, he negotiated a win-win solution with upper-level management: in exchange for not closing the plant and increasing its investment in his division, the organization would over time benefit from lower costs and higher profitability. Phillips thus worked with others and the organization to lead an inquiry and adopt an alternative ethical and cost-effective plan.

3. Lotus and Brazilian Software Importing.[21] Lotus, a software manufacturer, found that in spite of restrictions on the importing of much of its software to Brazil, many people there were buying and using Lotus software. On further investigation, the company discovered that Brazilian businessmen, in alliance with a Brazilian general, were violating the law by buying Lotus software in Cambridge, Massachusetts, and bringing it into Brazil.

Instead of blowing the whistle on the illegal behavior, sabotaging it, or leaving Brazil, Lotus negotiated a solution: In exchange for the Brazilians' agreement to stop illegal importing, Lotus helped set them up as legitimate licensed manufacturers and distributors of Lotus products in Brazil. Instead of working against them and the Lotus salespeople supplying them, the Lotus managers worked with these people to develop an ethical, legal, and economically sound solution to the importing problem.

And in at least a limited sense, the importers may have been transformed into ethical managers and business people. This case may remind you of the legendary "Old West," where government officials sometimes negotiated win-win solutions with "outlaw gunfighters," who agreed to become somewhat more ethical as appointed sheriffs. The gunfighters needed to make a living, and many were not interested in or qualified for such other professions as farming or shopkeeping. In some cases, ethical behavior may take place before ethical beliefs are assumed.

4. Insurance company office/sales manager and discrimination.[22] The sales-office manager of a very large Boston-area insurance company tried to hire female salespeople several times, but his boss refused to permit the hires. The manager could have acted against his boss and the organization by secretly threatening to blow the whistle or actually blowing the whistle, publicly or secretly.

Instead, he decided to try to lead a change in the implicit hiring policy of the organization.

The manager asked his boss why he was not permitted to hire a woman. He learned that his boss did not believe women made good salespeople and had never worked with a female salesperson. He found that reasoning with his boss about the capabilities of women and the ethics and legality of refusing to hire women was ineffective.

He inquired within the company about whether being a woman could be an advantage in any insurance sales areas. He negotiated with his boss a six-month experiment whereby he hired on a trial basis one woman to sell life insurance to married women who contributed large portions of their salaries to their home mortgages. The woman he hired was not only very successful in selling this type of life insurance, but became one of the office's top salespeople. After this experience, the boss reversed his policy of not hiring female salespeople.

Limitations to Leading Ethical Organizational Change

In the four cases described above, the individuals did not attack the organization or people within the organization, nor did they intervene against individuals and/or the organization to stop an unethical practice. Instead, they worked with people in the organization to build a more ethical organization. As a result of their leadership, the organizations used more ethical behaviors. The strategy of leading an organization toward more ethical behavior, however, does have some limitations. These are described below.

1. In some organizational situations, ethical win-win solutions or compromises may not be possible. For example, in 1975 a pharmaceutical company in Raritan, New Jersey, decided to enter a new market with a new product.[23] Grace Pierce, who was then in charge of medical testing of new products, refused to test a new diarrhea drug product on infants and elderly consumers because it contained high levels of saccharin, which was feared by many at the time to be a carcinogen. When Pierce was transferred, she resigned. The drug was tested on infant and elderly consumers. In this case, Pierce may have been faced with an either-or situation that left her little room to lead a change in organizational behavior.

Similarly, Errol Marshall, with Hydraulic Parts and Components, Inc.,[24] helped negotiate the sale of a subcontract to sell heavy equipment to the U.S. Navy while giving $70,000 in kickbacks to two materials managers of Brown & Root, Inc., the project's prime contractor. According to Marshall, the prime contractor "demanded the kickbacks. . . . It was cut and dried. We would not get the business otherwise." While Marshall was not charged with any crime, one of the upper-level Brown & Root managers, William Callan, was convicted in 1985 of extorting kickbacks, and another manager, Frank DiDomenico, pleaded guilty to extorting kickbacks from Hydraulic Parts & Components, Inc. Marshall has left the company. In this case, it seems that Marshall had no win-win

21. The person involved wishes to remain anonymous.

22. The person involved wishes to remain anonymous.

23. David Ewing, *Do It My Way or You're Fired.* New York: John Wiley, 1983.

24. E. T. Pound, "Investigators Detect Pattern of Kichbacks for Defense Business," *The Wall Street Journal,* November 14, 1985, pp. 1, 25.

alternative to paying the bribe. In some situations it may not be possible to lead a win-win ethical change.

2. Some people do not understand how leadership can be applied to situations that involve organizational-ethics issues. Also, some people—particularly those in analytical or technical professions, which may not offer much opportunity for gaining leadership experience—may not know how to lead very well in any situation. Some people may be good leaders in the course of their normal work lives, but do not try to lead or do not lead very well when ethical issues are involved. Some people avoid discussing ethical, religious, and political issues at work.

For example, John Geary was a salesman for U.S. Steel when the company decided to enter a new market with what he and others considered an unsafe new product.[25] As a leading salesman for U.S. Steel, Geary normally was very good at leading the way toward changes that satisfied customer and organizational needs. A good salesman frequently needs to coordinate and spearhead modifications in operations, engineering, logistics, product design, financing, and billing/payment that are necessary for a company to maintain good customer relationships and sales. Apparently, however, he did not try to lead the organization in developing a win-win solution, such as soliciting current orders for a later delivery of a corrected product. He tried only reasoning against selling the unsafe product and protested its sale to several groups of upper-level engineers and managers. He noted that he believed the product had a failure rate of 3.6% and was therefore both unsafe and potentially damaging to U.S. Steel's longer-term strategy of entering higher technology/profit margin businesses. According to Geary, even though many upper-level managers, engineers, and salesmen understood and believed him, "the only desire of everyone associated with the project was to satisfy the instructions of Henry Wallace [the sales vice-president]. No one was about to buck this man for fear of his job."[26] The sales vice-president fired Geary, apparently because he continued to protest against sale of the product.

Similarly, William Schwartzkopf of Commonwealth Electric Co.[27] did not think he could either ethically reason against or lead an end to the large-scale, long-time bid rigging between his own company and many of the largest U.S. electrical contractors. Even though he was an attorney and had extensive experience in leading organizational changes, he did not try to lead his company toward an ethical solution. He waited until he retired from the company, then wrote a secret letter to the Justice Department accusing the contractors of raising bids and conspiring to divide billions of dollars of contracts among themselves.

Many people—both experienced and inexperienced in leadership—do not try to lead their companies toward developing solutions to ethical problems. Often, they do not understand that it is possible to lead such a change; therefore, they do not try to do so—even though, as the cases here show, many succeed when they do try.

3. Some organizational environments—in both consensus-building and authoritarian types of cultures—discourage leadership that is nonconforming. For example, as Robert E. Wood, former CEO of the giant international retailer Sears, Roebuck, has observed, "We stress the advantages of the free enterprise system, we complain about the totalitarian state, but in our individual organizations we have created more or less a totalitarian system in industry, particularly in large industry."[28] Similarly, Charles W. Summers, in a *Harvard Business Review* article, observes, "Corporate executives may argue that . . . they recognize and protect . . . against arbitrary termination through their own internal procedures. The simple fact is that most companies have not recognized and protected that right."[29]

David Ewing concludes that "It [the pressure to obey unethical and illegal orders] is probably most dangerous, however, as a low-level infection. When it slowly bleeds the individual conscience dry and metastasizes insidiously, it is most difficult to defend against. There are no spectacular firings or purges in the ranks. There are no epic blunders. Under constant and insistent pressure, employees simply give in and conform. They become good 'organization people.'"[30]

Similar pressures can exist in participative, consensus-building types of cultures. For example, as mentioned above, Yoshino and Lifson write, "A Japanese leader, rather than being an authority, is more of a communications channel, a mediator, a facilitator, and most of all, a symbol and embodiment of group unity. Consensus building is necessary to decision making, and this requires patience and an ability to use careful cultivated relationships to get all to agree for the good of the unit."[31]

The importance of the group and the position of the group leaders as a symbol of the group are revealed in the very popular true story, "Tale of the Forty-Seven Ronin." The tale is about 47 warriors whose lord is unjustly killed. The Ronin spend years sacrificing everything, including their families, in order to kill the person responsible for their leader's death. Then all those who survive the assault killed themselves.

Just as authoritarian top-down organizational cultures can produce unethical behaviors, so can participative, consensus-building cultures. The Japanese novelist Shusaku Endo, in his *The Sea and Poison*, describes the true story of such a problem.[32] It concerns an experiment cooperatively performed by the Japanese Army, a medical hospital, and a consensus-building team of doctors on American prisoners of war. The purpose of the experiment was to determine scientifically how much blood people can lose before they die.

Endo describes the reasoning and feelings of one of the doctors as he looked back at this behavior:

> "At the time nothing could be done. . . . If I were caught in the same way, I might, I might just do the same thing again. . . . We feel that getting on good terms ourselves

---

28. See Footnote 3, p. 21.

29. C. W. Summers, "Protecting All Employees Against Unjust Dismissal," *Harvard Business Review,* 58, 1980, pp. 132–139.

30. See Footnote 3, pp. 216–217.

31. See Footnote 17, p. 187.

32. Shusaku Endo, *The Sea and Poison,* New York: Taplinger Publishing Company, 1972. See also Y. Yasuda, *Old Tales of Japan.* Tokyo: Charles Tuttle Company, 1947.

---

25. See Footnote 23. See also Geary vs. U.S. Steel Corporation, 319 A. 2nd 174, Supreme Court of Pa.

26. See Footnote 23, p. 86.

27. See Footnote 14.

with the Western Command medical people, with whom Second [section] is so cosy, wouldn't be a bad idea at all. Therefore we feel there's no need to ill-temperedly refuse their friendly proposal and hurt their feelings. . . . Five doctors from Kando's section most likely will be glad to get the chance. . . . For me the pangs of conscience . . . were from childhood equivalent to the fear of disapproval in the eyes of others—fear of the punishment which society would bring to bear. . . . To put it quite bluntly, I am able to remain quite undisturbed in the face of someone else's terrible suffering and death. . . . I am not writing about these experiences as one driven to do so by his conscience . . . all these memories are distasteful to me. But looking upon them as distasteful and suffering because of them are two different matters. Then why do I bother writing? Because I'm strangely ill at ease. I, who fear only the eyes of others and the punishment of society, and whose fears disappear when I am secure from these, am now disturbed. . . . I have no conscience, I suppose. Not just me, though. None of them feel anything at all about what they did here. The only emotion in his heart was a sense of having fallen as low as one can fall." [33]

WHAT TO DO AND HOW TO BE

In light of the discussion of the two approaches to addressing organizational ethics issues and their limitations, what should we do as individuals and members of organizations? To some extent that depends on the circumstances and our own abilities. If we know how to lead, if there's time for it, if the key people in authority are reasonable, and if a win-win solution is possible, one should probably try leading an organizational change.

If, on the other hand, one does not know how to lead, time is limited, the authority figures are unreasonable, a culture of strong conformity exists, and the situation is not likely to produce a win-win outcome, then the chances of success with a leadership approach are much lower. This may leave one with only the choice of using one of the intervention strategies discussed above. If an individual wishes to remain an effective member of the organization, then one of the more secretive strategies may be safer.

But what about the more common, middle range of problems? Here there is no easy prescription. The more win-win potential the situation has, the more time there is, the more leadership skills one has, and the more reasonable the authority figures and organizational cultures are, the more likely a leadership approach is to succeed. If the opposite conditions exist, then forcing change in the organization is the likely alternative.

To a large extent, the choice depends on an individual's courage. In my opinion, in all but the most extreme and unusual circumstances, one should first try to lead a change toward ethical behavior. If that does not succeed, then mustering the courage to act against others and the organization may be necessary. For example, the course of action that might have saved the Challenger crew was for Boisjoly or someone else to act against Morton Thiokol, its top managers, and NASA by blowing the whistle to the press.

If there is an implicitly characteristic American ontology, perhaps it is some version of William James' 1907 *Pragmatism,* which, for better or worse, sees through a lens of interactions the ontologies of being as an individual and being as a part. James explains our situation as follows:

"What we were discussing was the idea of a world growing not integrally but piecemeal by the contributions of its several parts. Take the hypothesis seriously and as a live one. Suppose that the world's author put the case to you before creation, saying: "If I am going to make a world not certain to be saved, a world the perfection of which shall be conditional merely, the condition being that each several agent does its own 'level best.' I offer you the chance of taking part in such a world. Its safety, you see, is unwarranted. It is a real adventure, with real danger, yet it may win through. It is a social scheme of co-operative work genuinely to be done. Will you join the procession? Will you trust yourself and trust the other agents enough to face the risk? . . . Then it is perfectly possible to accept sincerely a drastic kind of a universe from which the element of 'seriousness' is not to be expelled. Who so does so is, it seems to me, a genuine pragmatist. He is willing to live on a scheme of uncertified possibilities which he trusts; willing to pay with his own person, if need be, for the realization of the ideals which he frames. What now actually are the other forces which he trusts to co-operate with him, in a universe of such a type? They are at least his fellow men, in the stage of being which our actual universe has reached." [34]

In conclusion, there are realistic ethics leadership and intervention action strategies. We can act effectively concerning organizational ethics issues. Depending upon the circumstances including our own courage, we can choose to act and be ethical both as individuals and as leaders. Being as a part and leading ethical change is the more constructive approach generally. However, being as an individual intervening against others and organizations can sometimes be the only short or medium term effective approach.

ACKNOWLEDGEMENTS

I would like to acknowledge and thank the following people for their help with ideas presented in this article: the members of the Works in Progress Seminar of Boston College, particularly Dalmar Fisher, James Gips, John Neuhauser, William Torbert, and the late James Waters; Kenneth Boulding of the University of Colorado; Robert Greenleaf; and, Douglas Steere of Haverford College.

---

33. See Footnote 32.

34. William James, *Pragmatism: A New Name for Some Old Ways of Thinking.* New York: Longmans, Green and Co., 1907, pp. 290, 297–298.

After Social Responsibility

Paul H. Weaver

For about a century now, most U.S. corporations have acknowledged a responsibility to society that goes beyond what is required of them in the marketplace. This ethos, at first glance, looks like an expression of altruism; in fact, it is anything but. As part of its approach to doing business and conducting relations with competitors, customers, and the government, the corporation in the United States used the notion of social responsibility to justify corporate and governmental intrusions into the marketplace in the hope of managing it to its advantage and escaping the disciplines of competition. Thus, what seems like an expression of the corporation's benevolence is actually a reflection of its aggressiveness. The idea that business has social responsibilities has been a weapon wielded by the corporation in its war to wrest advantage from customers and the political system.

Today, the cozy, oligopolistic world described by John Kenneth Galbraith is crumbling under the intense pressures of an increasingly competitive market.[1] The political system that protected, subsidized, and otherwise aided business has become less solicitous of business interests, more influenced by antibusiness and promarket ideologies, and less stable and predictable. As a result, business gets less and less help from the political system—and the little it does get is of less and less benefit.

American business is entering a new era in which it must compete rather than try to rig markets and manipulate public policy to its advantage. Accordingly, corporations must abandon an old self-legitimation that subordinated economics to politics and concealed an appetite for privilege behind a facade of benevolence. They must now embrace a new concept of the corporation based on the original liberal tradition of individual right, limited government, rule of law, free markets, and peaceful, nonimperial international relations. They must accept the disciplines of competition and adopt public postures and policies that reinforce the marketplace and strengthen market institutions.

U.S. companies today are scrambling furiously to develop new strategies that will enable them to survive and prosper in a demanding new global economic environment. In doing so, they must learn new ways of thinking, talking, and acting in the social and political arenas.

THE MODERN CORPORATION

In the second half of the nineteenth century, railroads, life insurance companies, chemical and steel manufacturers, and other businesses began to grow. To manage increasingly far-flung operations, companies set up central offices, run by a widening array of new professionals—marketing experts, financial specialists, corporate communicators. Companies also began growing in new directions—backward toward the production of goods and services for use in their business, forward toward end-user markets, and horizontally to buy up or control competitors.

This was the beginning of the modern corporation, which was both generator and product of a little-understood revolution that transformed American politics and culture in the nineteenth century. It defines the watershed between the popular perception of the American political tradition—the world of Madison and Jefferson—and our own age, dominated by a corporatist ethos that has blurred distinctions between public and private, led government to grow, and established the quest for economic advantage and privilege at the heart of the political process.

The men who created the corporation had a negative attitude toward the marketplace. They thought it inefficient, a drag on progress, a source of difficulty. They intended the corporation to transcend these limitations—to grow faster, become bigger, be more efficient, and advance technologies more than traditional business structures were able to. They meant to realize these ambitions by building on an ethic of social harmony and hierarchy influenced by the philosophy of Auguste Comte, instead of the social bedrock of individual rights and free markets. "The spirit of cooperation is upon us," exulted George Perkins, a leading figure in corporate management and investment banking at the turn of the century. "It must . . . be the next great form of business development and progress." Agreed Frederick W. Taylor, the first great theorist of the corporation: "In the past the man has been first. In the future the system must be first."[2]

For the individualism, competition, and serendipity of traditional capitalism, the corporation substituted, in the phrase of business historian Alfred Chandler, the visible hand of management.[3] Management, in part, meant hierarchy and bureaucracy; as business organizations grew, elaborate chains of control emerged. The corporation curtailed market relationships and caused bureaucratic and political relationships to proliferate.

The corporation sought to extend the reach of the visible hand beyond the organization. Hardly a group, institution, or process relevant to a corporation's line of business was not subject to efforts to influence or control it. Advertising, product differentiation and product cycles to manage consumer demand, economic forecasting with production planning to increase manufacturing efficiency, financial communications and public accountancy to

"After Social Responsibility" by P. H. Weaver in *The U.S. Business Corporation: An Institution in Transition* edited by John R. Meyer and James M. Gustafson. Copyright © 1988 by Ballinger Publishing Company. Reprinted by permission of Harper Collins Publishers, Inc.

1. See John Kenneth Galbraith, *The New Industrial State* (Boston: Houghton Mifflin, 1967).

2. George W. Perkins, "The Modern Corporation" (pamphlet of an address given at Columbia University, New York, N.Y., February 7, 1908), p. 16; Frederick Winslow Taylor, *The Principles of Scientific Management* (New York: Harper and Brothers, 1919), p. 7.

3. See Alfred D. Chandler, *The Visible Hand: The Managerial Revolution in American Business* (Cambridge: Harvard University Press, 1977); see also idem, *Strategy and Structure: Chapters in the History of the American Industrial Enterprise* (Cambridge, Mass.: MIT Press, 1962).

improve the market for corporate debt and equity instruments all signaled attempts to shape the world outside the firm. Most important and characteristic were the corporation's closely related efforts to limit competition among producers and to influence to its own advantage the policy process defining the economic rules of the game.

CONTROL OVER THE MARKETPLACE

In the 1850s the first modern corporations, the big railroads, began lobbying for federal land and cash subsidies. Though, at first, they encountered fierce resistance, eventually they were highly successful, and by the 1870s the industry was a crazy quilt of cutthroat competition and strangulating monopoly. States created regulatory commissions to keep prices down in the uncompetitive markets, and railroads formed cartels to keep prices up in the competitive ones. But the cartels, which generally didn't last for long, did little to curb price competition. The railroads also tried merging; after the severe business downturns of the nineteenth century, waves of mergers swept the industry. But new railroads continued to start up, old ones continued to expand, and competition reappeared. Railroad executives searching for a better solution settled on the concept of a federal commission to set rates. With backing from the railroad lobby and agrarian and labor forces, the first federal regulatory agency, the Interstate Commerce Commission, was created in 1887.

A similar process transformed many manufacturing industries toward the end of the century. New technology and investment increased competition, precipitating efforts to fix prices, including the creation of cartels. When these came to naught, between 1895 and 1904 mergers folded more than 3,000 independent companies into vast new combines called trusts, which often doubled or tripled the market value of the companies involved. However, in many industries, these mergers were followed by an influx of new entrants, new efficiencies, an outburst of competition, falling prices, and dwindling profits. Borrowing a leaf from the railroads, many industries from meat packing to banking turned to regulation in the hope that it would curb competition or confer some other business advantage. The most dramatic examples were the telephone, electric, and gas companies, which began to lobby state governments for the status of official regulated monopolies around the turn of the century.

Despite variations from industry to industry, the overall pattern—of seeking to control the marketplace wherever possible—was remarkably consistent, as may be judged from the near universality of business support for tariffs in the period in question. The high, wide barriers to foreign competition erected by U.S. tariff laws constituted the fundamental anticompetitive industrial policy running across the entire panorama of American business life.

From the dawn of the modern corporation to its high noon—from just after the Civil War until just after World War II—the business lobby continued its campaign for public policies to keep prices high, provide subsidies and incentives, and control new entrants. This effort reached a climax in the 1920s and 1930s, when more businesses and trades than ever before or since joined the crusade for industrial policy and cartelization and their lobbying met with more success than ever before or since.

In the 1920s, amid an explosion of trade associations, business leaders spoke often of a "business commonwealth," in which industry groups, backed up by government power where required, would set standards and control the behavior of firms and the nation's economic life as a whole. The idea took root most firmly in state and local government, which became extremely active in regulating entry and pricing in a slew of professions and services from taxi cabs and barber shops to funeral homes and dentistry. At the national level, such quasi-cartelist programs sprang up around emerging industries such as broadcasting and air transportation and older ones like shipbuilding.

With the onset of the Depression, business efforts to get government to regulate economic activity grew more feverish. The business lobby's program to end the Depression emphasized a sharp increase in tariffs, a halt to immigration, regulations prohibiting wages and prices from falling further, a governmental authority with power to require producers to manufacture fewer goods, and low-cost federal loans to industry. This strategy was embodied in the National Recovery Act, the Roosevelt Administration's main initial effort to end the Depression. Business leaders were exultant. The president of the U.S. Chamber of Commerce hailed the NRA and pledged business's cooperation. Laissez-faire, he said, "must be replaced by a philosophy of planned national economy."[4]

THE BIRTH OF SOCIAL RESPONSIBILITY

One who scans the historical record for examples of executives acting like Daddy Warbucks without Annie searches largely in vain. Even in the nineteenth century, businessmen sought to downplay the self-interest embodied in corporate behavior and acknowledged what they called their social responsibilities to the community, the poor, and other groups and institutions. Not even railroad tycoon William K. Vanderbilt, the man who said, "The public be damned," turns out to be a good example.

Vanderbilt made the statement in 1882, in an interview with two reporters from the *New York Times*. Queried about his New York–New Haven line, Vanderbilt lamented that, though it wasn't profitable, he had to keep it running because competition from another railroad on the same route gave him no choice. "But don't you run it for public benefit?" one of the reporters asked. Vanderbilt took the bait:

> The public be damned. What does the public care for the railroads except to get as much out of them for as small a consideration as possible! I don't take any stock in this silly nonsense about working for anybody's good but our own because we are not. When we make a move we do it because it is in our interest to do so, not because we expect to do someone else some good. Of course we like to do everything possible for the benefit of humanity in general, but when we do we first see that we are benefiting ourselves. Railroads are not run on sentiment, but on business principles and to pay.[5]

4. In Robert M. Collins, *The Business Response to Keynes, 1929–1964* (New York: Columbia University Press, 1981), pp. 29–30.

5. In Richard S. Tedlow, *Keeping the Corporate Image: Public Relations and Business, 1900–1950* (Greenwich, Conn.: JAI Press, 1979), p. 5.

Vanderbilt was merely saying that self-interest and profit are the main motives in business and that altruistic objectives are secondary. Had an economist or journalist made such a statement, the reporters wouldn't have bothered to write it down. But, coming from a big railroad executive, the statement was a bombshell. The dominant theory of corporate behavior and corporate legitimacy was being revealed as a fraud by someone in a position to know.

The next day, when the *Times* printed the story, Vanderbilt, who was as interested in his public image as the next tycoon, was aware that he had blundered. He complained to the editors of the *Times* that he had been misquoted, that he had never said or meant any such thing, that the reporters had made it up. The man who is the source of the quote most widely accepted as typifying the businessman's point of view didn't mean what we imagine he meant and refused to admit that he said it.

The corporation was a tough sell in the nation of Jefferson, Madison, and Jackson, especially in the beginning. What the large majority of Americans believed in—individualism, limited government, free markets—the corporation scorned and worked against. What corporations wanted—subsidies, industrial policy, protection from competition, monopoly—most Americans hated. Unsurprisingly, the turbulent politics of the late nineteenth and early twentieth centuries revolved around the corporation, and, for a time, the corporation's ability to extract what it wanted from the political system and, indeed, its very survival were open questions. The founders' answer was to create a strategy of political self-definition of such subtlety and power that it not only enabled them to achieve their policy objectives but also reshaped the entire landscape of modern politics. They called it publicity—what we know as public relations. But, by any name, the idea of corporate social responsibility was at its heart.

There were three ways to organize relations between the corporation and society, the founders argued. At one extreme was a system of private ownership, private management, and free markets. This, of course, they considered undesirable and unrealistic. To them, competition was the problem, not the solution, and, anyway, they doubted that the public would trust markets to control corporations. At the other extreme was public ownership, public management, and public direction of the economy. The founders dismissed this possibility out of hand. They had shareholders to think of, they had no intention of becoming civil servants, and they were sure that public ownership would quickly self-destruct. "Imagine the Erie and Tammany rings rolled into one and turned loose on the field of politics," scoffed Charles Francis Adams, "and the result of State ownership would be realized."[6]

The founders preferred a middle course: private ownership, as in the first scenario, with broad governmental direction of the economy, as in the second. The corporation's conduct would be subject to public review and control through extensive disclosure of corporate information, supervision by government regulators, and potential legislative intervention on any outstanding problems. The corporation, in short, would be private property infused with public purpose, sanctified by public approval, disciplined by public authority, answerable to public scrutiny. Corporations were "taking the public into partnership," said Edward L. Bernays, the early-twentieth century inventor of public relations. In Bernays' illuminat-

ing oxymoron, the corporation would "make a majority movement of itself."[7]

From the beginning, then, executives defined the corporation as an institution dedicated mainly to the service of society and the welfare of others. "The great semi-public business corporations of the country . . . have in our day become not only vast business enterprises but great trusteeships," said George Perkins. "The larger the corporation becomes, the greater become its responsibilities to the entire community."[8]

To be sure, Perkins and his contemporaries were quick to admit, the corporation wasn't always and everywhere in perfect alignment with the public interest. Unbridled competition could break out; executives could make mistakes. When this happened, Perkins argued, it was usually the result of attitudes left over from the precorporate era. Executives who had once been "in business for themselves" found it hard "to cease looking at questions from the sole standpoint of personal gain and personal advantage, and to take the broader view of looking at them from the standpoint of the community of interest principle."[9]

But, for the most part, the corporation did embody social values—an almost endless list of them, according to the founders. Richard McCurdy, president of Mutual of New York at the turn of the century, said his industry "combined business with pleasure, business with sentiment, business with philanthropy, business with great and ennobling ideas of humanity." In the 1920s U.S. Steel, proud of its worker benefits and anxious to keep the union out, billed itself as "the corporation with a soul." To George Perkins, the corporation "develop[ed] men of a higher order of business ability . . 'influence,' so called, as an element in selecting men for responsible posts, has been rapidly on the wane. Everything is giving way . . . to the one supreme test of fitness."[10]

As corporations zeroed in on benefits or exemptions they sought from the political system, their identification with social purposes and their enthusiasm for social policy grew. In the early 1850s, when the Illinois Central was lobbying for federal land grants, the company met with stern opposition to its attempts to persuade the national government to break with the tradition of nonintervention. The *American Railroad Journal* said the Illinois Central's executives were offering a plan for "the public to furnish the means necessary to build the road, while they pocket the profits." Asked another opponent: "Where is the power in this Government to make a donation to A in a manner that pressed [sic] B into paying double price?"[11]

The Illinois Central's lobbying and public-relations team hit upon a brilliant response. At the time, slavery had risen to the top

6. In Thomas K. McCraw, *Prophets of Regulation* (Cambridge: Harvard University Press, 1984), p. 11.

7. Edward L. Bernays, *Propaganda* (New York: Horace Liveright, 1928), pp. 41, 62.

8. Perkins, "The Modern Corporation," pp. 10–11.

9. Ibid., p. 9.

10. Richard McCurdy is quoted in Morton Keller, *The Life Insurance Enterprise, 1885–1910: A Study in the Limits of Corporate Power* (Cambridge: Harvard University Press, 1963), p. 27; Perkins, "The Modern Corporation," pp. 5–6.

11. In Carter Goodrich, *Government Promotion of American Canals and Railroads, 1800–1890* (New York: Columbia University Press, 1960), p. 172.

of the national agenda, and fear was growing that the debate would end by destroying the Union. Cleverly, the Illinois Central turned the issue to its advantage. By giving it a subsidy, ran the argument, Congress would be creating the nation's first major north-south railroad. These trains would set up a pattern of intercommunication and interdependency binding North and South "together so effectually that the idea even of separation" would become unthinkable.[12] In other words, by giving the Illinois Central what it wanted, the federal government would be funding a social policy to save the Union. Surely, the nation's survival justified a one-time deviation from the traditional relationship between government and business.

This argument, together with some aggressive, expensive lobbying, carried the day. The Illinois Central became the first major railroad to receive federal subsidies. The corporation's new concept of business-government relations took a giant step forward.

Half a century later, when AT&T's share of the telephone market had dwindled alarmingly from 100 to 40 percent and continued to fall, AT&T president Theodore Vail launched his campaign for regulated monopoly status. Arguing that the American people deserved cheaper, better integrated, higher quality phone service than the market was providing, he committed his company to a bold new social policy: AT&T was prepared to meet the emerging social need, but this would require state governments to give AT&T the status of a regulated monopoly.[13]

In the campaign for regulated-monopoly status for electric power companies that was led by Chicago utility tycoon Samuel Insull the pitch was that competition in this industry was unworkable and would lead either to bankruptcy or to inadequate service. This would leave city governments no choice but to step in and take over the electric business—and that would be socialism. But why would Americans embrace that alien ideology when a superior alternative was available?

Today, though competitive electricity is both profitable for companies selling it and cheaper for people buying it, most U.S. markets are served by private monopolies, thanks, in no small part, to Insull's success in manipulating Americans into thinking that monopoly was the realistic alternative to socialism and that utility companies were suffused with the social mission of deflecting the nation from a noncapitalist future.

THE INVISIBLE GOVERNMENT

Government regulation of business was integral to the concept of publicity, and it enjoyed wide acceptance among the founders. George Perkins explained it this way:

> If the managers of the giant corporations feel themselves to be semi-public servants, and desire to be so considered, they must of course welcome supervision by the public. . . . The responsibility for the management of a giant corporation is so great that the men in control should be glad to have it shared by proper public officials.[14]

Regulatory commissions were established to free the corporation from the bondage of competition and free markets. Mere private interests would no longer control an industry's destiny; now, the public interest could be the decisive consideration. Someone would be in control; policy rather than personal preferences would prevail. Regulation represented the extension of the visible hand, and the idea of social responsibility, to the marketplace as a whole.

The founders of the corporation meant that hand to be their own. Charles Francis Adams, often cited as the father of regulation, stressed the fact-finding, issue-defining, opinion-leading, initiative-taking functions of the railroad commission he helped create in Massachusetts. It would not set rates but usher in

> a new phase of representative government. Work hitherto badly done, spasmodically done, superficially done, ignorantly done, and too often corruptly done by temporary and irresponsible legislative committees, is in future to be reduced to order and science by the labors of permanent bureaus, and placed by them before legislatures for intelligent action.[15]

The regulatory commission was to be, not a source of neutral expertise, but a lever to pry public opinion and public policy away from a legislature that believed in competition and refused to acknowledge Adams's "irresistible law" of economic concentration. Of course, control of the regulatory process could fall into wrong (antibusiness) hands. But the founders believed that risk could be minimized by publicity.

From the beginning, the corporation was a lavishly communicative institution, spending large sums and much energy to put out a flood of information. In the nineteenth century, some corporations owned newspapers, and many distributed canned features and editorials, often without disclosing their source. Bribes and freebies to journalists were commonplace. By 1905 a business group was organizing a program to persuade the current generation of college students of the evils of socialism and the merits of capitalism.

The goal was to create what Edward Bernays called an "invisible government" that would manage all aspects of the corporate environment.

> The conscious and intelligent manipulation of the organized habits and opinions of the masses is an important element in democratic society. Those who manipulate this unseen mechanism of society constitute an invisible government which is the true ruling power of our country. . . . It is they who pull the wires which control the public mind, who harness old social forces and contrive new ways to bind and guide the world.[16]

The idea that there were public and private interests that were largely opposed to each other; that private, profit-seeking business untempered by concern for the public interest would subvert democratic society; that society demanded of business a social responsibility going beyond the requirements of law and the disciplines of the marketplace; that if corporations wouldn't voluntarily

12. Ibid., p. 171.

13. See John Brooks, *Telephone: The First Hundred Years* (New York: Harper & Row, 1976), pp. 142–45.

14. Perkins, "The Modern Corporation," pp. 12–13.

15. In McCraw, *Prophets of Regulation,* p. 15.

16. Bernays, *Propaganda,* pp. 9–10.

satisfy such concerns, society would rightly force them to do so through the regulatory process—this was the theme of the "propaganda," as Bernays called it, with which business would control the use of public power over economic life and make regulation safe for business. The myth of social responsibility was an invention of breathtaking brilliance and power, and it has advanced business public policy interests for over a century now. It mobilizes Americans' natural hatred of privilege in support of policies whose very purpose is to create privilege.

THE RETURN OF FREE ENTERPRISE

From the end of the nineteenth century through the first third of the twentieth, business was an ambitious, high-profile, politically active, initiative-taking sector of society, its agenda often dominating the nation's. Since then, it has retreated from leadership and played an increasingly reactive and self-concealing role.

This retreat began in the aftermath of one of business's greatest public policy triumphs, the NRA. The program gave business much of what it had asked for in the way of powers to cartelize industry, but it also gave unions new powers to organize the labor force. The unions grew quickly. Businessmen were aghast, and, within months, a new theme began to stir the hearts of American businessmen: free enterprise.

By the mid-1930s the new mood seemed to have permeated the business community. The American economy was the most productive in the world, argued a new series of economic advertising campaigns. The credit for this achievement was business's. Now, however, false leaders, preaching redistribution, social policy, and interventionist government, were throwing the tradition of free markets and limited government to the winds and coming between the country and its natural leaders. If the planners gained control, the businessmen said, the nation's freedom would be in danger.

The promarket, antigovernment posture was disingenuous, of course. Businessmen remained as certain as ever of the need for cartels and more government spending. They lobbied for programs to regulate trucking, airlines, and broadcasting and to fund the Reconstruction Finance Administration. They said nothing about repealing the Smoot-Hawley tariff. Free enterprise was a weapon with which to fight New Deal policies whose vice was that they interfered with the marketplace to serve labor's interest, rather than business's.

Some historians write of this oppositional posture as if it reduced business to impotence and irrelevance in the 1930s. This is a misreading of history. Business's passionate crusading against the New Deal had a powerful impact. It helped direct many of the twists and turns of New Deal economic policy, which was notably erratic and contradictory, and was an important reason why domestic reform came to an end in 1938, when the prospect of war persuaded FDR that he had to establish more cordial relations with business. In the 1930s, business stood for something.

But the new antigovernment position did weaken business's ability to advance its interests. More and more, it said no to others' initiatives or it said nothing at all. More and more, when it said no, it did so by misrepresenting what businessmen really thought about fundamental political issues. Slowly, business lost influence over the political agenda.

A seeming exception was a loose group of about fifty executives of the biggest U.S. corporations, organized as a kind of business cabinet by Commerce Secretary Daniel C. Roper soon after FDR's inauguration. The Business Advisory and Planning Council (later, the Business Advisory Council and, later still, the Business Council) included the most dazzling luminaries of corporate America; most of them Republicans, as well as some executives from smaller companies who were liberals.

The members of the council were sophisticated exponents of the visible hand, and at times and on issues where the National Association of Manufacturers and U.S. Chamber of Commerce had begun opposing the New Deal, these executives supported it. In exchange for modest changes, the council backed the Social Security Act and the Wagner Act and supported the creation of the Securities and Exchange Commission.

In 1938, as a severe recession underscored the New Deal's failure to revive the economy and a desperate administration turned to spending and antitrust action, the group around the BAC, casting around for new solutions, commissioned a young economist named John Kenneth Galbraith to write a report on the new theories of British economist John Maynard Keynes. So delighted were these executives to discover an antidepression policy strategy that would boost sales right away without entailing punitive steps against big companies that the BAC printed Galbraith's report and began touting it.[17]

Naturally, free enterprisers held members of the BAC in contempt, and BAC people returned the favor. Yet, beneath the surface, the two groups had much in common, for the sophisticates of the BAC were being just as disingenuous and reactive as the free enterprisers. Where the free enterprisers gave up their ability to reform public policy in order to oppose the New Deal, the BAC gave up its ability to resist bad proposals in order to gain whatever concessions they could from the inside. Where free enterprisers misled the public with antigovernment, promarket rehetoric that was inconsistent with the entitlements they still wanted, accommodationists did so by backing policies that, fundamentally, they considered dangerous. Free enterprisers locked themselves out of the policy-reform process that governed their business prospects; accommodationists locked themselves into policies that were not reviving the economy or improving their bottom lines.

Organizational Reform

World War II reshaped the world largely to business's liking. It revived the economy, increased big companies' market shares, changed the government from an adversary into a partner, and expanded the government's role in managing the economy. In a real sense, business's basic agenda had been achieved; further policy leadership was unnecessary. This drift toward passivity was accelerated by a quiet shift in strategy and structure that swept the corporate world in the 1950s and 1960s and transformed the psychology of corporate managers.

In the beginning, the corporation was a unitary organization—it had what analysts today call a U-form structure. A U-form organization engages in a single line of business and has a single corporate hierarchy. At the top is management; below it are functional divisions contributing the necessary inputs. The top managers coordinate and rule on day-to-day business decisions, and they allocate resources and set broad corporate directions.

---

17. See Collins, *The Business Response to Keynes,* p. 65.

After World War II, corporations dropped the U-form in favor of the multidivisional or M-form. In an M-form company, there is a central corporate management, and reporting to it are independent divisions, each with its own functional subdivisions. Divisional managers are responsible for their divisions' bottom lines. The M-form thus diffuses profit-mindedness into the operating levels of corporations, giving middle managers no alternative but to pay attention to the bottom-line implications of their actions. By taking operating decisions out of top executives' hands, the M-form fixes their attention on overall profit and loss, on the relative returns of assets in different lines of business, and the rational allocation of corporate resources among them. It encourages them to think about which new businesses they should be getting into and which old ones they should be phasing out.

When M-form executives foresee trouble, they are likely to try solving the problem and, simultaneously, to ready a strategy of disinvestment. In this sense, an M-form organization is inherently more passive than a U-form company: In the face of damaging public policies, M-form managers have fewer incentives to stand and fight, more incentives to exit.

Thus, in the 1960s and 1970s, when an explosion in social policy and regulatory intervention led to a vast buildup of the business lobby in Washington, business's professions of corporate social responsibility were displaced and somewhat undercut by an increasingly reactive and opportunistic approach to policy. Business still sought entitlements in the name of social responsibility, but it did so in a very different manner. Instead of developing and campaigning for broad, interventionist public policies to advance its interests, business cagily played the angles, working to extract covert entitlements from other people's policy initiatives.

Discarding Social Responsibility

In the 1970s the corporatist, social-responsibility approach to business strategy and public policy began to unravel. The growing political influence of ideology and the news media made government a less generous and less reliable dispenser of corporate entitlements. And the United States' entry into the increasingly competitive world economy has turned what entitlements government does hand out from a boon to a burden. Subsidies, protection from competition, regulation of entry, management of pricing were music to corporate ears in the comfortable world described by John Kenneth Galbraith. But that world is a fading memory. In today's competitive world, corporate welfare is a recipe, not for success, but for disaster.

In the global marketplace, companies either compete or go out of business. There is no third alternative. The dream of an entitlement that will solve an uncompetitive company's problems without weakening its incentive to compete is a delusion. Our politics ensure that no entitlement will be sufficiently massive, long lived, and unconditional to neutralize the effects of the marketplace indefinitely. Sooner or later, even entitled companies have to compete. The landscape is littered today with companies whose sad stories show how entitlements not only don't help, but make a competitive disadvantage worse.

The U.S. corporation needs to unlearn outmoded, dysfunctional political behaviors and to learn new behaviors better suited to its new environment. Since this environment is characterized by markets and competition, the corporation needs public policies that support and assume competition and that help business get and stay competitive. It needs a public that understands the nature of business's environment and companies' need to respond to it. Perhaps above all, it needs to have executives who grasp and accept the logic of the marketplace and the overriding necessity to respond to its imperatives. In short, business must abandon its old, corporatist approach to business strategy and convert to capitalism.

Support Policies That Strengthen Markets and Oppose Policies That Weaken or Flout Markets

Rather than accommodate others in an effort to get subsidies, protection from competition, and other business advantages, capitalist corporations will seek mainly to reduce the competitive risks created by arbitrary, antimarket public policy and to promote policies that improve markets and make companies more efficient. Instead of supinely acquiescing, capitalist corporations will oppose policies that go against their interests and promote policies that help them, letting the political chips fall where they may. Capitalist corporations will accept compromises only in exchange for specific concessions and switch positions only for good reasons—not because they are about to lose or want to create goodwill.

Capitalist corporations will support markets, efficiency, and growth. They will advocate deregulation wherever a regulatory presence is not required. They will support lowering barriers to international trade. They will promote lower business income taxes and strongly urge tax policies that are neutral among industries and types of assets. They will oppose inflation and endorse steady, growth-oriented monetary policy.

Where regulation is needed, capitalist corporations will urge that it create incentives for efficiency, competition, and innovation. In general, broad bureaucratic mandates are the most stultifying, least incentive-creating forms of regulation and should be avoided whenever possible. Taxes, effluent charges, and user fees are better. Regulation should not create competitive advantages, as when it subjects new plants to rules that old ones do not have to meet. Public policy should permit failing companies to fail.

Communicate More and Lobby Less

Business needs a stable, promarket public policy backed by an understanding and supportive public. This is possible only if business has policy positions that will work for the public as well as for business—and only if these positions are communicated far and wide, honestly and tirelessly.

Capitalist corporations will scale back the lobbying, wire-pulling aspects of their public-affairs operations. They will cut back or eliminate Washington lobbying offices and work through business groups and think tanks to converge, not on fleeting entitlements for individual companies, but on long-term interests common to many companies. They will also be less subject to the salami tactics used to turn around individual companies by shaving away their resolve slice by slice.

Capitalist corporations will participate in policy discussion. They will give the same message to all audiences. The language should be clear and sharp, conveying passion, conviction, and earnestness, rather than caution or sophistication.

Capitalist corporations will own up to self-interest and bad news and use them in their advocacy. They will candidly and undefensively discuss the effects of different policy alternatives on the various interests at stake—those of shareholders, workers, customers, and the society as a whole—explaining what trade-offs they would make and why.

When there is bad news for shareholders, customers, workers, or the society as a whole—and particularly when the bad news is caused by public policy—capitalist corporations should clearly and vigorously explain it and what they propose to do in response. Even when the bad news is the result of a market process, executives should explain. What market-driven, profit-seeking institutions do in response to decline and failure is what really sets them apart from public-sector institutions and is a key element of their legitimacy, and capitalism's. Studies show that acknowledging error usually doesn't have any negative impact whatsoever on share prices and may even boost them.

Adopt a Private-Property Justification of Business

The time has come for the corporation to stop masquerading as public property and admit that it is the private property of its owners, an institution engaging in capitalist transactions with consenting adults. It is time, too, for the corporation to adopt the philosophy that justifies private property—the doctrine of classical liberalism: individual right, rule of law, limited government, representative democracy, progressive science, markets, and so forth. The corporation has a vital stake in the repute of these ideas and institutions; it prospers insofar as they do; if they languish, it will, too.

The first principle of corporations should be the primacy of the shareholder interest in its full breadth and complexity—not merely the interest in profit, nor yet that in the share price, but in the well-being of the institution of private ownership and all that goes with it.

This principle needs to be institutionalized. Executive perks should be sharply limited, and the grandiose style to which senior management has become accustomed in most big corporations should be phased out. Executives should pledge formally to put the shareholder interest first. They should also endorse formally the private-property concept of the corporation and the principles behind it. To increase identification with shareholders, profit- and stock-based forms of compensation should be used where possible, and straight salary should be reduced.

Conscientiousness should be the moral style of capitalist corporations. Things should be done for good reasons that can be explained and justified to others. A scrupulously honorable, truthful, customer-oriented, product-honoring approach should prevail.

Conscientiousness flourishes where there is self-knowledge and self-respect, and capitalist corporations should be at pains to encourage both. They should provide executives with extensive continuing-education programs on the industry, company, product, and on the market economy in general. They should also support original research on these topics. Business is a vast, important, and ill-understood subject, among businessmen themselves as well as in the lay public. As they seek to put themselves on a principled footing, capitalist corporations will want to dispel misunderstanding, shed light, and boost their members' morale.

Drop Apologetic PR Programs

Business should not give money to groups or causes that are hostile to market capitalism. Such groups have a right to exist and make an important contribution, but corporations should not support them.

Moreover, corporations should not fund the arts in most cases. Corporations should seek public support on the basis of what they are and, at their best, can be—not on the basis of what they aren't and can't and shouldn't be. Arts that bear some direct relation to a company, its people, or its products are appropriate objects of corporate support. Companies that are themselves involved in the arts can support the arts in all their forms. But corporations that make a point of associating themselves with the arts when these arts have nothing to do with their businesses and are cultivated to blur awareness of those businesses are cynical, manipulative, and dishonest. Such programs have no place in a capitalist corporation.

CONCLUSION

Social responsibility, as it was preached and practiced, was not an authentic business ethic, but propaganda. It misrepresented the actual relations between business and society for the purpose of manipulating citizens and the political system into giving business entitlements.

Most discussions of corporate social responsibility present the idea as new and unconventional, an alternative to older, discredited, market-oriented conceptions of corporate governance. In fact, social responsibility has been in currency for a century. Far from being an avant-garde business idea, it is the orthodox rationale for the corporation's legitimacy.

Most discussions of corporate social responsibility present the idea as an effort to moralize an economically driven institution. In fact, it represents an effort to protect politically bestowed privileges for business.

Most discussions present corporate social responsibility as a liberal idea that, in practice, benefits the poor and powerless. In fact, it is a corporatist and, in that sense, conservative idea that mainly benefits companies and managers. By and large, the practices it legitimates operate at the expense of the poor and powerless.

Most discussions present corporate social responsibility as an idea that justifies corporate responsiveness to external social conditions and public attitudes. In fact, it helps corporations avoid the tests of the marketplace and deflect social and political pressure.

By rejecting the dishonest, manipulative corporatist concept of the corporation and embracing a market-oriented idea of the business-society relationship, companies would free themselves, not merely to become competitive again, but also to be honest. Capitalist executives will be more alert to customers and workers on their own terms, more willing to find areas of mutual interest, more respectful of individual wishes and rights, more willing to acknowledge other views on public policy issues. The new capitalist corporation's sharpened sense of self-interest will make it a better, more thoughtful producer, employer, neighbor, and citizen.

Exercise: Four Cultures

PURPOSE

The purpose of this exercise is to increase your awareness of the behavioral expectations associated with different cultures. By the time you finish this exercise, you will

1. Explore expectations of cultural behavior

2. Experience a cross-cultural encounter

3. Become more sensitive to differences across cultures

INTRODUCTION

In this worldwide economy, managers today are expected to enter into international business deals easily and effortlessly. But learning how to do business in another culture is a complex matter. Differences in dress code, approach, and demeanor can make or break a business transaction. What you say and how you say it may have multiple meanings in different cultures.

It is important, therefore, that you become more sensitive to the behavioral expectations associated with different cultures. This exercise provides you with an opportunity to practice how you would approach an international business situation. The exercise is designed not to single out a particular culture but to become aware of the different mannerisms and approaches of four (anonymous) cultures.

INSTRUCTIONS

1. Form a small group of four to six people. You will be assigned to a particular area of the room for this exercise.

2. Read the Four Cultures Instruction Sheet. Read your group's description on the Four Cultures Traits Sheet.

3. Develop your approach to the six cultural activities and rehearse them quietly until your instructor tells you to begin interaction with other groups.

4. Your instructor will provide you with refreshments for your visitations with other groups. Follow the posted visitation schedule provided by your instructor. When the instructor tells you to begin, receive your first visitors (Round 1).

5. Bid farewell to your first group and participate in a brief group discussion.

6. Repeat the sequence in Round 2 and Round 3, according to the posted schedule, when your instructor tells you to do so.

7. Participate in a class discussion that includes the Discussion Questions that conclude this exercise.

Reprinted from I. D. Goodstein and J. W. Pfeiffer (eds.). *The 1983 Annual for Facilitators, Trainers and Consultants.* San Diego, CA: Pfeiffer and Company, 1983. Used with permission.

Four Cultures Traits Sheet

Trait Description

You are Group 1.

You are a lordly, martial, highly regimented people with a sense of superiority that shows in your gestures and speech. You like organization and you like things to be in their proper places.

When guests arrive, you take charge and, although you treat them well, you insist that they do things *your* way.

Trait Description

You are Group 2.

You are a gentle, meek, submissive people with much grace and movement in your gestures.

When guests arrive, you put them in a superior position and are apologetic in the way you treat them.

Trait Description

You are Group 3.

You are a very warm, friendly, expressive people with gestures that demonstrate your warmth and friendliness.

When guests arrive, you are open and free in the way you treat them, and you try hard to please.

Trait Description

You are Group 4.

You have a very calm, relaxed outlook on life—one that borders on being lackadaisical. You are unhurried in what you do.

When guests arrive, you acknowledge their presence and do get around to serving them, but hurry is abhorrent to you.

Four Cultures Instruction Sheet

I. The following is a fairly natural sequence of welcoming visitors. Your group is to create specific ways of expressing each activity below in accordance with the traits and characteristics that are distinctive of your group. Be as verbal as you want to be and create as many gestures as you wish, but be careful that the *way* in which you express yourself reflects your cultural traits. (This is a group activity.)

1. The equivalent of waving "Hello" as guests approach from a distance.

2. The equivalent of a close greeting, such as the custom of shaking hands.

3. The equivalent of inviting your guests to come in or to come with you.

4. The equivalent of inviting your guests to sit down (on a chair, the floor, and so on).

5. The equivalent of inviting your guests to partake of refreshments.

6. The equivalent of seeing your guests to the door and bidding them farewell.

Time will be allotted for you to develop and rehearse this sequence within your group.

II. The second part of this activity will be to act out your roles by conducting visits with other groups.

If you are the Host group: Demonstrate your traits and act out your host activities as you have designed and rehearsed them.

If you are the Visitor group: Maintain the traits and attitudes that are characteristic of your group, but allow your hosts to treat you according to the dictates of their own culture.

Four Cultures Discussion Questions

1. What were common themes in the groups' discussions following each round?

2. How did it feel to play the role of a member of another culture?

3. What were some of the most difficult or negative aspects of dealing with members of another culture?

4. What were some of the most enjoyable or positive aspects of dealing with members of another culture?

5. How did it feel to attempt to "go native"? Which was more comfortable, the role your group had been assigned or "going native"?

6. What were the reactions of the host groups when the visitors attempted to "go native"?

7. Which of the four cultures are most like our own? Which are like other cultures that the participants have experienced?

8. What implications do the reactions described have for real-life business encounters?

9. What other things did the participants learn about cross-cultural interactions?

10. What generalizations can be drawn from these insights and learnings?

Exercise: The Maquiladora Decision[1]

PURPOSE

The purpose of this exercise is to help you become more aware of the ethical dilemmas managers face when issues of social responsibility are involved. By the time you finish this exercise, you will

1. Explore an ethical dilemma, involving issues of social responsibility, for which there are no easy answers.

2. Understand the difference between "legal" and "ethical."

---

1. This exercise was developed as an ethical dilemma that happens to involve a maquiladora, not as an exercise about a maquiladora that happens to involve an ethical dilemma. I believe that this distinction is important in terms of emphasis. I have made every attempt to accurately portray the facts about maquiladoras and the perspectives of the groups involved. But, the exercise was developed as a vehicle for exploring the ethical and social responsibility issues that are outlined in the teaching guidelines, and a decision about a maquiladora was an efficacious framework within which to do that.

This exercise was developed by Cheryl L. Tromley and was presented at the Eastern Academy of Management, Baltimore, MD, 1992.

3. Explore the usefulness of organizational codes of ethics in promoting ethical behavior.

4. Discover the added complexities of ethics and social responsibility in international management.

INTRODUCTION

Organizations are focusing increasing attention on ethical issues. Many companies have developed codes of ethics. How useful are these codes for guiding decision makers through the ethical dilemmas endemic to organizational life? What happens when what is legal and what is ethical become uncoupled?

The tendency to equate legal and ethical makes it easy for the decision maker to say, "It's legal, so it must be all right." Such attitudes relieve the decision maker from the responsibility for ethical thinking. But what about situations where what is legal is not ethical or what is illegal is ethical? Taken to its extreme, this situation becomes the Nuremberg defense, "I was just following orders." The world is changing too quickly for us to be able to rely on the law as the final arbitrator of what is ethical.

In this exercise you will play the role of a member of the top management group of a manufacturing company that must decide whether to open an assembly facility in Nogales, Mexico, just across the border from Arizona. This will be an opportunity to explore an ethical dilemma that involves issues of corporate social responsibility for which there is no easy answer.

INSTRUCTIONS

1. Follow your instructor's directions about the role you will be portraying in this exercise.

2. Your instructor will divide the class into groups of five to seven.

3. Read The Situation, E-Z Open, Inc.: Background Information (including the mission statement and code of ethics), The Setting, and Folder Contents.

4. Participate in a 45-minute group decision-making discussion.

5. Follow your instructor's guidance in a general class discussion.

The Situation

You are a senior vice president of E-Z Open Inc., a manufacturer of automatic garage-door openers. You are about to attend a meeting of the top management team to decide whether E-Z Open should set up an assembly facility in Nogales, Mexico. The proposed plant would employ 1,500 workers who would assemble garage-door openers from parts manufactured in the United States. The president and CEO of E-Z Open is out of the country and has delegated the decision to you, the senior vice presidents.

Manufacturing plants on the Mexico border are known as maquiladoras[2] (from the Spanish for "grain mill"; it has also come to mean an assembly plant). There are over 1,300 U.S.-owned factories, employing over 400,000 workers, along the Mexican border, including ITT, IBM, Rockwell, United Technologies, Kodak, Memorex, Zenith, and Kimberly Clark. Parts and raw materials are shipped to Mexico, assembled at low cost—the cost of labor in Mexico is one of the lowest in the world—and returned to the United States under special tariffs. A proposed free-trade pact between Mexico and the United States would eliminate all duties. Both the Mexican and United States governments actively support this type of development. Organized labor in the United States as well as various international human rights and environmental groups are strongly opposed to the maquiladoras. You—the top management team of E-Z Open—have requested reports from these groups, as well as from your board of directors, on their position.

E-Z OPEN, INC.: BACKGROUND INFORMATION

E-Z Open makes automatic garage-door openers that retail for $149 to $349. These openers are sold under the E-Z Open label and through a major discount department store—Serviday—under the store label. Approximately 60 percent of E-Z Open's product is sold under Serviday's label. E-Z Open has five plants and employs over 4,000 hourly workers. The plants are located in different parts of the country. Two of the plants manufacture component parts and are located in New Britain, Connecticut (850 workers) and Kansas City, Kansas (700 workers). The remaining three plants assemble the component parts into the finished product. The assembly plants are located in Cheboygan, Michigan (750 workers), Little Falls, Colorado (1,000 workers), and Madison, Georgia (750 workers). The corporate headquarters is in Stamford, Connecticut.

E-Z Open is the market leader, but their market share has been slipping. This is due in part to a decline in sales by Serviday and in part to the relatively high price of their product. E-Z Open's major competitors are currently manufacturing their products overseas where they are able to take advantage of lower labor costs. E-Z's strategy has been to emphasize the quality of their product through increased advertising and a policy that allows customers to return the product for a full refund, for any reason at all, for up to three years. However, there is compelling evidence that

---

2. The facts about maquiladoras used in the exercise are based primarily on information from Tolan, S. with Kammer, J. 1989. Life in the low-wage boomtowns of Mexico, *Tuscon Weekly,* October 18.

this strategy may no longer be working. With the end of the free spending 1980s, consumers are more cost-conscious and E-Z is experiencing a slow but steady decline in market share.

Until recently, E-Z Open has been resistant to the idea of taking any of its manufacturing process outside the United States. E-Z's founder, Wilfred Shaw, was extremely patriotic. His parents fled Ireland during a period of famine. Wilfred was born in the United States and he believed that it was the finest place on earth and the only place where the son of poor immigrant parents could have achieved his level of success. Wilfred had little formal education and began his career in a General Motors' factory in Flint, Michigan. Because of this experience on the assembly line, he believed strongly in the American worker and would tell anyone who would listen that the downfall of the United States would come from U.S. business breaking its covenant with the American worker. Wilfred was proud of the quality of his company's product and the fact that the consumer associated E-Z Open with the slogan he had created—which was prominently featured in all its advertising—"Quality Born and Bred in the USA." As long as he was chairman of the board, no one would have dared to suggest taking part of the manufacturing process out of the United States. But Wilfred died in 1985 and his oldest son, Arnold, the current chairman, is less concerned about E-Z's covenant with the U.S. worker than he is about the company's profits and the possibility that lower profits may lead to an erosion in the value of his 28 percent stake in the company. It is Arnold Shaw, current chairman of the board and the company's largest stockholder, who has asked you to consider opening the plant in Nogales as a way of cutting costs. The idea was suggested to him by one of his old college friends who currently sits on the U.S.-Mexican Free-Trade Advisory Board to the president. Arnold is known to be open minded but ruthless in pursuit of his goals.

E-Z Open Mission Statement

To provide:

❐ the highest-quality garage-door openers for our customers

❐ the highest rate of return for our investors

❐ a high quality of work life for our employees.

We believe that the best way to achieve these ends is through high ethical standards in all of our dealings and a commitment to the United States and the ideals for which it stands.

E-Z Open Code of Ethics[3]

E-Z Open is dedicated to ethical behavior and corporate responsibility. Because we, as a company, believe this to be essential to our success we have developed the following code of ethics to ensure that our employees will uphold our high ethical standards.

---

3. The code of ethics used in this exercise is based on the research presented in D. R. Robin, M. Giallourakis, F. R. David, and T. E. Moritz. "A Different Look at Codes of Ethics," *Business Horizons,* January-February 1989.

Be a Dependable Employee, a Good Corporate Citizen,
and Show Concern for the Customer

1. Demonstrate courtesy, respect, honesty, and fairness in relationships with customers, suppliers, competitors, and other employees. Always exhibit standards of personal integrity and professional conduct, and dress in businesslike attire appropriate for your job.

2. Strive to provide products and services of the highest quality and convey true claims for products.

3. Perform assigned duties to the best of your ability and in the best interest of the corporation, its shareholders, and its customers.

4. Conserve resources and protect the quality of the environment in areas where the company operates.

5. Do not use abusive language or actions. Racial, ethnic, religious, or sexual harassment is prohibited. Do not request other employees to perform duties that fall outside of their normal job duties.

6. Directives from supervisors must be followed.

7. Be reliable in attendance and punctuality.

8. Comply with all laws and organizational rules regarding safety, health, and security.

9. Possession of firearms on company premises is prohibited.

10. Use of alcohol or illegal drugs on company premises is prohibited.

11. Report questionable, unethical, or illegal activities to your manager.

Avoid Behavior That Could Harm the Company

1. Maintain confidentiality of customer, employee, and corporate records and of information.

2. Avoid outside activities that conflict with or impair the performance of organizational duties.

3. Make decisions objectively without regard to friendship or personal gain.

4. The acceptance of any form of bribe is prohibited.

5. Payment to any person, business, political organization, or public official for unlawful or unauthorized purposes is prohibited.

6. Conduct personal and business dealings in compliance with all relevant laws, regulations, and policies.

7. Comply fully with antitrust laws and trade regulations.

8. Comply fully with accepted accounting rules and controls.

9. Do not provide false or misleading information to the corporation, its auditors, or a government agency.

10. Do not use company property or resources for personal benefit or any other improper purpose.

11. Each employee is personally accountable for company funds over which he or she has control.

12. Staff members should not have any interest in any competitor or supplier of the company unless such interest has been fully disclosed to the company.

13. Do not recommend attorneys, accountants, insurance agents, stockbrokers, real estate agents, or similar individuals to customers.

THE SETTING

You are at corporate headquarters in Stamford, Connecticut. You are in what is known as the Small Conference Room on the 20th floor. It is a room approximately $20' \times 20'$ in the center of which is a round mahogany table now cluttered with dirty dishes, which are being removed by a young man in a waiter's uniform whom you recognize as an employee in the mailroom. The table is surrounded by seven comfortable leather chairs, some of which are occupied by your colleagues in the top management group. One end of the room is taken up by a large picture window from which a magnificent view of Long Island Sound is still visible through the increasing darkness. Against the opposite wall sits a buffet table on which can still be seen the remains of trays of cold-cuts and salads along with several bottles of wine. It is 6:30 P.M. and you and the rest of the top leadership of E-Z Open have spent the last hour having a light dinner prior to making your final decision about the Nogales plant. The waiter removes the remaining dishes, wipes the table clean, and leaves. A secretary comes through the door with a stack of folders and places one in front of each chair explaining that they are copies of summaries of the reports that were submitted by groups with an interest in the Nogales plant. The members of the top management group take their places and begin to read through the folders.

FOLDER CONTENTS

From: Board of Directors

As you know, E-Z Open has slowly but steadily been losing market share. Our profit margin is eroding. This can be traced directly to our high manufacturing costs. We have instituted a number of cost-cutting programs, which have been very successful, thanks in large part to the cooperation of the union. However, these savings have not been sufficient to stop the decline in our market share and our profits. After a thorough investigation, it is evident that there are no remaining places to significantly cut our expenses within our current operational structure. Therefore, the board recommends that E-Z Open take steps to reduce our largest expense—labor. We can no longer compete against organizations who manufacture their product in the Pacific Rim. Because of our high labor costs we are pricing ourselves out of the market. If we cannot find a way to significantly cut our labor costs, we will be forced to reduce our operation and that would negatively impact everyone. We must think long term. This is the best way to hurt the fewest number of people. An assembly plant in Nogales will enable us to save millions of dollars in labor costs annually and thus lower the price of our product. This will help us increase our market share at home and be more competitive abroad. By reducing our costs we will be able to maximize profits, fight off foreign competition, and eventually expand our operation. Please keep in mind that the management of E-Z Open has a fiduciary responsibility to protect the investment of the stockholders. The only reasonable way to do this and ensure the long-term stability of the company is by improving our competitive stance through reduced labor costs.

Board of Directors, Finance Subcommittee Report

By moving a portion of our assembly process to Nogales, Mexico, E-Z Open will save up to $25,000 per worker per year—$37,500,000 per year. This savings will enable us to lower our price by 15 percent and make our product more competitive. This reduction will allow us to expand our market share. There is also a significant possibility that we will be able to secure contracts with at least two additional chains to market our product under their name.

The only way that these savings will be fully realized is by closing and selling the plants in Cheboygan, Michigan, and Madison, Georgia. Laying off a percentage of the workforce in all three assembly plants is not a viable financial option. Keeping the three plants open would significantly increase our overhead thereby reducing the cost savings from the Nogales plant and forcing us to raise the projected price of our product.

From Mexican Government

The Mexican government actively promotes the establishment of maquiladoras. It is an arrangement that benefits everyone, the Mexican worker, the Mexican economy, and the United States economy. The people who work in the factories make much more than they could ever hope to in their home villages, even if there were jobs, which there are not. Mexico has an under- and unemployment rate of 50 percent; over half the population is malnourished, and the situation is getting worse every day. The depths of the problem can be seen in the exodus of people illegally crossing the border from Mexico to the United States. E-Z Open's factory will provide employment for 1,500 assembly-line workers. This is the best way to help the people of Mexico, to provide jobs. Critics of the government's policy say that wages are too low. But wages will rise when the industrial base takes hold. It would be foolhardy to raise wages at this point. It would create massive inflation and chaos on the border and the industries that are currently providing the jobs would move to other parts of the world where labor is even cheaper—for example, in the Philippines wages are as low as $.18 per hour and in Bolivia the minimum wage is $.24. This is why the possibility of a free-trade agreement with your country is so important to Mexico. We want to maintain and build on what has begun on the borders so we can improve the standard of living for the Mexican people.

Maquiladoras are Mexico's second largest generator of foreign exchange—second only to oil and ahead of tourism. Maquiladoras are our most dynamic economic sector and therefore essential to our ability to repay our $108 billion foreign debt.

The Mexican and U.S. economies are interdependent. U.S. banks are our largest lenders, thus the health of the U.S. banking system is dependent on Mexico's ability to service its debt. Further, the world is realigning itself into large trading blocks. Because of our geographic proximity, Mexico and the United States are natural allies. A healthy Mexican economy will create a better trading partner. Maquiladoras are the leading edge of that economic integration. Finally, there is always the possibility that economic chaos could lead to political chaos. The elections of 1988 almost resulted in the election of Cuauhtemoc Cardenas, leader of a center-left coalition. Free market economics will bring prosperity to Mexico. But it cannot happen overnight. It is through the continued investment of companies like E-Z Open that Mexico will pull itself out of the Third World and remain a strong political and economic ally of the United States.

From United States Government, Department of Commerce

The United States government supports the development of what have come to be known as maquiladoras. We must use all means at our disposal to maintain Mexico's economic viability. Mexico is the United States' third largest trading partner and we hope to further strengthen our economic ties with Mexico when our free-trade pact is finalized. This will strengthen our trade position worldwide. Goods produced in Mexico are more competitive on foreign markets and can make a positive contribution to our balance of trade. An economically strong Mexico could also become a major market for U.S. goods, further improving our balance of trade.

We must not forget that Mexico is also a strategic source of foreign oil, a source that we cannot afford to jeopardize in any way. In addition, maquiladoras are a necessary ingredient in Mexico's strategy to repay its foreign debt, a disproportionate percentage of which is owed to our already troubled banks. Due to these considerations and the geographic positioning of our two nations, it is crucial that Mexico become as economically vigorous as possible and remain politically aligned with the policies of the United States.

Further, our domestic companies must be supported in their attempts to increase their profitability so that capital will become more readily available if we hope to get the economy growing once again for the benefit of all Americans.

From Human Dignity (an international human rights group)

Human Dignity spends 70 percent of its available resources fighting the human misery that maquiladoras have created for Mexican workers. Rich companies from the United States come to Mexico with the purpose of exploiting the poverty and desperation of the Mexican people. Poor people are lured north from their homes by the hope that factory work will enable them to pull themselves out of grinding poverty. But salaries are so low that they barely pay for food and clothing. At the high end of the pay scale, workers make $.55 per hour. Uninformed people sometimes say that that salary is not as bad as it appears because the cost of living is so low in Mexico. This is not true. Most of the maquiladora workers shop at the supermarkets on the U.S. side of the border where chicken, milk, and even beans are cheaper than they are on the Mexican side. And the situation is getting worse. Real wages have fallen in the last eight years—workers must now work 15 to 20 additional hours per week to match the standard of living they had six years ago. In addition, there are few laws that protect the workers and as a result accident rates in the factories are high and child labor is widespread.

There is no housing, no water, no heat, no sanitary facilities. Workers live in shacks made from discarded wooden pallets and cardboard boxes. They store water in whatever is available, usually the large toxic chemical drums discarded by the factories on which they cannot read the warnings printed in English. There are no sanitary facilities, so raw sewage runs through the squatter camps. The poor sanitary conditions combined with the lack of heat results in widespread illness, especially among the children. The more maquiladoras there are, the worse the situation becomes.

Board of Directors' Response to Human Dignity

E-Z Open cares about its employees; it always has. Concern for our employees is part of our Mission Statement. It is one of the core values on which Wilfred Shaw founded the company. We have every intention of extending this concern for our employees to those who will work in the facility in Nogales. We will pay all of our workers at the top of the pay scale. We will also provide vacation benefits, a cafeteria that will serve two free meals per day, and day-care facilities. We will give workers everything they are legally entitled to and more.

But clearly there is a limit to what we are able to do—to what business should be expected to do. It is not business's responsibility to solve all of the social problems of the world. Business's primary responsibility to the social order is economic. We have a responsibility to keep costs down so we can stay in business and compete effectively. E-Z Open cannot solve all of Mexico's problems and we should not be expected to. We will be socially responsive, but within reasonable limits.

From Environment Now (an international environmental group)

Maquiladoras are destroying the environment along the border between Mexico and the United States. They are contributing to the ecological destruction in two major ways: through the conditions in the workers' squatter camps that spring up around them and through the pollution and waste generated by the manufacturing process.

Because of the lack of sanitary facilities in the squatter camps and the lack of health regulations, raw sewage is contaminating the ground water and waterways. This sewage is not just confined to the Mexican side of the border. Because of the growing number of maquiladoras and the resultant increase in the populations of the squatter camps, raw sewage has begun to flow across the border. These camps are also creating significant air pollution from the tires the workers burn to keep warm. It is their only source of heat.

There is also a growing hazardous-waste problem along the border that is traceable directly to the maquiladoras. Recent tests on both sides of the border showed that groundwater is contaminated with high levels of cadmium, chromium, arsenic, and other dangerous chemicals. It is true that Mexico has recently strengthened some of its environmental policies, but they are still much too soft and even those soft policies are not being enforced. For example, companies now have two legal options for disposing of hazardous waste. They can ship it back to the United States or they can have it recycled by a licensed Mexican waste facility. However, Mexico does not have the resources to enforce these laws or the necessary facilities. Thousands of tons of toxic waste go unaccounted for.

Environment Now proposes a moratorium on development along the border until such time as enforceable strategies for dealing with these sources of pollution can be developed.

Board of Directors' Response to Environment Now

This is a nonissue for E-Z Open. We are being accused of misconduct before we have done anything. E-Z Open has an excellent record of environmental responsibility. We have always followed all laws pertaining to the environment and we plan to continue this policy in Mexico.

From Clyde Seeley, President, UMAWA (United Manufacturing and Assembly Workers of America—the union that represents E-Z Open's hourly workers)

Closing the assembly facilities in Georgia and Michigan would mean the loss of 1,500 jobs for American workers. This country cannot afford to keep losing jobs to cheap overseas labor. It is the American worker that made this country great. That was something that your founder, Wilfred Shaw, was adamant about. Wilfred did not wait for the union to come to him. He came to see me because he believed that a true partnership between management and labor was the key to a strong and successful company. Wilfred's legacy of respect for the value of the men and women who actually make and assemble the product is one of the cornerstones of the unusually trouble-free relationship E-Z Open has enjoyed with the UMAWA—a relationship based on trust, fairness, and an understanding of the interdependence between labor and management. It is a relationship that is the envy of your competitors and a relationship that is in jeopardy. You have an obligation to the men and women who created the extraordinary quality that sets E-Z Open garage-door openers above the competition.

However, we are not concerned only about the short term. If you follow the pattern of the many companies that have come before you, this will only be the beginning. You won't stop at one foreign facility. Taking the first step is the hardest. The first decision—this decision—will be the only time that you consider whether moving part of your operation out of the country violates the values on which Wilfred Shaw built this company. If you decide to go ahead with this factory in Mexico, you will violate those values; you'll change E-Z Open, what it stands for, and the relationship of trust and mutual benefit that has existed between the company and the union since the company was founded.

Board of Directors' Response to UMAWA

The UMAWA exaggerates the problem. United States workers will still be making the parts that will be assembled in Mexico and our largest assembly plant in Colorado will continue unaffected. Many more jobs would be lost if we were forced to move the entire process to the Pacific Rim, as most of our competitors have done, or if we are unable to compete and are forced to reduce our entire operation. Either of these are realistic possibilities if we are unable to reverse our loss of market share and declining profits. On the other hand, if we can increase our domestic market share and expand our exports we will actually be able to create more jobs in the manufacturing end of the business. The unions need to start looking toward the long-term good of their workers. It may be a little tough in the short run, but in the long run it should work out to everyone's benefit. We have not lost, nor will we ever lose, sight of our responsibility to our workers.

From Cheboygan, Michigan, Chamber of Commerce

As you know, we are a small town in the northern part of the state. Our unemployment rate is currently 22 percent because of the recent closing of Plymouth Industries and the Martin Paper plant. At this time E-Z Open is the largest single employer in Cheboygan. If you do decide to close the plant, there is no possibility that the town will survive. Now, when we talk to other companies about the possibility of locating in Cheboygan—maybe buying Plymouth Industry's facility—we can point to E-Z Open as an example of what the town has to offer. If you leave the town will die. This is not overstating the situation. Many of the stores on Main Street are closed and our only remaining supermarket has indicated that they may leave because of the rumor that you are going to close the E-Z plant. People are already being forced to leave their homes and families to find work. Our population shrinks daily. What is now a trickle of people leaving will become a flood if you close the E-Z plant. People have to eat and feed and clothe their children. People will be forced to abandon their homes because they cannot sell them. Who would buy them? We have never been a wealthy town. People have had to sacrifice to build their homes. Most people did not just buy a house. Most people could not afford to. Many times a family saves enough to buy a piece of land and put a house trailer on it. When they save more money, they dig the basement and finish that and live in it—just the basement—sometimes for years before they can afford to build another story.

As you know, your founder, Wilfred Shaw, opened the first E-Z plant here, as a way of helping the community. He owned a cottage on a nearby lake and he was concerned with the economic plight of the people in the community who had become his friends. He saw in them reflections of himself—immigrants and children and grandchildren of immigrants, people who unlike himself had not had the opportunity to prosper. He wanted to give them that chance and he did. His success in the community drew other enterprises and Cheboygan thrived. We plead with you to give us the opportunity to do so again. We cannot do it without you.

Board of Directors' Response to Cheboygan, Michigan, Chamber of Commerce

We at E-Z Open have always been grateful for the mutually beneficial relationship that we have enjoyed with Cheboygan. For the last 25 years we have provided jobs and security for a large percentage of Cheboygan's population, who have proven to be very competent, dependable, and productive employees. We are sorry that, because of financial imperatives, this relationship might have to end. When we were considering the options that were available to us, we did consider your previously offered suggestion that we cut back on the hourly employees throughout the company so that no one community would have to bear an undue part of the burden. After careful analysis we rejected this option for two reasons. The first is that if we open the Nogales plant, and keep all of our existing facilities operational, we would add to the company's overhead and thereby reduce the savings that we hope to realize from the Nogales plant. But our financial outlook is not the only consideration. We are also concerned that we make a decision that will be in the best interest of the community. With that in mind we concluded that the worst situation for Cheboygan would be for a significant number of its citizens to be indefinitely unemployed with limited hope for getting other jobs in the immediate area. Therefore, if we decide to open a facility in Nogales, we have decided to close the plant entirely with plans to sell the facility to a company that will be able to provide a more optimistic employment picture for the citizens of Cheboygan and provide a firm base for economic recovery.

DISCUSSION DIRECTIONS

You have 45 minutes to discuss your decision; keep your values and priorities in mind.

REFERENCES

R. A. Buchholz. *Fundamentals, Concepts and Problems in Business Ethics.* Englewood Cliffs, NJ: Prentice-Hall, 1989.

P. F. Drucker. *Management: Tasks, Responsibilities, Practices.* New York: Harper & Row, 1973.

S. W. Gellerman. "Why 'Good' Managers Make Bad Ethical Choices." *Harvard Business Review,* July-August 1986, 85–90.

T. M. Jones. "Corporate Social Responsibility Revisited, Redefined." *California Management Review,* 1980, *22,* 59–67.

M. C. Mathews. *Strategic Intervention in Organizations: Resolving Ethical Dilemmas.* Vol. 169, Sage Library of Social Research. Newbury Park, CA: Sage, 1988.

L. L. Nash. "Ethics Without Sermon." *Harvard Business Review,* November-December 1981, pp. 79–90.

D. R. Robin. M. Giallourakis, F. R. David, and T. E. Moritz. "A Different Look at Codes of Ethics." *Business Horizons,* January-February 1989.

Exercise:
Vanatin—Group Decision Making and Ethics

PURPOSE

The purpose of this exercise is to help you understand group decision making and ethics. By the time you finish this exercise you will

1. Understand the factors that contribute to decision making about ethical practices

---

This exercise was adapted by Roy J. Lewicki, Duke University, from an exercise developed by J. Scott Armstrong, University of Pennsylvania. It is reprinted from Douglas T. Hall, Donald D. Bowen, Roy J. Lewicki, and Francine S. Hall, *Experiences in Management and Organizational Behavior.* (2nd ed.) New York: John Wiley & Sons, 1982. The case is based on the research study by J. Scott Armstrong, "Social Irresponsibility in Marketing," published in *The Journal of Business Research,* 5, 1977, 185–213.

2. Participate in making a group decision about an ethical issue

3. Explore the aspects of group dynamics and leadership that affect ethical decisions

INTRODUCTION

The Vanatin case provides an opportunity for group members to struggle with questions of social responsibility and ethics in decision making. The case is constructed around a medical product, considered by experts to be injurious to the health of consumers—even to the point of possibly causing death. These consequences must be evaluated against the potential economic losses to the company, which would be substantial if sale of the drug were discontinued. The decision—not an easy one—is nevertheless common to many corporate and governmental groups that must consider both their own interest and the overall interests of society and public welfare.

INSTRUCTIONS

1. Your instructor will divide the class into groups and assign you to one of seven roles.

2. Read the Background Information for the Vanatin Case.

3. Read *only* your own role description and make notes on what you want to emphasize in the group discussion.

4. Read the directions for and complete the Vanatin role-play.

5. Participate in a class discussion.

BACKGROUND INFORMATION FOR THE VANATIN CASE

You are a member of the Booth Pharmaceutical Corporation board of directors. You have been called to a special board meeting to discuss what should be done with the product Vanatin.

Vanatin is a "fixed-ratio" antibiotic sold by prescription. That is, it contains a combination of drugs. On the market for more than 13 years, it has been highly successful. It now accounts for about $18 million per year, which is 12 percent of Booth Company's gross income in the United States (and a greater percentage of net profits). Profits from foreign markets, where Booth is marketed under a different name, is roughly comparable to that in the United States.

Over the past 20 years, numerous medical scientists (such as the AMA's Council on Drugs) have objected to the sale of most fixed-ratio drugs. The arguments have been that (1) there is no evidence that these fixed-ratio drugs have improved benefits over single drugs and (2) the possibility of detrimental side effects, including death, is at least double. For example, scientists have estimated that Vanatin is causing about 30 to 40 unnecessary deaths per year (that is, deaths that could be prevented if the patients had used a substitute made by a competitor of Booth). Despite recommendations to remove fixed-ratio drugs from the market, doctors have continued to use them. They offer a shotgun approach for doctors who are unsure of their diagnoses.

Recently, a National Academy of Science–National Research Council panel, a group of impartial scientists, carried out extensive research studies and recommended unaminously that the Food and Drug Administration (FDA) ban the sale of Vanatin. One of the members of the panel, Dr. Peterson of the University of Texas, was quoted by the press as saying, "There are few instances in medicine when so many experts have agreed unanimously and without reservation [about banning Vanatin]." This view was typical of comments made by other members of the panel. In fact, it was typical of comments that had been made about fixed-ratio drugs over the past 20 years. These impartial experts, then, believe that, while all drugs have some possibility of side effects, the costs associated with Vanatin far exceed the possible benefits.

The special board meeting has arisen out of an emergency situation. The FDA has told you that it plans to ban Vanatin in the United States and wants to give Booth time for a final appeal to them. Should the ban become effective, Booth would have to stop all sales of Vanatin and attempt to remove inventories from the market. Booth has no close substitutes for Vanatin, so that consumers will be switched to close substitutes currently marketed by rival firms. (Some of these substitutes apparently have no serious side effects.) It is extremely unlikely that bad publicity from this case would have any significant effect on the long-term profits of other products made by Booth.

The board is meeting to review and make decisions on two issues:

1. What should be done with Vanatin in the U.S. market (the immediate problem)?

2. Assuming that Vanatin is banned from the U.S. market, what should Booth do in the foreign markets? (No government action is anticipated overseas.)

Decisions on each of these issues must be reached at today's meeting. The chairman of the board has sent out this background information, and he also wanted you to give some thought as to which of the following alternatives you would prefer for the domestic market:

1. Recall Vanatin immediately and destroy it.

2. Stop production of Vanatin immediately, but allow what's been made to be sold.

3. Stop all advertising and promotion of Vanatin, but provide it for doctors who request it.

4. Continue efforts to most effectively market Vanatin until its sale is actually banned.

5. Continue efforts to most effectively market Vanatin and take legal, political, and other necessary actions to prevent the authorities from banning Vanatin.

A similar decision must also be made for the foreign market *under the assumption that the sale is banned in the United States.*

VANATIN ROLES

(Read only the role to which you have been assigned.)

Role of Elmer B. Parker, Ombudsman and Consumer Advocate

You have been hired by the board to represent the interests of the consumers of Booth's products, which in this case means both the doctors who prescribe the drugs and the patients who ultimately consume them. While you are aware that Vanatin makes life easier for some doctors, you feel that these doctors ought to know better. Any difficulty doctors might have if the drug is removed from the market is far outweighed by the deaths stemming from the use of the drug. Except for your vote, your ultimate weapon is to "blow the whistle" and give the Vanatin story to the newspapers. This would, however, cost you your job so that you could not continue to have the "moderating effect" that you have previously been able to exercise on board decisions.

Role of Cyrus Booth, M.D., Chairman of the Board

As chairman of the board, it is your job to have the board reach a decision on the two issues within the time allowed. You *must* reach a decision by the end of that time, since some of the board members have to leave to catch a plane.

Your general philosophy about meetings is to try to allow various sides of the issues to be discussed before a decision is reached. Legally speaking, a majority vote is required to reach a decision. You prefer a consensus decision, but a formal vote may be used at the end of the meeting if necessary. At the end of the meeting, you are to record the decision on the group decision form and hand it to the instructor.

Personally, while you are concerned about the effect that a cut in the sale of Vanatin will have on earnings, you are also concerned that this company, which you have led through its period of greatest growth, also maintain its image of honesty and integrity. This is more than just "corporate image." Both must be devoted to the maintenance of health and prevention of sickness, for in the last analysis that is how you and your family will be judged in history. You will make every effort to ensure that the decision reached today reflects a unified consensus of the board.

Role of Philip Brown, President, and Vice Chairman of the Board

You were the president of Booth when Vanatin was introduced into the market. Naturally, you feel that Vanatin was, and still is, a good product for both Booth and for the people who have used it. If you didn't feel this way, you wouldn't have put Vanatin on the market in the first place. A cut in the sales of Vanatin would bring about managerial dislocations and threaten to reverse the strong growth of profits under your command. Furthermore, it has become increasingly difficult to develop new products because of extensive testing requirements of the FDA. On the other hand, as chief executive officer of Booth, you are concerned about the kind of company that you lead.

Role of Jack Booth, Son of Cyrus Booth,
President, Booth Associates, Consultants

You and your two brothers manage a consulting firm that does most of its business with the Booth Company. You and your brothers control approximately 20 percent of Booth stock, and you are concerned with the potential effects of the proposed ban on corporate earnings. You have become increasingly disturbed recently at the responsiveness of management to the demands of labor, community, and governmental groups. You feel that management is hired by the stockholders, and that management through the board should be primarily responsive to them. In a well-publicized statement to *The Wall Street Journal,* you stated that "management seems to be more concerned with its own comfort and security than with corporate profits."

A suggestion was recently sent to you by the corporate lobbyist in Washington. He suggests that it might be possible to bring political pressure to bear on the FDA by securing the cooperation of the current Secretary of Health and Welfare. The secretary might be willing to overrule a proposed ban by the FDA, since the ban would represent a major precedent that increases the power of the FDA at the expense of drug companies and their rights to free enterprise. Getting the secretary to go along might require some major financial contributions to the president's reelection campaign.

Role of James Vance, Corporate Legal Counsel

You would prefer not to fight the FDA on Vanatin because you are convinced in the long run that Booth will lose. The FDA has respected research data to support its claim. Other legal tactics are necessary.

You have been checking out various ways of handling the problem with friends. One suggestion has been sent to you by another Booth attorney. He has seen the Vanatin issue develop over the past few years, and he thinks that it would be possible legally to delay any action by the FDA. He suggests that Judge Kent of Kalamazoo (a man whom you know personally) would be willing to serve an injunction on the FDA. This would prohibit the FDA from banning Vanatin until such time as a formal hearing can be held. The results of this hearing, if unfavorable, could then be appealed. In effect, the case could be tied up in the courts for three to five years. A similar move in international courts would not be likely to have an impact on Vanatin sales for five to ten years.

Role of John C. Gauntlett, M.D., Board of Directors

You have been aware of the bad publicity on Vanatin. As a practicing physician, you have been prescribing Vanatin for years, and you have seen nothing wrong with it. At the last AMA meeting, other doctors to whom you talked reported similar findings. Your thought is that an appeal should be sent to all doctors to protest the FDA, on the grounds that a ban by the FDA would be violating the physician's right to prescribe the most effective drugs. The fact that some of the doctors you talked to have been using Vanatin for 13 years indicated that it must have some value.

You have been a member of the board of directors for eight years and own 150,000 shares of Booth stock.

Role of Herb Phillips, M.D., Ph.D.

As head of Booth's research division, you are very aware of the deaths caused by Vanatin. Although it is the best product of its kind that Booth produces, products produced by Booth's competitors are just as effective and have fewer negative aftereffects. It is because of Booth's superior marketing, advertising, and drug distribution system that Vanatin has fared so well competitively. Still, the profits of drugs like Vanatin help finance new drug research and maintain your large and highly productive research laboratories.

VANATIN ROLE-PLAY

Directions: The chairman of the board will conduct the discussion of the Vanatin problem. By the end of 45 minutes, the group should reach a decision on what to do about *both* domestic and international distribution of Vanatin. At the end of the meeting, each chairman should record the decisions of the group on the Recording Form.

Recording Form

Group Decision on Vanatin

1. Check the category that most closely approximates your position with regard to the U.S. market (circle one letter only):

    a. Recall Vanatin immediately and destroy it.

    b. Stop production of Vanatin immediately, but allow what's been made to be sold.

    c. Stop all advertising and promotion of Vanatin, but provide it for doctors who request it.

    d. Continue efforts to most effectively market Vanatin until sale is actually banned by the FDA.

    e. Continue efforts to most effectively market Vanatin and take legal, political, and other necessary action to prevent the FDA from banning Vanatin.

2. Assume that the FDA did succeed in banning Vanatin but that it was still legal to sell Vanatin in foreign countries. What category most closely approximates your position with regard to foreign markets? (Circle one letter only.)

    a. Recall Vanatin immediately and destroy it.

    b. Stop production of Vanatin immediately, but allow what's been made to be sold.

    c. Stop all advertising and promotion of Vanatin, but provide it for doctors who request it.

    d. Continue efforts to most effectively market Vanatin until sale is banned in each particular country.

    e. Continue efforts to most effectively market Vanatin and take legal, political, and other necessary action to prevent the banning of Vanatin.

TABULATION OF RESULTS

Directions: The instructor will tabulate the types of decisions made by all the groups for the U.S. and foreign markets. You may record the decisions on the table below.

1. Record in columns 1 and 2 the actual decisions made by the discussion groups.

2. *Privately* note to yourself what you think Booth actually did in this case. The instructor will tally the predictions, and you may record these predictions in columns 3 and 4.

3. Record in columns 5 and 6 what Booth actually did.

Decision	Decisions Made By Groups*		What Do You Think Happened?		What Actually Happened?	
	U.S.	Foreign	U.S.	Foreign	U.S.	Foreign
a. Recall immediately						
b. Stop production						
c. Stop advertising and promotion						
d. Continue to market						
e. Block FDA						
	(1)	(2)	(3)	(4)	(5)	(6)

*Record the letter designation of the group decision in the proper place.

DISCUSSION QUESTIONS

1. What were the primary ethical parameters upon which you made your decision? Other groups?

2. Are you surprised at the general class results? Why or why not?

3. Did the nature of leadership in your group affect the decision-making process?

4. To what extent do you think the way in which decisions were made in this case model simulate real-life corporate decisions that require ethical considerations?

Memo Assignments

CHAPTER ONE

MEMO: MANAGING YOUR JOB

The purpose of this memo assignment is to help you manage the time demands in your job (or as a student). This assignment will teach you how you actually spend your time. By identifying your priorities and goals, you will be in a better position to more closely monitor your time management skills as a manager (or student).

Part I

Develop a daily diary record of your activities for a series of three (3) days. You may use the following Activity Record to record your activities.

Day One: Activity Record

Time	Activities
Time	*Activities*

7 A.M.

8 A.M.

9 A.M.

10 A.M.

11 A.M.

12 noon

1 P.M.

2 P.M.

3 P.M.

4 P.M.

5 P.M.

6 P.M. and beyond

Day Two: Activity Record

Time	Activities
Time	*Activities*

7 A.M.

8 A.M.

9 A.M.

10 A.M.

11 A.M.

12 noon

1 P.M.

2 P.M.

3 P.M.

4 P.M.

5 P.M.

6 P.M. and beyond

Day Three: Activity Record

Time	Activities
Time	*Activities*

7 A.M.

8 A.M.

9 A.M.

10 A.M.

11 A.M.

12 noon

1 P.M.

2 P.M.

3 P.M.

4 P.M.

5 P.M.

6 P.M. and beyond

Part II

Once your diary is complete, analyze how you spent your time by answering the following questions:

1. What proportion of time was spent performing specific job tasks (or specific educational tasks, such as preparing an exam)?

2. What proportion of time was spent involved in activities not directly related to your job or education?

3. Among the specific job or educational tasks listed, how much of your time was spent on people or interpersonal tasks?

4. Among the specific job or educational tasks listed, how much of your time was spent on technical tasks?

5. Is the proportion of time that you spent on specific tasks appropriate for the demands of your job (or your life as a student)? In other words, at what point during each day or with specific tasks did you waste time that could have been used for other, more worthwhile activities?

6. What are the current priorities of your job (or of your life as a student)? How much of your time was actually spent pursuing those priorities?

7. Describe your ideal work day—a day in which you complete the day feeling very productive and pleased with your accomplishments. What schedule would you follow to discipline your work?

8. How can you improve your time management skills so that your most important priorities can be fulfilled each day? Develop an action plan for improvement.

My Goals and Priorities	*Action Plan: What I Will Do*
1.	1.
2.	2.
3.	3.

CHAPTER TWO

MEMO: RESOLVING PERSONAL AND PROFESSIONAL CONFLICTS

For the purpose of this memo, it is important that you identify any problematic relationships that may be bothering you currently. One could be a relationship in your *personal* life; perhaps the relationship you have with your spouse, your girlfriend or boyfriend, your mother-in-law, your children. The other might be a relationship in your *professional* life; perhaps the relationship you have with your boss, a peer, or one of your employees.

Part I

Identify a conflict that you would like to work on in one of these relationships. The conflict may be minor, for example, a disagreement about housework between you and your spouse; or it may be quite serious, such as your decision to leave your place of employment due to your boss's negative attitude. What would you like to say to this person? What message should you communicate about your relationship? What suggestions might you have for improving the quality of your relationship?

Part II

Write a letter to the person with whom you have identified a conflict. In your letter, you should:

1. Describe the areas of disagreement and agreement—your viewpoint and what you believe to be the other's viewpoint on each

2. Define the root causes of the conflict (the subtext)—again, your viewpoint and what you believe to be the other's viewpoint

3. Outline the other person's strengths, weaknesses, expectations, and assumptions; outline yours

4. Suggest current circumstances that may be aggravating the conflict—from both perspectives

5. Illustrate differences (and similarities) in working style, and especially, in conflict-resolution styles

6. Identify how you are each dependent on each other

Part III

To conclude the letter, you should develop a plan for improving this relationship. Your plan for improving your relationship should

1. Include steps to maximize the strengths of your relationship and minimize the weaknesses—including, but not limited to, adaptations you plan to make

2. Be specific

3. Develop a mechanism to monitor and maintain your relationship on an ongoing basis

CHAPTER THREE

MEMO: REDESIGNING YOUR JOB

No job is perfect. Most jobs can benefit from redesign. How should your job be changed to allow you greater task variety, task identity, task significance, autonomy, and/or feedback from the job? The purpose of this memo is to help you think more creatively about your own job to identify ways in which you can make your job more motivating.

Part I: Your Own Job Redesign

Identify which of the scales identified in Hackman's (1977) article "Designing Work for Individuals and Groups" is *lowest* in your job. (*Note: You may wish to take the Job Diagnostic Survey as preparation for this memo if requested by your instructor.*) What areas could be improved?

1. Would you prefer more variety among tasks? If so, which ones?

2. Completion of a whole and identifiable piece of work? If so, how?

3. Greater appreciation of the work that you do? If so, how?

4. More autonomy, responsibility, and discretion in decision making? How?

5. Increased feedback from the job? If not your job, then from whom?

If you could design your ideal job, what elements would it include? How can you redesign your own job to fit such a model? Write out a description of your job and how it can be improved. You may want to use Hackman's (1977) principles for redesign for ideas.

My Current Job	*My Improved Job*

Part II: Redesigning Subordinates' Jobs

(Note: Complete this section only if you currently are managing subordinates for whom this task might apply.)

Think about the jobs held by your subordinates. How can you utilize this knowledge to improve the motivating potential of the jobs of people who work for you? Can you reorder the work? Split up work tasks among employees? Establish client relationships? Provide more project responsibility? Delegate more authority? Form natural work units? Open feedback channels?

Think about the work of your department *as a whole*. If none of the current jobs existed, how would you create jobs to organize tasks? Think about your own work as a manager. In what areas could you use more help? To whom could you successfully delegate more? How would such changes affect each job's motivating potential?

Identify the ways in which subordinate jobs could be improved. Make notes of your ideas in your memo.

CHAPTER FOUR

MEMO: PRACTICING EFFECTIVE LEADERSHIP

The purpose of this memo is to help you distinguish between effective and ineffective leadership practices. You will also have an opportunity to evaluate your own leadership qualities and skills and determine an action plan for improvement.

Part I

Think about the managers you have encountered who have impressed you with their abilities as leaders and as decision makers. To what extent did these leaders

1. Create enthusiasm in followers?
2. Delegate tasks to empower subordinates?
3. Possess effective communication skills?
4. Organize effectively?
5. Evidence an empowering attitude toward subordinates?
6. Set high standards for work performance?
7. Encourage follower participation in decisions directly affecting them?
8. Exhibit transformational qualities?

Now think about the managers whom you have observed who in your opinion have failed miserably as managers. What qualities do these managers have in common? What skills did they fail to demonstrate?

Part II

Based upon your analysis, identify a list of skills that are necessary for effective leadership. Review your list to determine which skills you may potentially demonstrate as a leader. Identify the skill areas that require further practice. Then develop an action plan to help you improve your leadership abilities.

Action Plan

Effective Leadership Skills I Demonstrate	*Skills I Lack*	*How I Can Improve My Skills*
1.	1.	1.
2.	2.	2.
3.	3.	3.
4.	4.	4.
5.	5.	5.

CHAPTER FIVE

MEMO: POWER AND DEPENDENCE ANALYSIS

The purpose of this memo is to help you become more aware of the sources of dependence and relative structural power of your job. If you are currently employed, use your current job as the focus for this memo. *Note: If you are not currently employed, think about a job you have held in the past and answer as many questions as possible that are pertinent to your analysis. Or complete Part II of the* Dependency Situations *questionnaire in its place.* Complete the following questions as a guide:

I. Dependency Analysis: Job Sources

1. To what extent are you dependent on others for the information and support necessary to perform the tasks associated with your job?

2. On whom are you dependent for information and/or support?

3. How dependent are you on each source of information and support?

4. How dependent are others on you for the information and support you provide that is necessary for them to perform their jobs well?

5. Discuss a typical situation in which you were dependent for information or support and you successfully empowered yourself using the strategies discussed in this chapter. Discuss another situation in which you were unsuccessful.

6. Relative to other jobs within your department, how important is your job? How aware is upper management of the work that you do in your job?

7. To what extent is the way you perform your job limited by company policies and procedures? To what extent does your job allow you to exercise your own initiative in carrying out your assignments?

II. Dependency Analysis: Departmental Sources

8. How critical is your department's work to the success of your organization?

9. Which departments in your organization have the most people and/or the largest budgets?

10. How important does upper management consider the work of your department?

Based on this analysis, do the following:

1. Determine the structural power of your job by assessing the lines of support and information that contribute to your ability to exercise power in your job or that render you powerless.

2. Identify the strategies you can use to handle dependency situations with peers, superiors, and subordinates so that you can be more effective in your job.

CHAPTER SIX

MEMO: ASSESSING YOUR TEAM

The purpose of this memo is to help you analyze and identify your group's interaction process. Think about a group that you know well and that is important to you (if possible, choose your work team or task force). Answer the following questions:

1. What are the goals and priorities of your group? Are those goals and priorities being effectively fulfilled? If not, why not?

2. What impairs the group's effectiveness? What contributes to the group's effectiveness?

3. Do members within the group communicate openly and honestly? Are conflicts aired without prejudgments?

4. Around which issues is conflict generated? Does your group have effective mechanisms for resolving conflicts among members?

5. Does the composition of the group affect the group's effectiveness? How?

6. How does the group normally make decisions? Authority rule? Majority or minority rule? Apathy? Consensus? What are the consequences of the group's decision-making style?

7. Describe the group's norms. Which norms are critical to group functioning? Which norms are dysfunctional for group productivity?

8. Is there a group deviant who routinely violates certain group norms? Which ones? How does the group respond to this deviant member?

9. Does the group capitalize on the assets of group problem solving? Does the group minimize the liabilities of group problem solving? If not, why not?

10. Has the group fallen into the trap of groupthink? How does this manifest itself?

Use this analysis to formulate an action plan for improving the effectiveness of your team. Be sure to include

1. What your group must do

2. How you plan to influence your group

3. How you expect your group to respond

CHAPTER SEVEN

MEMO: HANDLING INTERDEPARTMENTAL CONFLICTS

The purpose of this memo assignment is to help you manage intergroup relations among departments in your organization. Think about your department or a group in which you are currently a member and answer the following questions:

1. With which groups are the members of your group or department most frequently in contact? For what reasons?

2. What are the goals and priorities of your group or department? How do they differ from the goals and priorities of the group or departments you identified in the first question?

3. What are the attitudes of your group toward the groups with which you must work most frequently? What do you think the attitudes of these groups are toward your group?

4. How are resource allocations (such as staff, budget, and the like) different between your group and the groups with which you must most frequently work?

5. What are the most common conflicts that emerge between your group and the groups or departments on which you have focused?

6. What superordinate goals do your departments or groups share? How can such superordinate goals be used to increase the cooperation among departments or groups?

7. Based on the readings in this chapter, what methods or techniques, in your opinion, should be used to ensure more cooperative relations?

Use this analysis to formulate a plan for improving the effectiveness of your group and the relationship of your group and the groups with which you are in conflict. Be sure to include

1. What your group must do

2. What you expect the other group to do

3. What obstacles you might encounter

4. How you plan to overcome these obstacles

5. The support your organization must provide

CHAPTER EIGHT

MEMO: ANALYZING YOUR ORGANIZATION'S DESIGN

The purpose of this memo is to help you consider the fit between your current organization's design, its environment, and its culture. Consider your organization or, if you work for a very large firm, consider your division within it and answer the following questions:

1. What is the primary business or mission of your company/division?

2. Is the environment simple or complex? Static or dynamic? How much uncertainty is there in the environment?

3. What is the organization's stage of evolution/revolution? What indicators are you using to diagnose this stage?

4. What is your company's image of itself? How would you describe your company or division's image in the minds of competitors?

5. What is the general philosophy of management? Is management more oriented to human resource or budget objectives?

6. Describe your company's culture. What stories communicate what is expected of members? Who are your company's heroes?

7. How are new members hired and socialized? Is deviance tolerated well? If not, why not?

Use these questions to assess your organization. Determine whether or not your firm/division has

1. Evolved a culture appropriate to its stage of growth

2. Developed a design or structure appropriate to its environment

CHAPTER NINE

MEMO: CAREER PROGNOSIS

The purpose of this memo assignment is to help you think about your future. Develop a career plan for your next job by completing the following:

Part I: Background and Work History

❑ List all the jobs you have worked in the past (or provide a resume). Include the major jobs that you have had, as well as some of the minor jobs that may have been fundamental to your development.

Part II: Skill Analysis

❑ Review each job on your list. Identify the primary skills you learned while performing the activities associated with that job.

Part III: Target Job Identification

❑ Where do you want to be in one year? Five years from now? What do you want to have accomplished—careerwise—by the time you retire? Dream a little and determine the types of skills you need to improve to fulfill your career goals.

Part IV: Developmental Plan

❑ Develop a psychological contract with yourself to formulate a career plan for your future. Include how you will identify a mentor, the training workshops you will attend, the life-style constraints that might impact on your career goals, and how you will overcome the psychological barriers you must face to achieve your dreams. Will your career goals generate too much stress for you to cope with? If so, should you reconsider your goals?

CHAPTER TEN

MEMO: MANAGING DIVERSITY

In this memo, you will be asked to consider the culturally diverse groups with whom you are in contact in your firm, or may be in contact with in the next ten years. What contributions can these groups make to your firm? How might you *value* their different approaches to doing business?

Part I

1. Consider the characteristics of three culturally diverse groups with whom you are in contact (or expect to be in contact with during the next 10 years). What are the primary characteristics of how members of these groups do business?

Group I:

Group II:

Group III:

2. How may these characteristics be considered a contribution to how business in your firm is done? How might the members of these groups shape the norms of your firm to improve business dealings with others?

3. Imagine that you are chief executive officer of your firm in the year 2020. What key norms or cultural values would you like to emphasize as you shape the corporate culture? What programs might you put in place to enhance diversity management in your firm?

Key Cultural Values

Possible Programs

REFERENCE

Ideas for this memo were generated from a symposium presented at the Eastern Academy of Management, Baltimore, MD, 1992, "Diversity as Learning Opportunity." Presenters included M. Cecelia McMillen; Judith White; Ann Baker; Anne London; Patrice Kiernan; and Michael London.

INDEX